Baltic States
& Kaliningrad
a travel survival kit

John Noble

Baltic States & Kaliningrad – a travel survival kit

1st edition

Published by

Lonely Planet Publications

Head Office: PO Box 617, Hawthorn, Vic 3122, Australia
Branches: PO Box 2001A, Berkeley, CA 94702, USA
12 Barley Mow Passage, Chiswick, London W4 4PH, UK
71 bis rue du Cardinal Lemoine, 75005 Paris, France

Printed by

Singapore National Printers Ltd, Singapore

Photographs by

Miervaldis Balodis (MB)
Livijus Grigaliunas (LG)
Sulev Kalamäe (SK)
John Noble (JN)
Colin Richardson (CR)
Eduards Voitkuns (EV)
Gabrielius Žemkalnis (GZ)

Front cover: View of Tallinn from Toompea (SK)

Published

March 1994

Although the authors and publisher have tried to make the information as accurate as possible, they accept no responsibility for any loss, injury or inconvenience sustained by any person using this book.

National Library of Australia Cataloguing in Publication Data

Noble, John
Baltic States & Kaliningrad – a travel survival kit.

1st ed.
Includes index.
ISBN 0 86442 183 4.

1. Baltic States – Guidebooks.
2. Kaliningrad (RSFSR) – Guidebooks.
I. Title (Series: Lonely Planet travel survival kit).

914.7404854

John Noble

John was born and raised in the valley of the River Ribble, England, only about 1500 km from the Baltic states. But despite travelling Europe and the world on and off from his teens, and 1½ decades of journalism and Lonely Planet guide writing in numerous countries, his ignorance of the Baltic states was near-total till one day in the late 1980s, when he found himself agreeing to co-author a new Lonely Planet guide to the USSR.

Amazed then by the advanced stage the Baltic independence movements had already reached, he became hooked on every twist and turn of a saga which culminated, for him, in a small headline in a Mexican newspaper on 5 September 1991: 'La URSS reconoce la independencia de las repúblicas bálticas' ('USSR recognises Baltic independence'). John returned to the Baltics after independence to write this book.

Other Lonely Planet guides John has co-authored are *Australia*, *Indonesia*, *Mexico*, *Scandinavian & Baltic Europe*, and *Sri Lanka*. With his wife, Susan Forsyth, and their children, Isabella and Jack, he still has home base in the Ribble valley.

Dedication

For my parents.

From the Author

John gratefully thanks the dozens of individuals, offices, companies and organisations in the Baltic states and around the world who gave their time and effort to answer his questions and help him in all sorts of other ways with this book. It is impossible to mention them all, but special thanks go to Kārlis and Dace Einis, Livijus Grigaliunas, Julian Howden, Andrew Humphreys, Andrew Inkley-Leitch, Sulev Kalamäe, Tiina Koik, Viesturs Lucāns, Zita Makutienė, Algis Misevičius, James Morley, Margus Parve, Arvo Piir, Christina Quick, Colin Richardson, Vaclovas Sakalauskas and his daughter Jurga, Janis Šnepsts, Robert Strauss, Neil Taylor and colleagues at Regent Holidays, Jana Teteris, Valdis at Sporta Bāze Baiļi,

Māris Valtenbergs, Alexandr Vasilev, Esther Wettenhall and Gabrielius Žemkalnis.

John also thanks the producers of all the Baltic states' English-language papers and city guides, for making his task a great deal easier; the production team at Lonely Planet, especially Robert Flynn for consistently careful and constructive editing and Sandra Smythe for turning sometimes hard-to-follow diagrams into real maps; and last but not least, Estonia, Latvia, Lithuania and Susan Forsyth for making the book (in their different ways!) possible at all.

From the Publisher

This first edition of *Baltic States & Kaliningrad – a travel survival kit* was edited by Robert Flynn. Maps were drawn by Sandra Smythe with assistance from Matthew King and Michelle Stamp. Michelle also designed and illustrated the book. The cover was designed by Margaret Jung.

Frith Pike and Tom Smallman assisted with proofreading, and Ann Jeffree with the index. The fonts were created by Dan Levin. Thanks also to Sue Mitra and Rob van Driesum for editorial guidance.

Thanks go to the following readers of Lonely Planet's USSR travel survival kit who wrote in with information on the Baltics: William Blatt (USA), John & Kim Chesarek (USA), Derek Emson (UK), Roel Forceville (Belgium), Paul Geldhof (Belgium), Ruth & Drew Klee (USA/Switz), Gerald Marlow (Transworld Publishing), Roger Morgan (UK), Brooke Ratliff (USA), Anne-Sophie Redisch (Nor), Weld Royal (USA), Erik Slavenas (Aus), Julle Tuuliainen (Fin), Heleen van der Beek (Belgium).

Warning & Request

Throughout the Baltic states it's a period of great change, and this will continue. Prices,

schedules and phone numbers will alter, good new places to stay will keep appearing, bad old ones may disappear, transport services will develop, eateries will come and go, entertainment places will rise and fall – all even faster than they do in most other countries. So if you find things better or worse, recently opened or long since closed, please write and tell us and help make the next edition even better!

Your letters will be used to help update future editions and, where possible, important changes will also be included as a Stop Press section in reprints.

All information is greatly appreciated and the best letters will receive a free copy of the next edition or any other Lonely Planet book of your choice.

Contents

INTRODUCTION 9

FACTS ABOUT THE REGION 12

History 12
Geography 27
Climate 28
Flora & Fauna................. 30

National Parks & Reserves....... 31
Environment 31
Government 32
Economy 32

Population & People 33
Arts & Culture 36
Religion................................. 38
Language............................... 39

FACTS FOR THE VISITOR 40

Visas & Embassies 40
Documents............................. 44
Customs 45
Money................................... 45
When to Go 47
What to Bring 48
Tourist Offices 48
Business Hours & Holidays 48
Cultural Events 49
Post & Telecommunications.....50

Time......................................55
Electricity..............................55
Laundry.................................55
Left Luggage..........................55
Toilets...................................55
Weights & Measures................ 55
Books....................................55
Maps.....................................58
Media....................................59
Film & Photography 61

Health....................................61
Women Travellers 62
Dangers & Annoyances 63
Work.....................................64
Activities...............................64
Accommodation......................65
Food 69
Drinks...................................71
Entertainment.........................72
Things to Buy.........................73

GETTING THERE & AWAY 75

Travel Agencies 75
Air.......................................78
Bus......................................85

Train......................................88
Car & Motorbike 95
Bicycle..................................97

Hitching.................................97
Sea.......................................97
Tours.....................................102

GETTING AROUND...103

Borders 103
Information & Tickets 103
Air......................................104
Bus.....................................105

Train.................................... 106
Car & Motorbike 107
Bicycle................................ 109
Hitching 110

Boat.....................................110
Local Transport 111
Tours....................................111

ESTONIA

FACTS ABOUT THE COUNTRY 115

Geography 115
National Parks & Reserves......116

Government 116
People 117

Arts............................... 117

FACTS FOR THE VISITOR 119

Diplomatic Missions 119
Customs 119

Money 120
Cultural Events 121

Food 122

TALLINN 123

History 123
Orientation..............................124
Information.............................124
Things to See & Do 129

Festivals 137
Places to Stay 137
Places to Eat......................... 141
Entertainment........................ 143

Things to Buy........................145
Getting There & Away 145
Getting Around 148
Around Tallinn 149

NORTH-EAST ESTONIA 152

Lahemaa National Park 152
Lahemaa to Narva 157

Narva..................................... 158
Lake Peipus (North) 161

Paide 161
Around Paide 161

SOUTH-EAST ESTONIA 163

Tallinn to Tartu 163
Tartu 163
Tartu to Jõgeva 173
Lake Peipus (South) 174
Otepää 174
Elva & Võrtsjärv 177

Valga 177
Põlva & Taevaskoja 178
Võru 179
Suur Munamägi 181
Rõuge 182

Paganamaa, Mõniste &
Ähijärv 182
Vastseliina Castle 182
Hino Järv 183
Setumaa 183

WEST ESTONIA & THE ISLANDS 184

Haapsalu 184
Tuksi 190
Noarootsi 190
Around Haapsalu 191
Vormsi 192
Matsalu Nature Reserve &
Lihula 193
Virtsu 194
Hiiumaa 194

Getting There & Away 196
Getting Around 197
Heltermaa to Kärdla 197
Kärdla 198
Tahkuna Peninsula 200
Western Hiiumaa 200
Käina 201
Kassari 201
Southern Hiiumaa 202

Väinameri Nature Reserve 202
Saaremaa 202
History 204
Getting There & Away 204
Getting Around 206
Muhu 206
Eastern Saaremaa 206
Kuressaare 208
Western Saaremaa 213

SOUTH-WEST ESTONIA 215

Pärnu 215
Around Pärnu 223

Kihnu 224
Ruhnu 224

Viljandi 224
Around Viljandi 226

LATVIA

FACTS ABOUT THE COUNTRY 229

Geography 229
National Parks & Reserves 230

Government 230
People 230

Arts 231

FACTS FOR THE VISITOR 233

Diplomatic Missions 233
Customs 233

Money 233
National Holidays 234

Cultural Events 234
Food 235

RĪGA 236

History 236
Orientation 238
Information 238
Things to See & Do 242
Tours 250

Festivals 250
Places to Stay 250
Places to Eat 253
Entertainment 255
Things to Buy 256

Getting There & Away 256
Getting Around 259
Around Rīga 260
Salaspils 260
Jūrmala 260

VIDZEME 264

The Coast 264
Mazsalaca & Rūjiena 266
Sigulda 267
Līgatne & Around 270

Araiši 272
Cēsis 272
Valmiera 273
Around Valmiera 275

Valka 275
Vidzeme Upland 275

LATGALE 276

Daugava Valley 276
Rēzekne 276

Latgale Upland 280
Daugavpils 281

ZEMGALE 284

Iecava 284
Bauska 284

Rundāle 286
Mežotne 288

Jelgava 288
Tērvete 289

KURZEME 290

Tukums 290
Talsi 292
Northern Kurzeme 293
The Abava Valley.................... 295
Ventspils................................ 295
Ventspils to Liepāja 298
Kuldīga..................................298
Liepāja..................................301

LITHUANIA

FACTS ABOUT THE COUNTRY 307

Geography 307
National Parks & Reserves..... 308
Government 308
People 309
Arts..309

FACTS FOR THE VISITOR 311

Customs 311
Money.................................... 312
National Holidays................... 312
Cultural Events 312
Media.....................................313
Food 313

VILNIUS 314

History 314
Orientation............................ 316
Information 316
Things to See & Do 320
Festivals................................ 331
Places to Stay 331
Places to Eat......................... 335
Entertainment........................ 338
Things to Buy 339
Getting There & Away............ 339
Getting Around 342
Around Vilnius **343**
Paneriai 343
Trakai 344
Kernavė 346

EASTERN & SOUTHERN LITHUANIA..347

Aukštaitija National Park 347
Molėtai................................... 348
Jūžintai 350
Druskininkai 350
Around Druskininkai 353
The South-West.....................353

CENTRAL LITHUANIA...356

Kaunas 356
Around Kaunas...................... 365
Šiauliai 365
Panevėžys 369

WESTERN LITHUANIA 370

Žemaitija Upland 370
Salantai & Mosėdis 372
Palanga 372
Klaipėda 377
Courland Lagoon – East Coast 385
Neringa (Courland Spit) .. **385**
Juodkrantė.............................386
Juodkrantė to Nida.................387
Nida.......................................387

KALININGRAD REGION

KALININGRAD REGION..393

Government 393
People 393
Diplomatic Missions 395
Customs 395
Money.................................... 395
National Holidays................... 395
Kaliningrad **395**
History 398
Orientation............................ 399
Information............................. 399
Things to See & Do 400
Places to Stay 405
Places to Eat......................... 407
Entertainment........................ 408
Things to Buy 408
Getting There & Away............ 408
Getting Around 411
Other Destinations **412**
Svetlogorsk 412
Zelenogradsk 416
Sovietsk.................................417
Baltiysk 418
Yantarny 418
Kurshskaya Kosa 419
Gurievsk, Mordovskoe &
Polessk..................................419
Gvardeysk, Chernyakhovsk &
Gusev 419
Balga 420

LANGUAGE GUIDE 421

APPENDIX – Alternative Place Names 436

INDEX 438

Map Legend

BOUNDARIES

— · — · — · — .... International Boundary

— · · — · · — .... Internal Boundary

+++++++++++++ .... National Park or Reserve

— — — — — — .... The Equator

· · · · · · · · · · · · .... The Tropics

SYMBOLS

⊙ NATIONAL ....National Capital

● TOWN .... Major Town >50,000 Pop.

● Town ....Other Major Town

● Town ....Minor Town/Village

■ ....Places to Stay

▼ ....Places to Eat

⊠ ....Post Office

✈ ....Airport

ℹ ....Tourist Information

● ....Bus Station or Terminal

66 ....Highway Route Number

☾ ✝ 🛉 ♁ ...... Mosque, Church, Cathedral

∴ ....Temple or Ruin

✚ ....Hospital

※ ....Lookout

⚑ .... Camping Area

ᴦ .... Picnic Area

⌂ ....Hut or Chalet

▲ .... Mountain or Hill

⊢━━━⊣ .... Railway Station

═══ .... Road Bridge

⊢┼┼┼⊣ .... Railway Bridge

⇒ ⇐ ....Road Tunnel

↦ ↤ ....Railway Tunnel

ᴖᴖᴖᴖ ....Escarpment or Cliff

⌣ ....Pass

ᴨᴨᴨᴨ ....Ancient or Historic Wall

ROUTES

———————— ....Major Road or Highway

– – – – – – – – .... Unsealed Major Road

———————— .... Sealed Road

– – – – – – – – ..... Unsealed Road or Track

════════ ....City Street

++++++++++ ....Railway

⊏━⊙━⊐ ....Subway

– – – – – – – – ....Walking Track

– – – – – – – – ....Ferry Route

⊢⊣⊢⊣⊢⊣⊢⊣ .... Cable Car or Chair Lift

HYDROGRAPHIC FEATURES

⌒⌒⌒ ....River or Creek

- - - - - ....Intermittent Stream

⬭ ⬭ ....Lake, Intermittent Lake

⌒⌒ ....Coast Line

● ....Spring

≋ ∥ ....Waterfall

ᴗᴗᴗ ᴗᴗᴗ ᴗᴗᴗ ....Swamp

[shaded box] .... Salt Lake or Reef

[contour box] ....Glacier

OTHER FEATURES

[dotted box] Park, Garden or National Park

[crosshatched box] .... Built Up Area

[market box] ... Market or Pedestrian Mall

[plaza box] .... Plaza or Town Square

[+ + + box] ....Cemetery

Note: not all symbols displayed above appear in this book

Introduction

Estonia, Latvia, and Lithuania – the three Baltic states – burst on to the world scene almost from nowhere in the late 1980s. Previously they had been, in the awareness of much of the world, almost semi-mythical places that might have existed in an old atlas or a grandparent's stamp collection. Suddenly they were leading players in the break-up of the Soviet Union of which, the world learned, they had been unwilling members since the 1940s.

The Baltic states' dramatic – at times, heroic – campaigns for independence finally succeeded in 1991, and they quickly faded back out of the world's headlines as they set about the more mundane task of re-creating themselves as independent countries in the face of dire economic problems.

With Soviet restrictions on movement now ended, growing numbers of travellers are taking the opportunity to see for themselves what these three tiny countries are really like. What we find measures up, in a degree, to the fairy-tale image: castles everywhere; quaint folk costumes which still come out at festival times; countryside, forests and lakes inhabited by legends and myths. Even the trams that rattle round city streets seem relics of an earlier age.

Life for visitors is getting better and better. In contrast to the privations of the Soviet era it's now a joy to find true freedom of movement, a fast-growing supply of good places to stay and eat that don't cost the earth, friendlier people in service industries, more in the shops, an increasingly lively entertainments scene, and media and museums that no longer have to bend the truth.

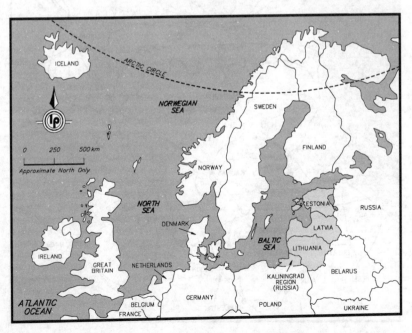

Baltic States &
Kaliningrad Region

Part of the fascination of visiting the Baltic states today is witnessing their transformation. Although independence has brought new opportunities for some with talent, initiative and energy, the everyday struggle for existence has been as tough as ever for the majority.

But change is happening surprisingly fast, and there's light at the end of the economic tunnel. It's impossible, however, to ignore the damage done to the appearance of city and country by the drab Soviet apartment blocks and dirty factories and to social harmony by divisive, initiative-sapping methods of political control and heavy immigration from Russia.

Apart, perhaps, from Lithuania's medieval golden age, the Baltic states have always been something of a backwater, tucked away in a remote corner of Europe – except of course to their own peoples and, in recent times, their hundreds of thousands of émigrés scattered round the world. For several centuries a succession of dominating foreign rulers pushed the native peoples almost entirely into the countryside, while the towns and cities – whose architecture is the region's main tourist magnet today – were created by incomers. Today, Estonian, Latvian and Lithuanian roots still lie very much in the countryside.

But the obscurity of the Baltic states makes them, in some ways, all the more intriguing. Here are whole nations with their own languages, customs, and a wealth of colourful, musical festivals to discover, and whole sweeps of history, little known outside the immediate region, to explore.

The Baltic landscape surprises, too. While rarely spectacular, it has a gentle, rolling beauty that gradually grows on you in summer (though in the dull days of winter it can seem bleak and dreary). The long sweeps of coast and, in Estonia, the many bays, promontories and islands add a further dimension to the region's scenic attractions. Ordinary Baltic people are now rediscovering their connection with the sea after

decades of being virtually banned from it by the Soviet authorities.

One aspect of travelling in the Baltic states that disconcerts some visitors is the rather glum, pessimistic outward bearing of many people – a product of perennial economic hardship and the dispiriting effect of Soviet rule. But once you break through this surface, you'll generally find people are surprisingly happy to be able to help Western visitors. Their growing knowledge of the English language makes this easier.

Though the outside world tends to view the three Baltic states as a single entity, they are three very different countries with separate languages, histories and traditions and noticeable general differences between their native peoples. Estonians are stereotypically reserved, efficient and polite; Lithuanians are more gregarious and less organised; and Latvians are somewhere between the two extremes. Discovering the contrasts between the three countries is part of the fascination of travel in the Baltic states.

In the south-western corner of the region lies a place that's in strong contrast to all three Baltic states. The Kaliningrad Region is a slice of Russian territory wedged between Lithuania, Poland and the Baltic Sea, disconnected from the rest of Russia. In many ways this region has the most bizarre story of any in the Baltics. Until 1945, when the Red Army took it, it had been German for seven centuries. Its main city, Kaliningrad (then known as Königsberg), was a focus of the Prussian state, which was at the heart of German history for so long.

Since WW II the city and region of Kaliningrad have been repeopled and rebuilt by Russians. The surviving traces of the German past amid the Soviet-created present are haunting evidence of the power of politics and war over ordinary people's lives. Because of Russian visa regulations, visiting the Kaliningrad Region may be a bit more costly and difficult than visiting the Baltic states, but if you can manage it, it's an instructive and surprising experience.

Facts about the Region

HISTORY

The story of the Baltic states, especially that of Estonia and Latvia, is one of centuries of rule by oppressive foreign powers in which the native peoples were reduced almost to non-peoples. After WW I the three Baltic states emerged from this unhappy history to enjoy just 20 years of existence as independent countries before falling back under the foreign boot with the Soviet takeover of 1940. In 1991 they again won their freedom. Is it any wonder they prize it so intensely?

In terms of ethnic origins the Latvians and Lithuanians are closely related to each other, but the Estonians belong to a completely different family of ancient peoples. However, in terms of the history of the past 800 years or so, Latvia and Estonia have much more in common with each other than with Lithuania.

Lithuania was once a powerful state in its own right – at its peak in the 14th to 16th centuries – but Latvia and Estonia were entirely subject to foreign rule from the 13th to the early 20th century. For much of this time the southern part of modern Estonia and most of modern Latvia were governed as one unit called Livonia (the concept of modern Latvia as a political entity in its own right didn't arise till the 19th century). By the late 18th century the entire region had fallen under Russian rule; and, until emancipation in the 19th century, most of its native people had been serfs for centuries.

Beginnings

Arrival Human habitation in the region which now constitutes the Baltic states goes back to at least 9000 BC in the south and 7500 BC in the north. The first forebears of the present inhabitants were Finno-Ugric hunting peoples from the east, who probably reached Estonia and parts of Latvia between 3000 and 2000 BC. Their descendants – the Estonians and the now almost-extinct Livs – are related to other Finno-Ugric peoples such as the Finns, Lapps and Hungarians (see People in the Estonia, Facts about the Country chapter). The ancestors of the modern Lithuanians and Latvians – known as 'Balts' – probably reached the area from the south-east some time around 2000 BC.

Outside Contacts All these newcomers settled sooner or later to agriculture. Well before the time of Christ the region became known as the source of amber – fossilised tree resin found along the south-east Baltic coast which was prized for making jewellery and ornamental objects. In the first few centuries AD, the tribes of the region achieved considerable cultural development and traded, particularly in amber, with German tribes and the Roman empire. Later they traded with (and fought) the Vikings from the west and the Russians from the east. The Viking trade route to Russia and Ukraine from the 8th or 9th century was along the Daugava River through modern-day Latvia and Belarus. Russian armies tried to invade Estonia and Latvia in the 11th and 12th centuries but were defeated. Orthodox Christianity, however, did penetrate parts of Latvia and Lithuania from the east. Many of the castle mounds and hill-fort sites which are scattered across the Baltic countryside date from this era.

Who Was Who By the 12th century the Finno-Ugric and Balt peoples in the region were split into a number of tribal groups – all practising nature religions. Of the Finno-Ugric peoples, the Estonians were divided into eight to 12 districts in Estonia, while the Livs inhabited northern and north-western coastal parts of Latvia. The Balts on the territory of modern Latvia were divided into the Latgals or Letts in the east, who were grouped into at least four principalities; the Cours or Couronians in the west, with five to seven principalities sometimes united under one king; the Zemgals or Semigallians in the

ESTONIA

E S T O N I A N S

Lake Peipus

RUSSIA

L I V S

L A T G A L S

LATVIA

C O U R S

L I V S

Z E M G A L S

S E L O N I A N S

Daugava

BALTIC SEA

SAMOGITIANS

LITHUANIA

Nemunas

RUSSIA

P R U S S I A N S

YOTVINGIANS

A U K Š T A I T I A I

BELARUS

POLAND

Vistula

Who Was Who

Approximate Distribution of pre-German Tribal Groups, 12th Century AD

0   100   200 km

centre, again sometimes united; and the Selonians in the eastern centre, south of the Daugava. The Cours, Zemgals and Selonians all fringed over into modern-day Lithuania.

Lithuania had two main groups of its own: the Samogitians (or Žemaičiai) in the west and the Aukštaitiai in the east and south-east. In what is now south-west Lithuania and neighbouring parts of Poland were the Yotvingians or Sūduviai – also a Balt people – later to be assimilated by the Lithuanians and Poles. A little further west, between the Nemunas and Vistula rivers, were the Prussians, the westernmost Balt people. (Other Balts to the east, in eastern Belarus and neighbouring parts of Russia, were already in the process of being assimilated by Slavs.)

German Conquest & Rule
Latvia & Estonia – the Knights of the Sword The region was dragged into written history by the *drang nach osten* (pull to the east) of German princes, colonists, traders, missionaries and crusading knights. Having overrun Slavic lands in modern-day eastern Germany and western Poland in the 12th century, the German expansionists turned their attention to the eastern Baltic. Traders

visited the mouth of the Daugava River, near Rīga, in the mid-century.

Following papal calls for a crusade against the northern heathen, German missionaries arrived in the area but achieved little until Albert von Buxhoevden was appointed Bishop of Rīga in 1201. Albert built the first German fort in the Baltics at Rīga, which was to become the region's leading city, and in 1202 established the Knights of the Sword – an order of crusading knights whose white cloaks were emblazoned with blood-red swords and crosses – to convert the region by conquest. The invaders gave the name Livonia (after the Liv people) to the area round the Gulf of Rīga and the territories inland from it.

Despite strong resistance, this unwholesome brood had subjugated and converted all of Estonia and Latvia within a quarter of a century – except for the Zemgals and Cours in western Latvia. Southern Estonia fell to the knights in 1217 with the defeat of the Estonian leader, Lembitu. Denmark, an ally of Bishop Albert, conquered northern Estonia about 1219, landing on the site of modern-day Tallinn. The knights took control of all of Estonia in 1227, having subdued the Estonian islands, too, in that year. The Livs had been conquered by 1207 and most of the Latgals by 1214.

Prussia – the Teutonic Order In the 1220s another band of German crusaders, the Teutonic Order, was invited into Mazovia (in modern-day central-northern Poland) to protect it against raids by the Prussians. Founded in Palestine in 1190 as a charitable organisation, the Teutonic Order had developed a military character and begun crusading in Europe. Its method of 'protecting' Mazovia was essentially to exterminate the Prussians and to bring in Germans to resettle their territory. The Prussians resisted till 1283, by which time all their lands were in the hands of the Teutonic Order. Among the forts the order founded on the conquered Prussian territory were Memel (now Klaipėda in Lithuania) in 1252, Königsberg (now Kaliningrad) in 1255, and Marienburg

Knight of the Teutonic Order

(now Malbork in Poland) where the order set up its headquarters in 1306. The few Prussians left were eventually assimilated by their conquerors: they ceased to exist as a separate people by the end of the 17th century. (For more on the history of Prussia see Where is Prussia? in the Kaliningrad Region chapter).

Final Subjugation of Estonia & Latvia The Knights of the Sword, meanwhile, had received a couple of setbacks. First they earned a ticking-off from the pope for their brutality, then, returning laden with booty from a raid into Samogitia in 1236, they were attacked and defeated by Zemgals and Samogitians at Saule (probably modern Šiauliai in Lithuania). The next year they were compelled to reorganise as a branch of the Teutonic Order and became known as the

Livonian Order. Northern Estonia was returned to Danish rule in 1238, and any dreams the knights might have had of eastward expansion were ended by their defeat on the ice of frozen Lake Peipus (in eastern Estonia) in 1242 by the Russian prince, Alexandr Nevsky of Novgorod.

In the 1260s the knights subjugated the Cours (whose strategy of making their own separate peace with the Pope failed to deter knightly conquest) and in 1290 they completed the conquest of Latvian territory by defeating the Zemgals. Eventually the Livonian Order settled its headquarters at Wenden (now Cēsis in Latvia). All the native tribes in the area now known as Latvia, with the exception of a few Livs, were assimilated into one group – the Latgals or Letts – by the 16th century.

The peoples of Estonia, meanwhile, continued to rise up in intermittent revolt, the last and biggest of which was the Jüriöö (St George's Night) Uprising of 1343-46. Denmark, unsettled by this, sold northern Estonia to the Livonian Order in 1346. This meant that Germans were in control of the Baltic seaboard from west of Danzig (modern Gdańsk in Poland) all the way to

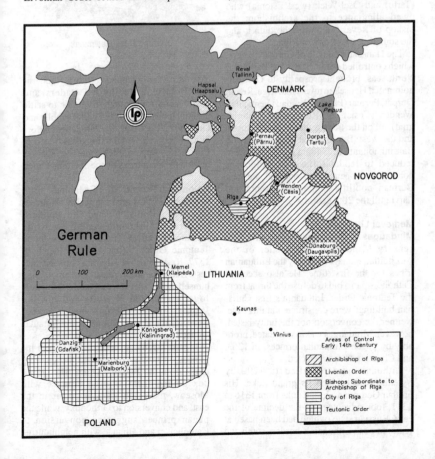

0   100   200 km

German Rule

Areas of Control
Early 14th Century

Archibishop of Rīga

Livonian Order

Bishops Subordinate to
Archibishop of Rīga

City of Rīga

Teutonic Order

DENMARK
NOVGOROD
LITHUANIA
POLAND

Reval (Tallinn)
Hapsal (Haapsalu)
Lake Peipus
Pernau (Pärnu)
Dorpat (Tartu)
Rīga
Wenden (Cēsis)
Dünaburg (Daugavpils)
Memel (Klaipéda)
Kaunas
Königsberg (Kaliningrad)
Vilnius
Danzig (Gdańsk)
Marienburg (Malbork)

Narva in north-east Estonia. In addition they controlled territory up to 250 km inland and the Estonian islands. The major gap in the German's Baltic domain was Lithuania which, protected by forests, was able to restrict the invaders to a thin coastal strip despite repeated attacks in the 14th century.

German Rule The German-dominated parts of the region were divided into a number of rival fiefdoms headed variously by the Prussia-based Teutonic Order; the Livonian Order; their vassals; the archbishop of Rīga; the bishops of Courland (Kurzeme), Dorpat (Tartu) and Ösel-Wiek (west Estonia) who owed allegiance to the archbishop; the bishop of Reval (Tallinn), who didn't; and the sometimes-free city of Rīga.

The Hanseatic League of German traders, which controlled commerce in the Baltic and North seas, brought prosperity to German-dominated Hanseatic towns like Rīga, Reval, Dorpat, Pernau (Pärnu), Windau (Ventspils), Wenden (Cēsis) and Königsberg (Kaliningrad), all on the trade routes between Russia and the West. But the local Finno-Ugric and Balt inhabitants of Estonia and Latvia were reduced to feudal serfs. The indigenous nobility had been wiped out and the new German nobility dominated Estonia and Latvia till the 20th century.

Medieval Lithuania
Mindaugas & Gediminas In the mid-13th century Mindaugas, the leader of the Aukštaitiai, managed to unify the Lithuanian tribes for the first time. He also accepted Catholicism in a bid to defuse the threat from the Teutonic Order. Lithuania's first Christian buildings were constructed at this time. Neither the conversion nor the unity lasted, however. Mindaugas was assassinated, probably by pagan Lithuanian princes, in 1263, and Christianity was rejected.

Lithuania was reunified in 1290 by Vytenis, who became its grand duke. His brother Gediminas, grand duke from 1316 to 1341, took advantage of the decline of the early Russian state (which had been based at Kiev) to push Lithuania's borders south and

Grand Duke Gediminas

east into Slav-inhabited territory (modern-day Belarus). He invited traders and landowners from around the Baltic to settle in Lithuania and protected both Catholic and Orthodox clergy. But, like Mindaugas before him, he found his own willingness to accept Christianity opposed by pagan kin. Nor was he able to stop attacks by the Teutonic Order.

Union With Poland After Gediminas' death two of his sons shared the realm. Algirdas, based in Vilnius, pushed the southern borders of Lithuania past Kiev while Kęstutis, based at Trakai, fought off the Teutonic Order. After Algirdas' death in 1377, Kęstutis drove Algirdas' son and successor, Jogaila, from Vilnius and proclaimed himself sole ruler of Lithuania. However Jogaila captured Kęstutis and his son Vytautas in 1382. Kęstutis died in prison, some say murdered by Jogaila, but Vytautas escaped.

Jogaila faced conflicting advice from his princes on how to respond to the growing threat from the Teutonic Order. The Orthodox among them advised alliance with Moscow, the rising Russian power in the east, and conversion to Orthodoxy, while the pagan princes suggested conversion to Catholicism and alliance with neighbouring

Poland. Jogaila's decision to take the latter path was a watershed in east European history. In 1386 he married Jadwiga, crown princess of Poland, forging a Lithuanian-Polish alliance against the German knights. Jogaila became Władysław II Jagiełło of Poland and a Catholic, initiating Poland's 200-year Jagiellon dynasty and a 400-year bond between the two states – which together became a major power and a rival to emergent Muscovy. The Aukštaitiai were baptised in 1387 and the Samogitians in 1413, making Lithuania the last European country to accept Christianity. Just a few years earlier, Jogaila's predecessors, Algirdas and Kęstutis, had been cremated according to the practices of the old religion: burnt on pyres with their treasures, weapons, horses and hunting dogs.

Defeat of the Teutonic Order Jogaila patched things up with Vytautas, who became Grand Duke of Lithuania on condition that he and Jogaila would share a common policy. Samogitia (occupied by the Teutonic Order in 1398) rebelled in 1408, which led to a decisive defeat for the Teutonic Order by Jogaila and Vytautas' combined armies at Grünwald (also called Tannenberg or Žalgiris), in modern-day Poland, in 1410.

Kazimieras IV of Poland (1447-92), also Grand Duke of Lithuania, went on to reduce the Teutonic Order's Prussian realm and to place it under firm Polish suzerainty. In 1525 the order was dissolved by its last grand master, Albert of Hohenzollern, and its lands became his own secular fiefdom under Polish hegemony – the Duchy of Prussia. Its territory was similar in extent to the area inhabited by the old Prussians before the order had arrived. Its capital was Königsberg, where the Teutonic Order's headquarters had been transferred in 1457.

Lithuanian Expansion Vytautas (who is called 'the Great') extended Lithuanian control further to the south and east. At his death in 1430 Lithuania stretched beyond Kursk in the east and almost to the Black Sea in the south – the greatest extent it was to reach. Lacking a big population to colonise its acquisitions or the military might to rule by force, Lithuania maintained its territories through diplomacy, allowing conquered lands to keep their autonomy and Orthodox religion.

Polonisation Lithuania sank into a junior role in its partnership with Poland, especially after the formal union of the two states (instead of just their crowns) at the Treaty of Lublin in 1569 during the Livonian War with Muscovy, and the end of the Jagiellon line in 1572. Lithuanian gentry adopted Polish culture and language; Lithuanian peasants became serfs. The joint state became known as the Rzeczpospolita (Commonwealth). The 16th century religious Reformation sent a wave of Protestantism across it, but in the 1570s this was reversed by the Counter-Reformation. Lithuania and Poland remain predominantly Catholic today.

Swedish, Polish & Russian Rule
Livonian War The loose confederation of Catholic Church, Livonian Order and semi-independent towns through which Germans controlled Latvia and Estonia became fatally weakened by the mid-16th century: the Hanseatic League was losing its hold over Baltic commerce; the Reformation threatened the Catholic ecclesiastical states from the 1520s onwards; the Livonian Order lost its military strength after the death of its last capable master, Walter von Plettenberg, in 1535; and peasant discontent was growing.

Poland and Lithuania began to cast interested eyes over Livonia and Estonia, but so did other growing regional powers – Muscovy, under Ivan the Terrible, and Sweden. It was Ivan, looking for access to the Baltic Sea, who invaded first. And so, in 1558, began the Livonian War – a 25-year spell of bloodshed, misery and devastation in which Ivan seemingly ravaged, occupied or besieged nearly every town in mainland Estonia and the eastern half of Latvia. Estonia lost nearly two-thirds of its popula-

Ivan the Terrible

tion during this and subsequent wars which lasted until 1629.

The Livonian Order, unable to resist the Russian invasion, disbanded. Its territories either sought the protection of neighbouring powers or were battled over by them. Poland-Lithuania fought Russia for Livonia proper (eastern Latvia and southern Estonia), eventually triumphing in 1582 – but not before Ivan had taken, then been expelled from, areas of Lithuania itself. Sweden took 20 or so years to finally expel the Russians from northern Estonia, also acquiring west mainland Estonia and the island Hiiumaa in 1582. The last master of the Livonian Order made Courland (western Latvia) and Zemgale (central Latvia) his own personal duchy, owing allegiance to Poland. Even Denmark joined in, taking possession of some ex-church lands in Courland and west Estonia for a while; it held on longest to the island Saaremaa which was finally transferred to Sweden in 1645. Rīga was independent from 1561 to 1582 then autonomous under Polish rule.

Swedish Dominance The Russian menace dealt with for the time being, Protestant Sweden and Catholic Poland-Lithuania settled down in 1592 to fight each other in the Baltic lands. By 1629 Poland had been forced to hand over Rīga and most of Livonia (eastern Latvia and southern Estonia) to Sweden. The only piece of Livonia that stayed in Polish-Lithuanian hands was Latgale, the south-east, which is why Latgale is the stronghold of Catholicism in Latvia today. Sweden successfully defended its gains against Russia and Poland in a couple more wars in the 1650s.

Swedish rule, which consolidated Lutheran Protestantism in Estonia and most of Latvia, is looked back on fondly as it was a relatively enlightened episode in the two countries' long history of foreign oppression. The 17th century Swedish kings, Gustaf II Adolf (Gustavus Adolphus) and Carl (Charles) XI, tried to raise Estonian and Latvian peasants from serfdom and introduced universal elementary education, translated the Bible into Estonian and Latvian, and founded Dorpat (Tartu) University – but their efforts were severely hampered by the frequent wars, plagues and famines.

Russian Wars Meanwhile, conflict between Poland-Lithuania and Muscovy continued. Rzeczpospolita forces briefly took Moscow in 1610 and besieged it again in 1617; but in 1654 it was Russia's turn to invade the Rzeczpospolita and take significant territory from it.

Russia finally succeeded in reaching the Baltic shores under its westward-looking tsar, Peter the Great, in the Great Northern War (1700-1721), which destroyed Sweden as a regional power. Sweden surrendered its Baltic possessions – Estonia and central and north-east Latvia – to Russia at the Treaty of Nystad in 1721. The war was another period of devastation for Estonia and Latvia. At the end of it, according to one Russian general, neither bark of dog nor crow of cock could be heard anywhere from Narva to Rīga.

Prussian Revival In 1618 Prussia was joined through royal marriage to the power-

SWEDEN

Stockholm

Reval
(Tallinn)

ESTONIA

LIVONIA

Swedish &
Polish Control

0   150   300 km

Areas of Control
Mid-17th Century

Polish

Swedish

Mitau
(Jelgava)   Riga

COURLAND

Smolensk

Königsberg
(Kaliningrad)   Vilnius

PRUSSIA

LITHUANIA
(RZECZPOSPOLITA)

RUSSIA

Warsaw

POLAND
(RZECZPOSPOLITA)   Kiev

Kraków

ful north-German state of Brandenburg, centred on Berlin. In 1660 Brandenburg purchased suzerainty over Prussia from Poland, and in 1701 the elector of Brandenburg was crowned as the first Prussian king at Königsberg. In the 18th century the Prussia-Brandenburg axis became a major European power, with a military and bureaucratic bent, under Frederick the Great; and cracks appeared in the Polish-Lithuanian Rzeczpospolita, where various factions called in Russian help from time to time.

Partitions of Poland Finally the Rzeczpos-

polita was so weakened that Russia, Austria and Prussia (as the Prussia-Brandenburg state was called) simply carved it up in the Partitions of Poland (1772, 1793 and 1795-96). Most of Lithuania, along with the Polish-Lithuanian possessions Latgale and Courland, went to Russia. A small chunk of western Lithuania went to Prussia, which now stretched uninterruptedly across northern Poland from its original core around Königsberg to its Brandenburg territories.

The 19th Century
National Revivals Russian rule brought

privileges for the Baltic-German ruling class in Estonia and Latvia but greater exploitation for the peasants. Finally the Estonian and Latvian peasants were freed, between 1811 and 1819, and permitted to move freely and own land from the mid-19th century. In Lithuania, which got involved in the Polish rebellion against Russian rule in 1830-31, the peasants were not freed till 1861, the same year as the rest of Russia. Lithuania was also involved in a second Polish rebellion against Russia in 1863. Later, tens of thousands of Lithuanians, and fewer Latvians and Estonians, migrated to the Americas.

The liberation of the serfs enabled the Baltic national revivals of the second half of the 19th century and early 20th century by allowing the native peoples to move into trades, professions, commerce and intellectual circles. In the north the revivals focused particularly around educated Estonians and Latvians at Dorpat (Tartu) University; Vilnius University had been shut down in 1832. Slowly the three native Baltic peoples crawled out from under the doormat of history. They began to express their cultures and senses of nationality; to teach, learn and publish in their own languages; to hold their own song festivals and stage their own plays. Railways were built from Russia to the Baltic ports. Rīga had become an important international port with over 500,000 people by 1914. It also grew, like Tallinn and Narva, into an industrial centre. In Estonia and Latvia there was almost total literacy by 1900.

Russification The national movements were strengthened, if anything, by the unpopular policy of Russification which was followed by the Russian authorities, especially towards the end of the century. Estonia, Livonia and Courland were governed as separate provinces, but Lithuania, after the rebellions, was treated as part of Russia itself. Russian law was imposed on the region (as early as 1840 in Lithuania) and the Russian language was used for teaching. Catholicism was persecuted in Latvia and

Lithuania. From 1864 books could only be published in Lithuanian if they used the Russian alphabet, while books, newspapers or periodicals in Polish (which was spoken by the Lithuanian gentry) were banned altogether. Lithuanian publishing continued among Lithuanians living in eastern Prussia (including the first newspaper in Lithuanian) and was smuggled into Lithuania.

Meanwhile in Prussia By the late 19th century the Prussian state formed the basis of a united Germany which stretched, uninterrupted, from the border of France to that of the Russian empire. The Prussian king Wilhelm I, crowned in Königsberg in 1861, was proclaimed the first kaiser (emperor) of this new empire, in Versailles in 1871 – thanks to his aggressive chancellor (prime minister) Otto von Bismarck.

Independence
Effects of Russian Revolutions Ideas of Baltic national autonomy and independence were first seriously voiced during the 1905 Russian revolution. When Estonian and Latvian revolutionaries started burning manor houses, there were harsh reprisals with about 1000 people being shot.

During WW I, Germany occupied Lithuania and western Latvia in 1915 but didn't reach Rīga, eastern Latvia or Estonia until late 1917 or early 1918. Baltic nationalists initially hoped the war would bring their nations some kind of improved status within Russia; only with Russia's February Revolution in 1917, which overthrew the tsar, did the idea of full independence really take off. But there were wars and some complicated comings and goings to negotiate first.

In March 1917 Russia passed a bill for Estonian self-government and the first Estonian parliament, the Diet Maapäev, met in July in Toompea Castle, Tallinn. Following the October Revolution in Russia, a communist administration was set up for Estonia, but when the German forces reached mainland Estonia in February 1918, the communists fled. On 24 February the Diet Maapäev declared Estonian independence. Next day, however, the Germans occupied Tallinn. In Lithuania, under German occupation, a Lithuanian national council, the Taryba, had declared independence on 16 February.

In March 1918 Russia's new communist government, desperate to get out of the war, abandoned the Baltic region to Germany in the Treaty of Brest-Litovsk.

Baltic Independence Wars On 11 November 1918 Germany surrendered to the Western allies. The same day, a Lithuanian republican government was set up. In Latvia, peasant, middle class and socialist groups declared independence on 18 November and the leader of the Farmers' Party, Kārlis Ulmanis, formed a government. The Estonian independence declaration of February was repeated in November. Soviet Russia now launched a military and political campaign to win back the Baltic states, but this was eventually defeated by both local opposition and outside military intervention – in Estonia's case a British fleet and volunteer fighters from Scandinavia and Finland. Estonia's prime minister, Konstantin Päts, was able to declare Estonia free of enemies in February 1919.

In Latvia, fighting continued until 1920

between nationalists, Bolsheviks, and lingering German occupation forces and Baltic Germans under the anticommunist General von der Goltz, who still hoped to bring the Baltic region back under German sway. The Ulmanis government had a communist rival in Valmiera headed by Pēteris Stučka. The Red Army took Rīga in January 1919 and the Ulmanis government moved to Liepāja, where it received British naval protection. In May, von der Goltz drove the Red Army from Rīga but he was then defeated at Cēsis by Estonian and Latvian troops, who also drove the Red Army from most of the rest of Latvia. Ulmanis returned to Rīga only to have another army attack the city in November 1919, this time of anticommunist Russians and Germans organised by von der Goltz and led by an obscure adventurer called Pavel Bermondt-Avalov. The Latvians, however, defeated it, and in December the last German troops left Latvia. The last communist-held area, Latgale, also fell to Latvia.

In Lithuania, things were complicated by the re-emergence of an independent Poland which wanted Lithuania either to reunite with it or to cede it the Vilnius area, which had a heavily Polish or Polonised population. The Red Army installed a communist government in Vilnius in January 1919 but was driven out of Lithuania by August. But it was Polish troops who took Vilnius, and Poland kept Vilnius – apart from three months in 1920 – right through till 1939. The 'Vilnius issue' was a constant source of interwar Lithuanian-Polish tension. Independent Lithuania's capital was Kaunas. German forces finally left Lithuania in December 1919.

In 1920 Soviet Russia signed peace treaties with the parliamentary republics of Estonia, Latvia and Lithuania recognising their independence in perpetuity.

The Independence Years The gentry's estates in the new Baltic states were redistributed to the peasants as small farms (the redistribution was less radical in Lithuania than in the two formerly German-dominated

Konstantin Päts

countries). The three new democracies made surprising economic progress despite war damage and the collapse of their traditional trade with Russia (Latvia for instance had lost about 40% of its population through death or emigration, factories had been evacuated to Russia, and trade through Rīga in 1926 was only one-tenth of what it had been in 1913). Britain and Germany were their main export markets. But come the world slump, they began to struggle politically in the face of the rise of fascism and fears of the communist USSR. The authoritarian regimes which emerged, however, were pretty mild as authoritarian regimes go, and the inter-war period is regarded with great fondness by most Estonians, Latvians and Lithuanians. It was still an agrarian age, with industry much less important than today, and big strides were made in education and culture.

In Estonia the anticommunist, anti-parliamentary 'vaps' movement easily won a constitutional referendum in 1933 but was outflanked in a bloodless coup by prime minister Päts, who took over as a fairly moderate and benevolent dictator. In Latvia from 1934, Ulmanis headed a nonparliamentary government of unity which tried to steer between the strong Nazi extreme and the left. Lithuania suffered a military coup in 1926 and from 1929 was ruled by Antanas Smetona along similar lines to Mussolini's Italy.

Meanwhile in Prussia (Again)

In the wash-up of WW I, Danzig (Gdańsk) became a free state while Poland gained a narrow corridor of land through to the coast between Gdańsk and Germany. This meant that East Prussia, as the original Prussian lands focused on Königsberg were now known, was cut off from the rest of Germany, though remaining German territory. Hitler's desire to reunite East Prussia with Germany was one of the sparks that lit WW II.

Memel (Klaipėda), an 'international territory' after WW I, was seized by Lithuania in 1923 and then by Germany in 1939 in Hitler's last land grab before WW II.

WW II & Soviet Rule

Soviet Occupation

On 23 August 1939, Nazi Germany and the USSR signed the Molotov-Ribbentrop non-aggression pact which also secretly divided Eastern Europe into German and Soviet spheres of influence. Estonia and Latvia were put in the Soviet sphere and Lithuania in the Nazi one. When Lithuania refused to join the Nazi attack on Poland in September 1939, it was transferred to the Soviet sphere. The USSR insisted on 'mutual-assistance pacts' with the Baltic states, gaining the right to station troops on their territory. Lithuania's pact regained it Vilnius in October 1939 (the Red Army had taken the city in its invasion of eastern Poland at the same time as Germany had invaded western Poland).

Those Baltic Germans who hadn't left for Germany during the 1920s land reforms departed in 1939 or 1940 in response to Hitler's *Heim ins Reich* (Home to the Reich) summons. By August 1940 Estonia, Latvia and Lithuania had been placed under Soviet military occupation, communists had won 'elections', and the three states had been 'accepted' as republics of the USSR.

The Soviet authorities began nationalisation and purges. Within a year or so of their takeover, according to various estimates, Estonia lost somewhere between 11,000 and 60,000 people killed, deported or fled; Lithuania about 45,000; and Latvia about 35,000. Many of the deportees were children or elderly. Many went in mass deportations to Siberia, beginning on 14 June 1941.

Nazi Occupation

When Hitler invaded the USSR and occupied the Baltic states in 1941, many in the Baltics initially saw the Germans as liberators. The Nazi-occupied Baltic states were governed together with Belarus as a territory called Ostland, which was eventually supposed to become part of the German Reich. Some local people collaborated to varying degrees with the Nazi occupation and a few joined in the slaughter of the Jews – gaining a reputation for cruelty at least as bad as that of their German masters. Nearly all Lithuania's Jewish population – between 135,000 and 300,000 people according to varying estimates – were killed in camps or ghettos. Latvia's Jewish population of perhaps 90,000 was virtually wiped out. An estimated 5000 Jews were killed in Estonia. Thousands of other local people, and Jews and others brought from elsewhere, were killed in the Baltic states by the Nazis.

An estimated 140,000 Latvians, 45,000 Lithuanians and 50,000 Estonians were enlisted in German military units – some voluntarily, some conscripted. Other people were conscripted for forced labour. There was also nationalist and communist guerrilla resistance against the Nazis. Somewhere between 65,000 and 120,000 Estonians and about 70,000 Estonians and 80,000 Lithuanians, succeeded in escaping to the West in 1944 and 1945 to avoid the Red Army's reconquest of the Baltic states. Many others were captured on the way and sent to Siberia. Altogether, Estonia lost something like 200,000 people during the war. Latvia lost 450,000 and Lithuania, 475,000.

Soviet Reoccupation The Red Army reconquered the whole of the Baltic states except Courland (which was still in German hands when Germany surrendered in May 1945) by the end of 1944. Cities such as Narva and Tallinn were badly damaged by the advancing Soviet forces. The battle for East Prussia in 1944-45 was one of the fiercest of WW II, with hundreds of thousands of casualties on both sides. Königsberg was nearly flattened by British air raids in 1944 and by the Red Army's final assault from 6 to 9 April 1945. Many of the surviving Germans were sent to Siberia: the last 25,000 were deported to Germany in 1947 and 1948. Königsberg was renamed Kaliningrad after a sidekick of Stalin and rebuilt and repeopled mostly by Russians. Since WW II, the northern half of East Prussia has formed Russia's Kaliningrad Region and the southern half has been in Poland.

Soviet Rule Between 1944 and 1952, with Stalinism re-established in the Baltic states,

agriculture was collectivised. Around a further 60,000 Estonians, 175,000 Latvians and 250,000 Lithuanians were killed or deported between 1945 and 1949, many of them in March 1949 during the collectivisation. Thousands of partisans known as 'forest brothers' put up some armed resistance to Soviet rule. They were effectively crushed by 1952 or 1953, but the last forest brother, an Estonian called August Sabe, wasn't cornered by the KGB until 1978. He drowned swimming across a lake trying to escape.

With post-war industrialisation, the Baltic republics received such an influx of migrant workers, mainly from nearby regions of Russia, Belarus and Ukraine, that the native Estonians and Latvians feared they would become minorities in their own countries. This further increased the Baltic dislike of Soviet rule. Resentment also grew over issues like the allocation of housing and top jobs. Industrialisation shifted the population balance from the countryside, on which the Baltic economies had been based before WW II, to the towns. Many of the new industries were technologically advanced by

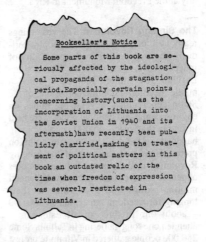

Bookseller's Notice

Some parts of this book are seriously affected by the ideological propaganda of the stagnation period. Especially certain points concerning history (such as the incorporation of Lithuania into the Soviet Union in 1940 and its aftermath) have recently been publicly clarified, making the treatment of political matters in this book an outdated relic of the times when freedom of expression was severely restricted in Lithuania.

Lithuanian bookseller's notice found in a book published during the Brezhnev era

Soviet standards and helped bring the Baltic states high living standards in Soviet terms but also brought environmental problems. In the Soviet era the Baltics also attracted people from other parts of the USSR with their supposedly 'Western' atmosphere and their relative tolerance for the arts. Religion was repressed and discouraged. Tourism was restricted.

Towards New Independence
First Steps In 1972 there were anti-Soviet riots in Kaunas after a student, Romas Kalanta, burnt himself to death in protest at Soviet rule. In 1980 fans of the Estonian punk band Propeller went on a rampage through Tallinn, shouting anti-Russian slogans after a concert had been called off halfway through. When Mikhail Gorbachev encouraged *glasnost* (openness) in the USSR in the mid-80s, pent-up bitterness in the Baltic republics came into the open and national feelings surged. The floods of emotion which were released swelled fast into tides for independence. One of the first significant public protests was on 14 June 1987 when about 5000 people rallied illegally at the Freedom Monument in Rīga.

The Singing Revolution The year things really took off, and the Baltic peoples seriously began to believe in the possibility of independence, was 1988. In March some Latvian government members joined a public meeting to commemorate one of the Stalin deportations. Several big rallies on environmental and national issues were held in Latvia that year – 45,000 people joining hands along the coast in one anti-pollution protest. This was the year of the Singing Revolution in Estonia, when huge numbers of people gathered to sing previously banned national songs and give voice to their longing for freedom. An estimated 300,000 – about one in three of all Estonians – attended one song gathering in Tallinn. Some 250,000 people gathered in Vilnius to protest on the anniversary of the Molotov-Ribbentrop Pact, 23 August.

Political Steps Popular fronts, formed in each republic to press for democratic reform, won huge followings. The local communist parties joined them in virtual alliance. Estonia's Popular Front, claiming 300,000 members, called for Estonian autonomy, democracy, and cuts in immigration at its first congress in October 1988. All three republics paid lip service to Gorbachev's new watchword, *perestroika* (restructuring), while actually dismantling Soviet institutions. In November 1988 Estonia's supreme soviet passed a declaration of sovereignty, announcing that USSR laws would apply in Estonia only if it approved them.

Lithuania came to lead the Baltic push for independence after candidates supporting its popular front, Sajūdis (The Movement), won 30 of the 42 Lithuanian seats in the March 1989 elections for the USSR Congress of People's Deputies.

On 23 August 1989, the 50th anniversary of the Molotov-Ribbentrop Pact, some two million people formed a human chain stretching from Tallinn to Vilnius, many of them calling for secession. In November Moscow granted the Baltic republics economic autonomy. In December the Lithuanian Communist Party left the Communist Party of the Soviet Union – a bold, pioneering act which was one of the most dramatic landmarks in the break-up of the USSR. Lithuania also became the first Soviet republic to legalise non-communist parties. Estonia and Latvia soon followed suit.

Lithuania Declares Independence Vast pro-independence crowds met Gorbachev when he visited Vilnius in January 1990. He could do nothing to dissuade Lithuania from its clear course towards independence. Sajūdis won a majority in the elections to Lithuania's supreme soviet in February, and on 11 March this assembly declared Lithuania an independent republic and stated that its 16 February 1918 constitution had never lost validity.

In response, Moscow carried out weeks of intimidatory troop manoeuvres around Vilnius, then clamped an economic blockade on Lithuania, cutting off fuel supplies. The pressure was finally removed after 2½ months, when Lithuania's gnomish music-professor-turned-president and Sajūdis leader, Vytautas Landsbergis, agreed to a 100-day moratorium on the independence declaration in exchange for independence talks between the Lithuanian and USSR governments. No foreign country had yet recognised Lithuanian independence.

Vytautas Landsbergis

Estonia and Latvia followed similar paths, but more cautiously. In spring 1990 nationalists were elected to big majorities in their supreme soviets (or parliaments) and reinstated their pre-WW II constitutions, but declared 'transition periods' for full independence to be negotiated. Estonia led the way towards a market economy by abolishing subsidies on some important everyday goods. But the momentum for independence flagged as the Baltic republics' economic reliance on the Soviet Union became clearer; Lithuania's talks with Moscow bogged down, and Soviet hardliners gained the ascendancy in Moscow in winter 1990-91.

The Events of 1991 In January 1991 Soviet troops and paramilitary police occupied and stormed strategic buildings in Vilnius and Rīga in apparent bids to pave the way for communist coups and Soviet crackdowns.

Thirteen people were killed in the storming of the Vilnius TV tower and TV centre, five in the storming of the Interior Ministry in Rīga, and hundreds were hurt. The parliaments in both cities were barricaded; the people stayed calm; the violence drew Western condemnation of Moscow; and the immediate threat subsided.

In referendums in February and March 1991, big majorities in all three states voted in favour of secession from the USSR. However the West, not wanting to weaken Gorbachev further, gave only lukewarm support to the Baltic independence movements.

Everything changed with the 19 August 1991 coup attempt against Gorbachev in Moscow. Estonia declared full independence on 20 August and Latvia on 21 August (Lithuania had done so back in March 1990). The Western world recognised their independence and so, finally, did the USSR on 6 September 1991.

Independence Again

On 17 September 1991 the three Baltic states joined the United Nations. Also that year they started issuing their own postage stamps. In 1992 they competed independently in the Olympic Games for the first time since before WW II (Romas Ubartas of Lithuania won a discus gold and Erika Salumäe of Estonia won a sprint cycling gold, but the greatest emotions were aroused by Lithuania beating the CIS in the basketball bronze medal play-off). In 1992 Estonia introduced its own currency to replace the Russian rouble. Latvia and Lithuania followed suit in 1993. The Pope visited all three states in September 1993. Such landmarks apart, the Baltics dropped out of the world's headlines except for coverage of their elections and strained ethnic relations.

With independence won, the states now had to get on with the more mundane job of making it work. Political leaders came and went as movements and parties splintered into factions. Life for ordinary people got tougher and tougher as the feeble condition of the Baltic economies made itself felt.

Living standards and morale slumped, but few wanted to return to Soviet times.

Estonia moved with greatest consistency towards free-market economics and a Western orientation and by 1993 was not far from an economic upswing. Latvia, too, was starting to pull through towards the light at the end of the economic tunnel. Lithuania seemed to be afflicted by more governmental muddle and hesitation than the other two countries. Not that everyone was unreservedly wild about capitalism – some people worried that the quest for the dollar would erode other values, and in any case most people couldn't afford many of the goodies capitalism offered.

All three countries set up new electoral systems and held general elections in 1992 or 1993. In Estonia and Latvia the vote in these first elections was denied to the large numbers of post-WW II immigrants from the USSR and their descendants because they were being made to wait for citizenship. One condition of citizenship was some knowledge of the Estonian or Latvian language which, in Estonia, looked likely to deter many Russians. Happily, despite the stresses and strains of ethnic relations, everyone seemed to agree that getting violent about the issue wouldn't help. (See the Government sections in the Facts about the Country chapters for more on this topic.)

In 1992 Estonia's voters chose the conservative Fatherland party led by a young historian, Mart Laar, with nationalist, anti-communist and free-market policies that were clear enough but more moderate than those of some of its rivals. In Latvia the moderately nationalist Latvian Way party, also committed to free-market economics, came out on top in the 1993 elections.

Lithuania provided the most dramatic reversal of fortunes. Vytautas Landsbergis, who had led the country to independence, was unable to inspire it with an equal sense of direction once that goal was achieved. By summer 1992 the Lithuanian parliament was divided into many small factions, some of which refused to attend sessions – which rendered parliament inquorate and therefore

unable to pass any laws. In one particularly absurd episode a prime minister named Gediminas Vagnorius was prevented from resigning because there weren't enough members present to vote on whether to accept his resignation! The more impressive former Sajūdis prime minister Kazimiera Prunskiene was found guilty in September 1992 of having consciously cooperated with the KGB.

In autumn 1992 the Lithuanian Democratic Labour Party (LDDP), the reformed pro-independence wing of the old Lithuanian Communist Party, was voted into power. The voters were fed up with squabbling politicians who couldn't even manage to switch on the country's heating and hot water for election time. They opted instead for people with some experience of practical government, in particular the popular LDDP leader Algirdas Brazauskas who, as leader of the Communist Party from 1988, had taken several big strides along the independence road before being dumped in favour of Sajūdis in the 1990 elections. Brazauskas went on to be elected president in early 1993. After a year in power his party, while enjoying a better relationship with Russia and pursuing a slower path towards market economics than the Latvian and Estonian governments, still looked the European-style social-democratic party that it professed to be, rather than the communist wolves in democrats' clothing that its opponents made it out to be. In May 1993 Lithuania and Estonia became the first ex-Soviet states to be admitted to the Council of Europe, a broadly based organisation promoting human rights, democracy and European integration. EC membership for all three Baltic states was the goal on the horizon.

The post-independence political fragmentation within each of the three countries was mirrored to some extent in their relations with each other. Whereas the shared goal of independence had tended to draw them together, after it was won their differences came more to the fore. There were differences over issues like economics and border controls, and the three states found themselves competing for some of the same foreign investment and aid. Baltic émigré communities in the West were an important source of investment for all three states, and influenced politics too. Germany took an active economic interest in all three countries, while Estonia also developed its links with Finland and Sweden, and Latvia looked to Sweden and Denmark. The quarrelsome Lithuanian-Polish relationship took up where it had left off in 1939 and Lithuania made more effort than Estonia and Latvia in its relationships with the CIS states, while also maintaining a Western orientation. Trade and other forms of cooperation between the three Baltic states, however, remained relatively minor.

The Baltic states set up their own armed forces and police but experienced problems with organised crime which, unlike the governments, still operated on a USSR-wide basis. With their porous borders the Baltics became conduits for drugs, illegal arms and other smuggling. Russian troops still stationed in the Baltic states after Baltic independence were not totally innocent in all this. While Russia had pulled all its troops out of Lithuania by the end of August 1993, in Estonia and Latvia it saw the troops issue as a way of putting pressure on the local governments over rights for their Russian populations. In autumn 1993 there were still about 16,000 Russian troops in Latvia and about 6000 in Estonia – far less than Soviet-era numbers but still enough to upset locals who continued to regard them as an occupation army.

And in Kaliningrad The Kaliningrad Region, with its military importance, remained closed to the outside world until 1991 when 50,000 German visitors flooded in during its first 'open' year. The region remains part of Russia but after the break-up of the USSR declared itself a free-trade zone.

GEOGRAPHY

It's tempting to sum up the geography of the Baltic states in two words: 'small' and 'flat'. From the northernmost point of Estonia to the southern tip of Lithuania is only 650 km – less than the length of England – and even at the snail's pace of the local trains you can traverse all three countries in well under a day. As for altitude, nowhere does the land rise much above 300 metres and in parts of Latvia it's even below sea level. The Baltic peoples do make quite a lot of their 'uplands', however, even though you may hardly notice as you travel across them.

The coastal regions are generally the lowest-lying. The whole of west Estonia, most of the Zemgale region of central Latvia, and most of the Kaliningrad Region are below 50 metres. Lithuania has a wide central lowland belt, running from north to south and up to 80 km across. The low-lying regions are generally the most fertile. However there's more of geographical interest than these basic facts suggest. The coasts vary from cliff to dune to low-lying marshy margins. The inland landscape is gently rolling as a result of deposits left behind on the bedrock of the North European Plain by the glaciers which covered the region before about 12,000 BC. And the region is crossed by many rivers, some of which have cut surprisingly deep valleys, and is dotted with thousands of lakes and a range of vegetation.

Estonia is the northernmost of the three Baltic states and is also the smallest, covering 45,200 sq km (slightly bigger than Switzerland or Denmark). Estonia borders Russia in the east and Latvia in the south. Its capital is Tallinn, on the north coast, just 80 km from Helsinki across the Gulf of Finland. Nearly 10% of Estonian territory is islands, the biggest of which are Saaremaa and Hiiumaa in the west.

Latvia, the middle Baltic state, is 63,700 sq km in area, a little smaller than the Irish Republic; it is much wider from east to west than from north to south. Latvia borders Estonia in the north, Russia and Belarus in the east, and Lithuania in the south. Its capital is Rīga on the Daugava River, just inland from the Gulf of Rīga. Latvia has four main regions: Vidzeme, the north-east; Latgale, the south-east; Zemgale, the centre; and Kurzeme, the west.

Lithuania is the southernmost Baltic state and, at 65,200 sq km, the biggest. It borders Latvia in the north, Belarus in the south-east and Poland and the Kaliningrad Region in the south. Its capital, Vilnius, lies in the south-east of the country. Its four main regions are: Aukštaitija (Upper Lithuania), the east; Žemaitija (Lower Lithuania), the west; Dzūkija, the south; and Suvalkija or Sūduva, the south-west.

In the south-west of the region, wedged between Lithuania and Poland, is the Kaliningrad Region which is an *oblast* (region) of Russia totally disconnected from the rest of Russia. It is 15,100 sq km in area and its capital is Kaliningrad which stands on the Pregolya River, just inland of the Kaliningrad Lagoon.

The Baltic states and the Kaliningrad Region between them have about 5000 km of coastline, the majority of it (3794 km) being around the indented fringes of Estonia's mainland and islands. Some stretches of coast are low-lying, reedy and wet – the kind of place where it's hard to tell where land ends and sea begins. There are also lengths of cliff or steep bank, over 50 metres high in parts, and long stretches of dunes often fronted by sweeping, sandy beaches and covered with pine woods. These create a really refreshing fragrance in combination with the salty sea air.

Little of this coast faces the open Baltic Sea, as much of it fronts the gulfs of Finland and Rīga or is protected from the open sea by islands. The most extraordinary feature of the coastline is the Courland Spit (Lithuanian: Neringa; Russian: Kurshskaya kosa) – a sandbar 98 km long and up to 66 metres high, but nowhere more than four km wide.

One thing the Baltic states don't lack is lakes. There are around 9000 of them according to some counts, though the distinction between a lake and a pond must be hard to make in some cases! Most of the lakes are small and shallow, and Latvia and Lithuania have the greatest numbers, especially in their south-east and north-east uplands respectively. Estonia has the biggest lakes: Lake Peipus and Võrtsjärv.

Lots of rivers wind their way across the land. The two biggest, both flowing in from Belarus, are the Daugava, which crosses Latvia from the south-east to enter the sea near Rīga, and the Nemunas, which crosses south-west Lithuania then forms the Lithuania-Kaliningrad border for its final 100 km or so to the Courland Lagoon. Other major rivers include the Narva flowing north from Lake Peipus to the Gulf of Finland and forming the Estonia-Russia border; the Gauja looping 440 km entirely within eastern Latvia; the 350-km Venta, rising in Lithuania and entering the sea in western Latvia; and the Pregolya which collects most of the waters of the Kaliningrad Region and enters the Kaliningrad Lagoon just west of Kaliningrad city.

Not surprisingly in such a low-lying region, there are a lot of bogs, swamps, fens and marshes. These occupy as much as one-fifth of Estonia and one-tenth of Latvia, though you see little of them as you travel those countries' roads. They're a useful resource for their peat.

CLIMATE

The Baltic states' climate is temperate, but on the cool and damp side of temperate. It verges on the continental as you move towards the inland extremities where, in winter, it's typically 2°C to 4°C colder than on the coasts but in summer may be a degree or two warmer. According to the statistics there's hardly any north-south temperature variation, but certainly the warmest weather I've experienced in the region was in Kaliningrad – so warm that one Saturday morning, seemingly by the wave of a bureaucrat's magic wand, crate upon crate of beer appeared for sale on the streets to keep everyone cool – and by evening the whole city was afloat on a sea of alcoholic happiness.

From May to September, the best time to visit (see When To Go in the Facts for the Visitor chapter), daytime highs throughout the region are normally between 14°C and 22°C. It's unusually warm if the temperature reaches the high 20s (°C). July and August, the warmest months, are also wet, with days

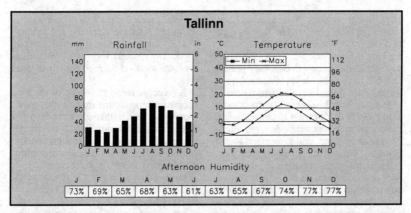

Tallinn

	J	F	M	A	M	J	J	A	S	O	N	D
Afternoon Humidity	73%	69%	65%	68%	63%	61%	63%	65%	67%	74%	77%	77%

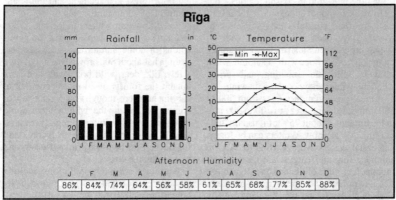

Rīga

	J	F	M	A	M	J	J	A	S	O	N	D
Afternoon Humidity	86%	84%	74%	64%	56%	58%	61%	65%	68%	77%	85%	88%

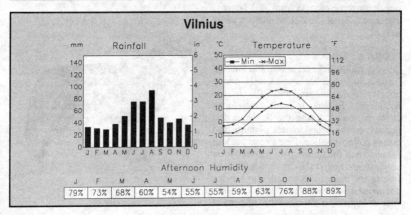

Vilnius

	J	F	M	A	M	J	J	A	S	O	N	D
Afternoon Humidity	79%	73%	68%	60%	54%	55%	55%	59%	63%	76%	88%	89%

of persistent showers. May, June and September are more comfortable. Late June can be thundery. At these northern latitudes days are long in summer, with a full 19 hours of daylight at midsummer in Estonia. April and October have cold, sharp, wintery days as well as mild springlike or autumnal ones.

In winter – November to March – temperatures rarely rise above 4°C and in parts of the region may stay below freezing almost permanently from mid-December to late February. Winter hours of daylight are short, and sometimes it never seems to get properly light at all. The first snows usually come in November, and there's normally permanent snow cover from some time in January to some time in March in coastal regions – but up to an extra month either side in the inland east. In some coastal areas, some recent winters have been much milder, with no lasting snow cover. Slush underfoot is something you have to cope with in autumn, when snow is falling then melting, and spring, when the winter snow cover is thawing.

Annual precipitation ranges from 500 to 600 mm in lowland areas to 700 to 900 mm in the uplands. About 75% of it usually falls as rain, 25% as snow. Winters can be foggy.

Coastal waters average 16°C to 21°C in summer: July and August are the warmest months. The gulfs of Finland and Rīga freeze occasionally, and the straits between Estonia's islands and the mainland usually freeze for three months from mid-January. The open Baltic Sea coast almost never freezes.

FLORA & FAUNA
Large portions of the region are still forested – about 40% of Estonia and Latvia, over a quarter of Lithuania, and 20% of the Kaliningrad Region. In some areas forest cover increased during the Soviet period because of the abandonment of farm land during collectivisation. Pine forests account for up to half the forest cover and tend to be concentrated nearer the coasts, while inland forests are more often mixed. Birch is the commonest deciduous tree. Juniper, a bushy type of cypress, is characteristic of parts of

Estonia, especially the islands and western mainland. Northern Kurzeme and northern Vidzeme are the most forested parts of Latvia. In Lithuania, the south – particularly the south-west – is the most densely forested area.

A favourite forest recreation of the local people is gathering the many edible mushrooms and berries that grow there in late summer and autumn. You'll see people returning laden with these from the countryside on weekend buses and trains and selling them in markets and on street corners.

Western coastal regions tend to have the greatest range of wild flowers because of their milder climate.

Loose forest management and the abandonment of some farm lands in the Soviet period, and warm winters in the late 1980s and early '90s have helped boost the populations of some animal and plant species. Estonia has about 800 brown bear and Latvia a few. Elk, deer, wild boar, wolf and lynx inhabit the forests of all three countries in varying numbers, though you're not likely to bump into any in the wild without some guidance. All are hunted legally though usually in limited numbers. In Estonia and Latvia there are beavers on inland waters and seals along the coasts.

Estonia's animal populations include 40,000 deer (of which 10,000 are shot by hunters annually), 400 wolves (also culled),

Wolf

Wild Boar

800 lynx, 2500 beavers, 10,000 wild boar (5000 shot a year) and several thousand elk.

Some of Estonia's islands and coastal wetlands and Lake Žuvintas in southern Lithuania are important breeding grounds and migration halts for water birds.

One species you're likely to encounter anywhere in summer is the mosquito.

NATIONAL PARKS & RESERVES

Each of the three Baltic states has one national park established in the 1970s, and Lithuania has four others designated more recently. There are also many nature reserves of varying degrees of strictness.

The national parks protect areas of natural, historical, architectural and archaeological importance. Some parts of them are strict reserves, off limits to everyone except a few specialists, but recreation is encouraged in other sectors. All are partly inhabited and can be reached by public transport. They have accommodation possibilities either within their territory and on their fringes. The nature reserves tend to be more remote and harder to reach, but still worth getting to if you're interested. Some have organised visitor facilities. There's detailed information on individual national parks and nature reserves in the relevant Facts about the Country chapters, and in the regional chapters.

ENVIRONMENT

Most problems of the Baltic environment stem from irresponsible management in the Soviet period, but the now-free states cannot immediately afford to upgrade or replace polluting factories and industries. Estonia put a stop to exploitation of its large phosphorite reserves; but the continued mining of oil shale in its north-east and its use in the production of electricity at thermal power plants in Narva causes great air and water pollution. Also in north-east Estonia there's radioactive pollution from wastes dumped on the coast of the Gulf of Finland at the Sillamäe Soviet military nuclear plant.

Life expectancy in the Baltic states is lower – and infant mortality higher – than European norms, and there are several cases of particular diseases cropping up with unusual frequency near particular factories. Two notorious black spots in Lithuania are the cement works at Akmenė and the fertiliser plant at Jonava – where a big escape of ammonia into the atmosphere killed seven people in 1989.

Though the Baltic Sea as a whole is gradually getting cleaner, virtually all the Baltic states' coastal waters are polluted – partly by chemical pollution washing out from rivers and partly by untreated sewage pumped straight into rivers or the sea. The biggest city in the region, Rīga, lacked any kind of modern sewerage system until 1991. Today Rīga has a treatment plant but it can only handle less than half the city's sewage. The rest still goes straight into the Daugava River only 15 km from its mouth – which is just a few km from Latvia's major coastal resort, Jūrmala. Jūrmala is also blighted by chemical wastes carried down the rivers from the town of Olaine, about 25 km to its south. Tap water in many parts of the Baltic states – including Rīga – should be boiled before being drunk.

Many rivers and ground waters are polluted not just by industrial wastes but also by run-off of fertilisers and pesticides. These were used too freely under the Soviet policy of collectivisation, which concentrated agriculture on smaller (and consequently over-worked) areas of each country's soil. Agriculture is now gradually returning to private ownership and smaller farms.

Lead-free petrol is virtually non-existent in the Baltic states and the motor engine is a major polluter as you can tell from a walk along any semi-busy city street.

The Ignalina nuclear power plant in Lithuania has reactors of the same type as Chernobyl, but so dependent is the country on its electricity that, far from closing it down, there's talk of adding a new reactor. Other types of power plant in the Baltics tend to be dirty, wasteful and expensive. Soviet-built heating and water supply systems are also inefficient.

GOVERNMENT

The three Baltic states are independent republics. Until 1990, as parts of the USSR, they were governed by soviets (councils) ranging in scope from district to city to republic to all-union – but always controlled by the Communist Party. The 1990 elections to the republic supreme soviets were held under reformed, more democratic conditions and in all three republics pro-independence groups won majorities. After independence in 1991, the three states moved to new political systems. In 1992 Estonia was the first to hold elections under its own system. It was followed later that year by Lithuania and by Latvia in June 1993.

The constitutional issue that has generated most steam is the terms on which the many Soviet-era immigrants from other parts of the USSR, and their descendants, are to be granted local citizenship – and therefore voting and other important rights. Lithuania has a more liberal policy on this than Estonia or Latvia, where most such immigrants were excluded from the first post-independence elections. There is more information on the government and citizenship requirements of each of the Baltic states in the relevant Facts about the Country chapters.

ECONOMY

The Baltic states had relatively high living standards in Soviet terms when they were in the USSR. They hope that independence will eventually bring them something like Western standards of living, but the transition from the centrally controlled Soviet economy to free-market capitalism has been proving exceedingly tough. Though a minority of people with skills, good contacts, entrepreneurial initiative, or criminal instincts are making money as never before, most people find their purchasing power falling rapidly. There is more in the shops (to the benefit of tourists) but local people can't afford to buy much of it. The winter of 1992-93 was probably the hardest economically since WW II. Hot-water supplies, for instance, were cut off much of the time in some areas, and central heating was kept at very low levels.

In 1992 the cost of living across the region multiplied by about 10 to 12 times (that's inflation of 900% to 1100%), while wages only doubled in Lithuania and quadrupled in Estonia and Latvia. This was the third or fourth year of such a decline in living standards. The average monthly wage in July 1993 was about US$80 in Estonia and Latvia and US$40 in Lithuania. By then Estonia and Latvia, with the help of stable currencies introduced the previous year, looked to have inflation under control but Lithuania was still struggling to slow the rise in prices.

Though there were differences of emphasis and speed, all three states followed broadly similar paths of economic restructuring – gradual privatisation of state-owned businesses, property and land; removal of state subsidies to industry, agriculture and consumers; and agreements on economic austerity with the International Monetary Fund and other world financial bodies to attract vital foreign loans and investment.

Before WW II, agriculture was at least as important as industry but during the Soviet era the Baltic states were turned into specialist makers of all sorts of industrial and technical products, receiving raw materials from other parts of the USSR and sending manufactured goods back. But by the time of independence, though their industries were often technically advanced in Soviet terms, they tended to be outdated and low-quality in world terms. And when the Soviet economy started collapsing and Baltic ties with the ex-USSR were disrupted, raw materials for many Baltic industries became more expensive or in short supply, or both. Plants in the Baltic states that had made single specialised products for large Soviet markets – eg sausages for the whole Leningrad region or bicycle chains for most of European Russia – suddenly found their markets had vanished. Such factories often employ largely Russian labour, which has added to the problems of the immigrant communities.

Other economic difficulties stem from the environmental hazards of some Soviet-era industries. In the 1980s, Estonia closed down its big phosphorite mines and rejected Moscow's plans for further development of its important electricity-producing oil shale fields in the north-east of the country for ecological reasons.

The Baltic states are short on natural resources, except for timber. Estonia and Latvia have useful reserves of peat in their bogs, and Estonia has its oil shale. Lithuania has an oil refinery and some small oil reserves. But virtually all oil and gas has to be imported, and the end of cheap fuel from Russia not only made petrol, diesel, water, electricity, heating, gas and virtually everything else dearer but also caused industrial and agricultural output to fall. By 1993, after about three years of swift decline, production in all three countries was down to the levels of 15 or 20 years earlier. It was expected to start growing again by 1994 in Estonia and Latvia and 1995 in Lithuania.

Registered unemployment was being held at relatively low levels – 20,000 to 40,000 people in each country in 1993 – but there were many more people, as many as 250,000 in Lithuania, on unpaid leave or shortened working weeks.

There was little regional unity on economic affairs, especially after the LDDP won power in Lithuania in 1992. Though the LDDP said it would keep Lithuania moving towards a market economy under its IMF-backed reform programme, it also wanted to continue subsidies to industry and agriculture. A free-trade agreement ending all import tariffs and most export tariffs on trade between the three Baltic states was signed in September 1993 and was seen as a big step forward. But intra-Baltic trade accounts for only a small percentage of each country's commerce. Agricultural exports to Belarus and Ukraine are important money-earners for Lithuania. Meanwhile, by late 1992, Finland had replaced Russia as Estonia's biggest trading partner. Estonia's main exports are timber, timber products, cotton textiles, dairy and farm products.

One of the brightest spots in the picture is tourism. Half a million Western visitors were expected in the Baltics in 1993 – albeit many of them Finns on shopping trips or other Scandinavians on brief cruise stops. Estonia seems particularly well attuned to the needs of Western visitors – and to the capitalist work ethic in general. It has pursued free-market goals with the greatest determination of any of the three states and, in 1993, a US-government adviser went so far as to describe it as an 'economic miracle'. Small service industries are playing a big part in this. There's an air of efficiency in Estonia which is rather lacking in Lithuania, where labyrinthine bureaucracy discourages some foreign investment. Latvia, as in so many things, seems to lie between the two extremes, but there's a tangible entrepreneurial atmosphere in Rīga – the former commercial powerhouse of the Baltics – which looks set to reclaim that title.

POPULATION & PEOPLE

According to the 1989 Soviet census, Estonia has 1.56 million people, Latvia 2.7 million and Lithuania 3.68 million. These figures have since dropped a little owing mainly to emigration of Russians to Russia. The Kaliningrad Region has about 900,000 people.

The bald population totals for the three

Baltic states conceal an inharmonious ethnic mix. In Estonia about 62% of the people are Estonian, 30% Russian and 3% Ukrainian. In Latvia 52% are Latvian, 34% Russian, 4.5% Belarussian and 3.5% Ukrainian. In Lithuania 80% are Lithuanian, about 9% Russian and 7% Polish. For more on what 'Estonian', 'Latvian' and 'Lithuanian' mean, see each state's Facts about the Country section. Other ethnic groups present in smaller numbers include Jews, Gypsies, Tatars, and Germans (in Lithuania), as well as nationalities of the ex-USSR. The population of the Kaliningrad Region is predominantly Russian.

Though there were quite a lot of Russians in the Baltic states before WW II (about 8% in Estonia, 10% in Latvia and 3% or 4% in Lithuania) their current numbers are chiefly a result of immigration during the Soviet period when many came to work in the new industries that were being set up in the Baltics. Before WW II two-thirds to three-quarters of the population of the Baltic states lived in the countryside; today only a quarter to one-third do.

Today the Russians' presence is the biggest social problem in the Baltic states, as their relations with the native Baltic peoples are strained – with the possible exception of Rīga where Russians have been established since the early 19th century. The Baltic peoples tend to see their Russian residents as colonists from an unwelcome imperial power, who rarely tried to integrate into local society or learn the local languages. Not surprisingly many of the Russians (though by no means all) were unenthusiastic about Baltic independence. Hard-line Baltic nationalists would no doubt like to see most of the Russians 'go home', even though many of them have lived all their lives in the Baltic states. What's actually happening is that most non-native residents in Estonia and Latvia are being required to learn the local language before they can become citizens of these states. Lithuanians, with a smaller Russian minority in their midst, do not have the understandable fear of being swamped that Estonians and Latvians feel, and

Lithuania's citizenship policy is more relaxed.

The Russians are typically working class and are mostly congregated in the main cities. They form about half the population of Tallinn, over half that of Rīga and one-fifth of that of Vilnius. The industrial towns of north-east Estonia are overwhelmingly Russian-populated. Latvians are a minority in all seven of Latvia's biggest cities.

Lost People

The history of the Baltic states in the 20th century is studded with groups of people who have disappeared. Emigration for straight economic reasons apart, war, Nazi and Soviet terror, and Soviet deportations have all caused horrifying drops in the countries' populations at various times. Estonia's population fell from 1.14 million in 1939 to 854,000 in 1945; Latvia's from 2.5 million in 1914 to 1.6 million in 1920; and Lithuania's from 3.1 million in 1940 to about 2.5 million in the mid-1950s.

In WW II the Nazis exterminated virtually all the Jews in the three states. Estimates vary, but they average around 200,000 to 300,000 Jews killed in Lithuania, 100,000 or so in Latvia, and fewer in Estonia.

The Baltic Germans, the upper class who had dominated Estonia and Latvia for centuries, left for Germany in the mid-1920s when they lost most of their lands in agrarian reforms and in 1939-40 when they were summoned 'home' by Hitler. They had numbered a few tens of thousands. Estonia lost virtually its whole Swedish population of about 8000 when they left for Sweden in 1943-44 under an agreement with the German occupiers.

Some 220,000 Poles, including most of the educated ones, left or were deported from Lithuania to Poland in 1945-58. Those 'Poles' who stayed in Lithuania were mostly Belarussian speakers living in rural areas with Polish Catholic churches – nearly all in the two south-eastern districts of Vilnius and Šalčininkai. They became the focus of controversy when their regional councils were accused of supporting the August 1991 coup

National Characteristics

It's always dangerous to generalise about 'national characters' but there *are* some clear general differences between Estonians, Latvians and Lithuanians.

Estonians and Lithuanians usually seem to be at the extremes, with Latvians somewhere in between. The stereotypical Estonian is reserved, efficient, short on praise, and polite. Lithuanians are stereotypically more gregarious, welcoming, and emotional – placing greater emphasis on contacts and favours than method and calculation.

Two episodes of recent history put the contrasts in a nutshell. One was the independence campaign of the late 1980s and early '90s. In Lithuania this was romantic, daring, cliff-hanging and risky, with at least 20 deaths. In Estonia it was cool, gradual, calculated and bloodless, leading to the unkind saying that 'Estonians would die for their freedom – to the last Lithuanian'. Latvia's path to independence lay, as usual, somewhere between the two extremes.

The other episode was the three countries' introduction of new currencies to replace the Russian rouble after they gained independence. Estonia brought in its *kroon* cleanly, efficiently and with minimum fuss over a single weekend in mid-1992. Latvia introduced its *lats* gradually in 1993 after an intermediate phase with a transitional currency called the Latvian rouble. Lithuania had to undergo two sets of transitional banknotes, a succession of postponements, and the sacking of the head of the national bank (amid reports that new banknotes had to be printed all over again because they were too easy to forge) before its *litas* finally appeared in June 1993.

But with a much smaller Russian minority in their midst than Latvia or Estonia and a grander history behind them, Lithuanians seem to have a greater confidence in their national identity. Some of them even think of Lithuania as a European bastion of the Roman Catholic faith. Such conservatism may explain why Lithuania is embracing capitalism more slowly than Estonia or Latvia.

Bureaucracy certainly seems its most Byzantine in Lithuania, and regulations, schedules and statistics at their vaguest. Latvians, in Rīga at least, have perhaps the best developed entrepreneurial sense of the three peoples and are the most at ease with foreigners – a legacy, maybe, of Rīga's commercial traditions.

Some people find the Estonian reserve frustrating. An invitation to an Estonian's home – unless you're a relative – is a rare treat. One Englishman living in Estonia told me his work colleagues felt they could never regard him as a real friend because they knew that sooner or later he would leave Estonia.

But such an attitude can also be seen as an admirable form of self-reliance. Certainly the Estonian modesty and embarrassment about advertising is a joy to anyone who likes to make up their own mind about where to stay, eat and so on. You'll hardly ever find anyone – even a travel agent – trying to pressurise you into some particular choice.

There are some traits which all three peoples share. One, which many visitors find disconcerting, is the outwardly glum, pessimistic, sometimes brusque bearing of many people. This can be put down to at least three things. One is that life has never been easy for the majority of people in this part of the world, and the early years of independence have been economically even harder than usual. Another is the weather: long, dark, cold winters never make anybody very happy (there's a marked brightening of everybody's mood in spring and summer). A third factor is the legacy of the Soviet era, when trust in strangers could be risky.

But in happy contrast to all this – and all the more pleasing because of it – you'll find that once you break the ice, people are often only too pleased to do what they can to help a Western visitor.

Another trait the Baltic peoples share is a very strong feeling for their land; even those who live in cities frequently abandon them to visit family, friends, or their own cottages in the country. The universal custom of taking flowers when visiting someone's home is one reflection of this love of nature; flower stalls and markets for the purpose are to be found in every town, often open at ridiculously late night-time hours, and travellers can be seen nurturing bunches of blossoms for hours on crowded buses in order to present them to their host on arrival.

Attachment to local roots is, perhaps, also a cause of the Baltic peoples' surprisingly sparse contact with each other. Though the outside world tends to think of the three Baltic states as one group, each is actually very much its own little world.

There are obviously neighbourly connections between the three states, but it's a lot less common than you might expect for Estonians, Latvians and Lithuanians to speak each other's languages; or do business with each other; or visit, have friends in – or even know much about – each other's countries. ∎

attempt in Moscow and collaborating with the KGB. The Lithuanian parliament imposed direct rule on the two districts in September 1991 dissolving the two regional councils, which caused tensions in Lithuania's relations with Poland. New councils were elected to office in 1993.

The Kaliningrad Region has seen the biggest ethnic change of the whole region. During and after WW II, virtually its entire German population disappeared: some fled, some were sent to Germany, some were deported to Siberia, and some were shot. They were replaced with people from the USSR – mainly Russia. In the last few years some ethnic Germans from Russia (mainly the Volga region) have made their way to Kaliningrad.

ARTS & CULTURE
Folk Culture
Native folklore survived the centuries of foreign dominance, thanks largely to a rich oral tradition of songs, verses and chants on subjects like the seasonal cycle, farming and the land, family life, love, and myths. It's widely thought that women composed most of these. The Latvian and Lithuanian verses, known as *dainas*, are often short and poetic and have been compared to the Japanese *haiku*. The oldest Estonian song type, going back to the first millennium BC, is the runic chant, based on lines of eight syllables with a theme gradually developing from line to line. Runic verses are still sung at weddings on the island of Kihnu.

In the 19th century, great collections of folk lyrics and tunes were made by people like Krišjānis Barons in Latvia and Jakob Hurt in Estonia; over 1.4 million folk lyrics and 30,000 tunes have been written down in Latvia alone. There's much interest in folk rhymes and music today with numerous societies and groups devoted to them, but they're also a living tradition with regional variations. Particularly unusual are the chants of the Setumaa region in south-east Estonia and those known as *sutartinės* in north-east Lithuania. Those I've heard aren't exactly catchy but they're obviously a source of fascination and amusement to those who can understand them properly.

More immediately impressive, and evidence of the age-old power of song in the Baltic cultures – though centred more on 19th and 20th century songs than the oldest traditions – are the huge five-yearly national song festivals which played a great part in awakening national feelings in the 19th century and keeping them alive in the Soviet period. The late 1980s independence movement was christened the Singing Revolution in Estonia because of extra song festivals held in 1988. One of them was attended by an estimated 300,000 people (around one in three of all Estonians) who sang previously banned songs and rekindled their national spark.

There are also quite a few folk festivals in the Baltics each year and these, particularly the annual Baltika festival, are probably your best bets for catching folk song, music and dance as well as the colourful traditional costumes which are one of the few instantly recognisable trademarks of the Baltic states. The costumes vary from region to region (in some places from parish to parish) but you can rely on the women to sport long and colourful skirts, embroidered blouses, jackets or shawls, and an amazing variety of headgear from neat pillboxes to vast, winged, fairy-tale creations. Male gear tends to be plainer and more obviously a product of peasant existence. The women's styles have been influenced by German and other fashions from the towns. See Cultural Events in the Facts for the Visitor chapter for more on song and folk festivals.

Folk music and dance performances are also regularly given at Rocca al Mare in Tallinn, the Open-Air Ethnography Museum in Rīga and the Lithuanian Country Life Museum at Rumšiškės near Kaunas.

A number of traditional musical instruments may accompany folk song. Each of the three states has its own version of the zither – the *kannel* in Estonia, the *kokle* in Latvia and the *kanklės* in Lithuania. Bells, pipes, flutes and fiddles also feature. In Lithuania you may see the *birbynė*, a pipe with an

Lithuanian Folk Costume

animal horn attached, or the long wooden trumpet called the *daudytė*, or the *skudučiai* from the north-east which is like a set of pan pipes with each note produced by a different player, playing a different pipe.

Arts

Few Baltic artistic figures or works, past or present, are internationally known. Until the 19th century, Estonian, Latvian and Lithuanian culture were largely foreign-dominated, and when they did emerge in their own right in the 19th and 20th centuries, they remained, with some exceptions, isolated by geographical, linguistic or political barriers or by their chiefly local relevance. In the Soviet years many leading writers and artists went into voluntary or forced exile and most other talent was stifled.

Literature Literature in the Baltic states draws heavily on the rich folklore heritage of

each of the native peoples. Modern Estonian and Latvian literature got going with the writing of national epic poems in the mid-19th century – *Kalevipoeg* (Son of Kalev) in Estonia and *Lāčplēsis* (The Bear Slayer) in Latvia. These epics were based on legends and folktales which had been part of the oral tradition over preceding centuries. The giants of 20th century literature in these countries are the Estonian novelist Anton Hansen Tammsaare and the Latvian poet and playwright Jānis Rainis, who spent much of his life in exile in Siberia and Switzerland for his trenchant criticisms of tsarist social and political oppression. He has been compared with Shakespeare and Goethe. More recently the Estonians Jan Kross, a novelist, and Jaan Kaplinski, a poet, have received international acclaim.

The first major fiction in Lithuanian was the poem *Metai* (The Seasons) describing the life of serfs in the 18th century. Jonas Mačiulis, known as Maironis, is regarded as the founder of modern Lithuanian literature for his poetry written around the turn of this century. Lithuania also shares the credit for some major Polish writers who grew up in Lithuania, including contemporary Nobel laureate Czesław Miłosz.

In recent years much of the literature of the region has reflected the oppression of the Soviet era, and the peoples' hope for a new beginning. The literature of each of the Baltic states is discussed in more detail in the relevant Facts about the Country chapters.

Visual Arts The art scene is pretty active in the Baltic states and there are lots of galleries and museums in the capital cities displaying past and present art, but few Baltic artists have managed to cause much of a stir internationally. The overall story is one of emergence of national artists in the 19th century, a flowering around the turn of the century under Western influences like Impressionism, followed by decades of experiment and uncertainty in the first decades of the 20th century and forced conformity in the Soviet era. Like some other art forms, the visual arts seem to be struggling to find new directions now that the Soviet straitjacket, which shaped their approach for so long even in rebellion, has been removed. Some good modern work is in the field of applied art and handicrafts, often influenced by folk art.

Music Rock thrives particularly in Estonia and Latvia where there are big annual festivals (see Cultural Events in the Facts for the Visitor chapter). Jazz is particularly popular in Lithuania.

The classical performing scene is busy in all three states though it has had funding problems since independence – see Entertainment in the capital city sections. The region's best known composer is the Estonian Arvo Pärt, who writes mainly choral works.

All three capitals have opera and ballet companies and several theatres. Drama played a part in the 19th century national revivals and Rīga was the pre-eminent performing arts centre before WW I and between the world wars. Its ballet, which produced Mikhail Baryshnikov, among others, goes back to the 1920s and was one of the best in the Soviet Union. Since independence there have been problems of funding and dwindling audiences for some companies.

For more information on the arts and culture of each of the Baltic states see the relevant Facts about the Country chapters.

RELIGION

After decades of persecution and discouragement under Soviet rule, religion – which chiefly means Christianity – enjoys full freedom again and is experiencing a revival. It was an important element in the national independence movements of the 1980s and '90s.

The leading faith among Estonians is Lutheranism but they are a rather irreligious people: only 23% of them reckoned to have religious convictions in an opinion poll held in 1991-92. Lutheranism is also the leading faith among Latvians but there's a significant Roman Catholic community too, especially in Latgale, the south-eastern region. Lithuanians are mostly Roman Catholics and more enthusiastic about their creed than the Lutherans to their north. The Catholic Church is a conservative force in Lithuanian society. Its head is the Archbishop of Kaunas, Cardinal Vincentas Sladkevičius. Russian Orthodoxy is the faith of most Russian believers throughout the region, which makes it important in places with big Russian populations such as Tallinn, north-east Estonia, Rīga and the Kaliningrad Region. There are also, particularly in Lithuania, some Old Believers – a schismatic sect of the Russian Orthodox church which has come in for intermittent persecution since it rejected a number of church reforms back in the 17th century.

The Baltic states were one of the last areas of Europe to be Christianised, and elements of their peoples' earlier nature religions survive to this day in the form of customs and beliefs connected with the land and nature and its cycles – perhaps most notably the 23 June midsummer celebrations. See Cultural Events in the Facts for the Visitor chapter for information on the midsummer events and the section on Rēzekne, Latvia, for more on the old religions.

Orthodoxy made some inroads into the region from the Slav regions to the east before Catholicism took over from the west in the 13th and 14th centuries (after desultory efforts since the 10th century). The brutal conversion of Estonia and Latvia by German crusaders, as well as the atheist influences of the Soviet period when even Christmas celebrations were banned for a long time, make it hardly surprising that support in those countries for the Lutheran church, to which the German ruling class turned with the Reformation in the 1520s, is still lukewarm. Lithuania fought off the German knights but its leaders eventually accepted Catholicism as part of the deal with Poland which led to the knights' long-term defeat. Still, as late as 1377 and 1382, the Lithuanian princes Algirdas and Kęstutis were cremated in rituals of the old religion – dressed in silver and gold and burnt on pyres together with their treasures, weapons, horses and hunting dogs.

The Reformation which swept across Europe in the 16th century triumphed in Estonia and most of Latvia, where Lutheranism became established under German or Swedish rule. But Catholicism survived in Lithuania and Latgale, controlled by Poland. The local churches – Lutheran and Catholic – endured oppression under Russian rule in the 19th century as well as in the Soviet periods.

LANGUAGE

You can just about get by with English in the Baltic states, and German and Finnish (in Estonia) are also useful; but getting to know a few words and phrases in the local languages will help you find your way around and will please any locals you utter them to. Things are complicated by the fact that there are four local languages – Estonian, Latvian, Lithuanian and Russian – and if you're travelling quickly between the different countries they tend to merge into a confused morass. In the Kaliningrad Region, German is probably more useful than English but local knowledge of both is poorer than in the Baltic states and some words of Russian are extremely useful.

Knowledge of English is on the way up in the three Baltic states now that they are no longer under Soviet rule. It is regaining the status of most-taught foreign language that it held between the world wars and may even be on the way to becoming a lingua franca.

Many people, especially in Estonia, already know a bit of English as a result of listening to Western rock music and receiving some English-language TV programmes. Waiters, hotel desk staff and other people who come into contact with tourists, often have enough English or German to make some communication possible, but in general only the best educated and those at higher levels in tourism have conversational English.

The one language that nearly everyone understands throughout the region is Russian. But Estonians, Latvians and Lithuanians have little fondness for the tongue of their former imperial rulers and can be touchy about being addressed in Russian. If you do know some Russian it's advisable to make the attempt to communicate in some other language first – try English, and if that doesn't work say you don't speak Estonian/Latvian/Lithuanian and ask if the other person understands Russian. The Russian minorities in the Baltic states, and of course people in the Kaliningrad Region, will be only too happy to be addressed in Russian. Quite a number of signs, timetables and so on throughout the region are in Russian as well as the local language, and in the Kaliningrad Region they're in Russian only – so it certainly helps to get on top of the Cyrillic alphabet used for Russian.

See the Language Guide at the back of the book for more information on the Baltic languages and Russian (including the Cyrillic alphabet) and for useful words and phrases.

Facts for the Visitor

VISAS & EMBASSIES

The three Baltic states all issue their own visas. They are still developing – if that's the right word – their visa policies, and the details of rules and procedures are constantly changing. So a check with your local Estonian, Latvian or Lithuanian embassy or consulate is the first step. But three basic facts are fairly constant:

- All three states have lengthening lists of nationalities that don't need visas.
- For citizens of Western countries, a visa for any one of the three Baltic states is good for the other two as well, for the term of its validity. So if you want to travel around all three states for a total of, say, three weeks, all you need is a three-week visa for any one of them.
- Visas are cheaper if obtained in advance at an Estonian, Latvian or Lithuanian embassy or consulate than at the border or airport when you arrive. The price difference is particularly marked for Estonia.

The Kaliningrad Region comes under the Russian visa system, which is discussed separately in this section.

Who Needs Visas for Where?

At the time of writing, all three Baltic states require visas from all nationalities *except* the following:

Estonia
Andorra, Australia, Bulgaria, Canada, Czech Republic, Denmark, Hungary, Japan, Latvia, Liechtenstein, Lithuania, Monaco, New Zealand, Poland, San Marino, UK, USA
Latvia
Estonia, Czech Republic, Hungary, Lithuania, Poland, UK
Lithuania
Bulgaria, Czech Republic, Denmark, Estonia, Hungary, Iceland, Latvia, Norway, Poland

This list of exempted nationalities is growing. Estonia is likely to start admitting Finnish, Swedish, Norwegian and Icelandic passport holders without visas in the near future. Remember that even if you don't need a visa for the country or countries you're visiting, you still need to carry your passport.

The three states established a 'common visa space' in 1992, meaning that a visa for one of them was good for the other two, but Estonia backtracked on this to a certain extent in March 1993 when it decided that it would only recognise Latvian and Lithuanian visas for the holders of passports of some 38 countries – including the Western countries. Citizens of other countries need a separate Estonian visa even if they have a Latvian or Lithuanian one. This move was prompted by what Estonia saw as over-relaxed policies by the other two states, particularly in relation to citizens of the other ex-Soviet states. Since then, Latvia and Lithuania have tightened up their visa regimes, so a genuine 'common visa space' may again become a reality.

Some cruises from Finland or Scandinavian countries calling at ports in the Baltic states are visa-free.

Types of Visa

Each Baltic state issues three main types of visa: transit, single entry, and multiple entry. The fees you have to pay for them veer about erratically and some issuing offices seem to add little charges of their own. The costs given here give a general idea of what you can expect to pay.

Latvian visas are free to US citizens.

Transit These visas are valid for 48 or 72 hours. Single-entry transit visas cost from US$5 to US$15, the cheapest being Estonian and Latvian visas issued at embassies or consulates. Estonia and Latvia will issue double-entry or multiple-entry transit visas, but these are dearer and may be available only from embassies and consulates, not on arrival.

Single Entry Embassies and consulates issue these visas for periods up to a usual maximum of six months for Estonia and 90 days for Latvia or Lithuania. Visas obtained on arrival may be subject to shorter time limits – reportedly 10 days for Lithuania and 30 days for Estonia – but can be extended. From embassies or consulates, single-entry visas cost between US$10 and US$25. On arrival in Latvia or Lithuania, they cost from US$20 to US$30. On arrival in Estonia they cost US$30 for 10 days or US$60 for 30 days if you have an invitation or accommodation confirmation but twice as much if you don't (see the following section for more on these conditions).

Because of the Baltics' common visa space, a single-entry visa for any of the three countries allows you to travel back and forth across the Estonian-Latvian and Latvian-Lithuanian borders as many times as you like within its term of validity, provided you don't leave the common visa space during that time. Some border officials reportedly don't understand this detail, however.

Multiple Entry These are issued for various periods up to 12 months but may only be available from embassies and consulates – not on arrival. They cost between US$30 and US$120.

Applying for Visas

You can get visas at Estonian, Latvian and Lithuanian embassies and consulates in most countries or at airports, main seaports and main land borders on arrival – though there's talk of Estonia ceasing to issue visas to travellers arriving at Tallinn seaport. Fees are lower if you get your visa in advance, and you may well save delays at the border if you do so. Estonia will only issue visas at borders to passport holders of 20 countries, which include all those in Western Europe whose citizens require visas for Estonia, plus South Africa, Israel and South Korea. Embassies and consulates usually process visa applications in a few days at most. The Lithuanian Embassy in Warsaw reportedly issues visas within one day. The busy Estonian Embassy and Latvian Embassy in Helsinki have an 'immediate processing' service at about double the normal cost.

When applying at an embassy or consulate you normally need to supply your passport (which should expire at least two months after your planned departure from the country in question), a completed application form, and sometimes one photo. For a transit visa you may have to show a visa for the country you're going on to.

Invitations & References This is the most confusing aspect of the Baltic states visa business. You will probably hear a different story every time you ask an embassy or consulate. The basic point seems to be that the states want to keep out 'undesirables' of various kinds. Thus the Estonian visa regulations state that applicants must have an invitation or confirmation of accommodation in Estonia, and the Latvian regulations say applicants may need to prove their means of support for their stay and the funds for onward travel.

In practice, however, the individual embassy, consulate or immigration official has discretion, and Westerners are regarded favourably. You will probably not be asked to show or prove anything, unless perhaps you want to stay a long time; or are requesting a multiple-entry visa; or are applying on a border between the Baltic states and Russia or Belarus, or at a Baltic embassy or consulate in a former Soviet country. If you are asked, and don't have an invitation on paper from a local resident or institution, or an actual hotel or homestay reservation, a return ticket or proof of funds may well be good enough. (Just what level of funds is 'sufficient' is a debatable point, but one traveller entering Estonia was told US$8 a day was enough.) Failing that, show anything indicating that you have contacts in the country in question or any paper with an accommodation address printed or written on it.

The case where you're most likely to fall foul of the regulations is if you're applying for a visa on arrival in Estonia. At the time of writing, Estonia has double fees for people doing this without invitation or accommodation confirmation. You may be able to talk your way round this or produce some piece of paper that could be accepted as an 'invitation' or 'confirmation', but it's really better to get the visa before you arrive.

Visa Extensions

Once in the Baltics you can extend a visa. In Estonia go to the National Migration Board at Lai 40, Tallinn (☎ 22-664 333). In Latvia go to the visa office at Raiņa bulvāris 5, Rīga (☎ 22-219 176) – you must apply at least three days before the expiry of your existing visa. In Lithuania go to the immigration office at Verkių gatvė 3, Vilnius.

Border Controls

Controls on the Baltic states' borders with Russia and Belarus have tightened since the early months of Baltic independence, when travellers could slip back and forth across those frontiers without visas.

Russians have needed visas for Estonia since 1992, and Estonians for Russia since 1993, so expect efficient passport control on this border. The same goes for the Latvia-Russia and Latvia-Belarus borders, where mutual visa requirements were introduced in 1993. The Lithuania-Belarus border is increasingly tightly policed, especially since Lithuania introduced a visa requirement for CIS citizens in late 1993, though controls have sometimes been lax on trains from Vilnius to Moscow via Belarus.

Lithuania's border with Poland and flights and ships between the Western world and all three states are subject to passport control.

The Kaliningrad Region's land border with Poland is still closed to all but Russian and Polish citizens at the time of writing. If and when it opens up to others, it will almost certainly be subject to strict passport control

as are the sea connections between the two places already.

For information on the Estonia-Latvia, Latvia-Lithuania and Lithuania-Kaliningrad Region borders, see the Getting Around chapter.

Baltic Embassies & Consulates

Some of the Baltic states' pre-WW II diplomatic missions remained in existence for decades after the states' de facto absorption into the USSR, only shutting up shop when their diplomats died. A very few managed to hold on until Baltic independence was again recognised by the world in 1991. Lithuania's man in London, Vincas Balickas, had by then reached his late eighties and was thought to be the oldest serving diplomat in Europe. Since 1991 the Baltic states have opened numerous new diplomatic missions. More will be added to the list, and some existing ones may move. Baltic missions are often open for limited hours, and smaller ones may also be a consul's home, so ring ahead and allow plenty of time to make contact.

Details of diplomatic missions for each of the Baltic states can be found in the relevant Facts for the Visitor chapters later in the book.

Foreign Embassies in the Baltic States

Many countries have set up their own embassies or missions in the Baltic capitals since 1991, while others cover the Baltic states from embassies in nearby countries. See the Tallinn, Rīga and Vilnius chapters for details.

Russian Visas

The Kaliningrad Region is part of Russia and you need a Russian visa to go there. You also need a Russian visa if you're travelling through 'mainland' Russia on the way to or from the Baltic states. A Russian visa is a separate document, not stamped in or attached to your passport, listing the cities you have been granted permission to stay in and the dates of your stay in the country. It's best obtained well in advance as procedures can be slow. A listing of Russian embassies can be found in the Kaliningrad Region chapter.

Types of Russian Visa There are basically three types of Russian visa: tourist, ordinary and transit. A tourist visa is intended primarily for tourism but can also cover business and some other trips. One of the things you're supposed to produce when applying for it is confirmation of already-booked accommodation, which can be complicated and expensive to get. Ordinary visas are intended for visits by private invitation. A transit visa is for 'passing through', which would probably only give you a day or two, if granted for Kaliningrad alone, but can be valid for as long as 10 days if, for instance, you're 'passing through' Russia on the Trans-Siberian railway.

Applying for a Russian Visa At some Russian embassies and consulates, especially busy ones in major capitals, getting any kind of visa can be a time-consuming, frustrating experience even once you have got all the paperwork together. At others it's quick and surprisingly easy. Specialist travel agents and worldwide branches of Intourist, the Russian state tourism organisation (which is more friendly and helpful nowadays than it used to be), should be able to give you information and advice on visa-getting. If there's any kind of travel agency involved in your trip planning it's usually easiest to let it look after your visa application even though an extra fee is charged. Some specialist agents have their own short cuts and arrangements which will greatly simplify things.

To apply yourself, you need a passport, three or four photos, a completed application form, a handling fee (typically US$25 or so), and proof of accommodation. This last item means, for a tourist visa, confirmation of hotel bookings – officially, but in practice not necessarily, for your whole stay; for a transit visa, a ticket or ticket voucher with confirmed times and dates; and for an ordinary visa, an invitation from an organisation or private person. Check with a specialist travel agent, Intourist, or a Russian embassy or consulate whether the invitation has to follow any particular format. Once your documents have been handed over you should receive your visa within 10 days. At some busy embassies you can pay more for quicker service but you may still have to wait several days. At the time of writing, the Russian Embassy in Vilnius reportedly issues visas quicker than those in Tallinn and Rīga. Tallinn is more expensive at US$30 for a tourist visa against about US$10 in the other cities.

Two US travellers obtained three-week visas from the Russian Embassy in Helsinki on the day they applied, on the strength of four nights accommodation at the St Petersburg Youth Hostel reserved quickly through SRM, the Finnish Youth Hostel Association. The same travellers reported the Warsaw office of Intourist as saying that only two nights accommodation needs to be pre-booked for each week on your visa.

The St Petersburg hostel, incidentally, is at 3-ya Rozhdestvenskaya ulitsa 28 (formerly 3-ya Sovetskaya ulitsa), about half a km from St Petersburg's Moscow station. For bookings and visa help, you can contact it direct at St Petersburg 193312, prospekt Solidarnosti 11, PO Box 57, Russian Youth Hostels (☎ 812-277 0569, fax 812-277 5102) or through Russian Youth Hostels, 409 N Pacific Coast Highway, Building 106, Suite 390, Redondo Beach, California 90277, USA (☎ 310-379 4316, fax 310-379 8420). Other forms of cheaper accommodation in Russia include campsites (ask Intourist about these) and homestays (organised by several outfits including some which also do Baltic states homestays – see Accommodation in this chapter).

Another possible way to avoid paying heavy accommodation costs in advance is to obtain the easiest, cheapest visa available to get you into Russia – for instance a transit visa or a short-period tourist visa using cheap accommodation – then try to extend it and/or have new cities added to it at the local office of OVIR (Otdel Viz i Registratsii), the Visa & Registration Department. Some travellers don't bother with the extension and just trust to luck that they won't get into any trouble. The only time you're really likely to be asked to show a visa once you're inside Russia is when you check in at some hotels or if you try to enter a restricted military zone.

Belarus Visas

Trains between Poland and Lithuania, unless they take the direct Suwałki-Šeštokai route, pass across about 60 km of Belarussian territory en route. If you're taking one of these trains or driving through Belarus to avoid delays on the Poland-Lithuania border you need a Belarus visa. (One route on which the visa requirement hasn't always been enforced – though this may change – is trains between Vilnius and Russia which pass through Belarus.)

Belarus transit visas, valid for three days, can be obtained at road borders or on the train on the way through for US$20 without accommodation bookings or an invitation. There may just be a few anxious moments when you have to leave the train to visit the immigration office at Grodno station, trusting to luck that the train won't pull out without you.

Russian embassies used to issue Belarus visas but seem to have stopped doing so since Belarus began to set up its own diplomatic missions in 1993. To date, however, there are no Belarus missions in the Baltic states. The Russian embassies in Rīga and Vilnius have advised travellers to obtain Belarus visas at the Belarus border. If you want to stay in Belarus more than three days, you'll probably need to show a hotel reservation or an invitation to get a tourist or ordinary visa.

Other Visas

Don't forget that you may need visas for other countries on your trip – such as Poland, where citizens of several Western nations still need visas at the time of writing – and make arrangements to get them in good time.

DOCUMENTS

Your number one document is your passport. Make sure its validity extends to at least two months after the end of your Baltic travels as this may be a requirement for some visas.

Driving Licences

If you're planning to drive to or in the region, an International Driving Permit (IDP) will be useful, though not necessarily essential – see the Getting There & Away and Getting Around chapters. It's obtainable, usually cheaply, from your local automobile association such as the AA or RAC in Britain. If you have don't have an IDP you must take your own national licence.

Student & Youth Cards

These are of very limited use in the Baltic states themselves so far, but they're useful in neighbouring countries (except Russia and Belarus) and can certainly cut the cost of getting to the Baltic states. Apart from youth air fares, there are youth rail tickets, youth rail discounts, and student discounts on the EstLine Stockholm-Tallinn ferry. See the Getting There & Away chapter. The two main cards are the International Student Identity Card (ISIC) and the International Youth Card of the Federation of International Youth Travel Organisations (FIYTO) card for people under 26. They're available from student unions and 'alternative'-style travel agencies.

Youth Hostel Card

An International Youth Hostel (IYHF) card currently brings discounts in only one or two places in the Baltic states, as the youth hostel scene there is still in its infancy and local hostel groups aren't yet affiliated to the IYHF. They have no serious membership requirements in any case. But things may change and it's worth asking your local youth hostels organisation whether any Baltic states have yet joined the IYHF.

Customs Form

This is a document you may get when you enter the Baltic states or the Kaliningrad Region of Russia and keep till you leave. See the following Customs section.

CUSTOMS

All three Baltic states ban the import or export of firearms, ammunition, explosives or narcotics without special permission. Beyond that the customs rules vary and are subject to change. Baltic embassies and consulates should be able to tell you the latest if there's anything you're concerned about.

If you're bringing into the Baltic states anything you think might be queried when you take it out again – such as an expensive camera, a lot of money, or works of art, furs or jewellery – it's wise to declare it on a customs form and get this stamped by customs officials, which will prove later that you're not trying to smuggle it out. Customs forms should be available at border points. If you're having language difficulties ask for a *deklaratsia* (the Russian word for them which should be understood everywhere).

If you think that a painting or other cultural object you want to buy in the Baltic states may attract customs duty or require special permission to export, check with the shop or seller before you buy.

Further details on customs restrictions for each of the Baltic states is given in the relevant Facts for the Visitor chapters later in the book. Customs restrictions for the Kaliningrad Region can be found in the Kaliningrad Region chapter.

MONEY

Baltic travel will improve your mental arithmetic because if you travel through all three states and the Kaliningrad Region you'll end up using at least four different currencies along the way.

Until 1992 the whole region used the Russian rouble. Then the three independent states started introducing their own separate currencies, partly out of national pride and partly to escape the raging inflation that went with the rouble. The Kaliningrad Region, however, had to stick with the rouble. In addition to the local currencies you'll very likely find yourself using US dollars or Deutschmarks here and there too.

Prices in the Estonian, Latvian and Lithuanian chapters of this book are given in local currency – Estonian *krooni* (EEK), Latvian *lati* and Lithuanian *litų* – whose values seem pretty settled at the time of writing. Prices in the Kaliningrad Region chapter are given in US\$ since the value of the Russian rouble was subject to fluctuation.

Currency information specific to each of the Baltic states can be found in the relevant Facts for the Visitor chapters later in the book. The Russian rouble is discussed in the Kaliningrad Region chapter.

What Money to Bring

Travellers' cheques can only be exchanged at relatively few places in the Baltic states and commissions are sometimes rather high. Things are slowly changing but for the next couple of years cash US dollars and Deutschmarks will remain the most useful money to carry. Other major Western currencies are usually acceptable but in a few places, such as Klaipėda and Kaliningrad, no one seems interested in anything but US\$ and DM.

A limited amount of travellers' cheques is also useful because of the protection they offer against theft. American Express cheques are among the best choices as they have a couple of offices in the Baltic states where you can get replacement cheques (ask for an up-to-date list of offices when you buy the cheques).

To date, only a limited number of mainly top-end establishments accept credit cards, but they're slowly becoming more widely used and any cards you have may prove useful. One thing they're virtually essential for is renting a car. Visa, MasterCard, Diners Club and American Express all crop up. You can get cash advances on a Visa card in Vilnius (see that city chapter for details) and this service may spread to other cities.

Get rid of Polish złoty, Russian roubles, Ukrainian currency and other east European money before you enter the Baltic states – unless (in the rouble's case) you're going to Kaliningrad. Exchange rates for them are poor. Similarly you don't get very good rates for the Baltic states' own currencies outside each home country – if you can change them at all, that is.

Changing Money

Throughout the region there is a variety of places where you can exchange cash and a more limited number of places that will change travellers' cheques. Every town will have somewhere you can at least change cash. Usually it's either a bank, or a special exchange office or kiosk doing nothing but currency exchange. The latter crop up in all sorts of places but particularly transport terminals – airports, bus stations and railway stations. They may not be obviously identifiable at first but the tell-tale sign is a list of exchange rates posted up outside. Major hotels often change money too. Other places where you may come across exchange kiosks include post offices and shops.

Exchange rates do vary from one outlet to another. Sometimes the posted rates take account of commission, sometimes they don't.

Banks generally open from about 9 am to 12.30 pm Monday to Friday, sometimes with an hour or two in the afternoon as well. Specialist money-changing offices may be open much longer hours.

In Kaliningrad there's also a black market. Individuals with money to change hang around stations, banks, markets, hotels and so on. You might get a slightly better rate from such people, but you might also get ripped off.

Costs

The costs of many goods and services are yet to settle down. New rises were taking place during the time this book was being written. These have been included where the information was reliable but not all were precise – hence the proliferation of 'approximately's and 'about's.

After the cost of your visa and of getting to the Baltics, your main expenses are likely to be accommodation, food and transport. At the time of writing Estonia is perhaps 25% more expensive than the other two states.

Accommodation On a middle-range budget you can get comfortable homestays for about US$15 per person a night or hotel rooms for US$30 to US$50 a double. You can go a lot cheaper too: at cheap hotels, youth hostels or camping grounds you'll rarely pay more than US$7 or US$8 and often a lot less. Some hotels have rooms for US$1.50 or US$2. Prices are similar at 'local' homestays – rooms in private homes normally rented out to travelling locals. Then again you can go up to more than US$200 a double at the very top hotels – though US$80 to US$100 is nearer the normal top-end mark.

Food Eating can be very cheap. If you avoid the establishments that are aimed at Western business customers or more affluent tourists, you'll rarely pay even US$5 for an evening meal with a drink or two. You can cut costs to the bone – US$1 or less – by eating at the cheap canteens or cafeterias, some of which serve perfectly adequate food, and by buying some of your own food at markets and shops. If you do patronise the top-end places, a meal will typically be in the US$8 to US$15 range.

Transport This is getting more expensive but is still cheap by Western standards. Fares vary a bit from country to country but, very roughly, US$1 will take you 150 km by bus or 200 km by train. A bus or train from Tallinn to Vilnius – the length of the region – is about US$6 at the time of writing.

Things get more expensive if you take to the air or use a lot of taxis or guided tours, but you probably won't need these much unless you're in a big hurry. Some travel agents add absurdly heavy commissions if you use them to get transport tickets for you, so check their prices before booking through them.

Petrol prices can change unpredictably. At the time of writing, a litre of 95-octane petrol, suitable for most Western engines, is about US$0.40 to US$0.50. Unleaded or super (99-octane) can cost double that. Local cars usually run on 93-octane, which costs less. Petrol prices may have neared their peak but there's no certainty.

Other Costs Most of the other little items you spend money on while travelling – maps, souvenirs, handicrafts, entertainment – are as cheap as everything else. But it's advisable to bring with you film, batteries and any medicines or toiletries you're going to need.

Two-Tier Prices Sometimes Westerners have to pay more than local people for things like air tickets and accommodation. In the case of air tickets this is an official policy to bring in extra foreign currency. There's little chance of avoiding foreigners' prices on air tickets because you usually have to show your passport when buying the ticket. Happily rail and bus tickets now seem to cost much the same for everybody – but if you employ a travel agency to get these tickets for you it may add on an almighty commission in the hope that you don't know the real level of local fares.

Some hotels may charge a Westerner US$20 or US$30 for a room which costs only US$5 or US$10 for locals. This may be as much a case of opportunism by the desk clerk as of management policy. It happens at the bottom end of the hotel range rather than at the top, where prices are equally high for everybody. You stand a greater chance of avoiding this if you use a bit of the local language, or even Russian, or if you have local friends who can help you.

Prices given in this book are those which travellers seem most likely to have to pay.

Tipping & Bargaining

It's fairly common, though not compulsory, to tip waiters 5% or 10% by rounding up the bill. A few waiters may try to tip themselves by 'not having' any change.

Some bargaining (but not a lot) goes on at markets. Traders from the Caucasus or Central Asia are more likely to enter into bargaining than locals, and savings are not likely to be more than 10% or 20% of the initial asking price.

WHEN TO GO

Summer and spring are far and away the best

times of year. There's better weather, longer daylight and more fresh food. People are happier, cottage gardens blossom with flowers, and there's generally more happening in the way of festivals and outdoor events during the warmer months. Summer starts some time in May, depending on the weather, and ends some time in September. It may extend a little longer in the south of the region than in the north. July and August, the warmest months, are also among the wettest and there can be days of persistent showers particularly in July – though summer weather is rarely very predictable. May, June and September, while a bit cooler, are often more comfortable.

July and August are also the months which bring the majority of foreign tourists, when top-end hotels in the capitals can get fully booked and some ferries to the Baltic states may also be full. Spring – April and May – has a magic to it as the land and the people open up after the long, dark winter. June is the month of the midsummer celebrations which bring home the Baltic peoples' close ties to nature and their land and remind us of their pagan past. It's no coincidence that the famous Baltic song festivals take place in late June.

Winter is very much a second best season. Though there'll usually be a picturesque sprinkling (or more) of snow on the ground and in the trees, there may also be only a few hours of semi-daylight every 24 hours. And you can't escape the fact that it's cold – which is made worse when economic austerity forces central heating and hot-water supplies to be switched off, as happened regularly in many places in the early years of independence! At these times only the top hotels are likely to keep their heating and hot water going while locals wash with small quantities of water boiled up on a stove. All the more reason to visit the Baltics in summer! If you dress warmly there's no reason you can't spend a reasonable length of time out of doors in winter. Locals enjoy skating and (wherever they can find a slope) tobogganing or skiing but also turn to indoor-based activities. Theatre and concert-going is at its peak in winter. This is also the season that explains why 'cosy' is such an important word in the Baltic states. If you have friends whose homes you can visit you'll probably find life a whole lot cosier.

The in-between seasons are, well, in between. April and October have cold, sharp, wintery days as well as mild, springlike or autumnal ones. There's often a lot of slush underfoot, particularly during the late-March and April thaw.

WHAT TO BRING

Don't bring too much! As far as luggage is concerned, if you're going to be doing much travelling around, a backpack is the easiest receptacle to carry your things in. A light day-pack is also extremely useful. Unless you plan to camp or sleep out, a sleeping bag is not necessary. A towel and soap will be useful if you're staying in cheap hotels, which don't always provide them. A universal sink plug is also very useful.

In summer bring clothes for the cool (but not cold) days you're likely to experience. A light waterproof garment or an umbrella will mean you don't have to keep ducking under shelter on rainy days. In spring and autumn there may be cold snaps, so take some warm headgear, gloves, warm and water-resistant footwear, a coat (or at least a warm leather or padded jacket) and either thermal underwear or some very warm trousers. In winter your coat should be able to keep out strong, biting winds and your headgear should cover your ears. A scarf is a very good idea. The rest of your clothing should be able to cope with permanent sub-zero temperatures: thermal underwear is essential. The essence of dressing is layers that you can put on or take off to adjust to the differences between indoors and outdoors, night and day, cold and less cold weather. Not that there's much difference between indoor and outdoor in winter when the heating is switched off because of an energy crisis!

Jeans and trainers are rejected in a few smart restaurants and nightspots, and in others you may feel ill at ease if you're not cleanly and tidily dressed (though you can

remain fairly casual) – so you might want to take one set of clothes for such occasions.

Bring film, batteries and any medicines or toiletries you'll need (including tampons and condoms) as supplies are haphazard and can be expensive. In summer bring mosquito repellent or coils. An electric water-heating element will enable you to purify suspect tap water by boiling it and to make your own hot drinks. For the latter it's worth buying a light plastic mug and a supply of tea, coffee, milk powder and sugar before you go. You can get these in the Baltic states but it'll usually be easier and probably cheaper beforehand. A few packets of soup may also turn out surprisingly welcome – they're more sustaining than tea or coffee. A Swiss army knife never goes amiss.

TOURIST OFFICES

To date, the Baltic states have not opened any tourist information offices in other countries but their embassies and consulates are often happy enough to answer questions relating to tourism and travel. Some even provide printed information. Baltic-specialist travel agencies in Western countries are also useful sources of information.

In the Baltic states themselves there are, to my knowledge, precisely two tourist information offices – one in the Estonian capital, Tallinn, which is helpful, useful and has some information on the rest of Estonia too, and one in the Latvian town of Valmiera, which doesn't have a huge amount to get excited about but tries hard! Over time, more tourist offices can be expected to appear. In the meantime there are travel agencies in most towns and cities which are often willing to give information on accommodation, transport, things to see and so on.

Whatever the shortcomings of the present situation it's already a big improvement on the Soviet system, which regarded all information as a security risk. Getting answers to the simple questions any traveller has in a new place was often infuriatingly difficult.

BUSINESS HOURS & HOLIDAYS

Throughout the Baltic states and the

Kaliningrad Region most shops are open from 8, 9 or 10 am to 6, 7 or 8 pm Monday to Friday; and 8, 9 or 10 am to some time between 1 and 5 pm on Saturday. They are closed on Sunday. Some close for lunch from 1 to 2 pm or from 2 to 3 pm. A few food shops stay open till 10 pm and open on Sunday. Some bookshops and department stores close on Monday.

Cafés are generally open from about 9 am to 8 pm, often with an hour or two's break after lunch. Restaurants usually open from noon to around midnight, with two hours break in late afternoon or early evening.

Normal working hours in offices are from 9 am to 1 pm and 2 to 6 pm Monday to Friday. Museums open for varying days and hours but almost always between 11 am and 4 pm on their opening days; Monday and Tuesday are the most common closing days. Banks generally open from about 9 am to 12.30 pm Monday to Friday, sometimes with an hour or two in the afternoon as well. Specialist money-changing offices may be open much longer hours.

Most places to eat, museums, and some shops have a regular monthly 'sanitary day' when the place gets a good scrub-up. This can throw the best-laid plans into confusion; information about it is usually displayed somewhere on site but that's little use if you don't know about it till you get there or, equally likely, can't understand the sign anyway.

National holidays vary from country to country (for details, refer to the relevant Facts for the Visitor chapters later in the book). In the Baltic states Soviet holidays began being replaced by local nationalist ones during the *perestroika* period. There may be more changes yet to come, especially in the Kaliningrad Region, which has Russian holidays.

CULTURAL EVENTS

All three Baltic states have fat festival calendars encompassing religion, music, song, art, folk culture, handicrafts, film, drama and more. Summer is the busiest time of year. Some festivals are annual, others one-off.

Tickets, if needed, are often easy enough to get, and some events are open to everyone for free. Just keep your eyes open for what's on when you arrive. Three regular events stand out: the Baltic song festivals, the midsummer celebrations, and the Baltika folk festival.

Song Festivals

The national song festivals held every five years in each of the Baltic states are the most emotive events on the calendar. So strong is the power of song, particularly in Estonia and to a slightly lesser degree in Latvia, that the campaign for independence from the USSR became known as the 'Singing Revolution'. During the Soviet period the song festivals and similar gatherings became the focus of great surges of national feeling which kept Baltic identities alive and provided a great deal of the momentum for independence. The first Estonian song festival was held in Tartu in 1869, during the Estonian national awakening, and helped to show that Estonians could emulate their German overlords. The first Latvian song festival followed in 1873 but Lithuania didn't begin till 1924.

The song festivals climax with giant choirs of 10,000, 20,000 or 30,000 people, from several hundred choirs, singing in huge open-air amphitheatres in the national capitals to vast audiences of 100,000 or more. Often they're accompanied by simultaneous dance festivals, with thousands of dancers creating huge, intricate patterns. They're an experience not to be missed if you have the chance. Normally they're held every five years, simultaneously, over one weekend around the end of June, as happened in 1990. But independence seems to be disrupting the cycle and the 21st Latvian Song Festival was held in 1993. Estonia is holding its next in 1994, the 125th anniversary of its first, while Lithuania appears to be sticking to 1995.

For the 1994 Estonian song festival, tens of thousands of singers and dancers will perform in Tartu on 18 and 19 June, then move to Tallinn for rehearsals and preliminary concerts in churches and concert halls, along with an international choir competition from 26 June to 1 July. A parade of singers and dancers from the city centre to the Tallinn Song Bowl will precede the first of the two climactic concerts which starts at 7 pm on 2 July. There's a second concert at 2 pm the next day. The dance festival performances will be on 1 and 3 July at 11 am and 3 pm.

In Estonia, large children's and youth song and dance festivals are held in the years between the main festivals. Some 26,000 singers and dancers took part in the seventh Estonian youth song and dance festival held over six days in mid-June 1993.

At all these festivals you'll see many people in the picturesque traditional dress of the Baltic states' various regions.

Midsummer

In a part of the world with such a short summer and long, dark winters it's only natural that midsummer, when night barely falls at all, should be an important festival time. The festivities are reminders of the Baltic peoples' strong ties to nature and their land, and of their pagan roots. The night of 23 June, preceding what's known as Jaanipäev in Estonia, Jāni or Jānu Diena in Latvia, and Rasos or Joninės in Lithuania (all meaning St John's Day, 24 June), is the climax of events. It's considered a night with magical powers, and the traditional way of celebrating it is to head out into the countryside to dance, sing and make merry round bonfires and to seek the mythical fern flower which, it's said, only blooms this night and brings luck to any who find it. Another belief is that if you go to sleep on this night the spirits abroad cast an evil spell over you. Nowadays many people seem to ignore the tradition but still make the occasion an excuse for a party. In Latvia people traditionally hang wreaths made of grasses, flowers and herbs gathered on 23 June (known as Ligo or Jānu Nakts) around their homes for good luck, and special beer, cheese and pies are prepared. Water and dew are held to have a purifying force on this night. However it's celebrated, the festival is the focus of an extended midsummer break which in Estonia lasts about a week.

Baltika

The Baltika annual international folklore festival, which has taken place in each Baltic state in turn since 1987, is a week (usually in mid-July) of music, dance, exhibitions and parades focusing on Baltic and other folk traditions. It's a colourful event and well worth catching if you're in the region. You'll see many people wearing the picturesque traditional dress of each of the Baltic states and their neighbours. The national capitals are the centre of things. In 1994 the Baltika will be held in Latvia; in 1995 it's due in Estonia, and in 1996 in Lithuania.

Other Festivals

Listings of other festivals and events for each of the Baltic states can be found in the country-specific Facts for the Visitor chapters later in the book. More detail on some of them is also given in the relevant city and town sections. One date which spans all three Baltic states is 23 August. This is not a festival but the anniversary of the 1939 Molotov-Ribbentrop Pact and is still marked by demonstrations and other events – though no longer to the extent of 1989 when an estimated two million people formed a human chain across all three countries, many calling for secession from the USSR.

POST & TELECOMMUNICATIONS

With the cost of mail, telephone, faxes and telegrams in the various Baltic states all swivelling around like demented spinning tops, there are some unusual bargains to be had. At one point in 1993, Lithuania's mail rates were so much lower than Estonia's and Latvia's that some organisations with large foreign-mailing loads found it cheaper to transport their mail to Vilnius and post it there, than to mail it in their own countries. As a visitor you may not need to go to such lengths, but it may pay to try to keep track of where parcels and international phone calls are cheapest.

If you come up against any problems

remind yourself that until a couple of years ago all mail and telecommunications had to be routed through Moscow and took far longer (if they got through at all).

Sending Mail

It typically takes up to seven days for mail to reach other European countries from any of the Baltic states and 10 to 14 days to more distant countries – though there are still cases when it takes several weeks. From Kaliningrad things can still be much slower – about three weeks on average to Western Europe. Buy your stamps at a post office (Estonian: *postkontor*; Latvian: *pasts*; Lithuanian: *paštas*; Russian: *pochta)*, and post your mail there too.

The table at the bottom of the page shows the cost of sending a post card or a letter up to 20 grams at the time of writing.

A one-kg air-mail parcel costs about US$5 to anywhere in the world from Lithuania, US$5 to US$9 from Estonia, and US$6 to US$10 from Latvia. Surface mail is typically half the cost of air mail.

Expensive international express-mail services for letters and parcels are available in the capital cities (see the city sections for where).

Receiving Mail

Delivery times for mail sent to the Baltic states from other countries are generally similar to those for outward mail but can be a bit more erratic. There are poste restante services in Tallinn and Rīga – see those city chapters.

In the Soviet era, addresses were essentially written in reverse order, for example:

Russia
654321 g. Kaliningrad
ulitsa Gorbachova
d. 85 kv. 91
Ivanov, Alexey Vladimirovich

The 654321 is the postcode, g stands for *gorod* (city or town), d for *dom* (house) and kv for *kvartira* (flat). This style is still followed in the Kaliningrad Region, but the Baltic states are changing over pretty rapidly to the Western order of doing things, for example:

Kazimiera Jones
Veidenbauma iela 35-17
Ventspils LV-5432
Latvia

Veidenbauma iela 35-17 means Veidenbaum Street, building No 35, flat No 17. Postcodes in Estonia are the letters EE plus four digits, in Latvia LV plus four digits, and in Lithuania LT plus four digits (though in Lithuania most people don't bother with the two letters).

Telephone

Telephone services in the three Baltic states have improved quickly since the end of the

Comparative Postal Rates from the Baltic States				
	Domestic	To CIS	To Europe	To USA
Estonia	US$0.04	US$0.17	US$0.17	US$0.17
Latvia	US$0.08	US$0.08	US$0.16	US$0.24
Lithuania	US$0.05	US$0.16	US$0.16	US$0.16

era, with new internal networks and and t connections to the Western world steadily replacing the slow and decrepit Soviet system routed through Moscow. You can dial direct to anywhere else in the Baltic states, most of the rest of the ex-USSR, and to a good proportion of the rest of the world. The Kaliningrad Region is still locked into the Russian phone network where international direct dialling hasn't arrived.

There are three basic types of phone call, each with a different procedure: local (within the city or area code that you're already in); long-distance (to anywhere else in the Baltic states or the former USSR); and international (to the rest of the world). In the three Baltic states, call charges are already not far off general world levels though there are bound to be some further changes. Phone numbers, unfortunately, seem to change with alarming frequency.

Where to Call From Most hotel rooms have a phone, and where they don't you can usually use one at the reception. You can also make long-distance calls at telephone offices, where it typically takes about 10 minutes to order a call then 30 minutes or so waiting for it to be connected – though things may happen much quicker or much slower. International calls can be made in the same way but waiting time is usually longer (in Latvia you still had to order 24 hours ahead, then wait some more once the appointed hour had rolled around). In the capital cities and some larger towns there are a few special offices, or desks in regular telephone offices, offering quicker service for a higher than normal price.

Public pay phones can be a problem because they're often out of order or incomprehensible to operate. There are different types of pay phone for local and long-distance calls and none (except a few special ones in hotels) for international calls. Hotel lobbies and telephone offices are good places to look for local and long-distance pay phones. On the whole, finding someone who'll let you use their private or office

phone can be less trouble than messing around with public pay phones.

Locations of telephone offices and other tips are given in city and town sections.

Local Calls From a private phone you just dial the number, which is six figures in Tallinn, Rīga, Vilnius, Kaunas and Kaliningrad, and five figures elsewhere. From hotel rooms you may have to use a dialling-out digit or go through the hotel switchboard.

Public local-call pay phones in Estonia are due to be converted to a phonecard system. In the meantime they're free but most don't work (and if you do get through, the person on the other end may sound as if they're trying to talk from under 20 feet of snow with a blizzard going on).

In Latvia local-call pay phones work on tokens *(žeton)* which you can buy at post and telephone offices, some news kiosks, the information booth at Rīga airport and elsewhere.

In Lithuania and Kaliningrad they still take Russian 15-kopeck coins. In Lithuania these are no longer legal tender but are sold at post offices for around US$0.01 each; conversion to tokens *(žetonas)*, which are already in use for long-distance pay phones, is in the offing.

On some phones you have to put the coin or token in the slot before you lift the receiver, on others you must wait till you hear the dial tone before you deposit your coin or token. The cost of a local call is minuscule.

Long-Distance Calls To make a long-distance call from a private phone dial 8, wait for a new dial tone, then dial the area code and number. (In Estonian a long-distance call is a *kaugekõne*; in Latvian a *tālsaruna* or a *starppilsētu telefona saruna*; in Lithuanian a *tarpmiestinis pasikalbėjimas*; and in Russian a *mezhdugorodnyy vyzov*.)

If you don't have a private or hotel phone, you can either book a long-distance call at a telephone office (see Where to Call From), or you can try to find a long-distance pay phone. (In Estonian these phones are called *kaugekõneautomaadid*; in Latvian, *starppilsētu telefonu automāti*; in Lithuanian, *tarpmiestiniai telefonai automatai*; and in Russian, *mezhdugorodnye telefonye avtomaty*.) These are most often found in or outside telephone and post offices, which is handy because you can often get supplies of whatever is needed to operate them on the spot (currently 20-sent coins in Estonia,

tokens in Latvia and Lithuania and 15-kopeck coins in Kaliningrad). The routine is: lift the receiver, put a coin or token in, wait for the dial tone, dial 8, wait for a new dial tone, dial the area code and number, and if the number answers press the button. Feed in new coins as you go along.

Costs In Estonia, a one-minute long-dis-

Area & Country Codes

It's very important to note that the area code for any Baltic states number changes if you are dialling from a different country, even another of the Baltic states.

Local Calls The area codes given in the city and town sections in this book, which all begin with 2, are the ones to use for calls *within* Estonia, *within* Latvia, *within* Lithuania, or *within* the Kaliningrad Region.

Long-Distance Calls If you are calling from one Baltic state to another, or between one of the Baltic states and the Kaliningrad Region, or to one of the Baltic states or the Kaliningrad Region from elsewhere in the ex-USSR, replace the initial 2 of the area code given in this book with:

014 if you are calling an Estonian number
013 if you are calling a Latvian number
012 if you are calling a Lithuanian number
011 if you are calling a Kaliningrad Region number.

For example, the area code for Vilnius is 22 if you are calling from elsewhere in Lithuania, but 0122 if you are calling from Estonia, Latvia, Kaliningrad or elsewhere in the ex-USSR. The area code for Ventspils, Latvia, is 236 if you're calling from elsewhere in Latvia, but 01336 if you're calling from Estonia, Lithuania, Kaliningrad or elsewhere in the ex-USSR.

International Calls For calls originating *outside* the ex-USSR, new country codes for the three Baltic states were introduced in 1993. The old codes were to remain in simultaneous use until all changes were completed. They should no longer be needed by the time you read this, but if you're having difficulties with a new code you could always give the old one a go.

	New Country Code	Old Country Code
Estonia	372	7-014
Latvia	371	7-013
Lithuania	370	7-012

Follow the country code with the area code given in this book – *without its initial 2* – then the number. For example, to call Vilnius you dial your international access code, then the Lithuania country code 370, then 2 for the Vilnius area code, and then the number. In Rīga some new seven-digit numbers have started being allocated for international calls. With these, you leave out the city code: just dial the country code then the number.

For international calls to the Kaliningrad Region dial 7 (the Russia country code), then 011, then the area code as given in this book *minus its initial 2*, and then the number.

Area codes for CIS cities include St Petersburg 812; Moscow 095; Kiev 044; and Minsk 0172 for six-digit numbers or 01722 for five-digit numbers. ■

tance call costs 0.45 EEK (US$0.035) within Estonia; 3 EEK (US$0.25) to Latvia, Lithuania or western European Russia; and 4 EEK (US$0.33) to the rest of European Russia, including Moscow. In Latvia it's US$0.03 within Latvia; US$0.30 to Estonia or Lithuania; and US$0.50 to European Russia. In Lithuania it's US$0.01 or US$0.02 (depending on when you call) within Lithuania; US$0.22 to Latvia or Estonia; and US$0.33 to Russia. In all three countries there are discounts for calls between midnight and 6 am. In the Kaliningrad Region calls to the Baltic states or European Russia are still all under US$0.03 a minute, which surely can't last. Rates to other parts of the ex-USSR are up to double the rates to Russia.

International Calls Calls to anywhere within the former USSR, including the Baltic states, aren't classed as international and are covered in the Long-Distance Calls section. At the time of writing you can already dial virtually all European and other Western countries direct from most private phones and hotels in Lithuania and Estonia. Finland, Sweden, Poland, Hungary, the Czech Republic and Slovakia can be dialled direct from some phones in Latvia. It shouldn't be too long before all phones in all three Baltic states are hooked up to the whole of the Western world, though things look likely to take longer in Kaliningrad.

To call an international number direct from Estonia or Lithuania: dial 8, wait for a new dial tone, then dial 10 followed by the country code, area code and number. For countries you can't dial direct, the international operator is on 007 in Estonia and 8-wait-194 in Lithuania. In Latvia the international operator is on 8-wait-15 if you want your call routed through Stockholm (the better option if you can reach this number) or 8-wait-194 for calls routed through Moscow. In Latvia and Lithuania you can request 'priority' or 'urgent' service, costing 50% to 100% extra to most countries, from the international operator.

If you don't have access to a private, hotel or office phone you need to go to a telephone office to make an international call as already described. Reverse-charge calls will remain impossible for the near future, as will the use of home-billed calling cards.

Costs The table at the bottom of the page shows the cost, at the time of writing, of a one-minute call to various parts of the world. (Calls from Estonia are 25% cheaper between 11 pm and 7 am.)

Fax & Telegraph
Many hotels and organisations in the Baltic states are contactable by fax. There are reasonably priced public fax services, both outgoing and incoming, in the main cities throughout the region. In Latvia you can send or receive domestic or international faxes from the main post office in about 25 of the biggest towns. Some hotels or travel agents will also let you use their fax machine.

Telegrams are a cheap way of contacting the outside world. From Estonia, for instance, they're US$0.08 a word to Western Europe. They can be sent from any post or telegraph office and reach most European countries well within 48 hours. Telegraph is *telegraaf* in Estonian, *telegrāfs* in Latvian, *telegrafas* in Lithuanian, and *telegraf* in Russian.

International Telephone Call Charges (per minute)				
	To Finland or Sweden	To Poland	To Elsewhere in Europe	To North America	To Australia
Estonia	US$0.35 to 0.45	US$0.70	US$0.70	US$1.10	US$1.55
Latvia	US$0.70	US$0.70	US$0.70	US$1.40	US$1.60
Lithuania	US$1.25	US$0.55	US$1.25	US$2.30	US$2.70
Kaliningrad	US$0.20 to 0.35	US$0.20 to 0.35	US$0.20 to 0.35	US$0.40 to 0.75	US$0.45 to 0.65

TIME

Estonian, Latvian, Lithuanian and Kaliningrad time is GMT/UTC plus two hours, except from 2 am on the last Sunday in March to 2 am on the last Sunday in September when daylight saving is in force and it's GMT/UTC plus three hours. When it's noon in the Baltic states it's 1 pm in Moscow, noon in Helsinki, 11 am in Warsaw, 10 am in London, 8 pm in Sydney, and 5 am in New York – though variations in daylight saving schedules may alter that by an hour at certain times of year.

The 24-hour clock is used for rail, bus and air timetables. Kaliningrad still follows the old Soviet practice of using Moscow time *(Moskovskoe vremya)* for air timetables but has changed to local time *(mestnoe vremya)* for train timetables – but you should always double check on this in case further switches are made.

ELECTRICITY

The Baltic states and Kaliningrad run on 220 V, 50 Hz AC. Most appliances that are set up for 240 V will handle this happily. Sockets require a European plug with two round pins.

LAUNDRY

There's laundry service in the better hotels. It normally takes two days. If you're staying in a private flat or house you may be able to use a washing machine there. Otherwise you're on your own. Laundromats are rare.

LEFT LUGGAGE

You can leave luggage at many railway and bus stations throughout the region for a small fee. Often there are supervised baggage rooms where your things should be safe – take a note of their opening times. In some places there are just lockers, which may be risky unless they're in a supervised hall. Be suspicious of anyone who offers to help you stow your baggage in a locker. The normal locker procedure is as follows: find out what coins or tokens you need to lock and unlock the locker (often nearby ticket windows or kiosks will sell these if you don't have any); find an open locker and put your bags in; turn the inner knobs to your chosen combination of letters and/or numbers, and make a note of the combination and of the number of the locker; turn the outer knobs to a different combination; put the right coins or tokens in the slot and shut the door. To open the locker: turn the outside knobs to your combination and put the right coins or tokens in the slot.

TOILETS

Many public toilets, even some of those in good restaurants, are vile, stinking black holes. Always bring your own paper and be prepared to squat. The few public toilets that are up to decent standards of cleanliness have a small admission fee. You pay on entry and pick up paper, if you need it, at the same time. Many Baltic sewerage systems can't cope with toilet paper. If a bin or basket is placed in the toilet, put the paper in there. The letter **M** marks a men's toilet in Estonian or Russian, **V** in Latvian or Lithuanian. **N** indicates a women's toilet in Estonian, **S** in Latvian, **M** in Lithuanian and **Ж** in Russian.

WEIGHTS & MEASURES

Estonia, Latvia, Lithuania and Russia all use the metric system. Drinks are sometimes served by weight: a standard shot of spirits is 50 grams and a glass of wine is 200 grams.

BOOKS

The Baltic states have lots of bookshops but foreign books are a comparative rarity in them. Some of the following books will crop up but it's better to try to get the ones you want before you go. In any case the more you read in advance, the better you'll be prepared. Take any other reading matter you want with you, too, as the choice on the spot is strictly limited.

General

Until recently there was a dearth of modern non-specialist books in English on the Baltic states. But the gap has been well and truly filled by *The Baltic Revolution* by Anatol Lieven, published in 1993 by Yale University Press (hardback, US$30). The author, who is half Irish and half Baltic German (of a family which traces its lineage back to Germanised Liv chieftains), grew up in London but spent the early 1990s as the Baltic states correspondent for *The Times*. His book entertainingly and thoroughly surveys both the past and present of the region, with the unique insights of the simultaneous insider and outsider; it has a lively style and a grasp of the big sweeps of history as well as excitement about detail.

The Singing Revolution by Clare Thomson (hardback, Michael Joseph, London) traces the Baltic states' path towards their new independence through an account of travels there in 1989 and 1990. It also provides background on the Soviet and earlier periods of outside rule. The author is a British journalist of Estonian extraction.

The 1980 winner of the Nobel prize for literature, Czesław Miłosz, who grew up in Vilnius in a part-Polish, part-Lithuanian family, occupies a leading position in modern Polish literature. The last chapter of his *The Captive Mind* (Penguin), written in 1951-52, deals with the Soviet occupation of the Baltic states.

The Baltic States: A Reference Book, published jointly in 1991 by Estonian, Latvian and Lithuanian Encyclopaedia Publishers of Tallinn, Rīga and Vilnius respectively, is 260-plus pages of dense and useful facts, including information on history, arts and culture, politics, places to visit, organisations, and who's whos of important people in each country. You can get it at some Baltic embassies and some outlets in the Baltic states themselves – the price ranges from about US\$2 to US\$20 depending where you find it. It contains phrase lists for all three Baltic languages.

For an introduction to Estonia alone, there's *Estonia and the Estonians* by Toivo Raun (Hoover, California, 1991).

Travel

Among The Russians by Colin Thubron (Penguin), an Englishman's account of driving everywhere he could in the pre-*glasnost* Soviet Union, takes in Tallinn and Rīga, and captures the gloomy, resigned mood of the time.

A Guide to the Baltic States edited by Ingrīda Kalniņš (Inroads, Merrifield, Virginia, USA, 1990) was the first modern guide in English to concentrate exclusively on the Baltics. Though good on background and covering more places than other guides available at that time, it inevitably became rapidly outdated on practical matters. An update is reportedly in the pipeline. The first edition was much stronger on Latvia and Lithuania than on Estonia.

A *Baltic States* guide in the well-illustrated Insight series was published in 1993. This series contains a lot of cultural and historical background.

The only two locally produced English-language guides I've come across to date are the good *Tallinn – A Practical Guide* (Revalia Publishing, Tallinn) and *Visit Lithuania* (Lithuanian Information Institute, Vilnius) which is less of a guidebook than a slim but worthwhile little reference book, including among other things a list of hotels in provincial towns. Latvian Encyclopedia Publishers of Maskavas iela 68, Rīga, have started to publish a series of guides to Latvia's regions. They are in Latvian, but the first volume, *Kurzeme*, also includes a 20-page summary in English. The magazines *Tallinn This Week*, *Vilnius In Your Pocket* and *Klaipėda Today* (see Media) also serve quite well as guides.

If you can manage to track it down, *Russia* by J G Kohl includes a quite lengthy section on the Baltic states among its German author's account of his travels in the tsarist empire in the 1840s. It's both informative and amusing, as much for Kohl's attitudes to what he finds in these outposts of civilisation as for the scenes he describes. The book is a 19th century translation and abridgement of the original.

History

The classic works in English on Baltic history are two weighty tomes: *The Baltic States: The Years of Independence 1917-40* by Georg von Rauch (University of California Press, 1974), and *The Baltic States: Years of Dependence 1940-1980* by Romualdas Mišiunas and Rein Taagepera (C Hurst, London, 1983), covering the Soviet era. These books have lengthy bibliographies if you're interested in following things up further.

The Baltic States and Europe by two British scholars, John Hiden and Patrick Salmon (Longman, hardback, 1991), focuses on Baltic diplomatic history but also gives accounts of the Soviet era and of the reform movement which saw it out. *Northern Europe in the Early Modern Period* by D G Kirby (Longman, 1990) also covers the Baltic states.

Fiction & Arts

Like many writers living under repressive governments, Estonia's most celebrated novelist, Jaan Kross, who was exiled to Siberia for eight years under Stalin, has used historical tales to address contemporary themes. *The Czar's Madman*, first published in 1978, was among the first Baltic writing to become available in English when published by Harvill in 1992. One strand of the work is woven around the true story of Timotheus von Bock, an Estonian German noble whose honesty compelled him to write to Tsar Alexandr I suggesting changes in the way Russia (of which Estonia was then part) was governed. Von Bock was locked away for his pains. At the same time the book explores the German/Estonian class barrier and the semi-mystical feelings aroused by the Estonian countryside.

The Estonian poet Jaan Kaplinski has had two collections, *The Same Sea in Us All* and *The Wandering Border*, published in English, also by Harvill. His work expresses the feel of Estonian life superbly. Both Kaplinski and Kross are thought to have been not far off a Nobel prize – and both were elected to the Riigikogu, Estonia's parliament, for centre parties in 1992.

One of the very few recent novels in English dealing with the Baltic states is *The Good Republic* by William Palmer (hardback, Secker & Warburg, London, 1990). It tells the story of a young man in a Baltic country who, more by accident than design, gets involved in a minor way in the Nazi bureaucracy during WW II then escapes to exile in London but returns 'home' decades later to suffer unexpected nightmare consequences from his past. The book conjures up well the atmosphere of the pre-WW II Baltics, the Soviet and Nazi occupations, and the feel of émigré life. It also lays bare the moral dilemmas facing the occupied peoples in the war years.

Bohin Manor (hardback, Faber & Faber, UK; Farrar, Straus & Giroux, USA) by Tadeusz Konwicki, a leading modern Polish writer who was born in Lithuania, is set in Lithuania in the aftermath of the 1863 uprising. Using the past to comment on more contemporary events (like Jaan Kross), Konwicki evokes the tensions between locals, their Russian rulers and a Jewish outsider, as well as the foreboding and mysterious nature of the Lithuanian backwoods.

For a sense of the atmosphere of 1930s Latvia and Estonia, track down *Venusburg*, one of Anthony Powell's early novels. Published in 1932, it tells the amusing tale of an English journalist trying unsuccessfully to make his name as a foreign correspondent amid the exiled Russian aristocrats, Baltic German intellectuals, and earnest local patriots of the era.

Vytautas Landsbergis' *M K Čiurlionis – Time and Content* (hardback, Lituanus, Vilnius, 1992) is a product of the former Lithuanian president's other great interest in life apart from politics – Mikalojus Konstantinas Čiurlionis, early 20th-century Lithuania's artistic and musical giant. Well illustrated with many of Čiurlionis' paintings and scores, the book contains many of his letters and writings as well as Landsbergis' account of Čiurlionis' rather tragic life and absorbing times.

Dictionaries & Phrasebooks

There's a handy little paperback *Sõnastik Eesti-Inglise* (Estonian-English Dictionary) by Mart Repnau available in Estonia but, unfortunately, it doesn't have an English-Estonian side. In the same series is a *Vestnik* (Conversation Guide) by Mart Aru and Maila Saar which, though primarily designed for Estonians learning English rather than vice versa, will still enable you to say anything in Estonian from 'rampant corruption' to 'Are there any new singles by Cliff Richard?'.

Dictionaries I've found of the other Baltic states' languages are all hardback. The *Lietuvių-Anglų Kalbų Žodynas* (Lithuanian-English Dictionary) (Mokslas, Vilnius, 1991) is again one-way – it has no English-Lithuanian half – but is certainly comprehensive at over 800 pages, and it cost me just under US$0.40, brand new, in the Turistas bookshop at Pilies gatvė 10 in Vilnius. The *Latviešu-Anglu Vārdnica* (Latvian-English Dictionary) (Avots, Rīga, 1989) is a two-way volume but a lot smaller and more easily carried than the Lithuanian one – and it cost me about 20 times as much. Some handier dictionaries and phrasebooks will probably appear in the near future.

Collins Gem Russian Dictionary and Lonely Planet's *Russian Phrasebook* by James Jenkin are both handy and portable.

Non-English-Language Books

There's an enormous amount published on the Baltic states and Kaliningrad in German, including a few dozen guide and travel books since the late 1980s. If you're going to Kaliningrad I particularly recommend *Königsberg Kaliningrad* by Henning Sietz (1992, Edition Temmen). Any decent bookshop in Germany should have a selection but enthusiasts could try writing for catalogues to Baltic-specialist booksellers and publishers such as Edition Temmen, Hohenlohestrasse 21, 2800 Bremen 1; Harro von Hirschheydt, Postfach 810 253, 3000 Hannover 81; Mare Balticum, Helker Pflug, Rubensstrasse 7, 5000 Köln 1; Neuthor-Verlag, Postfach 3402, Neuthorstrasse 3, 6120 Michelstadt; and Verlag Gerhard Rautenberg, Blinke 8, Postfach 1909, 2950 Leer.

There are also guides to the Baltics and numerous other books in Swedish and Finnish. One of the best books I've come across is in French: *Pays Baltes: Estonie, Lettonie, Lituanie: Le Réveil* (Baltic States: Estonia, Latvia, Lithuania: The Awakening), edited by Yves Plasseraud; it's a fascinating collection of essays, articles and interviews covering history, culture, modern life and politics. This book was the January 1991 edition of Série Monde published by Editions Autrement of 4 Rue d'Enghien, 75010 Paris – price FFr 95.

You may also want to pick up the odd book in local languages as a souvenir. There are some attractive, if expensive, coffee-table-type photo essays available.

MAPS

Thankfully the age of deliberately distorted Soviet maps is over. Good, accurate town and national maps are now sold cheaply and fairly widely by bookshops, kiosks and hotels in the Baltic states. Some of them are available in the West too, but at much higher prices. The exception is Kaliningrad where no accurate street map is available locally at the time of writing. Apart perhaps from a Kaliningrad map, the only map you really need to buy in advance is one of the region as a whole.

City & Town Maps

Good accurate street plans, often highlighting places of visitor interest, are available cheaply in many Baltic cities and towns. Try to avoid any street map from before about 1990 since it's likely to contain Soviet 'mistakes' – and also because a good half of its street names will be out-of-date, now that the Baltic states have jettisoned communist and Russian-inspired names. Publication dates are usually in the small print at the bottom or on the back of these maps.

For Kaliningrad the German publishers Verlag Gerhard Rautenberg (see Books) put out an *Aktueller Stadtplan* (Up-to-Date City Map) in 1993. The scale is 1:10,000 (1 cm = 100 metres). The map may not be easily available in Kaliningrad itself. You can order it by post from the publishers: excluding post and packing, it costs DM 26.80, but it's best to write for their free catalogue and order form first. They also publish a 1938 map of the city, showing its pre-WW II layout with Nazi street names, and other Kaliningrad Region maps, atlases and guide books.

Country Maps

The excellent *Eesti Maanteed* (Estonian Roads) paperback atlas, covering the whole of Estonia at 1:200,000 (1 cm = 2 km), is invaluable to anybody spending any time beyond Tallinn. It tells you exactly which stretches of road are paved and which are dirt and accurately marks a host of other features from food shops to archaeological sites. It will, for instance, help you to pinpoint many of the pre-German Estonian fortresses dotted around the countryside. It's blue-covered and fairly widely available in Estonian bookshops and kiosks for up to 50 EEK.

For Latvia there's a 37-page *Road Atlas of Latvia* at 1:200,000 (1 cm = 2 km), published in 1993 by Vade Mecum of Rīga, with text in English, Latvian and Russian. If you prefer a single-sheet map, there's the widely available 1992 *Latvijas Republika* map at 1:600,000 (1 cm = 6 km), cheekily including the Abrene/Pytalovo area in the north-east which has been under Russian rule since WW II but which Latvia claims. Also widely available and cheap (about US$0.50) is the soft-cover *Latvijas Ceļu Karte* (Latvian Road Map) atlas, which reproduces 50-odd pre-WW II maps covering the whole country at 1:200,000 (1 cm = 2 km), plus 40 town maps of the same era. This is still a useful atlas if you bear in mind its limitations – there aren't all that many new roads and many towns' central street lay-outs are little changed. With many street names now back to what they were in the 1930s it scores better than Soviet-era city plans. The atlas also gives lots of good unchanging information about the countryside – locations of pre-German castle mounds *(pilskalns)*, high points of the landscape with good views and so on.

The *Lietuvos Keliai* (Lithuanian Roads) map, published in 1991, covers the whole of Lithuania in useful detail at 1:400,000 (1 cm = 4 km). It's quite widely available in bookshops and kiosks for around US$0.20. Sometimes it comes in three separate sections, sometimes all in one.

In Kaliningrad you can pick up the 1991 *Kaliningradskaya Oblast* map of the Kaliningrad Region, in Russian, cheaply and readily. It's at 1:400,000 (1cm = 4 km) and seems accurate. Verlag Gerhard Rautenberg (see the City Maps section) has published *Das nördliche Ostpreussen* (Northern East Prussia), a map of the Kaliningrad Region with old German place names given beside the new Russian ones.

Regional Maps

A good map of the whole Baltic states is useful for planning and needs to bought in advance. *Lithuania Estonia Latvia* (Cartographia, Budapest), *Estonia, Latvia, Lithuania* (Bartholomew, Edinburgh) and *Baltische Staaten* (Ravenstein Verlag, Bad Soden am Taunas, Germany) are very similar 1:850,000 (1 cm = 8.5 km) maps of the three countries plus most of the Kaliningrad Region, which will be adequate for most travellers.

MEDIA

Newspapers & Magazines

English-Language A surprising number of good English-language publications are produced in the Baltic states, all newcomers since 1990. Their proliferation is partly a result of the growth of English as a common language.

First there's a clutch of city handbook-cum-guidebook-cum-what's-on magazines, each costing US$1 or so. *Vilnius In Your Pocket*, updated five times a year, is as good as any similar publication you'll find within several thousand km. It's a really comprehensive, honest and up-to-date guide to survival and enjoyment in and around the Lithuanian capital. The same publishers put out the similar *Klaipėda Today*, covering western Lithuania, in German and English. Almost as good is *Tallinn This Week* which has parallel text in Swedish and, despite its

name, comes out six times a year. All these guides are among the best single investments you can make in their respective cities. *Riga This Week*, published four times a year with parallel text in German, is less comprehensive but getting better. There's also a similar, rival publication, *Riga Success Guide*. *What? When? Where? In Tallinn* is a free monthly pamphlet listing concerts, theatre, exhibitions, festivals and sports events.

Tallinn City Paper is a quarterly colour magazine with some absorbing features and honest, up-to-date pages of accommodation, food, entertainment, travel and other listings of things visitors need to know. It's called *Estonia Magazine* when mailed to foreign subscribers.

Then there are the several weekly English-language newspapers published in the Baltic states. Best is *The Baltic Independent*, published in Tallinn but giving bright, intelligent coverage of all three states, including entertainment, arts and sport as well as heavier topics. Its Upcoming Events and Visitors' Guide sections are both useful. In 1993 it launched a monthly colour supplement designed for visitors, *The Baltic Outlook*, with lots of useful practical information and bright feature articles.

The Rīga-published *The Baltic Observer* is much less slick and professional than the

Independent but also full of informative material on all three states. *Baltic News*, based in Vilnius, emphasises business and economic news and analysis, while the slim *Lithuanian Weekly*, also from Vilnius, covers Lithuania only. All these papers can be picked up at news kiosks, hotels, and some bookshops. Their prices range from 2 EEK (US$0.15) for the *Independent* to US$1.

Imported English-language newspapers and magazines are much harder to find, for some reason, in Tallinn and Vilnius than in Rīga, where you can get *The Guardian*, *The Times* or the *International Herald Tribune* easily on the day of publication or the next day. The same story goes for *Time* and *Newsweek*. Typically one of these newspapers will cost US$2, one of the magazines US$3.50. German papers are available in Rīga and Vilnius, Finnish ones in Tallinn.

Local-Language Judging by its variety, the local-language press is thriving, though it hasn't really shaken off the Soviet habit of 'hiding the news in a cloud of verbiage', as *Tallinn City Paper*'s editor Mihkel Tarm once put it. Though some papers have been hit by the rising cost of newsprint and postage, there's still a great variety of them in Estonian, Latvian, Lithuanian and Russian. Most of their sales are by subscription. Details of local-language publications available in each of the Baltic states are given in the country-specific Facts for the Visitor chapters later in the book.

TV & Radio

All middle and top-end hotel rooms, and some bottom-end ones too, have a TV. Those in top-end hotels often receive CNN or other Western satellite stations, but in cheaper hostelries you'll probably only get one channel in the local language and one or two in Russian. MTV is screened in dozens of cafés and restaurants. There's quite a lot of English-language broadcasting if you know when and where to tune in. Further details are given in the relevant Facts for the Visitor chapters later in the book.

FILM & PHOTOGRAPHY

Sunlight is sometimes a rarity in the Baltic states, even in summer, so take advantage of whatever you get. Some fast film, ASA 400 or more, is useful if you want to try taking photos in dim light. Carry spare camera batteries, especially in winter when the cold can make them sluggish.

Kodak, Agfa and Fuji film and a few basic accessories like batteries are available from special outlets, which are noted in the city and town sections of this book, and from some hotels and import shops. But you're unlikely to find even slightly unusual types of film such as Kodachrome and prices are liable to be higher than back home, so on the whole it's advisable to take what film you need with you. But beware of the sometimes antiquated x-ray machines at Baltic airports (and any other ex-Soviet airport for that matter): these can fog your film. The best defence against fogging is to carry all your film, unexposed as well as exposed, in a lead-lined pouch which costs only a few US$ from photo shops.

There are a few quick print-processing outlets, also noted in city and town sections.

HEALTH

The Baltic states are, on the whole, pretty healthy places to travel around. Though medical care is not up to Western standards your chances of needing any are low.

Predeparture Preparations

Bring with you all medicines and pharmaceuticals you think you'll need on the trip – even aspirin, tampons or sanitary towels, and condoms or other contraceptives. These things are only patchily available (chiefly in the main cities) and you can't rely on getting any particular thing where and when you feel like it. Take mosquito repellent in summer.

Insurance A travel-insurance policy covering theft, loss and medical problems is a very good idea. Travel agents, including student travel agencies, can help you arrange one. Read the conditions before buying insurance and check to see if it covers ambulances or a flight home. If it's a policy on which you have to pay out for your treatment first, then reclaim the money later, make sure you keep all relevant documentation.

Medical Kit A small, basic medical kit is a wise thing to carry, particularly if you are going off the beaten track. Consider aspirin or paracetamol for pain or fever; an antiseptic for cuts; bandages and Band-aids; antihistamines – which are useful for allergies, as decongestants for colds, to ease itching from bites or stings, and to help prevent motion sickness; something for diarrhoea such as a kaolin preparation like Pepto-Bismol, or Imodium or Lomotil; scissors; insect repellent; a broad-spectrum antibiotic; and, to avoid possible contamination through dirty needles if you have to have an injection, a sterile pack of disposable syringes, available from medical-supply shops. If you use the antibiotics, follow the prescribed dosage and intervals exactly.

Immunisations No immunisations are required for any of the three Baltic states or Kaliningrad. You might consider a gamma-globulin jab to reduce the chances of contracting hepatitis A, which is spread by contaminated food or water. If you travel a lot, a course of Havrix injections, which give long-term protection against Hepatitis A, is worth considering.

Basic Rules

Water Take care with water – both the tap and sea varieties. Tap water in several places smells (and *is*) unclean. Definitely in Rīga, and probably in Vilnius, it needs to be boiled before you drink it, which is why an electric water-heating element is a good thing to have in your luggage. In other places always check with locals whether the tap water is safe to drink or not. Try to make sure they're not just saying 'yes' to keep you happy. If in any doubt boil it or drink something else (mineral water is a cheap, widely available substitute). To purify water thoroughly you should boil it for 10 minutes. Alternatively, you can do it chemically. Chlorine tablets kill many but not all pathogens. Iodine is very effective and is available in tablet form (such as Potable Aqua) but follow the directions carefully. Too much iodine can be harmful.

Sea water is similarly dodgy because of pollution, chiefly untreated sewage though there's chemical pollution as well. In 1991 and 1992 the Estonian government advised people not to swim anywhere along the Estonian coast, and there are similar warnings at Latvia's main beach resort, Jūrmala. According to one press report, only one small beach along the whole Latvian coast is pollution-free. The situation seems similar along Lithuania's coast where equally few of the many beachgoers venture into the water. In 1993, however, the local authorities at Estonia's main coastal resort, Pärnu, declared that the waters there were now harmless. Many of the inland lakes in all three Baltic states are cleaner than the sea waters, but you should take local advice anywhere.

Food & Nutrition Food is generally OK but if in any doubt – for instance if you're suspicious about the piece of meat hidden under the sauce on your plate – leave it. Wash fruit and other things from markets if you can, but make sure you dry off any unboiled tap water. The basic guide is your own good sense – if you're dubious about something then don't eat it. Ice cream from street vendors is sometimes a potential hazard, but there really are few cases of travellers contracting stomach problems in the Baltic states. More of a potential problem is the possibility of getting run-down through poor nutrition if you're eating irregularly and poorly. Try not to go hungry, and eat as much and as varied vegetable matter as you can. This isn't always as easy as it sounds because the Baltic diet is fairly stodgy and meat-based. Get fresh fruit from markets. Especially in winter it's a good idea to take along vitamin pills. Women may want to take iron pills to replace iron lost through periods.

Medical Treatment

Ordinary pharmacies may contain more local traditional remedies – herbal and so on – than medical preparations of the type the West is used to. However there are now quite a few pharmacies in the capitals and other towns stocking imported Western medicines – see the town and city sections.

There are few alternatives to the dismal local medical system, which is short on both facilities and training, if you do need serious attention. There aren't even many private clinics or surgeries. In an emergency seek your hotel's help first (if you're in one) – the bigger hotels may have doctors on call. Emergency care is free in all three states. Secondly, your embassy or consulate may be able to recommend a doctor or hospital, but if things are serious be prepared to go straight home or to Scandinavia.

WOMEN TRAVELLERS

The Baltic peoples have some fairly traditional ideas about gender roles, but on the other hand they're fairly reserved and rarely impose themselves upon other people in an annoying way. If anything, Western women are likely to find less aggravation from men in the Baltics than at home. Unaccompanied women may want to avoid a few of the sleazier bars and beer cellars. In some tourist hotels prostitution is a fact of life, and a woman sitting alone in a lobby, corridor or café might be propositioned.

DANGERS & ANNOYANCES
Crime
Crime in the Baltic states has increased markedly since independence, but that's starting from a pretty low level. You should certainly guard against theft from hotel rooms, particularly in cheap or slackly run hotels lacking much supervision, by keeping valuables with you or in a hotel safe. Carrying your own padlock can be a help. You should also be careful when walking along poorly lit city streets at night. Some of the prostitutes working in tourist hotels rob their customers.

If you're driving your own or a hired vehicle in the Baltic states don't leave anything valuable in it when parked. Lock-up car parks are fairly common and quite a few hotels have them on the spot.

You're sure to hear about the 'mafia' while you're in the Baltic states. These are not Sicilians but the ex-USSR's own version of organised crime. They're not one organisation but many different gangs, stereotypically hailing from the former southern areas of the Soviet Union – Georgia, Azerbaijan, Armenia and the Russian parts of the Caucasus – but in reality from anywhere in the ex-USSR including the Baltic states. It seems their tentacles extend into such high places that little can be done to control them. Even the local press seems unwilling to do exposés for fear of reprisals. The mafia is into any sort of third-rate activity that will turn a few bucks including arms dealing, drugs, metals smuggling, prostitution, buying up state businesses on the cheap by frightening off other potential buyers and extortion from any profitable business they can get their claws into.

The mafia should not hold any terrors for the average visitor. You're most likely to come across it as a slob-like presence – a small knot of thick-set, five-o'clock-shadowed men wearing track suits or cheap leather jackets – at a taxi rank or in a restaurant or café that they frequent. But more worryingly, in 1993 there were a few cases of bombings at restaurants (one in Rīga, one in Jūrmala, and one in Vilnius), thought to be mafia reprisals on owners who refused to pay extortion money. Reportedly no one was hurt in the restaurant attacks but it's certainly to be hoped they don't become a habit.

Service
In the Soviet era, a combination of bureaucracy and apathy turned a lot of people in 'service' industries into rude, obstructive goblins. Most of these people have miraculously changed character now that pleasing the customer has become worthwhile, but there are still one or two hangovers from the bad old days – including some railway booking clerks and telephone-office staff. All you can do is grit your teeth and quietly persist until you've got what you need.

Rip-Offs
Taxi drivers may cheat foreigners the world over and those in the Baltic states, especially at airports and outside the main tourist hotels, are no exception. A few tips on avoiding rip-offs are given in the city sections.

Drunks
Drunks on the streets and in hotels can be a nuisance in the evenings, especially at weekends. In Tallinn they're as likely to be foreign tourists as locals. Steer clear and don't get involved!

Smoke
Smoking is just beginning to go out of fashion in the Baltic states and it's not appreciated in some restaurants. People who want to smoke at these eateries go out for a smoking break between courses. But many public places such as waiting rooms, bars and lobbies are wreathed in tobacco smoke and some cheaper hotel rooms retain a semipermanent aroma of it.

Ethnic Relations
A number of Estonians, Latvians and Lithuanians have what can only be called racist attitudes towards the Russians and other ex-

Soviet nationalities in their midst. While it's easy to understand the resentment the Baltic nationalities feel towards Russia, and even towards Russian people, from whom they have some clear cultural differences, it's not clear what possible good could come from some people's 'send 'em home' mentality. You may find these sort of ideas a barrier to communication with some people. On the other hand, when it comes to action rather than words, the Baltic governments have been pretty careful to avoid provoking any serious trouble with their legislation in these fields.

To avoid falling foul of local ethnic suspicions, in some situations it may pay to make absolutely clear you're a Westerner. In one incident in Tallinn an uncomprehending British tourist was stabbed by a Russian who thought he was an Estonian refusing to answer in Russian. In another, a resident of Tallinn was mugged by two Russians who promptly handed back the stolen goods, and apologised, when they realised he was British!

WORK
The Baltic states have enough difficulties keeping their own people employed so there's not much temporary work for visitors. Most Westerners working here have been posted here by companies back home. However these *are* times of change and opportunity, and there is some scope for people who want to stay a while and carve themselves a new niche – though, in Western terms, you couldn't expect to get rich doing so. The English language is certainly in demand, and you might be able to earn your keep (or part of it) teaching it in one of the main cities. It's better still if you speak Estonian, Latvian or Lithuanian (or even German, Russian, or a Scandinavian language). You might be able to turn this to profit with one of the growing number of international trading, shipping or travel firms, or a bank – especially if you have another relevant skill. You'll have to convince your prospective employers/partners

that you can do something special for them which will significantly help their business.

Just occasionally, jobs for English speakers are advertised in the local English-language press.

ACTIVITIES
Cycling
Cycling is an enjoyable way of getting around virtually anywhere in the predominantly flat Baltic states. If you want to cycle independently bring your own bike; there are only a few places where you could rent one. However it's also possible to take an organised cycle tour with all the equipment provided for you in the Baltics. See the Bicycle section in the Getting Around chapter for more information.

Canoeing
Canoeing is a quite popular activity locally. Latvia and Lithuania have some of the most interesting possibilities. In Latvia the Gauja, Salaca and Abava rivers and the Latgale lakes region all offer uninterrupted routes of several days. The Gauja and Latgale would be the prime choices. Two organisations offering trips for small groups are the Latvian University Tourist Club (Latvijas Universitātes Tūristu Klubs, LUTK) (☎ 22-223 114, fax 22-225 039, 22-227 411) at Raiņa bulvāris 19, LV-1098 Rīga and the Tourist Club of Latvia (Latvijas Tūristu Klubs, LTK) (☎ 22-221 731, 22-227 680) at Skārņu iela 22, LV-1350 Rīga. The LUTK, much the cheaper of the two, charges an average of about US$15 a day including canoe and food (see the Vidzeme and Latgale chapters for more on its programmes). You can contact either organisation in advance for more information, including what you need to bring (possibly a sleeping bag and waterproof clothing and baggage).

In Lithuania the north-eastern Aukštaitija National Park is a good canoeing area with another big network of interconnected lakes. There are canoes to rent at the Kaltanėnai youth hostel in the park. Lithuanian Youth Hostels in Vilnius (see the Vilnius Information and Places to Stay sections) can help you set up a trip.

Sailing

The most appealing waters are around the Estonian coast and islands. Most sailors come in their own craft from elsewhere on the Baltic but there are also a couple of charter possibilities in Estonia itself. See the Sailing Yourself section in the Getting There & Away chapter for some information on harbours and the Getting Around chapter for charter outfits.

Winter Sports

Skiing (mainly cross-country), ice skating and tobogganing are all popular, though there's little if anything on an organised basis for foreign visitors. You'll need to take your own gear or borrow it. Otepää in south-east Estonia is probably the main skiing centre – there are some downhill runs in the district as well as a ski jump. Otepää is also the start of the annual Tartu ski marathon in mid-February. In Latvia the Gauja valley is a winter sports centre: there's a bobsleigh run at Sigulda and a ski jump at Valmiera.

Sauna

A number of hotels, particularly in Estonia, have saunas, and there are also some public bath-houses with saunas. The basic sauna is a wooden room with benches and a hot stove, usually surrounded by bricks or stones, on which you toss water to produce clouds of steam. More modern saunas have more modern forms of heating. A sauna is relaxing, cleansing, said to be good for the lungs and also a close, personal experience. An invitation to share a sauna is a hospitable and friendly gesture. Lightly switching the body with a bunch of birch twigs increases perspiration and tingles the nerve ends.

Courses

Language and culture courses are held at Tartu and Vilnius universities though they can be pretty expensive. For information write to TU Advanced Training Centre or TU Information Service at Tartu Ülikool,

Ülikooli 18, EE2400 Tartu, Estonia; or to the Praktinės lietuvių kalbos katedra (Practical Lithuanian Language Department) at Vilniaus Universitetas, Universiteto gatvė 3, 2734 Vilnius, Lithuania.

Organisations

Apart from those organisations already mentioned, one organisation which may be helpful is the Lithuanian Travellers' Union – see the Vilnius Information section.

ACCOMMODATION

There's a big range of accommodation in the Baltic states and you'll probably get most out of your trip by trying out a variety of types. A few nights in private homes will bring you as close to the people and their way of life as a couple of weeks in hotels.

Hotels

Hotels range from almost the cheapest accommodation of all to easily the most expensive.

Cheap Cheap hotels are still getting used to the idea of Westerners, who in the Soviet era were steered very clear of these less-than-shining examples of the communist way of life. Receptionists and managers often think – or pretend to think – that their premises are so poor that any Westerner prepared to contemplate staying there will want the best, most expensive room available. These hotels are typically ageing, gloomy places whose staff speak no English and whose stereotypical customer is a man in a vest, lying on his bed quaffing vodka, chain-smoking and watching TV. In times of energy shortage, these are the hotels where hot water and heating fail first. Every middle-sized town has at least one.

However some cheap hotels are much better kept than others and the better ones can be quite a bargain: you may get a spacious and clean (if not exactly jovial) room with TV and private bathroom for as little as US$4 a double. A 'lux' room or 'suite' – with a sitting room as well – won't be very much more.

Once they realise that Westerners are interested, some hotels cash in with special high prices – perhaps five or 10 times their regular rates – for foreigners. And for every decently kept, cheap hotel there'll be another that's dark and decaying. At these you may get a room for as little as US$1 or US$1.50 but the showers and toilets will be shared between all the rooms on the floor and will probably be pretty filthy. A few of the very cheapest hotels rent not rooms, but beds in a room which you'll share with a handful of strangers. These places are often unwilling to take Westerners, however.

Middle-Range & Expensive These are basically the hotels that Westerners were lodged in during the Soviet era, plus the new breed of comfortable or luxury hotel that has emerged, often with Western money and management, in the 1990s. At the very top of the range – places like the Palace in Tallinn or the de Rome in Rīga – a double room is in the US$200 region, but at the other end of the scale there are, particularly in Estonia, some pleasant, clean and modern little establishments in the US$15 to US$25 range. In between there's a whole range of prices and types of hotel.

Hotels surviving from the Soviet era are mainly either large 'prestige' establishments from the 1970s or '80s – often tower blocks built with Western tour groups in mind (and still, in many cases, getting this type of customer) – or older, dowdier places now rarely used by Western groups, which used to host East European tourists or youth, student or trade-union groups from the West. Some Soviet-era hotels, especially those that have been privatised, have adapted to the new era quite well and can be agreeable places to stay, but on the whole it's the new hostelries, in all parts of this price spectrum, that are more comfortable, cosy and friendly.

Some top-end hotels in the capitals can get fully booked in summer. At such times you may need to enlist the help of a travel agent to find a room – though it's nearly always cheaper to steer clear of travel agents. In a couple of places, retired cruise ships have been moored on rivers or harbours to alleviate the shortage of middle-range accommodation.

Campsites

In the Baltic states or Kaliningrad, a campsite (Estonian: *kämping*; Latvian: *kempings*; Lithuanian: *kempingas*; Russian: *kemping*) is not normally what we understand by a campsite in the West. Though there are a few tent-only sites and other sites usually (though not always) have space for tents to be pitched, most campsites consist mainly of permanent wooden cabins or, occasionally, brick bungalows. They're a very basic but also very cheap form of accommodation, suitable if all you're really looking for is a roof over your head at night. They're often in quite out-of-the-way country or coastal places which may be hard to reach unless you have a vehicle. The cabins vary in shape and size but are usually small one-room affairs with three or four beds. Showers and toilets are nearly always communal and not very clean. Some sites have a bar and/or cafeteria, or a sauna.

Campsites are usually open only in summer, from some time in May or June to the end of August or mid-September. Though Estonia is quite well provided with campsites (perhaps 40 or 50 are dotted around the country) there are fewer in the other states, especially Latvia.

A night in a campsite cabin typically costs US$1 per person but there are a few superior new places which charge up to US$10. Take special care with security in campsites. Camping in the countryside is possible but if it looks like the land belongs to somebody don't hesitate to ask permission.

Hostels

Youth and backpacker hostels are a new concept in the Baltic states. Estonia has the most advanced network, followed by Lithuania, while Kaliningrad has none at all. Things can be expected to develop everywhere. What Baltic hostels provide isn't quite what you'd expect from a hostel in the West but, in most cases, the enthusiasts who run them deserve all the encouragement they can get. None of the hostel groups is yet affiliated to the International Youth Hostel Federation (or its new incarnation, Hostelling International), but it's always worth asking your own national youth hostel organisation for up-to-date information on the Baltics.

Estonia The Estonian Youth Hostels Association (Eesti Puhkemajade Organisatsioon), launched in 1991, currently has two hostels in Tallinn and one each in Tartu, Otepää and Taevaskoja (south-east Estonia); Klooga (north); Virtsu (west); and Kabli (south-west). The situation is still fairly fluid, with hostels going on and off the list, but you can get up-to-date information – and make bookings if necessary – at the hostels office (☎ or fax 22-441 096) at Room 114, Liivalaia 2, Tallinn.

Prices in the Estonian hostels range from about US$1.50 to around US$15 per person but most are in the US$5 region. No card or membership is currently needed. The type of accommodation is a rather ragbag assortment, from hotels with which the association has an arrangement to wooden country houses. Most rooms hold three or four people, with bedding provided. Showers and toilets are usually shared and there are usually cooking facilities. More information on particular hostels is given in the town/city sections.

The Estonian Youth Hostels Association cooperates with the Finnish Youth Hostel Association (SRM) of Yrjönkatu 38B, SF-00100 Helsinki (☎ 90-694 0377, fax 90-693 1349), the Eurohostel at Linnankatu 9, SF-00160 Helsinki (☎ 90-66 4452, fax 90-65 5044) and the St Petersburg Youth Hostel at 3-ya Rozhdestvenskaya ulitsa 28 (formerly, 3-ya Sovietskaya ulitsa 28), St Petersburg (☎ 812-277 05 69, fax 812-277 51 02, postal address: St Petersburg 193312, prospekt Solidarnosti 11, PO Box 57). You can get information on and make bookings for Estonian hostels through any of these organisations, and vice versa. Advance bookings are particularly advisable for the popular Agnes hostel in central Tallinn.

Latvia Hostels in Rīga come and go but the YMCA has one summer hostel which looks likely to last – see the Rīga chapter.

Lithuania Lithuanian Youth Hostels (Lietuvos Jaunimo Nakvynės Namai) of PO Box 12, Vilnius 2000 (☎ 22-756 650, fax 22-260 631) began life in 1992 with a successful tent hostel in a Vilnius park which it plans to repeat each summer. The friendly people here help their guests in all sorts of ways from renting bikes and setting up national-park canoe trips to advice on ways of crossing into Poland or the Kaliningrad Region. They are establishing a network of hostels in rural and coastal Lithuania and have set up a year-round, budget-travel information office in Vilnius. By 1993 there were hostels at Juodkrantė and Palanga on the coast; and Aukštaitija National Park, Molėtai and Jūžintai in the north-east; as well as Vilnius itself. See Information and Places to Stay in the Vilnius chapter and the other relevant sections for more.

BATS (Baltic Accommodation & Travel Service) is a loose-knit grouping of three rather dissimilar hostels in Vilnius, Kaunas and near Trakai, all costing around US$10 a night. BATS used to have an office in Tallinn and a hostel in Rīga, too, but at the time of writing these are no more. See the relevant city/town sections for information.

Colleges

Universities in Tallinn, Tartu, Rīga, Vilnius and possibly Kaunas have rooms available in student hostels and the like for typically US$5 to US$10 per person per night. Most of the rooms are quite clean, have two or three beds, and share showers and toilets with two or three other rooms. In some cases you're asked to make contact with the relevant office in advance but they'll often be able to accommodate you if you arrive out of the blue. See city sections for details.

Private Homes

Renting a room in a private home is one of the most interesting types of accommodation as you see more of what local life is really like. You'll often – though you may have to pay extra for it – get to sample home cooking, which can be amazingly good after the uninspired fare of many restaurants. Most of the rooms are in flats, since most homes are flats.

In a few mainly rural places, old traditions of hospitality linger and if you're asking around for a room you may be offered one for nothing. In such cases a parting gift of a dollar or two, offered 'for the children' or in some other way to avoid giving offence, can be a good way of saying thank you.

In many homes everybody takes their shoes off once inside the door to keep the floors clean. You'll be offered a pair of slippers to wear indoors.

Local Room Agencies Paying to stay in a private home is a quite regular practice among people from all parts of the former Soviet Union when they travel to a strange town. It's often cheaper, cleaner, friendlier and more secure than a cheap hotel. Locals typically pay under US$1 a night. At this price you may be sharing a small room with a stranger and sharing the bathroom and toilet with everyone in the flat, which may be in an outer suburb. There are networks of such guesthouses – in the true sense of the term – in most towns. The only difficulty may be tapping into them as they're known chiefly by word of mouth. Sometimes they advertise at rail or bus stations with phrases like 'Flat Bureau', 'Hotels in Homes', 'Express Flats', 'Express Hotels' or 'Visit Cooperative' – but normally only in the local language or Russian, since few Westerners use them. Rarely does anyone speak English in their little hole-in-the-wall offices.

If it comes to asking around, the most universal phrase, which most people will understand, is the Russian *kvartirnoe byuro* (flat bureau), pronounced 'kvarr-TIRR-na-yeh byu-ROH'. The Estonian equivalent is *korteri büroo*; the Lithuanian, *butų biuras*. Or simply try words like the Estonian *korter* (flat); Latvian *istaba* (room or flat), *dzīvoklis* (flat) or *mājoklis* (lodging); Lithuanian *viešnagė* (staying-with), *nakvynė* (lodging),

butas (lodging or flat), or *būstas* (lodging, room or flat); or Russian *kvartira* (flat).

Travel agencies can often find you private-home accommodation but may charge a foreigners' price which could triple or quintuple the cost.

Rooms-for-Westerners A number of agencies both in the Baltics and the West specialise in providing private-home accommodation for Westerners in the Baltics. Their prices vary wildly. Cheaper ones may book you into much the same homes as the local flat bureaus but they charge more than the local bureaus – basically because you're a Westerner but also because their staff speak reasonable English or German, which does help. More expensive homestay organisations may provide larger, more comfortable or more central accommodation, English-speaking hosts, more meals, even city tours or intercity transport. Those based in the USA, in particular, tend to be at the luxury end of the market. Some agencies can also offer stays in Russia and other ex-Soviet states.

Information on agencies dealing only with the cities where they are located is given in the relevant city/town sections. The following all cover a number of different cities and towns:

American-International Homestays, 1515 West Penn St, Iowa City, IA 52240, USA (☎ 319-626 2125 or toll-free 1 800 876 2048, fax 319-626 2129) – two-week homestay tours combining Baltic and Russian cities, with full board in English-speaking homes and hosts off-work, from about US$2000; also customised trips

CDS Reisid, PO Box 3443, EE0090 Tallinn, Estonia or Raekoja plats 17, EE0001 Tallinn (☎ 22-445 104 or 22-445 262, fax 22-313 666) – bed & breakfast with English-speaking families in Tallinn, several other Estonian towns, Rīga or Vilnius, US$25/35 a single/double; full board with city tours and host always available US$55/90

Family Hotel Service, Mere puiestee 6, Tallinn, Estonia (☎ & fax 22-441 187) – rooms in flats throughout Estonia including the islands, mostly US$10 to US$15 per person per night; also a few unoccupied flats

Gateway Travel, 48 The Boulevarde, Strathfield, NSW 2135, Australia (☎ 02-745 3333, fax 02-745 3237) – Baltic homestays from around US$200 a week including some meals

Home & Host International, 2445 Park Ave, Minneapolis, Minnesota 55404, USA (☎ 612-871 0596, fax 612-871 8853) – homestays in any Baltic city from US$45/59 a single/double per day for bed & breakfast with non-English-speaking hosts to US$149/199 for 'deluxe homestay' with all meals, entertainment, and English-speaking host off-work to act as guide

IBV Bed and Breakfast Systems, 13113 Ideal Drive, Silver Spring, MD 20906, USA (☎ 301-942 3770, fax 301-933 0024) – bed & breakfast in Baltic capitals, US$75/85 a single/double a night

Patricia Ltd, Elizabetes iela 22-4A, Rīga, LV-1011 Latvia (☎ 22-284 868) – rooms in private flats throughout Latvia between US$6 and US$15 per person

Schenker-Rhenus Reisen, Hohe Brücke 1, 2000 Hamburg 11, Germany (☎ 040-36 135 448, fax 040-36 135 434) – bookings for Eesti Kodu Turism (see Westra Travel, below)

Tourist Club of Latvia (Latvijas Tūristu Klubs), Skārņu iela 22, LV-1350 Rīga, Latvia (☎ 22-221 731, 22-227 680) – rooms in homes in a few Latvian and Lithuanian towns, about US$13 to US$15 per person

Westra Travel, PO Box 67, EE3170 Haapsalu, Estonia (☎ 247-45 648, fax 247-45 191) – handles bookings for Eesti Kodu Turism (the Estonian Guesthouse Association) which offers rooms for around US$9 to US$15 per person per night (including continental breakfast) in several dozen private homes and small hotels of reasonable standard – many of them detached houses – in south-east and west Estonia including the islands; bookings can also be made through regional associations in Haapsalu, Kärdla, Kuressaare and Võru (see those town sections); many houses are only open from 1 May to 31 August; further regions may become available

Holiday Homes, Tourist Bases & Sanatoriums

Many of the holiday homes that in Soviet times were reserved for members of particular organisations are being opened up to general trade now, and while some are tatty and institutional, others are as good as decent hotels. The better ones give an idea of the rewards that awaited those who succeeded in the communist system. Prices in such places range widely but often include full board. A holiday home is likely to be called a

puhkebaas, puhkekodu, puhkemaja, or *pansion* in Estonia; a *pansionāts* in Latvia; a *poilsio namai* in Lithuania; and a *pansionat* in Kaliningrad and elsewhere in Russia.

A rung down the ladder from holiday homes are 'tourist bases' (Latvian: *tūristu bāze*; Lithuanian: *turistinė bazė*; Russian: *turistskaya baza* or *turbaza*), which were established as cheap accommodation in popular Soviet holiday locales. Their standards are similar to those of cheap hotels and in a few of the more remote areas they're the only accommodation available. They can be very cheap.

In some places you can even stay in sanatoriums, now functioning in part as middle-range straight hotels.

FOOD

Things have changed quite rapidly on the Baltic eating scene since the late 1980s when getting a half-decent meal involved a great deal of planning and patience. There are now many human-scale restaurants with good food and good service. Some are new and privately run, others are older but have made a successful transition to the new era. The three Baltic capitals, and Estonia in general, are particularly well endowed with enjoyable eating places, but things can still be pretty basic in provincial Latvia and Lithuania.

The Language Guide at the back of the book includes words and phrases you will find useful when ordering food and drink.

Types of Eatery

The stereotypical Soviet-style restaurant, with its surly door attendant, invisible waiters, ear-splitting pop group and parties of drunken revellers, is on the decline. However it's still usually a good idea to speak in English or another Western language at the door of many restaurants; this decreases your chances of a surly response.

Eating is still relatively cheap, though improved standards have brought higher prices, notably in Estonia. There are numerous restaurants with food and service of Western quality where you can get a three-course meal for US$5 or less – indeed a lot less in some of the older places in Latvia and Lithuania. There are only a handful of restaurants in the whole region where you'd pay over US$15 for a meal. At the other end of the scale are canteens and cafeterias, where you can fill up for less than US$1. These places, incidentally, are also useful for avoiding language problems as most of what's on offer is on display and you can just point at what you want. Their food is no gourmet's delight but it's usually quite palatable and filling.

Fast food is slowly nosing its way into the region as another low-effort method of feeding. Estonia has two small chains of its own – Bistro (burgers, salads etc) and the good Peetri Pizza. In Rīga you can find US-style fried chicken and even a Latvian version of fish and chips. Local pizzerias are also popping up here and there though their offerings may be idiosyncratic. At all these places you can expect to eat for round about US$1 – perhaps a bit more in Estonia. McDonald's is on its way to Rīga and Tallinn.

There are many good cafés, too. The three capitals in particular have excellent café scenes with a variety of places serving up good coffee, pastries and, as often as not, alcoholic drinks and light hot meals. In Estonia a *baar* will often serve light meals as well as drinks.

Ordering

What you actually get to eat in a restaurant is still a bit of a lottery at times. But a growing number of places now have legible multi-lingual menus which accurately describe what they've got for you to eat. If not, there are more and more waiters able and willing to explain the choices in reasonable English. If prices are written beside only a few items on a menu, it means that only those items are 'on' that day. If you're faced with pages covered in items typed on, written in, or crossed out in an illegible hand and unintelligible language, don't spend ages trying to decipher it. The chances are that nothing you've chosen will be 'on' in any case.

Instead, simply find out what the waiter recommends.

The Russian custom of consuming large helpings of *zakuski* (hors d'oeuvres) such as tomato, beetroot or cucumber salads, smoked fish, or cold meats is alive and well in many Baltic restaurants. Where a menu has a heavy weighting towards these items it's a good idea to order two or three of them as the later courses in such places tend to be small and not very carefully prepared. A full dinner in this mould would consist of zakuski followed by soup, possibly followed by a fish course, then a meat-and-veg course, and then a dessert (usually ice cream) with a range of beverages along the way. The menu will be divided on the lines of all these courses. However there's also a growing number of (mainly Scandinavian or German-influenced) eateries where, in the Western style, the main course really is the main course and the starters and soups are genuine preliminaries.

What You Get

There's increasing variety in the types of meal available. A growing number of European-style eateries, even good Chinese and Indian restaurants, have opened up. Try to budget for a good meal in one of these not too infrequently. But a typical main course in an ordinary restaurant still consists of a piece of grilled or fried meat or fish, along with chips and small amounts of a couple of boiled vegetables. This is only a fairly pallid reflection of real local diets. You won't truly experience what Baltic people eat unless you're lucky enough to enjoy some home cooking. If you do, the care with which it's prepared and the variety of tastes and textures which can be extracted from some pretty ordinary ingredients will be a pleasant surprise. Notes on some local specialities are given in the Estonia, Latvia and Lithuania Facts for the Visitor.

Common food items throughout the region include pancakes, which come with all manner of different fillings – fruit, meat, curd, cheese, jam, sour cream etc – and in a variety of sizes; sausage, usually cold and sliced; and dairy products – milk is turned to curd, sour cream and cottage cheese as well as plain old butter, cream and cheese.

Four common ways of cooking meat of almost any kind are as a shashlik (kebab), carbonade (officially a chop but in practice it could be almost any piece of grilled meat), 'beefsteak' (any piece of fried meat), and stroganoff (cubes of meat in sauce or gravy).

Nutrition & Self-Catering

While no one needs to go hungry travelling in the Baltic states or the Kaliningrad Region, you need to think a little bit about getting enough variety of food, particularly fresh fruit and vegetables, to stay healthy. This applies especially to vegetarians, whose existence is only on the fringe of being recognised. To avoid any misunderstanding, vegetarians should specify precisely what items they want – a waiter who speaks your language makes a big difference.

Estonian and Russian at least have words for 'vegetarian' (Estonian: *taimetoitlane*; Russian: *vegetarianets* (male), *vegetarianka* (female)), but the concept isn't always very well understood. Even if you get across the message 'no meat' or 'vegetables only' you may fall foul of the notions that chicken isn't meat and potatoes aren't vegetables.

Salad starters can supply some of the nutrients everyone needs from vegetable matter but it's a good idea to supplement restaurant fare by buying some of your own food in markets and shops. This is an inexpensive way of at least partly feeding in any case. Most towns have a market, open every day, with a surprising range of fruit and vegetables often brought from the southern states of the former USSR and sold at what, by Western standards, are good prices (though they may be beyond the pockets of many locals). Bread is easy to get from bakeries at under US$0.20 a loaf. Food shops may not have a great variety but they'll have something worth buying. A kg of cheese from a shop or market will normally be in the US$1 to US$2 range. Sausage and tinned fish are other staples. There are also shops specialising in Western imports – more

expensive but tempting for a few familiar food items.

DRINKS
Non-Alcoholic Drinks

Tap water can be dodgy – see the Health section. A good cheap substitute (a few US cents a bottle) is mineral water, of which there are numerous brands. Estonia's best is Värska. Tea and coffee are easy to get throughout the region. 'Juice' is not usually what we understand by the term in the West: it's more like a cordial, a concentrate diluted with water. *Kvas* is a refreshing drink made from fermented bread. Sometimes in summer it's dispensed on the street from big cylindrical wheeled tanks. In Lithuania it's called *gira*. Coke, Fanta etc also crop up.

The Language Guide at the back of the book contains words and phrases you will find useful when ordering drinks.

Alcoholic Drinks

Good beer is brewed in the Baltic states but little of it can be had in restaurants – presumably because it's much cheaper than imported German or Scandinavian beer which, at US$1 or US$1.50 a can, can double the cost of a meal! Local beer is sold in shops, kiosks, some bars and the occasional beer cellar, which is about the nearest thing to a pub – if usually a pretty rough pub – that you'll find in the Baltic states. Beer normally comes in half-litre bottles which cost between about US$0.10 and US$0.35. You can also buy the mostly inferior draught ale with which people fill cans at kiosks, some shops, and breweries. Most Baltic beer is light, fairly flat, and of medium strength. Utenos alus, brewed in Utena, north of Vilnius, is one of Lithuania's best brews; the heavy Saare beer from the island of Saaremaa is Estonia's first choice; Gambrinus is one of Latvia's most popular. Here and there you can get good strong stout – known in Latvia as *tumšais* and in Lithuania as *porteris*. A few quality, more-Western-style brews are starting to be produced, mostly in smaller bottles with bigger prices – among them the Estonian Saku Reval Luksus,

Latvia's Aldaris Luxus, and the Utena brewery's new GJ beer. The Rīga state brewery has relaunched an old light ale, Kummel, using a pre-WW II recipe.

Vodka, brandy and champagne, all from various areas of the ex-USSR, are easier to get than local beer in bars and restaurants, where they're usually sold by weight: a normal shot of spirits (bigger than the average Western measure) is 50 grams, a glass of champagne or wine, 200 grams. All these drinks are available in shops and kiosks too; champagne is around US$1.25 to US$2 a bottle.

Some Estonian cafés and bars serve tasty, warming *hõõgvein* (mulled wine). Latvia's speciality is Rīga Black Balsam (Rīgas Melnais Balzāms), a thick, dark, bitter and potent liquid with supposedly medicinal properties. Its recipe is secret but the ingredients include orange peel, oak bark, nutmeg, peppermint, brandy, ginger, nutmeg and valerian. It can be drunk 50/50 with vodka, or in coffee. In Lithuania you may find mead (*midus*) or jolly little fruit liqueurs called *likeriai* – about US$0.25 for 50 grams in a café or bar.

All manner of imported Western drinks are sold in import shops, top restaurants, and some bars and cafés.

ENTERTAINMENT

There's plenty of entertainment to be had in the Baltic states, if you can find out about it.

The Entertainment sections of this book's city chapters give pointers to what to expect and how to find it. Posters, local media, and word-of-mouth are the three main sources of what's-on information.

The three capital cities are the centres of entertainment though university cities like Tartu and Kaunas and, in summer, resorts like Pärnu, Jūrmala and Palanga can also be active. Regular live-music venues are fairly few and, of course, this is a changing scene. The jazz scene in Vilnius, the club scene in Rīga and, at the time of writing, the excellent Eeslitall in Tallinn are the highlights. One-off concerts of rock, pop, folk, jazz and blues – by visiting foreign stars as well as local artists – are fairly frequent but you have to study the posters and media to find out about them. There are a number of good music festivals including the Tallinn Rock Summer, FiESTa in Pärnu, the Liepāja rock festival in Latvia and the biennial jazz festival in Birštonas, Lithuania – see the Cultural Events sections.

Classical music, opera and ballet are all very active and there are plenty of opportunities to take in a performance or two. Vilnius seems to get quite a few big-name visiting performers from other countries. The Rīga Ballet is perhaps the region's best known company but was suffering from lack of a permanent home while its theatre was being rebuilt. See the city Entertainment sections for more information on this field. Virtually all theatre is in local languages which limits its interest for many visitors.

The commonest form of nightlife remains restaurants with live music and dancing. Often the music is bland, over-loud middle-of-the-road pop which doesn't appeal much to visitors, but that doesn't stop many locals from having a good night out. Some of the smarter establishments reject jeans and trainers. Discos crop up with irregular regularity. In Tallinn, Rīga, Jūrmala and probably one or two other places there are (mainly small) casinos.

Festivals of music, dance, theatre, drama and so on are an integral part of the entertainment and arts calendar so keep your eyes and ears open for what's on at the time of your visit.

THINGS TO BUY

The Baltic states may not be among the world's shopping meccas, but what is available is often pretty good value. The end of the Soviet era has released on to the market many of the best handicrafts and other products which could previously be seen only in museums. If you're considering buying anything of much monetary, artistic or historic value ask about the rules on exporting things of that kind as there are some restrictions. Some information on this subject is given in the Customs section of this chapter.

Amber

Amber – pine resin fossilised 40 to 55 million years ago – is one of the most distinctive souvenirs of the region. It washes up on beaches and is brought up in fishing boats' nets – especially in the southern half of the region – and alluvial deposits from rivers are mined in the Kaliningrad Region. This translucent, surprisingly light material has been made into jewellery in the region for thousands of years. Amber artisanry probably reached its zenith in the 18th century Amber Room of the Russian royal palace at Tsarskoe Selo (formerly Pushkin) near St Petersburg. The Amber Room was plundered by the Nazis in WW II; the treasure disappeared in Kaliningrad in 1945 and has been the subject of much speculation ever since. There are interesting museums of amber in both Palanga and Kaliningrad.

Modern amber jewellery, particularly necklaces, is widely available today in Lithuania (especially), Latvia and the Kaliningrad Region. It's sold in a variety of shops, markets, and privately. The biggest selection I've seen anywhere is in the market at Palanga. Klaipėda, Vilnius, Liepāja, Rīga and Kaliningrad are other places you'll find it on sale. The cheapest necklaces, made with small pieces of poor colour, cost little over a dollar while the best in city shops go for over US$50, sometimes up to US$100.

Amber pieces come in a variety of shades and sizes and some are a result of a heat and compression treatment which combines small pieces into bigger ones. More old-fashioned ways of treating it include boiling in honey to make it darker, or in vegetable oil to make it lighter. Pieces with 'imperfections' such as grains of dirt or vegetation inside are more likely to be original and may also be more valuable.

Handicrafts

Some really excellent and original pottery and ceramics are made in the Baltic states and there's quite a boom in shops selling them and other craft products. Prices are nearly always quite reasonable. Some attractive stained-glass panels are also available. Easier to get home in one piece than either pottery or glass are woodcarvings and leatherwork.

If you fancy a Baltic national costume to take home there are shops in the capitals selling them – not cheap though. Perhaps more practical are some of the quite attractive hand-knitted woollen garments from Estonia.

Rīga stages a big crafts fair, the Gadatirgus, with much of Latvia's best produce on sale, on the first weekend in June. Vilnius has a similar event, the Kaziukas Fair, around St Kazimieras' Day, 4 March.

Art

Paintings and prints galore are on offer at galleries, shops and open-air art markets throughout the region. You can buy some quite attractive little city views or landscapes, if you just want an easily portable reminder of the Baltics to hang on your wall back home, or the latest in local avant-garde outpourings if you're a connoisseur or speculator. Prices range widely.

Other Souvenirs

Books and maps can be good souvenirs. Among other things, some quite lavish coffee-table-type photo books and interesting reproductions of historic maps are starting to appear in a few Baltic bookshops. Antiquarian books are starting to come out of the woodwork too. Cassettes and records of local music are usually pretty cheap in Baltic music shops, but the selection is often limited. There are also a lot of cheap Russian pirate CDs circulating.

The number of antique shops is mushrooming; icons, old silver and medals are three of their stocks-in-trade. Typical Russian souvenirs like *matryoshka* dolls and flower-printed scarves are also sold not just in the Kaliningrad Region but in the Baltic states too.

Getting There & Away

If anyone needed convincing that the Baltic states really were independent (perhaps an Estonian, Latvian or Lithuanian who had freshly returned from a few years of astral travelling having finally despaired of the Soviet system in the mid-1980s), you'd only need to take them to an airport or major seaport in their country. The evidence that you can travel, with minimal fuss, direct to the Baltics' western neighbours would be proof enough that Soviet writ no longer runs here.

Until 1989 the only direct passenger transport between the Baltic states and anywhere outside the USSR was a single ferry plying between Tallinn and Helsinki. Now there are dozens of direct services by plane, train, ship, hydrofoil, and bus. If your transport service turns out to be slow or uncomfortable, remind yourself that just a few years ago it didn't exist at all!

There are now so many ways of travelling into the Baltics that the choice is almost mind-boggling. The situation will continue to change rapidly as travel companies compete for new routes and find out just how much demand there is. Schedules change, prices yo-yo, routes go in and out of action almost every month – so bear this in mind when making your plans and treat the information in this chapter as a starting point for your own enquiries. Fares in this chapter have been converted to US$ for ease of comparison but are subject to currency fluctuations as well as general price rises.

There's no need to stick with the same form of transport all the way to the Baltics: it's perfectly feasible to fly or take a bus to Warsaw and then enter Lithuania by train; or fly to Helsinki and sail from there to Estonia, for example. Travelling this way you can take in another country on your trip. Lonely Planet's travel survival kits to *Poland* and *Finland* have much more information on ways of reaching those countries than there's room for here.

Distances within the Baltic states are relatively small; if there's no suitable transport direct to where you want to go, just enter the Baltics somewhere not far away and travel overland.

TRAVEL AGENCIES

Here's a sampler of places to start asking about transport to or from the Baltic states and neighbouring countries. Some are travel agencies specialising in the region (who may have some of the cheapest air tickets), others are general budget, student, or youth travel agencies. Also look at the ads in the travel pages of newspapers and 'what's on' magazines. You could try the *Independent*, the *Observer*, the *Sunday Times*, *Time Out*, or *TNT* in Britain; Berlin's *Zitty*; the *New York Times*, *LA Times*, *Chicago Tribune*, or *San Francisco Chronicle Examiner* in the USA; Toronto's *Globe & Mail* in Canada; the Melbourne *Age* or the *Sydney Morning Herald* in Australia; or the *South China Morning Post* in Hong Kong. *Travel Unlimited* newsletter (PO Box 1058, Allston, MA 02134, USA) publishes details of cheap airfares and courier opportunities to worldwide destinations from the USA, Britain and elsewhere. One monthly issue costs US$5; a year's subscription costs US$25 (US$35 outside USA).

Estonian, Latvian, and Lithuanian embassies, consulates, and émigré organisations may be able to help with information on charter flights or other economical ways of getting to the Baltic states (look in capital or major-city phone books).

Information on travel ticket outlets within the Baltic states is given in the relevant city and town sections of this book.

Australia
Contal Travel, 72 Campbell St, Sydney, NSW 3000 (☎ 02-212 5077) – Polish-run travel agency with fares to the Baltics; also has offices in other major cities

Eastern Europe Travel Bureau, 5th floor, 75 King St, Sydney, NSW 2000 (☎ 02-262 1144) – Russia, Eastern Europe, Trans-Siberia specialist; offices in other state capitals

Gateway Travel, 48 The Boulevarde, Strathfield, NSW 2135 (☎ 02-745 3333, fax 02-745 3237) – Baltics, ex-USSR and Trans-Siberia specialist

Red Bear Tours, 320B Glenferrie Rd, Malvern, Victoria 3144 (☎ 03-824 7183, fax 03-822 3956) – Russia budget-travel specialist; cheap Trans-Siberia packages

STA – student/youth/discount travel specialist with offices in major Australian and world cities

Austria

ÖKISTA, 9 Garnisongasse 7, Vienna (☎ 0222-401 480) – student travel agency also open to non-students

Belgium

Acotra, Rue de la Madeleine 51, Brussels (☎ 02-5128607) – student travel

Connections Travel Shop, Rue du Marché-au-Charbon 13, Brussels (☎ 02-5125060) – useful ticket agent

Canada

FB On Board Courier Services (☎ 416-671 1614) – courier flights

Finncharter, 20 York Mills Rd, Suite 402, North York, ON M2P 2C2 (☎ 416-222 0740, fax 416-222 5004) – Baltic tours including Estonia

Pedersen World Tours, Park Place Corporate Centre, 15 Wertheim Court, Suite 402, Richmond Hill, Toronto, Ontario, L4B 3H7 (☎ 416-882 5470, fax 416-882 5472) – flights to the Baltics via Copenhagen; also tours

Travel CUTS – student/youth/discount travel agency with branches in major cities

Denmark

FremadRejser, Vesterbrogade 43, 1, DK-1620 Copenhagen V (☎ 31 22 04 04, fax 31 22 22 77) – hotel and travel bookings and tours to the Baltic states and Kaliningrad

Kilroy Travels, Skindergade 28, DK 1159 Copenhagen K (☎ 33 11 00 44, fax 33 32 32 69) – budget travel agency; especially useful for tickets if you're a 'youth' (under 26) or a student under 35; offices in other cities

Pedersen World Tours, H C Andersens Blvd 12, 1553 Copenhagen V (☎ 33 93 86 87) – part-charter flights between the Baltics and Canada via Copenhagen

Transalpino, Skoubogade 6, Copenhagen (☎ 33 14 46 33) – student, youth, discount specialist

Finland

Kilroy Travels, Mannerheimintie 5, 00100 Helsinki (☎ 90-624 101; fax 90-651 528, 90-602 917) – budget travel agency; useful for tickets if you're a 'youth' (under 26) or a student under 35; offices in other cities

France

Council Travel, 31 Rue Saint Augustine, Paris 2ème (☎ 1-42.66.20.87) – branch of USA's biggest student and budget travel agency

Selectour Voyages, 29 Rue la Huchette, Paris 5ème (☎ 1-43.29.64.00) – discount air tickets

Voyages et Découvertes, 21 Rue Cambon, Paris (☎ 1-42.61.00.01) – cheap tickets

Germany

Alternativ Tours, Wilmersdorfer Strasse 94, Berlin (☎ 030-8 81 20 89) – discount flights

ASTA-Reisen, Amalienstrasse 73, München (☎ 089-50 06 05 40 ext 544) – student travel

Baltisches Reisebüro, Bayerstrasse 37/1, D-8000 München 2 (☎ 089-59 36 53 or 089-59 36 94; fax 089-52 59 13) – big range of tours to all three Baltic states and Kaliningrad Region

Bavaria Studentenreisebüro, Augustusplatz 9, Leipzig (☎ 041-7 19 22 67) – youth and student tickets

Deutsches Reisebüro, Emil-von-Behring Strasse 6, 6000 Frankfurt am Main 50 (☎ 069-95 88 00, fax 069-95 88 10 10) – tours to Baltic states and other parts of ex-USSR

Greif Reisen A Manthey, Universitätsstrasse 2, 5810 Witten-Heven (☎ 02302-2 40 44, fax 02302-2 50 50) – tour company specialising in Kaliningrad Region, Neringa and Klaipėda; also covers other Baltic states and Poland

Ost-Reise Service, Artur Ladebeck Strasse 139, 4800 Bielefeld 14 (☎ 0521-14 21 67, fax 0521-15 25 55) – Baltics, Kaliningrad & Eastern Europe specialist

Rautenberg-Reisen, Blinke 8, Postfach 1909, 2950 Leer (☎ 0491-41 43) – group trips to the Kaliningrad Region and former German areas of Lithuania and Poland

Reisebüro Alainis, Revalweg 4, 8940 Memmingen (☎ 08331-35 82) – tours and individual bookings to Baltic states and Kaliningrad Region

Schnieder Reisen, Harkortstrasse 121, 2000 Hamburg 50 (☎ 040-380 20 60) – big range of tours and individual bookings to Baltic states and Kaliningrad Region

SRID Reisen, Berger Strasse 1178, Frankfurt (☎ 069-43 01 91) – cheap tickets

SRS Studenten Reise Service, Marienstrasse 23, Berlin (☎ 030-2 81 50 33) – student (under 35) and youth (under 26) airfares

Ireland

USIT Travel Office, 19 Aston Quay, Dublin (☎ 01-679 8833) – specialising in youth and student travel

Italy

CTS, Via Genova 16, off Via Nazionale, Rome (☎ 06-46 791) – discount and student/youth travel agency; offices throughout Italy

Netherlands

ILC Reizen, NZ Voorburgwal 256, Amsterdam (☎ 020-620 51 51 for flights; 020-622 43 42 for other matters) – flights, trains, buses

Malibu Travel, Damrak 30, Amsterdam (☎ 020-623 68 14) – long-established cheap flight specialist

NBBS, Rokin 38, Amsterdam (☎ 020-624 0989) – Dutch nationwide 'student' travel agency

New Zealand

Sun Travel, 407 Great South Rd, Penrose, Auckland (☎ 09-525 3074) – Trans-Siberian packages; individual travel bookings

Norway

Kilroy Travels, Nedre Slottsgate 23, 0157 Oslo (☎ 22 45 32 00, fax 22 42 97 09) – budget travel agency; especially good if you're a 'youth' (under 26) or a student under 35

Poland

Biuro Turystyki Cliff Tour, ulica Dabrowszczaków 37, 80 365 Gdańsk Przymorze (☎ 0-58-56 35 13; ☎ & fax 0-58-53 49 32) – ferry, hotel, and chauffeur-car bookings for Kaliningrad

Spain

TIVE, Calle José Ortega y Gaset 71, Madrid (☎ 91-401 1300) – student/youth travel

Sweden

Estlandsresor, Runebergsgatan 3, S-216 11 Malmö (☎ 040-15 22 66, fax 040-15 36 16) – Baltics specialist

Kilroy Travels, Kungsgatan 4, Box 7144, S-10387 Stockholm (☎ 08-23 45 15, fax 08-10 16 93) – budget travel agency; especially worth trying for tickets if you're a 'youth' (under 26) or a student under 35

Nordisk Reseservice, Engelbrektsgatan 18, S-10041 Stockholm (☎ 08-791 50 55, fax 08-791 40 90) – travel and tour agency knowledgeable on Baltics

Switzerland

GIB, Eigerplatz 5, CH-3007 Bern (☎ 031-45 81 51) – tours to the Baltic states and Kaliningrad

SSR, Leonhardstrasse 5 & 10, Zürich (☎ 01-261 29 56) – budget travel specialist; branches in other cities

UK

ACE Study Tours, Babraham, Cambridge, CB2 4AP (☎ 0223-835055) – art and architecture-oriented tours etc

Campus Travel, YHA Adventure Shop, 174 Kensington High St, London W8 7RG (☎ 071-938 2188) – student and youth travel specialist with about 30 branches in university towns

Council Travel, 28A Poland St, London W1 (☎ 071-437 7767) – branch of USA's biggest student and budget travel agency

Finlandia Travel, 227 Regent St, London W1R 7DB (☎ 071-409 7334) – cheap flights to the Baltics

Martin Randall Travel, 10 Barley Mow Passage, Chiswick, London W4 4PH (☎ 081-994 6477, fax 081-742 1066) – tours focusing on art, architecture etc

Progressive Tours, 12 Porchester Place, London W2 2BS (☎ 071-262 1676, fax 071-724 6941) – tours and individual bookings, some cheap flights

Regent Holidays, 15 John St, Bristol, BS1 2HR (☎ 0272-211711, fax 0272-254866) – leading British Baltic specialist; tours, individual bookings, cheap flights

Rochdale Travel Centre, 66 Drake St, Rochdale, OL16 1PA (☎ 0706-31144, fax 0706-526668) – flights, packages, individual bookings to Baltic states and Ukraine

Scantours, 8 Spring Gardens, London SW1A 2BG (☎ 071-839 2927) – flights to Scandinavia; Baltics and Scandinavian tours

STA Travel, 74 Old Brompton Rd, London SW7 (☎ 071-937 9962) – branch of worldwide student/budget travel agency; branches in major British and European cities

Trailfinders, 194 Kensington High St, London W8 (☎ 071-938 3232) – discount tickets, travel bookshop, visa service; also offices in Manchester and Glasgow

USA

Airhitch (☎ 212-864 2000) – New York-based specialist in cheap one-way airfares to Europe

American-International Homestays, 1515 West Penn St, Iowa City, IA 52240 (☎ 319-626 2125, fax 319-626 2129) – homestay tours or customised homestays in the Baltic States and ex-USSR

Baltic-American Holidays, 501 Fifth Avenue, Suite 1605, New York, NY 10017 (☎ 212-972 0200, fax 212-972 0208) – specialist in group and individual trips to the Baltics

Baltic Tours, 77 Oak St, Suite 4, Newton, MA 02164 (☎ 617-965 8080, fax 617-332 7781) – flights, individual and group tours

Council Travel – student/youth/discount travel agency with offices in many cities including New York (☎ 212-661 1450) and Los Angeles (☎ 310-208 3551)

GT International, 9525 South 79th Avenue, Hickory Hills, Il 60457-2259 (☎ 708-430 7272, fax 708-430 5783) – Baltics specialist; tours and individual bookings

Home & Host International, 2445 Park Avenue, Minneapolis, Minnesota 55404 (☎ 612-871 0596) – homestays in Baltics and ex-USSR; accompanying travel arrangements

IBV Bed and Breakfast Systems, 13113 Ideal Drive, Silver Spring, MD 20906 (☎ 301-942 3770) – Baltic homestays with or without flights

STA Travel – student/youth/discount travel agency with offices in many cities

Union Tours, 79 Madison Ave, New York, NY 10016 (☎ 212-683 9500, fax 212-683 9511) – group and individual flights and packages to the Baltics

Way To Go – information on courier flights in Los Angeles (☎ 213-466 1126) or San Francisco (☎ 415-864 1995)

Air

Until 1989 there were no scheduled international flights into the Baltic states. Now you can fly direct from a dozen or so Western countries, and with a single change of plane from a great many more. Finnair, Swissair, Lufthansa (Germany), SAS (Scandinavia), Lot (Poland), and Austrian Airlines are among the airlines flying into the Baltics that have worldwide connections to their home countries.

As well as scheduled flights there are also charter flights from some countries. Another option is to fly to a nearby country (Finland, Poland and Sweden are the most convenient) and do the last leg by sea or overland. This may work out both cheaper and more interesting. Flights to Warsaw on Lot, the Polish airline, are often sold at deep discounts all over the world.

New routes are opening all the time, and services will become more frequent on some existing routes and reduced on others. Fare information given here is very much subject to change. Check out the field before buying your ticket.

Travel agents, as well as the airlines themselves, should be able to sell you tickets for any of the scheduled flights. SAS, Lufthansa and Finnair are among airlines offering cheap 'youth' fares for under-26s on some routes. Like other cheaper fares these may only be bookable a week or two before departure. Many airlines also have 'general sales agents' appointed to sell discounted tickets for certain routes. In the case of the Baltics, these are often travel agents who specialise in the region. See the preceding Travel Agencies section for details of some of these. Also get quotes from student, youth, and general discount ticket agents.

One-way flights at regular fares are sometimes as expensive as returns, but 'open-jaw' tickets (on which you fly into one city and out of another) are quite widely available for the Baltic capitals and St Petersburg. On SAS, one-way youth fares between Scandinavia and the Baltic capitals can be combined to form the equivalent of open-jaws.

The Baltic Airlines

Since 1992 each Baltic state has had its own state airline carved out of the old Soviet Aeroflot monopoly. These are Estonian Air, Latvian Airlines (Latvijas Aviolīnijas or Latavio), and LAL (Lithuanian Airlines, or Lietuvos Avialinijos). In addition, there are

Baltic International Airlines (a Latvian-US joint venture which flew initially between Rīga and Germany, then launched London flights, too); Rīga Airlines Express (an independent Latvian airline due to start Oslo and Amsterdam flights in late 1993); and Air Lithuania (Aviakompanija Lietuva, an independent Lithuanian enterprise flying mainly in and out of Kaunas).

While clearly a boost to national pride, the Baltic airlines have proved costly and problematic to get up and running, tending to be overambitious while lacking in the experience and attitude to succeed in a competitive market. The émigré Lithuanian businessman Balys Stankunavičiaus, who was brought in from Australia to get LAL on its feet commercially, resigned in frustration after about a year.

The idea of a united Baltics airline has been raised (along the lines of Scandinavia's SAS), but there are big hurdles of national pride to be jumped before such a prospect could become a reality.

The airlines' initial handicaps included poor Soviet-style service, primitive customer information and advertising, and Soviet-made planes which weren't popular with some passengers. These things are gradually changing.

With a few exceptions, fares on the Baltic airlines are no cheaper than on their Western rivals – except for Baltic citizens who often have to pay only a fraction of what foreigners must pay. The consequence is that where a Baltic airline shares a route with a Western rival, the rival often gets the lion's share of the passengers. How long the little Baltic airlines can survive – if they don't start filling their planes with more passengers soon – is a serious question.

Ticket Offices You don't always go to an airline itself for the cheapest fares on its flights. But it may be useful to know that the Baltic airlines are gradually setting up their own ticket outlets in other countries. Otherwise, Aeroflot sells tickets in some countries on their behalf. Estonian Air has opened the following offices:

Denmark
    Nyhavn 31J, Copenhagen K (☎ 33 32 00 23, fax 33 32 15 99)
Sweden
    Drottninggatan 65, S-11136 Stockholm (☎ 08-233 666, fax 08-233 669)
    Gustav Adams Torg 47, PO Box 4026, S-20311 Malmö (☎ 040-7 97 55)
Ukraine
    Ploshchad Pobedy 2, Kiev

LAL tickets are sold in the UK by Flight Representation (☎ 0293-551737) of Ocean House, Hazelwick Ave, Three Bridges, Crawley, West Sussex. LAL has an office in Germany at Frankfurt Airport Kabinet Nr 200.3323 (☎ 069-69 45 79 or 069-69 45 80). In Warsaw, LAL's tickets are sold by Lot.

Latvian Airlines is at World Trade Centre, A-1300 Vienna Airport, Austria (☎ 71110 6178).

Baltic International is on ☎ 071-828 4223 in London; at Cullen Center, 601 Jefferson, Suite 3742, Houston, Texas 77002 (☎ 713-651 8730, fax 713-651 8750) in the USA; and at Valter Colp Strasse 9-11, Frankfurt (☎ 069-62 80 28, fax 069-61 06 37).

TO/FROM FINLAND
Estonia
Finnair and Estonian Air both fly from Helsinki to Tallinn, and vice versa, at least once a day. The flight is only 35 minutes but often ends up being no quicker than a hydrofoil (which is much cheaper) because of the time spent getting to and from the airports. The cheapest returns are around US$90 with either airline. Finnair has a one-way youth fare of around US$40, bookable no more than seven days before you fly.

Latvia & Lithuania
Finnair flies Helsinki-Rīga-Helsinki three times a week, and Latvian Airlines flies Rīga-Helsinki-Rīga twice a week. An Apex return from Helsinki was around US$200 with Finnair, but US$360 with Latvian Airlines. Latvian Airlines had the cheaper Rīga-Helsinki one-way fare – US$110 at the time of writing. Air Lithuania flies three times weekly between Helsinki and Kaunas.

Air Travel Glossary

Apex Apex, or 'advance purchase excursion' is a discounted ticket which must be paid for in advance. There are penalties if you wish to change it.

Baggage Allowance This will be written on your ticket: usually one 20 kg item to go in the hold, plus one item of hand luggage.

Bucket Shop An unbonded travel agency specialising in discounted airline tickets.

Bumped Just because you have a confirmed seat doesn't mean you're going to get on the plane – see Overbooking.

Cancellation Penalties If you have to cancel or change an Apex ticket there are often heavy penalties involved; insurance can sometimes be taken out against these penalties. Some airlines impose penalties on regular tickets as well, particularly against 'no show' passengers.

Check In Airlines ask you to check in a certain time ahead of the flight departure (usually 1½ hours on international flights). If you fail to check in on time and the flight is overbooked, the airline can cancel your booking and give your seat to somebody else.

Confirmation Having a ticket written out with the flight and date you want doesn't mean you have a seat until the agent has checked with the airline that your status is 'OK' or confirmed. Meanwhile you could just be 'on request'.

Discounted Tickets There are two types of discounted fares – officially discounted (see Promotional Fares) and unofficially discounted. The lowest prices often impose drawbacks like flying with unpopular airlines, inconvenient schedules, or unpleasant routes and connections. A discounted ticket can save you other things than money – you may be able to pay Apex prices without the associated Apex advance booking and other requirements. Discounted tickets only exist where there is fierce competition.

Full Fares Airlines traditionally offer first class (coded F), business class (coded J) and economy class (coded Y) tickets. These days there are so many promotional and discounted fares available from the regular economy class that few passengers pay full economy fare.

Lost Tickets If you lose your airline ticket an airline will usually treat it like a travellers' cheque and, after inquiries, issue you with another one. Legally, however, an airline is entitled to treat it like cash and if you lose it then it's gone forever. Take good care of your tickets.

No Shows No shows are passengers who fail to show up for their flight, sometimes due to unexpected delays or disasters, sometimes due to simply forgetting, sometimes because they made more than one booking and didn't bother to cancel the one they didn't want. Full-fare passengers who fail to turn up are sometimes entitled to travel on a later flight. The rest of us are penalised (see Cancellation Penalties).

On Request An unconfirmed booking for a flight, see Confirmation.

Open-jaws A return ticket where you fly out to one place but return from another. If available this can save you backtracking to your arrival point.

Overbooking Airlines hate to fly empty seats and since every flight has some passengers who fail to show up (see No Shows) airlines often book more passengers than they have seats for.

TO/FROM SWEDEN

Estonia

SAS has daily flights both ways between Stockholm and Tallinn, and Estonian Air flies the same route six times a week. The regular one-way youth fare on SAS is about US$115. The cheapest return tickets from either airline are around US$225. If you are under 26 (or a student under 35) Kilroy Travels has one-year return fares for as low as US$165.

Latvia

SAS flies Stockholm-Rīga-Stockholm four times weekly, and Latvian Airlines flies Rīga-Stockholm-Rīga three times weekly. The cheapest returns from Stockholm are around US$225 with SAS. A one-way youth fare on SAS is half that. Latvian Airlines' one-way Rīga-Stockholm fare is about US$160. There are also flights between Jönköping in central Sweden and Rīga.

Lithuania

LAL flies twice weekly each way between Vilnius and Stockholm. The Scandinavian airline Taffo and Air Lithuania both fly twice a week each way between Kristianstad in

Usually the excess passengers balance those who fail to show up but occasionally somebody gets bumped. And guess who it is most likely to be? The passengers who check in late.

Pex and Superpex Variations on Apex fares, usually with tighter restrictions on when they can be booked, when you must pay, and how long you can stay.

Promotional Fares Officially discounted fares like Apex fares which are available from travel agents or direct from the airline.

Reconfirmation At least 72 hours prior to departure time of an onward or return flight you must contact the airline and 'reconfirm' that you intend to be on the flight. If you don't do this the airline can delete your name from the passenger list and you could lose your seat. You don't have to reconfirm the first flight on your itinerary or if your stopover is less than 72 hours. It doesn't hurt to reconfirm more than once.

Restrictions Discounted tickets often have various restrictions on them – advance purchase is the most usual one (see Apex). Others are restrictions on the minimum and maximum period you must be away, such as a minimum of 14 days or a maximum of one year. See Cancellation Penalties.

Stand-by A discounted ticket where you only fly if there is a seat free at the last moment. Stand-by fares are usually only available on domestic routes.

Sunday or Weekend Rule Applies to some return tickets – you must spend one Sunday or weekend in your destination before returning.

Tickets Out An entry requirement for many countries is that you have an onward or return ticket, in other words, a ticket out of the country. If you're not sure what you intend to do next, the easiest solution is to buy the cheapest onward ticket to a neighbouring country or a ticket from a reliable airline which can later be refunded if you do not use it.

Transferred Tickets Airline tickets cannot be transferred from one person to another. Travellers sometimes try to sell the return half of their ticket, but officials can ask you to prove that you are the person named on the ticket. This is unlikely to happen on domestic flights, but on an international flight tickets may be compared with passports.

Travel Agencies Travel agencies vary widely and you should ensure you use one that suits your needs. Some simply handle tours while full-service agencies handle everything from tours and tickets to car rental and hotel bookings. A good one will do all these things and can save you a lot of money, but if all you want is a ticket at the lowest possible price, then you really need an agency specialising in discounted tickets. A discounted ticket agency, however, may not be useful for other things like hotel bookings.

Travel Periods Some officially discounted fares, Apex fares in particular, vary with the time of year. There is often a low (off-peak) season and a high (peak) season. Sometimes there's an intermediate or shoulder season as well. At peak times, when everyone wants to fly, not only will the officially discounted fares be higher but so will unofficially discounted fares or there may simply be no discounted tickets available. Usually the fare depends on your outward flight – if you depart in the high season and return in the low season, you pay the high-season fare. ■

southern Sweden and Vilnius. Air Lithuania also has flights between Kaunas and Kristianstad via Palanga. Six days a week there are also flights by SAS or LAL between Vilnius and Copenhagen, where SAS connects with main Swedish cities. Stockholm-Vilnius returns start about US$450 on SAS, and the one-way youth fare is about US$225.

TO/FROM DENMARK
Estonia
Estonian Air makes direct flights between Tallinn and Copenhagen four times a week,

taking 1½ hours. Four days a week SAS links both Copenhagen and Oslo with Tallinn (up to 2½ hours) with a change at Stockholm. Kilroy Travels in Copenhagen has youth or student fares for as low as US$160 one way and US$320 return. A standard one-month return fare on SAS, bookable seven to 14 days in advance, is about US$400; the one-way youth fare is half that. Estonian Air's cheapest Tallinn-Copenhagen fare, one way or return, is about US$370.

Latvia
SAS has five direct flights a week each way

between Copenhagen and Rīga, and Latvian Airlines has three flights a week. The cheapest SAS returns from Copenhagen are around US$320; the one-way youth fare is about US$160. A one-way Latvian Airlines ticket from Rīga to Copenhagen is around US$220.

Lithuania

SAS has four direct flights a week each way between Copenhagen and Vilnius. LAL has three. The cheapest returns from Copenhagen on SAS are around US$320, and the one-way youth fare is about US$160. Vilnius-Copenhagen costs about US$460, one-way or return, with either airline.

Kaliningrad

SAS was due to start flights between Copenhagen and Kaliningrad in late 1993.

TO/FROM NORWAY

The independent Latvian airline Rīga Airlines Express (RIAIR) was due to start flights between Oslo and Rīga in late 1993. With SAS, you can connect at Copenhagen or Stockholm. Kilroy Travels has youth and student fares for around US$160 one way, US$320 return to Tallinn; or US$220 one way, US$440 return to Rīga or Vilnius.

TO/FROM POLAND

Latvia

Latvian Airlines and Lot both fly twice a week from Warsaw to Rīga and vice versa.

Lithuania

Three times a week (on different days) LAL and Lot both fly from Warsaw to Vilnius and vice versa. A one-way ticket or a one-month return from Warsaw is around US$100 (though it'll probably cost a lot less if you fly into Warsaw from elsewhere with Lot). From Vilnius it's the same one-way fare, but about US$125 return. In Warsaw find out whether your flight will leave from the domestic or the international airport terminal. They're far enough apart to make you miss your plane if you turn up at the wrong terminal at the last minute.

Kaliningrad

Warsaw-Kaliningrad flights are planned.

TO/FROM GERMANY

In addition to the scheduled flights mentioned here, charter flights may be an economical option from Germany to any Baltic state. Baltisches Reisebüro, Greif Reisen, Ost-Reise Service and Schnieder Reisen have all offered charters in the past. Lufthansa has open-jaw youth fares combining Baltic capitals at similar rates to there-and-back youth fares.

Estonia

Lufthansa and Estonian Air both fly three days a week (each airline on different days) to/from Frankfurt. Regular return fares from either end start at around US$450.

Latvia

Lufthansa flies Frankfurt-Rīga-Frankfurt five times weekly; Baltic International flies Rīga-Frankfurt-Rīga three times weekly, and Rīga-Hamburg-Rīga and Rīga-Berlin-Rīga twice a week each. An independent German airline, Hamburg Airlines, flies to/from Berlin (Tempelhof) and Hamburg three times a week. Baltic International may start Munich-Rīga flights. Return fares from either Germany or Latvia generally begin around US$460, though Lufthansa's youth fare is in the US$400 region, and there have also been some cheap promotional fares on these routes.

Lithuania

Lufthansa and LAL each fly between Frankfurt and Vilnius, and vice versa, three times a week. LAL also flies to/from Berlin (Schönefeld) three times weekly. Germany's Hamburg Airlines flies Hamburg-Berlin (Tempelhof)-Vilnius and back, twice a week. Apex returns on the LAL Berlin route are around US$300, departing from either end. Returns to/from Frankfurt or Hamburg start at around US$500, but Lufthansa's Frankfurt youth fare is about US$420. Air Lithuania Hamburg-Palanga-Kaunas flights were due to start at the end of 1993.

Kaliningrad

In 1993, Baltisches Reisebüro and Schnieder Reisen started to fly groups from Hamburg to Kaliningrad on direct twice-weekly Aeroflot charters. Tickets on these flights may become available to individual travellers. There are also, reportedly, plans for scheduled Berlin-Kaliningrad flights by Lufthansa or Aeroflot.

TO/FROM THE UK

Latvian Airlines and Baltic International both fly Rīga-London-Rīga three times weekly. The cheapest return fares with either airline were initially around US$470 but these may change. LAL flies three times a week from Vilnius to London and back. In Britain you can pick up one-month LAL return tickets to Vilnius for about US$360 from Flight Representation (see the earlier Baltic Airlines section). Direct flights between London and Tallinn are talked about, but for the moment it's necessary to make a connection en route, usually in Scandinavia with SAS or Finnair. Other air routes to the Baltics from Britain include via Warsaw with Lot, via Vienna with Austrian Airlines, and via Zürich with Swissair.

For all three Baltic capitals, the fares offered by specialist agents are often cheaper than the airlines' own. Some of the best are on SAS or Finnair flights via Scandinavia. Regent Holidays, for instance, has some return fares to Tallinn or Rīga on Finnair for as low as US$320. Regent also offers returns from London or Manchester to Tallinn or Rīga on SAS for about US$440. Progressive Tours has London-Vilnius return fares with Lot via Warsaw starting around US$400.

Another option is to fly to Scandinavia or Poland and complete the trip by sea or land. Scantours has interesting fares to Helsinki from around US$340 return; Progressive Tours has London-Warsaw returns at around US$300. Also worth checking for fares to or through Warsaw are the Polish tourist office, Polorbis, (☎ 071-637 4971) at 82 Mortimer St, London W1N 7DE; or Polish-run travel agents like Fregata Travel (☎ 071-734 5101) at 100 Dean St, London W1, and (☎ 061-226 7227) 117 Withington Rd, Manchester; and Travelines (☎ 071-370 6131) at 154 Cromwell Rd, London SW7 4EF.

TO/FROM ELSEWHERE IN EUROPE

Other direct flights to/from countries west of the Baltics include:

Amsterdam-Tallinn
  Estonian Air, three times weekly
Amsterdam-Vilnius
  LAL, three times weekly
Budapest-Kaunas
  Air Lithuania, twice weekly
Budapest-Vilnius
  Malev, twice weekly
Paris-Vilnius
  LAL, twice weekly
Prague-Kaunas
  Air Lithuania, twice weekly
Prague-Rīga
  CSA, twice weekly
Vienna-Rīga
  Latvian Airlines, twice weekly
Vienna-Vilnius
  Austrian Airlines, twice weekly
Zürich-Vilnius
  Swissair, twice weekly

New services proposed or talked about by the Baltic airlines include: Paris to Tallinn and Rīga; London, Athens, Rome and Vienna to Tallinn; and Amsterdam, Vienna and Zürich to Rīga. Where there isn't a direct flight there'll usually be reasonable one-stop options using the airlines that do fly into the Baltics. For instance, on the days that Estonian Air doesn't fly from Amsterdam, you can still reach Tallinn from Amsterdam by SAS, with a change in Stockholm, in 3¾ hours.

Or again, you could fly into Helsinki, Warsaw or Stockholm and do the last leg by sea or land. For discount fares to or through Warsaw, try Polish tourist offices (which go under the names Orbis or Polorbis) or any Polish-specialist travel agencies.

TO/FROM RUSSIA, TRANSCAUCASIA & CENTRAL ASIA

There are up to three flights daily between Moscow and each of the Baltic capitals including: Estonian Air from Tallinn; Latvian Airlines and Transaero, an independent Russian airline, from Rīga; LAL from Vilnius; and the Russian state airline, Aeroflot, from Tallinn and Kaliningrad. In Moscow all flights use Sheremetevo airport, except Kaliningrad flights which use Vnukovo.

The three Baltic state airlines also fly two or three times a week between Tallinn, Rīga, Vilnius, and St Petersburg; Aeroflot flies around 10 times a week from Kaliningrad to St Petersburg and vice versa. Latvian Airlines flies between Liepāja and St Petersburg, and LAL links Palanga with Moscow (Sheremetevo) – both up to five times a week. You can also get to and from dozens of other places in Russia, Transcaucasia or former Soviet Central Asia via a connection at Moscow with Aeroflot or one of its successors – you should be able to book all the way through in one go. Some direct flights pop up but they're on/off affairs so far.

At the time of writing there's considerable fare variation between the three Baltic state airlines on flights to Russia, though this may not last very long. Flying Estonian Air – the most likely of the three to be pointing the way to future fare patterns – the cheapest one-way or one-month return tickets are US$254 to Moscow and US$140 to St Petersburg; but if you're booking less than seven days before departure it goes up to US$307 one way or US$466 return to Moscow, and US$188 one way or US$280 return to St Petersburg. Latvian Airlines charges just US$83 one way to Moscow and $67 to St Petersburg (from either Rīga or Liepāja). LAL charges US$150 to Moscow (US$200 from Palanga) and US$120 to St Petersburg, with return fares double in each case. In Russia go to Aeroflot offices for tickets to the Baltics; the foreigner's fare from Moscow to any Baltic capital is about US$80 at the time of writing. You normally need your passport to buy an air ticket in Russia.

Aeroflot's fares from Kaliningrad to Moscow or St Petersburg were both around US$2 (yes, that's two dollars!) for Russians at the time of writing. But they're almost certain to increase and, as a foreigner, you'll probably have to pay many times the locals' fare in any case.

TO/FROM BELARUS & UKRAINE
Estonia
Estonian Air flies Tallinn-Minsk-Tallinn three times weekly and Tallinn-Kiev-Tallinn four times. One-month returns are from US$168 for Minsk and from US$268 for Kiev.

Latvia
Latvian Airlines and local Belarussian or Ukrainian airlines fly Rīga-Minsk-Rīga six times weekly, and Rīga-Kiev-Rīga two to four times a week. Rīga-Minsk is US$61 one way. In summer there are Liepāja-Minsk and Liepāja-Kiev flights.

Lithuania
LAL flies Vilnius-Kiev-Vilnius four times weekly for US$100 one way, US$200 return. Vilnius-Odessa flights are in prospect.

Kaliningrad
Aeroflot flies seven times a week to/from Minsk, and three times a week to/from Kiev. For Russians, fares from Kaliningrad are US$1.50 to Minsk and US$3.50 to Kiev.

TO/FROM ISRAEL
At one time LAL did schedule weekly flights between Vilnius and Tel Aviv for US$230 one way, US$460 return. Last time I checked they weren't actually flying, but they may be revived. Estonian Air has also talked about Tel Aviv flights.

TO/FROM NORTH AMERICA
In 1993 the US airline, American TransAir, began direct flights twice weekly between New York and Rīga with return fares from US$680 (winter, midweek). Tickets can be bought through travel agents, or direct (☎ 1-800-382-5892). There are also plenty of connections through countries near the Baltics on Finnair, SAS, Lot, CSA, Lufthansa and so on, plus some charter possibilities. Or you can fly to Scandinavia or

Warsaw and finish the trip by sea or overland.

From New York, most return fares to the Baltic capitals through Baltic specialist firms are between US$700 and US$1000, but these can go down in winter, or up to US$1200 in peak summer weeks. These firms can fix flights from cities throughout the USA and in some cases Canada. Baltic Tours offers summer charter flights to Kaunas from Chicago (US$850 return) and Newark (US$800). Baltic-American Holidays offers open-jaw fares, and Union Tours has one-way fares in either direction.

The weekend edition of the Polish newspaper *Nowy Dziennik* has lots of ads for flights from the USA to Poland, and there are several Polish travel agencies in Manhattan, Brooklyn, Chicago and elsewhere. There's a lot of competition on US-Scandinavian routes which should keep prices down; you should get a New York-Stockholm return for US$500 to US$600 low season, US$700 to US$800 high season. Airhitch can get you a one-way stand-by fare from the USA to Europe for around US$160 to US$270 depending where you start in the USA. Call Council Travel or Way To Go for information on courier flights – two to three months in advance, at the start of the calendar month.

Pedersen World Tours of Toronto and Copenhagen offers charter flights between Toronto and Copenhagen combined with Estonian Air or LAL flights to/from Tallinn or Vilnius; these are mostly in the US$950 to US$1100 range, down to around US$700 in the off-season. They'll throw in Vilnius-Rīga coach transfers for US$40. They also do tickets from west Canada, or tickets starting in the Baltics (US$40 to US$80 cheaper).

CSA claims to be the only airline that can fly you from Rīga to Canada in under 12 hours.

TO/FROM AUSTRALIA

There are no direct scheduled flights from Australia to the Baltics. Aeroflot, or Russian International as it now calls itself overseas, flies from Sydney to Moscow for US$1200

to US$1300 return. Another airline flying to both Australia and the Baltics is Lufthansa. Among the specialist agents, Gateway Travel offers return fares from Sydney, Melbourne or Brisbane to the Baltics from around US$1100 to US$1500. Or you could fly to Scandinavia, Warsaw or Moscow then finish the trip by sea or overland. Discounted return fares to Scandinavia on mainstream airlines – through a reputable agent like STA – range from around US$1100 (low season) to US$1750 (high season).

TO/FROM ASIA

There are no direct flights between Asia and the Baltics although there has been talk of a service starting between Taipei and Rīga after Taiwan and Latvia made friends with each other in 1992 (causing China to close its embassy in Rīga).

Some of the cheapest flights from Asia are with East European airlines, such as via Moscow using Aeroflot, via Prague with CSA, or via Warsaw with Lot. Helsinki with Finnair and Stockholm with SAS are other possible routes.

Land

BUS

With a few exceptions, buses are the cheapest but least comfortable method of reaching the Baltic states. There are direct buses from Denmark, Germany, Poland, Sweden, Finland, Russia and Belarus. From much of the rest of Europe you can reach the Baltics with a single change of bus in Warsaw, though buses from Warsaw into Lithuania do have a couple of potential snags. One is delays on the border (which are even worse when leaving Lithuania), though scheduled buses seem to be spared the very long waits that some private motorists have to endure. A second is that some of the buses between Warsaw and Vilnius can get booked up.

Motorists have had to queue as long as four days at the border between Ogrodniki (east of Suwałki, Poland) and Lazdijai (Lithuania), which to date is the only regularly functioning road crossing between Poland and Lithuania. Most buses, however, seem to get through in two to four hours. A second border point, on the road from Suwałki, Szypliszki and Budzisko (Poland) to Kalvarija and Marijampolė (Lithuania), was due to open in 1993 but had already been subject to several postponements. If you're thinking of taking a bus across this border, it pays to find out how long it will *really* take to reach its destination. Ask other travellers, youth-hostel workers, and Lithuanian or Polish embassies as well as bus companies. An alternative to the direct crossing is to take one bus from Poland to Belarus then another from Belarus to Lithuania, but you'll be up for a Belarus transit visa charge of US$20. If the buses from Poland to Kaliningrad become open to non-locals, then yet another way into the Baltics will be open.

In general you should book as far ahead as you can for any bus into or out of any of the Baltic states.

Poland-Lithuania

The Polish state tourist company, Orbis, runs a fairly reliable and comfortable daily service from Warsaw to Vilnius and back. The overnight trip takes about 11 hours. The fare is US$18 one way or US$26 return from Warsaw; US$25 one way or US$35 return from Vilnius. In Warsaw you can get tickets from the Orbis offices at ulica Puławska 31 and ulica Marszałkowska 142 – which are usually closed Saturday and Sunday. In Vilnius, tickets are sold by Turistinė Firma Erelis (see the Vilnius Getting There & Away section) and departures are from the Hotel Lietuva.

There are a further two daily buses each way between Warsaw and Vilnius (a scheduled 10-hour trip), costing US$11 to US$16 one way – departures and tickets from Warsaw Central bus station or Vilnius bus station. The international (*miedzynarodowa*) ticket window at Warsaw Central bus station (which is a few km west of the city centre – take bus M from Warszawa Centralna rail-way station to Dworzec Zachodni) is closed on Saturday afternoon and all day Sunday.

There's also a thrice-weekly night bus between Gdańsk and Vilnius (10 to 12 hours; US$20 one way, US$25 return). Turistinė Firma Erelis is the ticket outlet in Vilnius. The Vilnius terminus is the Hotel Lietuva.

Other buses, between Poland and Vilnius bus station, include:

Białystok-Vilnius
    two or three daily; seven hours; US$11 or US$13
Gdańsk-Olsztyn-Elblag-Vilnius
    one daily; 12 hours; US$18
Olsztyn-Vilnius
    four a week; US$15
Suwałki-Vilnius
    four or five daily; six hours; US$8 to US$11

Buses between Poland and other places in Lithuania include:

Augustów-Druskininkai: two daily
Gdańsk-Olsztyn-Suwałki-Kaunas: three weekly
Suwałki-Druskininkai: one daily
Suwałki-Kaunas: three weekly

Poland-Belarus

There are buses from Warsaw Central bus station to Brest and Grodno daily (both about US$8), and to Minsk four times weekly. These might be useful if you want to approach Lithuania through Belarus.

Poland-Latvia/Estonia

The twice-weekly Warsaw-Rīga-Pärnu-Tallinn bus run by the Estonian company Mootor (Tallinn ☎ 22-211 409, 22-444 484 or 22-422 549) gets through the Polish-Lithuanian border pretty quickly and reaches Rīga (US$20) in 14 hours and Tallinn (US$30) in 19 hours. In Warsaw you can get tickets at the Central bus station (see Poland-Lithuania). Departures at present are on Wednesday and Sunday mornings from Warsaw; Monday and Thursday mornings from Tallinn. The schedule may change. In Tallinn you can get tickets from the main bus station or the bus ticket office at Pärnu maantee 24. In Rīga some ticket clerks don't seem to know about this bus, but it does exist.

There's a daily bus each way between Warsaw Central bus station and Daugavpils (Latvia), costing about US$15.

Poland-Kaliningrad

In 1992 a number of bus services started up between north-eastern Polish towns and Kaliningrad, operated jointly by König Auto of Kaliningrad (☎ 22-430 480) and various Polish companies. Initially these were only open to Polish and Russian residents, but they may become more generally available. With new road borders being developed between Poland and the Kaliningrad Region, Warsaw-Kaliningrad and other services may also start. The initial routes are:

Olsztyn-Bartoszyce-Bagrationovsk-Kaliningrad: twice daily each way, 4¼ hours; US$6 Olsztyn-Kaliningrad, US$4 vice versa; Polish operator: PKS

Białystok-Augustów-Suwałki-Bartoszyce-Bagrationovsk-Kaliningrad: twice weekly each way, 11¼ hours; US$11 Białystok-Kaliningrad, US$6 vice versa; Polish operator: Biatra, Białystok

Elblag-Braniewo-Mamonovo-Kaliningrad: once daily each way, four hours; US$5 Elblag-Kaliningrad, US$3 vice versa; Polish operator: ZKS Olimpia (☎ 0-50-24503), ulica Agrikola, Elblag

Gdańsk-Elblag-Braniewo-Mamonovo-Kaliningrad: once daily each way, five hours; US$7 Gdańsk-Kaliningrad, US$4.50 vice versa; Polish operator: PPKS (☎ 0-58-316276), ulica Wałowa 19, Gdańsk

See the Kaliningrad Getting There & Away section for information on ticket outlets for these buses in Kaliningrad.

To/From Western Europe

A bus trip through Poland is probably the cheapest way into the Baltics from Western Europe.

Direct Buses One direct weekly service runs between Copenhagen and Vilnius via Berlin and Warsaw. It takes about 25 hours to Vilnius from Copenhagen and 17 hours from Berlin. At present it leaves Copenhagen on Friday mornings and Vilnius on Saturday evenings. The one-way fare is about US$115

between Copenhagen and Vilnius; about US$75 between Berlin and Vilnius; and about US$45 between Warsaw and Vilnius. In Copenhagen tickets are sold by Royal Rejser (☎ 33 91 91 15, fax 33 91 91 85) of Store Kongensgade 94, 1264 Copenhagen K; in Vilnius tickets are available at the bus station. The bus stops in Berlin or Warsaw only if prior reservation is made by telephone to Copenhagen.

A twice-weekly service between Copenhagen, Stockholm and Tartu, Estonia, is run by the Tallinn company Mootor. Tartu-Copenhagen costs US$73; round trip, US$131. In mid-1993 a weekly service was due to start from Munich, Cologne and Hamburg to Tallinn (stopping in Nuremberg, Essen, Hannover, Berlin, Rīga and Pärnu) with a round-trip fare from Cologne or Munich to Tallinn of US$170. There has also been talk of a weekly Kiel-Hamburg-Berlin-Tallinn service run by the Tallinn Bus Company (☎ Tallinn 532 063) which would cross from Poland into the Kaliningrad Region at Mamonovo.

Via Warsaw From many other cities in Europe you can get a bus to Warsaw and pick up another bus or a train from there into Lithuania. There are useful youth or student discounts on some international European buses. From London the trip takes one to 1½ days and costs around US$90 to US$110 one way, US$150 to US$180 return. One of the main operators to Warsaw is the Polish bus company Pekaes, with services from London, Manchester, Brussels, Cologne, Frankfurt, Hamburg, Oslo, Paris and Rome.

Other buses are run by Eurolines (☎ 071-730 0202) of 52 Grosvenor Gardens, London SW1, which is a major European bus line with continent-wide connections and agents in many cities including: Amsterdam (☎ 020-627 51 51); Brussels (☎ 02-217 0025); Budapest (☎ 1-262 800); Frankfurt (☎ 069-79 03 240); Milan (☎ 02-80 11 61); Munich (☎ 089-59 18 24); and Paris (☎ 1-43.54.11.99).

Some buses are run by Polish-specialist travel firms: Travelines has a 25-hour service from London; Fregata Travel sells bus tickets to Warsaw from London and Manchester. See Air – To/From Britain for contact numbers of these firms.

In Western capitals most regular travel agents (including Polish tourist offices, which go under the name Orbis or Polorbis) and some youth/student travel agents will also be able to supply information on buses to Warsaw and should be able to do bookings. Traveller's Check In at 35 Woburn Place, London WC1, is another sales point for bus tickets to Poland.

In Warsaw you can get tickets for buses to the west both at the Central bus station and at the Orbis offices at ulica Marszałkowska 142 and ulica Bracka 16.

To/From Belarus

Remember that if you travel through Belarus you will need a Belarus visa – see Visas & Embassies in the Facts for the Visitor chapter.

Services (all run both ways) include:

Brest-Rīga: daily
Brest-Vilnius: daily
Grodno-Druskininkai-Kaunas-Rīga: daily
Grodno-Lazdijai-Chernyakhovsk-Kaliningrad: daily (10 hours)
Grodno-Druskininkai-Kaunas: three daily
Minsk-Daugavpils: daily
Minsk-Druskininkai: daily
Minsk-Vilnius-Chernyakhovsk-Kaliningrad: daily (11½ hours, US$1.50)
Minsk-Vilnius-Kaunas: twice daily
Minsk-Vilnius-Klaipėda: daily
Minsk-Vilnius-Rīga: twice daily
Minsk-Vilnius: three expresses (3¼ hours) and three other buses (five hours) daily

To/From Russia

Estonia was the only Baltic state with bus links to anywhere in Russia (apart from the Kaliningrad Region) at the time of research. More services may appear if petrol shortages ease and relations thaw. There's a nightly bus both ways between St Petersburg and Tallinn, taking eight hours for around US$2. You have to get off the bus for border formalities in the middle of the night. Departure in St Petersburg is from bus station No 2 on

the corner of Ligovsky prospekt and Obvodny kanal.

There are also nightly buses both ways between St Petersburg and Tartu, taking eight hours for about US$1.50; and between St Petersburg and Pärnu. There are also a few cross-border services to/from Narva, and there's a daily bus between Tartu and Pechory.

The Kaliningrad organisation Turism (☎ 22-446 656, 22-442 352) at ulitsa Sudostroitelnaya 13 was advertising daily 'soft' buses from Kaliningrad to Moscow (US$3) and 'Leningrad' (St Petersburg; US$2.25), departing from the tourist bus park at Kaliningrad Yuzhny Vokzal (South Station).

To/From Finland

The Baltia-Express or 'Gold Line' bus runs Helsinki-Tallinn-Rīga and vice versa three times a week (Thursdays, Fridays and Sundays both ways at the time of writing). The trip takes 10 hours and the fare includes the Helsinki-Tallinn ferry crossing. Fares are approximately US$22 Helsinki-Tallinn (US$41 return), and US$37 Helsinki-Rīga (US$71 return). Departure points are the South Harbour (Eteläsatama) in Helsinki, the harbour in Tallinn, and the bus station in Rīga. In Finland you can ring ☎ 90-153 7332 for information; in Rīga tickets are currently sold at window 13 in the waiting room area of the bus station.

TRAIN

Travelling by train can be an interesting way of reaching the Baltic states: cheaper than flying, generally less boring than by bus. Two of the world's most memorable rail journeys figure among the approaches to the Baltic states: the Trans-Siberian and the briefer – but unforgettable – Suwałki-Šeštokai railway from Poland to Lithuania.

If you plan to do a lot of train travel around Europe, the *Thomas Cook European Timetable*, updated monthly, gives full intercity timetable listings and indicates where reservations are necessary or supplements payable. It covers as far east as Moscow (the *Thomas Cook International Timetable* continues across Siberia and Central Asia) and is available from Thomas Cook outlets around the world.

Rail Passes & Youth Tickets

The Baltic states are not, at present, included in the Inter-Rail, Eurail, ScanRail or Nordturist rail passes, so if you're travelling with one of these you won't get any benefits in the Baltics. There have been talks about the Baltic states joining Inter-Rail sometime in the future.

Meanwhile, there are rail passes available for the Baltic states and Kaliningrad alone, but you need to buy them before you arrive. One of them, the Baltic Card, includes some discounts on travel into and out of the Baltic states from nearby countries. Information is given in the Getting Around chapter.

Travellers under 26 can make worthwhile savings with BIJ (Billets Internationales de Jeunesse) tickets to Vilnius or Rīga – available from various outlets in Europe including those of Eurotrain, the youth rail discount agency, and in Britain from Campus Travel or other student travel offices. A London-Vilnius BIJ ticket, for instance, is around 25% cheaper than a full fare. BIJ tickets are valid for two months and permit stopovers en route – which means that a BIJ ticket to Moscow or St Petersburg could also be used to visit the Baltics, provided the route is through Vilnius or Rīga.

To/From Germany

There are two daily trains between Berlin and Vilnius, one with a through-carriage to/from Rīga. In 1993 a weekly summer charter train ran between Berlin and Rīga. Another possibility is to travel to Warsaw first and then take a direct train to Kaunas, Rīga or Tallinn (see To/From Poland). Direct trains between Berlin and Kaliningrad are expected to start once an agreement has been worked out between Germany, Poland and Russia.

Berlin-Vilnius/Rīga The *Petersburg* train leaves Berlin Lichtenberg in the evening and reaches St Petersburg's Warsaw Station

some 33 hours later. It travels via Warsaw Central (nine hours from Berlin); Białystok in Poland (12 hours); Grodno in Belarus (17 hours); Vilnius (20½ hours); and Daugavpils, Latvia (24 hours). The through-carriage for Rīga is uncoupled at Vilnius where it waits a few hours before being hitched to another train to reach Rīga 33½ hours after leaving Berlin. The return journeys follow similar schedules, though precise times change fairly often.

Another daily train leaves Berlin Lichtenberg in the morning and follows the same route as the *Petersburg* in about the same time, but only travels as far as Vilnius. Going back, it leaves Vilnius in the late afternoon.

On both trains the cheapest class for international travel is a four-berth couchette. From Vilnius to Berlin this costs about US$100, from Rīga to Berlin about US$138. In Vilnius you can only book for the *Petersburg* on the day of travel, but you can book in advance for the other train.

Since these trains pass through Belarus you also have to pay US$20 for a Belarus transit visa. See Visas & Embassies in Facts for the Visitor for more information. At the Poland-Belarus border the train sits motionless for hours – apart from an incredible amount of lurching, vibrating and clanking – while the bogeys are changed to fit the broader gauge of the ex-USSR. You'll probably be checked by at least four different sets of officials as you go through Belarus – so don't hope for much sleep if you're on a night train!

Berlin-Rīga Charter Train The weekly *Baltic Express* charter train – not to be confused with the daily Warsaw-Tallinn train of the same name – ran between Berlin and Rīga in summer 1993. Whether it will continue in following summers is uncertain. Departures in 1993 were on Sunday from Berlin, and Tuesday from Rīga; the journey time is 25 hours. Couchette fares were about US$240 one way, US$360 return or US$300 youth return. The use of the Suwałki-Šeštokai line between Poland and Lithuania necessitated a change of train at Šeštokai where the gauge broadens. For information and bookings contact the German Baltic-specialists Schnieder Reisen and Baltisches Reisebüro.

To/From Poland

There are direct trains between Poland and all three Baltic states and the Kaliningrad Region.

Estonia & Latvia The daily *Baltic Express* between Warsaw and Tallinn began in summer 1993. It uses the Suwałki-Šeštokai route between Poland and Lithuania, which means everyone has to transfer to a different train at Šeštokai because the gauge changes there. The route is Warsaw-Šeštokai-Kaunas-Rīga-Valga-Tartu-Tallinn. Departures from both ends of the route are in the afternoon and the full trip takes 22 hours. Four carriages with sleeping accommodation are included from Šeštokai to Tallinn and vice versa. The Tallinn-Warsaw fare is US$40 in compartment class (equivalent to a Western four-berth couchette), US$62 in soft class (1st class), and US$30 in non-sleeping accommodation.

It's also possible to travel between Warsaw and Tallinn and Rīga on daily through-carriages which switch trains at Vilnius. The Tallinn through-carriage leaves Warsaw in the afternoon as part of a Moscow-bound train. Returning, departure from Tallinn is around 6 or 7 am. Since the wait in Vilnius is long, the whole trip takes about 30 hours. The Rīga through-carriage forms part of a Berlin-St Petersburg train between Warsaw and Vilnius – see To/From Germany. Fares are similar to the *Baltic Express* but the cheapest class is compartment class.

At Warsaw Central station the international booking office is upstairs from the main concourse.

Lithuania The *Baltic Express* (see the preceding section) stops at Kaunas, where you can change to another train for Vilnius or Klaipėda. There are four daily trains between Warsaw and Vilnius via Grodno in Belarus. At the time of writing, there is also a single daily train which runs between Suwałki, a small town in north-east Poland, and Šeštokai, an even smaller one in south-west Lithuania.

The Warsaw-Grodno-Vilnius route is covered by the two Berlin-Warsaw-Vilnius trains (see To/From Germany), plus one daily Warsaw-Moscow train and one daily Warsaw-St Petersburg train. All have the same Belarus visa requirement and the same bizarre bogey-changing operation. The Warsaw-Moscow service leaves Warsaw in the afternoon and takes about 11 hours to Vilnius. Returning, departure from Vilnius is after midnight. The Warsaw-St Petersburg service takes 13 hours between Warsaw and Vilnius, departing from Warsaw eastbound after midnight, and from Vilnius westbound about 5 am. On all these trains the cheapest class for international travel is compartment class (four-berth couchette). At present this costs around US$25 either way between Warsaw and Vilnius. At Warsaw Central station the international booking office is upstairs from the main concourse.

Suwałki-Šeštokai The Suwałki-Šeštokai trains are cheap but chaotic – in fact they're a classic example of the mayhem resulting from the collapse of the Soviet Union, and for that reason highly recommended to travellers with an interest in post-Soviet reality and strong nerves. It's uncertain, however, how long this short cross-border service will stay in operation now that the Warsaw-Tallinn *Baltic Express* uses the same line, enabling travellers from Warsaw to get all the way to Kaunas on a single service. (For a personal account of the Suwałki-Šeštokai experience, see the Eastern & Southern Lithuania chapter.)

The 50-odd km of track between Suwałki and Šeštokai was built before WW II (some say before WW I), but was closed (and expunged from maps) throughout the Soviet era. The line is the same gauge as Polish and west European railways, narrower than those of the Baltic states and the ex-USSR. It's said that the only reason it wasn't broadened was because the Soviet Union's central planners didn't know the line was there – because they had removed it from the maps!

In 1992 the line was revived and quickly became a main artery for smugglers and a chaotic, bewildering experience for everybody. The little four-carriage trains became crammed with travellers: Poles going to the Baltics or the CIS to sell Western goods; Lithuanians and CIS citizens travelling to Poland to sell cheap Baltic or Russian cigarettes, drink and textiles; and everybody going back to Lithuania or the CIS to sell Western goods they had bought in Poland with the proceeds. The compartments were piled high with suitcases, boxes, packing cases and the teams of people needed to carry them all. Lesser mortals who simply wanted to travel between Poland and Lithuania were left with standing room only – if they could get on the train at all, that is, for ticket queues were seething, silent and motionless. Many people despaired of getting a ticket but boarded the trains anyway and spent the trip dodging, bribing or arguing with ticket inspectors.

A trip between Warsaw and Kaunas or Vilnius using the Suwałki-Šeštokai service involves at least three separate trains: Warsaw-Suwałki, Suwałki-Šeštokai, and Šeštokai-Kaunas/Vilnius. You can get timetable information at Warsaw Central, Vilnius, and Kaunas train stations, but don't assume your source has come to grips with the Polish-Lithuanian time difference. The schedule changes from time to time but at present is as follows (times are given in 24-hour notation):

Depart Warsaw Central 2302; Białystok 0203; arrive Suwałki 0535 (all Polish time)
Depart Suwałki 0650 Polish time (0750 Lithuanian time); arrive Šeštokai 1015 Lithuanian time (0915 Polish time)
Depart Šeštokai 1140; Kaunas 1315; arrive Vilnius 1500 (all Lithuanian time)

Depart Vilnius 0810; Kaunas 0945; arrive Šeštokai 1115 (all Lithuanian time)
Depart Šeštokai 1250 Lithuanian time (1150 Polish time); arrive Suwałki 1445 Polish time (1545 Lithuanian time)
Depart Suwałki 1512; Białystok 1725; arrive Warsaw Central 2007 (all Polish time)

If the Šeštokai-Suwałki train is late you'll probably miss the Suwałki-Warsaw train departing at 1512 – but there are later trains

or combinations of trains which will get you to Warsaw in the end. Any of the six daily Suwałki-Sokółka trains will probably do for starters. Going in the other direction, there's more time to catch the Kaunas and Vilnius train at Šeštokai – if you don't, there are three other trains daily to Kaunas only, plus some to Alytus.

At the time of writing you need three separate tickets for the three legs of the trip. You probably won't be able to buy all three before you start. Get two together wherever possible. You can reportedly buy both Suwałki-Šeštokai tickets and Šeštokai-Vilnius tickets (and returns) at Suwałki. In Vilnius you can buy Vilnius-Šeštokai and Šeštokai-Suwałki tickets together but, currently, only from the travel bureau (Kelioniu Biuras) in the sunken plaza beside the Hotel Lietuva, which charges the high prices of US$8 Vilnius-Šeštokai and US$4 Šeštokai-Suwałki. Normal fares are: Warsaw-Suwałki or vice versa about US$5 2nd class, US$6.50 1st class; Suwałki-Šeštokai or vice versa about US$2.25 (2nd class only); and Šeštokai-Vilnius or vice versa US$0.70 (2nd class only). No sleeping accommodation is available.

If you end up having to get each ticket stage by stage along the way, it will involve lots of queueing and anxiety – and you may not be successful in any case. Passengers take up position near carriage doors long before the trains pull into Suwałki and Šeštokai ready to run for tickets for the next stage of the journey. Even if you get near the front of the queue, you may not get a ticket before your train leaves. You'll still probably be able to board the train but you'll have to spend the trip either dodging ticket collectors or paying fines or bribes. Fines for travelling without a ticket are much steeper in Poland than in Lithuania: from Šeštokai to the border it's about US$2, but from Suwałki to the border (which is a similar distance) it's over US$20.

The motto is: if in doubt, get on the train! And take food and a major Western currency – there's an exchange office at Šeštokai station, but it won't accept złoty.

Kaliningrad A regular train service may now be running between Gdańsk and Kaliningrad using Western European gauge all the way. But, at the time of research, the only service across this border was one or two trains daily each way between Kaliningrad and Braniewo in north-east Poland, just six km from the Kaliningrad Region border – a 65-km trip that took 3½ hours. The one-way Kaliningrad-Braniewo fare for foreigners was about US$6.50, and passports had to be shown when buying tickets. Between Braniewo and Warsaw, a trip of five or six hours, you need to change trains at Olsztyn. The Braniewo-Warsaw fare is about US$5.50 in 2nd class, US$8 in 1st class.

To/From Hungary, the Czech Republic & Bulgaria

There are daily trains or through-carriages to Vilnius from Budapest, Prague and Sofia, taking 36 to 41 hours and passing through Ukraine and Belarus. There's also a three times weekly through-carriage between Sofia, Rīga and Tallinn, taking 38 hours between Sofia and Tallinn. Couchette fares from Vilnius are around US$133 to Budapest, US$60 to Prague and US$65 to Sofia.

To/From Western Europe

If you're coming from west of Germany, you can reach the Baltics with a change of train in either Berlin or Warsaw. There are direct services to Warsaw from London, Paris and elsewhere. From countries south of Germany you can head for Warsaw, or for Prague, Budapest or Sofia and take a train to Vilnius through Ukraine. Tickets to Vilnius bought in Western Europe will route you through Belarus. See the earlier To/From Germany section, and Visas & Embassies in the Facts for the Visitor chapter for comments on Belarus visas.

London-Vilnius takes a little under two days with a change of trains in Warsaw. The basic one-way 2nd-class fare is US$180; a couchette costs US$66 as far as Warsaw, and US$35 from Warsaw to Vilnius if you book it in London. At present, you can save a few dollars by booking initially only as far as Poland, then buying another ticket there.

To/From Russia

The old Soviet rail network still functions, with little change, over most of the ex-USSR. Trains linking Moscow and St Petersburg with all the main Baltic cities enable you to combine the Baltics with a Trans-Siberian trip or other Russian or Central Asian travels. One major improvement since Soviet days is that foreigners can now usually get tickets on more or less any train in Russia for the same price as locals. For information on types of train, classes of accommodation, how to understand time-tables and so on, see the Getting Around chapter.

All the services mentioned here will have compartment-class (*kupeynyy*) sleeping accommodation, but some will lack either the more expensive soft class (*myagkiy* or *lyuks*), or the cheaper reserved-place class (*platskartnyy*).

At the time of writing, fares from Moscow to the Baltics are around US$2 kupeynyy, US$4 myagkiy, and US$1.50 platskartnyy; from St Petersburg to Tallinn they are about half this; and from St Petersburg to the main Latvian or Lithuanian cities or Kaliningrad about two-thirds. Travelling in the opposite direction, fares from Latvia to Russia are similar to those above, but fares from Estonia and Lithuania are about double. If you are making a round trip from the Baltics to Russia, ask for a round-trip ticket before you set off: this will save queueing in Russia. In St Petersburg there's an office reportedly selling train tickets to foreigners at local prices; it's at naberezhnaya Kanala Griboedova 24 near the Kazan Cathedral.

Services from Russia to the Baltics and Kaliningrad include:

Moscow (Belorussia Station)-Kaliningrad
19 to 29 hours; three or four trains each way daily; the *Yantar* (No 29 westbound, No 30 eastbound) via Vilnius and Kaunas is the quickest, No 243/244 via Klaipėda is the slowest

Moscow (Belorussia Station)-Kaunas
15 to 18 hours; three or four trains each way daily, some terminating at Kaliningrad

Moscow (Belorussia Station)-Klaipėda
21 to 24 hours; one or two trains each way daily, some terminating at Kaliningrad

Moscow (Rīga Station)-Rīga
16 hours; three fast trains each way nightly, plus some slower ones (up to 23½ hours)

Moscow (St Petersburg Station)-Tallinn
16 to 20 hours; two trains each way daily via Narva (16 hours), one via Pskov and Tartu (20 hours)

Moscow (St Petersburg Station)-Tartu
17 hours; one train each way daily

Moscow (Belorussia Station)-Vilnius
13 hours; five fast trains each way daily, some terminating at Kaliningrad, Kaunas or Warsaw.

Pskov-Kaliningrad
14 hours; one train each way daily, terminating at St Petersburg

Pskov-Kaunas
10 hours; one train each way daily, terminating at Kaliningrad and St Petersburg

Pskov-Rīga
six hours; two fast trains each way daily, terminating at St Petersburg

Pskov-Tallinn
6½ hours; one train each way daily, terminating at Moscow

Pskov-Tartu
four hours; one train each way daily, terminating at Tallinn and Moscow

Pskov-Vilnius
eight or nine hours; several trains daily, terminating at Vilnius, Kaliningrad, Lvov, Chernovtsy, Warsaw, Berlin or St Petersburg

St Petersburg (Warsaw Station)-Kaliningrad
19½ hours; one train each way daily, via Pskov, Vilnius and Kaunas

St Petersburg (Warsaw Station)-Kaunas
15½ hours; one train each way daily, terminating at Kaliningrad

St Petersburg (Warsaw Station)-Rīga
10 or 11 hours; two fast trains each way nightly

St Petersburg (Warsaw Station)-Tallinn
8½ to 9¾ hours; two trains each way nightly, both often heavily booked; lyuks only available on the quicker one (No 17 from St Petersburg, No K22 from Tallinn); when the train stops for border formalities, get off quickly with your baggage – otherwise it may leave with your baggage but without you

St Petersburg (Warsaw Station)-Vilnius
14 hours; four fast trains each way daily terminating at Kaliningrad, Chernovtsy, Warsaw and Berlin; three slower ones terminating at Vilnius or Lvov

Other places in the Baltics with direct rail services to/from Russia include: Daugavpils and Rēzekne in Latvia (Moscow, Pskov, St Petersburg); Sigulda in Latvia (Pskov, St Petersburg); Narva in Estonia (St Petersburg, Moscow); and Valga and Võru in Estonia (Pskov, St Petersburg).

To/From Belarus & Ukraine

The old Soviet rail network still functions between the Baltic states and Belarus and Ukraine. Remember that timetables often list only the start and end points of a train's journey: for instance, some trains listed at stations as Lvov-St Petersburg or Kiev-Rīga will take you to Vilnius. Services include:

Grodno-Druskininkai
1¼ hours; one train each way daily

Grodno-Vilnius
3½ hours, four trains each way daily

Kiev-Rīga
22 hours; one to three trains daily each way; terminating Rīga northbound, Kiev or Simferopol southbound

Kiev-Vilnius
16 hours; one to three trains each way daily; terminating Rīga northbound, Kiev or Simferopol southbound

Lvov-Rīga
21 hours; one train daily; terminating Rīga northbound, Lvov southbound

Lvov-Vilnius
15 hours; four trains each way daily; terminating Rīga or St Petersburg northbound, Lvov or Chernovtsy southbound

Minsk-Kaliningrad
10 hours; three or four trains each way daily; terminating Kaliningrad westbound, Moscow eastbound

Minsk-Kaunas
5½ hours; three or four trains each way daily; terminating Kaliningrad westbound, Moscow or Gomel eastbound

Minsk-Rīga
eight hours; two or three trains each way daily; terminating Rīga northbound, Minsk or Kiev southbound

Minsk-Tallinn
17 hours; one train each way daily; terminating Tallinn northbound, Minsk southbound

Minsk-Tartu
14 hours; one train each way daily; terminating Tallinn northbound, Minsk southbound

Minsk-Vilnius
3½ hours; six to eight trains each way daily;
terminating Vilnius, Kaliningrad, Rīga or Tallinn
northbound, Gomel, Kiev, Minsk or Moscow
southbound

To/From China & the East

If you have the time and inclination for it, the
Trans-Siberian railway will carry you much
of the way between the Baltics and eastern
Asia, Australasia, or even Alaska. The 9300-
km Trans-Siberian proper runs between
Moscow's Yaroslavl Station and Vladivostok on Russia's Pacific coast. In summer at
least, there are steamers between Vladivostok and Niigata in Japan. Straight through
without stopping, the ride takes 5½ to 6½
days, but you can break it at places like
Irkutsk, Ulan-Ude and Khabarovsk and
make side-trips to beautiful Lake Baykal and
interesting regions like remote Yakutia or
Buddhist Buryatia. Branches of the Trans-
Siberian with their own names are the Trans-
Mongolian which goes via the Mongolian
capital, Ulaan Baatar, to Beijing; and the
Trans-Manchurian which goes to Beijing via
Harbin and north-east China.

The cost of a Trans-Siberian trip varies
enormously, depending among other things
on which direction and what class you travel,
what time of year, where you book, who you
book through, and the overall geopolitical
situation. Through a Western-world travel
agent, expect to pay US$350 or more all the
way from Moscow to Beijing or Vladivostok
or US$600 if you include the boat to Niigata.
From Beijing to Moscow, CITS (China International Travel Service) offers tickets for
US$185 in hard class, but book well in
advance as these trains, especially the Trans-
Mongolian, are currently very popular with
Russian and Chinese business folks who
compete for tickets and like to conduct business from the carriages.

Obtaining local-price tickets in Russia is
a hit-and-miss matter but offers incredible
bargains if you succeed – for instance the
Moscow-Irkutsk fare in kupeynyy (compartment class) is around US$7.50. To get such
tickets you have to be prepared to stand in
queues for hours at ordinary Russian railway
ticket offices (not Intourist, which charges
much more). A good command of Russian,
or help from Russian friends or local travel
agencies, improves your chances of success.
You still need to go to Intourist for international tickets (eg Irkutsk-Beijing around
US$70). At the time of writing, tickets from
Russia to the Baltic states aren't counted as
international. One risk with buying your
tickets on the spot is that there's absolutely
no guarantee there'll be vacancies on the
trains when you want them.

There are almost as many variations of a
Trans-Sib itinerary as there are Trans-Sib
travellers, and equally as many ways of
setting up a trip. Lonely Planet's *USSR* travel
survival kit has lots of Trans-Sib ideas and
detail; a comprehensive resource is *The
Trans-Siberian Rail Guide* by Robert Strauss
(Compass Publications, London, 1993).
Also useful is Bryn Thomas' *Trans-Siberian
Handbook* (Trailblazer Publications, UK).

Trans-Kazakhstan In 1990 a new rail link
was completed between Ürümqi in Xinjiang,
north-west China and Alma-Ata in Kazakhstan, ex-Soviet Central Asia. With Ürümqi
linked to Beijing and elsewhere in China,
and Alma-Ata to Moscow and elsewhere in
the ex-USSR, this opens a whole new route
from east to west through fascinating Central
Asia – tentatively being called the Trans-
Kazakhstan. In 1992 regular weekly trains
started between Ürümqi and Alma-Ata.
Reportedly it's a wild trip with frayed tem-
pers and fights that can make the
Suwałki-Šeštokai railway seem like arm-
chair travel. At the time of writing it seems
you have to make your way to Ürümqi or
Alma-Ata to buy the ticket, so allow plenty
of flexibility in your travel plans. There's
also a bus service between Alma Ata and
Yining (Gulja) in north-west Xinjiang, about
700 km west of Ürümqi. The visa situation
for the Central Asian states is changeable.
Robert Strauss' *The Trans-Siberian Rail
Guide* includes material on the Trans-
Kazakhstan.

CAR & MOTORBIKE

Having your own vehicle has the great advantages of convenience and comfort in the Baltic states, as long as there's enough petrol and you take care of your vehicle. One option is to rent a car for all or part of your stay, but it's perfectly feasible to take your own vehicle too. If you do, get it in good condition before you start off and carry a large petrol can, supplies of engine oil and some basic spares. A fire extinguisher, first-aid kit and warning triangle are also advisable as they might just be insisted on by border guards. Motoring clubs like Britain's AA and RAC are worth checking with for information on regulations, border crossings, petrol supplies and so on – as are Baltic states' embassies and, if you're going to drive in the Kaliningrad Region, worldwide branches of the Russian state tourist company, Intourist. For information and tips on driving once you're in the Baltic states, see the Getting Around chapter.

Documents

You need to bring your vehicle's registration document. If you can get it in the form of an international motor vehicle certificate, which is a translation of the basic registration document, so much the better. Motoring associations should be able to provide one. An International Driving Permit (also obtainable from motoring associations) is recommended, but if you don't have one, your own licence (if from a European country) will suffice in most situations. Estonia is the only Baltic state with compulsory accident insurance for drivers, and even these payouts are low, so you really need comprehensive insurance in case of damage done by another driver.

At the time of writing, the Green Card – a routine extension of domestic motor insurance to cover most European countries – is not valid in the Baltic states or Russia, so you must organise insurance separately. If you have difficulty doing so through your regular insurer, try Black Sea & Baltic General Insurance (☎ 071-709 9202) of 65 Fenchurch St, London EC3M 4EY. Insurance policies with limited compensation rates can be bought at the border when you enter Estonia, for around US$20 a car. The Russian state insurer, Ingosstrakh, which has an office at Salomonkatu 5C, 00100 Helsinki, and other offices at main Russian frontier posts, can provide insurance cover for Russia. Remember that you'll also need appropriate documentation for all the countries you pass through on the way to or from the Baltics – motoring associations should be able to advise you.

To/From Scandinavia

If travelling from Scandinavia, you can put your vehicle on a ferry or drive to the Baltics through Russia.

Ferries There are four vehicle-ferry crossings from Helsinki to Tallinn most days; a car and two people will cost around US$50 to US$60 one way. From Stockholm there are direct services to Tallinn and Rīga but, at the time of writing, you'll save quite a lot on ferry fares if you sail with Viking Line from Sweden to Finland, then take a second ferry from Helsinki to Tallinn. There's also a car ferry service to Rīga from Copenhagen and Karlskrona in southern Sweden. See the following Sea section for more on these services.

Through Russia From the Finnish/Russian border at Vaalimaa/Torfyanovka to St Petersburg is about 220 km; from St Petersburg to the Russian/Estonian border at Ivangorod/Narva is 140 km. You could do it in a day but there's little point coming this way unless you want to look at St Petersburg on the way through. Don't delay on the Finland-St Petersburg road as it's said to be plagued by bandits.

See Facts for the Visitor for information on Russian visas.

To/From Germany & Poland

Bringing a vehicle into the Baltics from the south is less straightforward than from Scandinavia. At present there are three main ways of doing it, with Kaliningrad offering a future fourth possibility.

Ferries To/From Germany The Mercuri ferries between Kiel and Klaipėda (Lithuania) or Rīga, a voyage of 30 to 42 hours, are expensive at around US$500 or more one way for two people and a car, and can get booked up months ahead. The Mukran-Klaipėda link is cheaper and quicker but with even smaller capacity. A Kiel-Tallinn vehicle ferry service began in 1993. See the Sea section for details.

Poland-Lithuania This border, virtually closed during the Soviet era, opened up with Lithuanian independence but became notorious for interminable delays, making a mockery of the much talked-about *Via Baltica* – a proposed fast road route from central to northern Europe through Poland and the Baltic states. Only one road crossing was open at the time of writing. There's also a reported danger of highway robbery on the Polish side of the border.

Queues at the crossing point between Ogrodniki, Poland (east of Suwałki), and Lazdijai, Lithuania, are much longer and more chaotic on the Lithuanian side than the Polish side so it should be easier to enter Lithuania by this route than to leave it.

A two-km queue on the Lithuanian side is short, and movement is extremely slow due to the number of people trying to smuggle cheap cigarettes, alcohol and textiles into Poland and the extreme lack of urgency among the border officials. In a car you should count on at least half a day's wait, but remember that it has been four days at its worst. One traveller wrote to say that motorcyclists can go to the front of the queue. Toilets have been installed and roadside kiosks have sprung up to serve the waiting travellers. Track-suited black-market 'mafia' types have been selling car places at the front of the queue for around US$60. Those who couldn't or wouldn't pay this had to wait even longer as the rich went in front of them.

Even the Lithuanian Embassy in Tallinn admitted that 'no legal or moral norms' applied at the Lazdijai crossing, after an Estonian children's choir was held up for two days there in 1993. A Western car and an important manner might help, but letters from Lithuanian and Polish (preferably both) government ministers or embassies stating that your journey is urgent are apparently the only sure way to get through quickly without bribery.

A second crossing point being constructed between Szypliszki (Poland) and Kalvarija (Lithuania), on the Suwałki-Marijampolė road, was supposed to open in 1993 but had already been postponed several times. Obviously it pays to sound out the situation beforehand if you're thinking of crossing the Poland/Lithuania road border.

Through Belarus An alternative to the direct Poland-Lithuania crossing is to go from Poland to Lithuania via Belarus. The most direct route is from Białystok, Poland, to Grodno in north-west Belarus, then to Merkinė, Lithuania. This route takes you across only about 60 km of Belarus territory and adds little to the length of a Warsaw-Vilnius trip. Other possible routes are Brest-Lida-Vilnius or Brest-Minsk-Vilnius. If you'll be staying less than 72 hours in Belarus you shouldn't need anything more complicated than a Belarus transit visa, which is available at the border (see Visas & Embassies in Facts for the Visitor). Drive past any lines of stationary trucks waiting at the borders. Intourist should be able to put you in the picture on visas, driving regulations, insurance and so on.

Poland-Kaliningrad At the time of writing, the Braniewo-Mamonovo and Bartoszyce-Bagrationovsk crossings from Poland to the Kaliningrad Region are open to Polish and Russian citizens on local bus services, and to some tour coaches. It seems only a matter of time before these or other Poland-Kaliningrad border points open to general traffic. A section of the old German autobahn between the Polish border and Kaliningrad city has been rebuilt and may now be open, and a second new crossing between Goldap and Gusev is reportedly being prepared.

BICYCLE

Bicycles can be carried cheaply on the ferries from Scandinavia and Germany to the Baltic states, but of course the passenger fare depends on which route you take – see the Sea section for details. Overland riders through Poland face the same choices as drivers – see the Car & Motorbike section – but can reportedly go to the front of the queue at the Ogrodniki-Lazdijai crossing.

HITCHING

Look upon hitching as a method of getting part-way to or from the Baltics; it's fairly widely practised in Finland, Germany and Poland, but Sweden and Denmark aren't so good for hitching. Many German towns have organisations called Mitfahrzentrale which put people willing to pay for lifts together with drivers willing to take them. There's a similar organisation in Rīga, organised by the VAK, the Latvian Environmental Club, which has an office on Smilšu iela. If you're considering hitching from Poland to Lithuania, take advice on safety as there have been reports of highway robbery on roads leading to the Polish side of this border. You reportedly can't cross the Ogrodniki-Lazdijai border as a pedestrian – you must be in a car. Keep in mind that hitching is never a totally safe way of travelling. Even though we explain how to do it, we don't recommend it.

Sea

The number of ferries to the Baltic states has mushroomed since 1990, and you can now sail direct from Finland to Estonia; Sweden to Estonia or Latvia; Germany to Latvia or Lithuania; and Poland to Kaliningrad. This can be one of the most enjoyable ways to reach the Baltic states. It can be surprisingly cheap on some routes, but expensive on others. The Helsinki-Tallinn route has so many competing services that you should

have no difficulty getting a passage any day, but some of the other services – notably EstLine from Stockholm and Mercuri from Kiel – can get booked up far in advance.

TO/FROM FINLAND

A small fleet of varied shapes and sizes now ferries nearly two million people each year back and forth across the 80-km Gulf of Finland between Helsinki and Tallinn. There are fewer services from September to April, but at least three or four crossings are made each way every day. Ships cross in $3\frac{1}{2}$ to four hours, hydrofoils in $1\frac{1}{2}$ to two. In Helsinki they all sail from the large South Harbour (Eteläsatama), which has four different terminals. The Ageba agency (☎ 90-669 193 or 90-661 123, fax 90-174 280 or 90-602 848) has ticket and information booths in the Olympia and Katajonakan terminals. You can also get tickets from other outlets including those mentioned in the rundown of main services that follows. Prices change fairly frequently. There's a travel tax of about US$5 on tickets bought in Finland.

Eminre (Tallink & Estonian New Line)

In late 1993 the two main operators on the Helsinki-Tallinn route, Tallink and Estonian New Line, announced a merger of their passenger services. A new company, Eminre, using the Tallink logo, is due to take over ticket sales and there may be changes to the following schedules and fares.

Tallink runs the large passenger and vehicle ferries *Tallink* and *Georg Ots* which both make one crossing in each direction daily. Service is year round but there may be a slight slackening of frequency around Christmas and New Year. One-way deck fare is US$17 Monday to Thursday, US$20 Friday to Sunday; a car is US$25, a motorbike US$9, and cabins for two to four people are US$13 to US$21. Buffet lunch or dinner is US$12. In the Soviet era the *Georg Ots* was the only direct transport link between the Western world and any of the Baltic states. It was rebuilt in 1992-93.

Helsinki departures are from the Olympia Terminal. You can get tickets there within two hours of departure, otherwise from the Tallink office (☎ 90-602 822, fax 90-635 311) nearby at Eteläranta 14, or from travel agents worldwide.

Estonian New Line operates the large passenger and vehicle ferries *Roslagen* and *Corbiere*, each with a capacity of about 1000 people and 250 cars. From early April to the end of October it also runs three fast hydrofoils with capacities of 120 to 200 passengers: the *Liisa*, *Jaanika* and *Monika*.

The *Roslagen* and *Corbiere* between them make one morning and one evening sailing in each direction daily, year round. They're cheaper than the Tallink ships at US$12 one-way (deck) and US$9 for a four-person cabin. Meals are also a little cheaper. Cars and motorbikes are the same prices as with Tallink. After an evening crossing you can have a cabin overnight at Tallinn for an extra US$9. From mid-May to mid-August the hydrofoils make four crossings each way daily, fewer during the rest of their season. Fare is US$17 one way (the same as the Tallink ships), US$31 return.

In Helsinki, the *Roslagen* and *Corbiere* sail from the Olympia Terminal and the hydrofoils currently from the Magazine Terminal (Makasiiniterminaali). You can get tickets at the terminals (for the ships only, within two hours of departure) or from ticket offices at Fabianinkatu 12 or Kalevankatu 1 C 51 (both ☎ 90-680 2499). In Tallinn the ships use the main ferry terminal, but the hydrofoils dock at the quay behind the Linnahall.

Helta Line

The Finnish Helta Line operates the *Sinilind* and *Luik* hydrofoils (capacity 94 each), making up to two trips a day each way from April to September or October; fares are US$20 one way, US$31 return. Helta was also reportedly planning to introduce a new 200-seat hydrofoil. At the time of writing Helsinki departures and tickets (☎ 90-664 141, fax 90-660 551) are from the Magazine Terminal; Tallinn departures are from the main ferry terminal.

Cruises

You can take 24-hour or half-day cruises from Helsinki to Tallinn on Tallink, Estonian New Line, Kristina Cruises (☎ 90-629 968) of Korkeavuorenkatu 45, Helsinki, or aboard the luxurious *Sally Albatross* of the Silja Line. These are basically floating parties for Swedes and Finns. Kristina Cruises are probably cheapest, at around US$30 and up.

TO/FROM SWEDEN

Estonia

There are direct sailings from Stockholm to Tallinn; alternatively you can go via Finland with Viking or Silja Line, which needn't take much longer and can work out cheaper.

EstLine The joint Swedish-Estonian company EstLine operates the modern passenger and vehicle 'cruise-ferry' *Estonia* which makes one Stockholm-Tallinn-Stockholm journey every two days. Departures are from the Tallinnterminalen at the Frihamn in Stockholm, and from the EstLine terminal next door to the main ferry terminal in Tallinn. The ship sails overnight and takes 15 hours each way. The normal one-way fare is approximately US$55 (US$42 for students and senior citizens), but there's a US$14 surcharge on Friday sailings from Stockholm and Saturday sailings from Tallinn. Cabin charges per person range from US$17 in a four-person cabin below the car deck (with toilet and shower in the corridor) to US$280 for a luxury single outer cabin. A car costs about US$50 one way; breakfast is US$7, and smorgasbord dinner US$20. A connecting bus service, EstLine Express, will transfer you from Tallinn to Pärnu for US$10, to Tartu for US$14, or to Rīga for US$22 – with 30% discount for students. In Stockholm there's also a bus service between the city centre and the port.

EstLine's address is Box 1215, S-111 82 Stockholm. You can book on ☎ 08-667 00 01, fax 08-660 74 39 or through travel agents or at the terminal. In the past, EstLine has been heavily booked so make your reservation a month or two ahead if possible.

Viking & Silja Lines You can combine a voyage between Sweden and Finland on Sweden's Viking Line with a Helsinki-Tallinn passage to travel surprisingly cheaply between Sweden and Estonia. Viking Line sails once or twice daily from Stockholm to Helsinki, from Stockholm to Turku (Finland), from Kapellskär (Sweden, 90 km north of Stockholm) to Naantali (Finland, 12 km west of Turku), and vice versa in each case. The crossings take 10 to 15 hours and some are made in vast 2500-capacity ships like the *Cinderella* and *Mariella* which would be better described as floating pleasure palaces. The really good news is for motorists: at the time of writing, cars and motorbikes are carried *free* on all three routes.

Basic passenger fares are US$11 Kapellskär-Naantali, US$15 Stockholm-Turku, and US$18 Stockholm-Helsinki; these double from late June to early August and as much as quadruple on Friday, but there are Inter-Rail, student, and pensioner discounts of about one-third on non-Friday sailings. Cabins range upwards from US$7.50 per person. The fares are so low because the line makes a lot of money from duty-free shopping on board. Viking Line sails from the Stadsgården pier at Stockholm and the Katajanokan terminal in the South Harbour, Helsinki. For information ring Stockholm ☎ 08-644 07 65 (fax 08-641 32 72), or Helsinki ☎ 90-123 51 (fax 90-175 551).

The Silja Line also has some interesting fares on its high-class ferries between Stockholm and Helsinki/Turku. If you're travelling from the Baltic states to Sweden, you can buy Viking or Silja Line tickets in Estonia or Latvia to avoid Finnish travel tax – see the Tallinn and Rīga Getting There & Away sections.

Baltic Star In 1993 the Ånedin Linjen-owned *Baltic Star* began twice-weekly cruise sailings between Stockholm and Kuressaare on Saaremaa which is linked by frequent ferries to the Estonian mainland.

For information in Estonia contact Baltic Tours in Tallinn (☎ 22-440 760).

Latvia
At present, there are weekly overnight sailings to Rīga from Stockholm (17 hours) by the Scandinavian-owned Baltic Line. If you want to cut costs it will probably pay to go via Tallinn with EstLine (which has a direct bus connection from Tallinn to Rīga) or even via Finland and Tallinn, starting on Viking or Silja Line.

The cheapest fare on the Stockholm-Rīga ferry is around US$100 one way in a two-person E2-class cabin, with dinner and breakfast included. A car costs around US$80, and a motorbike US$30. There are advance-booking reductions on return fares for vehicles. Baltic Line has a booking office (☎ 08-20 27 95, fax 08-10 07 41) at Vasagatan 4, 11120 Stockholm. You can also book by calling ☎ 020-72 50 50, 020-29 00 29 or 011-16 44 45, or faxing 0752-1 91 95. Departures are from the Balticterminalen at the Frihamn, Stockholm.

In 1993 a cargo and vehicle ferry with 12 places available for people travelling with their vehicles or cargo began a twice-weekly service from Copenhagen to Rīga via Karlskrona in southern Sweden. It's operated by LSA Hanza of Smilšu iela 14, Rīga in a joint venture with Denmark's Dan-Transport. Sailing time to Rīga is about 36 hours from Copenhagen and about 26 hours from Karlskrona. You can contact LSA Hanza in Rīga on ☎ 22-329 893 or fax 22-325 540.

Kaliningrad
A planned (or maybe just rumoured) ferry service from Karlskrona to Gdynia (Poland) and to Kaliningrad by Sweden's Corona Line hasn't got going at the time of writing, but it's worth checking. Corona Line is on ☎ 0455-4 66 00 in Karlskrona and 0-58-217072 in Gdynia. There are other ferries from Sweden (Ystad, Oxelösund, Karlskrona) to Gdynia or neighbouring Gdańsk

which you could use a stepping stone to Gdańsk-Kaliningrad buses, trains and boats.

Cruises

Ånedin Linjen has cruises from Stockholm combining Tallinn, Rīga and Klaipėda. One Kristina Cruises route combines Rīga with Helsinki and the medieval port of Visby on Gotland island. There are cruise packages on Baltic Line too.

TO/FROM GERMANY
Estonia

A weekly vehicle ferry service between Kiel and Tallinn on the *Cap Afrique* began in summer 1993 for an initial six-month period. One-way fares are in the region of US$35 a metre for vehicles, and US$150 for a driver. Contact Estma, the Estonian Maritime Agency, in Tallinn – see Tallinn Getting There & Away for details.

You can also sail to Latvia or Lithuania and travel to Estonia overland, or sail to Helsinki and take a ferry to Tallinn. Silja Line's *Finnjet*, sailing between Travemünde (Germany) and Helsinki, is claimed to be the fastest passenger ferry in the world. It sails nine to 12 times a month, making the trip in 22 hours or more, and costs around US$160 one way. There's also the *Translubeca* vehicle ferry sailing Lübeck-Helsinki-Lübeck three times a fortnight – and there are several Germany-Sweden ferries if you want to go that way round.

Latvia & Lithuania

In 1993 the *Mercuri-I* and *Mercuri-II* vehicle ferries began twice-weekly service on both the Kiel-Rīga-Kiel and Kiel-Klaipėda-Kiel routes. The sailing to Rīga takes 42 hours and to Klaipėda 30 hours. One-way fares on either route range from about US$170 to US$675 depending on the type of cabin. A car costs US$145, a motorbike US$60, and a bicycle US$15. Full meals are US$55 extra to/from Rīga, US$40 to/from Klaipėda; round-trip fares are well under double. You can sail into Klaipėda and back from Rīga or vice versa, if you wish.

These ferries enable motorists to avoid the clogged-up Polish-Lithuanian border, but they're not very big (about 100 passengers each) so you may need to book several months in advance. Sailing frequency and fares may be reduced in winter.

For Mercuri information and tickets in Germany, contact Schnieder Reisen in Hamburg or Baltisches Reisebüro in Munich.

There's also a weekly ferry between Travemunde, Germany, and Rīga, taking 38 hours for a minimum of US$180 one way.

Cheaper and quicker (20 hours), if you can get on to it, is the daily cargo ferry plying between Klaipėda and Mukran (near Sassnitz on the eastern German island of Rügen), which has limited cabin space – due to be expanded – but does carry vehicles. Cars are around US$50 one way, motorbikes US$30, and bicycles US$15. Contact Deutsche Seereederei-Lines (☎ 038392-33135, fax 038392-35141) in Mukran.

Another possible alternative is a Baltic Express ferry from Kiel to Nynäshamn, Sweden (25 hours), then Baltic Line from Stockholm to Rīga. Nynäshamn is between Stockholm and Norrköping. Baltic Express and Baltic Line are part of the same group so you should be able to make a through booking.

A Lübeck-Klaipėda link has also been talked of.

Kaliningrad

A Kiel-Kaliningrad ferry service began on a trial basis in 1993. Schnieder Reisen and Baltisches Reisebüro should have information on developments.

TO/FROM POLAND
Kaliningrad

The twin Polish ports Gdańsk and Gdynia are natural stepping stones to the Kaliningrad Region, only 80 km away across the Gulf of Gdańsk. But the uncertainty over Kaliningrad's future has meant that passenger shipping services have a habit of being short-lived. Watch for posters advertising the latest developments.

One ferry service that looks more durable

than most is the Alexandr Line, whose ferry *Dagomys* sails three times a week each way in summer (winter schedule uncertain) between Gdańsk Nowy Port and Svetly, 25 km west of Kaliningrad city. The trip takes 4½ or five hours and costs US$25 one way. Bus No 105 runs four or five times an hour between Kaliningrad bus station and Svetly. In Gdańsk you can book Alexandr Line tickets through Biuro Turystyki Cliff Tour (see the Travel Agencies section earlier in this chapter).

In summer at least, the hydrofoils of Baltic Foils also sail once or twice daily from Gdańsk Nowy Port to Svetly. This is a 2½-hour trip and costs US$20 one way; tickets go on sale at the port 1½ hours before departure. The Baltic Foils representative in Gdańsk is on ☎ 0-58-479735.

If you get to Gdańsk and find that all ferries are off, you can always reach Kaliningrad by train, or even bus if they're open to third-country citizens.

Another possible service is a hydrofoil link to Svetly from Elblag, near the south end of the Kaliningrad Lagoon. Enquire from Przedsiębiorstwo Zeglugowe Zulawy (☎ 0-50-27319, fax 0-50-26997) at ulica Bulwar Zygmunta Augusta 1, 82 300 Elblag. A service from Karlskrona in Sweden to Gdynia and Kaliningrad has also been mooted (see To/From Sweden).

The Orbis office (☎ 0-58-314944) at ulica Heweliusza 22 in Gdańsk runs US$140 day trips to Kaliningrad using a catamaran from Gdynia. There may be other day cruises from Gdynia.

Elsewhere

There are currently no direct sailings between Poland and the Baltic states, but Polferries' service between Gdańsk and Helsinki might be a way of approaching Estonia.

TO/FROM DENMARK

There's a vehicle and cargo ferry service between Copenhagen and Rīga via Karlskrona in southern Sweden. See the To/From Sweden section for more informa-tion. A Copenhagen-Klaipéda link has also been discussed.

TO/FROM OTHER COUNTRIES

From Britain or the Netherlands there are Scandinavian Seaways sailings to Sweden. There are no ferry services from Russia at the time of writing.

SAILING YOURSELF

The Baltic states – particularly Estonia with its many islands and deeply indented coast – are now attracting hundreds of private yachts a year, mainly from Finland and Scandinavia. The EJL, the Estonian Yachting Union (☎ & fax 22-238 044), based at the Pirita marina, Regati puiestee 1, Tallinn, recommends the following harbours:

Estonian mainland
  Pirita (☎ 22-238 044), Milduranna and Aegna near Tallinn; Dirhami (☎ 247-97 221); Haapsalu (☎ 247-45 582); Rohuküla (☎ 247-91 138); Virtsu (☎ 247-75 520); Pärnu (☎ 244-41 948)
Estonian islands
  Lehtma (☎ 246-99 214), Heltermaa (☎ 246-94 252) and Orjaku (☎ 246-92 127) on Hiiumaa; Sviby on Vormsi; Nasva (☎ 245-75 140), Roomassaare, Triigi, Veere (☎ 245-76 223) and Mõntu on Saaremaa; Kuivastu (☎ 245-98 435) on Muhu; Kihnu; Ruhnu

(The area codes given above are those to be used if you are dialling from within Estonia – see the Post & Telecommunications section in the introductory Facts for the Visitor chapter for telephone codes to be used from other countries.)

Customs facilities are available at Pirita, Dirhami, Haapsalu, Pärnu, Lehtma, Nasva, Roomassaare and Triigi. Approaches to Orjaku, Triigi, Mõntu, Kihnu and Ruhnu should only be made in daylight.

The Tallinn firm Esail (☎ 22-527 366 or 22-238 145, fax 22-237 945) offers a useful information, harbour-berth booking, and visa service for yachties.

It's also possible to rent yachts in Tallinn and on Saaremaa – see the Getting Around chapter.

Tours

With independent travel in the Baltics now fairly straightforward, there's no need to take a tour or package just to get there or to help you get around. A tour is unlikely to take you anywhere you couldn't easily reach yourself. But if you want to stay in the better hotels all the time, a package may save you money.

Although tours can insulate you from the reality of local life, a possible advantage if your time is limited is that they take care of the practicalities of food, bed and transport so that you can concentrate on more interesting things. Or you may just want the expertise or experience of a guide to draw on. There are plenty of options if you can afford them.

Some group trips visit only one of the Baltic states or the Kaliningrad Region – or even just one city. Others visit a mixture of countries or maybe all of them. Yet others combine a visit to the Baltic states with St Petersburg and maybe Moscow. See the Travel Agency section earlier in this chapter for contact details of some tour operators.

Germany's Baltic-specialist travel agents are well abreast of developments. In 1993 a 10-day Schnieder Reisen or Baltisches Reisebüro trip taking in all three Baltic states plus either Kaliningrad or St Petersburg – with flights to/from Germany – was typically around US$1400. At the other end of the scale, 10 days in Kaliningrad with travel by bus was about US$500. Both trips used good-class hotels. There are also organised self-drive trips which include a ship passage to the Baltics and back, accommodation, and, if you want, a hire-car laid on. Greif Reisen has some of the less expensive regular tours and includes parts of Poland in some of them, while Deutsches Reisebüro will take you to all three Baltic states, Kaliningrad, St Petersburg *and* Moscow on one 15-day US$1750 trip.

From Britain, Regent Holidays runs tours for 12 nights to the three Baltic capitals, typically in the US$1400 region. It's also a good firm to contact for one-off special interest tours. Martin Randall Travel offers Baltics tours focusing on art, architecture and related subjects.

From the USA, Union Tours offers eight-day, two-Baltic-capital packages for US$1079 or 'long weekends' with three nights in the Baltics for US$699 to US$949 – both good value. Baltic Tours has quite a big range of Latvia and Lithuania packages with 10 to 12-day trips costing between US$1150 and US$1600.

Intourist, the Russian state travel company, still does Baltic tours. For information, contact its many branches worldwide. A seven-day Intourist tour of the three Baltic capitals with flights from London is about US$900.

Getting Around

Buses and trains go just about everywhere throughout the Baltic states – except at times of fuel shortage when bus services may be curtailed. Both are cheap, if fairly slow. Since distances are small, flying is rarely a necessity – though it can be fun. Driving or riding your own vehicle is an attractive option if you can afford to bring or rent a motor vehicle, or have the time to tour by bicycle.

Whether to choose a bus or a train for a particular journey depends entirely on the route in question. Buses tend to be a bit quicker than trains, but on the whole – except in Estonia at present – a place in the reasonably comfortable compartment class on a train is a bit cheaper than a seat on a bus. General seating on trains is certainly cheaper than buses. Other factors are the frequency of service, departure times – and comfort. You obviously get more chance to stretch your legs on a train but, for obscure reasons, some carriage attendants try to ensure that all windows remain firmly shut which can make things stuffy to say the least. You stand equal chances of freezing or baking, depending on whether the heating is turned on or not. If you have to travel overnight, sleeping accommodation on a train is likely to be less uncomfortable than on a bus. You may even be served tea if you're in soft or compartment class.

The transport scene is still very much in flux. New services will appear, some old ones will vanish. Schedules and prices will change. Even price ratios may be reversed sooner or later. In general, both trains and buses are dearer in Estonia and Latvia than in Lithuania and the Kaliningrad Region – but they're still pretty cheap everywhere. Some improvements in service standards have been made since independence in 1991, and this will probably continue, but problems arising from shortages of fuel and funds may crop up at any time.

BORDERS
At road borders between Estonia and Latvia, and Latvia and Lithuania, you normally have to wait half an hour or so as there are usually queues of vehicles waiting. Trains across these borders should cross without delays as customs and immigration checks can be made while in motion.

The Kaliningrad Region's road and rail borders with Lithuania are now strictly supervised, and you can't get into the Kaliningrad Region without a visa, though there have reportedly been cases of Russian border officials issuing 'instant' visas for under-the-counter payments of up to US$50 per person. The main road crossing is at Sovietsk, with the Klaipėda-Zelenogradsk road down the Neringa peninsula a scenic alternative. The Kybartai-Nesterov road is reportedly meant for commercial traffic, though cars may be able to use it too.

INFORMATION & TICKETS
Bus and train stations usually have pretty full timetables posted up. They may need some careful decoding but if you can manage this they are helpful. The bus stations in most of the main cities have information windows whose staff often speak a little English and can tell you which are the best services to your destination. Railway ticket clerks may be less helpful, and at main stations it can be difficult to work out which of the many ticket windows sells the ticket you want. The problem is compounded if there are queues at all windows and you don't want to waste time queueing at the wrong one. However, despite such difficulties and the seemingly confusing range of classes of bus and train, in practice things usually work out fairly straightforwardly. If you're in difficulties it's usually easy enough to find someone who will help you out. Some information on the best places to go for certain types of ticket – which occasionally are separate booking

offices away from the station – is given in the city and town Getting There & Away sections.

Timetables

Bus and train timetables will tell you a lot if you can decipher them. Since fuel shortages and other problems can mean unannounced changes to posted schedules, you should try (though it's not always easy) to check that what they tell you is correct – at least if you have looked at the timetable you should be able to ask a pertinent question. Some timetables give not only departure times but also arrival times, return journey schedules, and even the number of minutes a train waits in your station or the time a bus or train left the place it began its journey. Trains have numbers which are almost always listed on timetables, and it's worth noting the number of your train. The small print on timetables is worth studying too: it will tell you if a bus runs only on certain days, or a train only between certain dates.

Bus and train timetables don't usually list intermediate stops, which means there may be more services to your destination than at first appears. For instance, Rīga-Vilnius trains stop at Šiauliai but the only mention of Šiauliai on timetables at Rīga station is for the few trains that terminate at Šiauliai without going on to Vilnius. In this book some information on terminal points is given in city Getting There & Away sections to help you work out which services stop at intermediate places.

In the Language Guide at the back of this book you'll find some of the words that crop up in transport terminology in the different countries. Some of them may appear on timetables in abbreviated form.

AIR

Distances within the region are short, so flying only needs to come into play if you're short of time. Internal flights within the Baltic states still haven't settled to a regular pattern owing to disappointing passenger levels on existing flights, and a strange lack of advertising of what is surely a useful transport option for business, official, and some tourist travellers. So you must expect schedules and fare structures to change and routes to appear and disappear.

At the time of writing, Estonian Air flies Tallinn-Vilnius-Tallinn four times a week; there are no flights between Rīga and either Tallinn or Vilnius. Domestic flights within Estonia are in the process of being transferred from Estonian Air (which has been losing money on them) to a company called Ergon, which plans to fly between Tallinn and Tartu, Pärnu, Kuressaare (Saaremaa), and Kärdla (Hiiumaa). In Lithuania there are flights between Vilnius and Palanga by LAL and between Kaunas and Palanga by Air Lithuania. Liepāja in Latvia has an airport, but currently its only flights are to/from St Petersburg. Future possibilities include flights between Rīga and Kaunas by Latvian Airlines. There are currently no flights between Kaliningrad and any of the Baltic states.

As with international flights, tickets on local flights with the Baltic states' airlines are mostly much more expensive for foreigners than for locals. Another oddity: as a result of the varying speeds at which the different countries have been jettisoning Soviet-style cheap-transport policies, one-way fares on the Estonian Air flights to/from Vilnius are a lot lower at present if you buy them in Lithuania rather than in Estonia. The cheapest fare available in Tallinn is US$190, but for the reverse trip you pay only US$120 in Vilnius. This anomaly may change, of course. Internally, Estonian Air's fare from Tallinn to either of the island airports, Kuressaare or Kärdla, is about US$25. LAL charges US$70 on the Vilnius-Palanga route.

See city and town Getting There & Away sections for more information.

I flew twice with Estonian Air in its difficult first year of operation – once from Tallinn to Rīga and, several months later, from Rīga to Tallinn. (This route has since been abandoned.) The first trip was memorable for the sight of a Western businessman who had been sold an Estonian Air ticket for a flight from Tallinn to Vilnius, only to discover at Tallinn airport that the route was Tallinn-Rīga-Minsk and that, at that time,

Estonian Air didn't fly to Vilnius at all! Steam poured from his ears; all Estonians were held responsible for the error; and he vanished in search of a long-distance taxi.

Later in the year, the Rīga ticket clerk started off by denying the existence of the flight I wanted. I had seen it advertised in a newspaper, which I thought a fairly reliable source, but the clerk's schedule listed no Tallinn flight on the day in question. Finally she realised her information was out of date and agreed to sell me a ticket. All went well enough till I was out on the tarmac about to step on to the plane. Hadn't I heard? There was bad weather in Tallinn: the flight was delayed.

Back in the terminal, information on the chances of flying that day was scanty; officials were waiting for a telex from Tallinn about the weather there. Eventually I phoned Tallinn airport myself to find out: the prognosis was good. Finally, five or six hours late, having become familiar with every inch of Rīga airport and friendly with several of its staff, I made it on to the plane – to find I was the only passenger! Perhaps I had been the only person in Latvia who knew about the Rīga-Tallinn flight that day. My reward was a personal, face-to-face chat with the cabin attendant about altitudes, flying time and smoking rules for the one-hour flight.

A couple of days later in Tallinn, I asked an Estonian Air official why the airline didn't advertise its Rīga-Tallinn service more enthusiastically. After all, under normal circumstances it wiped several hours off the overland journey time between the two cities – surely something many business people would appreciate. The official looked blank, as if he didn't really understand what I meant.

Things have got better since those early days as the Baltic airlines gradually sort themselves out – and Estonian Air seems the best organised of them all! For one thing, its cabin crew have been trained by SAS. Generally, service is improving and information and ticketing are better organised. If you're not put off by fears that cost-cutting might lead to corner-cutting on maintenance, flying Estonian, Latvian or Lithuanian can be fun. It's certainly a 'Baltic' experience.

BUS

There are reasonably good bus services throughout the region. Apart from buses within each of the three Baltic states and the Kaliningrad Region, there are direct buses linking all the four major cities – Tallinn, Rīga, Vilnius and Kaliningrad – as well as other cross-border services between main towns. Buses are cheap but mostly rather slow – it's worth getting an 'express' or 'fast' bus if you can as they make fewer stops. On a few routes there are small microbuses, holding just 15 or 20 passengers, which also stop only a few times. Service frequencies are usually adequate for the number of travellers – extra buses are put on to popular destinations in summer – but if there's a fuel shortage (which is always possible unless the Baltic states manage to break free of dependence on Russian oil) bus services are among the first victims, and services are reduced.

One thing to watch out for is the route a bus takes, as some go by roundabout routes which can add several hours to a journey. Buses travelling longer distances are generally more comfortable and in better condition than local ones – but when it's raining or snowing watch out for leaky windows on any bus. In winter the only form of heating may be the body warmth of the other passengers.

Unless a bus is very crowded you'll normally be able to carry all your baggage on board with you. If you have to put some of it in the underneath baggage compartment you may have to pay a small sum.

Detail on specific service frequencies, journey times and fares is given in town and city Getting There & Away sections.

Tickets

For longer-distance buses starting their trips where you are, you can buy tickets in advance and this is worthwhile though not always essential. You will normally get a seat number written on your ticket. For local buses to nearby towns or villages, or for long-distance buses which are in mid-route ('in transit'), you normally pay on board. This may mean a bit of a scrum for seats if there are a lot of people waiting.

Costs

Fares vary a bit between the different countries and can be expected to rise everywhere – but they'll remain comparatively cheap. For a 100-km trip you currently pay around

US$0.60 in Estonia, US$1 in Latvia, US$0.55 in Lithuania, and US$0.30 in the Kaliningrad Region. International services within the region are a bit more expensive from Estonia (US$1 per 100 km) and Latvia (US$1.10) but not from Lithuania or Kaliningrad. 'Express' or 'fast' services or microbuses may be marginally dearer than other buses.

TRAIN

The Baltic states and the Kaliningrad Region are fairly well covered by railways and you can reach most parts of them – if not quite every main town – by train. Like the buses, the trains are cheap and slow.

The railway network is one area of Baltic life that seems to be dominated by Russian speakers, and the Russian names for types of train and classes of accommodation are given in the following section. Tickets on long-distance trains may still be printed in Russian.

Routes

The most important line through the Baltics runs from Tallinn to Vilnius through Tartu, Valga, Valmiera, Cēsis, Sigulda, Rīga, Jelgava, and Šiauliai. The daily *Baltic Express* between Tallinn and Warsaw follows this route as far as Šiauliai, but then branches off through Kaunas and Šeštokai to the Polish border (see the Getting There & Away chapter for more on this train).

Just one daily train, the *Seagull* (Estonian: Kajakas; Latvian: Kaija; Lithuanian: Žuvėdra; Russian: Chayka), runs the full distance from Tallinn to Vilnius and vice versa. Other trains cover sections of the route including Tallinn-Rīga and Rīga-Vilnius. The *Seagull*'s southern terminus is actually Minsk in Belarus, 3½ hours south of Vilnius. It takes a full 13½ hours to trundle between Tallinn and Vilnius, leaving Tallinn southbound at 6.50 am and Vilnius northbound at 10.11 am at the time of writing. Tallinn-Rīga takes 7½ hours and Rīga-Vilnius six hours.

Other lines include Tallinn-Narva (which continues to St Petersburg); Tallinn-Haapsalu; Tallinn-Pärnu; Tallinn-Viljandi; Valga-Võru (which continues to Pskov in Russia); Rīga-Ventspils; Rīga-Rēzekne; Rīga-Liepāja; Rīga-Daugavpils; Vilnius-Druskininkai; Vilnius-Kaunas-Kaliningrad; Vilnius-Daugavpils-Rēzekne (continuing to Pskov); Šiauliai-Sovietsk-Kaliningrad; and Klaipėda-Šiauliai-Panevėžys-Daugavpils. There are several other local railways fanning out from the main cities.

Types of Train

The basic distinction is between long-distance trains, which link main towns and cities and stop at a limited number of stations between, and local trains which stop at every station. There are three main types of long-distance trains : 'fast' *(skoryy)*, 'passenger' *(passazhirskiy)*, and 'diesel' *(dizel)*. 'Fast' trains are less slow than the others, but the only ones to be found in the Baltic states or Kaliningrad Region are some of those travelling to or from Russia, Ukraine or Poland – though you can, of course, use these for trips just within the Baltic region. Local trains are usually described as 'suburban' *(prigorodnyy)* – even though some of them travel 100 km or more – or sometimes 'electric' *(elektrichka)*.

At main stations there are often separate booking halls, and sometimes separate sets of platforms, for long-distance and local trains.

Classes

There are four main classes of train accommodation, only some of which will be found on any one train. In descending order of comfort and cost, they are: soft class *(myagkiy)*, compartment class *(kupeynyy)*, 'reserved-place' *(platskartnyy)*, and general seating *(obshchiy)*.

Soft Soft class is only available on some 'fast' trains. Compartments have upholstered seats and convert to comfortable sleeping compartments for two or four people. Your beds are usually made up for you. Myagkiy may also be called 1st-class, *lyux* or *spalny vagon (SV)*, which means 'sleeping carriage'.

Compartment Compartment class is the equivalent of a Western couchette, with leather or plastic seats. Bedding is provided for the bunks at an extra charge which is usually collected by the carriage attendant. 'Fast' and 'passenger' trains have compartment carriages and you can get places in them even if you're not travelling at night; in daytime they provide a numbered seat in a space that shouldn't be too crowded. Compartment and reserved-place classes together are sometimes referred to as 2nd-class or 'hard' *(zhyostkiy)* sleeping accommodation.

Reserved-Place These carriages have three tiers of hard bunks in sections that are partitioned, but not fully closed off from each other. Travelling in them is certainly a communal experience and can be pretty grubby and stuffy. They're normally only found on 'passenger' trains.

General Seating This is the only class on local trains and usually on 'diesel' trains too. It also appears on some 'passenger' trains. It consists of unreserved bench-type seating.

Tickets

Since trains are, on the whole, cheaper than buses, they are more popular and you should book in advance if you want any kind of sleeping accommodation. Queues at ticket offices are usually shorter in the early morning and in the evening than during the day, and on weekdays than on Saturdays and Sundays. Some cities have special advance-booking offices selling tickets up to 24 hours before departure.

Costs

As with buses, rail fares vary from one country to another and are constantly being changed. In compartment class you can go 100 km for about US$1 in Estonia, US$0.70 in Latvia, US$0.40 in Lithuania, and US$0.20 in the Kaliningrad Region. In general seating, 100 km costs about US$0.45 in Estonia and Latvia, US$0.15 in Lithuania, and US$0.12 in the Kaliningrad Region. Generally, soft class costs about twice as

much as compartment class, while reserved-place fares are between general-seating and compartment-class fares, but nearer general seating. Sometimes there are minor differences in the cost of compartment and reserved-place classes between fast and passenger trains, or in the cost of general seating between passenger, diesel and local trains.

Rail Passes

Two types of rail pass for the Baltic states were introduced in 1993. Their costs and conditions may change if they continue in future years. Since rail fares in the region are low in any case, you'd have to be doing a fair bit of rail travel to make the passes worthwhile.

Baltic Rail Explorer Pass This offers unlimited 2nd-class rail travel in the three Baltic states and the Kaliningrad Region at US$20 for seven days, US$30 for 14 days, or US$40 for 21 days, and includes any sleeping and bedding supplements. It's sold by Campus Travel branches and other student travel offices in the UK, and in continental Europe by outlets of Eurotrain, the discount youth rail-ticket specialist. The card is available to ISIC holders, people under 26, teachers and academic staff, and accompanying spouses and children.

Baltic Card This offers unlimited 2nd-class rail travel in Estonia, Latvia and Lithuania, plus some discounts on connecting travel from Sweden, Denmark, Finland, Poland and Germany. An eight-day card is about US$55 for 'adults', US$40 for 'youth' (age 12 to 25), and US$27 for 'children' (age four to 11). For 15 days it's about US$105 adult, US$80 youth and US$55 child. The card is available to non-residents of the Baltic states and is sold in Scandinavia by branches of the student travel agency, Kilroy Travel, and possibly elsewhere.

CAR & MOTORBIKE

Driving or riding in the Baltic states can be really enjoyable as roads are good, traffic light, and distances not too great. Some country roads are dirt or gravel but reasonably smooth. This way of getting around enables you to get off the beaten track, explore hidden corners that others can only reach with difficulty, and appreciate the gentle beauty of the Baltic countryside and coasts. It's also more comfortable than buses and trains, though it may give you less contact with the local people. Getting petrol can be difficult, but not impossible, at times of fuel shortage. There are Western-run petrol stations at various points on the main north-south trunk route through the Baltics which seem to have permanent supplies of good-quality fuel. Take a spare petrol can with you and keep it full, in any case. Most towns have service stations, though only a few specialists have parts for Western makes.

You can take your own vehicle to the Baltics from the West by ferry from Finland, Sweden, Denmark or Germany; or by road from Poland, Belarus or Russia – though the direct Poland-Lithuania border crossing is to be avoided if possible owing to long delays and other shenanigans. The slight detour through Belarus might be easier. The Kaliningrad Region is likely to open up as another land entry point to the region; you can already drive into it from Lithuania. See the Getting There & Away chapter for detail on all these routes.

Alternatively you can rent a car in Estonia, Latvia or Lithuania, though this is not cheap.

Rental
The three capital cities, especially Tallinn, are the easiest places to rent cars although there are possibilities in a growing number of other places. International chains like Avis, Hertz and Europcar-InterRent have opened offices in the capitals. In addition to the hire firms themselves, you can arrange rentals through most top-end hotels and some travel agencies. You usually need to pay with a major credit card.

The cheapest cars are Russian-made Ladas, which have the added advantage of running on cheap, easily available 93-octane petrol. They typically cost US$50 or US$60 a day with unlimited mileage. Their petrol

tanks usually hold 40 litres and they do about 10 km a litre. Ladas are only available from a few outlets and tend to be heavily booked, so plan ahead if you want one. Western makes of car usually cost US$90 or more a day with unlimited km, though you can get them for less if you're only doing a short distance and choose a per-km deal. One-way rentals are often possible – at a price. See city and town Getting There & Away sections for specific information on car rental firms.

Documents
If you're renting a car you need a passport and a suitable driving licence – normally an International Driving Permit but a national licence from a European country is often acceptable. Some rental companies have minimum ages (usually 19 or 21, but 22 at some places in Estonia) and stipulate that you must have held your licence for at least a year. A major credit card is almost essential too, as some companies insist on it as the method of payment. Even if they don't, you'll have to leave a very large deposit or make a heavy cash prepayment. See the Car & Motorbike section in the Getting There & Away chapter for more on licences, and on other documents you need if you bring your own vehicle.

Road Rules
The whole region drives on the right. Except in Latvia, driving with any alcohol at all in your blood is illegal – don't do so after even a sip of a drink. A blood alcohol level of 0.05% has been permitted in Latvia since 1992. Seat belts are compulsory for drivers and front-seat passengers. Speed limits in built-up areas are 50 km/h in Estonia and the Kaliningrad region, 60 km/h in Latvia and Lithuania. Limits outside vary from 70 to 110 km/h. Definitely in Estonia, and probably in the rest of the region, you're supposed to use your headlights on highways even in daytime. Traffic fines are usually collected on the spot by the police officer who books you (always ask for a receipt).

There are small fees for driving into the

old cities in Tallinn, Rīga and Vilnius, though these are not always enforced.

Take care with trams, trolleybuses and buses in towns. Passengers may run across the road to catch them while they're still in motion. Traffic behind a tram must stop when it opens its doors to let people in and out. Trolleybuses often swing a long way out into the road when leaving a stop.

Fuel
Since the Baltic states are still largely dependent on Russia for their petrol, shortages can occur either when Russia hikes the price higher than the Baltics are willing to pay or when supplies just don't get through. The situation seems to be settling down, however, and severe shortages are becoming rare. Petrol stations are fairly common but even when there's plenty of fuel to go round, long queues may form because they either have only one pump working or everybody's filling up a spare can as well as their main tank to save queueing up again next time! Things are further slowed down by the usual rule that you must pay for your petrol before the pump is switched on for you.

Sometimes petrol is sold 'direct to the customer' by tankers standing at roadsides with a sign out saying what grade of petrol they're offering – A-93, A-76 etc.

Regular petrol comes in four grades, all with lead: 76, 93, 95 and 98, marked on pumps as A-76, AI-76 etc. However, grades higher than 93 are often unavailable at most petrol stations. This is inconvenient for drivers of Western cars, which mostly prefer 95-octane or higher. But help is at hand in the form of about a dozen Western-run petrol stations around the Baltic states, many of them open 24 hours, which have seemingly continuous supplies of higher grades (sometimes including 99-octane – the equivalent of Western 'Super') and also of unleaded fuel.

Petrol prices were still on the way up everywhere at the time of research but a litre of 93-octane cost about US$0.30 in Estonia and slightly more in Latvia and Lithuania. Regular 95-octane was about 15% dearer,

and 95-octane unleaded (95-E), 98 and 99-octane, where available, were all about three times the price of 93-octane. Diesel is about two-thirds the price of 93-octane.

Western-run petrol stations that are definitely open at the time of writing are:

Tallinn
    Neste: Pärnu maantee 141
    Neste: Regati puiestee 1, Pirita
    Statoil: corner of Sadama and Mere puiestee
    Statoil: Tartu maantee (next to airport)
Pärnu
    Neste: Riia maantee 110A
Rīga
    Traffic Service (Neste): Brīvības gatve 386
    Traffic Service (Neste): Pērnavas iela 78
Vilnius
    Litofinn (Neste): Erfurto gatvė 41, Lazdynai

Other stations are likely to open. Locations planned or proposed by Neste or its local partners include Narva; Saulkrasti, 40 km north of Rīga on the Tallinn road; Ķekava, 20 km south of Rīga on the Vilnius road; and Kryžkalnis, Klaipėda, Mažeikiai, Panevėžys and Marijampolė in Lithuania.

Security
Take normal precautions when you leave your vehicle unattended: lock it and don't leave anything of any value in it. Western makes of vehicle will attract attention. There are fenced-in parking lots in many towns which are worth finding if you're not staying in a hotel with lock-up facilities.

BICYCLE
The flatness and small scale of the Baltic states and the light traffic on most roads make them good cycling territory. Even in the first full year of independence, 1992, several dozen foreigners toured the Baltics independently by bike. Most bring their own bikes but there are also a few places where you can rent a bicycle – including Kärdla, Rīga, Vilnius and Palanga for local use, and Rīga, Vilnius and Valmiera for touring (see the city and town sections and the introduction to the Vidzeme chapter for details). Cyclists should certainly bring waterproof

clothing, and perhaps a tent if you're touring since you may not find accommodation in some out-of-the-way places.

Two Latvian organisations offer organised small-group cycle tours with a guide and all equipment provided. They are the Latvian University Tourist Club (Latvijas Universitātes Tūristu Klubs, LUTK) (☎ 22-223 114, fax 22-225 039 or 22-227 411) of Raiņa bulvāris 19, LV-1098 Rīga, and the Tourist Club of Latvia (Latvijas Tūristu Klubs, LTK) (☎ 22-221 731, 22-227 680) at Skārņu iela 22, LV-1350 Rīga. Both are small, friendly set-ups but the LUTK is very much cheaper. It has suggested routes of five to nine days in all the regions of Latvia – Vidzeme, Latgale, Zemgale and Kurzeme – for around US$15 a day per person including bike, food, tent and guide. Accommodation is in tents. These trips are well worth considering as they'll take you right off the beaten track in the company of someone who can explain a lot of what you see. The LTK offers a nine-day riding itinerary round Vidzeme and Latgale (eastern Latvia) plus three days in and around Rīga, with accommodation in a mixture of cheaper hotels, tents and farmhouses. All food, equipment and an English-speaking guide are provided, for US$670 per person (maximum eight people). You can write to either club for information. Both would probably set up trips for just a couple of people if that's all there are of you, and maybe a tailor-made itinerary if you had particular requirements. Latvia Tours (see Travel Agencies in the Rīga chapter) may also have cycle-camping possibilities.

HITCHING

Hitching is an accepted, if not especially common, way of getting around the three Baltic states. It's customary to pay your share of the petrol.

BOAT

Combined passenger and vehicle ferries sail from the Estonian mainland to the islands of Muhu (which is linked by a road causeway

to Estonia's biggest island, Saaremaa), Hiiumaa and Vormsi. There are through-buses from Tallinn to Saaremaa and Hiiumaa, and from Tartu and Pärnu to Saaremaa, which use these ferries. Fares are low, but traffic can be heavy in summer – especially on Saturdays and Sundays when sailings may be fewer; if you're driving it's worth trying to reserve a place in advance. You should also book your return passage off the island as early as possible. The ferry from Virtsu on the mainland to Kuivastu on Muhu goes 10 to 12 times daily. From Rohuküla near Haapsalu to Heltermaa on Hiiumaa there are sailings nine or 10 times a day Monday to Friday, but only three to five sailings daily at weekends. From Rohuküla to Sviby on Vormsi there are three sailings a day Monday to Friday, two on Saturdays, and one on Sundays. Full details of the services are given in the West Estonia & The Islands chapter.

It's possible to take boat excursions from Pärnu to the smaller Estonian islands of Kihnu and Ruhnu – see the South-West Estonia chapter.

In Lithuania during summer, a hydrofoil service plies daily along the Nemunas River and the Courland Lagoon between Kaunas and Nida, with some sailings to Klaipėda, too.

Sailing Yourself

Private yachting is an increasingly popular way of getting around the Baltic coasts – particularly Estonia's with its many islands and bays. TopSail (☎ 22-237 055, fax 22-237 044) at the Pirita marina, Regati puiestee 1, Tallinn EE0019, charters out British Westerly yachts with or without a skipper. There are also yachts for hire at the Nasva Yacht Club on Saaremaa island and possibly other main yacht clubs such as Haapsalu and Pärnu. See the Sailing Yourself section in the Getting There & Away chapter for information on recommended harbours in Estonia.

Canoe

There are some good canoeing rivers and lakes in the Baltic states. Information is given under Activities in Facts for the Visitor.

LOCAL TRANSPORT
Bus, Tram & Trolleybus

A variety of trams, buses, and trolleybuses (buses run by electricity from overhead wires) provide pretty thorough, if often very crowded, public transport around towns and cities in the Baltic states and the Kaliningrad Region. They run from 5 or 6 am to about midnight, though they thin out in outlying areas after about 7 pm. You pay for your ride by punching a flat-fare ticket in one of the ticket-punches fixed inside the vehicle. Tickets are sold from street kiosks displaying them in the window (the kiosks can be hard to locate), and by some drivers (who are easier to find). Buy five or 10 at once – they're very cheap at between US$0.01 and US$0.04 depending on the town. The system depends on honesty and obviously lends itself to cheating, but there are occasional inspections with fines of up to US$0.60 levied on the spot if you're riding without a punched ticket.

All airports are served by regular city transport as well as by taxis.

A further type of city transport is the route-taxi (Estonian: *liinitakso* or *marsruuttakso*; Latvian: *maršruta taksometrs*; Russian: *marshrutnoe taksi*), though most visitors needn't bother about it. These are minibuses that will drop you anywhere along their fixed routes for a flat fare.

Taxi

Taxis are plentiful and should be cheap, as officially they cost US$0.17 a km in Estonia, US$0.12 in Latvia and Lithuania, and about US$0.10 in Kaliningrad at the time of writing. But there are lots of attempted rip-offs, especially by the mafia types who seem to run most main taxi ranks including those at airports and outside main tourist hotels. Absurd prices are often asked of unsuspecting foreigners. State-run taxis – often large Volga cars, usually with a little chequered strip on the side – tend to be more honest than private-enterprise taxis with no recognisable insignia. Taxi drivers in Kaliningrad also seem more honest than their Baltic states counterparts.

One way to avoid rip-offs is to insist on the meter running, but a problem with this is that in some places, owing to inflation, meters turn over at out-of-date speeds. In such cases the price showing on the meter has to be multiplied by a fixed figure – but until you find out what that figure is, you're at a disadvantage. Failing all else, agree a fixed price before you get in and take no notice of claims that where you want to go is 10 times the distance it really is. In some places you can also avoid rip-offs by ordering a cab by phone.

Train

Suburban trains serve the outskirts of the main cities and some surrounding towns and villages. They're of limited use as city transport for visitors as they mostly go to residential or industrial areas with little to see. But some are useful for day trips to destinations outside the cities.

TOURS

There are a lot of single-city, two or three-city, country, island and so on tours and excursions available in the Baltic states. Most are advertised by travel agencies. Some possibilities are mentioned in city and town sections of this book.

Estonia

Facts about the Country

Estonia (Eesti) is the northernmost of the three Baltic states and the most Scandinavian in atmosphere – Helsinki is just 80 km away across the Gulf of Finland.

Estonia seems to be adapting to capitalism and independence faster than its Baltic siblings, which makes visiting it perhaps less of a shock to a Westerner and a good starting point for a trip through the Baltic states.

Estonia's German-influenced past lingers in the medieval heart of Tallinn, the capital, which is a highpoint of any visit to the Baltic region. Tallinn is the hub of Estonian life, but Tartu, the second city; Lahemaa National Park; and the islands off the west coast are among other appealing destinations.

This chapter contains information specific to Estonia. For a more general introduction to the history, geography and culture of the Baltic states, see Facts about the Region at the front of the book.

GEOGRAPHY

Estonia is the smallest Baltic state, at 45,200 sq km – slightly bigger than Switzerland or Denmark. It borders Russia in the east and Latvia in the south. Tallinn is situated on the north coast. Nearly 10% of Estonian territory is islands, the biggest of which are Saaremaa and Hiiumaa to the west.

Northern Estonia faces the Gulf of Finland, the narrow eastern arm of the Baltic that leads into St Petersburg, while much of Estonia's west coast is shielded by its islands.

Like the other Baltic states, Estonia is mainly flat. The main upland area is the south-east where the hill Suur Munamägi, at

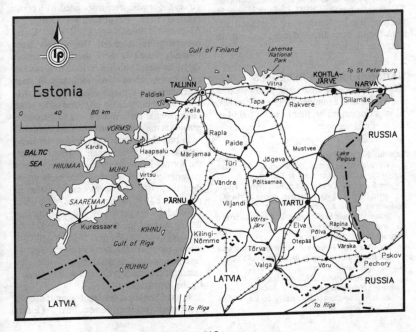

317 metres, is the highest point in the Baltic states.

Estonia has the biggest lakes in the Baltic region: Lake Peipus, which straddles the Estonian-Russian border, is the fourth-biggest in Europe, at 3548 sq km (though its maximum depth is only 15 metres). Võrtsjärv, in southern Estonia, is the biggest lake lying entirely within the Baltic states, covering 270 sq km (but just six metres deep).

Borders

Estonia does not accept its existing borders with Russia. Two areas which were part of Estonia under the terms of the 1920 Estonia-Russia peace treaty have been under Russian control since WW II, and Estonia does not recognise Russian rule over them. One is a thin slice of land east of the Narva River. The other is a larger area around Pechory (Estonian: Petseri), across Estonia's existing south-east border. Pechory is the traditional 'capital' of the distinctive Estonian region of Setumaa, more than half of which is now in Russian hands. Numbers of Estonian citizens live in both disputed areas and vote in Estonian elections.

NATIONAL PARKS & RESERVES

Estonia has one national park, established in the 1970s, and a number of nature reserves. More information on them can be found in the regional sections.

Lahemaa National Park
   Estonia's only national park comprises 649 sq km of typical Estonian coast and unspoiled hinterland east of Tallinn – beaches, rivers, lakes, waterfalls, walking trails; park centre at Viitna
Endla State Nature Reserve
   around the lake Endla järv, east of Paide – boggy area, nature trails
Matsalu State Nature Reserve
   on west coast – wetland and major water bird habitat; visitor centre; guided trips available
Nigula State Nature Reserve
   in the south-west near Latvian border – bog
Väinameri Nature Reserve
   islets off south-east Hiiumaa – bird and plant habitat; permit needed

Viidumäe State Nature Reserve
   on Saaremaa – forested area around the island's highest point; observation tower
Vilsandi State Nature Reserve
   small islands off western Saaremaa – bird sanctuary; closed to visitors

GOVERNMENT

Estonia's present constitution was approved in June 1992 by a referendum of citizens of the pre-1940 republic and their descendants. The law-making body is a 101-seat parliament called the Riigikogu ('National Council'), elected every four years. The head of state is the president, but the government is headed by the prime minister, who is nominated by the president and has to be approved by the Riigikogu. The prime minister chooses the cabinet.

The first elections under the new constitution were held in September 1992. The Fatherland Alliance won a narrow majority after campaigning under the slogan 'Cleaning House', which meant removing from power those who were associated with communist rule. Fatherland's leader, a 32-year-old historian called Mart Laar, became prime minister. The alliance later formally united as the Fatherland (Isamaa) Party. Its stated policies include free-market economics, privatisation, reduction of state bureaucracy and monopolies, and liberalisation of the citizenship law. One of its most controversial early moves was to introduce prayers at the start of parliamentary sessions!

In presidential elections held at the same time as those for parliament, Arnold Rüütel, the former head of Estonia's Soviet puppet government, and who had also been president under the semi-democratic system in place since 1990, won most votes (42%). But since he did not get the overall majority that the election rules required, the choice of president was handed over to the Riigikogu, which plumped for the writer and former foreign minister, Lennart Meri. Under the constitution, future presidents will be chosen by the Riigikogu.

In the Riigikogu, the right-wing Estonian National Independence Party (Eesti

Rahvusliku Sõltumatuse Partei) and the Moderates (Moodukad) are broadly aligned with Fatherland. The main opposition comprises the Centrist Party, led by former prime minister Edgar Savisaar; the right-of-centre Safe Home (Kindel Kodu) coalition; some extreme nationalist members; and the eccentric Royalists (Sõltumatud Kuningriiklased), who have seven seats and want to put a member of the Swedish royal family on a newly created Estonian throne.

The Greens (Rohelised) have one member of parliament.

Citizenship

People who were citizens of the pre-1940 Estonian Republic (and their descendants) are automatically citizens. Other people, basically, must have lived in Estonia for two years after 30 March 1990 and be able to write, read, and converse in the Estonian language. Applications take a year to go through. Only citizens may vote in parliamentary elections.

The citizenship rules were approved by the referendum in 1992 and made law by the Riigikogu in 1993. Few of the Russians, Ukrainians, or Belarussians who make up about 35% of Estonia's population seem interested in applying for citizenship, no doubt partly because many of them live and work in immigrant enclaves where Estonian is rarely heard.

PEOPLE

Of the approximately 1.5 million people who live in Estonia, only around 62% are ethnic Estonians. About 30% of the population is Russian, and about 3% is Ukrainian. These ethnic populations are not evenly distributed throughout the country. About half the people of Tallinn, for instance, are Russian, and the industrial towns of north-east Estonia are overwhelmingly Russian-populated.

The Estonians themselves are one of the Finno-Ugric peoples, an ethno-linguistic group whose members are scattered from the Arctic to central Europe, halfway across Siberia, and along the River Volga. This sets them apart from the Latvians and Lithuanians, who are Indo-European. It's reckoned that the ancestors of the present Estonians reached Estonia from the east from about 2500 to 2000 BC. Within the Finno-Ugric group, the Estonians are closely related to such peoples as the Finns, the Lapps, the Karelians (who live in Finland and neighbouring parts of Russia) and the Livs, who used to inhabit much of coastal Latvia but are now reduced to tiny numbers and are on the verge of extinction as a separate people. Other Finno-Ugric peoples include the Samoyeds along the Russian shores of the Arctic Ocean; the Ostyaks and Voguls, east of the Urals; the Magyars (Hungarians); the Votyaks and Zyryans, west of the Urals; and the Mordvins and Cheremis, along the Volga.

An estimated 60,000 Estonians live in Russia and 80,000 in other countries mainly as a result of emigration around the turn of the 20th century and following the outbreak of WW II. The main overseas Estonian communities are in North America and Sweden but there are others in Britain, Australia and elsewhere.

ARTS
Literature

Estonian literature began with the poems of Kristjan Jaak Peterson in the early 19th century. The national epic poem *Kalevipoeg* (Son of Kalev) was written between 1857 and 1861 by Friedrich Reinhold Kreutzwald, who was inspired by Finland's *Kalevala*, a similar epic created a few decades earlier. Kreutzwald put together hundreds of Estonian legends and folk tales to tell the adventures of the mythical hero Kalevipoeg, which end with his death and his land's conquest by foreigners, but also hope for a future freedom. Kalevipoeg must have travelled pretty widely round Estonia, as there's barely a big boulder in the country which wasn't apparently once tossed by him or a lake he didn't once jump across.

Lydia Koidula (1843-86) was the poet of Estonia's national awakening, while Eduard Vilde (1865-1933) was an influential turn-of-the-century novelist and playwright. Oskar Luts is reckoned to be a kind of Estonian Mark Twain for his school and childhood tales including *Kevade* (Spring), written in 1912-13. Anton Hansen Tammsaare is considered the greatest Estonian novelist for his *Tõde ja Õigus* (Truth and Justice), written between 1926 and 1933. A five-volume saga of village and town life, it explores Estonian social, political and philosophical issues.

More recently the novelist Jaan Kross has won acclaim for his historical novels in which he managed to tackle contemporary Soviet-era subjects at one remove. His best known book, *The Czar's Madman*, has been translated into English – see Books in the introductory Facts for the Visitor. Another leading novelist is Arvo Valton who, like Kross, spent some time as an exile in Siberia. His *Masendus ja Lootus* (Depression and Hope) deals with that experience.

Estonia also has a number of outstanding contemporary poets. Jaan Kaplinski (see Books) is one who has works published in English. Paul-Eerik Rummo is considered by many the leading Estonian poet – a judgement which predates his elevation to the post of Minister of Culture in 1992. Kross and Kaplinski were also elected to parliament the same year – and both have been mentioned as Nobel prize candidates.

Music
Rock thrives in Estonia and there are big annual festivals (see Cultural Events). The Estonian R&B/soul band Compromise Blue (nine-piece, at the time of writing) has been gaining a growing army of fans since it formed in Tartu in 1988 and shouldn't be missed if you get the chance – see the Tallinn Entertainment section. Röövel Ööbik (Thieving Nightingale), whose influences range from My Bloody Valentine to oriental and Islamic music, have won the attention of Britain's John Peel. Alo Mattiisen's use of Estonian folk chants in some of his rock songs was a powerful force in the Singing Revolution. Other leading Estonian bands are the U2-style Mr Lawrence and the folk rockers Jää-äär.

Estonia's Arvo Pärt is the Baltics' most widely acclaimed serious composer though he emigrated to Germany in 1980. His works are chiefly choral and classified as 'minimalist'. Veljo Tormis, another leading Estonian choral composer, writes striking music based on old runic chants. His best known works include the difficult-to-perform *Curse Upon Iron* and *The Ingrian Evenings*, mainly folk-dance song, which is one of a series of cycles of songs of disappeared or disappearing Finno-Ugric peoples called *Forgotten Peoples*.

The Estonian Rudolf Tobias wrote influential symphonic, choral and concerto works around the turn of the century.

Visual Arts
Kristjan Raud (1865-1943) who illustrated *Kalevipoeg* was a leading figure of the 19th century in Estonia. Contemporary Estonian art leans towards geometrical abstraction. Leading exponents include Raul Meel, Leonhard Lapin and Siim-Tanel Annus.

Facts for the Visitor

This chapter contains visitor information specific to Estonia. For details on obtaining visas for the Baltic states, Russia and Belarus and for more general information on travelling in the Baltic states see the introductory Facts for the Visitor chapter at the front of the book.

DIPLOMATIC MISSIONS

Since 1991, Estonia has opened many diplomatic missions throughout the world. More will be added to the list, and some may move. Some missions operate for limited hours or from the consul's home, so it pays to ring ahead and to allow ample time to make contact.

Estonian diplomatic missions include:

Australia
    Consulate: 141 Campbell St, Darlinghurst, Sydney, NSW 2010 (☎ 02-212 1207)
Austria
    Consulate: Reichenhallerstr 10A, A-5020 Salzburg (☎ 0662-848 4961)
Belgium
    Embassy: Avenue Isidore Gerard 1, 1160 Auderghem (☎ 02-7790755)
Canada
    Consulate: 958 Broadview Ave, Toronto, Ontario, M4K 2R6 (☎ 416-461 0764)
Denmark
    Embassy: Admiralgade 20, DK-1066, Copenhagen K (☎ 33 15 18 62)
Finland
    Embassy: Fabianinkatu 13 A-2, Helsinki 13 (☎ 90-179 528)
    Consulate: Kasarmikatu 28, Helsinki (☎ 90-179 719)
France
    Embassy: 14 Boulevard Montmartre, 75009 Paris (☎ 1-48.01.00.22)
Germany
    Embassy: Fritz-Schäffer-Strasse 22, 53113 Bonn (☎ 0228-91 47 90)
Israel
    Honorary Consul: 6 Hadassah St, Tel Aviv (☎ 03-527 9386)
Latvia
    Embassy: Nometņu iela 62, LV-1002 Rīga (☎ 22-601 014)
Lithuania
    Embassy: Turniškių gatvė 20, 2016 Vilnius (☎ 22-769 848)
Norway
    Consulate: Schwensens gate 5, N-0170, Oslo (☎ 22-69 88 73)
Russia
    Embassy: Sobinovsky pereulok 5, 103009 Moscow (☎ 095-290 50 13)
    Consulate: Bolshaya Monetnaya ulitsa 14, 3rd floor, St Petersburg (☎ 812-233 55 48)
Sweden
    Embassy: Storgatan 38, 1 tr, S-11455 Stockholm (☎ 08-665 65 50)
Switzerland
    Consulate: 8 Chemin des Aulx, CH-1228 Planles-Ouates, Geneva (☎ 022-706 1111)
UK
    Embassy: 16 Hyde Park Gate, London SW7 5DG (☎ 071-589 3428)
USA
    Embassy: 1030 15th St NW, Suite 1000, Washington DC 20005 (☎ 202-789 0320)
    Consulate: 630 Fifth Ave, Suite 2415, New York, NY 10111 (☎ 212-247 1450)

CUSTOMS

Customs regulations vary between the Baltic states and are subject to change. Some general pointers are given in the introductory Facts for the Visitor chapter. Estonian embassies and consulates should be able to tell you the latest if there is anything you are concerned about.

Alcohol & Tobacco

People aged 21 years or over can bring in or take out, duty-free, 10 litres of beer; 200 cigarettes or 20 cigars or 250 grams of tobacco; and either one litre of strong alcoholic drinks (up to 58% volume) and one litre of mild alcoholic drinks (up to 21% vol), or two litres of mild alcoholic drinks.

The duty-free allowances for people aged between 18 and 21 years are the same except that no strong alcoholic drinks are included.

Money

Hard currency worth more than DM1000 should be declared on arrival, and you cannot take out more than you brought in.

Other Items

There's duty on bringing in furs, fur articles, precious metals and jewellery above certain limits which very few people will exceed.

Purchases up to a total value of 5000 EEK can be exported duty-free. Above that there's 100% duty. There are also export duties on some cultural objects such as paintings and sculptures, furs and fur articles over 500 EEK in purchase price, more than 20 litres of petrol, and gold and silver jewellery above the duty-free import limits.

Without special permission you cannot import or export the following items: poisons, mint postage stamps, precious stones or metals, or hunting trophies. On some of these there are duties even if you do get permission.

Customs Information

In Tallinn the customs department is at Rävala puiestee 9 (☎ 22-444 662 or 22-691 827). You can also call ☎ 22-691 805 for information on customs regulations.

MONEY

Estonia's currency is the *kroon* (pronounced 'krohn'). The kroon is written in this book, and commonly elsewhere, as EEK which stands for Eesti Kroon (Estonian Crown) and distinguishes it from Swedish, Danish, Norwegian and other crowns. It is divided into 100 *sents* (cents).

The kroon is the only legal tender in Estonia. It's illegal to buy or sell with any other currency. The kroon was the first new Baltic currency to be introduced, coming in over the weekend of 20-22 June 1992. Its value is held within 3% of a rate of eight to the Deutschmark. Exchange rates in late 1993 included:

US$1	=	12.89 EEK
DM1	=	8.01 EEK
UK£1	=	19.62 EEK
C$1	=	9.65 EEK
A$1	=	8.21 EEK
1 Fmk	=	2.24 EEK
1 SKr	=	1.62 EEK

The kroon comes in notes of 1 EEK, 2 EEK, 5 EEK, 10 EEK, 25 EEK, 50 EEK, 100 EEK and 500 EEK. There are coins of 5 sents, 10 sents, 20 sents, 50 sents and 1 EEK. The notes, handsomely designed by Vladimir Taiger who won a competition in 1990, were printed in the UK and USA. Each shows a national hero on the front and a symbolic scene on the back.

Estonia's pre-WW II currency, displaced by the rouble in 1940, was also called the kroon but was an entirely different system.

NATIONAL HOLIDAYS

National holidays vary from country to country in the Baltic states, and there may be

Estonian Banknotes

Denomination	Front	Back
1 EEK	Kristjan Raud (artist)	Toompea Castle
2 EEK	Karl Ernst von Baer (scientist)	Tartu University
5 EEK	Paul Keres (chess player)	Narva and Ivangorod
10 EEK	Jakob Hurt (folklorist)	Tamme-Lauri oak at Urvaste
25 EEK	Anton Hansen Tammsaare (novelist)	Vargamäe
50 EEK	Rudolf Tobias (composer)	
100 EEK	Lydia Koidula (poet)	Limestone cliffs
500 EEK	Carl Robert Jakobson (national awakener)	Barn swallow (national bird)

more changes to come. National Holidays in Estonia include:

New Year's Day, 1 January
Independence Day (anniversary of 1918 declaration), 24 February
Good Friday – Easter Monday is also taken as a holiday by many people; some shops, offices and even restaurants also close on the Thursday before and the Tuesday after Easter
May Day, 1 May
Victory Day (anniversary of Battle of Võnnu, 1919), 23 June
Jaanipäev (St John's Day), 24 June – taken together, Victory Day and Jaanipäev are the excuse for a week-long midsummer break for many people
Rebirth Day (anniversary of 1988 sovereignty declaration), 16 November
Christmas (Jõulud), 25 December
Boxing Day, 26 December

CULTURAL EVENTS

Estonia has a long list of festivals and cultural events, especially during the summer months. Three major events are worth making time for: the national song festival, the midsummer celebrations, and the Baltika folk festival. For some background to these events, see Cultural Events in the introductory Facts for the Visitor chapter at the front of the book.

Tartu Ski Marathon – mid-February
Old Tallinn Days – Tallinn old-town festival; early or mid-June
FiESTa music festival & Baltoscandal drama days – Pärnu, late June
Rock Summer – the Baltics' biggest rock-music festival, with big foreign names as well as local favourites; at Tallinn Song Bowl, early/mid July
Viru Säru – folk music and dance festival; Palmse Manor, Lahemaa National Park, first weekend in July, even-numbered years
Visual Anthropology Festival – film festival and conference focusing on issues of cultural survival; Pärnu, variable dates (has been mid-July in some years, early September in others)
Lillepidu – international flower festival with thousands of spectators; Tallinn, early September
Jazzkaar – jazz festival; Tallinn, October
NYYD – international new-music festival; Tallinn, November
Time of Spirits – a period of quietness for remembering the past and the dead, when spirits are believed to be abroad; roughly a month from 2 November

MEDIA
Local-Language Press

The most popular Estonian papers are *Postimees*, *Rahva Hääl*, and *Paevaleht*, all published five or six days a week with circulations of 50,000 to 90,000; and the more sensationalist colour weekly *Eesti Ekspress*.

A new daily, *Hommikuleht*, was founded in 1993 by leading journalists from other papers with the aim of combining the best of all its rivals. Details of English-language newspapers and magazines published in the Baltics are given in Facts for the Visitor – Media at the front of the book.

TV & Radio

With special aerials it's currently possible to pick up six TV channels in Tallinn – state-run Eesti TV plus one from Moscow and four from Finland. But a bog-standard hotel room set is only likely to offer Eesti TV and the Moscow channel. This may change when new independent stations come on air. In among its mainly Estonian-language output, Eesti TV shows a few British programmes with subtitles and some locally made Russian-language ones. News in Estonian is at 9.30 pm.

State-run Eesti Raadio broadcasts 10 minutes of news about Estonia in English from Monday to Friday at 1620 GMT/UTC (in Estonia that's 6.20 pm from October to March, 7.20 pm at other times of the year) and the Estonia Today magazine programme, also in English, on Mondays and Thursdays from 2130 to 2200 GMT/UTC. Its frequencies are 1035 kHz medium wave, 69.3 MHz FM, and 5.925 MHz short wave. The independent Radio Kuku on 100.7 MHz FM has good music and some news and features in English between 2 and 4 pm daily.

You can get Voice of America on 70.28 MHz from 0700 to 1100 GMT/UTC and 2200 to 2400 GMT/UTC.

FOOD

The Estonian diet relies heavily on red meat, chicken and sausage. Fish is not as widespread as you might expect: it appears most often as a smoked or salted starter. *Suitsukala* means smoked fish. Smoked trout *(forell)* is one good speciality. Estonian sausage varieties include *suitsuvorst* (salami) and *viiner* (frankfurter).

General information on eating in the Baltic states is given in the introductory Facts for the Visitor chapter at the front of the book. The Language Guide at the back of the book includes words and phrases you will find useful when ordering food and drink.

Tallinn

Tallinn (population: 495,000) fronts a bay on the Gulf of Finland and is dominated by Toompea, the hill over which it has tumbled since the Middle Ages. In few places in Europe does the aura of the 14th and 15th centuries survive intact as it does in Tallinn's jumble of medieval walls and turrets, needling spires, and winding, cobbled hills. Tallinn's Old Town is judiciously restored, fascinating to explore, and about the most picturesque square kilometre in the Baltic states.

Tallinn is also a lively capital city with Estonia's government, embassies, culture, entertainment, commerce and industry all headquartered here – and some chic fashions are to be seen on its streets and in its shops. It's a far brighter, more welcoming place than it was in the Soviet era, with cosy cafés, good restaurants, and good accommodation all easy to find now. There's also much more in the shops for those who can afford it, along with a friendlier disposition among the people you'll encounter in such places. All this and a coastal location that the other two Baltic capitals lack make Tallinn probably the most magnetic, not-to-be-missed hub in the whole of the Baltic states.

But the glossy sheen imparted by Tallinn's modern restaurants and shops, and by the Finns and other Westerners who flock into the town at weekends and during summer, is to some extent misleading. Though a percentage of Tallinners are earning a much better living than they used to, for many others life is probably harder than ever – witness the subdued, anxious people squeezing into trams, scouring the market for cheap food, or queueing at cheap canteens. Among Tallinn's poor are many of the Russians who form about half its population. A visit to one of the drab apartment-block suburbs where the Russians are congregated, such as Kopli or Lasnamäe, will show you a very different side of Tallinn from the carefully preserved charms of the old central area.

Tallinn is on a similar latitude to St Petersburg and shares that city's warm summer 'white nights' and short, cold, dark winter days. In summer it comes alive with local and international festivals.

HISTORY

The site of Tallinn is thought to have been settled by Finno-Ugric people about 2500 BC. There was probably an Estonian trading settlement here from around the 9th century AD, and a wooden stronghold was built on Toompea in the 11th century. The Danes under King Waldemar II (who conquered northern Estonia in 1219) met tough resistance at Tallinn and were on the verge of retreat when, so the story goes, a red flag with a white cross fell from the sky into their bishop's hands. Taking this as a sign of God's support, they summoned new energy and went on to win the battle; the flag became their national flag. The Danes set their own castle on Toompea. The origin of the name

Tallinn is thought to be from *Taani linn* which is Estonian for 'Danish town'.

The Knights of the Sword took Tallinn from the Danes in 1227 and built the first stone fort on Toompea. German traders arrived from Visby on the Baltic island of Gotland and founded a colony of about 200 people – the beginnings of the Lower Town – beneath the fortress. In 1238 Tallinn returned to Danish control, but in 1285 it joined the German-dominated Hanseatic League as a channel for trade between Novgorod, Pskov and the west. Furs, honey, leather, and seal fat moved west; salt, cloth, herring and wine went east.

By the mid-14th century, when the Danes sold northern Estonia to the Teutonic Order, Tallinn was a major Hanseatic town with about 4000 people. A conflict of interest with the knights and bishop on Toompea led the mainly German artisans and merchants in the Lower Town (who dominated the town council) to build a fortified wall to separate themselves from Toompea. However, Tallinn still prospered and became one of northern Europe's biggest towns. Many of its characteristic Hanseatic buildings were constructed in the 14th and 15th centuries. Tallinn's German name, Reval, coexisted with the local name until 1918.

The prosperity faded in the 16th century. The Hanseatic League had weakened; and Russians, Swedes, Danes, Poles and Lithuanians fought over the Baltic region. Tallinn survived a 37-week siege by Russia's Ivan the Terrible. It was held by Sweden from 1561 to 1710 until, decimated by plague, it surrendered to Russia's Peter the Great. Old Tallinn remains so little changed today because no one in those days could afford to rebuild it.

In the late 19th century a railway was built from St Petersburg, and Tallinn became a chief port of the Russian empire. Freed peasants converged on the city from the countryside increasing the percentage of Estonians in its population from 52% in 1867 to 89% in 1897. By WW I Tallinn had big shipyards, and a large working class in its population of over 100,000.

Tallinn suffered badly in WW II, with thousands of buildings destroyed during Soviet bombing in 1944. After the war, under Soviet control, large-scale industry was developed in Tallinn – including the USSR's biggest grain-handling port – and the city expanded fast: its population growing to nearly 500,000 from a 1937 level of 175,000. Much of the new population came from Russia, and new high-rise suburbs were built on the outskirts to house the new workers.

ORIENTATION

Tallinn spreads south from the edge of Tallinn Bay (Tallinna Laht) on the southern shore of the Gulf of Finland. At the city's heart, just south of the bay, is the Old Town (Vanalinn), which divides fairly neatly into two parts: Toompea (the hill which dominates Tallinn) and the Lower Town, spreading out from Toompea's eastern side. The Lower Town is centred on Raekoja plats (Town Hall Square), and is still surrounded by most of its 2.5-km medieval wall. Around this old core is the 'New Town', dating mainly from the 19th and early 20th century. Stretching several km in every direction from the edges of the New Town are the Soviet-era suburbs, mixed up with industrial areas.

The majority of places to stay, the railway station, and the harbour are all in the New Town within walking distance of the Old Town. The Hotell Palace on Vabaduse väljak and the tall slab of the Hotell Viru, just outside the eastern edge of the Old Town, are good landmarks.

INFORMATION
Tourist Office

There's a good, helpful tourist information centre on Raekoja plats on the corner of Kinga. Open at least from 9 am to 5 pm Monday to Friday and 10 am to 3 pm Saturday and Sunday, it deals mainly with Tallinn but also has some information on other places in Estonia. It sells a good selection of regional maps and some guides. When it opened in 1992, this was the first tourist information office, as such, in the Baltic states.

Money
There are exchange counters at the airport, the main ferry terminal, the railway station, the bus station, the main post office, banks, major hotels (including the Viru, Palace, Pirita, Olümpia, and Tallinn), and the Tallinna Kaubamaja department store. The exchange counters at the Hotell Viru and the Põhja-Eesti Aktsiapank at the airport were the only ones I found that would accept travellers' cheques, but this will probably change. Estonian Tours (☎ 442 034) at Roosikrantsi 4B will replace lost American Express travellers' cheques or cards.

Post & Telecommunications
The central post, telegraph and telephone office is at Narva maantee 1 on the north side of Viru väljak; the post and telegraph section, upstairs, is open from 8 am to 8 pm Monday to Friday, and 8 am to 5 pm Saturday. There are poste restante and express mail (letters or parcels) services here; in one corner is an information desk where some English is spoken. Have poste restante mail addressed like the following example:

Jane SMITH
Poste Restante
Central Post Office
Narva maantee 1
Tallinn
ESTONIA

There's a public fax service in the telephone office (open Monday to Friday from 8 am to 7 pm) at Gonsiori 10 near the corner of Tartu maantee (Gonsiori is still widely known by its old name Lomonossovi, even on some street signs). Telephone queues are usually shorter at this office and at the airport post office (open from 6 am to 7 pm daily) than at Narva maantee. There are service bureaus with faxes at the Viru and Palace hotels.

If you have Finnish marks you can dial Finland direct from a phone booth behind the Tallink window at the main ferry terminal for 3 Fmk a minute. There's also a quick (but expensive) international radio-phone service next to the Inreko ticket office in the terminal.

Tallinn's main telephone code (for calls made from elsewhere within Estonia) is 22. Some numbers connected to a new digital exchange introduced in 1993 use the code 26. Telephone numbers in this chapter all take the 22 code unless otherwise stated.

Foreign Diplomatic Missions
Foreign embassies and missions in Estonia are quite a novelty. The first ambassadors since the 1940s only started setting up shop after Estonia's independence was recognised in 1991. At present, some still don't have permanent premises, so a few of the Tallinn missions listed here may move. Some countries cover Estonia from their embassies in nearby countries, including: Australia, Iceland and Ireland from Stockholm; Belgium from Rīga; New Zealand from Moscow; and the Netherlands, South Africa and Switzerland from Helsinki.

Austria
    Consul: Pikk 58 (☎ 442 428)
Canada
    Embassy Office: Toom-Kooli 13 (☎ 449 056)
China
    Embassy: Haigru 22 (☎ 477 325)
Denmark
    Embassy: 6th floor, Rävala puiestee 9 (☎ 691 494)
Finland
    Embassy: Liivalaia 12 (☎ 311 411)
France
    Embassy: Toomkuninga 20 (☎ 453 784)
Germany
    Embassy: 7th floor, Rävala puiestee 9 (☎ 455 606)
Italy
    Embassy: Müürivahe 3 (☎ 441 572)
Latvia
    Embassy: Tōnismägi 10 (☎ 681 668)
Lithuania
    Embassy: Vabaduse väljak 10 (☎ 666 634)
Norway
    Embassy: Pärnu maantee 8 (☎ 441 680)
Poland
    Embassy: Pärnu maantee 8 (☎ 440 609)
Russia
    Embassy: Pikk 19 (☎ 443 014)

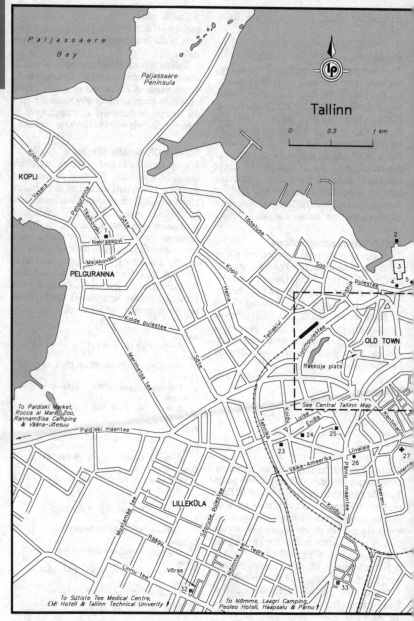

Tallinn

0   0.5   1 km

Paljassaare Bay

Paljassaare Peninsula

KOPLI

Kopli

Vasara

Pelguranna

Taakoski

Säte

Nekrassovi

Majakovski

PELGURANNA

Kolde puiestee

Töostuse

Kopli

Heina

Soo

Pöhja Puiestee

2

3

4 5

Merimetsa tee

Säte

Telliskivi

Toompuiestee

OLD TOWN

Raekoja plats

See Central Tallinn Map

To Paldiski Market,
Rocca al Mare, Zoo,
Rannamõisa Camping
& Vääna–Jõesuu

Paldiski maantee

Tehnika

Koidu

Luise

Endia

Kentmanni

24   25

23

Väike-Ameerika

Vaike-Ameerika

26

Liivalaia

Pärnu maantee

Veerni

Herne

27

Koidu

LILLEKÜLA

Mustamäe tee

Sõpruse puiestee

Raagu

Nõmme tee Tedre

Linnu tee

Võrse

32

To Sütiste Tee Medical Centre,
EMI Hotell & Tallinn Technical Univerity

To Nõmme, Laagri Camping,
Peoleo Hotell, Haapsalu & Pärnu

33

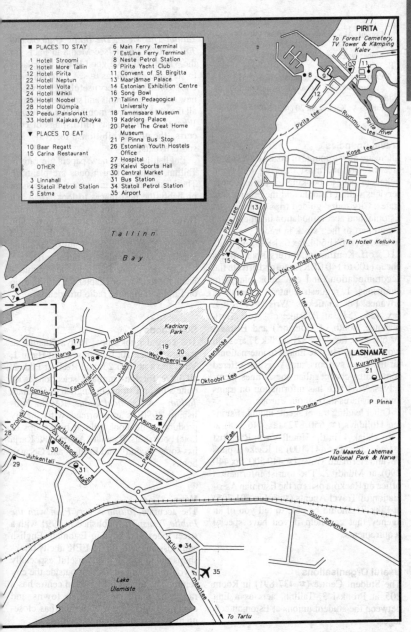

PLACES TO STAY
1 Hotell Stroomi
2 Hotell More Tallin
12 Hotell Pirita
22 Hotell Neptun
23 Hotell Volta
24 Hotell Mihkli
25 Hotell Noobel
28 Hotell Olümpia
32 Peedu Pansionatt
33 Hotell Kajakas/Chayka

PLACES TO EAT
10 Baar Regatt
15 Carina Restaurant

OTHER
3 Linnahall
4 Statoil Petrol Station
5 Estma
6 Main Ferry Terminal
7 EstLine Ferry Terminal
8 Neste Petrol Station
9 Pirita Yacht Club
11 Convent of St Birgitta
13 Maarjämae Palace
14 Estonian Exhibition Centre
16 Song Bowl
17 Tallinn Pedagogical University
18 Tammsaare Museum
19 Kadriorg Palace
20 Peter The Great Home Museum
21 P Pinna Bus Stop
26 Estonian Youth Hostels Office
27 Hospital
29 Kalevi Sports Hall
30 Central Market
31 Bus Station
34 Statoil Petrol Station
35 Airport

ESTONIA

Spain
    Consul: Akadeemia tee 70-29 (☎ 539 315)
Sweden
    Embassy: Endla 4A (☎ 450 350)
UK
    Embassy: 2nd floor, Kentmanni 20 (☎ 313 353 –
    use area code 26 for calls from outside Tallinn)
USA
    Embassy: Kentmanni 20 (☎ 312 021)

Travel Agencies

There are now a couple of dozen travel agencies in Tallinn, most offering outbound tickets as well as bookings, tours and other services within Estonia and the other Baltic states. City tours, guided trips to provincial Estonia, and accommodation in other towns are all part of their stock in trade.

Eutour (☎ 681 644, fax 681 893) at Sakala 11C, off Kentmanni, offers some fairly cheap (100 to 140 EEK) hotel and private flat accommodation, and can book places in campsites. It requests contact a month in advance. For air tickets, Wris (☎ 441 364, fax 426 251) at Pääsukese 1 (off Tartu maantee, south of Gonsiori) and Estravel (☎ 601 886, fax 444 882) at Pikk 37 are both worth trying. They're linked to international air-ticketing systems, and Wris has offered some fares cheaper than the airlines themselves. Wris also has information on trains and their fares throughout Europe.

Other leading travel agents include Estonian Holidays (☎ 650 872, fax 446 188) at Viru väljak 4 (in the Hotell Viru); Raeturist (☎ 444 333, fax 441 100) at Raekoja plats 18; and Hermann Travel (☎ 440 500, fax 440 290) at Mündi 2. The tourist information office on Raekoja plats or the Estonian Association of Travel Agents (☎ & fax 601 705) at Pikk 71 should be able to tell you of an agency that can help if you have special requirements.

Useful Organisations

The Student Centre (☎ 437 891) in Room 205 at Pronksi 3, Tallinn, acts as a link between the student unions at Estonian colleges.

Media

Tallinn This Week, *The Baltic Outlook* and *Tallinn City Paper* (see Media in Facts for the Visitor) all have good listings of places to stay and eat, things to see, entertainment and so on. They're very useful in a city where new hotels, restaurants and so on are opening all the time. The free monthly *What? When? Where? In Tallinn* has full listings of concerts, theatre, exhibitions, festivals and sports events.

English-language newspapers are rare in Tallinn, though Finnish ones are plentiful. The Viru and other main tourist hotels are probably the best places to look. *Time* and *Newsweek* are sold for about 40 EEK in the Hotell Palace's downstairs shop. The National Library on the corner of Endla and Toompuiestee has some English-language publications. A single-visit ticket is free.

Also see TV & Radio in the Estonia – Facts for the Visitor chapter for information on English-language radio broadcasts.

Bookshops

The central bookshops, Rahva Raamat at Pärnu maantee 10, Lugemisvara at Harju 1, Viruvärava at Viru 23, and R&E at Pikk 2, all have foreign-language selections with quite a lot on Estonia in English or German. *Tallinn – A Practical Guide* (Revalia Publishing, 1990) is an informed, witty locally produced guidebook sold at bookshops or hotel bookstalls. Raamatu Äri on Suur Karja has some second-hand English and German books.

Maps

The accurate *Tallinn – City Plan with the Public Transport* (published in 1991 with a street index and keys in Estonian, English and Russian) sells for 15 EEK in city bookshops and kiosks. It's very useful, especially if you're staying or visiting outside the city centre. The tourist information centre has a range of maps of Estonian towns and regions. Lugemisvara bookshop has close-up maps of some Estonian regions.

Left: Alexandr Nevsky Cathedral, Tallinn, Estonia (SK)
Right: Estonian boy (SK)
Bottom: Lower Town walls, Tallinn, Estonia (SK)

Top: Raekoja plats, Tallinn, Estonia (JN)
Bottom: Fat Margaret bastion & Oleviste Church, Tallinn, Estonia (SK)

Health & Medical Services

If you are desperate, there are emergency medical centres at Sütiste tee 19 in Mustamäe, a south-western suburb (☎ 525 652; open 24 hours, seven days a week), and in the hospital at Ravi 18 near the Hotell Olümpia (Monday to Friday, 9 am to 6 pm). The Sütiste tee centre has ambulances.

The pharmacy at Rävala puiestee 7 sells German medicines and toiletries. The one at Tõnismägi 5 has an information counter telling you where you can find a particular medicine in Tallinn. The Baltic Medical Partners dental practice (☎ 602 200 and 666 009), open daily at Toompuiestee 4 and also present on the 4th floor of the Hotell Olümpia, is Western-run to Western standards – at 'modest' rates.

Tallinn water is reckoned to be safe to drink and I have had no problems with it.

Left Luggage

There's a left-luggage room (*pakihoid*) behind the Tallink office in the main ferry terminal (open 7 am to noon and 2 to 9 pm) which charges 2 EEK an item for 24 hours. Other left-luggage rooms are at the bus station – where it's called 'käsipakkide hoiurruum' (open from 5 am to 12.30 pm and 12.50 to 11.40 pm) – and the railway station.

Film & Photography

Kodak Express on the corner of Narva maantee and Pronksi sells a range of Kodak film but not Kodachrome. It can process print film in a day for 45 EEK plus 5 EEK a print, and can do four passport photos for 70 EEK. The Agfa shop a few doors further along Narva maantee also does processing. There's a Fuji film shop on Suur-Karja in the Old Town, and a passport-photo booth in the main ferry terminal.

WALKING TOUR

A good place to start exploring old Tallinn is the **Viru Gate** in the east side of the Lower Town walls. Flower stalls line the eastern approach to the twin towers which are all that remain of the gate, once one of six entries in the Lower Town walls. From the gate continue along Viru to the corner of Vene (known as **Vana turg**) which is surrounded by a particularly impressive group of tall 15th to 17th century houses and warehouses; continue into **Raekoja plats**, the wide square which is the heart of the Lower Town. From Raekoja plats you can climb the street Pikk jalg to **Toompea**. As you wander round Toompea, use the look-out points off Toom-Kooli, Kohtu and Rahukohtu to get your bearings and decide where to go when you descend. Particularly interesting are the streets north of Raekoja plats in the Lower Town where you can walk north up Pikk to the **Fat Margaret** bastion, the northern bastion of the Lower Town, then return south along Lai or Laboratooriumi.

RAEKOJA PLATS

Wide Raekoja plats (Town Hall Square), dominated by the only surviving **Gothic town hall** in northern Europe, has been the centre of Tallinn Lower Town life since markets began to be held here, probably in the 11th century (the last was in 1896). Today it's the place all Old Town streets lead to: a meeting place, and the setting for open-air concerts in summer. The **Raeapteek** (Town Council Pharmacy) on the north side of the square is an ancient Tallinn institution; there has been a pharmacy or apothecary's shop here since at least 1422, and the present façade is 17th century.

Town Hall

Built between 1371 and 1404, the Town Hall was the seat of power in the medieval Lower Town. Its minaret-like tower is supposedly modelled on a sketch brought back by an explorer from the orient. **Vana Toomas** (Old Thomas), the warrior-and-sword weather vane at its top, has guarded Tallinn since 1530. The arches at ground level along the north side of the hall were a trading place in the Middle Ages. The interior of the hall is open from 10 am to 5 pm Monday to Friday – knock on the door to enter. Inside, the **Citizens' Hall** has an impressive vaulted roof, while the fine 1374 bench-ends in the **Council Hall** are Estonia's oldest woodcarv-

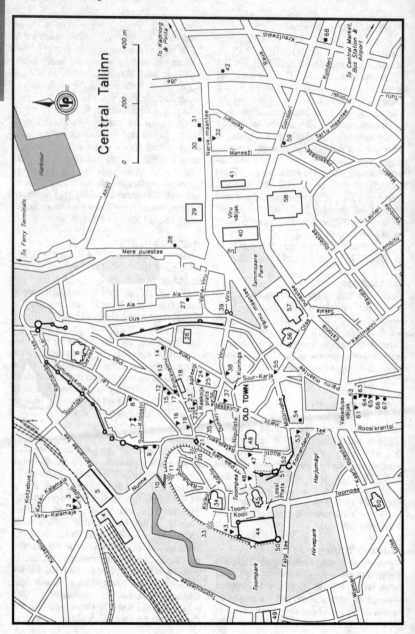

Central Tallinn

To Kadriorg & Pirita

To Ferry Terminals

Harbour

OLD TOWN

Toompark

Hirvepark

Harjumägi

Toompea

To Central Market, Bus Station & Airport

■ PLACES TO STAY

9   Imperial Hotell
30 Agnes Hostel
31 Hotell Vitamiin
40 Hotell Viru
49 Hotell Tallinn
62 Hotell Palace
68 Hotell Kungla

▼ PLACES TO EAT

2   Peetri Pizza
3   Peetri Pizza
16 Peetri Pizza
17 Maiasmokk Kohvik
23 Vana Toomas Restaurant
24 Maharaja Restaurant
25 Rosalie Bar
32 Bistro
35 Eeslitall Restoran
37 Kullassepa Kelder
38 Gnoom Grill
43 Toomkooli Restoran
46 Bogapott Café
47 Sub Monte Restoran
51 Kohvik Neitsitorn
53 George Brown Pub
55 Vesi Veski Café
61 Astoria Restaurant
63 Pizzeria Margareta
65 Finest Restaurant
66 Peetri Pizza

    OTHER

1   Great Coast Gate &
    Fat Margaret Tower
4   Railway Station
5   Local Bus Station

6   Oleviste Church
7   St Michael's Convent
8   Applied Art Museum
10 Patkuli Trepp (steps)
11 Lookout Point
12 Russian Embassy
13 Brotherhood of Blackheads Building
14 City Museum
15 Great Guild Building &
    State History Museum
18 Pühavaimu Church
19 Kohvik Pärl
20 Lookout Point
21 Pikk Jalg Gate Tower
22 Tourist Information Office
26 Dominican Monastery
27 EstLine Office
28 Family Hotel Service
29 Post, Telephone & Telegraph Office
33 Lookout Point
34 Toomkirik
36 Town Hall
39 Viru Gate
41 Teenindusmaja Shop
42 Student Centre
44 Toompea Castle
45 Alexandr Nevsky Cathedral
48 Niguliste Church
50 Pikk Hermann
51 Neitsitorn
52 Kiek-in-de-Kök
54 Estonian Air
56 Estonia Drama Theatre
57 Estonia Theatre & Estonia
    Concert Hall
58 Tallinna Kaubamaja Shop
59 Telephone Office
60 Kaarli Kirik
64 Tallink Office
67 Bus Ticket Office

ings. Sometimes chamber concerts are held in the town hall. In the town hall cellar (Raekelder) is a small **museum** of Tallinn history up to 1710 – open Wednesday to Sunday from 10.30 am to 5.30 pm. The old **Town Jail** (Raevangla) at Raekoja plats 4/6 (in the alley behind the town hall) is now the Town Hall Museum (Raemuuseum), open from 10.30 am to 5.30 pm daily, except Wednesday.

NEAR RAEKOJA PLATS
Pühavaimu Church

An arch beside the Raeapteek on Raekoja plats leads into short, narrow Saia kang (White Bread Passage), at the far end of which is the 14th century Gothic Pühavaimu (Holy Spirit) church, used by Lutherans. Its clock is the oldest in Tallinn, with carvings dating from 1684, and the tower bell (1433) is the oldest in Estonia. Inside are a fine 1483 wooden altarpiece, 16th century carved bench-backs and a 17th century pulpit.

City Museum

A medieval merchant's home at Vene 17 (on the corner of Pühavaimu) houses the City Museum (Linnamuuseum), devoted mainly to Tallinn in the 18th and 19th centuries, with paintings to help tell the story. There's an account of the building's history in English. The museum is open 10.30 am to 6 pm daily, except Tuesday.

Dominican Monastery

Also on Vene, look for an 1844 Catholic church set back from the street with the Latin inscription 'Hic Vere Est Domus Dei' on its wall. A small door in the corner of the courtyard leads into the Dominican monastery (Dominiiklaste klooster), founded in 1246. The monastery was home base for Scandinavian monks who played a big role in converting Estonia to Christianity and starting education in Tallinn. Once wealthy, with its own brewery and hospital, the monastery was ruined by plunder during the Reformation in 1524-25 and by a fire in 1531; today only the cloister and a few rooms are open. Its **St Catherine's Church** (Katariina kirik) on the south side of the cloister, once the biggest in Northern Europe, has not been restored and is closed. But the open areas contain a wealth of lovely 15th to 17th century stonecarving – open in summer only, 11 am to 4.30 pm daily except Monday.

Niguliste Church

A minute's walk south of Raekoja plats, the early-Gothic north doorway of Niguliste church (named after St Nicholas of Bari, patron saint of sailors) proves the church's ancient origins – it was the hub of the 13th century German settlement – but most of Niguliste dates from the 15th century. It is now used for organ recitals and as a museum of art from medieval Estonian churches. It is open as a museum on Wednesday from 2 to 9 pm, and Thursday to Sunday 11 am to 6 pm, unless there's a concert on.

The foot of the small slope on which Niguliste stands looks like an abandoned demolition site. What you're looking at is the carefully exposed wreckage of the buildings that stood here before the Soviet bombing of Tallinn on 9 March 1944. A sign facing Harju details the damage done to the city that night.

TOOMPEA

Toompea ('TOM-pe-ah'), the hill on which Tallinn is centred, is covered in winding, cobbled old streets and is protected on the north, south and west by steep slopes, now with parks at their feet. In German times this was the preserve of the feudal nobility and bishop, looking down on the traders and lesser beings of the Lower Town. The most impressive – and until the 17th century the only – approach to Toompea is through the red-roofed **Pikk jalg gate tower** (dating from 1380) at the west end of Pikk in the Lower Town. From here Pikk jalg ('Long Leg') slopes up the hill between high walls; where it curves right, a passage down to the left (beneath a 15th century gate tower) emerges onto Lühike jalg ('Short Leg'), which leads down to Niguliste church.

The name Toompea is a corruption of the German *Domberg* (Cathedral Hill). According to legend, Toompea is the burial mound of Kalev, the heroic first leader of the Estonians, built by his widow Linda – herself commemorated by a statue in Hirvepark on the southern side of the hill.

Lossi Plats

The 19th century Russian Orthodox **Alexandr Nevsky Cathedral** dominates Lossi plats at the top of Pikk jalg. In such a focal location it's an imposing testament to the Russian imperialist urge, but is rather out of place among its older neighbours.

A path leads down from Lossi plats beneath the uppermost stretch of the Lower Town wall into an open space where, in summer, artists set up their easels and paint portraits. One of the towers here, **Neitsitorn** (Virgin's Tower), has been turned into a popular café-bar, and has good views. Its name must be ironic: it's said to have been a prison for medieval prostitutes.

Toompea Castle

Estonia's parliament, the Riigikogu, meets in Toompea Castle at the west end of Lossi plats. Nothing remains of the 1219 Danish castle here, but three of the four corner towers of its successor, founded by the Knights of the Sword in 1227-29, still stand. The castle's mainly Baroque appearance dates from the 18th century when, under Catherine the Great, it was rebuilt and had its moat filled in. The finest of the towers is the 1371 **Pikk Hermann** (Tall Hermann) at the south-west corner, topped by the national flag. Sixteenth century shell scars are visible on its walls. The two other surviving towers, plus most of the north wall of the old castle, can be seen from the yard of Toom-Kooli 13.

Pikk Hermann

Toomkirik

Toompea is named after the Lutheran Toomkirik (Cathedral), founded in 1233, which is at the north end of Toom-Kooli. Most of this interesting building's existing structure dates from the 15th and 17th centuries (it was largely rebuilt after a fire in 1684) but the tower was built in 1779. Among other things, the church served as a burial ground for the rich and noble. Among the finest of the many **carved tombs** inside are those on the right as you approach the altar, including life-size figures of the 16th century Swedish commander, Pontus de la Gardie, and his wife. The Swedish siege of Narva, where de la Gardie died, is shown on the side of their sarcophagus. Also here are the tombs of two other Swedish commanders of the same period, Karl Horn and Otto Üxküll. The marble Greek-temple-style sarcophagus belongs to Admiral Samuel Greigh, an 18th century Scot who joined the Russian navy and became a hero of Russo-Turkish sea battles. Admiral Adam Johann von Krusenstern, a German Estonian who was the first Russian citizen to sail round the world, has another elaborate tomb.

Estonian Art Museum

Only a tiny fraction of the 59,000-item collection of the Estonian Art Museum (Kunstimuuseum) is on show at the museum's temporary quarters in an 18th century noble's house at Kiriku plats 1 near the Toomkirik. The rest of the collection will have to wait till Kadriorg Palace is reopened (in 1995 or later) and a proposed new main building is designed and built. The Kiriku plats premises are open from 11 am to 6 pm Wednesday to Sunday.

Kiek-in-de-Kök

The tower south of Neitsitorn is the tall, stout Kiek-in-de-Kök, built about 1475. It's now one of Tallinn's most interesting museums, for its setting as much as its exhibits. You have to enter from Komandandi tee, on the outer side of the town wall. The name Kiek-in-de-Kök is Low German for 'Peep into the Kitchen': from the upper floors a watch could be kept over the entire Lower Town, even the kitchens. Kiek-in-de-Kök has several floors of maps, weapons, models of old Tallinn – and great views. It's opening hours vary, but it's always open at least between 11 am and 4 pm daily (except Monday and Thursday).

Look-out Points

There are look-out points off Toom-Kooli, Kohtu and Rahukohtu. From the Rahukohtu platform the Patkuli Trepp steps lead down to **Toompark**, largest of the city's central parks, with a lake which used to be part of

ESTONIA

Toompea's moat. From down here you get a good sense of the might of Toompea Castle from the angle which appears on the back of the 1 EEK note.

LOWER TOWN – NORTH
Pikk

Running north from Raekoja plats towards Tallinn port, the street Pikk ('Long') is lined with the houses of medieval German merchants and gentry. Many were built in the 15th century, usually with three or four storeys, the lower two being living and reception quarters and the upper ones used for storage. Some top storeys still have the hatch to which goods were lifted by pulley.

Museum & Guild Buildings On Pikk are the buildings of several old Tallinn guilds (associations of traders or artisans, nearly all German-dominated). At Pikk 17 is the Gothic doorway of the Great Guild, to which the most important merchants belonged, and which supplied all the members of the town council. The building dates from 1410 and one of its fine vaulted halls retains its original appearance. Today it houses the State History Museum (Ajaloomuuseum), devoted to Estonian history up to the mid-19th century. This small museum has labelling in English and is the best place in Tallinn to get a feel for Estonian history – open daily from 11 am to 6 pm except Wednesday.

Pikk 20, on the east side of the street, with statues of Martin Luther and St Canute on the front, dates only from the 1860s, but the site had already housed St Canute's Guild for several centuries. Its members were master-artisans. Pikk 24 and 26 are the adjoining buildings of the Brotherhood of Blackheads and the Oleviste Guild – both closed to the public except for concerts. The Blackheads were unmarried merchants who took their name from their patron saint, Maurice. His head is between two lions on one of the stone reliefs on the building's façade (1597). The Oleviste Guild – probably the first guild in Tallinn – began in the 13th century, and

developed a membership of mostly less important, non-German artisans and traders.

Oleviste Church Further north on Pikk, this church was the focal point of old Tallinn's Scandinavian population. It's dedicated to the 11th century king Olaf II of Norway but is linked in local lore with another Olaf, its legendary architect, who fell to his death from the tower. It's said a toad and snake then crawled out of his mouth. The incident is shown in one of the carvings on the eastern wall of the 16th century Chapel of Our Lady, adjoining the church, which shows a skeleton with a toad on its chest and a snake round its skull. The 124-metre **Oleviste tower** is a chief Tallinn landmark. Most of the church was rebuilt in something close to its original Gothic form after an 1820s fire.

Fat Margaret At the north end of Pikk is the **Great Coast Gate**, the medieval exit to Tallinn port. It's joined to Fat Margaret (Paks Margareeta), a rotund 16th century bastion which protected this entrance to the town. Fat Margaret's walls are more than four metres thick at the base. Inside is the **Sea Museum** (Meremuuseum), open daily from 10 am to 6 pm except Monday and Tuesday.

Lai & Laboratooriumi

The street Lai ('Wide') is roughly parallel to Pikk. No 29 near the corner of Suurtüki and No 23 opposite Vaimu both have fine 15th to 17th century façades. The **Natural History Museum** (Loodusmuuseum), devoted to Estonia's wildlife and countryside, occupies the back of a nice little courtyard at No 29, open daily except Tuesday from 10 am to 5 pm. The **Applied Art Museum** (Tarbekunstimuuseum), in a 17th century barn at Lai 17, has a collection of excellent modern woven rugs, ceramics, glass, metal and leather work. It's open from 11 am to 6 pm daily except Monday and Tuesday.

Suur-Kloostri leads past the former St Michael's Convent to the longest standing stretch of the **Lower Town wall**, with nine towers marching back along Laboratooriumi to the north end of Lai.

EAST OF THE CENTRE

Kadriorg

Park & Palace The park at Kadriorg, two km east of the Old Town along Narva maantee, is pleasant and wooded, with oak, lilac, and horse chestnut trees. Together with the Baroque Kadriorg Palace (Kadrioru Loss), it was designed for the Russian tsar, Peter the Great, by the Italian Niccolo Michetti, soon after Peter's conquest of Estonia in the Great Northern War.

The palace, at Weizenbergi 37 along the road from the Kadriorg tram stop, was built between 1718 and 1736 with Peter himself laying an amazing three bricks! They were left bare for visitors to marvel at. The palace was the residence of the president of independent Estonia in the 1930s. Today the palace is part of the Estonian Art Museum (Kunstimuuseum), but is closed for major reconstruction till about 1995. When reopened, Kadriorg Palace will display only Russian and Western European works; a new home is to be built for the bulk of the museum's 59,000-item collection, including Estonian art. In the meantime a small part of the collection is on show in a temporary home at Kiriku plats 1, on Toompea.

Behind the palace, at Mäekalda 2, is the cottage Peter the Great occupied on visits to Tallinn while the palace was being built. In summer it's open as the **Peter the Great Home Museum** (Peeter Esimese Majamuuseum). You may examine his clothes and the boots he made.

The wooden house at Koidula 12A, just west of the park, was the last home of the great Estonian novelist Anton Hansen Tammsaare, and now contains a museum of his work – open from 11 am to 6 pm daily except Tuesday.

Song Bowl The Tallinn Song Bowl (Lauluväljak), site of the main gatherings of Estonia's national song festivals, is a natural amphitheatre officially said to hold about 150,000 people. In September 1988 some 300,000 squeezed in for one sing-song during the Singing Revolution. The song bowl is on the left side of Narva maantee, a short distance past the fork where Pirita tee heads off to the left, up the side of Tallinn Bay.

Maarjamäe

Two km north of Kadriorg Park, at Pirita tee 56, Maarjamäe Palace (Maarjamäe Loss) contains the mid-19th-century-onwards section of the **Estonia History Museum**; it's open Wednesday to Sunday from 11 am to 5 pm. The neo-Gothic limestone palace was built in the 1870s as a summer cottage for the Russian General A Orlov-Davydov. To its south at Pirita tee 28 is the Estonian Exhibition Centre (Eesti Näitused).

Pirita

Some 1½ km beyond Maarjamäe, just before Pirita tee crosses the Pirita River, a short side road leads down to Pirita Yacht Club and the **Olympic Sailing Centre** near the mouth of the river. This was the base for the sailing events of the 1980 Olympics, and international regattas are still held here.

In summer you can rent rowing boats beside the road-bridge over the river. North of the bridge is the suburb of Pirita, six km from the city centre, with a **beach** backed by pine woods. Beside the river is the ruined **Convent of St Birgitta**, built in the early

Convent of St Birgitta

15th century but destroyed in the Livonian War in 1577. It housed nuns of the Swedish-based Birgittine Order, which reportedly now wants it back. Currently the ruins are open to visitors from 11 am to 6 pm daily except Monday.

Forest Cemetery & TV Tower

Two km east of Pirita along Kloostrimetsa tee is the Forest Cemetery (Metsakalmistu) where many Estonian national heroes are buried including singer Georg Ots, writer Anton Hansen Tammsaare, and poet Lydia Koidula. A km further on is the 300-metre TV tower with, they say, views as far as Finland from the café halfway up.

Getting There & Away

Tram No 3 from anywhere along Pärnu maantee in the city centre, and No 1 along Narva maantee, go to the 'Kadriorg' stop right by Kadriorg Park. Bus Nos 1, 8 and 34 all run between the city centre and Pirita, stopping at the Kohvik Kadriorg, on Narva maantee near Kadriorg Park, and at Maarjamäe. You can catch No 1 on Pärnu maantee in front of Tammsaare Park; No 8 at the Pronksi stop on Narva maantee, 350 metres east of the Hotell Viru; and No 34 at the Viru Väljak stop beside the main post office. No 34 goes on to the Forest Cemetery and TV tower. You could also walk along the seafront from Kadriorg to Pirita, or back.

WEST OF THE CENTRE
Paldiski Market

A giant flea-market-cum-car-boot sale, with many imported and, at best, semi-legal goods, is held on Saturdays and Sundays till early afternoon at Mustjõe, three km west of the Old Town on the north side of Paldiski maantee. A water pistol placed on a car bonnet apparently means there are weapons for sale in the boot.

Rocca al Mare

About four km out along Paldiski maantee, Vabaõhumuuseumi tee branches right to Rocca al Mare, 1½ km away, where wooden buildings from 18th and 19th century rural

Estonia, including a windmill, farmstead and chapel, have been collected in the **Estonian Village Museum**. The site's Italian name ('Rock by the Sea') was coined by a merchant who built his country house here in 1880. There are views back to the city and you can walk in the woods or down to the sea. The museum is open Wednesday to Sunday 10 am to 5, 6 or 7 pm, from May to September or October. On Sunday mornings there are folk song and dance shows.

Zoo

Just past the Rocca al Mare turning, at Paldiski maantee 145, is the Tallinn Zoo with over 3500 animals of 370-plus species. It's open daily from 9 am to 3 pm.

Getting There & Away

Bus No 21 from the railway station and No 45 from Vabaduse väljak go to Paldiski market, Rocca al Mare and the zoo. Trolleybus No 6 and bus No 46 from Vabaduse väljak, and trolleybus No 7 from the railway station, go to the market and zoo.

OTHER SIGHTS
Old Town Museums

The **Adamson-Ericu Museum** at Lühike jalg 3, just up the hill from Niguliste Church, is devoted mainly to the varied art and crafts of Erich Karl Hugo Adamson (1902-68). It's open daily except Monday and Tuesday. For something a bit different look into the **Fire-Fighting Museum** (Tuletõrjemuuseum) at Vana-Viru 14, open Tuesday to Saturday, or the **Theatre & Music Museum** (Teatri-ja Muusikamuuseum) at Müürivahe 12, open daily except Tuesday.

Exhibitions

Many of the museums stage temporary exhibitions along with their permanent displays, and there are also a couple of dozen specialist art galleries. Listings are published in *Tallinn This Week*, *Tallinn City Paper*, the Upcoming Events section of the *Baltic Independent*, and *What? When? Where? In Tallinn*. Some of the best shows are at **Draakoni Galerii** at Pikk 18 (concentrating on graphics), **Vaal** at

Väike-Karja 12, **Galerii-G** at Vabaduse väljak 6 and Narva maantee 2, and **Kunstihoone Galerii** at Vabaduse väljak 6.

Soviet Nostalgia

Rävala puiestee, a block south of the Estonia Theatre, was called Lenini puiestee in Soviet times and a statue of Lenin stood in the middle of it, between the corners of Lembitu and Lauteri. Rävala puiestee 9, which now houses some foreign embassies, was the Estonian Communist Party headquarters. Opposite the railway station on Toompuiestee (then called Gagarini puiestee) stood a five-piece monument to the 1924 'armed uprising of the Tallinn proletariat'. The local joke was that this was the only monument in the world which managed to represent individually every participant in a 'mass' uprising.

Suburbs

Nõmme is a wealthy garden suburb of detached houses seven km south of the centre, down Pärnu maantee. Bus Nos 14 and 18 from Tammsaare Park and Vabaduse väljak run there. **Kopli** is a working-class Russian suburb five km north-west of the centre, reached by tram No 1 or 2 from behind the railway station or from the stop on Mere puiestee just north of the Hotell Viru. **Lasnamäe** is a high-rise Russian suburb six km east of the centre – bus Nos 19, 44 and 56, among others, will take you there from Narva maantee.

Lake Ülemiste

Across the road from the airport, Ülemiste was filled, so the story goes, by the tears of the legendary Linda as she wept for Kalev – and is guarded by an old man called Järvevana who threatens to flood Tallinn if its people stop building.

FESTIVALS

In summer Tallinn comes alive with festivals. There are often three or four going on at the same time and many of them involve music. Every five years or so there's the All-Estonia Song Festival in late June or early July. Youth or children's song and dance festivals, or the Baltika folk festival, often fill the gap in intervening years. In early or mid-June there are several days of jollification in the Old Town, with lots of music and dance, called the Old Tallinn Days; in July there's the Tallinn Rock Summer rock festival; and in October the Jazzkaar jazz festival. For more on all these regular events see Cultural Events in Facts for the Visitor. There are numerous one-off happenings too.

PLACES TO STAY – BOTTOM END

In summer it's worth trying to book ahead for most types of Tallinn accommodation, including the youth hostels, as there still aren't enough rooms to go round when things are at their busiest.

Campsites

It's always worth trying to ring ahead to check on vacancies, prices and opening dates for campsites. All of them are usually open at least from 1 June to 1 September. *Laagri Camping*, also known as *Leevike*, is about 13 km south of the city centre on the Pärnu road. There are 30 cabins of 10 or 20 sq metres, plus space for tents, a kitchen, cold showers and a bar. Bus No 18 from Viru väljak terminates on Pärnu maantee about a km before the site. Laagri's operator, Silvest Motel Group (☎ 557 059 or 556 525) of Viljandi maantee 16, runs several other campsites within 60 km of Tallinn (see Around Tallinn).

Kämping Kalev (☎ 238 686) is at Kloostrimetsa tee 56A in the shadow of the TV tower, nine km north-east of the city centre and three km east of Pirita. It's shabby, but its 136 places include tent spaces as well as small cabins, and there's a café. Bus No 34 will get you there from Viru väljak.

Eutour (see Travel Agencies in the Tallinn Information section) can arrange campsite places for 60 to 100 EEK a person.

Hostels & Colleges

Estonian Youth Hostels has two hostels in Tallinn and a third in preparation. You can get up-to-date information at the hostels office – Room 114, Liivalaia 2 (☎ & fax 441 096) – from 10 am to 4 pm, Monday to Friday. You can also book Estonian hostels from Helsinki or St Petersburg (see Accommodation in Facts for the Visitor at the front of the book).

The *Agnes Hostel* (☎ 438 870) at Narva maantee 7 is centrally located and has quite comfortable two or three-bed rooms, each sharing shower and toilet with two or three others. Price is 80 EEK a night. It's advisable to book ahead as the Agnes is very popular. Go through to the back of the building to find the entrance. The *Kuramaa 15 Hostel* (☎ 327 781) is out of the centre at Kuramaa 15 in the high-rise eastern suburb of Lasnamäe – you'll get an insight into Estonia's Russian population if you stay here. For 70 EEK you get a place in a two or three-bed room, sharing toilet, shower and kitchen with two other rooms. Numerous buses make the 15-minute trip to Lasnamäe including Nos 19, 31, 35 and 44 from in front of the Teenindusmaja shop on Viru väljak or just round the corner on Narva maantee. Get off at the P Pinna stop on Punane in Lasnamäe, then walk along P Pinna. Kuramaa is the first cross street.

The Foreign Relations Department (☎ 422 088, fax 425 339) of *Tallinn Pedagogical University* (Tallinna Pedagoogika-Ülikool), the city's teacher-training institution at Narva maantee 25, a km east of the Hotell Viru, can provide some clean, quite spacious single or double rooms for around 70 to 150 EEK per person in a college building close-by – you need to contact the department a couple of weeks in advance. Each room shares two bathrooms and a kitchen with three others. The department office in the university building is room 215 on the first floor, with the sign 'Välissuhted' on the door.

The student union of *Tallinn Technical University* (Tallinna Tehnikaülikool) (☎ 532 961, fax 537 334) at Ehitajate tee 5 in the south-western suburb of Mustamäe also has some rooms available, but again you should contact it in advance. These are three-bed

rooms sharing facilities with two others. Bus No 36 going south along Pärnu maantee in the city centre will take you to the Tehnikaülikool stop by the college.

Private Homes

Tallinn-based agencies like Family Hotel Service and CDS Reisid, as well as several overseas organisations, can arrange homestays in Tallinn and other parts of Estonia at a variety of prices – see Accommodation in Facts for the Visitor. Eutour (see Travel Agencies under Tallinn, Information) offers places in private flats in Tallinn for 100 to 140 EEK a person.

Hotels

The *Hotell Vitamiin* (☎ 438 585) is handily placed at Narva maantee 7, and has six clean doubles with attached toilet and shower, TV and phone for 250 EEK. There are also some rooms sharing facilities with one or two other rooms, which may be cheaper. The hotel has no sign: go through the door next to the Vitamiin shop, up the stairs and through the door on the first floor landing.

The *Hotell Volta* (☎ 451 340) at Endla 31, 600 metres west of Toompuiestee, has small, perfectly clean doubles, sharing toilet and washbasin with one other room, for an amazing 10 EEK. The management speaks no English, isn't used to Westerners, and may need a bit of convincing to find you a room. Endla 31 is a large pink block: enter at the back and look inside for the small 'gostinitsa' ('hotel') sign in Russian.

The *EMI Hotell* (☎ 521 611, fax 521 625) at Sütiste tee 21 in the south-western suburb of Mustamäe, about five km from the city centre, is attached to an economics institute but open to the public. It's good value: rooms sharing shower and toilet with one or two others are under 100 EEK a double. Bus Nos 17 and 17A from Vabaduse väljak go to the Tervise stop by the hotel.

An intriguing find is the *Hotell Kajakas/ Chayka* (☎ 555 892), 2½ km south of the centre at Pärnu maantee 123. This is a chalet-like building skulking behind Pärnu maantee 123A, an unpromising four-storey block of flats. The sign over the door says 'Kajakas Hotell' in Estonian and 'Gostinitsa Chayka' in Russian. Both mean 'Seagull Hotel'. Inside you enter a homely warren of cosy wood-panelled rooms, each seemingly a different size and shape. Most are around 100 EEK a person, with attached toilet and basin, and sometimes shower. The management speaks little English but is friendly enough. The chances of a room will increase as the Russian army officers who have been its main clientele go home. Tram No 3 or 4, or bus No 18, will get you there from Vabaduse väljak.

Ship

If you come to Tallinn on an Estonian New Line evening sailing from Helsinki, you can have a two to four-person cabin on the ship overnight in Tallinn for 50 Fmk (about 140 EEK) – but you have to clear out early in the morning before the ship goes back to Helsinki.

PLACES TO STAY – MIDDLE
City Centre

Perhaps convenient if you've arrived in Tallinn by sea, though unlikely to stay where it is for ever, is the *Hotell More Tallinn* (☎ 601 502, fax 602 182) which is actually the cruise ship *Vissarion Belinsky* moored behind the Linnahall concert hall, 10-minutes walk from the main ferry terminal. It holds 360 people in very small cabins with just enough room for beds and a tiny bathroom at around 275 EEK a single, 420 EEK a double or 565 EEK a triple. On board are a bar, restaurant, nightclub and casino for all the revellers from Finland. Some English is spoken. In Helsinki you can book at the Ageba agency (☎ 90-669 193 or 90-661 123, fax 90-174 280 or 90-602 848) at Pohjoisranta 4, or in the Olympia and Katajonakan terminals at the South Harbour. *More* is Russian for 'sea'.

The small *Hotell Mihkli* (☎ 453 704) at Endla 23, 400 metres down the hill from Toompuiestee, has clean, bright doubles for 430 EEK and a snack bar. It's fair value but short on atmosphere. *Pension Maria* (☎ 666

304) opened in 1993 at Roosikrantsi 10 A-8, 200 metres from Vabaduse väljak, and has three double rooms with showers for about 390 EEK and a four-bed room at about 130 EEK per person. Prices include breakfast, and the owners can make bookings for homestays or hostels elsewhere in the Baltic states. The pension will only stay open after the end of September if there are enough visitors to make it worthwhile. It's on the third floor of a yellow four-storey house – don't be put off by the dilapidated staircase.

The *Hotell Tallinn* (☎ 604 332), at Toompuiestee 27 on the western edge of the Old Town, charges 400/600 EEK for singles/doubles, with suites at 800 EEK. It's reasonably comfortable but has a gloomy Soviet-era air, but it will surely improve now that it has been privatised and is to be renovated. The 300-bed Soviet-built *Hotell Kungla* (☎ 427 040) at Kreutzwaldi 23 has small, fading rooms with attached bathroom for 400/500 EEK – poor value.

Pirita

The 400-bed *Hotell Pirita* (☎ 238 598, fax 237 433) at Pirita, six km north-east of the city centre, was originally designed as accommodation for the yachting events of the 1980 Olympics, which were held at Pirita. The hotel is on the seafront at Regati puiestee 1, just south of the Pirita River. The Olympic Sailing Centre is adjacent. The hotel's rooms are clean, modern, already renovated and have balconies – those on the sea side look back across Tallinn Bay to the city centre. They're good value for Tallinn at 360/530 EEK for singles/doubles (including breakfast) from May to September, 320/480 EEK the rest of the year. The *Galerie Bar* at the top of the building serves good meals. Bus No 8 from the railway station and Nos 1 and 34 from the Pronksi stop on Narva maantee, 400 metres east of the Hotell Viru, all stop on Pirita tee a minute's walk from the hotel.

Also at Pirita, at the time of writing, is a second More ship-hotel. The *Hotell More Pirita*, moored on the river just below the bridge, has cabins for 300 guests and a restaurant and bar. Prices and contact booking numbers are the same as for the Hotell More Tallinn (see City Centre) but the prices also include breakfast, and at Pirita you can take a four-person cabin for the same price as a three-person.

Other Suburbs

Five km north-west of the centre at Tšaikovski 11 in the suburb of Pelguranna on the Kopli peninsula is the *Hotell Stroomi* (☎ 495 219, fax 495 255) which was renovated in 1992 and has 150 clean rooms with private shower and cable TV for 230/380 EEK including breakfast in its restaurant. The management is friendly. Bus No 3 from the Linnahall stop or Mere puiestee stops virtually outside the door.

The *Hotell Kullervo* (☎ 557 553, fax 527 212), about three km out at Tedre 27/29 in the western suburb of Lilleküla, has just 11 comfortable rooms at 400 EEK a single or double (extra for suites). Also in Lilleküla, at Võrse 22, is another small, comfortable hotel in a similar bracket, the *Peedu Pansionaat* (☎ or fax 530 872). The Peedu has a bar and restaurant. Bus No 17 or 17A from Vabaduse väljak will take you along Nõmme tee, close to both places. For the Kullervo get off at the Koolimaja stop on the corner of Tedre; for the Peedu get off two stops later at Linnu tee and walk to the right (west) along Linnu tee – Võrse is the third street on the right.

The 330-bed *Hotell Neptun* (☎ 215 431) is a large, drab Soviet-style place at Asunduse 15 on the edge of an estate of flats 2½ km south-east of the centre. Dowdy, if clean enough, singles/doubles with private bath cost foreigners 236/462 EEK – no great deal. You may have to ward off guests from the CIS who might be excessively keen to share a few vodkas with you. Bus No 39 goes there from the corner of Tartu maantee and Pronksi. On foot, take the footbridge to Asunduse over the Oktoobri tee dual carriageway from the southern tip of Kadriorg Park.

PLACES TO STAY – TOP END

Two comfortable modern places on the out-skirts might interest motorists in particular. One is the Scandinavian-style *Peoleo Hotell* (☎ 556 566, fax 771 463), built in 1990 on the Pärnu road just outside the city at Pärnu maantee 555, about 14 km from the centre. The 44 rooms with private bathroom and satellite TV cost around 600/800 EEK for singles/doubles. There's a good restaurant with a live group at night, a café and a sauna. The Peoleo is a member of the Best Western chain and you can book through any Best Western office worldwide. In a similar price bracket is the friendly, well-run *Hotell Kelluka* (☎ 238 811, fax 237 398), eight km east of the centre at Kelluka tee 11, in a residential area just north of Narva maantee. There's a restaurant, a bar, and a sauna too. Bus No 5 from Pärnu or Narva maantee in the city centre reaches the Kelluka.

The *Hotell Viru* (☎ 650 300 or 652 093, fax 444 371), towering 22 storeys at Viru väljak 4 just east of the Old Town, dates from 1972 and was one of the better Intourist hotels in the USSR – but still a byword for prostitution and sullen service. It has shaken off much of its past now (including the prostitutes), and isn't a bad place to stay if you're into this price range, though service can still be a mite grumpy. The Viru holds over 800 guests. Comfortable pine-panelled rooms cost about 880/1145 EEK from June to September, 800/1040 EEK the rest of the year. There are also some renovated rooms about 30% dearer – and a long list of eateries and drinkeries.

The *Hotell Olümpia* (☎ 602 600 or 602 436, fax 602 492) about 700 metres south of the Old Town at Liivalaia 33, is another Soviet (1980) creation, even taller than the Viru with 26 floors, but less lively and with mostly smaller rooms which cost about 785/960 EEK from May to September, 700/870 EEK at other times. There are great views from the top-floor sauna!

Tallinn's top hotel is the 91-room *Hotell Palace* (☎ 444 761, fax 443 098), just outside the Old Town at Vabaduse väljak 3, which was renovated to 'international four-star standard' by Scandinavian companies in 1989. The elegant, if not huge, rooms had international direct-dial phones long before anywhere else in Estonia and also boast Sky TV. There's a nightclub and casino on the premises, and two good restaurants. Regular room rates are around 2150/2650 EEK including breakfast, but from Friday to Sunday there's currently a special rate of about 1350/1950 EEK. In Finland you can book through Arctia Hotel Partners (☎ 90-694 8022, fax 90-694 8471) of Iso-Roobertinkatu 23-25, 00120 Helsinki; in other countries through Finnair Hotels or SAS Associated Hotels.

The only place of similar standard to the Palace at present is the small *Hotell Noobel* (☎ 683 713, fax 444 889) at Tuvi 14B, a wooden house in a little street just off Tõnismägi, half a km south of Toompea. Rooms have satellite TV and air-conditioning and cost 2500 EEK a double including breakfast. There's a bar, restaurant, sauna, and massage room.

A second old hotel being renovated to the same standard as the Palace – by the same Scandinavian-Estonian joint venture, the Finest Group – is likely to be open by the time you read this. It's the *Imperial Hotell* (☎ 446 919, fax 440 386) at Nunne 12-14 in the Lower Town. There are 61 rooms (all with bath or shower, and satellite TV) and a restaurant and a sauna.

A Sheraton hotel is planned on a site near the Hotell Tallinn.

PLACES TO EAT

Tallinn's eating-out scene has improved beyond recognition since the grim Soviet years when you had to bribe or barge your way into most restaurants – and still be disappointed with what you were served. There are now several quality restaurants which *really* have what's on their menus, plus a number of other places where the choice is more limited but which can still provide a reasonable meal. And the only time they'll hinder you from entering is when the place is full. Restaurant opening hours are normally from noon to 11 pm or midnight, with an hour's break around 6 pm. In summer,

reservations are sometimes needed at a few of the best places.

The Old Town's café *(kohvik)* scene is a big plus, too – a large number of places sell good coffee and tempting pastries, cakes and open sandwiches. Most cafés close around 7 pm.

New places are opening all the time – *The Baltic Outlook*, *Tallinn City Paper* and *Tallinn This Week* will have good tips.

The Central Market (Keskturg) at Keldrimäe 2 between Lastekodu and Juhkentali, out beyond the Hotell Olümpia, is a source of fresh fruit and vegetables. One handy shop for basic foodstuffs like bread, fruit, cheese, tinned fish or milk is on Narva maantee a few doors east of Viru väljak. Tallinn also has a number of shops stocked with imported Western food, drink, tobacco, chocolate and other luxuries at Western prices. These include *Comex*, which stays open till 11 pm every night, at Pärnu maantee 19 opposite the Tallink office.

Fast Food

McDonald's is on its way to Tallinn and will probably get there before you do. You may be glad of its convenience at some stage during your stay, even if the chips are lukewarm and the burger soggy. A local face of capitalism, *Peetri Pizza*, already has five outlets in Tallinn. They dole out tasty pizzas for 4 to 8 EEK (small) or 9 to 14 EEK (big) at almost any hour you might need one. Don't bother with the small pizzas because they really are small. If you're truly hungry you'll need two big ones, as the pizza base is crisp but light. The Peetri locations are: Pärnu maantee 22 near the Hotell Palace (open from 10 am to 3 am, take-away only); Lai 4 in the Old Town (10 am to 11 pm, take-away or sit-down); Vana-Kalamaja behind the railway station (11 am to 10 pm sit-down, 11 am to 2 pm in the take-away section round the corner at Kopli 2C); Liivalaia 40 near the Hotell Olümpia (11 am to 11 pm take-away, 11 am to 10 pm sit-down); and Pargi 8 in Viimsi, a north-eastern suburb three km beyond Pirita (11 am to 10 pm, take-away or sit-down). In the sit-down

141

can add a help-yourself salad for
a glass of hõõgvein for 10 EEK.
run by the Finest Group which
brought Tallinn the Hotell Palace and almost
has a monopoly on the city's best catering
too.

Bistro, at Narva maantee 6 and Estonia
puiestee 5, serves up pasta, burgers of a kind,
and fresh vegetable salads. A grillburger has
no bun but comes with tomato sauce, grated
carrot and a helping of pasta, for 10 EEK.
Both Bistros are officially open from 9 am to
9 pm but may close early if business is slow
– and won't live up to their name (which is
Russian for 'fast') when there's much of a
crowd in. But they do have genuinely quick
ice-cream counters.

There's a reasonable stand-up snack bar in
the east end of the railway station (enter
through the suburban ticket hall), serving
chicken legs (around 3 EEK), beetroot salad,
bread and so on.

Cafés & Bars

Tallinn has a couple of dozen reasonable
cafés. Some of the best are on Toompea. One
is the *Bogapott* at Pikk jalg 9, a Finnish-
Estonian joint-venture with natty design,
very tasty snacks, real coffee and a nice little
shop. The *Pika Yala Baar*, a café-bar across
the street, is OK too. *Kohvik Neitsitorn*,
occupying a tall tower in the old city wall just
off Lossi plats, serves good hõõgvein (10
EEK a glass), coffee and snacks. You buy at
the counter then find a table on one of several
floors upstairs. The views are great, and it's
open from 11 am to 10 pm, but some customers gulp down a few too many hõõgveins.
The *Kuller* bar by the Alexandr Nevsky
Cathedral serves draught Estonian beer at 6
EEK a tankard, but closes at 8 pm.

In the Lower Town, *Kohvik Pärl* at Pikk 3
has good fare and lots of tables. The
Maiasmokk Kohvik (Sweet-Tooth Café) at
Pikk 16 does good pastries and has a place
of honour as it was also a café during
Estonia's pre-WW II period of independence. The *Vesi Veski* at Suur-Karja 17/19 is
a pleasant small coffee-house.

The *Eeslitall* restaurant at Dunkri 4 has

both a *Keldribaar* (cellar bar), open till the
early hours, which doubles as Estonia's top
live music spot, and a convivial little upstairs
bar where one vodka or konjak has a way of
leading to another. The *George Browne* at
Harju 6 is also very popular – it's an Irish
pub, with Guiness at 45 EEK a pint. The
Corrida at Vabaduse väljak 5, next to the
Hotell Palace, is a haunt of Tallinn's fashionable young. The *Von Krahli Theatre* bar at
Rataskaevu 10 serves Estonian beer. *Rosalie*
on Vene is a pleasant little bar with hõõgvein,
open till 11 pm. In summer a few pleasant
open-air bars spring up around the Old
Town.

There's a reasonable café-bar, the *Pubi
Baar ja Kohvik*, in the rear of the ground
floor of the Hotell Viru (go down the stairs
beside the main restaurant to find it), and a
huge café in the *Hotell Olümpia* (turn left
inside the main entrance and go up one
floor). Pancakes in all sorts of guises are the
speciality at the Olümpia.

Restaurants

Old Town There's a range of good restaurants on and around Raekoja plats, and
another good place up on Toompea.

The *Maharaja Restaurant* (☎ 444 637) at
Raekoja plats 13 is one of the best restaurants
in the Baltic states, serving excellent Indian
food. You pay for the pleasure: soups and
starters are 50 to 100 EEK, main courses 100
to 200 EEK, but there's also a three-course
'businessman's lunch' at 120 EEK. At
Raekoja plats 8 is the *Vana Toomas* – a large,
much cheaper, cellar restaurant serving a
number of Estonian dishes. It's one of the
few survivors from the Soviet era that can
still hold its head up, even if the waiters are
as cool as ever. A large plate of hors
d'oeuvres (külmad road) is around 25 EEK,
and main courses are about 15 to 20 EEK.
Try praetud sealiha seentega (roast pork with
onion and mushroom garnish, and vegetables) or praetud kala (a fried-fish and
vegetable dish).

The much newer *Eeslitall Restoran*
(☎ 448 033), just off Raekoja plats at Dunkri
4, has similar prices to the Vana Toomas but

also one of the lightest and brightest atmospheres in Tallinn. The menu is short but the choice is appealing to Westernised tastes: soups or starters (including a vegetable platter) are from 6 to 14 EEK, while main courses are from 10 to 25 EEK (chicken and spaghetti at the lower end of the range, fish and meat at the top). You'll probably need a reservation for dinner here – and in summer even for lunch. The Eeslitall stays open till 2 am on Saturday and Sunday mornings. There are two bars in the same building: the one downstairs is Tallinn's top music spot (see Entertainment).

Just off Raekoja plats in another direction, the *Kullassepa Kelder* at Kullassepa 9 concentrates on grilled chicken and does it very well – 38 EEK a shot with vegetables. Go down the stairs from the ground-floor café.

The *Gnoom* grill, also a few steps from Raekoja plats at Viru 2, has a fine spacious 15th century stone interior but the service and fare are no more than acceptable – chicken, pork or beef with vegetables are all 20 to 25 EEK. There's also a bar and an upstairs café. You pay a couple of EEK for an entry ticket.

The *Sub Monte Restoran* (☎ 666 871), in a medieval cellar at Rüütli 4 by Niguliste church, is a more up-market place (verging on the snotty) serving excellent international and Estonian fare. It's another Finest Group place. Meat or fish main courses are in the 50 to 60 EEK region. For vegetarians there's a token vegetables braised in butter with mushroom for 28 EEK. The Sub Monte gets busy in summer.

The popular *Toomkooli Restoran* (☎ 446 613) at Toom-Kooli 13 is right on the edge of Toompea looking out over western Tallinn. It's cleanly arranged inside and has outdoor tables in summer. The only question mark is over the service which can be grumpy. The choice of food is wide and good, though the portions aren't huge. I enjoyed fish soup and sweet cream from the long list of starters, and the stuffed chicken-fillet main course. Weightier appetites might choose hunter's sausage cooked in alcohol to start their meal, while vegetarians could get

by on vegetables braised with butter in cheese sauce, the cheapest of the main courses at 13 EEK. Fish and meat mains are 18 to 36 EEK. The Toomkooli is yet another Finest Group establishment.

Vabaduse Väljak & Around The *Pizzeria Margareta* in the side of the Hotell Palace, entered from Pärnu maantee, does the best pizzas in town – about 30 cm wide – for 25 to 40 EEK, plus hot meat and fish dishes for 80 to 100 EEK. A few doors along at Pärnu maantee 18 is yet another Finest Group eatery, seemingly without an official name but generally known just as the *Finest*. This is a grill-bar with fare ranging from plain sausages at 6 EEK or pikkpoiss (roast minced meat) with chips and beetroot for 12 EEK, to grilled chicken at 15 EEK or grill liha (meat) with chips and beetroot for 25 EEK. The liha isn't quite steak but I still enjoyed it; the cheaper dishes don't get very good reports.

In the Hotell Palace itself is the ground-floor *Restaurant Linda* with reportedly top-class international and Estonian cuisine.

Elsewhere The *Hotell Viru* has a top-floor restaurant with good food and even better views, where meat or fish main courses are 18 to 25 EEK. Prices are similar in the main restaurant on floor two. The all-you-can-eat buffet breakfast in the main restaurant is 55 EEK for non-residents. The hotel has a special desk for restaurant reservations on the ground floor of the rear section of the hotel – go down the stairs by the main restaurant.

Other restaurants that get good reports include the *Carina* at Pirita tee 26 and the *Vana Saku* in the Peoleo Hotell.

ENTERTAINMENT
Consult *Tallinn This Week*, *Tallinn City Paper*, *What? Where? When? in Tallinn* and the Upcoming Events section of the *Baltic Independent* to find out what's on.

Rock, Blues, Jazz & Folk
The Keldribaar (Cellar Bar) at the Eeslitall

restaurant at Dunkri 4, a few steps off Raekoja plats, is about the grooviest little night spot in Estonia. How long it will remain that way is anyone's guess but it certainly has a popular recipe – good R&B, jazz or folk every night from 10 pm till the early hours. The bar, open from 4 pm to 4 am, is a rambling multi-caverned dungeon but still gets packed to bursting on Friday and Saturday nights. Estonia's excellent R&B band, Compromise Blue, plays here fairly often. Officially the bar is a club, but non-members can get in. After 8 pm you may have to pay a 10 EEK admission charge.

The Von Krahl at Rataskaevu 10 also has live music most nights. It's open till 2 am; admission is 10 EEK. Other blues, rock, jazz etc gigs pop up at various venues around town – watch for posters. *The Baltic Independent* is a good source of information on these as they're often organised at too-short notice to get into the other publications.

Classical Music, Opera & Ballet
The large building at Estonia puiestee 4 houses both the Estonia Theatre, which stages ballet, opera and musicals, and the Estonia Concert Hall (Kontserdisaal) where you'll hear classical music and choral works. Several different classical and modern works are staged in repertory at the Estonia Theatre and there's one on nearly every night. At the time of writing, the ballet has an innovative choreographer, Mai Murdmaa. *Kuritöö ja karistus*, a ballet version of Dostoevsky's *Crime and Punishment* with music by Arvo Pärt, is one of the big successes of recent years. The theatre, like several other Baltic arts institutions, has lost some performers to the lure of higher earnings in other countries. Tickets are fairly cheap and the box office (☎ 449 040) is open from 1 to 7 pm daily except Tuesday.

Concerts at the Estonia Concert Hall are usually held two or three times weekly, though there may be fewer in summer when the resident Estonian State Symphony Orchestra takes a bit of a break. The Tallinn Conservatoire Symphony Orchestra and a variety of visiting orchestras and choirs also perform.

Chamber, organ, solo and other smaller-scale concerts are held in the Estonia Theatre café and several halls around town – many of which are architectural gems. They include Niguliste church, the Town Hall (Raekoda) on Raekoja plats, the House of Blackheads at Pikk 24, the Olavi Saal in the Oleviste Guild building at Pikk 26, and the Dominican monastery on Vene. The Hortus Musicus Early Music Consort and the Estonia Philharmonia Chamber Orchestra and Choir are Tallinn's leading smaller musical ensembles. Some big events are held at the 4200-seat concert hall in the Linnahall at Merepuiestee 20 near the harbour. Concert tickets are cheap and for most concerts they're sold at the Estonia Concert Hall box office (☎ 443 198), open from 1 to 7 pm daily except Sunday, though the Linnahall and Niguliste have their own box offices too.

Theatre
Tallinn has several companies all staging a number of dramas (including translations of Western plays) in repertory from September till the end of May. There are also some alternative-theatre groups who can be a lot brighter than the mainstream companies. Everything is in Estonian (except at the Russian Drama Theatre). Theatre is very popular, though the withdrawal of state financing may prove disastrous for some of the permanent companies.

The main theatre is the Estonia Drama Theatre (Eesti Draama teater) at Pärnu maantee 5, not to be confused with the opera and ballet-purveying Estonia Theatre next door. The Von Krahli Theatre at Rataskaevu 10 is a lively alternative place.

Nightlife
Tallinn has quite a few discos, mainly on Friday and Saturday nights. *Tallinn This Week* lists them. There are also several restaurants and a couple of bars with music (which may be live) and dancing. The restaurants include the quite expensive 1920s-style Astoria at Vabaduse väljak 5

which has live music – you can buy tickets for the evening from 1.30 to 3.30 pm – and the Gloria at Müürivahe 2 which has a cabaret show too. The bars include the Eeslitall Keldribaar at Dunkri 4 (see Rock, Blues, Jazz & Folk) and the Karikabaar at Kuninga 3, both in the Old Town, and the Baar Regatt at Merivälja tee 1, Pirita, which is open from 7.30 pm to 1 or 2 am. Several hotels including the Palace, Viru, Olümpia, Tallinn and Kungla have night clubs or restaurants with cabaret and dancing. Lucky Luke's at the back of the Linnahall is a big dance hall, sometimes with live country music, open from 11 am to 3 am. The Palace and Viru hotels have small casinos where you can play roulette or blackjack.

Sports

Tallinn's basketball team, Kalev, is among the best in Europe and plays to capacity crowds at the Kalevi sports hall at Juhkentali 12. Ice hockey matches are played at the arena in the Linnahall. A great many sporting events are staged year-round in Tallinn – *Tallinn This Week* lists many of them.

THINGS TO BUY

Tallinn's shops may not look like a Western city's yet, but they're far more interesting than in the dire last years of Soviet rule. For one thing, far more of Estonia's best handicrafts find their way into shops, and fewer into back pockets, than they used to. The Old Town has quite a lot of handicraft, art and antique shops, and even a couple of fashion houses. Prices are still fairly low by Western standards. If you're looking for something more mundane like a toothbrush or an envelope, start looking in the Tallinna Kaubamaja department store on Viru väljak. You might also find a few handicrafts there.

In the clothing line look for some of the fine knitted jumpers, gloves and socks. Linen tablecloths and napkins can also be good value. Firma Kauplus at Pikk 9 is one shop selling this kind of stuff plus some Estonian national costumes – which are interesting to see, at least. The Ars shops at Pikk 18 and Vabaduse väljak 8, and Uku at

Pikk 9 have similar stuff plus some jewellery, leather work and attractive ceramics. *Tallinn This Week* and *Tallinn City Paper* will tell you of numerous other outlets.

A rather random assortment of records and tapes of Western, Baltic and Russian music – rock, jazz, classical, choral, folk – can be found in Heli at Raekoja plats 15, Meloodia at Kuninga 4, and in the Kaubamaja. They're cheap at typically 10 to 20 EEK, but you'll be lucky to find leading contemporary Estonian music of any kind. The only CDs tend to be expensive Western imports or cheap Russian fakes.

GETTING THERE & AWAY

This section concentrates on transport between Tallinn and other places in Estonia, Latvia, Lithuania or Kaliningrad. See the Getting There & Away chapter for detail on links with countries outside the Baltic states, which include ferries to/from Finland and Sweden, flights to/from several Western and CIS cities, trains to/from Russia, Poland and Belarus, and buses to/from Germany, Russia and Poland.

The Tallinn Information section has information on some useful travel agents, including Wris, which may offer reduced air fares.

Air

At the time of writing, Estonian Air flies four times weekly to/from Vilnius. Tickets are much cheaper in Lithuania than in Estonia – though this wrinkle may be ironed out before long if Lithuania follows Estonia's move to international fare levels. In Tallinn, tickets are sold by Estonian Air and the cheapest are 'superpex' returns which must be bought seven to 14 days before flying. These are US$190 (2400 EEK). Straight one-way fares are US$258 (3300 EEK). In Vilnius, tickets to Tallinn are sold by LAL for US$120 one way.

In 1993 the rights to domestic flights within Estonia were transferred from Estonian Air, which had been operating them at a loss, to a Tartu-based company called Ergon. Ergon said it would start flights between

Tallinn and Tartu, Pärnu, Kuressaare (Saaremaa), and Kärdla (Hiiumaa). Estonian Air's one-way fare to the islands was 310 EEK, with flying time 45 minutes.

Tallinn airport is three km south-east of the city centre on Tartu maantee. It has a café, shops, car-rental desks, exchange counters and a post office where you can make international phone calls. For airport information in Tallinn call ☎ 211 092. Airline offices in Tallinn include:

Estonian Air
    Vabaduse väljak 8 (☎ 446 382 or 440 295, fax 211 624)
    Endla 59 (☎ & fax 490 679) – this office advertises reductions for foreigners on flights to Rīga, Vilnius and CIS cities and will take bookings by phone
    Airport (☎ 211 092)
Finnair
    Liivalaia 12 (☎ 683 771)
    Airport (☎ 423 538)
Lufthansa
    Airport (☎ 215 557)
SAS
    Airport (☎ 212 553, fax 210 354) (city centre office due to open 1993)

Bus

For bus information and advance tickets, go to the ticket office at Pärnu maantee 24, just down the street from the Hotell Palace. It's open from 8 am to 2 pm and 3 to 6 pm daily, and has a big, easily understood timetable and an information desk. Buses to places within 40 km or so of Tallinn, and some buses to Pärnu, go from the local bus station beside the railway station. For buses to other places, and the remaining Pärnu services, use the long-distance bus station (Maaliinide Autobussijaam) at Lastekodu 46, a km along Juhkentali from the Hotell Olümpia. Tram Nos 2 (from the railway station, Linnahall, Mere puiestee and Tartu maantee) and 4 (eastward along Pärnu maantee in the city centre) go to the Autobussijaam stop on Tartu maantee 200 metres from the bus station. At the bus station is another timetable (with a big route map on its reverse, showing which bus numbers go where), another information

desk, more ticket windows and a left-luggage room.

Services within the Baltic states to/from Tallinn include:

Haapsalu
    100 km, 2½ hours, 10 buses daily, 7 EEK
Kaliningrad
    690 km, 13½ hours, one bus nightly, 105 EEK
Kärdla
    160 km, five hours, one bus daily, 11 EEK
Kaunas
    575 km, 12 hours, one bus nightly, 72 EEK
Kuressaare
    220 km, 4½ hours, four fast buses daily, 17.50 EEK
Narva
    210 km, four hours, five buses daily, 15.30 EEK
Pärnu
    130 km, 2½ hours, about 12 buses daily, 9 to 25 EEK
Rakvere
    95 km, 1½ hours, nine buses daily, 7.50 EEK
Rīga
    310 km, six hours, six buses daily, 38 EEK
Tartu
    190 km, three hours, about 14 buses daily, 13 EEK
Viljandi
    160 km, 2½ hours, three buses daily, 12.50 EEK
Vilnius
    600 km, 12 hours, one bus nightly, 74 EEK
Võru
    250 km, 4½ hours, four to six buses daily, 18 EEK.

Train

The main railway station is the Baltic Station (Balti jaam) at Toompuiestee 35, just outside the north-west edge of the Old Town. Tram Nos 1 and 2 go from Kopli street at the back of the station and travel to the Linnahall stop near the ferry terminals, continuing to the Mere puiestee stop near the Hotell Viru. Tram No 1 then heads east along Narva maantee to Kadriorg, and No 2 goes south down Tartu maantee to the Autobussijaam stop near the bus station.

Ticket window 26 (☎ 624 058), by the platform round the back of the main long-distance booking hall, sells tickets for Latvia, Lithuania, Belarus, Poland and Russia. It's open from 8 am to 1 pm and 2 to 8 pm daily – and is used to dealing with foreigners so it may be worth trying for tickets to domestic destinations too. 'Suburban trains' *(linnalähedased rongid)* have their own ticket office at the rear, east end of the station. Some (but not all) trains going to places as far away as Tartu, Narva or Pärnu are classed as 'suburban'.

If you're planning much rail travel in Estonia, a copy of the cheap *Reisirongide Sõiduplaan* (Railway Timetable) booklet may be useful. A few shops around Tallinn sell it – look for 'Sõiduplaan' signs in windows.

The daily Tallinn-Warsaw *Baltic Express* (Balti Ekspress), leaving Tallinn at 5.10 pm at the time of writing, runs via Tartu, Valga, Rīga and Kaunas. The other most important train within the Baltic states is the *Seagull* (Estonian: Kajakas; Russian: Chayka), which trundles daily from Tallinn to Minsk (and vice versa) in 17½ hours, stopping at Tartu, Sigulda, Rīga, Jelgava, Šiauliai, Vilnius and a dozen or two other places en route. There's also an overnight train from Tallinn to Rīga (and vice versa), taking 9½ hours and making the same intermediate stops. The Tallinn-Rīga fare in compartment class is about 40 EEK at the time of writing.

The main services within Estonia, with approximate fares in general seating, include:

Haapsalu
   104 km, one through-train daily, three hours, 5 EEK (see the Haapsalu section for more information)
Kloogaranna
   39 km, nine trains daily, one hour, 2 EEK
Narva
   210 km, six trains daily, 3¼ to 4½ hours, 12 EEK (see the Narva section for more information)
Paldiski
   48 km, five or six trains daily, 1¼ hours, 2 EEK
Pärnu
   141 km, four trains daily, 2¾ to four hours, 7 EEK
Tartu
   190 km, seven or eight trains daily, 2½ to 3¾ hours, 11 to 15 EEK (see the Tartu section for more information)
Viljandi
   151 km, three trains daily, 2½ to 3¼ hours, 8 EEK

All these services make stops at small places along the way. Some trains on the Narva and Tartu lines are international services on which there is only sleeping accommodation, costing 15% to 150% more than general seating, depending on class.

Car & Motorbike
There are Norwegian-run Statoil petrol stations on the corner of Sadama and Mere puiestee near the ferry port, and on Tartu maantee by the airport, and Finnish-run Neste petrol stations at Pärnu maantee 141 and Regati puiestee 1, Pirita (on the harbour front down past the Hotell Pirita – look for the blue and green flags). Their stock includes 99-octane and unleaded petrol and a few basic supplies and parts for Western vehicles. The Sadama/Mere puiestee and Pärnu maantee stations are open 24 hours; the latter has a café open from 7 am to 11 pm.

The Tallinn traffic police (Tallinna Liikluspolitsei) (☎ 445 450) at Lastekodu 31 supposedly have some English-speaking staff who can give information about motor-repair workshops and other car matters.

Rental Avis (☎ 215 602, fax 212 735) at Tallinn airport, Lennujaama tee 2, rents self-drive Ladas for 664 EEK a day, 1776 EEK for three days, or 3872 EEK for a week (all with unlimited km), which is a reasonable deal by Baltics standards – especially as these cars will run on cheap 93-octane petrol. A Toyota Corolla is 496 EEK a day plus 4.96 EEK per km, or 3504 EEK for three days with unlimited km, or 6304 EEK for a week with unlimited km. You can limit your damage liability for an extra 160 or 200 EEK a day. Avis also has more expensive cars up to a Volvo 940 GL or a Pontiac Firebird. In Sweden you can make bookings on ☎ 063-12 78 60 or fax 063-12 19 15.

Europcar-InterRent, which rents Corollas and Volvos, operates through AS Refit at Mere puiestee 6 (☎ 441 637, fax 431 667) and also has a desk (☎ 219 031) at the airport. You can book through Europcar-InterRent offices in other countries. Balt Link (☎ 421 003) at Tartu maantee 13 rents Volvos. Finest

Auto (☎ 666 719) at Pärnu maantee 22 rents Peugeots, Mercedes, Chevrolets etc. Also in the more expensive bracket is Hertz (☎ 421 003, fax 450 893) at Tartu maantee 13.

Boat

Tallinn's main ferry terminal *(merevaksal)* is at the east end of Sadama, about a km north-east of the Old Town. This is used by almost all passenger shipping except EstLine, which has its own terminal next door, and one or two other services which dock not far away near the Linnahall. The main terminal has a café, bar, shops, and left-luggage room. Tram Nos 1 and 2 and bus Nos 3, 4 and 8 go to the Linnahalli stop at the west end of Sadama, five-minutes walk from all the terminals. The shipping lines' main booking offices are:

EstLine
  Aia 5A (☎ 666 579, fax 441 219) or EstLine terminal (☎ 602 010)
Estma (Estonian Maritime Agency)
  Sadama 17 (☎ 433 738)
Estonian New Line
  Inreko ticket office (☎ 428 382) in main ferry terminal or Baltlink office (☎ 445 967) at the Linnahall terminal
Helta Line
  Main ferry terminal (☎ 428 701)
Silja Line
  Baltic Tours (☎ 430 663) in Teenindusmaja shop, Viru väljak
Tallink
  Pärnu maantee 16 (☎ 442 440) or main ferry terminal (☎ 601 960)
Viking Line
  Estravel, Pikk 37 (☎ 601 886)

You can also buy tickets from a number of travel agents around town.

Yacht Charter TopSail (☎ 237 055, fax 237 044) at the Pirita marina, Regati puiestee 1, rents out British Westerly yachts with or without a skipper.

GETTING AROUND
To/From the Airport

Tallinn Airport is on the Tartu road three km south-east of the centre. Bus No 22 runs every 20 to 30 minutes to and from the bus station, the Tallinna Kaubamaja department store near the Hotell Viru, Vabaduse väljak near the Hotell Palace, and the railway station. A taxi from the airport to the city centre should cost 25 to 30 EEK but beware of rip-offs by the mafia sharks who have taken over the airport taxi scene at various times.

Buses, Trams & Trolleybuses

The Old Town is best explored on foot (trams, buses and trolleybuses circumvent it, and cars need a permit to enter it). The railway station, ferry terminals and many hotels are an easy walk from the Old Town. Buses, trams and trolleybuses will take you everywhere else from 5 or 6 am to about midnight, though they're often crowded and you may have to wait a long time to travel outside the centre after 7 or 8 pm. The *City Plan with the Public Transport* map shows all their routes. Tickets are 0.40EEK at the time of writing. One kiosk selling them is on Vabaduse väljak opposite the Astoria Restaurant. Look for 'Sõidupiletid' ('Transport tickets').

Route-Taxis

From 3 pm to 1.30 am there are also route-taxis *(liinitaksod)*: minibuses with a flat fare of about 2 EEK (pay the driver). They have an illuminated roof sign to show when they have empty seats, and will drop passengers anywhere along their fixed routes. Their terminal is beside the Hotell Viru. No 1 runs to Pirita.

Taxis

Taxis are plentiful and should cost 2 EEK a km, but you have to watch out for rip-offs. Drivers of the yellow state-owned Volga cabs tend to be more honest than private cabbies. Insisting on having the meter running is one way to avoid being cheated. Otherwise fix a price before you get in. Main taxi ranks around the city centre include those at the railway station and Viru väljak, but sometimes mafia thugs manage to get a monopoly on the most lucrative ranks, turning away honest drivers and demanding absurd fares. If you're faced with this scum, you have no option but to pay up, look elsewhere, or order a taxi by phone. There are three 24-hour firms you can call: the state-owned Taksopark (☎ 444 856), and the privately run Taksokeskus (☎ 603 044) and Esra (☎ 602 340).

Trains

Few of the suburban rail services from the main station in Tallinn go to places of much interest in the city, and buses cover most of the same routes anyway. The one line that may be a little more useful than the others heads south to Nõmme, Pääskula and Laagri. There are about 40 daily trains along this line from 5.20 am till after midnight. Most continue beyond the city bounds to Keila, Paldiski or Kloogaranna, but some only go as far as Pääskula.

Around Tallinn

Countryside and unspoiled coast are not far from Tallinn and there are several places worthy of an outing if you have time. Accommodation includes a number of campsites which offer a relatively cheap alternative to a night in the city for those with vehicles. It's advisable to check in advance with campsites about vacancies, prices and opening dates – though all of them are usually open at least from 1 June to 1 September. Several of the campsites are run by the Silvest Motel Group (☎ 557 059) of Viljandi maantee 16, Tallinn.

WEST OF TALLINN
Beaches
The coast west of Tallinn is a favourite summer escape for city folk and the first long, sandy beach is at **Vääna-Jõesuu**, 24 km from the city centre. From the main coast road it's about 600 metres down a side track to the beach. The beach continues south across the mouth of the Vääna River, where there's a stretch of 30-metre cliff, one of the highest on the Estonian coast. The road runs

right along the cliff top soon after the Naage bus stop. There are more beaches further west at **Lohusalu**, and at **Laulasmaa** and **Kloogaranna** on Lahepera Bay, all 35 to 40 km from Tallinn. Kloogaranna is reckoned to be the cleanest beach in Estonia and is very popular as it has a rail link with Tallinn – though it may not be quite the 'Estonian Miami' that some advertising talks of!

Paldiski
The port of Paldiski, 50 km west of Tallinn, was founded by Peter the Great. It was turned into a nuclear-submarine base, along with a rocket base, an airport and a submariner-training school, by his Soviet successors, who also made it off-limits to civilians. Several ships were scuttled here during the Russian military withdrawal from Estonia, and the submarine and patrol-boat harbours were wrecked. The two nuclear reactors that had provided fuel for the subs were due to be dismantled but, according to the latest reports, the Russian military had not made the reactors accessible to the Estonian government or to international inspectors.

All but about 1500 of the 10,000 ex-Soviet military at the base had left by mid-1993, and many of the mostly Russian civilian population of 5000 can also be expected to leave. In mid-1993, access to the town remains restricted, with a permit needed from the Estonian authorities.

Padise
At Padise, about 15 km south of Paldiski on a back road between Tallinn and Haapsalu, is an atmospheric Cistercian monastery-fortress dating from the 14th to 16th centuries with a cemetery dating back to the 13th century. It was damaged in the Livonian War in the 16th century and again in a 1766 fire. Padise is four km west of Rummu on the route of Haapsalu-Rummu-Keila-Tallinn buses.

Places to Stay & Eat
Klooga Youth Hostel (☎ 22-743 242) is near Lahepera Bay 200 metres from the Klooga II bus stop on the Kloogaranna-Laulasmaa

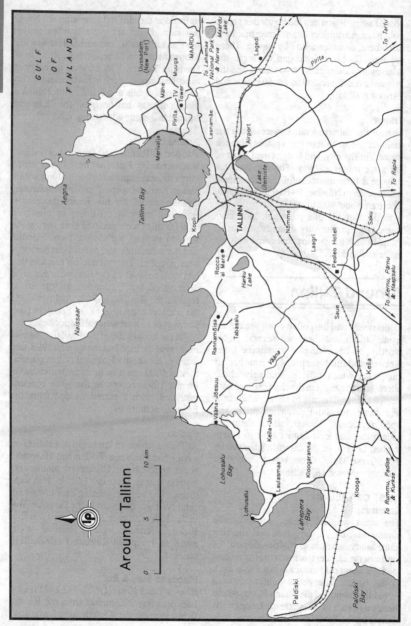

Around Tallinn

road. Its opening dates in its first year were 1 April to 1 December. There are 25 beds plus 18 quite large three-bed 'camping' cabins. The nightly cost is 50 to 60 EEK per person. Meals can be supplied. Kloogaranna railway station is about one km south.

Silvest's *Rannamõisa Camping* is 13 km west of Tallinn, 200 metres from sea. It has 100 places in cabins plus tent sites, hot showers, kitchen, tennis court, sauna and bar. The turning from the main road is just after Mere Tee bus stop which is just beyond Tabasalu village. Go 700 metres towards the coast. The popular *Merepiiga* (Mermaid) restaurant is near a cliff top a few hundred metres west.

Silvest's *Vääna-Viti Camping* is among forest 200 metres from Vääna-Jõesuu beach, 24 km from the city. The Vääna River is half a km away. It has tent places, a few cabins, kitchen, sauna and cold water. Silvest's *Kurkse Camping* is about 60 km from Tallinn, at the harbour of Kurkse on the southern shore of Paldiski Bay. There are 10 rooms, as well as tent and caravan sites and a sauna. The last 10 km or so to Kurkse are along dirt road – turn right at Padise.

Getting There & Away
Buses travelling west along the coast, including Nos 108 and 126 to Rannamõisa, Vääna-Viti and Vääna-Jõesuu, go from the terminal beside Tallinn railway station. For Kloogaranna and Klooga hostel there are 10 daily suburban trains from Tallinn's Baltic station to Kloogaranna, a ride of one hour. There are also suburban trains to Paldiski.

SOUTH OF TALLINN
Kernu & Ruunavere
At Kernu, 40 km south of central Tallinn on the road to Pärnu and Rīga, is the 1991-built *Kernu Kämping* (☎ 22-215 696) with modern wooden cabins from 100 to 150 EEK per person. Showers and toilets are shared. There's a classical-style manor house by a nearby lake.

Some 10 km further south on the Pärnu road, the former Ruunavere relay station is being renovated into what looks like an unusual and comfortable middle or top-end hotel which should be open by the time you get there. The *Ruunavere Hotell* (☎ 244-771 167) will have 13 double rooms and four suites. A quality restaurant and a bar with music and dancing are already open.

There's another *Kämping* about 30 km along the Tartu road from Tallinn, 300 metres to the right, 3½ km before the 'Kohila 21' turning.

EAST OF TALLINN
Maardu
On Tallinn's eastern border, the Tallinn-Narva highway crosses the Maardu area which is an industrial wilderness thanks to phosphorite mining and other industries which raged unchecked here in the Soviet era. A notoriously polluting chemical plant is still operating at the time of writing, but phosphorite mining in Estonia was stopped in 1991 and some innovative plans are being hatched to clean up Maardu and turn it to recreational use.

As early as 1987, 30 sq km to the east and south of Maardu Lake (which lies beside the highway) were declared the **Rebala Farming History Reserve**. Within this area are numerous traces of historic and prehistoric settlements and cultures including the Maardu manor founded in 1397, sites of pre-Christian cults, and 'sliding rocks' said to cure infertility in women who slide down them bare-bottomed. Trips round some of these spots and ex-industrial sites are being organised by the Green Maardu Association (Ühendus Roheline Maardu) (☎ 22-239 733, fax 22-440 963) of Kärestiku 10, Tallinn; and trips on horseback by Ain Unt (☎ 22-420 671) of Lohu 6 in Lagedi, a village eight km south-west of Lake Maardu.

Places to Stay
Silvest's *Kämping Must Kass* (Black Cat) (☎ 22-723 881) is in woods 400 metres south of the Tallinn-Narva highway at Kodasoo, 30 km east of Tallinn and 15 km east of Maardu. It has room for 50 in two-person cabins, as well as tent sites and a café. Signs on the highway indicate the entrance.

North-East Estonia

You travel across north-east Estonia if you approach Tallinn from St Petersburg. Lahemaa National Park, about a third of the way from Tallinn to the Russian border, is well worth a visit. The border town of Narva is of interest chiefly for one or two historic remains and because it's one of the two main centres of Estonia's Russian minority (the other is Tallinn).

LAHEMAA NATIONAL PARK

Estonia's only national park *(rahvuspark)*, Lahemaa, takes in a stretch of deeply indented coast with several peninsulas and bays plus 649 sq km of hinterland with 14 lakes and numerous rivers and waterfalls. The Tallinn-Narva road enters the park 50 km east of Tallinn and leaves it nearly 30 km further east. The park is a peaceful, unspoiled section of rural Estonia with a variety of attractive coastal and inland scenery. There's historical, archaeological and cultural interest as well as the natural attractions of the coast, forests, lakes, rivers, bogs and walking trails. About 30% of the park landscape is human-influenced, 65% is forest or heath, and 5% is bog. Roads crisscross the park from the Tallinn-Narva highway to the coast, and several parts of the park are accessible by bus.

Information

Lahemaa National Park Visitor Centre (Lahemaa Rahvuspark Külatuskeskus, ☎ 232-45 659 or 232-93 651, fax 232-45 759) is in the small village of Viitna, near the eastern boundary of the park, about 75 km from Tallinn on the Tallinn-Narva highway. Information and guides in several languages (including English) are available here, as is accommodation. See Getting Around for more on guides. The centre is open year round although most people visit the park between April and September. To reach the visitor centre, go about 400 metres east (towards Narva) along the main road from the bus stop in the middle of Viitna, almost opposite the Võsu junction. The entrance is marked by a small 'Lahemaa RP Külatuskeskus' sign and a wooden gate marked 'LRP Külatuskeskus'. The national park offices are also at Viitna, but it's planned to transfer them to Palmse, where a library will also be set up.

When it was founded in 1971, Lahemaa was the first national park in the Soviet Union. It was chosen partly because it contains many typically Estonian natural and cultural features. Its stated functions include protecting and popularising the natural and cultural heritage of its territory and contributing to public leisure and ecological thinking. Some 8% of its area is occupied by five strict reserves which only scientists may enter.

Geography

The landscape is mostly flat or gently rolling, with the highest point just 115 metres above

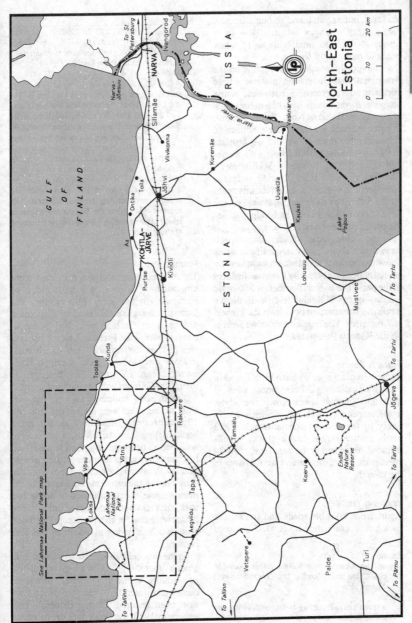

North-East Estonia

sea level, but as you travel through the park the scenery changes constantly – from forests to fields to small villages to sandy beach to rocky coast to bog.

Geologically, much of the park is on the North Estonian limestone plateau whose northern edge, stretching east-west across the park, forms a bank up to 56 metres high known as the Baltic or North Estonian Glint. In parts, the bank is a short, barely noticeable slope; in other places it's a cliff. At **Muuksi** in the west of the park it forms a 47-metre-high coastal bank (a site of Midsummer's Eve festivities). Rivers flowing over the bank become waterfalls, as at **Nõmmeveski** on the Valgejõgi river and **Joaveski** on the River Loobu. The Loobu and Valgejõgi are the park's major rivers.

Stone fields, areas of very thin topsoil known as 'alvars', and large single rocks known as 'erratic' boulders, brought here by glacial action, are typically Estonian features of the park. The biggest boulder (at 580 cubic metres) is the **Majakivi** (House Boulder), while the **Tammispea** boulder is the highest at 7.8 metres. The best known stone field is on the **Käsmu Peninsula**.

Flora & Fauna

Some 838 plant species have been found in the park (including 34 rare ones), plus 37 mammals (among them brown bear, lynx and European mink, none of which you're likely to see without specialist help), 213 birds (mute swan, black stork, black-throated diver and crane nest here), and 24 species of fish. Salmon and trout spawn in the rivers.

Walking Trails

Apart from hikeable roads and tracks, the park has several nature trails which include:

Käsmu
an 11-km circuit from Käsmu village, taking in coast, pine forest, 'erratic' boulders and the lake Käsmu järv

Viitna
a seven-km path starting at the visitor centre and taking in lakes and forest

Nõmmeveski
A 6.5-km waterfall trail. In addition, a two-km vehicle track leads two km east from Nõmmeveski to a pretty series of low waterfalls at Joaveski on the River Loobu.

Viru Rapa
A five-km trail across the 1.5-sq-km Viru Bog, starting at a car park on the road between Tallinn and Loksa. When the Baltic Sea was a lake, the Viru Bog was a smaller lake behind dunes on its shore. It began to fill with vegetation about 5000 years ago. The Viru Bog is a raised bog – separated from the soil by accumulations of peat moss (here the peat layer is about six metres deep). In a raised bog almost all the water comes from precipitation and is very low in mineral content, so the bog can only support plants with low mineral needs such as heather, bilberries and ledum (which gives the bog its characteristic smell). Trees growing here are stunted because of the high moisture.

Palmse

The restored manor and park at Palmse, eight km north of Viitna, is a showpiece of Lahemaa. In the early 13th century the Danish king gave the land to Cistercian monks from Gotland who had come to convert north-east Estonia. Later it became one of over 200 manors into which rural Estonia was divided under German land-owners. From 1674 to 1923 it belonged to the Baltic-German von der Pahlen family.

The existing buildings are restored versions of those that were built in the 18th and 19th centuries. The fine Baroque main house, dating from the 1780s, is decked out with period furniture. It's open from 10 am to 3 pm daily except Monday (also closed on Sunday in winter). At other times you can walk around the estate without entering the manor house. Behind the manor house is a park, first laid out in medieval times, when ponds were dug for fish breeding. The forest section of the park was added in the 19th century.

In the von der Pahlens' time, Palmse had, among other things, its own brewery, distillery, smithy, orchard, granaries, limestone quarry and water mill – many of which have now been restored. During Estonia's land reform in 1923, the estate was expropriated

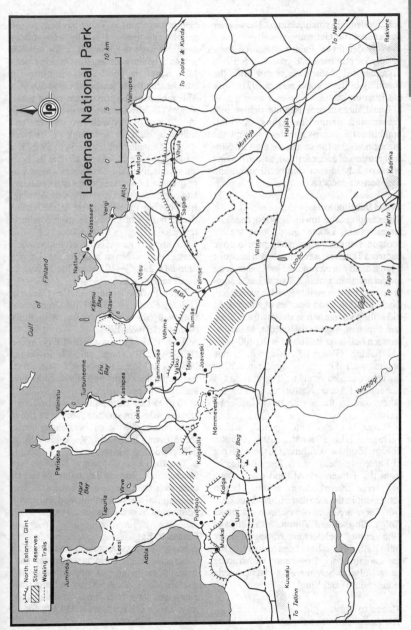

Lahemaa National Park

Legend:
- North Estonian Glint
- Strict Reserves
- Walking Trails

Gulf of Finland

and divided into smallholdings. The von der Pahlens left for Germany.

In Soviet times, Palmse was used for a variety of purposes but gradually fell into disrepair till restoration began after the founding of the national park in 1971. Work is still going on.

The Lahemaa area is quite rich in folk music and dance traditions. A small amphitheatre (across the lake behind the manor house) is the setting for the Viru Säru folk music and dance festival, held in the first week of July in even-numbered years, and for open-air concerts.

Other Destinations

The small coastal towns of **Võsu** and, to a lesser extent, **Loksa** are popular seaside spots in summer, when many people drive out from Tallinn at weekends. Võsu has quite a long, sandy beach and the bay it stands on is cleaner than Loksa's. Loksa has a ship-repair yard with a mainly Russian workforce. There are also good beaches at **Käsmu**, an old sailing village across the bay from Võsu, and between **Altja** and **Mustoja**. Many old wooden buildings still stand in the 400-year-old fishing village of Altja, which thus retains much of its original appearance. Altja is a centre of Midsummer's Eve festivities in Lahemaa. Käsmu, **Natturi** and **Virve** are other coastal villages with an old-fashioned flavour.

Inland, old farm buildings still stand in villages like **Muuksi**, **Uuri**, **Vatku**, **TõluguTõugu** and **Võhma**. On the small hill of Tandemägi, near Võhma, four stone tombs from the 1st century AD and earlier have been reconstructed after excavation. Human settlement in the area dates from about 2000 BC. There are more old German manors at **Kolga**, **Sagadi** and **Vihula**, with 18th and 19th century architecture. At Sagadi many Baroque buildings have been restored, as has the adjoining park. Restoration is also going on at Kolga (where there's a classical-style manor house) and Vihula.

Places to Stay

The *Lahemaa National Park Visitor Centre*

(see Information) at Viitna has beds for 36 people, and there are usually a few places available even at the height of the summer season. The site is among trees beside a clean lake which is good for swimming (in summer the water reaches the mid-20s °C). The pine-panelled rooms are either small singles (27 EEK) or doubles (44 to 49 EEK) in 12-room blocks with two showers and toilets in each, or four-bunk or six-bunk rooms in smaller houses for 54 to 59 EEK a room. The only drawbacks are that the beds are seemingly made for dwarves – mine was only about 1.68 metres long – and that noisy late-night carousers may stop you sleeping. It's possible to pitch a tent at the visitor centre, but ask in advance as space for this is restricted. There's a sauna too.

About 400 metres east of the visitor's centre, on the Narva road, is the *Kadaka Motell* (☎ 232-49 419) which has 20 beds in small cabins.

Near Palmse manor is the *Ojaäärse Holiday Centre* (☎ 232-34 108), run by the national-park visitor centre, with bunk rooms at 18 to 22 EEK.

The *Võsu Puhkekodu* holiday home (☎ 232-99 279), a large, unlovely Soviet-era building at Mere 21 on Võsu's main street, has reasonable rooms with private bathroom, for 200 EEK per person. Meals are available at 15 to 35 EEK. The puhkekodu also runs a smaller, 40-room summer place even closer to the beach. There's another holiday home, the *Käsmu Puhkekodu* (☎ 22-438 818 or 232-99 133), at Käsmu.

The *Must Kass* camping at Kodasoo (see Maardu under Around Tallinn) could also be used as a base for visiting Lahemaa. Tent camping in the park is allowed only with permission from the visitor centre.

Places to Eat

A bar with snacks, a canteen, and a shop all congregate in the building across the road from the eastbound-bus stop at Viitna. The *Kadaka Motell*, about 800 metres further east along the Narva road, has a bar doing quite good meals (eg soup, meat and veg for 15 EEK). An 18th century inn on the roadside near the middle of Viitna is being restored as a restaurant.

At Võsu there are a couple of restaurants plus a few cafés and bars.

Getting There & Away

Your own transport – car or bike – is the best means for exploring Lahemaa as it will enable you to travel easily around the park once there. Another possibility is to take a tour from Tallinn – several travel agents offer these, or you might be able to tag along with a group on a day trip.

To/From Viitna To reach Viitna from Tallinn by public transport, take one of the nine daily buses heading for Rakvere, 25 km beyond Viitna. These take an hour to Viitna, for 5 EEK. Tallinn-Narva and Tallinn-St Petersburg buses don't stop at Viitna. From Narva to Viitna take a bus or train to Rakvere (about six of each daily taking two to 2½ hours), and then a bus to Viitna (nine daily, 20 to 30 minutes). There are also a few trains and buses between St Petersburg and Rakvere, but they tend to depart or arrive at inconvenient night-time hours. From Tartu there's an early afternoon bus to Võsu, which stops at Viitna (3½ hours, 11 EEK) on the way, and three daily buses to Rakvere (2½ to three hours, 9 EEK). The daily bus from Võsu and Viitna to Tartu leaves in the early morning.

To/From Other Places There are buses from Tallinn to several places in the park including Käsmu, Võsu, Loksa, Pärispea, Viinistu and Leesi. All go and return two or three times a day in summer (in winter and at times of petrol shortage there are fewer services). You could, for instance, do a day trip from Tallinn by taking the 6.40 am bus to Käsmu (a 1¾-hour trip) and returning from there by the 7.20 pm bus.

Some days (Sunday, Monday, Wednesday and Friday at the time of writing) a bus leaves Rakvere for Võsu via Viitna at about noon, returning from Võsu at 2.30 pm. You could occupy a full day by taking the 6.40 am bus from Tallinn to Käsmu, spending six hours around Käsmu and Võsu then travelling down to Viitna on the 2.30 pm bus, giving you time for the Viitna lakes walking trail before overnighting at Viitna or heading out.

There's also the Tartu-Võsu bus already mentioned, taking four hours and costing 13 EEK if you go all the way.

Getting Around

A bicycle or motor vehicle is ideal. If you're not too pressed for time, walking is also a possibility, at least some of the time, as the distances are not too great. You can also use the buses running to the coastal villages (see Getting There & Away) to get around the park.

The visitor centre at Viitna provides guides for tours of the park, but not vehicles. Guides for one to three people cost 125 EEK for four hours and 187 EEK for eight hours; for four to 10 people they're 172 EEK and 258 EEK respectively. Try to book ahead if you want one. If you don't have your own vehicle the helpful park staff may be able to arrange for you to tag along with a group trip if you wish.

LAHEMAA TO NARVA

Much of Estonian territory east of Lahemaa is blighted by industries developed in the Soviet era. Some 40% of Estonian industrial output is produced here. Extraction of oil shale and phosphorite has scarred the landscape from west of Kohtla-Järve to beyond the Russian border, though phosphorite production was stopped in 1991 after a four-year public protest campaign that had been one of the seeds of Estonia's independence movement. Uranium waste from a nuclear plant at Sillamäe threatens to pollute the Baltic Sea. The towns in this north-eastern corner of Estonia have a predominantly Russian-speaking population – people who moved here in the Soviet era from elsewhere in the USSR to work in the new industries.

On a headland at **Toolse**, eight km west of the polluted town of Kunda, are the evocative ruins of a castle built in 1471 by the Livonian Order as defence against pirates. At **Purtse**, 10 km north of Kiviõli, there's a picturesque restored 16th century castle

Toolse Castle

open to visitors. The coast between Aa and Toila is lined by cliffs where it coincides with the edge of the Baltic Glint. At **Ontika**, north of **Kohtla-Järve**, these cliffs reach their greatest height: 55 metres.

Kohtla-Järve usually refers not just to the two adjoining settlements of Kohtla and Järve but to a whole string of other towns and villages on or just south of the highway, from Kiviõli in the west to Jõhvi and Viivikonna in the east. This area, with a population of about 90,000, is the centre of large-scale extraction and processing of oil shale, a kind of combustible stone used as fuel for power stations in and around Narva. The Ida-Virumaa Tourism Centre (☎ 233-62 260), which is trying to promote tourism in the area between Lahemaa and the Russian border and between the sea and Lake Peipus, is at Pargi 15 in Jõhvi.

Sillamäe, on the coast between Kohtla-Järve and Narva, was built after WW II to support a military nuclear-chemicals plant. Its 20,000 population is almost entirely Russian-speaking. According to press reports, the plant's waste dump contains several tonnes of radioactive and highly toxic wastes, surrounded only by an earth wall 10 metres wide and 20 metres high, and is already contaminating ground water and the Baltic Sea. By 1992 a joint Swedish, Finnish and Estonian team was looking into ways of safeguarding the wastes.

NARVA

Estonia's easternmost town, Narva, lies on the Tallinn-St Petersburg road and railway, 210 km from Tallinn and 140 km from St Petersburg. Only the Narva River separates Narva from Ivangorod (Estonian: Jaanilinn) in Russia. Whether you'll break your journey to take a look at Narva depends on your interest in its history and its unusual present-day status as the centre of an enclave of Russians: the town's 84,000 people are almost entirely Russian-speakers. With an industrial base that has particularly suffered from Estonia's economic problems, Narva has some of the highest unemployment in the country and is a centre of Russian political discontent. Over 90% of the population was not eligible for automatic Estonian citizenship after independence and, initially at least, few bothered to apply for it. Occasional political strikes occurred, and talk of a 'special status' – even secession for Narva –

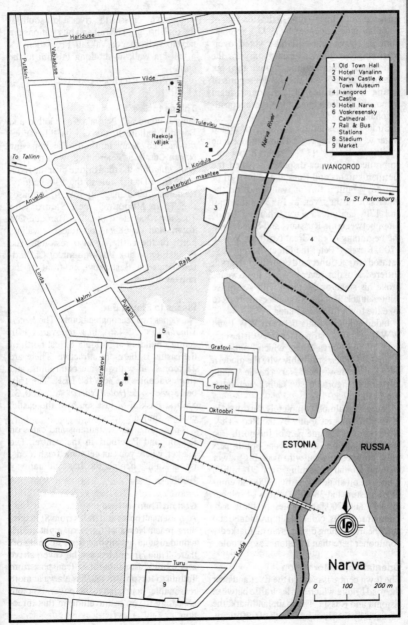

1 Old Town Hall
2 Hotell Vanalinn
3 Narva Castle &
  Town Museum
4 Ivangorod
  Castle
5 Hotell Narva
6 Voskresensky
  Cathedral
7 Rail & Bus
  Stations
8 Stadium
9 Market

Hariduse
Puškini
Vabaduse
Vilde
Mahmastäl
Tuleviku
Raekoja
väljak
Koidula
To Tallinn
Peterburi maantee
IVANGOROD
Anveldi
To St Petersburg
Narva River
Linda
Malmi
Raja
Puškini
Bastrakov
Grafovi
Tombi
Oktoobri
ESTONIA
RUSSIA
Turu
Kalda
Narva
0   100   200 m

ESTONIA

surfaced from time to time in the first year of Estonian independence. In 1993 a referendum in Narva and Sillamäe voted overwhelmingly in favour of autonomy for the two towns within Estonia, though turn-out was only 50-60% and there were reports of voting irregularities. The Estonian legal authorities had declared the vote unconstitutional.

Strategically sited on a system of inland waterways, Narva was a Hanseatic League trading point by 1171. Later it became embroiled in border disputes between the German knights and Russia, and Ivan III of Muscovy built a fort at Ivangorod, on the other side of the river, in 1492. In the 16th and 17th centuries, Narva changed hands often between the Russians and Swedes. At the beginning of the Great Northern War in 1700, Russia's Peter the Great, having devastated the countryside around Narva, suffered a major reverse when the Swedes broke his siege of the town with a surprise winter attack. But the Russians came back to take the town four years later.

Independent Estonia between WW I and WW II included a strip of territory on the east bank of the Narva River which contained Ivangorod. This is probably why the modern 5 EEK note shows both Narva castle (on the left) and Ivangorod castle facing each other across the river.

Narva was almost completely destroyed in 1944 during its recapture by the Red Army. Afterwards it became part of the north-east Estonian industrial zone and one of Europe's most polluted towns, with four big power stations around it burning over 20 million tonnes of oil shale a year by 1990 and emitting an estimated 380,000 tonnes of sulphur dioxide and 200,000 tonnes of toxic ash. Premature births, child health problems, and adult heart and lung diseases are all markedly commoner here than in Estonia as a whole.

Orientation & Information
The town centre is close to the river and near the road bridge which carries traffic between Estonia and Russia. The main landmark, the castle, is by the river, just south of the bridge.

The railway crosses the river a km south of the road bridge. The rail and bus stations are next to each other on Vaksali. From them it's a half-km walk north along Puškini to the castle.

The Narva telephone code is 235.

Things to See
Only a couple of Narva's fine Gothic and Baroque buildings survived its 'liberation' by the Red Army in 1944. The imposing **Narva Castle** at Peterburi 2, with its stout walls guarding the road bridge over the river, dates from Danish rule in the 13th century. Restored after damage in WW II, it houses the **Town Museum**, open Saturday to Tuesday 10 am to 6 pm. The Baroque **Old Town Hall** (1668-71) on Raekoja väljak, north of the castle, is also restored. The Russian Orthodox **Voskresensky Cathedral** stands on Bastrakovi, in front of the railway station.

Places to Stay & Eat
Narva has two reasonable hotels. The *Hotell Vanalinn* (☎ 22 486), in a renovated 17th century building at Koidula 6, just north of the castle, is the more attractive. There are 28 rooms, all with private bathrooms, and singles/doubles are 360/480 EEK. The 160-bed Soviet-style *Hotell Narva* (☎ 22 700, 31 552) at Puškini 6, just south of the castle, charges similar prices.

There are a few restaurants and cafés on Puškini and Peterburi in the centre. The market, where you can get some fresh foods, is on Kalda, behind the bus and railway stations.

Getting There & Away
At present all buses and trains from St Petersburg reach Narva at times of night which would discourage anyone from stopping off there. Trains from Moscow, however, arrive at a more reasonable time. Transport from Tallinn to Russia also reaches Narva at more reasonable hours, so a stopover is more appealing if you're travelling in that direction.

Top: Folk dancers, Rocca al Mare, Tallinn, Estonia (SK)
Bottom: Birch wood at Pirita, Tallinn, Estonia (SK)

Top: Town Hall, Tartu, Estonia (JN)
Bottom: 17th & 19th century houses, Pärnu, Estonia (JN)

Bus There are five daily buses each way between Tallinn and Narva, passing through Rakvere. They take four hours and cost 15.30 EEK one way. The overnight Tallinn-St Petersburg (and vice versa) bus goes through Narva about 1.30 am. There are two or three buses daily to/from Tartu, taking 3½ to 4½ hours for 12.90 EEK.

Train Six trains daily run from Tallinn to Narva and vice versa, taking 3¼ to 4½ hours, and all stop at Rakvere on the way. From Tallinn, the only train that reaches Narva with much daylight left is the first of the day, the 7.30 am, which arrives at 11.45 am. All the others leave Tallinn after 3 pm. Two go on to St Petersburg (4½ hours from Narva) and two to Moscow (11 hours), all leaving Narva in the night. The two nightly trains from St Petersburg to Tallinn also reach Narva during the night, while the two nightly trains from Moscow reach Narva about 6 and 8 am. The one-way Tallinn-Narva fare in general seating is about 12 EEK, at the time of writing, but is only likely to be available on the first two daily trains out of Tallinn and the last two from Narva; the other trains are all going to/from St Petersburg and Moscow, usually with sleeping accommodation only, which costs between about 15% and 150% more depending on class.

Car & Motorbike A Finnish-run Neste petrol station is due to open on the Tallinn road at Tallinna maantee 55A.

LAKE PEIPUS (NORTH)
The 1892 Russian Orthodox Pühtitsa Convent at **Kuremäe**, just over 20 km south-east of Jõhvi, draws some visitors. On holy days thousands of Russian Orthodox believers converge here.

There's a sandy beach along much of the northern shore of Lake Peipus, at its best at **Kauksi**, where the Narva-Jõhvi-Tartu road reaches the lake. At **Vasknarva**, where the Narva River flows out of the north-east corner of the lake, are ruins of a Teutonic Order castle. At **Lohusuu**, on the lake 12 km west of Kauksi, a Russian fishing community has lived in harmony with Estonians for centuries. The Tartu road diverges from the sometimes desolate lake shore after passing a string of villages south of **Mustvee**. For information on the southern part of Lake Peipus see the South-East Estonia chapter.

Places to Stay
There's a *Tent-Camping Site* (Telklaager) (☎ 233-93 840) at Kauksi and another (☎ 233-93 163) at Uusküla, six km east along the lake shore, and a *Kämping* (☎ 233-93 708) with wooden cabins at Uusküla. At Mustvee is a basic hotel, the *Mustvee Võõrastemaja* (☎ 237-24 276), on the Tartu road at Tartu maantee 58.

PAIDE
Paide lies on the main road between north-east and south-west Estonia, four km west of where that road crosses the Tallinn-Tartu road. Paide dates from 1260 when the German knights founded a fortress, whose main tower, Pikk Hermann, has recently been restored. The town centre has many 19th century classical-style buildings. The local museum is at Lembitu 5. There's a small (12 beds), basic hotel, the *Paide Võõrastemaja* (☎ 238-21 227), at Telliskivi 8. Several buses a day run to/from Tallinn and Tartu.

NEAR PAIDE
Vetepere (Vargamäe)
In a marshy area 30 km north of Paide, about 12 km west off the Paide-Tapa road, is the village of Vetepere, immortalised under the name Vargamäe in Anton Hansen Tammsaare's five-volume *Tõde ja Õigus* (Truth and Justice) which is generally acknowledged as the greatest Estonian novel. The people on whom its characters are based are now buried in the churchyard but many of the buildings and scenes are the same. There's a Tammsaare House Museum too. Tammsaare and Vargamäe both appear on the 25 EEK note.

ESTONIA

Endla Nature Reserve

The Endla Nature Reserve (Endla Looduskaitseala), covering a boggy area whose inhabitants include beavers, begins south of Koeru, about 25 km east of Paide, and extends nearly 20 km east to include the lake Endla järv and the five-metre-deep spring (Estonia's deepest) from which the Oostungu River flows. Nature trails lead to a couple of the more interesting spots.

South-East Estonia

The focus of south-east Estonia is the amiable, historic university town of Tartu, Estonia's second city. Beyond Tartu is an attractive region of gentle hills and lakes which includes the highest point in the Baltic states and some of Estonia's prettiest countryside. Some areas are accessible by bus or train but your own bike or car is the ideal means of exploring this rural region.

TALLINN TO TARTU

Paide (see the North-East Estonia chapter) is just off the Tallinn-Tartu road. Drivers could consider breaking the Tallinn-Tartu trip at **Adavere**, 70 km before Tartu, where the Finest group, which runs Tallinn's Hotell Palace and Tartu's Taru Hotell, has converted a windmill into the *Adavere Tuulik* restaurant (☎ 237-57 311), with some Estonian specialities on the menu – open daily from 7 am to midnight.

Ten km nearer Tartu, at Jõe 1 in Põltsamaa, is the basic 20-bed *Põltsamaa Võõrastemaja* (☎ 237-51 460).

TARTU

Tartu, 190 km south-east of Tallinn, is an enjoyable place. Its history, its fine classical architecture, the large number of students in its 115,000 population, and its active cultural life make for plenty to see and do, yet it's small enough to maintain a relaxed atmosphere. A number of parks in the hilly city centre, and the river Emajõgi flowing through Tartu on its way from Võrtsjärv to Lake Peipus, lend the place a pleasantly spacious feel.

Tartu was the cradle of Estonia's 19th century national revival and is the site of the country's original and premier university. It's still regarded as Estonia's spiritual capital, and a measure of its importance is that All-Estonia Song festivals often begin here. A big event in the local calendar, revived in 1993 after a four-year gap, is the Tartu ski marathon, a 60-km cross-country

trek from Otepää made by hundreds of skiers in mid-February.

History

There was an early Estonian stronghold on Toomemägi hill around the 6th century AD. In 1030 Yaroslav the Wise of Kiev, ruler of the Russian ancestor-state Kievan Rus, is said to have defeated the Estonians and founded a fort here called Yuriev. The Estonians regained control, but in 1224 were defeated by the Knights of the Sword who placed a castle, cathedral and bishop on Toomemägi. The town that grew up between the hill and the Emajõgi became a successful member of the Hanseatic League. It was known as Dorpat until the end of the 19th century.

In the 16th and 17th centuries Dorpat suffered repeated attacks and changes of ownership as Russia, Sweden and Poland-Lithuania all vied for control of the Baltic region – though the period of Swedish

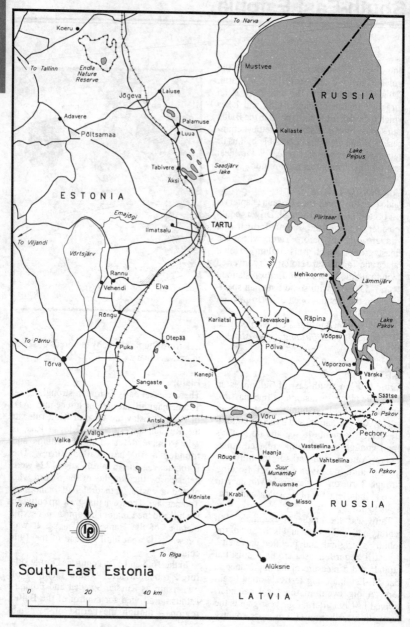

South-East Estonia

0   20   40 km

control, 1625-1704, was one of peace and it was then that the university (on which the city's importance and place in Estonian history is based) was founded. In 1704 during the Great Northern War, Peter the Great took Tartu for Russia. In 1708 his forces wrecked it and most of its population was deported to Russia. The town stayed under Russian control for over two centuries. Central Tartu's predominantly classical architecture stems from a comprehensive rebuilding after a fire engulfed it in 1775.

In the 19th century, Tartu – and especially the university – became the focus of the Estonian national revival. The first Estonian Song Festival, held in Tartu in 1869 to show that Estonian songs and singers could match their German counterparts, was an important step in raising Estonian national conscious-ness, as were the launching of an Estonian-language newspaper and the founding of the first Estonian societies, also in Tartu.

The peace treaty between Soviet Russia and Estonia by which the Russians acknowl-edged Estonian independence was signed in Tartu on 2 February 1920. During WW II Tartu was severely damaged both when Soviet forces retreated in 1941 – blowing up the 1784 Kivisild stone bridge over the river – and in 1944 when they retook it from the Nazis. Both the Nazi occupiers and the Soviet regime committed many atrocities, with thousands dying. The Nazis massacred 12,000 people at Lemmatsi on the Valga road, where there's now a monument.

In the Soviet period Westerners were not allowed to stay overnight at Tartu because of the supposed security risk to a military air base near the town – a ban which hampered, among other things, the development of the university. Since 1951 Tartu has also housed the Estonian Agricultural University, and it's home to several scientific-research insti-tutes, giving a total student population of over 10,000.

Orientation
The focus of Tartu is Toomemägi hill and the area of older buildings between it and the river Emajõgi. At the heart of this older area is Raekoja plats (Town Hall Square), with a footbridge over the river at its east end. The bus station is half a km south of Raekoja plats, at Turu 2 beside the main road bridge. The rail station is 750 metres west of Toomemägi at Vaksali 6.

Information
Money Places you can change cash include the bus station and the bank at Munga 18 on the corner of Vabaduse puiestee.

Post & Telecommunications The post office is on Rüütli just north of Munga, and the central telephone and telegraph office is at Lai 29 on the corner of Rüütli.

Tartu's telephone code is 234.

Travel Agencies Travel agencies that should be able to fix a tour or book transport or accommodation for you, if you can't do it yourself, include E-Tour (☎ 32 123, fax 77 766) of Kalevi 59, 600 metres south of Riia, Teele (☎ 31 517, fax 34 564) at Lai 35, and Pro Studiorum (☎ 61 853, fax 31 481), at the Hotell PRO.

Film & Photography The photo shop on the corner of Rüütli and Küütri, a block north of Raekoja plats, sells Kodak, Fuji and Agfa print film, Fuji and Agfa slide film, and a good range of batteries. It will also do four passport photos in one minute for 45 EEK. There's also a Fuji shop at Tiigi 6.

Shopping There's a supermarket on Küüni two blocks south of Raekoja plats, a flea market across Soola from the bus station, and a department store (kaubamaja) half a block up the hill from the bus station on Riia. Other shops are dotted round the central area.

Raekoja Plats & Around
Raekoja Plats The centre of the lower part of the town, between Toomemägi and the river, is Raekoja plats (Town Hall Square). Many of Tartu's shops, restaurants and offices are on or near the square. The older streets are to its north, while the area to its

south has been redeveloped since 1944, when it was flattened by Soviet bombardment. The square was rebuilt after a fire in 1775; its dominant feature is the finely proportioned **Town Hall** (1782-89), topped by a tower and weather vane, which its German architect, J H B Walter, based on the design of Dutch town halls. The buildings at Raekoja plats Nos 6, 8, 12 and 16 are also neoclassical, but No 2, one of the first to be built after the 1775 fire, is in an earlier style – late Baroque.

University The impressive main building of Tartu University (Tartu Ülikool) a block from the town hall at Ülikooli 18, with its six Corinthian columns, dates from 1803-09. The university's departments, student residences and other buildings are scattered around the town. For more information visit the Students' Union (Üliopilaskonna Edustus) on the top floor of Ülikooli 20 – open 11 am to 3 pm Monday to Friday – or contact the university's information service (☎ 35 421) or public relations office (☎ 31 968).

The university was founded in 1632 by the Swedish king, Gustaf II Adolf (Gustavus Adolphus), to train Protestant clergy and government officials. It was modelled on Uppsala University. A restored statue of Gustaf Adolf, unveiled by Carl XVI Gustaf of Sweden on his 1992 visit to Estonia, stands at the rear of the main university building. The university closed about 1700 because of the Great Northern War but reopened in 1802, developing into one of the Russian empire's foremost seats of learning, with an emphasis on science – which continues today. Those who worked here in the 19th century included physical-chemistry pioneer W Ostwald, physicists H F E Lenz and M H Jacobi, and natural historian Karl Ernst von Baer who, like the main building on Ülikooli, appears on the 2 EEK note.

The university's teaching language was originally Latin, then German for most of the 19th century, and then Russian until 1920, but that didn't stop it becoming the cradle of the Estonian national revival in the 19th

century. Developments since 1991 have included the re-opening of the theology faculty, the opening of a new classical and romance-languages department and a social-sciences school, and the launch of degree courses in Scandinavian languages. In 1992 over 60% of the university's students were women.

Other Sights North of the university on Jaani (the continuation of Ülikooli), the Gothic brick **Jaani Kirik** (St John's Church), founded in 1330 but ruined by Soviet bombing in 1944, is being restored. It has rare terracotta sculptures in niches around the main portal.

The nearby **botanic gardens** (Botaanikaaed) at Lai 40, open daily from 9 or 10 am to 4.30 or 5 pm, May to September, are worth a look. They include an impressively tall glass palmhouse.

Toomemägi
Toomemägi (Cathedral Hill), rising behind the town hall, was the original reason for Tartu's existence, having functioned on and off as a stronghold since the 5th or 6th century. It's the site of several important university buildings and a pleasant tree-shaded park created when the university revived in the 19th century. The approach to the hill from Raekoja plats is up Lossi, at the foot of which stands a **statue of Nikolai Pirogov** (a Tartu University graduate who pioneered field anaesthesia in the 19th century) and the university's new humanities building. Lossi passes beneath the 1836-38 **Angel's Bridge** (Inglisild) with its Latin inscription 'Otium reficit vires' ('Rest restores strength').

Toomemägi's most imposing structure is the ruined brick Gothic **cathedral** (Toomkirik) on the top. Originally built by the German knights in the 13th century, it was rebuilt in the 15th century, despoiled during the Reformation in 1525, used for a while as a barn, and partly rebuilt in 1804-07 when the university library was installed in the choir at its east end. The library has now moved to modern premises in the town and its place is taken by the **Museum of University History**, open from 11 am to 5 pm Wednesday to Sunday.

North of the cathedral, on the top of the hill, are a couple of small 17th century Swedish cannon and a **sacrificial stone** of the ancient Estonians, standing by a small bridge in front of a rocky mound thought to have been part of a defensive bastion but now known as **Musumägi** (Hill of Kisses). Nowadays students burn notes and drafts on the sacrificial stone after exams. Also on this top part of the hill are **monuments** to the Estonian poet Kristjan Jaak Peterson and the Baltic-German natural scientist Karl Ernst von Baer, both of whom studied at Tartu University in the 19th century; and to Johann Karl Simon Morgenstern, founder of the university library.

On the eastern part of the hill and dating from the early 19th century are the **observatory** (now also an astronomy museum open daily except Tuesday) on the old castle site (a sculpture commemorates the 19th century astronomer Georg Struve) and the still functioning semi-circular **Old Anatomical Theatre**. The 1913 **Devil's Bridge** (Kuradisild) crosses the road on the south side of the hill, around which the street Vallikraavi follows the line of the old castle moat.

Other Sights

The **Estonian National Museum** (Eesti Rahva Muuseum), at Veski 32 just west of the hill Toomemägi, is open Wednesday to Sunday from 11 am to 6 pm. Since its former home, the Raadi Manor in the north of Tartu, was destroyed in WW II, it has lacked proper space to show its full 850,000-piece collection which ranges from ancient farm tools to modern national costume. A fund-raising campaign is under way to pay for a new purpose-built home for the museum. In the meantime the limited displays on view at any one time are well worth a visit if you're interested in the history, life and traditions of the Estonian people.

The **Estonian Agriculture Museum**

(Eesti Põllumajandusmuuseum), with a machinery collection that includes some of Europe's oldest steam tractors, alongside historical displays on dairy farming, grain growing and animal breeding, is in the village of Ülenurme, six km south of the town centre, just off the Võru road. The airport bus No 12, about hourly from the bus station, goes through Ülenurme; times are posted in the bus station.

Tartu has more than its fair share of other museums. There's a **City Museum** (Linnamuuseum) telling Tartu's history at Oru 2, open daily from 11 am to 6 pm except Tuesday. The **Estonian Sports Museum**, open Wednesday to Sunday 11 am to 6 pm, is at Riia 27A and there's an **Art Museum** at Vallikraavi 14, open daily from 11 am to 6 pm except Monday. The home of Karl Ernst von Baer at Veski 4 is now the **K E von Baer House Museum**, open Monday to Friday from 9 am to 5 pm. On the literary side, there's the **Kreutzwald Literature Museum** (Kreutzwaldi Kirjandusmuuseum) at Vanemuise 42, open Monday to Friday from 8 am to 5 pm, and the **Oskar Luts House Museum** at Riia 38, open various hours daily except Tuesday. Kreutzwald and Luts are also honoured by **statues** in the riverside park north of Raekoja plats.

In 1990 a monument of a **Weeping Cornflower** was put up in front of the former KGB headquarters on Riia, almost opposite the main building of the **Estonian Agricultural University** (Eesti Põllumajandus Ülikool or just PU) to commemorate Estonian deportation and repression victims. (The blue cornflower is Estonia's national flower.)

Another monument worth a look at is found in a small park on Kalevi almost opposite the end of Vallikraavi. It commemorates **Barclay de Tolly**, an exiled Scot who settled in Livonia and distinguished himself in the Russian army's 1812 campaign against Napoleon.

The large modern **University Library** is on Struve between Tiigi and Vanemuise. The Song Festival grounds, also a site for 23 June bonfires, are in **Tähtvere-Park** at the north end of Tähtvere, two km north of the centre.

ESTONIA

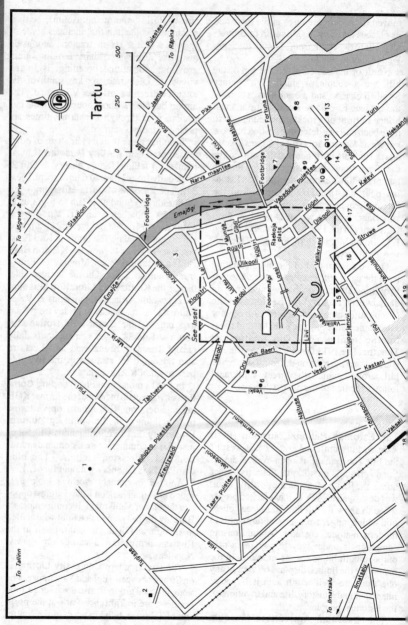

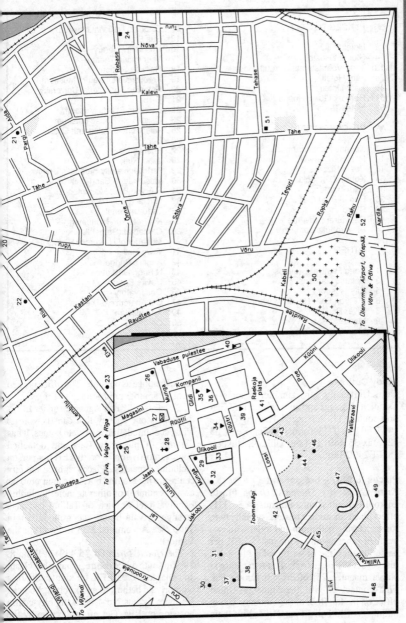

ESTONIA

■   PLACES TO STAY

2   Hotell PRO
4   Student Hostel
13   Tartu Võõrastemaja / Youth Hostel
24   Taru Hotell
48   Park-Hotell
51   Remark Guest House
52   Hotell Tarim

▼   PLACES TO EAT

7   Kaunas Restaurant
14   Restoran Tarvas
15   Peetri Pizza
34   Kohvik Dietsöökla
35   Gildi Trahter
36   Humal Beer Cellar
39   Bistro
40   Restaurant Taverna
44   Püssirohukelder

OTHER

1   Song Festival Grounds
3   Botanic Gardens
5   City Museum
6   K E von Baer House Museum
8   River Port
9   Market
10   Main City Bus Stop

11   Estonian National Museum
12   Bus Station
16   University Library
17   Vanemuine Theatre
18   Railway Station
19   Kreutzwald Literature Museum
20   Estonian Agricultural University
21   E-Tour
22   Estonian Sports Museum
23   Oskar Luts House Museum
25   Telephone & Telegraph Office
26   Bank
27   Post Office
28   Jaani Kirik
29   Tartu University Student's Union
30   Musumägi & Sacrificial Stone
31   K E von Baer Monument
32   Gustaf II Adolf Statue
33   Tartu University
37   K J Peterson Monument
38   Cathedral (Ruins) &
      Museum of University History
41   Town Hall
42   Angel's Bridge
43   N Pirogov Statue
45   Devil's Bridge
46   Observatory
47   Old Anatomical Theatre
49   Art Museum
50   Cemetery

Study Courses

Tartu University runs summer schools in Estonian language and culture – for information contact TU Advanced Training Centre (☎ 70 502) or TU Information Service (☎ 35 421, fax 35 440) at Tartu Ülikool, Ülikooli 18, EE2400 Tartu.

Places to Stay – bottom end

Tartu University Students' Union (Tartu Ülikool Üliopilaskonna Edustus, ☎ 35 331) offers places in student hostels – usually twin rooms sharing bathroom and toilet with two or three other rooms – for just 5 EEK per person at the time of writing. One hostel is just across the river from the town centre at Narva maantee 25; others are further out. First contact or visit the Students' Union office on the top floor of the Students' Union building at Ülikooli 20 – and try to give them

as much notice as possible. The office is open from 11 am to 3 pm Monday to Friday.

E-Tour (see Travel Agencies under Information) is one agency that can fix you up with accommodation in private homes. It has a range of places in flats and detached houses, mostly for 70 or 80 EEK per person including breakfast. Places right in the city centre are hard to find but some aren't too far away. A number of other agencies including Family Hotel Service of Tallinn can also arrange private-home accommodation in Tartu (see Accommodation in Facts for the Visitor).

The *Hotell Tarim* (☎ 75 433) at Rahu 8, 2½ km south of the centre, is basic but clean, and charges 70/95 EEK for singles/doubles with private bathroom and kitchen. You can get there by bus No 4 from the city-centre bus stop on Riia. Get off at the stop by the cemetery gates on Võru, just after you cross a railway, and walk a little further south to Rahu, which turns east off Võru; the hotel is part of a five-storey block on the south side of Rahu.

Tartu Youth Hostel (☎ 33 041) is actually part of the Tartu Võõrastemaja (see Places to Stay – middle). There's a slight reduction on regular room rates, with singles at 100 EEK.

Places to Stay – middle

The cheapest though least inviting place in this range is the *Tartu Võõrastemaja* (Tartu Inn, ☎ 32 091), a drab Soviet-era place next to the bus station at Soola 3. Singles are 140 EEK, doubles 180 to 240 EEK. Most rooms have to share bathrooms with others.

If your budget will go higher, there are three much better places. Best value among them are the two 280 EEK rooms (the price is the same for single or double occupancy) in the *Park-Hotell* (☎ 33 663) at Vallikraavi 23. This pair of large, comfortable, very well-kept rooms with TVs, share a bathroom. Rooms with their own bathrooms in this small, pleasant, central hotel are from around 400 EEK to 700 EEK. There's a bar and a good café-restaurant, with breakfast included in the room prices.

The *Hotell PRO* (☎ 61 853, fax 31 481), sometimes called the Pro Studiorum, is just as good, but less handily located at Tuglase 13, two km north of the centre. It's a recently converted section of an apartment block, with 13 clean, modern, reasonably sized rooms at 350/490 EEK a single/double, plus three two-room flats for four people at 720 EEK. Rooms have radios but no TV; there's a good restaurant in the basement, and breakfast is included in the price. To reach the hotel by bus, take No 5 from Vabaduse puiestee a few steps north of Raekoja plats, to the first stop on Tuglase – the hotel is then a two minute walk ahead, on the right.

The *Remark* guesthouse (☎ 77 720), just over two km south of the centre at Tähe 94, has only three rooms – a single for 480 EEK, a double for 640 EEK and a double suite for 800 EEK, but it's very comfortable with private bathrooms and breakfast included.

The Remark is a single-storey white building on the corner of Tähe and Tehase, 1¾ km south of Rīga – bus No 9 from the city centre stop on Riia goes there.

The *Motell Tare* (☎ 99 145), beside a reservoir at Ilmatsalu, 10 km west of Tartu, has three double rooms at 175 EEK including breakfast.

Places to Stay – top end

The *Taru Hotell* (☎ 73 700, fax 74 095) is inauspiciously located on the edge of a housing estate at Rebase 9, 1½ km south of the centre, but it's the top hotel in town, built in 1989 and operated by the Finest group which runs Tallinn's Hotell Palace. It's aimed mainly at business people. Comfortable and modern (though not huge) rooms cost from 680/880 to 880/1080 EEK for singles/doubles depending on season. Breakfast is included. The hotel has a bar, restaurant and small shop. Rebase is west off Turu, 1¼ km south of the bus station. The hotel is a few metres along Rebase, on the south side. You can book in Finland through Arctia Hotel Partners (☎ 90-694 8022, fax 90-694 8471) of Iso-Roobertinkatu 23-25, 00120 Helsinki.

Places to Eat

Raekoja Plats & Around There's one of the *Bistro* fast-food chain on Rüütli half a block off Raekoja plats, with the same fare and prices as in Tallinn. *Restaurant Taverna* (☎ 31 222) at Raekoja plats 20 is a smart Italian restaurant – no jeans permitted in the evening – with some Estonian dishes on its menu as well as a good range of Italian food. It's open from noon to 6 pm and 6.30 pm to 1 am; main courses are 15 to 30 EEK, starters up to 25 EEK. The entrance is actually just off the square, towards its east end.

The *Tartu University Students' Union* at Ülikooli 20 has a ground-floor *söökla* (canteen), open Monday to Friday from 10 am to 5 pm, where you can get lunch for 5 EEK or so, and a quite good *kohvik* (café) one floor up, open from 11 am to 9 pm daily except Sunday.

The *Humal* beer cellar at Küütri 12, which

also serves hot food and hõõgvein, is popular with students and has plenty of women customers. It's open from 11 am to 3 pm and 4 to 10 pm. Enter through the door beneath the 'Õlletare' sign. The *Gildi Trahter*, a block further back at Gildi 7, serves plain but good, plentiful, and not-too-expensive food – open from noon to 5 pm and 7 pm to midnight. A block west of the Humal on Küütri is the *Kohvik Dietsöökla*, a rather gloomy semi-dietetic café with much of its fare based on dairy products. Soup, a main course, dessert and a drink will cost 6 to 9 EEK – open till 8 or 10 pm.

The *Püssirohukelder* (☎ 34 124) at Lossi 28 behind the Town Hall began life as a gunpowder store, dug out of the Toomemägi hillside for Russia's Catherine the Great in the 18th century. Now it's a cavernous restaurant with pretty average food and service, open from 2 to 7 pm and (except Sunday) 8 pm till midnight or 1 am. A variety show is staged on Wednesday, Friday and Saturday at 10 pm. There's also a busy *Baar*-cum-café here, open 9 am to 7 pm.

Elsewhere The ever-reliable *Peetri Pizza* has a branch at Tiigi 11, near the university library at the back of Toomemägi, open from 11 am to 11 pm daily. Pizzas are 10 to 13 EEK (1 or 2 EEK cheaper if you take away) and there's a 4 EEK help-yourself salad bar – but, as usual, if you're really hungry you'll need two pizzas.

All the better hotels have good restaurants or cafés, the most central being at the *Park-Hotell* which is café-style with lighter dishes, and not open in the evenings. Soup and a light, hot meal cost around 10 or 12 EEK. The reportedly good *Restaurant Fox* in the Hotell Taru includes some Estonian specialities as well as international fare on its menu – open from 1 to 6 pm and 7 to 11 pm. The basement *Baar* in the *Hotell PRO* is actually a reasonable little pine-panelled restaurant with main courses at 9 to 15 EEK – nothing spectacular but good portions and good service.

The *Restoran Tarvas* at Riia 2 on the corner of Turu, opposite the bus station, is reckoned to be another of the town's better restaurants. It's open from 1 to 6 pm and, except Sunday, 7 pm to midnight or 1 am.

The *market*, a source of fresh fruit, cheese and so on, is a block from the bus station on Vabaduse puiestee.

Entertainment

Look at the posters in the entrance of the main university building at Ülikooli 18 for what's on in the way of music and student theatre. There are usually one or two interesting things coming up. Students at both Tartu University and the Agricultural University put on regular discos which are advertised here too.

Tartu's Vanemuine Theatre, named after the ancient Estonian song-god, was the first Estonian-language theatre when founded in 1870. Today it's housed in a modern building at Vanemuise 6 and has a professional company performing various operas and musicals in repertory. Other events including concerts are also staged here. The theatre has a second, smaller hall higher up Vanemuise at No 45A near the corner of Kastani.

Getting There & Away

Most trains and buses to/from Tallinn take 2½ to 3½ hours: buses are more frequent but trains tend to be cheaper. Tartu is linked with several other places in south-east Estonia by bus or train or both (information is given under each particular destination). For most of the rest of Estonia, buses are the only public transport option.

At the time of writing there are no buses between Tartu and Latvia or Lithuania. Trains are the only option. But this situation may change if fuel supplies become more plentiful. Heading for Russia, there's a train and a bus to/from Pechory (Petseri), a train to/from Pskov (Pihkva) and Moscow, and a St Petersburg bus.

Air Flights between Tartu and Tallinn (and possibly other places in Estonia) were due to be started by a Tartu-based company, Ergon, after Estonian Air pulled out of the domestic flight scene.

Bus About 14 buses a day run to/from Tallinn, taking about three hours for 13 EEK. Tartu bus station has a left-luggage room (*pakihoid*) off the booking hall on the ground floor and an information (*teated*) desk upstairs. Other services to/from Tartu include:

Haapsalu
  one bus daily, 5¾ hours, 18.60 EEK
Kuressaare
  one bus daily, eight hours, 23.80 EEK
Narva
  two or three buses daily, 3½ to 4½ hours, 12.90 EEK
Pärnu
  seven to 10 buses daily, three to 4½ hours, 11 EEK
Pechory (Petseri)
  one bus daily, three hours, 7.70 EEK
Rakvere
  three buses daily, 2½ to three hours, 9.70 EEK
  two route taxis daily, two hours, 10 EEK
St Petersburg
  one overnight bus via Kallaste, 7¾ hours, 18 EEK
Viljandi
  nine buses daily, 1½ to two hours, 4.70 EEK
  two to four route-taxis daily, 2¼ hours, 6 EEK
Virtsu
  two buses daily, six hours, 19.60 EEK

Train There are seven or eight trains daily to/from Tallinn, taking 2½ to 3¾ hours; the 6.50 am, 4.25 and 5.50 pm trains from Tallinn and the 7.54 am, 3 and 9.15 pm from Tartu all take less than three hours. The fare in general seating is about 11 EEK one-way, but 15 EEK on the fast 5.50 pm from Tallinn and 3 pm from Tartu. General seating is not available on the 6.50 am, 4.25 or 10.50 pm from Tallinn or the 6, 7.54 am or 9.15 pm from Tartu, which are international sleepers costing 15% to 150% extra.

The Tallinn-Warsaw *Baltic Express* (Balti Ekspress) comes through Tartu in the early evening southbound and in mid-morning northbound. Its other stops include Rīga and Kaunas but not Vilnius.

The daily Tallinn-Rīga-Vilnius-Minsk *Seagull* (Kajakas) leaves Tartu at 9.40 am southbound and 9.15 pm northbound, taking five hours to/from Rīga, 11 hours to/from Vilnius and 14½ hours to/from Minsk. Another daily train to/from Rīga leaves Tartu at 2.23 am and Rīga at 11.40 pm, taking about six hours. All these trains stop at Valmiera, Cēsis, and Sigulda in Latvia's Gauja valley; further *Seagull* stops include Jelgava (Latvia) and Šiauliai (Lithuania).

There's one daily train to/from Moscow, leaving Tartu at 7.21 pm and Moscow at 1.17 pm and taking 18 hours. Stops in Russia include Pechory (Petseri), 2½ hours from Tartu), Pskov, Staraya Russa, and Tver. Two other daily trains used to run between Tartu and Pechory but they were stopped by the Russians in 1993.

River In Soviet days there was a cheap hydrofoil service to/from Pskov (Pihkva) daily except Sunday, via the river Emajõgi and lakes Peipus and Pskov, but at the time of writing the craft are beached at Tartu river port and the only river trips available are by private hire – try contacting a travel agent such as E-Tour.

Getting Around
To/From the Airport Bus No 12 runs between the airport and bus station 14 times daily between 6 am and 7.30 pm, a 25-minute trip costing 0.40 EEK. The airport is seven or eight km south of the city centre, a km or so west off the Võru road.

City Transport Most of what's interesting or useful in Tartu is within easy walking distance of Raekoja plats. The main exceptions are some of the hotels – buses to those are mentioned in Places to Stay. The central stop for city buses is opposite the market, between Riia and Vanemuise.

TARTU TO JÕGEVA
There are a number of places of interest on (and not far off) the road from Tartu to **Jõgeva** (population: 7000), 60 km north. This is an alternative road route between Tartu and Tallinn or Narva. Jõgeva, and **Tabivere** at the north end of **Saadjärv**, a six-km lake 20 km north of Tartu which is one of the beauty spots of the region, are also

ESTONIA

on the Tartu-Tallinn railway, with several trains daily.

A large rock at **Äksi** on the west side of Saadjärv is said to have been tossed there from several leagues away by the legendary Kalevipoeg, in a rock-throwing contest with his two brothers.

Fourteen km north of Saadjärv is a fine manorial park at **Luua**. In **Palamuse**, four km beyond Luua, is a handsome 13th century three-naved stone church. Also in Palamuse is the **Oskar Luts House Museum** which documents the life and work of author Oskar Luts who grew up here and wrote the *Kevade* (Spring), Estonia's most loved novel of youth. **Kuremaa**, eight km further north, has a lovely lake and sandy beach, and a classical manor house with a terraced park. Six km further north, at **Laiuse**, are the fairly scanty remains of a castle of the German knights, ruined in the Great Northern War. Laiuse is on the road from Jõgeva to Mustvee on Lake Peipus.

Places to Stay & Eat

The *Motell Kukulinna* (☎ 234-19 526), located in a manor dating back to 1299 at the south end of Saadjärv, has five doubles at 120 EEK and two triples at 150 EEK, plus a few places in summer 'cottages' at 25 EEK a person. Breakfast is available if ordered and for other meals there's the *Restaurant Kukulinna*, open Tuesday to Thursday from 5 to 11 pm, Friday and Saturday noon to 2 am, and Sunday noon to 11 am. Boats and a sailboard can be rented. The *Äksi Puhkemaja* (☎ 234-36 318) on the west side of Saadjärv has seven doubles for 30 EEK, and breakfast is available if ordered.

There's a windmill-restaurant at Tabivere. At Jõgeva is a small hotel, the *Jõgeva Võõrastemaja* (☎ 237-21 454) at Jaama 4.

LAKE PEIPUS (SOUTH)

Much of the southern half of the Lake Peipus coast is marshy, but there are quite a number of villages. Russian Old Believers, a persecuted sect of the Orthodox Church, took refuge in Kallaste, the main town, in the 18th

and 19th centuries and founded several of the coastal villages.

The island Piirisaar, due east of Tartu, marks the south end of Lake Peipus. It used to be a refuge for young men fleeing from conscription into tsarist armies. The lake south of Piirisaar, Lämmijärv, narrows to only two km wide at Mehikoorma, where it may be possible to find a boat to Piirisaar. Further south, opposite Räpina, the waters widen out into Lake Pskov (Pihkva järv), which is mostly surrounded by Russian territory. The northern half of Lake Peipus is covered in the North-East Estonia chapter.

OTEPÄÄ

The small hilltop town of Otepää, 44 km south of Tartu, is the centre of a pretty, rural area, part farmed, part forested, with many small hills and lakes. The district is popular among Estonians for country breaks, and is a good place to enjoy the Estonian countryside. You can set off in almost any direction from the town for a day out on foot or bike. There are places to stay both in the town and in the surrounding country. Otepää is also Estonia's winter sports centre. Most skiing is cross-country (the 60-km Tartu ski marathon begins at Otepää every February) but a ski jump looms out of the forest a km or two east of the town, and there's downhill skiing on the hills Kuutsemägi (10 km west) and Väike-Munamägi. Bring your own skis – there are very few to rent.

In one of the more unlikely events of post-Soviet history, in March 1992 Otepää signed a friendship and economic cooperation agreement with Grozny, capital of the breakaway Muslim republic of Chechnia in the Russian north Caucasus. The idea was for Estonia to have access to Chechnian oil while Chechnia would obtain food and consumer goods from Estonia. The Chechnian leader, Dzhokhar Dudaev, had been a long-time chief of the Soviet air base at Tartu.

Orientation & Information

The centre of town is the triangular main 'square', Lipuväljak, with the bus station just off its east corner. The post office, bank and main food shop are beside the bus station. The main road from Tartu enters Lipuväljak on its north corner. On Lipuvaljäk you'll find the classical-style town hall and at least three travel bureaus – Otepää Tourist Information (☎ 55 364) at No 9, Otepää Reisibüroo (☎ 54 060) at No 11, and Real Reisid (☎ 55 009 or 54 042) at No 5. All three bureaus can be reached by fax on 55 293.

Otepää is included in the Valga telephone area code: 242.

Church

Otepää's pretty little 17th century church is on a small hilltop across the fields about 400 metres north-east of the bus station. The first church on this site was built in 1224. There's some fine timberwork and a large 1863 organ inside. The choir sometimes gives public performances. It was in this church in 1884 that the Estonian Students' Society conse-crated its new blue, black and white flag – which went on to become the flag of inde-pendent Estonia. Facing the church's west door is a small mound with a monument to Estonia's dead of the 1918-20 independence war.

Linnamägi

The tree-covered hill south of the church is the Linnamägi (Castle Hill), a major strong-hold of the old Estonians in about the 10th to 12th centuries. There are traces of old forti-fications on top, and good views of the surrounding country. Archaeological finds indicate that the area around the hill was inhabited as early as the 6th century.

Pühajärv

The islets and indented shore of 3½ km-long Pühajärv (Holy Lake) on the south-west edge of Otepää provide some of the area's prettiest views. The lake is circled by tracks and walkable roads. Its northern tip is just over two km along the Kääriku road from Otepää centre. The lake has a mystical atmo-sphere that no doubt accounts for its name, and was blessed by the Dalai Lama when he came to Tartu in 1992 for a conference of small nationalities. The Dalai-Laama

külaskaigu mälestusmärk (Dalai Lama Visit Memorial) stands on the east side of the lake. Pühajärv, legend has it, was formed from the tears of a mother whose five sons had all died in war. Its islands are their burial mounds.

Places to Stay

There's a 30-bed youth hostel, the *AS Kabli Otepää Puhkebaas* (☎ 55 934, fax 244-40 230), open year-round at Kastolatsi tee 3, 1½ km from Otepää centre. The price is 60 EEK a night and there are showers and a sauna. From the traffic lights on Tartu maantee on the north side of Otepää, go 800 metres west down Palupera tee, then turn right on to Kastolatsi tee. The hostel is a cosy-looking low red-brick building on the left after half a km.

The *Hotell Otepää* (☎ 55 431), 1¼ km south-east of the centre, is actually a sports training centre known locally as the 'Pentagon' because of its architectural style and because it's partly built into a hillside. But anyone who fancies it can stay here in quite reasonable rooms with their own shower and toilet for 26/52 EEK a single/double. To find it go to the far (east) end of the bus station, turn right along Valga maantee, then turn first left and go 600 metres. A probably much costlier new hotel is being built on the approach road. I was told that holiday lodges *(puhkebaasid)* belonging to art and pedagogical institutes, a km or two along the road past the Pentagon, are also open to the public if they're not full.

Out at the northern tip of Pühajärv, two km from the town centre, the *Pühajärve Puhkekodu* (☎ 55 103) is a large, rather insti-tutional place with 180 beds at 29/58 EEK for singles/doubles. The rooms are fair enough, with private bathrooms, but the hot water was only turned on when groups were in residence. There's a *Tent-Camping Site* (Telkimiskoht) on the south-east side of Pühajärv. At Kääriku, beyond the south end of the lake and about 11 km from Otepää, is a *Tartu Ülikool Puhkebaas* (Tartu University Holiday Lodge) with accommodation for the public, and meals available if ordered.

1 Traffic Lights
2 Church
3 Town Hall
4 Real Reisid
5 Bus Station
6 Bank
7 Post Office
8 Food Shop
9 Hotel Under
  Construction
10 Hotell Otepää

To AS Kabli Otepää Puhkebaas
(Youth Hostel)

To Tartu

Kastolatsi tee

Hurda

Palupera tee

Piiri

Lille

Pärna

Pikk

Virulombi

Tartu maantee

Lipuväljak

Kopli

Pühajärve tee

Kääriku

Koolitare

Mäe

Valga maantee

To Võru

Võru

Linnamägi

Otepää

0   150   300 m

To Pühajärv, Mäha,
Kääriku, Sangaste &
Valga

To Tent-Camping Site

Sangaste Loss (Sangaste Castle) (☎ 242-91 335), about 15 km south-west of the south end of Pühajärv and about 25 km from Otepää, is one of the most unusual places to stay in the whole Baltics. This almost fairy-tale brick castle, erected in Tudor-cum-Gothic style between 1874 and 1881, is said to be modelled on Britain's Windsor Castle. Recently it has been opened up as a hotel at prices of 93 EEK a person in double, triple or four-person rooms (with breakfast included), or 15 EEK (breakfast not included) in bunk rooms holding five to eight people. All meals are available. The castle is surrounded by a park with some rare trees, and you can go horse or pony riding. For more information and bookings contact Real Reisid (see Otepää Information). At the time of writing there are buses from Otepää to Sangaste at 8 am and 3.30 pm. Note that Sangaste railway station on the Tartu-Valga line is actually at Tsirguliina, 12 km from Sangaste.

Another of the most inviting places in the district is the *Mäha Puhkebaas* (☎ 242-54 003) at Mäha, about five km west of central Otepää. This is a well-built, well-kept pine-panelled place with 30 places in rooms holding three to five people each. The price is a reasonable 100 EEK per person. Everybody has to share two showers and two toilets, but that's no hardship unless there's a crowd in. The puhkebaas is by a small lake where you can swim or boat. Breakfast is available and there's a bar. To reach it by car, fork right on to a dirt road soon after the Pühajärve Puhkekodu, then watch for the building and lake on the right (there's no sign) after about three km. The manager says there are three buses a day from Otepää along this road.

There's a *Kämping* by Pangodi järv, a pretty lake by the roadside just over halfway from Tartu to Otepää. The Estonian Tourist Board lists another *Kämping* at Annimatsi, near Mähe, and the 36-place *Kuutsemäe Pansion* (☎ 242-57 263) at Kuutsemägi.

Places to Eat

Seemingly the only sizeable restaurant in the area is the reasonable *Restoran Pühajärv*, opposite the Pühajärve Puhkekodu at the northern tip of Pühajärv. Main dishes are around 15 EEK. There are also a few bars where you can get snacks – one is in the basement of Lipuväljak 5 and another is at the *Mäha Puhkebaas*. Otherwise you can order meals where you're staying (if they're available) or cater for yourself.

Getting There & Away

Buses and route-taxis are Otepää's only public transport. To and from Tartu there are five or six direct buses and three or four route-taxis daily. Buses take 1 hour 10 minutes for 2.10 EEK, route-taxis 45 minutes for 3 EEK. Avoid other buses going by Elva or Kanepi unless you fancy a roundabout trip.

There's a daily Tallinn-Otepää and vice versa bus via Tartu taking 4½ hours for 17.40 EEK. Other places served by bus to/from Otepää include Kanepi twice or three times daily, Kääriku, Sangaste and Valga twice daily, Võru and Pärnu twice daily, and Põlva and Viljandi once daily.

ELVA & VÕRTSJÄRV

Elva, a small town in a hilly, forested landscape on the Tartu-Valga road, has a pretty lake, Artsi järv, in the middle of the town. About a dozen trains and a few buses daily go from Tartu to Elva.

The eastern shore of Võrtsjärv, Estonia's second biggest lake (nearly 40 km long), is 35 km west of Tartu but only 15 km west of Elva.

Places to Stay

The *Puhkebaas Vaikne* (☎ 234-56 582) in a pine forest two km from Elva has double, triple and four-person rooms with shared showers at 12 EEK a person for Estonians or 24 EEK for foreigners. There's room for 35 people in winter and 100 in summer, when outdoor cabins are used.

The reportedly good *Motell Vehendi* (☎ 234-54 556) is on the eastern shore of Võrtsjärv, due west of Elva and 43 km from Tartu. It's a converted old farmhouse, 600 metres from a swimming beach. There are six rooms at 75/120 EEK a single/double for Estonians but the EEK equivalent of US$25/40 for foreigners. Prices include breakfast and other meals are available if ordered. You can book through the Taru Hotell in Tartu.

You can rent rooms in a number of private homes in Rannu, a hamlet with a couple of pretty little lakes of its own on the Elva-Vehendi road six km before Võrtsjärv. Contact the *Võru Taluturismi Ühendus* (Võru Farm Tourism Association) ; see Võru – Places to Stay for information or bookings.

VALGA

The border town of Valga (population: 18,000), contiguous with Valka in Latvia (8000), is where the Rīga-Tartu road and the main railway from Rīga and the south enter Estonia. There's not very much to stop for. Though Valga dates from the 13th century, it's unusual in never having had a castle. The most eye-catching building is the Jaani kirik (St John's Church), built between 1787 and 1816, on Sepa tänav opposite the town hall (1865). The church has fine acoustics and is the setting for a youth choral festival each spring. There's a local museum (Valga Koduloomuuseum) at Pärnu puiestee 11. An estimated 30,000 people were murdered at the Nazi death camp Stalag-351, in converted stables at Priimetsa on Valga's outskirts. The railway station was built after the war by German prisoners.

The German traveller Johann Georg Kohl, commenting in the 1840s, evidently received a poor impression of Valga, which was then known by its German name Walk:

...the grass...grows so high in its streets that it is said the little cowherds sometimes cut it as fodder for their cattle. In Walk the Lettish dialect is still spoken, but just beyond it begins the territory of the Esthonians. The Lettes and Esthonians are two very different races, and they hate one another with all the bitter animosity of contiguous nations...The best Lettes inhabit the south, and the best Esthonians the north; the frontier country, it is said, contains the worst of both.

Places to Stay & Eat

The *Vallai* (☎ 242-40 975) at Kuperjanovi 76 has two to four-bed rooms at 59 EEK a person. There's also the *Säde Hotell* (☎ 242-41 650) at Jaama puiestee 1, with 40 beds and a restaurant.

Getting There & Away

Bus There was only one bus (daily except Sunday) running between Tartu and Valga, leaving Tartu at 9.30 am and Valga at 12.30 pm, and taking 1¾ hours for 5.40 EEK. There are two buses daily (evening and early morning) between Otepää and Valga via Sangaste.

Train Seven trains run daily each way between Tartu and Valga, most taking about two hours. Three in each direction are on the way between Tallinn and Rīga. Valga is also on the Rīga-Pskov-St Petersburg route (which diverges from the line to Tartu and Tallinn on the east edge of the town) with two trains daily in each direction. There are also two other daily trains each way just between Valga and Rīga (3¼ hours). The three daily local trains each way between Valga and

Võru (1¼ hours) no longer continue across the Russian border to/from Pechory but might start to do so again some day.

PÕLVA & TAEVASKOJA

Põlva (population: 7000) lies in an attractive valley 50 km south-east of Tartu. Its typical country church dates from 1452.

Taevaskoja, seven km north of Põlva, is in the picturesque valley of the Ahja river which is noted for rapids and sandstone cliffs up to 20 metres high. You can walk up the river to Kiidjärve, six km north of Taevaskoja, where there's a working water mill built in 1909.

At Karilatsi, 15 km north-west of Põlva on the Tartu road, is the **Põlva Museum of Peasant Life**.

The Põlva telephone code is 230.

Places to Stay & Eat

The *Hotell Pesa* (☎ 90 086, fax 90 087), centrally located in Põlva at Uus 5, is a 1991-built hotel with good service, good food in its own restaurant, and 24 singles/doubles with private bathroom and TV at 450/600 EEK from May to September, 375/525 EEK the rest of the year. Everything's stylishly pine-panelled though the rooms are on the tight side; double suites, twice as big, cost 880 EEK from May to September, 800 EEK at other times. All prices include breakfast. There's a cheaper, older little hotel, the *Põlva Võõrastemaja* (☎ 95 374) at Võru 12. The *Põlva Restoran* and *Hämariku Baar* at Kesk 10 provide other eating possibilities.

At Taevaskoja there's a youth hostel, the *Taevaskoja Puhkebaas* (☎ 22-447 274), with 20 beds, two to four to a room, at 50 EEK per person. It's a wooden building, with showers and a sauna, about half a km east along the road from Taevaskoja railway station. A reservation is necessary if you want to stay – either through the hostel's phone number or the Estonian Youth Hostels office in Tallinn. In the first year of operation this hostel was only open from 1 May to 15 September and 15 December to 1 January.

Getting There & Away

From Tartu you can reach Põlva by bus (six times daily, 1¼ hours, 3.70 EEK) or train (three daily, 3/4 to 1¼ hours). The 9.52 am and 5.35 pm trains from Tartu also stop at Taevaskoja shortly before Põlva, as do one morning and one afternoon train in the other direction. Taevaskoja is two km east of the Tartu-Põlva road, which is the nearest a bus would get you. There are three buses daily between Põlva and Võru, one between Põlva and Otepää and one between Põlva and Tallinn (4½ hours, 17 EEK).

VÕRU

Võru (population: 18,000), 64 km south of Tartu, is a rather ordinary small town, but it's a possible base for visiting some interesting points in Estonia's far south-east, such as Suur Munamägi or the German knights' castle at Vahtseliina.

Orientation

Võru stands on the eastern shore of Tamula järv. The main streets, both running roughly north-south and parallel to the lake, are Jüri and, lower down nearer the lake, Kreutzwaldi. The central square, on Jüri, is dominated by the Lutheran church. The bus station is half a km east of this square along Tartu. Kreutzwaldi crosses the Valga-Pechory (Petseri) railway 2½ km south of the centre; Võru station is a few hundred metres east of this crossing, along Jaama.

Information

You can change money at the Võru Tourist Centre (see Places to Stay). The leaflet *Haanjamaa kutsub* (Haanjamaa Calls), which may be available at the Võru Tourist Centre, has an insert detailing places of interest in the Võru region in several languages including English.

The Võru telephone code is 241.

Things to See & Do

Võru's main claim to fame is that it was the home of Friedrich Reinhold Kreutzwald (1803-82), regarded as the father of Estonian literature for his folk epic *Kalevipoeg*.

Kreutzwald was Võru's town doctor for most of his adult life. His home at Kreutzwaldi 31, an 18th century wooden building where he wrote *Kalevipoeg*, now houses the **Kreutzwald Memorial Museum** which includes displays on his work and career as well as rooms preserved in 19th century style. It's open Wednesday to Sunday from 11 am to 6 pm. There's a **monument to Kreutzwald** in the lakeside park at the foot of Tartu. Võru also has a **local history museum** (Võru Koduloomuuseum) at Kreutzwaldi 16. There's a 1793 Lutheran church on the central square on Jüri.

People staying at Võru Turismikeskus can rent bicycles or canoes to explore the area. Just north of the town on the bank of the Võhandu River are the ruins of the Kirumpää fortress, founded by the Germans in 1322. Verijärv, four km south-east of the town on the Vastseliina and Pskov road, is a fine, steep-sided lake.

Places to Stay & Eat

The *Võru Taluturismi Ühendus* (Võru Farm Tourism Association) (☎ 42 469, fax 22 928) at Lembitu 2 offers rooms in a half-dozen private homes in and around Võru from 1 May to 31 August for 135 to 225 EEK per person including breakfast. It has about another 30 places elsewhere in the far south-east, only a few of them farms and some of them open all year, for similar prices. The association is part of Eesti Kodu Turism (the Estonian Guest House Association) – see Private Homes under Accommodation in Facts for the Visitor.

The small, shabby *Hotell Võru* (☎ 21 226) is on Tartu just west of Jüri in the town centre, but more inviting is the *Võru Turismikeskus* (Võru Tourist Centre, ☎ 31 757, ☎ & fax 42 498), four km south of the town centre at Männiku 43. The tourist centre consists of a reasonably good Soviet-era hotel and some small wooden cabins in a summer 'camping' area, all in a pine wood near the small lake Kubija järv. There's a reasonable restaurant in the hotel basement. Though the hotel can't quite throw off that air of drabness and faint decay that seems

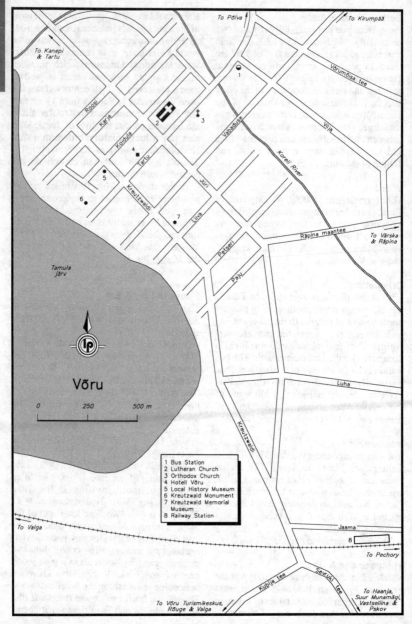

Võru

0   250   500 m

1 Bus Station
2 Lutheran Church
3 Orthodox Church
4 Hotell Võru
5 Local History Museum
6 Kreutzwald Monument
7 Kreutzwald Memorial
  Museum
8 Railway Station

To Põlva
To Kirumpää
To Kanepi & Tartu
Võrumõisa tee
Vilja
Koreli River
Vabaduse
Jüri
Liiva
Räpina maantee
To Värska & Räpina
Roosi
Karja
Koidula
Tartu
Kreutzwaldi
Patseri
Paju
Tamula järv
Luha
Kreutzwaldi
To Valga
Jaama
To Pechory
To Haanja, Suur Munamägi, Vastseliina & Pskov
Kubija tee
Sevuki tee
To Võru Turismikeskus, Rõuge & Valga

built into Soviet-era institutions, its rooms have private bathroom and balcony and are reasonably comfortable. Singles/doubles cost 265/300 EEK in June, July or August, 220/250 EEK in other months – unless you're Estonian, in which case you pay about one-third of those prices. The summer cabins, 18 EEK each, hold two to four people.

Võru Turismikeskus is not signposted from the town; to reach it, follow the main road south out of Võru, turn right immediately after crossing the railway line, then take the second left after about 750 metres. This is Männiku, and the centre is another 750 metres along on the left. Bus Nos 1 and 5 going south on Kreutzwaldi will take you to the Kubija stop on Männiku, which is almost outside the door.

Places to eat in the town include the *Pizzabaar Katariina* at Katariina 4, the *Restoran Võru* at Vabaduse 8, and the *Kohvik Wõro* at Jüri 11 which also sells handicrafts.

Getting There & Away
Bus There are five or six buses daily to/from Tartu via Kanepi, taking 1½ hours for 5 EEK, four to six daily to/from Tallinn (4½ hours, 18.10 EEK), three daily to/from Põlva, two to/from Otepää, and two to/from Pärnu (four to 4½ hours, 12.30 EEK).

Train Võru is about an hour from Valga by train, with five trains each way daily. Two trains in each direction stop on their way between Rīga (four hours from Võru) and St Petersburg (6½ hours). Other stops on this route include Valmiera, Cēsis and Sigulda in Latvia, and Pechory (Petseri) and Pskov in Russia – but all these trains go through Võru at unholy night-time hours. The local trains also used to run across the border to/from Pechory but this was stopped – perhaps temporarily – in April 1993 by Russian customs.

You can travel between Tartu and Võru by train in a minimum three hours, or between Tallinn and Võru in 5¾ hours or more, by changing at Valga on the way.

SUUR MUNAMÄGI
Suur Munamägi, 17 km south of Võru, is the highest hill in the Baltic states at 317 metres. It's part of the Haanja Upland lying between Võru and the Latvian border, which has three other hills over 290 metres. Suur Munamägi literally means Great Egg Hill, and indeed from a distance it looks not unlike the top of an eggshell. It's covered in trees, which makes it excusable that there's an ugly 29-metre observation tower plonked on its very summit.

Without the tower, which has stood here since 1939, you wouldn't be able to admire the long-distance views that the hill commands. It's said that in clear weather you can see the towers of Pskov in Russia, nearly 80 km to the east. Pechory monastery is a mere 40 km east. Unfortunately this hilly area has Estonia's wettest weather, with over 800 mm of rain a year.

The summit and tower are a 10-minute climb from the Võru-Ruusmäe road, starting about a km south of the village of Haanja. Near the start of the path is a monument to the dead of the Battle of Munamägi in Estonia's 1918-20 independence war. Like so many similar monuments, it was pulled down in the Soviet era but restored in 1988.

The observation tower has probably the most complicated opening hours of anywhere in all the Baltic states: from 5 May to 15 September it's open on Saturday and Sunday from 8 am to 9 pm, on Monday from 10 am to 1 pm and 2 to 7 pm, and on other days from 9 am to 8 pm; from 16 to 30 September it's closed on Monday but open every other day from 10 am to 1 pm and 2 to 6 pm; from 1 to 31 October it's open on Saturday and Sunday only, from 10 am to 1 pm and 2 to 6 pm; from 1 November to 4 May it's closed full stop. But don't despair if you want to visit on a closing day: 'closed' may mean open. The keeper lives 600 metres down the hill towards Haanja (a green sign near the foot of the path points down the road towards his home) and apparently he's usually willing, for a tip, to open the tower up if you don't come too late in the day – say if you arrive by 4 pm.

ESTONIA

Places to Stay

The *Võru Taluturismi Ühendus* (Võru Farm Tourism Association) offers rooms in several farmhouses and other homes within a few km of Haanja for 120 to 170 EEK per person including breakfast, from 1 May to 31 August. See Võru – Places to Stay for contact information.

Getting There & Away

There are a few buses a day from Võru to Haanja, just north of Suur Munamägi, or Ruusmäe.

RÕUGE

Ten km west of Suur Munamägi by dirt road, or reachable by paved road from Võru, the village of Rõuge stands on the edge of the Ööbikuorg (Nightingale Valley), which is strung with a chain of seven lakes. Suurjärv, near the village, is Estonia's deepest lake at 38 metres. Rõuge's Linnamägi (Castle Hill), by the lake Linnjärv, was an ancient Estonian stronghold in the 8th to 11th centuries. Nightingales gather near it in spring and there's a good view along the valley. Opposite Rõuge's simple village church, dating from 1730, there's a monument to the local dead of Estonia's 1918-20 independence war.

Places to Stay

The *Võru Taluturismi Ühendus* (Võru Farm Tourism Association) offers rooms in private homes in and near Rõuge for 120 to 175 EEK per person including breakfast, from 1 May to 31 August. See Võru – Places to Stay for contact information.

Getting There & Away

There are a few buses a day between Võru and Rõuge.

PAGANAMAA, MÕNISTE & ÄHIJÄRV

Along the Latvian border just south of the village of Krabi, which is some 20 km beyond Rõuge by paved road, Paganamaa (Devil's Land) is another scenic area with four lakes strung along the Estonian side of the border in the Piiriorg valley. There's an observation tower and bathing spot at Liivajärv, one of the lakes.

Mõniste, on the Võru-Valga road and 15 km west of Krabi, has an open-air village museum (Mõniste Külamuuseum), open from 10 May to 1 October except Monday, displaying 19th century country life.

About 12 km along dirt roads north of Mõniste is an area of rounded wooded hills dotted with many small lakes. The highlight is Ähijärv, a three-km-long lake with several bays, inlets and promontories. This area can also be reached from Antsla, a similar distance to its north.

VASTSELIINA CASTLE

The picturesque ruins of Vastseliina Castle (Vastseliina linnus), founded by the Germans on their border with Russia in the 14th century, stand on a high bluff above the Piusa River on the eastern edge of the village of Vahtseliina (pronounced: 'Vochtselina'), five km east of the small town of Vastseliina. All that's left of the castle is a couple of corner towers, a length of wall, a ditch, a rampart and a few other unexplained mounds, but on their dramatic perch in this remote corner of Estonia, these ruins are quite evocative. German, Russian and Swedish soldiers fought repeated battles over the centuries for control of this stronghold. If you visit at dusk you may leave half-expecting to come upon the encampment of some ghostly Teutonic host over every new rise in the landscape.

The castle stands behind a long, low 19th century inn building on the Meremäe road out of Vahtseliina. In the valley bottom, down to the left as you walk from the former inn to the castle, is the park of the old Vastseliina manor.

From the castle you can take a walk north up the Piusa valley, which has several sandstone cliffs. The valley from Vahtseliina to Tamme (10 km north as the crow flies but further if you follow the wiggles of the river) is a protected landscape reserve.

Vastseliina town has a big classical-style town hall in its centre.

Getting There & Away

To reach Vahtseliina turn east off the Võru-Pskov (Pihkva) road a km south of the southernmost turning to Vastseliina (which is just west of the road), and go two km. Several buses daily from Võru go to Vastseliina and some, including most of those to Misso, continue along the Pskov road to the Vahtseliina turning and beyond.

HINO JÄRV

Hino järv, two km south of Misso which is on the A212 Pskov-Rīga road, is one of southern Estonia's most picturesque lakes, with eight islands dotting its three-km length. There are a few buses from Võru to Misso. Near Hino järv is the Kõõgumägi stronghold, a fortification probably raised by the native tribes in the late 13th or early 14th century.

SETUMAA

Setumaa is the name of an area in far southeast Estonia, stretching over into Russia, whose people, the Setu, have a mixed Estonian-Russian culture and speak a dialect quite distinct from mainstream Estonian. Setumaa is particularly known for its women folk singers who improvise new words each time they chant their verses. All of Setumaa was in independent Estonia between 1920 and 1940 but the greater part of it is now in Russia. The town of **Pechory** (Estonian: Petseri), two km across the border in Russia and famous for its cave-monastery, is regarded as the 'capital' of Setumaa. Estonian Setumaa, roughly speaking, is the area east of a line extending north from

Vahtseliina to the small town of Võõpsu, just east of Räpina near Lake Pskov.

The town of **Värska** is known for its mineral water, drunk throughout Estonia, and its healing mud baths. **Võporzova** and **Tona** a few km north of Värska on the west side of Värska Bay, are classic Setu villages. In Võporzova there's a monument to the folk singer Anne Vabarna who knew 100,000 verses by heart. Võporzova homesteads typically consist of a ring of outer buildings around an inner yard – a formation which has defensive purposes – while Tona's houses all face the lake from which its people derive their livelihood. There's a Setu museum at **Säätse**, right in the corner of Estonia near the Russian border.

Getting There & Away

There are three buses a day each way between Tartu and Värska, taking two hours via Räpina. At the time of writing one of these, the 9 am from Tartu, goes on to Pechory, where it arrives at noon and waits two hours before making the return journey. You will probably need a Russian visa to visit Pechory. A daily Tallinn-Moscow train (and one vice versa) runs through Tartu, Põlva and Pechory; and two daily trains travelling in each direction between Rīga and St Petersburg run through Valga, Võru and Pechory – but all come through the area at night. Other trains from Tartu and Valga used to run to/from Pechory but were stopped (perhaps just temporarily) from crossing the Russian border by Russian customs in April 1993.

West Estonia & the Islands

West Estonia is, in many ways, the most intriguing part of provincial Estonia. The large islands Hiiumaa and, particularly, Saaremaa, with their windmills, juniper groves, old-fashioned rural pace and coastal vistas stretching gently away into infinity, are close to the Estonian idea of an earthly paradise. They're also historically interesting and claim to enjoy more sunshine than the mainland. Other islands and much of the mainland coast, including the historic town of Haapsalu and the Matsalu Nature Reserve, an important water bird sanctuary, are also rewarding to explore.

The whole region is extremely low-lying. In fact when the Baltic Sea was formed about 7000 years ago most of the region still lay beneath the waves. A bit of Saaremaa and a small part of the mainland existed as land but Hiiumaa was still sea-bed. Since then the region has been gradually rising from the sea – currently by about three mm a year – owing to a slow lifting of the earth's crust.

HAAPSALU

Haapsalu (population: 15,000) stands on a peninsula jutting out into Haapsalu Bay, a 15-km inlet in Estonia's west coast. It has been the dominant settlement in west Estonia since the 1260s, when it was chosen as the centre for the Ösel-Wiek (Estonian: Saare-Lääne) bishopric, through which the Archbishop of Rīga controlled most of west Estonia and its offshore islands.

Today Haapsalu, with a fine castle and cathedral to remind us of its powerful past, is a pleasant place to stop for a few hours or a night on your way to or from Hiiumaa. It's also a good base for visiting Vormsi island, Noarootsi, Matsalu Nature Reserve or other places in west Estonia.

History

Following the Knights of the Swords' conquest of this region in 1224, the Ösel-Wiek bishopric, covering west Estonia and its off-

shore islands, was formed in 1228. For over 300 years the bishops ruled the region, except for a few areas on the islands and one small mainland area which belonged to the knights under a 1238 deal with the bishop.

Haapsalu became the bishop's residence in the 1260s and a bishop's fortress and cathedral were built soon afterwards. The town around it developed with Germans as merchants and artisans, Estonians and Swedes as the lower classes. At the start of the Livonian War in 1559 the last bishop sold his territory to the Danish king Frederick II who in turn gave it to his brother Duke Magnus. During the war, which lasted till 1583, west Estonia lost two-thirds of its population. During the 17th century most of the region ended up in Swedish hands and some of the war damage was reversed.

At the beginning of the 18th century the region fell under Russian control during the Great Northern War. In the 19th century Haapsalu became a spa when the curative

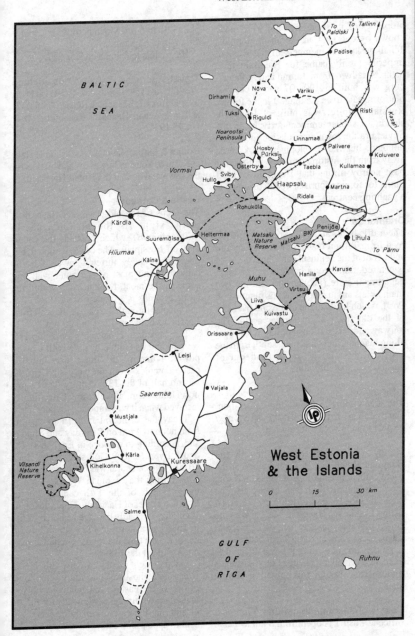

BALTIC

SEA

To
Paldiski

To Tallinn

Padise

Nõva

Variku

Dirhami

Risti

Tuksi

Riguldi

Kasari

Noarootsi
Peninsula

Linnamäe

Palivere

Koluvere

Hosby
Pürksi

Kullamaa

Österby

Taebla

Vormsi

Hullo

Sviby

Haapsalu

Martna

Ridala

Rohuküla

Matsalu
Nature
Reserve

Matsalu Bay

Penijõe

Kärdla

Heltermaa

Lihula

Suuremõisa

To Pärnu

Hiiumaa

Käina

Muhu

Hanila

Karuse

Liiva

Virtsu

Kuivastu

Orissaare

Leisi

Valjala

Saaremaa

Mustjala

Kärla

Vilsandi
Nature
Reserve

Kihelkonna

Kuressaare

West Estonia
& the Islands

0   15   30 km

Salme

GULF

OF

RIGA

Ruhnu

properties of its shoreline mud were made known by one Dr Carl Abraham Hunnius. Tchaikovsky and members of the Russian imperial family came for Haapsalu mud baths. A railway from Tallinn and St Petersburg was built in 1904-07 and a covered platform, said to be the longest in the former Russian empire, was built at Haapsalu station to shelter eminent arrivals. In the Soviet era the town's population more than doubled, but the development took place away from the historic centre. A military air base nearby meant that Haapsalu was off limits for foreign tourists. Today the town is a yachting centre.

Orientation

The traffic lights at the crossroads where the road from Tallinn reaches central Haapsalu, at the foot of the peninsula on which the town is centred, are a good landmark. The main department store (kaubamaja) and the two main hotels are just north of this junction on Posti, which leads to the castle and the heart of the old town a km further north. The railway and bus stations are half a km west along Jaama. Lihula maantee, south from the traffic lights, is the main road out of Haapsalu in that direction.

Information

The area's tourism promotion association, Haapsalu Turism (☎ 45 248) at Posti 34, may be able to help with information.

Money You can change money in the Haapsalu Hotell, the Pipi Pansionaat or the yacht club, or in a number of banks on Karja, the street leading south from Lossiplats. The banks include Haapsalu Hoiupank at Karja 4 facing Lossiplats; Haapsalu Maapank on the corner of Vaba, opposite the post office; and Lääne Eesti Pank at Karja 27 in between.

At the time of writing it's still difficult to exchange travellers' cheques on the islands themselves, though this situation should alter.

Post & Telecommunications The post office at Posti 1 is open from 8 am to 12.30

pm and 1 to 6 pm Monday to Friday, and 9 am to 4 pm on Saturday.

Haapsalu's telephone code is 247.

Travel Agencies Travel firms include Westra Travel (☎ 45 648, fax 45 191) at Posti 39, PO Box 67, Läänemaa Reisid (☎ 45 037) at Karja 2, and Haapsalu Reisibüroo (☎ & fax 45 193).

Books & Maps The main bookshop is Helk at Karja 6. You can buy maps and leaflets on the town and area at the Hotell Haapsalu.

Castle & Cathedral

The focus of the old town and Haapsalu's main 'sight' is the bishop's castle (piiskopilinnus), which contains the cathedral, off Lossiplats. The castle is ruined, but one picturesquely turreted tower plus the cathedral, and most of the outer wall and some of the moat, remain. Also within the castle grounds is a modern song stage. You can wander through the gate in the wall from Lossiplats between 7 am and 10 pm.

The cathedral, Haapsalu's most impressive building, is Gothic in style with a plain, powerful interior. Its integration into the castle complex from the very start (in the second half of the 13th century) shows just how lukewarm a welcome Christianity received when it was imported to these parts.

Today the cathedral is open to visitors from noon to 4 pm on Saturday and Sunday and, according to a notice in English on the door, 'Everi Sunday God service the clock 10 00'. The cathedral was badly damaged in 1563 during the Livonian War, restored in the first half of the 17th century by the Swedish owner of Haapsalu, Count Jakob de la Gardie, and badly damaged again by a fire in 1688 and a storm in 1726 which tore off its roof. This time the funds to repair it were not found till the 1880s.

On the night of the August full moon, Haapsalu's ghostly White Lady – the lover of one of the castle's inhabitants, who was walled up within the castle walls for the sin of entering the castle, a male preserve – is said to appear in a cathedral window.

Museum

The Haapsalu Museum at Kooli 2, in the former town hall at the east end of Lossiplats, built in 1775, is small but gives an informative glimpse of the town's and area's history from prehistoric times to the present. It's open from 11 am to 5 pm daily except Monday and Tuesday. There's some explanatory material in English.

Other Sights

The narrow, winding streets in the area round the castle are the hub of the old town, though there's nothing particularly special about them. On Neidude is a former courthouse built in 1787; the house at Saue 11 dates from 1782. Between Kooli and Jaani, east off Lossiplats, is the 16th century **Jaani kirik** (St John's Church).

On the shore north of here is a **park** with what's known as the **Aafrikarand** (Africa Beach) at its east end, the 1905 **Kuursaal** (Spa Hall) at its west end, and a **promenade** that once led as far north as the **yacht club**, one of Estonia's main yachting centres. In Haapsalu's fashionable era this area was the centre of the resort. You can still walk much of the way up the promontory, which has a lake in the middle and two separate points at the northern tip.

On the west edge of the town, beyond the railway station, is the **Paralepa forest park** with a beach frontage which is good for walks. Also out this way, near the air base,

are the ruins of **Ungru Castle** which, according to legend, had such fine gardens that Peter the Great came to see them.

Festivals

Haapsalu puts on a number of musical, cultural and sports events under the name Valge Daami Päevad (Days of the White Lady) around August full-moon time. On and around the full-moon night a drama, *Valge Daam* (The White Lady), is staged in the castle grounds. Afterwards the crowd waits for the White Lady to make her appearance at the cathedral window.

Yachting regattas are also held in summer. In July 1993 the first world reunion of west Estonians was due to be held. Whether this would become a regular event was uncertain.

Places to Stay – bottom end

The *Lääne Maakonna Koduturismi Assotsiatsioon* (Läänemaa Guest House Association) (☎ 44 543, fax 45 101) managed by Mrs Ene Kiisküla from her home at Lahe 34, offers rooms in a wide range of private homes in Haapsalu, and a few elsewhere in west Estonia, from around 100 EEK up to 200 EEK per person. The association is part of Eesti Kodu Turism (the Estonian Guest House Association) – see Accommodation in Facts for the Visitor.

Westra in Haapsalu (see Travel Organisations under Information) also handles bookings for Eesti Kodu Turism.

For other rooms in private homes, you could try the other travel organisations mentioned under Information.

The *Sanatoorium Laine* (☎ 45 639) on Sadama beside Väike-viik lake, about 600 metres north of the castle, has singles/doubles with private bath for 115/150 EEK. The doubles in particular are quite roomy and pleasant. You don't have to be in poor health to stay here, though the atmosphere can be gloomy. The sanatorium is a large, grey, stone-faced building with no signs. There's a canteen on the premises. Bus No 2 comes up here from Pipi Pansionaat about every 45 minutes.

Swedish Influence

West Estonia was home to most of Estonia's small Swedish population, who began settling along the coasts of the mainland and islands in the 13th century.

In 1934, 5312 of Estonia's 7641 Swedes lived in this region, mostly as fishers and peasants. However the Estonian Swedes left en masse for Sweden in 1944 before the Red Army occupied Estonia.

It was partly in recognition of the region's historical link with their country that Sweden's King Carl XVI Gustaf and Queen Silvia came to Haapsalu in April 1992 on the first royal visit to independent Estonia. ∎

ESTONIA

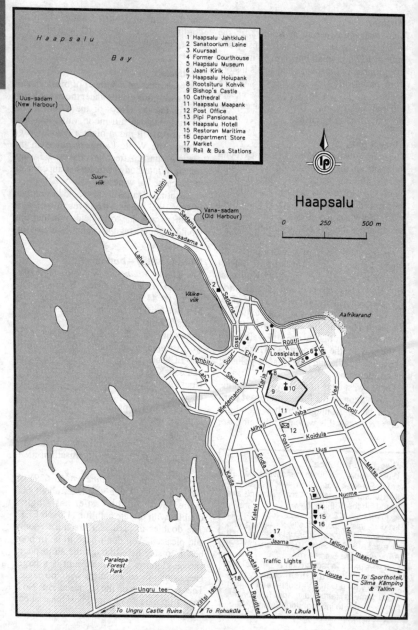

1 Haapsalu Jahtklubi
2 Sanatoorium Laine
3 Kuursaal
4 Former Courthouse
5 Haapsalu Museum
6 Jaani Kirik
7 Haapsalu Hoiupank
8 Rootsituru Kohvik
9 Bishop's Castle
10 Cathedral
11 Haapsalu Maapank
12 Post Office
13 Pipi Pansionaat
14 Haapsalu Hotell
15 Restoran Maritima
16 Department Store
17 Market
18 Rail & Bus Stations

Haapsalu

0   250   500 m

There's a *Kämping* at Silma, 1.2 km off the Tallinn road, a few km east of Haapsalu.

Places to Stay – middle & top end

Haapsalu's two main hotels are almost side by side on Posti, just north of the central traffic lights. The smaller *Pipi Pansionaat* (☎ 45 174, fax 45 191) at Posti 37 has 10 comfortable and immaculately clean rooms, sharing equally pristine showers and toilets, in a well-kept building designed as an inn in the 1930s. It bills itself as 'intimate' and 'romantic' and most rooms are in shades of pink and red. The national flags of everyone staying in the hotel stand on the reception counter for the length of their stay. Prices for singles/doubles, including breakfast in the good in-house café/restaurant, range from 200/280 EEK in January or February to 400/480 EEK between mid-May and the end of August.

The *Haapsalu Hotell* (☎ 44 847, fax 45 191), a few metres south of the Pipi at Posti 43, is a bright modern establishment, reopened in December 1991 after major renovation. Spacious Swedish-decorated rooms with private bathroom, phone and satellite TV cost from 400/480 EEK in January and February to 640/800 EEK from mid-May to the end of August. The hotel has a restaurant, and breakfast is included in the room rates.

A third place where you can get comfortable rooms is the *Haapsalu Jahtklubi* (Haapsalu Yacht Club, ☎ 45 582, fax 45 536), at Holmi 5A, just over a km north of the castle, right on Haapsalu's eastern bayside. Accommodation is not restricted to yachties but may be in short supply during busy yachting periods. Pleasant, if not huge, wood-panelled rooms each with two beds and one double bunk cost 220 EEK per person. Bathrooms are shared but are good and clean. There is a bar and a summer café here too. Bus No 2 comes to the nearby Holmi stop about every 45 minutes from the Pipi Pansionaat.

Active types might like to check out the *Sporthotell* (☎ 56 773), at Ehitajate tee 3A in the eastern suburb of Uuemõisa, which advertises tennis, basketball, bike rides, body building and hunting as well as rooms, restaurant and sauna. Ehitajate tee is south off the Tallinn road, 2½ km east of Haapsalu's central traffic lights.

Places to Eat

The *Rootsituru Kohvik* (Swedish Café) at Karja 3, with tables both indoors and outdoors beneath the castle wall, serves generous portions of good, inexpensive food in clean, tasteful surroundings – and you can't ask for much more than that! There's a variety of choices including some to suit vegetarians. Main courses are 4 to 7 EEK and salads are 1 to 4 EEK. What turned out to be a huge meal of cucumber salad, cabbage salad, sausage omelette, pancakes and coffee cost me just 16 EEK. Opening hours are from 10 am to 10 pm, except Sunday when they're from 2 to 10 pm.

Another very good place to eat, if more expensive, is the kohvik in the *Pipi Pansionaat* at Posti 37. The praad Pipi at 20 EEK is steak with about 10 types of fruit and vegetable – a really excellent main meal for the hungry. Another good choice is tursamaksalat (seafood salad) for 5 EEK.

The *Haapsalu Hotell* has a restaurant too, as well as the *Monika Baar* which seems to be the town's fashionable meeting spot. The *Restoran Maritima* next to the hotel is a large place redolent of the Soviet era, open from noon to 8.30 pm Monday and Tuesday, noon to 5 pm and 7 to 11.30 pm on other days. There are a couple of other bars and cafés along Posti and Karja, and one of the good *Peetri Pizza* chain is due to open near the castle at Karja 18. The market is on Jaama.

Getting There & Away

By car Haapsalu is an easy 105-km drive (about 1½ hours) from Tallinn along a good road. Otherwise you can reach it by bus or train. Haapsalu's train and bus stations are both at Jaama 1, with the buses out the front of the station building. Both ticket offices are inside.

Bus There are around 10 buses daily to/from Tallinn, the quickest taking 1¾ hours. Avoid the ones going by Keila (2¾ hours) or Nõva (3½ hours) unless you want a roundabout trip. The fare is 7 EEK. Buses between Haapsalu and other main destinations include:

Kärdla
    two buses each way daily, 2¾ hours, 5 EEK
Pärnu
    one or two buses each way daily, three hours, 7 EEK
Tartu
    one bus each way daily, 5¾ hours, 18.60 EEK
Virtsu
    two buses each way daily, two hours, 5.50 EEK

Local buses within west Estonia are mentioned under the relevant places.

Train There's one daily through-train each way between Tallinn and Haapsalu, departing from each town about 6 pm and taking about three hours. The one-way fare was about 5 EEK in general seating. You can also make the trip by changing trains at Riisipere, which is about halfway; two or three trains run each way daily, taking about three hours.

Boat Ferries to the islands of Hiiumaa and Vormsi leave from Rohuküla, nine km west of Haapsalu. Information is given in the Hiiumaa and Vormsi sections.

Getting Around

Haapsalu itself is small enough for most people to walk around, unless perhaps you're staying up at the sanatorium or yacht club, which you can reach by bus No 2, about every 45 minutes from the Pipi Pansionaat. Bus No 1 runs about hourly (though less often at weekends) between Lossiplats, the railway station, and Rohuküla which is the harbour for ferries to Hiiumaa, and is several km out of Haapsalu. Bus No 1 timetables are posted at Lossiplats and the railway station. Bus No 3 goes about hourly between the railway station and the cinema in the old town, near the castle.

TUKSI

In a pine forest beside Estonia's northernmost stretch of open-Baltic-facing coast, but somewhat removed from everywhere else, *Roosta Puhkeküla* (Roosta Holiday Village, ☎ 247-97 230, fax 247-57 875) at Tuksi is a comfortable, attractive, but expensive Swedish-built holiday-cottage complex, open year round. The 27 two-bed wooden cottages, with mini-kitchen, living room, TV, phone, shower and verandah, each cost 600 EEK a day in June, July or August but 400 EEK in May and 320 EEK the rest of the year. There are also a few four and six-person cottages, which are better value per person, two cottages for disabled people, as well as caravan places for 160 EEK; discounts apply if you stay a week or more. On site are a restaurant, bar, sauna, tennis and mini-golf – and you can rent a car for 12 EEK an hour plus 1.50 EEK a km, a bicycle for 40 EEK a day, a sailboard for 32 EEK, or a rowing boat for 16 EEK.

Getting There & Away

By road, Roosta is about 40 km north of Haapsalu and 130 km from Tallinn. You turn north off the main Tallinn-Haapsalu road seven km west of Palivere, and continue about 30 km through Linnamäe and Riguldi. Roosta will transfer up to eight people to or from Tallinn for 560 EEK. It's well off the beaten track and the only buses reaching it seem to be Haapsalu-Dirhami buses which at the time of writing go twice in each direction on Monday, Wednesday, Friday and Saturday and once on Sunday, taking one or 2¼ hours depending whether they go direct or via Nõva and Variku. On Tuesday and Thursday there's an early morning bus between Haapsalu and Riguldi, five km south of Tuksi.

There's a harbour (☎ 247-97 221) at Dirhami, a few km further north.

NOAROOTSI

The Noarootsi peninsula is only two km across the bay from Haapsalu but around 35 km away by road. Until the exodus of Estonian Swedes in 1944, it was populated mainly by Swedes for several centuries. There's an old church from the Swedish era at **Hosby**, a fine manorial park at **Pürksi**, and views over to Haapsalu from the old Swedish village of **Österby**. The name Pürksi is a corruption of Birke, the name of the Swedish trading town to which it was linked. The Noarootsi landscape is a combination of meadows, pine forests, juniper stands and reedy bays. Though a peninsula now, Noarootsi was an island a few centuries ago. It has joined the mainland because of the gradual rise of the land in west Estonia (one to two metres in the last 1000 years).

Getting There & Away

There are two buses a day in each direction between Haapsalu and Österby via Pürksi, taking 1¼ hours. A day trip from Haapsalu using these would give you about eight hours on Noarootsi.

AROUND HAAPSALU
Taebla

A km south of the Haapsalu-Tallinn road, about 10 km from Haapsalu and two km west of Taebla, is the eccentric house of the artist Ants Laikmaa (1866-1942) who, among other things, walked nearly 2000 km from Estonia to Düsseldorf to learn art there. His house has been turned into a gallery-museum which is worth a visit. The reed-thatched house is full of eccentric angles and unusual light. The exhibits display Laikmaa's life and work, as well as other work.

Ridala

Ridala is about 10 km south of Haapsalu on the Lihula road. The church at Ridala is typical of those built in west Estonia in the second half of the 13th century, the early years of the Ösel-Wiek bishopric. Tall and plain, these churches were based on the design of churches in Westphalia, Germany. Some of the finest of the type are on Saaremaa. Ridala church has a simple main body of two square bays, with a smaller square presbytery at the east end. The towers on the south and north sides and the buttresses at the west end were later additions. The stonework of the west doorway is particularly fine, and there's some good wood carving inside including a 1650s pulpit

---

The Baltic Sea

The Baltic Sea is very low in salt as seas go, being fed by so many rivers and with only one narrow, shallow opening to the oceans (between Denmark and Sweden) – a factor which also makes it relatively tideless. The Baltic is also a very young sea, having attained its present character only about 6500 years ago.

The Scandinavian ice sheet of the last ice age covered the whole Scandinavian-Baltic region as far south as the Polish-German coast till about 12,000 BC. The melting of the southern part of the ice sheet created what's called the Yoldia Sea, which by about 7500 BC stretched from the North Sea across southern Sweden, southern Finland and most of the present Baltic (except the Gulf of Bothnia between Finland and Sweden), and along the Gulf of Finland to Lake Ladoga, east of St Petersburg.

By about 6500 BC, with the ice sheet almost completely melted and no more meltwaters flowing off it, water levels in what is now the Baltic Sea had sunk. This left a land bridge between Sweden and Denmark/Germany and, behind it, the freshwater 'Ancylus Lake' which covered the present area of the Baltic plus a bit extra round some of the edges. The land bridge was breached around 4500 BC, opening up the Baltic to the oceans once more.

At that time nearly all of the Estonian islands and the western Estonian mainland, along with a slice of Latvia's west coast, were still under the sea. The earth's crust here has been gradually rising ever since – hence the proliferation of very low-lying islands off Estonia's coast and the flat, low nature of western Estonia. Currently the rate of rise is about one metre every 350 years. In a few more millennia, if this continues, Estonia's present islands will be part of the mainland and new islands will have appeared further offshore.

The Baltic Sea is called Läänemeri (Western Sea) in Estonian, Baltijas jūra in Latvian, Baltijos jūra in Lithuanian, and Baltiyskoe More in Russian. ■

made in Tallinn. In the graveyard are some 13th and 14th century tombstones.

Also at Ridala are the remains of an ancient Estonian stronghold called Tubrilinn.

Places to Stay

The *Lääne Maakonna Koduturismi Assotsiatsioon* (Läänemaa Guest House Association) has places at Taebla, and at Asuküla and Parila near Ridala, with rooms at 130 to 160 EEK per person. See Haapsalu – Places to Stay for contact details.

Getting There & Away

Taebla is a stop for all trains to or from Haapsalu. Buses along the Tallinn-Haapsalu road will also drop you at Taebla. Ridala is 20 minutes south of Haapsalu on the route of buses running to/from Lihula, Haeska or Puise.

VORMSI

Vormsi, Estonia's fourth-biggest island at 93 sq km, lies just three km off the Noarootsi peninsula. Ferries, however, make a 10-km crossing to Sviby on Vormsi's south coast from Rohuküla, nine km west of Haapsalu. Like Noarootsi, Vormsi had a mainly Swedish population until 1944, when nearly all of the Swedes left. It became a bit of a ghost island until mainlanders started to recolonise it for holidays. Nowadays it has about 400 permanent residents and lots of summer houses belonging to mainlanders. It's still a place where nature is largely undisturbed. There are small food shops at Sviby and Hullo.

Things to See

Sixteen km from east to west and averaging six km from north to south, Vormsi is a good place to wander round by bicycle, but you could also take a car or walk. There are about 10 km of paved road. Landmarks to head for include the 14th century church at **Hullo** (Vormsi's largest village) which has a fine Baroque pulpit and a collection of old Swedish-style wheel-shaped crosses in the graveyard; the southern **Rumpo peninsula**

dotted with juniper stands; the lighthouse at **Saksby** on the island's western tip; and the 5.8 metre-high boulder, Kirikukivi (Church Rock), near **Diby** in the north-east.

Places to Stay

Leili Allik's house in Hullo has rooms to rent at 120 EEK per person from 1 May to 31 August. The *Pension Vormsi* (☎ 247-44 173 or 247-92 309) on the coast at Suuremõisa in the south-west has seven rooms at 160 EEK per person and is open all year. Both places can be booked through the Lääne Maakonna Koduturismi Assotsiatsioon (Läänemaa Guest House Association); see Haapsalu – Places to Stay for details.

Getting There & Away

At the time of writing, the ferry leaves Rohuküla for Sviby at 7 am, and 1 and 6 pm Monday to Friday; 7 am and 6 pm on Saturday; and 9.30 am and 6 pm on Sunday. The ferry returns from Sviby an hour later in each case. It carries motor vehicles as well as bicycles and passengers. If you're taking a vehicle, particularly in summer or at a weekend, buy your outward ticket from the Rohuküla terminal as early as possible and make sure to check on the availability of return tickets (which you probably won't be able to buy until you reach Sviby). It will probably help to get someone to telephone the terminal (☎ 247-91 138) in advance to try to reserve places for you.

Haapsalu town bus No 1 runs about hourly (a bit less often at weekends) to Rohuküla from Lossiplats and the railway station, where its timetables are posted. All the Vormsi ferries wait for this bus except on Sunday morning . There are also daily buses from Tallinn at noon and 3.15 pm, reaching Rohuküla two hours later. From Rohuküla there are buses to Tallinn at 7 am and 6 pm.

Estonian Tours (☎ & fax 22-442 034) of Roosikrantsi 4B, Tallinn, organises trips to Vormsi from the capital. Haapsalu Reisibüroo (☎ & fax 247-45 193) can organise bicycle trips and guided tours from Haapsalu.

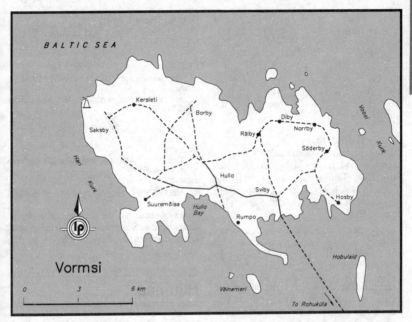

MATSALU NATURE RESERVE & LIHULA

Matsalu Bay, the deepest inlet in the west Estonian coast at over 20 km long, is an important water bird habitat protected as the Matsalu Nature Reserve (Matsalu Looduskaitseala) which comprises the bay, the islands around its mouth, and the coasts and wetlands along its edges and around the mouth of the Kasari River at the bay's east end. Water meadows surround the Kasari for several km inland from its mouth, while reed beds stretch some way out into the bay. The reserve also includes coastal pastures and hay meadows. Around 350,000 water birds stop here on migratory flights from mid-April to mid-May and mid-August to mid-October. This includes about 40,000 swans – numbering 10,000 together during the peak migration period. Some 300 pairs of greylag geese, 55 of mute swan, and 12 to 15 of bittern are among over 100 species nesting in the 486 sq km reserve or its 90 sq km surrounding buffer zone. Marsh harriers are also present and there are big colonies of various ducks, coot and black-headed gull.

The reserve centre, with a small bird museum, is at Penijõe on the reserve's southern border, three km north of the Tallinn-Virtsu road, near Lihula. From here you can take guided boat trips into the reserve. Some guides speak English. It's advisable to contact the reserve centre in advance: ☎ & fax 247-78 413, or write to Matsalu Riiklik Looduskaitseala (Matsalu State Nature Reserve), Lihula, EE3170. A company called Branta Ltd (also ☎ & fax 247-78 413) advertises comfortable accommodation for visitors to the reserve, and can provide meals.

Lihula

The small town of Lihula is worth a look if you have time to spare. It's strategically placed on a small hill and has been fought over several times down the centuries.

There's a memorial stone to the 1220 battle in which the local Estonians ejected the garrison placed here by an occupying Swedish king. Also to be seen are the ruins of a medieval castle, a manor house, and a Russian church. Karuse, 10 km along the road to Virtsu, and Hanila (16 km), also have early churches. Hanila's church is in the Gothic style.

Getting There & Away

Lihula is just off the main road to Virtsu and Saaremaa and is served by several buses daily from Tallinn (2½ hours, 9 EEK); Haapsalu (1¼ hours, 4 EEK); Virtsu (30 to 40 minutes, 2.50 EEK); and Pärnu (1¾ hours, 5 EEK).

VIRTSU

The village of Virtsu, 135 km from Tallinn, is the mainland terminus for ferries to Muhu island which is joined by a causeway to Saaremaa. The Virtsu ferry terminal is where the main road ends, so you can't miss it. You can change money in the main café in the terminal. The village has a youth hostel which you could use a cheap base for visiting Matsalu Nature Reserve or even Saaremaa. The heavily indented peninsula on which Virtsu stands was, like Noarootsi further north, an island a few centuries ago.

Places to Stay & Eat

There's a 12-bed *Youth Hostel* (☎ 247-75 527) in a quite large wooden house with a garden, just back from the south side of the main road, 600 metres from the ferry terminal. Nightly cost here is just 20 EEK. Breakfast can be ordered and there are cooking facilities too. You can make reservations on ☎ 22-624 562 or through the Estonian Youth Hostels office in Tallinn. A few metres along the side road beside the youth hostel are a *Kämping* with a few small cabins, and the *Trahter Werder*, a beer bar. There's a reasonable *Kohvik* (café) in the ferry terminal, open from 9 am to 3.30 pm and 4.30 to 9 pm, doing small 'pizzas' for 3.40 EEK, open sandwiches and other light bites.

Getting There & Away

Buses between Virtsu and mainland towns include:

Haapsalu
    two buses each way daily, two hours, 5.50 EEK
Lihula
    several buses each way daily, 30 to 40 minutes, 2.50 EEK
Pärnu
    two to four buses each way daily, 1½ to 2¼ hours, 6 EEK
Tallinn
    four to six buses each way daily, 2¼ to three hours, 10 EEK
Tartu
    two buses each way daily, six hours, 19.60 EEK

Some of these are on the way to or from Kuressaare on Saaremaa. More on these, and information on the ferries, is given in the Saaremaa & Muhu section.

Hiiumaa

Hiiumaa, Estonia's second-biggest island (1023 sq km) is quiet, sparsely populated, and gently beautiful with some lovely stretches of coast and pretty inland areas. Like nearby Saaremaa, Hiiumaa retains some of the atmosphere of pre-Soviet Estonia, being little touched by industry or Russian immigration. It is a favourite Estonian holiday retreat, dotted with summer homes. Sixty km from east to west and 45 km from north to south, it supports just 11,500 people, most of whom live near the coast, the inland being mainly forest or bog. Much of the soil is sandy and poor for cultivation. Before WW II there were 16,500 people. Low-lying like the rest of Estonia (its highest point, 63 metres, is on the western Kõpu peninsula), Hiiumaa is not quite visible from the mainland, 22 km away. Its old name, Dagö (Swedish for 'Day Island'), allegedly comes from the fact that it used to take a day to reach it from the mainland.

Like Saaremaa, Hiiumaa was out of bounds to foreign tourists in the Soviet era but it's now trying to catch up. Many new

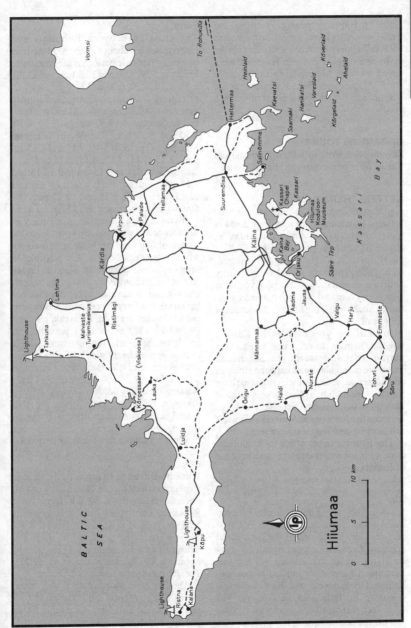

Hiiumaa

places to stay are opening up around the island – contact travel agents mentioned in the Kärdla Information section to find out the up-to-date range of choices. The island has a strong tradition of hospitality and if you're stuck in some out-of-the-way place as the afternoon draws on, locals might offer you a bed.

ORGANISED TOURS

Several travel firms in Tallinn, Haapsalu and Kärdla offer or can arrange Hiiumaa tours.

GETTING THERE & AWAY

A passenger and vehicle-ferry service runs between Rohuküla on the mainland, nine km west of Haapsalu, and Heltermaa at Hiiumaa's east end. A few buses from Tallinn via Haapsalu run right through to Hiiumaa, with a ferry crossing included in the trip. Other buses will drop you or pick you up at either ferry terminal. It's also common practice to hitch or ask for lifts off the ferries at either end.

In addition you can fly to Kärdla, Hiiumaa's main town, from Tallinn and maybe from Kuressaare (on Saaremaa). There are no regular boats between Hiiumaa and Saaremaa, which at their closest are only 5.5 km apart, but a few travellers have managed to organise private crossings between the harbours at Söru on Hiiumaa's southern tip and Triigi on Saaremaa.

The Estresor ticket office in Kärdla can book all manner of transport tickets in or out of Estonia.

Air

Estonian Air pulled out of flights between Tallinn and the islands in 1993 but new services were due to start by the Tartu-based company Ergon, which was awarded domestic flying rights in Estonian Air's place. Estonian Air flew daily to Kärdla from both Tallinn (45 minutes) and Kuressaare (20 minutes); its Tallinn-Kärdla fare was 310 EEK. Its ticket office in Kärdla was on Põllu, just off the central square, Keskväljak.

Ferry

The crossing between Rohuküla and Heltermaa takes about 1½ hours. At the time of writing ferries leave Rohuküla Monday to Friday at 5.30, 8.30 and 10.30 am and 12.30, 2.30, 4.30, 5.30, 6.30 and 8.30 pm, with an extra ferry at 10 pm on Friday. On Saturday they sail at 10.30 am and 2.30 and 6.30 pm, and on Sunday at 10.30 am and 2.30, 4.30, 6.30 and 8.30 pm. They leave Heltermaa Monday to Friday at 5.45, 7.15 and 8.15 am and 12.15, 1.15, 3.15, 4.15, 6.15 and 8.15 pm, on Saturday at 8.15 am and 12.15 and 4.15 pm, and on Sunday at 8.15 am and 12.15, 2.15, 4.15, 6.15 and 10.15 pm. The fare is 1 EEK per person and 5 EEK for a car.

If you're taking a vehicle, particularly in summer or at a weekend, try to get someone to telephone one or both terminals in advance to check times and, if possible, to reserve places. Ferries to the island on Friday and from it on Sunday are usually the busiest, and without an advance ticket you may not get on the first ferry of your choice. Buy your outward ticket from the Rohuküla terminal (☎ 247-91 138) as soon as possible and check on the availability of return tickets (which you probably won't be able to buy until you reach Heltermaa). The Heltermaa ticket office (☎ 246-94 212 or 246-94 252) is a small building on the right as you leave the pier. Ferry departure times are also posted in the bus ticket office at Haapsalu station.

There's a café in the Rohuküla terminal.

Bus

Through-Buses to Hiiumaa At the time of writing, two buses leave Tallinn daily at 4.10 pm and catch the 6.30 pm ferry from Rohuküla. One, which calls at Haapsalu at 5.55 pm, goes on to Kärdla, arriving at 8.40, and Viskoosa (Kõrgessaare) at 9.15; the other, calling at Haapsalu at 5.45 pm, goes to Käina (8.30), Emmaste and Õngu (9.25). The Tallinn-Kärdla fare is 11 EEK.

Another bus, Monday to Friday only, leaves Tallinn at noon and Haapsalu at 1.55 pm, catches the 2.30 ferry and reaches Käina at 4.20 and Kärdla at 4.45 pm.

Through-Buses to the Mainland Daily buses leave Viskoosa at 6.35 am, Kärdla at 7.25, Õngu at 6.30, Emmaste 7.00 and Käina at 7.35, catching the 8.15 am ferry to reach Haapsalu at 10.10 am and Tallinn at 11.50. Another, Monday to Friday only, leaves Kärdla at 4.30 am and Käina at 4.55, catching the 5.45 am ferry to reach Haapsalu at 7.10 am and Tallinn at 9.10 am.

Mainland – to/from Rohuküla Haapsalu town bus No 1 runs about hourly (a bit less often at weekends) to/from Rohuküla: its timetables are posted at Lossiplats and Haapsalu station, its two main stops in the town. There's also a daily bus leaving Tallinn at 3.15 pm, calling at Haapsalu at 5 pm and reaching Rohuküla in time for the 5.30 or 6.30 pm ferry; returning, this leaves Rohuküla for Tallinn at 6 pm after the arrival of the 4.15 pm ferry from Heltermaa. The buses running between Hiiumaa and Tallinn can also be picked up at Rohuküla.

Hiiumaa from Heltermaa If you take the 10.30 am or 2.30 pm ferry from Rohuküla, you can continue straight on to Kärdla on buses from Heltermaa at 12.15 or 4.15 pm. From Heltermaa to Kärdla takes 45 to 90 minutes depending whether the bus makes any detours. There are also buses to Kärdla meeting the 4.30 pm ferry Monday to Thursday and the 6.30 pm ferry Friday to Sunday. Off the 5.30 am ferry you have to wait an hour or so for a bus to Kärdla. Buses from Tallinn to Kärdla travel on the 2.30 pm ferry Monday to Friday and the 6.30 pm ferry daily – you should be able to hop on these if you need. The bus on the 6.30 pm ferry goes on to Viskoosa (Kõrgessaare).

A bus to Käina and Valgu meets the 2.30 pm ferry daily at Heltermaa. A Tallinn-Käina bus also uses this ferry from Monday to Friday, and the Tallinn-Käina-Õngu bus uses the 6.30 pm ferry.

Hiiumaa to Heltermaa Buses leave Kärdla for Heltermaa at 7.05 and 11.15 am and 2.30 pm daily, for passengers to catch the 8.15 am, 12.15 and 4.15 pm ferries from Heltermaa.

From Monday to Thursday there's a 5.20 pm bus to catch the 6.15 pm ferry, and on Friday and Sunday there's a 7 pm bus for the ferries at 8.15 pm (Friday) and 10.15 pm (Sunday). There are also Kärdla-Haapsalu-Tallinn buses on the 5.15 am ferry Monday to Friday and the 8.15 am ferry daily, the latter starting at Viskoosa (Kõrgessaare).

A daily bus leaving Valgu at 6.35 am and Käina a few minutes later reaches Heltermaa in time for the 8.15 am ferry. The Monday-to-Friday Käina-Tallinn bus takes the 5.45 am ferry; the daily Õngu-Käina-Tallinn bus goes on the 8.15 am ferry.

GETTING AROUND

Paved roads almost circle Hiiumaa and cover several side routes, so it's a good island to drive or cycle on. Estresor travel agency (see the Kärdla Information section) has Finnish Helkama bikes for rent at 50 EEK a day and a large Volga car at about 350 EEK a day. There are petrol stations at Kärdla and Käina.

Buses, nearly all radiating from Kärdla, get to most places on the island, though in some cases not very often. You could use them to make day trips to most parts of the island from Kärdla. A comprehensive if complicated timetable is posted in Kärdla bus station; if your destination is not mentioned by name, it may still be on one of the bus routes. Information on buses to and from the ferry port, Heltermaa, has been given under Hiiumaa, Getting There & Away. Hitching is fairly common on the roads to and from Heltermaa.

HELTERMAA TO KÄRDLA

At **Suuremõisa**, six km inland from Heltermaa, you can visit the chateau-like late-Baroque manor and park, created in the mid-18th century, that used to belong to the rich baronial Ungern-Sternberg family. Two brothers of the family founded the Kärdla cloth mill. Another member was supposedly responsible for the infamous false lighthouse of Kõpu in western Hiiumaa. The nearby **Pühalepa Church** dates back to the 13th century. Legends surrounding a mound of rocks known as the **Stones of the Ancient**

Agreement (Põhilise leppe kivid), about a km north-east of the manor, suggest that they mark the grave of a ruler of Sweden. At Palade, 12 km north towards Kärdla, then a km north-east along a side road, is the **Soera Farm Museum** (Soera Talumuuseum) in a traditional long, low wooden building.

KÄRDLA

Hiiumaa's 'capital' (population: 4000) grew up around a cloth factory founded in 1829 and destroyed during WW II. It's a green town full of gardens and trees, with a sleepy atmosphere, nothing historic, and little of great interest except that it's Hiiumaa's centre for services of all kinds.

Orientation

The town's main focus is Keskväljak, a long plaza half a km north of the main Heltermaa-Kõrgessaare road. On and near here are the town hotel, the market and main shops, and a couple of restaurants and bars. About 700 metres further north along Võidu and Sadama, where the cloth factory used to stand, is another square, Vabriku väljak, with a park either side – to the east Linnapark, with the town's Lutheran church built in 1861-63, to the west Rannapark running down to the sea.

Information

The travel agency Estresor (☎ 91 093, fax 96 350) at Vabaduse 4 has a range of accommodation around Hiiumaa. It also has a car, bicycles and camping gear to rent, and offers tours of the island and other parts of the Baltic states, and fishing or hunting trips. Estresor's ticket office at Kalda 3, about 100 metres from the bus station, will change money and can book travel tickets within or from Estonia. There's also Dagö Travel (☎ 98 885) at Uus 1. The Hiiumaa Taluturismi Ühendus (Hiiumaa Farm Tourism Association) (☎ 91 154, fax 91 030) at Leigri plats 5 has details on some rural accommodation possibilities on the island. *Hiiumaa Reisijuht*, which you may find in the news kiosk on Keskväljak or elsewhere, is a useful

leaflet-guide to the island, with text in English and Estonian.

The post office, at Posti 7, is open from 8 am to 4.30 pm Monday to Friday, 9 am to 1 pm Saturday, and is closed Sunday. Kärdla's post code is EE3200. There's a large food and drink shop at the north end of Keskväljak and a department store at Uus 2.

The telephone code for all Hiiumaa, including Kärdla, is 246.

Places to Stay

See the preceding Information section for details of travel agencies that can fix you up with accommodation in Kärdla or around the island. Estresor has a big range of accommodation available including about 20 cottages at 95 to 190 EEK per person a night, rooms in flats at 50 to 120 EEK per person, rooms in boarding houses at 120 EEK per person, tents at 95 EEK a night, and rooms in Hotell Liilia at Käina.

The only hotel in Kärdla is the *Võõrastemaja Kärdla* (Kärdla Inn) (☎ 91 481) at Vabaduse 13 near the corner of Valli, about 300 metres from Keskväljak. Decent clean rooms go for 35 EEK a single, 70 EEK a double, and the common toilets and washrooms are OK. However you might have to go to the town sauna, in another entrance of the same building, if you want hot water or a shower when the water supply is playing up.

Places to Eat

The *Kohvik Rannapargi* in Rannapark has both an upstairs café-bar and a downstairs restaurant where you can get a good meal for 15 to 20 EEK. Romsteek with veg at 10 EEK is a good choice. On weekend evenings there may be a folk group and dancing, for which you have to pay a few EEK extra. You can also get meals at the *Restoran Kärdla* on Keskväljak, normally open from 11 am to 9 pm daily except Wednesday and Thursday. It also has a bar with MTV. There's a third restaurant-cum-bar with highly erratic hours on Valli.

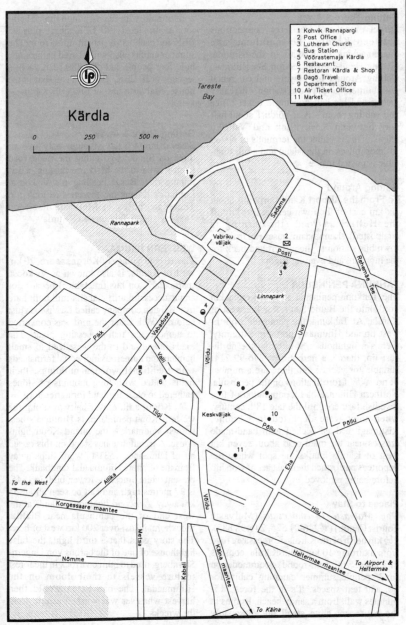

Kärdla

Tareste Bay

0   250   500 m

1 Kohvik Rannapargi
2 Post Office
3 Lutheran Church
4 Bus Station
5 Võõrastemaja Kärdla
6 Restaurant
7 Restoran Kärdla & Shop
8 Dagö Travel
9 Department Store
10 Air Ticket Office
11 Market

Rannapark

Vabriku väljak

Posti

Linnapark

Saadama

Rehemäe Tee

Uus

Vabaduse

Pikk

Valli

Võidu

5

6

7   8

g

Keskväljak

10

Põllu

Põllu

11

Tiigi

Allika

Eha

Hiiu

To the West

Korgessaare maantee

Metsa

Nõmme

Kabeli

Kaina maantee

Võidu

Heltermaa maantee

To Airport & Heltermaa

To Käina

Getting There & Away

Direct plane and bus/ferry connections between Kärdla, the mainland, and Saaremaa are dealt with in the Hiiuma, Getting There & Away section. See Hiiumaa, Getting Around for bicycle and car rental possibilities. Kärdla's bus station – in reality just a roadside halt housing a ticket office and waiting room – is at Võidu 1 about half way between Keskväljak and Vabriku väljak. This is either the terminus or a stop for most buses on the island and a full time-table is posted inside.

Getting Around

To/From the Airport Kärdla airport is about six km east of the town centre, 2½ km off the Heltermaa road (the turning is signposted). 'Lennujaam' buses run from the town bus station to the airport and back for the morning and evening flights.

TAHKUNA PENINSULA

The Tahkuna peninsula stretches eight km north into the Baltic Sea a few km west of Kärdla. At Tahkuna, the peninsula's north-west tip and Hiiumaa's northern extremity, there's a lighthouse; at Lehtma, the north-east tip, there's a harbour (☎ 246-99 214) suitable for yachts; and there are a number of pre-WW I fortifications on the peninsula. Northern Hiiumaa had a population of free Swedish farmers until the late 18th century, when they were deported to Ukraine. Ristimägi, a dune decked with hand-made crosses near the main road about seven km west of Kärdla, marks the spot where the deportees performed their last act of worship before being removed.

Places to Stay

The *Malvaste Turismikeskus* (Malvaste Tourist Centre) (☎ 246-91 525, 246-98 885), 2½ km north of the Kärdla-Kõrgessaare road from a turning 10 km from Kärdla, consists of a house with year-round accommodation for 35 people, summer 'camping' cabins for 50, and tent spaces. It's in the forest, 15-minutes walk from a sandy beach. Rooms in the house are quite small but reasonably comfortable, with clean-enough shared bathrooms; they cost 190 EEK single plus 95 EEK for each extra person up to four. The summer cabins, also with shared bathrooms, hold four people and cost 380 EEK each; a tent site is 20 EEK. There's a café-bar in the house. Malvaste has an office in Kärdla at Uus 1.

Getting There & Away

Several buses a day (though only two or three on Sunday) go along the main road from Kärdla to the Malvaste turning, a 15-minute ride. Buses heading for Viskoosa, Luidja or Kalana are the ones to look for. There are buses to Malvaste itself on Tuesday and to Tahkuna on Saturday.

WESTERN HIIUMAA

The harbour village of **Kõrgessaare**, 20 km west of Kärdla, is also known as Viskoosa (particularly on bus timetables) because of an unsuccessful artificial silk mill built here by a Belgian company called La Viscosa just before WW I. Later the mill was converted to a meat and fish-processing plant. The roads inland and to the west lead to small hamlets and numerous individual farmsteads with traditional wooden buildings, their fields dotted with long mounds of stones gathered to clear the land for agriculture.

At **Kõpu**, a little over halfway along the western Kõpu peninsula, is Hiiumaa's best known landmark – the inland Kõpu light-house. A lighthouse has stood on this raised bit of land since 1531 to warn ships away from the offshore Hiiumaadal sandbank. The present white limestone tower, built in 1845, is 37 metres high and can be seen about 55 km away. A second lighthouse stands at the west end of the peninsula near **Ristna**. Stockholm is just over 200 km west of here. The story goes that a third light, the false lighthouse of one of the barons von Ungern-Sternberg, used to burn on a rock in the forest to lure vessels to their doom on the Hiiumaadal. The bad baron would then harvest whatever was washed ashore from the wrecks.

Getting There & Away

Kärdla buses run several times most days to/from Kõrgessaare (Viskoosa) and Luidja at the start of the Kõpu peninsula, and two or three times a day to/from Kalana near the end of the peninsula. Kalana is about 1½ hours from Kärdla.

KÄINA

Hiiumaa's second-biggest settlement – not quite big enough to merit the label 'town' – stands in the south of the island near the shore of Käina Bay, a bird reserve which is virtually cut off from the open sea by the twin causeways to Kassari island. Käina is a fairly nondescript place, apart from the ruins of a fine 15th century stone church, wrecked by a WW II bomb, near the main road in the middle of the village. On the western edge of Käina is the house-museum of Rudolf Tobias, composer of some of the first Estonian orchestral works around the turn of the century.

Places to Stay & Eat

The *Hotell Liilia*, opened in 1993 at Hiiu maantee 22 in Käina, is Hiiumaa's best hotel; an inn-style place, it is a member of the international Best Western chain. Its 13 rooms, all with private bathroom and satellite TV, cost 225 to 265 EEK a single or 250 to 300 EEK a double in its first year, which is good value especially for the doubles. The Liilia has a restaurant with an Estonian and international menu including fish and vegetarian options; there's also a bar. You can book through any Best Western office worldwide or the Estresor travel agency in Kärdla.

There are a couple of rooms available in *Heido Ülev's* house (☎ 246-92 485) at Luige 8, for 175 EEK per person.

Getting There & Away

A good paved road runs 20 km across the island from Kärdla to Käina. There are five or six buses between Kärdla and Käina on weekdays, a couple fewer on Saturday and Sunday. Some are heading south or west to Aadma, Valgu, Tohvri, Nurste or Õngu.

Buses also run to Kassari – see the Kassari section.

KASSARI

The eight-km-long island of Kassari, off Hiiumaa's south coast opposite Käina, has a gentle beauty which, perhaps, makes it Hiiumaa's most attractive spot. The eastern half of Kassari is thickly covered with mixed woodland. At each end it's linked to the mainland by a causeway which supports a paved road. There's a harbour at Orjaku at the west end of the island run by the Dagö Yacht Club (☎ 246-92 127). Kassari is popular with Estonians and it may not be long before attractive new places to stay open up here.

Southern Kassari narrows to a promontory with some unusual vegetation and ends in a thin three-km spit of land whose tip, Sääre Tirp, is five km from Kassari's single main road. It's well worth making the trip to Sääre Tirp and allowing enough time to savour the unusual environment. There's a tent camping site about halfway with absolutely no facilities, not even water. The turning, roughly halfway along Kassari, is marked 'Sääre Tirp 2'. After 750 metres you pass a red and white barrier; after a further 1¾ km is a car park – beyond which vehicles are not allowed. The camping site is beside the car park. You can walk on to Sääre Tirp.

Just inland of the main road, a short distance west of the Sääre Tirp turning, is the single-storey **Hiiumaa Koduloomuuseum**, formerly servants' quarters on the Kassari estate, with a large collection of artefacts and exhibits on Hiiumaa's history, nature and ethnography.

Another enjoyable walk, ride or drive is to a pretty, whitewashed 18th century **chapel** at the east end of Kassari. A sign 'Kassari Kabel 2' directs you down a dirt road from the easternmost point of the island's paved road. In fact it's just 1½ km to the lovely little 18th century chapel which stands among trees, with a graveyard around it. A path continues nearly two km to a small bay in Kassari's north-east corner.

Getting There & Away

Only a few buses go to Kassari. At the time of writing, they leave Käina at 6.25 am and about 5 pm Monday to Friday, and Kärdla at 6 am Monday and 4.15 pm Monday to Friday. From Kassari to Käina buses go at 6.42 am and 5.19 pm Monday to Friday, and from Kassari to Kärdla at 6.42 am Monday to Friday and about 5.45 pm on Sunday. By changing buses in Käina (maybe with a bit of a wait) you can get from Kärdla to Kassari and back most days, but the times certainly aren't very convenient. Alternatively it's a six or seven-km walk (or hitch) to the middle of Kassari across either causeway from the main Valgu-Käina-Heltermaa road (which is used by buses), or about 10 km from the middle of Käina.

SOUTHERN HIIUMAA

The main paved road from Käina runs south-west through Valgu and Harju, villages separated from the coast by a three-km-wide marshy strip. Harju has two restored windmills. At Emmaste the main road turns north-west to end at Haldi just past Nurste. Hamlets and isolated farmsteads dot the west-facing stretch of coast and its hinterland. The southern tip of Hiiumaa around the harbour of Sõru is bleaker with few trees. North of Haldi, dirt roads continue through Õngu to the western Kõpu peninsula and to Luidja, the end of the paved road west from Kärdla.

Getting There & Away

There are buses from Kärdla and Käina to Valgu, Harju, Emmaste, Tohvri (in the south near Sõru), Nurste and Õngu every day. Their timings vary with the days of the week but most days they would enable you to make some kind of day trip.

VÄINAMERI NATURE RESERVE

Saarnaki, Hanikatsi, Kõrgelaid and other islets off south-east Hiiumaa form the Väinameri Nature Reserve. The reserve is a breeding place for avocets, eider ducks, goosanders, greylag geese and other birds, as well as a migration halt for swans, barnacle geese and other species. Over 600 plant species – almost half Estonia's total – grow here including the rarely found red helle-borine, wild apple and shining geranium.

The islets were inhabited until the 1960s or '70s and two of them even had inns, since this was the winter route to the mainland. They were depopulated, like many other Estonian coastal villages, because of Soviet bans on seagoing boats, which meant people could no longer earn a living from fishing.

A permit is needed to visit the reserve today – contact travel agents for information and ways of getting there.

Saaremaa

Mainland Estonians say Saaremaa, the country's biggest island at 2668 sq km, is 'like the old Estonia'. Soviet industry and immigration barely touched the place, and it retains the appearance and old-fashioned pace of agricultural pre-WW II Estonia, even though its famous windmills no longer work and its 'typical' reed-thatched roofs aren't so typical any more.

Saaremaa has always had an independent streak and was usually the last part of Estonia to fall to invaders. Its people have their own customs, songs and costumes, speak Estonian with a strong accent and never spoke much Russian at all. They brew a clear, dark beer widely reckoned to be the best in Estonia. They don't respect mainland Estonia's Kalevipoeg myth: Saaremaa has its own legendary hero, Suur Tõll, who fought numerous battles around the island with devils, fiends etc.

Though Saaremaa has long been a popular Estonian holiday retreat (with June and July the favourite months), during the Soviet era it was closed to foreigners, and even mainland Estonians needed an invitation to visit because of the siting of an early-warning radar system and rocket base here. The island now open to us is a thinly populated place of unspoiled rural landscapes with wooden farmsteads dotted among the forests that still

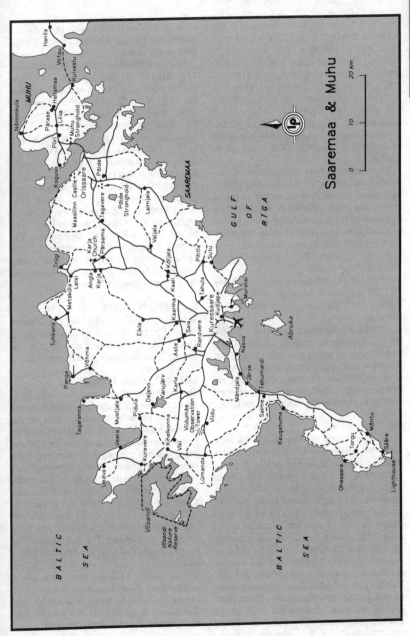

Saaremaa & Muhu

cover nearly half the land. Saaremaa is flat but has a deeply indented 1300-km coast of bays and peninsulas (and some sandy beaches). There are many remains from its intriguing past including pre-German strongholds, fine fortress-like early churches, windmills and, not least, the attractive old capital, Kuressaare, which has a mighty castle. Though known for its juniper groves, Saaremaa is also home to four-fifths of Estonia's roughly 1300 other plant species.

There are numerous accommodation possibilities around the island including private homes and some attractive, recently opened motels and hotels. Saaremaa is joined by a causeway to the neighbouring island, Muhu, to which ferries run from Virtsu on the mainland. Sailings to Saaremaa from Stockholm began in summer 1993 (see the Getting There & Away chapter).

At the time of writing, visitors have to pay 50 EEK on arrival, a charge which seems nothing but a piece of opportunism by the island authorities.

Historically the name Saaremaa ('islandland') sometimes referred to the whole archipelago of Estonia's western islands, and the same ambiguity goes for its old name Ösel. In Swedish *Ö* means island and *sel* means sieve. 'Island-sieve' could, perhaps with little imagination, mean 'archipelago'.

HISTORY
Human settlement on Saaremaa dates back to the 4th millennium BC. The early coastal settlements now lie some way inland owing to the rising of the land by about 15 metres in the last 5000 years. In the 10th to 13th centuries AD Saaremaa and Muhu were the most densely populated parts of Estonia. Denmark tried to conquer Saaremaa in the early 13th century but failed, and it wasn't till 1227 that the Knights of the Sword subjugated it. The knights and the church divided the islands between them in 1238. The knights got Muhu and relatively small eastern and north-western parts of Saaremaa, setting up their headquarters at Pöide in eastern Saaremaa. The Haapsalu-based

bishop of Ösel-Wiek got the rest of Saaremaa, making Kuressaare his stronghold on the island.

Saaremaa rebelled against German rule in 1236-41, 1260-61, and again in 1343 when the Germans were thrown off the island and the knights' castle at Pöide destroyed. In 1345, however, the Germans returned and forced the islanders to surrender.

All Saaremaa became a Danish possession in 1573 during the Livonian War, and in 1645 it was transferred to Sweden by the Treaty of Brömsebro. It was taken by Russia in 1710 during the Great Northern War and made part of the Russian province of Livonia, governed from Rīga. Saaremaa was occupied briefly by Germany from 1917 to 1918 before Estonia became independent. The population reached 60,000 around the turn of the century but is only 42,000 today, partly because of Stalinist and Nazi repression and the mass emigration of 1944.

ORGANISED TOURS
Several travel firms offer or can arrange tours of a day or more to Saaremaa from Tallinn. Ask around the agents there or contact some of those on Saaremaa itself.

GETTING THERE & AWAY
The usual way of reaching Saaremaa from mainland Estonia is the ferry service across the seven-km strait between Virtsu on the mainland and Kuivastu on the east coast of Muhu. You can use this service as a pedestrian, as a bus passenger, or with your own vehicle. Buses from Tallinn (and even Pärnu and Tartu) run right through to Saaremaa, with a ferry crossing included in the trip. These are obviously the most straightforward buses to use but if they don't suit you other buses will drop you or pick you up at either ferry terminal. It's not unusual for people to hitch lifts off the ferries at either end.

You can fly to Kuressaare from Tallinn and possibly from elsewhere. Twice-weekly cruise sailings between Stockholm and Kuressaare began in 1993 (see the introductory Getting There & Away chapter).

Air

Estonian Air stopped flying to the islands in 1993 but Ergon, which was awarded domestic flying rights in Estonian Air's place, was due to start new services. Estonian Air flew daily to Kuressaare from both Tallinn (45 minutes) and Kärdla (20 minutes) and there were also flights from Tartu (45 minutes): the Tallinn-Kuressaare fare was 310 EEK. The ticket office in Kuressaare was in the bus station on Pihtla tee.

Boat

Ferry The crossing between Virtsu and Kuivastu takes about 25 minutes. At the time of writing, ferries leave Virtsu at 7, 8.30, 9.50 and 11.20 am and 1.30, 3.30, 5.20, 6.40, 8.10 and 9.40 pm daily, with additional 5.40 am and 11 pm ferries from Monday to Friday. Daily sailings from Kuivastu are at 5, 6.20, 7.40, 9.10 and 10.30 am and 12.30, 2.20, 4.20, 6, 7.20, 9 and 10.20 pm. On Saturday and Sunday the 5 and 6.20 am ferries don't go. But on Saturday there's an extra ferry at 7 am, and also one at 8.30 pm instead of 9 pm. The one-way fare from Virtsu is 0.45 EEK per person and 2.25 EEK for a car; coming back, it's 0.30 EEK per person and 1.50 EEK for a car.

Each ferry takes about 25 vehicles including trucks and buses. If you're taking your own vehicle, particularly in summer or at the weekend, try to get someone to telephone the terminal in advance to check times and if possible reserve places. Ferries to the island on Friday (and from it on Sunday) are usually the most in demand and you may have to wait one or two sailings before you get a place. In any case buy your outward ticket as soon as you reach the Virtsu terminal and check on the availability of return tickets (which you may not be able to buy until you reach Kuivastu). The Virtsu terminal phone number is ☎ 247-75 520; the ticket office at Kuivastu (☎ 245-98 435) is a small building on the left just after you leave the pier.

There are cafés at both terminals. You may be able to buy the useful *Saare Maakond* tourist map of Saaremaa and Muhu, with text in English and Estonian, at the Virtsu terminal. The 50 EEK Saaremaa entry fee is collected when you land at Kuivastu.

Sailing Saaremaa is becoming quite popular with visiting yachties. Probably the best harbour facilities are at the Nasva Yacht Club (Nasva Jahtklubi) (☎ 245-75 140, fax 245-55 257), nine km west of Kuressaare. See the introductory Getting There & Away chapter for a list of other harbours on the island.

Bus

Through-Buses – to/from the Mainland
Four *kiir* ('fast') buses daily travel each way between Tallinn and Kuressaare, taking 4½ hours for the 220-km trip for a fare of 17.40 EEK. Departures from Tallinn are at 7.20 and 11 am, 2.50 and 5.40 pm, and from Kuressaare at 6 and 10.50 am, 2.40 and 5.40 pm. From Monday to Friday there's also a bus leaving Tallinn at 7.10 pm which does a circuit of Saaremaa through Leisi and Kihelkonna on its way to Kuressaare (arriving at 1 am). This bus leaves Kuressaare at 4 am for the six-hour return trip to Tallinn. There's also a bus from Tartu (1 am) via Pärnu (4.50 am) which reaches Kuressaare at 9 am. The return bus leaves Kuressaare at 2.40 pm. The Tartu-Kuressaare fare is 23.80 EEK. Another one or two buses go to/from Pärnu daily except Tuesday.

Other Buses If the through-buses don't suit you, you can get separate buses to and from the ferry, perhaps using one of the through-buses for part of its trip only. Saaremaa-bound through-buses cross on the 9.50 am and 1.30, 5.20, 8.10 and (Monday to Friday) 9.40 pm ferries from Virtsu; mainland-bound through-buses use the 5.40 (Monday to Friday only) and 7.40 am and 12.30, 4.20 and 7.20 pm ferries from Kuivastu.

There's a five-times-daily bus service each way just between Kuivastu and Kuressaare: a 1½-hour trip timed to connect with ferry arrivals and departures. First and last buses from Kuivastu are at 7 am and 6 pm; from Kuressaare they're at 4.45 am and

3.50 pm. Information on mainland buses to/from Virtsu is given in the Virtsu section.

GETTING AROUND

There are around 400 km of paved roads on Saaremaa and many more of reasonable dirt road so car, motorbike or bicycle is the ideal transport. Hitching is not uncommon on the main routes (but there's not much traffic on minor roads). Buses from Kuressaare get to many places and you could use them to make day trips to several parts of the island. Schedules are posted in Kuressaare bus station; if the place you want to go to is not mentioned by name, it may still be on one of the routes, so check your map and ask. Information on buses to/from the ferry port Kuivastu can be found under Saaremaa, Getting There & Away.

MUHU

Muhu, which you might hardly notice as you cross it in a few minutes from Kuivastu, is actually the third-biggest Estonian island and famous for its painstakingly worked folk costumes. Near the main road about halfway across the island is the 13th-14th century **Liiva church**, with some unusual ship murals. Just east of the road, shortly before the 2.5-km causeway to Saaremaa, is the **Muhu stronghold** of the old Estonians. It was here that the islanders surrendered to the Knights of the Sword on 3 February 1227, marking the end of Estonian resistance to the German invasion. The nearby **Eemu Tuulik** (Windmill) is now a small museum. **Koguva** on the western tip of Muhu, six km off the road, is an exceptionally well-preserved old-fashioned island village and all its 105 houses are protected as an open-air museum. They were mostly built between 1880 and 1930 but some date from the mid-18th century.

Places to Stay

The *Saare Maakonna Koduturismi Ühendus* (Saaremaa Guest House Association) has farm accommodation available at Pärase, near Hellamaa on Muhu. See Kuressaare

Places to Stay – out of town for contact details.

Getting There & Away

You can use the Kuivastu-Kuressaare buses, or hitch, to reach the points along the main road. There are occasional buses to Koguva too.

EASTERN SAAREMAA

The causeway from Muhu reaches Saaremaa near Orissaare on the north-east coast. The main road to Kuressaare goes past Tagavere and Valjala.

Orissaare

The village of Orissaare is probably the second-biggest settlement on Saaremaa. It has a shop or two. The German knights built the Maasilinn castle just north of Orissaare in the 14th to 16th centuries. It was blown up in 1576 but there are ruins to see.

Pöide

Three km south of the main road and not very far inland (on an alternative good route to Kuressaare) Pöide was the German knights' headquarters on Saaremaa. Their fortress was destroyed in the 1343 St George's Night Uprising, but Pöide church, a short distance east of the road, remains a starkly imposing reminder of their influence. Built by the Germans in the 13th and 14th centuries, it's still impressive even though currently in disrepair and held up by a forest of scaffolding. About 1½ km west of the road here, at Kahutsi, is the Pöide stronghold of the old Estonians.

Valjala

There's another early German church and old Estonian stronghold pairing at Valjala, just off the main Kuivastu-Kuressaare road 25 km out of Kuressaare. The church, in the village centre, is said to date from the 1230s which makes it the oldest on Saaremaa. It has a strikingly arched main façade. To reach the stronghold take the right fork at the church as you come from the main road. After 800 metres take a turning to the right marked

'Valjala Maalinn 1' and go 500 metres. The stronghold, an oval of stone ramparts, was where the people of Saaremaa were baptised after their surrender at Pöide in 1227.

Kaali

The **meteorite crater** at Kaali (2½ km north of the Valjala-Kuressaare road from a turning 10 km from Valjala) is over 100 metres wide and maybe 30 metres deep – and well worth detouring for. Look for it behind the wooden shop in the village with a 'Kauplus' sign. Trees have grown over the banks, and steps lead down to a pond in the bottom. The crater was blasted into existence in about the 8th century BC. At nearby Kõljala there's a classical 17th-19th century manor house.

Angla, Karja, Triigi & Tuhkana

This group of places in the northern part of eastern Saaremaa can be reached from Kuressaare or from other places in the east, to which they're linked by several paved roads.

Angla, 40 km from Kuressaare on the main road to the north coast, is the site of the biggest and most photogenic grouping of **windmills** on Saaremaa – five of them of various sizes, none now in use, lined up together on the roadside. Opposite the windmills is the turn-off to **Karja church**, two km east which, with the blank, fortress-like gaze of its façade, is one of the most evocative of Saaremaa's 13th-14th century German churches. There's a fine crucifixion carving on one of its walls. The church incidentally is not in Karja hamlet which is two km south of Angla on the Kuressaare road.

North of Angla the road continues 5½ km to Leisi, from where it's 3½ km to the tiny **harbour** of Triigi on Triigi laht, a picturesque bay on Saaremaa's north coast with views across to Hiiumaa. You might be able to find a boat that will take you to Hiiumaa from Triigi – there are a couple of shops in Leisi where you could start asking – but try to make enquiries about the chances before coming up here. To reach Triigi turn right in the middle of Leisi, then turn left (north) after two km and go 1½ km.

There's a sandy beach at Tuhkana, three km north of Metsküla, which is 10 km west of Leisi, mostly by unpaved roads.

Kaarma

There's another fine **13th century church** at Kaarma, 12 km north of Kuressaare. Both the church and the almost equally old par-sonage *(pastoraat)* next door are the subject of a research and rebuilding programme. On the other side of the main road from the church are the remains of an old **Estonian stronghold**. Kaarma is a centre of dolomite mining, one of Saaremaa's very few indus-tries.

Places to Stay

The *Saare Maakonna Koduturismi Ühendus* (Saaremaa Guest House Association) has rooms available in private homes at Oris-saare, Leisi and Laimjala. *Motell Tare* at Sutu might be convenient if you have been touring the east of the island. See Kuressaare, Places to Stay – out of town for more on all these. *Kämping Kadakas* (☎ 245-95 566), on the south side of Orissaare at Kuivastu maantee 44, has room for 32 people in summer cabins.

Getting There & Away

Buses between Kuressaare and the mainland usually take the main road passing within a km of Valjala (but always confirm this) while the local Kuressaare-Kuivastu service takes the more southerly road through Laimjala and within a km of Pöide. There are several buses daily between Kuressaare and Oris-saare, taking about 1¼ hours, and several, mostly in the morning, between Orissaare and Kuivastu.

Up to seven buses daily run between Kuressaare and Leisi, a trip of about an hour, passing right by Angla windmills and close to Karja church. Those via Pärsama go right by Karja church. Those via Eikla will prob-ably go through Kaarma, which is also served by buses 4½ hours apart in morning and early afternoon, via Aste.

Kaali is halfway between the Kuressaare-Valjala and Kuressaare-Leisi roads, two to

ESTONIA

three km from each, so you could use a bus along either road to get within walking distance.

KURESSAARE

Much of Saaremaa's capital, on the island's south coast 80 km by road from Kuivastu on Muhu, retains its historic appearance and atmosphere. Not only the imposing Kuressaare castle but also numerous other town-centre buildings date from past centuries. It's a small, pleasant, relaxed place of 17,000 people with a holiday atmosphere in summer. Kuressaare is Saaremaa's transport hub and a natural base for a visit to the island – though there's also good accommodation elsewhere.

A castle was founded at Kuressaare (originally named Arensburg) in the 13th century as the Haapsalu-based Bishop of Ösel-Wiek's pied-à-terre in the island-part of his diocese. The settlement that grew around it was given the rights of a town in 1563 by Duke Magnus, the Danish noble to whom it passed from the church in the mid-16th century. Kuressaare became Saaremaa's main trading centre, developing quickly after passing into Swedish hands in 1645. In the 19th century it became a health spa because of the curative properties of its coastal mud. In the Soviet era Kuressaare was named Kingissepa, after Viktor Kingissepp, an Estonian communist of the 1920s.

Orientation

The road from Kuivastu and the mainland enters Kuressaare as Tallinna, passing southwestward through modern suburbs to the central square Kesk väljak. Kuressaare castle and its surrounding park, which reaches down to the coast, are 500 metres beyond Kesk väljak, along Lossi. The bus station at Pihtla tee 25, and most other places you're likely to want to go, except some outlying accommodation, are within a short walk of Kesk väljak or the castle.

Information

Money At the time of writing it's still diffi-

cult to change travellers' cheques on Saaremaa, though that should be corrected soon. You can certainly change cash at the bus station till 6 pm and at the Kuressaare Maapank – the building with a 'Pank' sign at Tallinna 27, almost opposite the bus station – from 9 am to 12.30 pm, Monday to Friday.

Post & Telecommunications The post office at Torni 1 is open from 9 am to 2 pm and 3 to 9 pm Monday to Friday, 9 am to 2 pm and 3 to 4 pm Saturday and Sunday. The telephone and telegraph offices in the same building are open from 6 am to midnight daily.

The telephone code for Kuressaare and all Saaremaa is 245.

Travel Agencies Mardi Ltd (☎ 54 875, fax 56 241) at Tallinna 4 and Thule Ltd (☎ 59 686, 57 470, fax 54 104) at Pargi 1, in the Kuursaal building in the park, are two friendly travel agencies which can fix you up with a variety of accommodation, tours in several languages including English, and other services. Other agencies include Complex Ltd (☎ 54 349, 55 391, fax 57 448) at Kitsas 3, and Saaremaa Reisibüroo (☎ 55 079, fax 57 448) at Pihtla tee 2.

Left Luggage There's a left-luggage room in the bus station.

The Castle

Kuressaare castle stands at the south end of the town, on an artificial island with four pointed bastion-corners, ringed by a partly filled moat which is surrounded by a park. It's very well preserved and one of the most impressive castles in the Baltic states. You should be able to find an Estonian map of it, and/or an English leaflet, in the town or at the castle ticket office. The castle is 'unique in its northern ponderosity and utmost selfabsorbedness', according to one of these publications.

A castle was founded on this site as the bishop of Ösel-Wiek's island base by the 1260s, but the mighty square fortress of locally quarried dolomite that stands today

Kuressaare Castle

at the centre of the several rings of fortification was not built till 1338-80. It was designed as an administrative centre as well as a stronghold. The slenderer of its two tall corner towers, Pikk Hermann at the east, is separated from the rest of the castle within by a shaft crossed only by a drawbridge, so it could function as a last refuge in time of attack.

Interior The inside of the castle is a warren of chambers, halls, passages and stairways which will meet anyone's fantasies about Gothic fortresses. It houses the Saaremaa Regional Museum (Saaremaa Koduloomuuseum), open from 11 am to 7 pm Wednesday to Sunday, with some contemporary exhibitions as well as a large collection on the island's history and culture including some useful material in English. On the ground floor look for the hypocaust (hüpokaust) on the south-west side. This was a furnace which fed a medieval central-heating system of nine ducts conveying warm air to the chapter house one floor above, where you'll find nine corresponding holes in the floor, which could be opened and shut as comfort demanded.

From the chapter-house floor of the castle an interior cloister looks down into the inner courtyard. The beautifully vaulted chapter house – originally used as both dining hall and clergy meeting hall and now sometimes as a concert hall – and the adjacent chapel (in the south corner) are the castle's finest rooms. The bishop's living quarters were along the north-western side of this floor; in one of the rooms is a stone plate listing all the Ösel-Wiek bishops.

The massive seven-storey defence tower at the castle's north corner has been much rebuilt over the centuries but the narrow medieval staircases in its walls are original.

Outer Works The wall around the outer edge of the castle island was built at the end of the 14th century, and the cannon towers added later. The greatest of the cannon towers, completed in 1470, is at the island's north corner. The bastions and moat were created by the Danes in the 17th century. Later that century and in the following century, Swedes and Russians improved the bastions and added three ravelins (defence islands in the moat), one of which is crossed by the modern entrance road. There's a former gunpowder cellar in the south bastion.

Park The shady park around the castle moat and running down to Kuressaare Bay was laid out in 1861 and there are some fine wooden resort buildings from the turn of the century in and around it, notably the 1889 Kuursaal (Spa Hall). There's a Citizens' Museum (Linnakodaniku Muuseum), open from 10 am to 6 pm Wednesday to Sunday, at Pargi 5 nearby.

Other Sights
Town Centre Kuressaare's other best old buildings are grouped round the central square Kesk väljak, notably the **town hall** (linnavalitsus) on the east side with a pair of fine stone lions at the door, and the **weigh-house** opposite it on the corner of Kohtu, both 17th century Baroque. There's a handsome **Lutheran church** at the north-east end of Kesk väljak, and an **Orthodox church** on Lossi.

Beaches The best beach in the Kuressaare area is Järverand at Järve, about 14 km west, a couple of km past Mändjala. On the way – at Nasva – there's a yacht harbour with a few yachts for charter. There's also a beach at Sutu, 12 km east. There are accommodation options at Mändjala, Nasva and Sutu (see Places to Stay – out of town), but the beaches themselves, though sandy, are nothing very special. Salme, Torgu, or Sääre buses from Kuressaare go to Järverand.

Places to Stay – in the town

The Thule travel agency (see Information) can fix you up with accommodation in private flats in the town for 20, 40 or 60 EEK per person. Mardi travel agency offers similar for 110 EEK, breakfast included. Family Hotel Service of Tallinn (see Private Homes under Accommodation in Facts for the Visitor) also has options in Kuressaare.

Kuressaare hospital (haigla), a vast white building at Aia 25, a km from Kesk väljak, has a little five-room hostel, the Haigla Pansionaat, intended for visiting medics but open to anyone, out the back of its main buildings. Clean rooms with shared shower and toilet, plus use of a kitchen and a comfortable sitting room with TV, cost just 16 EEK a double or 24 EEK a triple. Go between 10 am and 1 pm when there'll be someone on duty at the hostel.

The Võõrastemaja Lossi (Castle Inn, ☎ 54 443), an old wooden building at Lossi 27 (on the island crossed by the road over the castle moat), has clean singles/doubles with shared bathrooms for 120/200 EEK.

The Panga Pansionaat or Hostel Pangamaja (☎ 57 989) at the back of the bank ('Pank') building at Tallinna 27 is a small, modern place where good clean rooms with spotless shared showers and toilets cost 60 EEK a single or double – or so the staff on the spot, who attend in the morning and late afternoon, told me. Travel agents Complex and Mardi, however, quote much higher prices such as 299 EEK double for bed and breakfast. You reach the entrance by walking up either side of the bank.

You can have a room with private bathroom in the Sanatoorium Kuressaare (☎ 59 250) at Kastani 20, a km west of the town centre, without taking any treatment, for 140 EEK a person.

Mardi travel agency has information on various other options including two places near the town centre – the six-bed Hotell Tarsa (☎ 57 293) at Kauba 10, charging 99/125 EEK with shared showers, and a Privat Hotell at Koidu 6 charging 130 EEK a person.

Places to Stay – out of town

These places are mainly aimed at people with their own vehicles, though some are on bus routes.

The Saare Maakonna Koduturismi Ühendus (Saaremaa Guest House Association) (☎ 77 269, fax 54 104), run by Õie Kivi from her home in Saia, on the Aste road 10 km north of Kuressaare, offers rooms from about 120 to 160 EEK per person, including continental breakfast, in about 12 private homes around Saaremaa, plus a few whole houses for around 700 EEK a day. Those in the Kuressaare area are at Nasva, Mändjala, Muratsi and Saia. The association is part of Eesti Kodu Turism, the Estonian Guest House Association, and bookings can also be made from elsewhere – see Private Homes under Accommodation in Facts for the Visitor.

The Tahula Motell (☎ 57 410), which opened in 1992 on the Kuivastu and Tallinn road 10 km from central Kuressaare, is an excellent, modern place with friendly staff. Good clean rooms with private bath and plenty of hot water cost 180 EEK a single or double. There's also a restaurant (open till 11 pm) where breakfast or a good evening meal will cost you around 15 EEK (unless of course you have an imported beer which will more than double the cost), and a bar open to midnight.

Kämping Saare or Kämping Mändjala, open in June, July and August in woods behind a sandy but ordinary beach at Mändjala, 10 km along the coast road west of Kuressaare, has quite big cabins, so-so showers (with warm water) and toilets, a bar and a restaurant. It's run by Saaremaa Reisibüroo (see Information) which charges

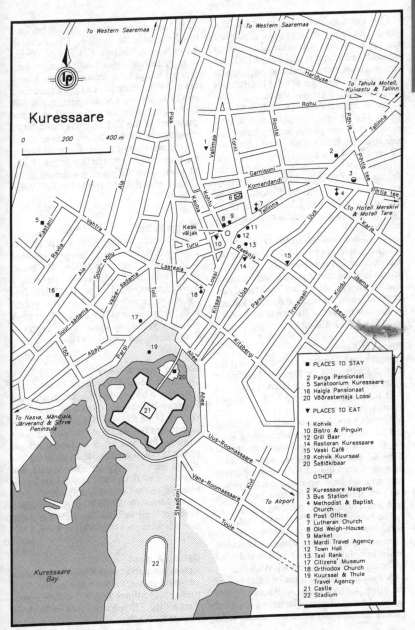

Kuressaare

0   200   400 m

To Western Saaremaa
To Western Saaremaa
To Tahula Motell,
Kuivastu & Tallinn

To Hotell Merekivi
& Motell Tare

To Nasva, Mändjala,
Järverand & Sõrve
Peninsula

To Airport

Kuressaare
Bay

■ PLACES TO STAY
2 Panga Pansionaat
5 Sanatoorium Kuressaare
16 Haigla Pansionaat
20 Võõrastemaja Lossi

▼ PLACES TO EAT
1 Kohvik
10 Bistro & Pinguin
12 Grill Baar
14 Restoran Kuressaare
15 Veski Café
19 Kohvik Kuursaal
20 Šašlõkibaar

   OTHER
2 Kuressaare Maapank
3 Bus Station
4 Methodist & Baptist
   Church
6 Post Office
7 Lutheran Church
8 Old Weigh-House
9 Market
11 Mardi Travel Agency
12 Town Hall
13 Taxi Rank
17 Citizens' Museum
18 Orthodox Church
19 Kuursaal & Thule
   Travel Agency
21 Castle
22 Stadium

62 EEK a person for bed and breakfast. You may get a slightly cheaper price if you just turn up at the site. There are also caravan sites at 50 EEK and tent sites at 4 EEK per person. Buses from Kuressaare to Torgu or Sääre (three a day) go to the Mändjala bus stop, about half a km past the site.

The *Hotell Männikäbi* (☎ 75 106, 55 680, fax 57 341 'Hotel'), which opened in 1992 about 600 metres past Kämping Saare, has nice spacious rooms with private bath and TV for 270/540 EEK including breakfast in its restaurant. It's 300 metres off the road; the turning is just past the Mändjala bus stop. Also on the west side of Kuressaare, the *Nasva Jahtklubi* (Nasva Yacht Club) (☎ 75 140) is building a hotel due to open by summer 1994.

The 50-bed *Hotell Merekivi* (☎ 57 651) at Kudjape, three km east of the town centre, was built in 1991 and charges 170 EEK a person in rooms with private bathrooms. It also has a restaurant and bar. The *Motell Tare* (☎ 90 125) near the beach at Sutu, 12 km east of Kuressaare, takes 20 people in sizeable rooms at 300 EEK double.

Places to Eat

Probably the best restaurant in the town is the *Kohvik Kuursaal* in the Kuursaal building in the castle park, with main courses from 7 to 9 EEK, salads from 1 to 3 EEK. It's open from noon to 5 pm and 6 to 11 pm.

There's a good *Kohvik* (café) on Vallimaa just a couple of minutes walk north of Kesk väljak. It serves soups and salads for around 2 EEK, and main courses such as biif-strogonoff for 5 or 6 EEK, in clean, spacious surroundings from noon to 7 pm daily. You can't see it from the street: look for the sign with a cat, on a nearby building.

The basement *Grill Baar* in the south end of the town hall building, open from noon to 4 pm and 6 pm to midnight, serves drinks and well-filled plates of grilled chicken and salad to the accompaniment of rock videos.

A *Pinguin* ice cream parlour and one of the *Bistro* fast food chain, with only a limited range of eat-in offerings including good hot cheese, sausage and salad sandwiches for 4

EEK, have popped up side by side on Turu on the corner of Kauba. The *Restoran Kuressaare* at Raekoja 1 is a large Soviet-style restaurant, open from noon to midnight; it has a *söökla* (canteen), open from 8 am to 3 pm, where you can get a meal for 5 or 6 EEK. There's a *Šašlõkibaar*, or shashlik (kebab) bar, with its own entrance, at the castle end of the Võõrastemaja Lossi, and a reasonable *Kohvik* in the bus station.

One place you can get Saaremaa beer is the *Veski* café, in a windmill at Pärna 19. Out of town there are good restaurants at the *Tahula Motell* and reportedly the *Hotell Männikäbi*.

Things to Buy

Several shops around Kesk väljak and on Lossi sell Saaremaa textiles, juniper-wood beer mugs and other souvenirs. The bookshop on Lossi has some attractive reproductions of old maps. You'll also find souvenirs, as well as food and other goods, at the little market off the north side of Kesk väljak. You can buy some film at a shop on Pargi, facing the west side of the castle park.

Getting There & Away

Direct plane and bus/ferry connections between Kuressaare, the mainland and Hiiumaa island are covered in Saaremaa, Getting There & Away. Kuressaare's gleaming modern bus station at Pihtla tee 25 is the terminus for most buses on the island and schedules are posted inside. Also in the bus station are a left-luggage office, a café, and offices for air tickets and some of the ferries from Tallinn to Finland and Sweden.

AS Metra (☎ 59 363) at Aia 25 has a Moskvitch car for rent. The Refit car rental firm has a branch (☎ 55 994) at Rohu 5.

Getting Around

Kuressaare airport is at Roomassaare, three km south-east of the town centre. Bus No 2 runs about 15 times daily to/from the central Kesk väljak. There's a taxi rank on Raekoja, just off Kesk väljak.

WESTERN SAAREMAA

Viidumäe

Saaremaa's highest point (54 metres) at Viidumäe, about 25 km west of Kuressare, is crowned by a tall observation tower with views of forest, more forest and the sea in the distance. The tower is two km along a dirt road off the Kuressaare-Lümanda road. The surrounding area is a nature reserve.

Viki & Kihelkonna

At Viki on the Kuressaare-Kihelkonna road, about 30 km from Kuressaare, an old farm has been preserved as the Mihkli Talumuuseum (Mihkli Farm Museum) with wooden buildings and farm and household implements from several generations on show. Kihelkonna, three km beyond, has a tall, austere, early German church. There's a fishing harbour, usable by yachts, at Veere on the east side of the Tagamõisa peninsula north of Kihelkonna. Vilsandi island, west of Kihelkonna, is the focus of a nature reserve and sanctuary for resident and migratory birds. It's not open to human visitors.

Karujärv

About 10 km east of Kihelkonna, but reachable by paved road from Kuressaare through Kärla, Karujärv is a popular forest lake with islands and indented shores. Dejevo by the road near its north shore is a Russian village built for Soviet military families who were stationed on Saaremaa.

North Coast

The 22-metre cliff known as Panga pank (bank) or sometimes Mustjala pank, at Panga on the north coast, is a big attraction for Estonians, though less so for people from hillier lands. This is Saaremaa's highest cliff though there are others, such as the Ninase pank on the next headland west.

Sõrve Peninsula

More cliffs, such as the Kaugatuma pank and Ohesaare pank, rear up along the west coast of the 32-km south-western Sõrve peninsula. There are good views from the lighthouse at Kaugatuma. Tehumardi at the neck of the peninsula, shortly west of the beach at Järve (see Kuressaare), was the site of a fierce night battle in October 1944 between retreating German troops and an Estonian Rifle Division. There's a big sword monument there now. About halfway down the narrow peninsula are remains of the Lõpe-Kaimri defence line also from WW II. Mõntu on the east coast has a small harbour usable by yachts in daylight. From Sääre at the peninsula's southern tip it's possible to see the Latvian coast, over 25 km away, in clear weather. Here are a lighthouse and coastal artillery positions built by the Red Army early in WW II.

Places to Stay

Among the trees on the east side of Karujärv lake, *Kämping Karujärv* (☎ 245-72 681) is a basic place with cabins at 15 EEK per person, and toilets but no showers. You can put a tent up too. You're a long, long way from urban life here. There's also a tent site *Kämping* at Kihelkonna.

Kämping Tagaranna (☎ 245-54 875), known in English as Cottage Village Tagaranna, is a modern Swedish-built place of five comfortable double cabins, sharing showers and toilets, on the north coast about 10 km north of Mustjala. The cost is 150 EEK per person.

On the Sõrve peninsula there's *Nõgu Talu* (Nõgu Farm) (☎ 245-70 421, fax 245-56 944) at Mõisaküla, a km north of Torgu, with a house that functions as holiday accommodation from 15 May to 1 September and as a hunting lodge in other seasons. There are three double rooms at 298 EEK and a suite at 483 EEK, breakfast included. Other meals are available but expensive at 90 EEK or more. For more information in English telephone ☎ 245-53 191.

The *Saare Maakonna Koduturismi Ühendus* (Saaremaa Guest House Association) has places on the Sõrve peninsula and at Võhma near Panga. There are also places to stay at Nasva and Mändjala, on the coast a few km west of Kuressaare. See Kuressaare Places to Stay – out of town for more information on all these.

ESTONIA

Getting There & Away

Buses between Kuressaare and western Saaremaa are a bit more limited than to the east. There are several buses daily to/from Kihelkonna (about an hour) by various routes. Three of these a day, Monday to Friday, go via Lümanda and will stop at Viidu, the turn-off for Viidumäe. Three daily go on to Undva and Veere on the Tagamõisa peninsula north of Kihelkonna.

There's a midday bus to Karujärv but you couldn't use it for a day trip to the lake because it turns round and comes straight back. Similarly a bus runs via Mustjala to Võhma some days and to Panga other days but it doesn't linger at the destination before heading back. There are three daily buses to Torgu on the Sõrve peninsula, two of them going on to Sääre at the tip, 1½ hours from Kuressaare.

South-West Estonia

The main town of south-west Estonia, the coastal resort Pärnu, only comes really alive at summer festival times. Otherwise it's a quiet but amiable place worth a halt if you're not in a hurry. Elsewhere in the region you might explore the isolated coast west of Pärnu, or venture out (if you can afford it) to the remote islands Kihnu or Ruhnu. The main road from Tallinn to Rīga runs through south-west Estonia. On the way from Tallinn, there's a fine Gothic church at **Märjamaa**.

PÄRNU

Pärnu (population: 53,000; pronounced: 'pair-nu'), 130 km south of Tallinn on the main road to Rīga, has been Estonia's leading seaside resort since before WW II. In the Soviet era the pleasures of its long, sandy beach were reduced by pollution which rendered swimming inadvisable. But new water-purification equipment had removed any health risk by 1993, according to the local environmental authorities. Still, 40% of the town's waste continues to flow directly into the Pärnu River. Meanwhile, Pärnu is making energetic efforts to attract visitors in other ways by hosting a succession of festivals every summer and opening several casinos. Though not exactly the 'Estonian Las Vegas' that some in the tourist business like to imagine, Pärnu can get fairly lively at festival times. At other times it's still pleasant to visit with some good places to stay, an agreeable environment of clean, wide, leafy streets, sea air, many parks and an attractive old town area. It can feel a little forlorn outside the main June - August tourist season.

History

Stone age objects from around 7500 BC found at Pulli, near Sindi on the Pärnu River about 12 km inland, are the oldest human artefacts found in Estonia. At that time the mouth of the river was at Pulli and the site of Pärnu was still sea-bed.

There was a trading settlement at Pärnu before the German crusaders arrived, but the place only entered recorded history when the Pärnu River was fixed as the border between the territories of the Ösel-Wiek bishop (to the west and north) and the Livonian knights (to the east and south) in 1234. In 1251 the bishop even came to live on his bank of the river here, promoting the church to a cathedral, but he moved north to Haapsalu after a Lithuanian raid in 1263. Meanwhile the knights had built a fort on the east side of the river. The town that grew up around the knights' fort, joined by rivers to Viljandi, Tartu, and Lake Peipus, became the Hanseatic port of Pernau in the 14th century. (Sinking water levels have since cut this link.) Pernau/Pärnu had a population of largely Lübeck origin till at least the 18th century. It suffered typical wars, fires, plagues, and switches between German, Polish, Swedish and Russian rule down the centuries – apparently taking an upswing in

ESTONIA

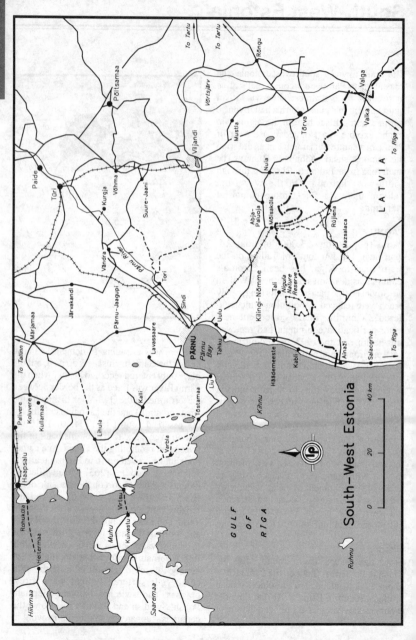

South-West Estonia

the 17th century under Swedish rule but having its trade devastated by the Europewide blockades that accompanied the Napoleonic wars.

From 1838 the town gradually revived as a resort: mudbaths proving a draw, as well as the beach and relatively good weather. By the late 1930s Pärnu was attracting Swedes and Finns as well as local visitors. Only the resort area was spared severe damage in 1944 as the Soviet army drove out the Nazi occupiers, but many bits of the old town have since been restored. In the Soviet era all the guesthouses, hotels and villas were turned into sanatoriums, and sea pollution damaged Pärnu's standing as a resort. But after independence, new hotels and other tourism initiatives happened quite quickly.

Orientation

Pärnu lies either side of the estuary of the Pärnu River, which empties into the northeast corner of the Gulf of Rīga, known as Pärnu Bay. The southern half of the town, a roughly 1½-km-wide neck of land between the river and the bay, is the centre of things. The central square is on the corner of Ringi and Rüütli, with the bus station half a block to the north on Pikk, and the old town with its relatively narrow streets stretching to the west. Rüütli is the main shopping street. Southward towards the sea the streets are younger and wider, opening out into a wide, treed park backing the beach.

Information

Tourist Office The Pärnu Tourism Development Centre (Pärnu Turismiarendus) (☎ 45 533 or 45 633, fax 45 266 or 45 633) at Supeluse 18B is primarily a promotional and development organisation but it can also help with some information.

Money Pärnu Kommertspank at Rüütli 51 on the south side of the main square, open Monday to Friday from 9 am to 1 pm and 2 to 3 pm, will change travellers' cheques. Pärnu Maapank on the north side of the square, and also at Rüütli 39, would only change cash, but stays open till 5 or 6 pm on

weekdays and is also open on Saturday till 2 or 3 pm.

Post & Telecommunications The main post office, open from 8 am to 7 pm Monday to Friday and 9 am to 3 pm Saturday and Sunday, is at Akadeemia 7; the telephone and telegraph office is at its rear on Rüütli.

Pärnu's telephone code is 244.

Media Pärnu Radio on 100.3 MHz has news bulletins on the hour alternately in Estonian, Russian, English and Finnish.

Travel Agencies Reiser Travel Agency (☎ 44 500, fax 44 885) at Rüütli 35 is a leading agent.

Health Pärnu tap water is often a brackish colour and best boiled before drinking.

Other Services There's a left-luggage office (pakihoid) next to the bus ticket office on Ringi. The best bookshop is Looming at Rüütli 41, with some publications in Western languages; it also sells Agfa film. The market is on the corner of Karja and Suur-Sepa.

Town Centre & Old Town

In an hour or two's stroll you can get the feel of modern Pärnu and also discover some surprising corners and snippets of its history. The old area stretches about 700 metres west of the central square along streets like Malmö, Rüütli and Kuninga.

The oldest building in Pärnu is the **Red Tower** (Punane Torn) on Hommiku. Originally bigger, this was the south-east corner tower of the medieval town wall, of which no more remains. At one stage the tower was used as a prison. The ground floor is a small museum, open Tuesday to Saturday from noon to 5 pm. Upstairs is an art shop.

Two blocks west, on Pühavaimu, is a fine pair of large **17th century houses** joined by a columned structure built in 1877. The in-between bit also has the date 1741 which was when the Pärnu merchant Hans Dietrich Schmidt, who owned both older wings in the 18th century, founded his general store.

ESTONIA

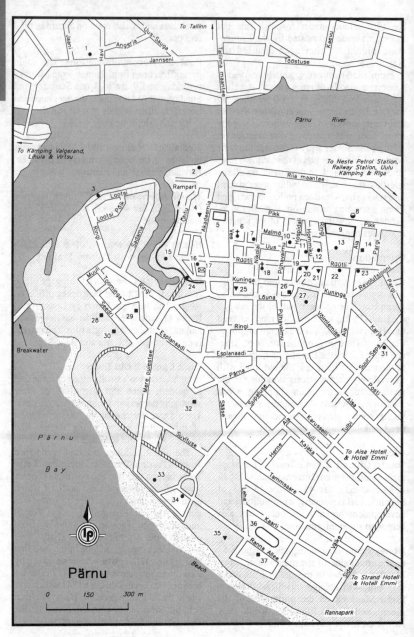

To Tallinn

Pärnu River

To Kämping Valgerand,
Lihula & Virtsu

To Neste Petrol Station,
Railway Station, Uulu
Kämping & Rīga

Riia maantee

Rampart

Breakwater

Pärnu
Bay

To Aisa Hotell
& Hotell Emmi

To Strand Hotell
& Hotell Emmi

Beach

Rannapark

Pärnu

0   150   300 m

■ PLACES TO STAY

14 Hotell Pärnu
26 Hotel Victoria
28 Hotell
29 Hotell Villa Del Mar
30 Hotell Kajakas
32 Hotell Leharu
37 Estonia Sanatorium
    (Under Reconstruction)

▼ PLACES TO EAT

4   Restoran Tallinn
20 Bristol Kohvipood
21 Bistro
25 Trahter Postipoiss
35 Rannahoone Restaurant
    (Under Reconstruction)

    OTHER

1   Lydia Koidula Museum
2   Port

3   Yacht Club
5   Theatre
6   Catherine Church
7   Town Hall
8   Taxi Stand
9   Bus Station
10 17th Century Houses
11 Red Tower
12 Bus Ticket Office
13 Pärnu Maapank
15 Open-air Auditorium
16 Telephone & Telegraph Office
17 Post Office &
    Sidesõlm Bus Stop
18 Elisabeth Church
19 Looming Bookshop
22 Pärnu Kommertspank
23 Pärnu Museum
24 Tallinn Gate
27 Lydia Koidula Statue
31 Market
33 Rannasalong
34 Mud Baths
36 Stadium

One block further west, on Nikolai on the corner of Uus, is the former **Town Hall** (Raekoja Hoon), a yellow-and-white classical edifice originally built in 1788 as the home of the town police chief. The grey-and-white Art Nouveau north wing with its little spire, opposite the corner of Malmö, was added in 1911. For some reason it features on a great number of postcards and photos of Pärnu. Across Nikolai from the main town-hall building there's a half-timbered house dating from 1740, and a block down the street on the corner of Rüütli is the Baroque Lutheran **Elisabeth Church**, also from the 1740s, named after the Russian empress of the time. Another block west at the corner of Uus and Vee, the Russian Orthodox **Catherine Church** (Ekatarina kirik) from the 1760s is named after another Russian empress, Catherine the Great.

If you now head to the far west end of Rüütli you'll find an embankment along an inlet of water from the river. This is a stretch of Pärnu's **Swedish ramparts** overlooking the **moat** which defended the west side of the old town. Where the rampart meets the west

end of Kuninga it's pierced by the tunnel-like **Tallinn Gate** (Tallinna Värav), one of three gates in the ramparts that the Swedes built as part of their 17th century strengthening of Pärnu's defences.

From here you can start back east along Kuninga, where there's a **17th century house** at No 21, with a shoe hanging from its eaves which is said to have been lost by Sweden's King Carl XII in this street in 1700. Nearby are an 18th century stone warehouse at Kuninga 24 and an 18th century house at Kuninga 28. The **Hotel Victoria** at Kuninga 25, a fine 1930 Art Nouveau building, stands on the site of the old Swedish Rīga Gate. Kuninga ran from the Tallinn Gate to the Rīga Gate. In Koidula väljak, the park opposite the hotel, stands a symbol of Pärnu: the **statue of Lydia Koidula**, the poet of Estonia's national revival whose likeness appears on the 100 EEK note. There's also a **Lydia Koidula Museum** at Jannseni 37 in Ülejõe on the north side of the river, open 10 am to 4 or 5 pm Wednesday to Sunday.

Pärnu Museum (Pärnu Rajoonide Vaheline Koduloomuuseum) is on the corner of the central square at Rüütli 53, open from 11 am to 5 or 6 pm Wednesday to Sunday. Its displays of handicrafts and local history include some stone-age artefacts.

Resort Area

The resort area begins just south of the old town and most of it is closed to vehicles. A band of green parkland known as Rannapark backs the long, wide beach. From its northern end you can walk along the two-km breakwater at the mouth of the river, but take care with the tides. The eye-catching 1927 classical structure at the sea end of Supeluse is the mud baths, where you can still take a mud bath. Bus No 1 comes to the Rannasalong stop here from Pärnu post office. Just to the west is the Rannasalong, a cultural centre and casino. A lot of reconstruction has been going on in the seafront area including at the large Rannahoone restaurant and the 1930s luxury Ranna Hotel (in Soviet times the Estonia Sanatorium).

Festivals

FiESTa International, a week-long splurge of live jazz, blues, new age and world music, has been celebrated yearly in the second half of June, around the Jäänipaev holiday, since 1986. In recent years FiESTa has also been accompanied by the Baltoscandal drama festival. Together the events bring about 40 musical acts and 20 mainly avant-garde theatre groups from around the world to Pärnu, filling the bars, cafés and streets with all sorts of weird and wonderful poseurs and generally turning the town into a kind of 'Womad meets Edinburgh on the Baltic'.

Another interesting Pärnu event is the Visual Anthropology Festival (Visuaalse-antropoloogia festival), a week-long international film festival and conference which focuses on threatened cultures. Its dates are movable: some years it has been held in July, others in early September.

The first 10 days of July are given over to a classical-music festival. The Astrijooks women's run, preceded by an international gymnastics event, is usually held on a Satur-day around 20 August. Other events include a children's festival in early June, a junior soccer tournament in early July and so on.

Places to Stay – bottom end

The *Hotell Kajakas* (☎ 43 098), in a green part of town a km from the bus station at Seedri 2, has singles/doubles for 20/40 EEK with private bathroom and TV, or 10/20 EEK with shared bathrooms. The one-storey building has reached its use-by date but the rooms are clean enough and the staff friendly despite being unused to Westerners. There's a café too. Next door at Seedri 4 another similar *Hotell* has rooms for 22 EEK a single or double, all with shared toilets and showers.

Kämping Jõekääru (☎ 41 121) should be operating in summer at Sauga Põhikool (Sauga Elementary School) in Sauga on the north side of the Pärnu River. Ten km west of central Pärnu among pleasant pine woods by the coast, *Kämping Valgerand* (☎ 64 231), open from mid-May to the end of September, has 40 reasonably sized two or four-person cabins for 50 or 80 EEK. There's space for tents too. Baths and toilets are shared. There's a canteen on the site. Valgerand means 'white beach' and there is indeed a small sandy beach out front of the site. You turn south off the Lihula road six km from Pärnu then go three km. *Uulu Kämping* (☎ 60 661), near the coast 13 km south of central Pärnu, has more cabins and a bar. The turn-off from the main Rīga road is just south of the turning to Valga, north of Uulu village.

Places to Stay – middle

Pärnu has quite a few hotels in the 200 to 350 EEK price range, though some of them are little more than recycled Soviet holiday homes. Definitely one of the best choices, despite being oddly located at Laine 2 in a housing estate two km east of the town centre, not far off the Rīga road, is the *Hotell Emmi* (☎ 22 043, fax 45 472). It's small, friendly and modern with singles/doubles at 225/320 EEK including a big smorgasbord breakfast. The rooms are comfortable, well decorated, a good size, and have their own bathrooms. The Emmi is easy to reach from the centre by bus or taxi; bus Nos 7, 19, 21 and others departing from the Sidesõlm stop at Pärnu post office go to the U Haigla stop on 9 Mai, a couple of minutes walk from the hotel.

At Tammsaare 27D in the same part of town as the Emmi, the 60-room *Strand Hotell* (☎ 24 243, 22 502), opened after conversion in 1992, has singles/doubles including breakfast at 150/215 EEK, and suites at 335 EEK. There's a restaurant, bar and conference centre, and the hotel offers a shuttle bus to/from the town centre – or you can take the same town buses as for the Emmi. Also towards this east side of town is the *Aisa Hotell* (☎ 43 186, fax 45 932) at Aisa 39, where comfortable singles/doubles with private bath, balcony and satellite TV go for 250/360 EEK. There's a restaurant and bar (room prices include breakfast), but the desk staff can be none too friendly.

The *Hotell Pärnu* (☎ 43 100, fax 42 944), on the central square at Rüütli 44, is a 1970s Soviet concrete block where light and clean but characterless rooms with TV and private bathroom cost 220 to 270 EEK a single, 300 to 380 EEK a double. There are also a few doubles with private toilet (but shared shower and no TV) for 250 EEK. All prices include breakfast.

Between the centre and the beach are a couple more middle-bracket hotels. The *Hotell Villa Del Mar* (☎ 43 534, fax 42 743) at Esplanaadi 42A has just a handful of quite pleasant, newish rooms with private bath and TV for about 250 EEK a double including breakfast. There's a swimming pool – though no certainty that it'll be in use – and bar. The *Hotell Leharu* (☎ 45 874) in a concrete-and-glass cube at Sääse 7 charges 200/350 EEK, including breakfast, for pretty average singles/doubles but offers car rental for 10 EEK an hour plus 2.50 EEK a km, or boat trips to Ruhnu or Kihnu islands for 132 EEK an hour.

Places to Stay – top end

The *Hotel Victoria* (☎ 43 412, fax 43 415) in the town centre at Kuninga 25 is easily the best hotel in Pärnu and among the top few in the Baltic states. A fine 1930 Art Nouveau building renovated in 1991, it's owned jointly by Pärnu town council and Swedish partners. The 21 singles/doubles are as tasteful and comfortable as you'd expect, with satellite TV, minibar, bathroom etc. They normally cost around 1300/1650 EEK including breakfast. At the time of writing there's a 30% discount from 15 June to 15 August (when the business travellers who are the hotel's main customers take their holidays) and at weekends. The Victoria is part of the Best Western chain so you could book through any Best Western office worldwide.

Places to Eat

One of the *Bistro* fast food chain, open from 8 am to 8 pm, is handily placed in the centre of town on the corner of Rüütli and Ringi. You can put together a meal of burger with spicy tomato sauce and pasta (but no bun), plus salad, coffee and juice, for around 15 EEK. It shouldn't be long before *Peetri Pizza* reaches Pärnu too.

A block west of Bistro along Rüütli there's the *Bristol Kohvipood* doing snacks, soups, and cheaper light meals such as frankfurter, potatoes and salad. There are several other cafés and numerous bars around the town centre and you can bet that the rebuilding work at the beach will give rise to a couple of good new places there. The *Trahter Postipoiss* at Vee 12 is a 19th-century post office turned into a tavern-restaurant, with a relaxed atmosphere, fairly good food and local beer. Starters are 2 or 3 EEK, main courses (typically meat and a few veg) from 7 to 9 EEK, and a big mug of beer is 1.80 EEK. The Postipoiss is open from 11 am to 3.30 pm and 5 to 10 pm.

The *Hotel Victoria* has easily the best restaurant in town and a meal there will cost less than you might expect, provided you avoid the expensive back part of the menu. The food is mixed Estonian and international. 'Assorted appetisers' at the high end of the starters price range (20 EEK) turns out to be a very good-sized plate full of cold meats, smoked fish, paté and vegetable trimmings. Main courses such as trout or roast beef in wine sauce, with vegetables, are 35 to 50 EEK. From 11 am to 2 pm there's a hot dish of the day for 15 EEK. The restaurant is open from 11 am to 11 pm. The hotel also has an outdoor café open in summer.

There's a reasonably good (and cheaper) restaurant at the *Hotell Pärnu*. You can play blackjack there too.

Getting There & Away

Air Pärnu has an airport on the northern edge of town, west off the Tallinn road. Flights to/from Tallinn were promised by the Tartu-based company, Ergon, which was awarded domestic flying rights in Estonia in 1993.

Bus The terminal for out-of-town buses is at the north end of Ringi, just off Pikk. The ticket office, open from 4.45 am to 9 pm, is a short distance south on the opposite side of Ringi. About 20 buses daily make the 130-km trip to/from Tallinn, some of them departing from beside the railway station in Tallinn instead of the main bus station used by other buses from the capital. Some are *ekspress* taking just over two hours; slower ones may take 2¾ hours. Fares range from 9 to 25 EEK. Some buses going from Pärnu to Tallinn, and most of those going south to Latvia and beyond, do not originate in Pärnu so you can't buy advance tickets – you have to take a chance on getting a seat when they arrive. Other buses to/from Pärnu include:

Haapsalu
one or two buses each way daily, three hours, 7 EEK
Kaliningrad
one overnight bus each way daily, 11 hours, 90 EEK
Kaunas
one overnight bus each way daily, 9½ hours, 60 EEK
Klaipėda
one overnight bus each way daily, 9½ hours, 60 EEK

Kuressaare
one bus each way daily and another one or two every other day except Tuesday, 4¼ hours, 10 EEK
Otepää
two buses each way daily, 3½ to four hours, 12 EEK
Rakvere
one bus each way daily, 4½ hours, 12 EEK
Rīga
one bus each way daily terminating in Pärnu and Rīga, and three others in transit each way daily, 3¾ hours, 12 to 20 EEK
St Petersburg
one overnight bus each way daily, 10 hours, 35EEK
Tartu
seven to 10 buses each way daily, three to 4½ hours, 11 EEK
Viljandi
five buses each way daily, 1¾ to 2¼ hours, 6EEK
Vilnius
one overnight bus each way daily, 9½ hours, 60 EEK
Virtsu
two to four buses each way daily, 1½ to 2¼ hours, 6 EEK

Train Four trains a day run each way between Tallinn and Pärnu, a trip of 2¾ to four hours. The fare in general seating is about 7 EEK at the time of writing. Pärnu station is five km east of the town centre along the Rīga road, at Riia maantee 116. There's a central ticket office on the south side of Rüütli between Hospidaali and Hommiku. South of Pärnu the railway heads inland to Kilingi-Nõmme and crosses into Latvia just south of Mõisaküla, but passenger trains on this line don't cross the border. One or two trains daily run between Pärnu and Mõisaküla (50 minutes).

Car & Motorbike The Neste petrol station at Riia maantee 110A is open 24 hours and has both 99 (super) and unleaded petrol. You can rent cars from Kalev Holzberg (☎ 41 051) at Haapsalu maantee 13. The Hotell Leharu also rents cars to its guests.

Boat It's possible to take trips from Pärnu to Kihnu and Ruhnu islands – see the sections on those islands. Pärnu Yacht Club (Pärnu

Jahtklubi) (☎ 41 948) at Lootsi 6 has a harbour suitable for visiting yachts.

Getting Around

A main local bus stop in the town centre is the Sidesõlm stop on Akadeemia in front of the main post office. Bus Nos 1, 2, 3, 5, 6, 7, 9, 10, 11, 12, 14, 16, 18, 18A, 19, 21, 40 and 57 stop here. There's a taxi stand on Pikk, across from the bus station.

AROUND PÄRNU
Lavassaare

Railways are used in the peat extraction industry at Lavassaare in an area of bogs 25 km from Pärnu, and there's a **railway museum** close to the peat fields with a couple of little old steam engines and narrow-gauge trucks. To reach Lavassaare turn north off the Lihula road 13 km west of central Pärnu, then go 12 km or so north. Reiser travel agency organises trips from Pärnu that include a ride on a 1960s train at Lavassaare.

Tori

There has been a stud farm at Tori, 20 km north-east of Pärnu on the Pärnu River, since 1856 when attempts began to breed bigger, stronger Estonian farm and cart horses. It went into decline in the Soviet period but is being revived. There's a **horse-breeding museum** here too, in a 250-year-old house. Reiser travel agency can arrange trips from Pärnu.

Kurgja

At Kurgja, on the Pärnu River 15 km east of Vändra and 65 km north-east of Pärnu, there's a **farm** still operated by 19th century methods and machinery, even with old-fashioned Estonian breeds of cow, pig and horse. It was founded in 1874 by Carl Robert Jakobson, a much revered leader of the Estonian national movement, as a model farm with the latest ideas in crop rotation, cattle feeding and so on. Here too is a museum to Jakobson, who was also an educationalist and edited the radical newspaper *Sakala*. If you should ever possess a 500 EEK banknote you can see what he looked like.

PÄRNU TO THE LATVIAN BORDER

The M12 highway from Pärnu to the Latvian border, a 65-km stretch, runs through forest much of the way, usually two or three km inland. An alternative if you have your own transport is the older road along the coast itself from Häädemeeste, 40 km from Pärnu, to the border.

Things to See

Konstantin Päts, the president of independent Estonia before WW II, was born at **Tahku**, 20 km down the coast from Pärnu. His statue here was the first **political monument** to be restored in post-Soviet Estonia. Estonia's biggest dunes line the coast at **Rannametsa**, about three km north of Häädemeeste. The **Nigula bog** (Nigula raba), just north of the Latvian border about 10 km east of the M12 highway, is a nature reserve the Nigula Looduskaitseala.

Places to Stay

A comfortable stopover on this coast is the *Lepanina Motell* (☎ 244-98 477 or 244-40 773, fax 244-40 230), a bright brick place with both middle-range and cheaper accommodation, right on the coast just 13 km from the Latvian border. All 32 motel rooms have private shower, toilet and balcony and cost 305/380 EEK for singles/doubles with breakfast from May to September, 225/305 EEK the rest of the year. There are also some four-person summer cottages in the forest back from the beach, at 80 EEK per person including breakfast, and caravan sites at 110 EEK including one person's breakfast. The motel has a restaurant (where a full meal costs around 40 EEK), a bar and a billiard room. It's on the Estonian Youth Hostels list as the *Kabli Hostel* but prices don't appear to be any lower for hostellers. The motel is just south of the hamlet of Kabli which is on the old coast road 10 km south of Häädemeeste. From the main highway turn down a paved road towards the coast 15 km from Häädemeeste, go 2½ km to the coast road then two km north.

WEST OF PÄRNU

The main road west from Pärnu heads straight across country to Lihula, where it meets the main road from Tallinn to Virtsu, the port for ferries to the island Saaremaa. The coast round this corner of Estonia is scenic with numerous bays, islands and some wild, isolated stretches – it's worth detouring along if you have time to spare. There's a paved road from Pärnu to beyond Tõstamaa, around halfway to Virtsu, and mainly reasonable dirt roads after that. A few buses come along this coast but it's easier to reach with your own transport.

KIHNU

Six-km-long Kihnu island, in the Gulf of Rīga 40 km south-west of Pärnu, is one of the most traditional places in Estonia, with colourful striped skirts still worn every day by most of the women in its population of 550. It's flat, and covered mainly by forests and grain fields. There are three main villages plus a school, church, and combined village hall-cum-bar in the centre of the island. Kihnu people are among the few Estonians who follow the Orthodox Church.

Many of the island's first inhabitants, centuries ago, were criminals and others exiled from the mainland. Kihnu men traditionally lived by fishing and seal hunting. The most famous of them was the sea-captain, Enn Uuetoa (better known as Kihnu Jõnn), who became a symbol of lost freedom for Estonians during the Soviet period when they were virtually banned from the sea. Kihnu Jõnn, said to have sailed on all the world's oceans, drowned in 1913 when his ship sank off Denmark on what was to have been his last voyage before retirement. He was buried in the Danish town of Oksby but in 1992 his remains were brought home to Kihnu and reburied at the island's church.

There's a museum near the church, and a lighthouse in the south with good views of the whole island from its top.

Getting There & Away

Reiser travel agency and the Hotell Leharu both offer boat excursions from Pärnu to Kihnu. The crossing is about two hours each way. A day trip with Reiser is about 230 EEK. You might also be able to organise a trip by asking at the harbour at Kalda 2, or the yacht club at Lootsi 6, in Pärnu. Liu on the west side of Pärnu Bay is the nearest mainland harbour to the island.

RUHNU

Ruhnu island, a little smaller than Kihnu, is 100 km south-west of Pärnu and nearer to the Latvian than the Estonian mainland. For several centuries Ruhnu had a mainly Swedish population of 200 or 300 but most of them left on 6 August 1944 to avoid the advancing Red Army, abandoning homes, animals and boats. Ruhnu has some sandy beaches and a 1644 wooden church which is the oldest wooden building in Estonia. It's flat but there's a forest of 200 to 300-year-old pines on its eastern dunes.

Getting There & Away

Reiser travel agency and the Hotell Leharu offer boat trips from Pärnu – see Kihnu. You might also be able to charter a boat from Saaremaa.

VILJANDI

Viljandi (population: 24,000) is a quiet country town 160 km south of Tallinn en route to Valga on the Latvian border. It's a green, hilly, quite pretty place on the north shore of the four-km-long lake Viljandi järv, over which there are good views. In summer it becomes a bit of a holiday centre. Many of the houses are decorated with small turrets, windmills or bay windows. Viljandi is 60 km east of Pärnu as the crow flies, but much of the area between is bog which the main Pärnu-Viljandi road skirts to the south, running about 110 km through Kilingi-Nõmme. The large, clean lake Võrtsjärv lies between Viljandi and Tartu.

The Knights of the Sword founded a castle at Viljandi (known in German times as Fellin) when they conquered this area in the

Top: Kuressaare Castle, Saaremaa, Estonia (JN)
Left: Bishops' castle, Haapsalu, Estonia (JN)
Right: Kiek-in-de-Kök, Tallinn, Estonia (JN)

   Top: Windmills at Angla, Saaremaa, Estonia (JN)
Bottom: Boats at Triigi, Saaremaa, Estonia (JN)

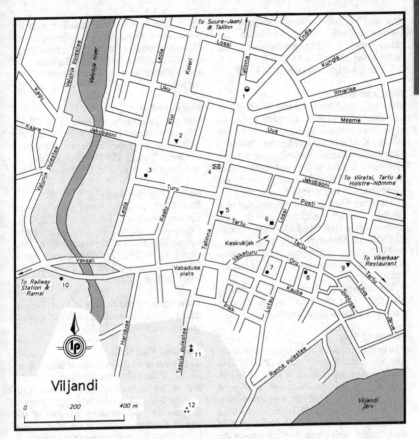

Viljandi

0   200   400 m

1   Bus Station
2   Menu Viljandi
3   Market
4   Post Office
5   Mulgi Kelder Café
6   Hotell Viljandi
7   Viljandi Museum
8   Town Hall
9   Draakon Café
10 Ugala Theatre
11 Jaani Kirik
12 Castle Ruins

13th century. The town around it later joined the Hanseatic League, then was subject to the usual comings and goings of Swedes, Poles and Russians.

Orientation & Information

The centre of town is about half a km back from the lake shore. The central square is Keskväljak, where Tartu meets Lossi, leading south to the castle park on the edge of the centre. The bus station is half a km north of the centre on Tallinna, past the main post office which is at Tallinna 11 on the corner of Jakobsoni. The market is at the west end of Turu, which leads west off Tallinna just south of the post office. The railway station is 750 metres west of the centre along Vaksali, at Metalli 1.

Viljandi's telephone code is 243.

Things to See
The ruins of **Viljandi Castle** overlook the lake from a hill in the castle park, just south of the town centre. The corner tower known as Villu Kelder is named after the leader of a 14th century Estonian rebellion who died a captive in it. Also in the castle park are the medieval **Jaani kirik** (St John's Church) and a **suspension footbridge** built in 1931.

There are few other buildings earlier than the 19th century. An exception is the 18th century **Town Hall** (Raekoda) in the centre. The **Viljandi Museum**, open from 10 am to 5 pm Thursday to Monday, is in a classical building on Laidoneri plats, in the old market square.

The surprisingly large **Ugala Theatre** at Vaksali 7 near the little Valuoja River is Estonia's most modern theatre.

Places to Stay
The better places are several km out of town. The Soviet-era *Hotell Viljandi* (☎ 53 852) in the centre on Keskväljak at Tartu 11 has 26 rooms with private toilet and shower at around 180/350 EEK for singles/doubles, but is rather dilapidated. Better if you have transport is the *Sammuli Puhkebaas* (☎ 54 463, fax 53 104) about five km out, on the far lake shore at Männimäe 28 in Viiratsi. Bare but comfortable rooms with balconies overlooking the lake cost 220/380 EEK. Bathrooms are shared. Meals, drinks, rowing boats and tennis are available. The friendly *Kivi Farm* (☎ 91 457), in Ramsi village seven km south of Viljandi, has rooms for 35/75 EEK in a separate building with its own shower, sauna, sitting and dining room. *Viljandi Kämping* (☎ 52 371), sometimes called *Viiratsi Kämping*, is at Tallinna 6 in Holstre-Nõmme about 10 km south-east of the town.

Places to Eat
You can get a reasonable meal in the *Hotell Viljandi* restaurant or in the *Vikerkaar* at Roo 5. Among the better cafés are the *Mulgi Kelder* at Tartu 5, the *Draakon* at Tartu 34 and the *Menu Viljandi* at Jakobsoni 11.

Getting There & Away
Bus There are four buses daily to/from Tallinn, taking 2½ hours for 12.50 EEK. Other services include five buses daily to/from Pärnu (two to 2½ hours, 6 EEK), and nine daily to/from Tartu by various routes (1½ to two hours, 5 EEK). There are also buses to/from Valga.

Train Three trains run daily to/from Tallinn, taking 2½ to 3¼ hours. The fare in general seating was around 8 EEK.

AROUND VILJANDI
At **Lõhavere** on the east side of Suure-Jaani on the Viljandi-Vändra-Pärnu road, is the site of the fortress of Lembitu, the 13th century Estonian leader who put up most resistance to the invading Knights of the Sword. He was defeated at the Madisepäev battle in 1217. A mKnights of the Swordonument of red stone blocks stands on a rise in the forest.

Vaibla is a bathing beach at the north end of Võrtsjärv, just off the Viljandi-Tartu road.

The Viljandi-Valga road crosses an area of slightly higher ground known as the **Sakala kõrgustik** (Sakala heights).

Latvia

Facts about the Country

Latvia (Latvija) is perhaps the least known of the Baltic states, lacking Estonia's close links to Western countries (Finland and Sweden) or the fame Lithuania achieved on its path to independence. Even those who visited Latvia under Soviet rule usually saw less than in Estonia or Lithuania, since travel was restricted to just a few places around Rīga, the capital.

Rīga remains Latvia's chief visitor magnet, being the biggest, most vibrant city in the Baltic states. Several other attractive destinations lie within day-trip distance of Rīga – including the coastal resort Jūrmala, the Sigulda castles overlooking the scenic Gauja river valley, and the Rastrelli palace at Rundāle. And now that Soviet-era restrictions are no more, there's plenty of off-the-beaten-track country to explore – such as the dune-lined coast and historic towns of Kurzeme (western Latvia) or the remote uplands of the eastern half of the country.

This chapter contains information specific to Latvia. For a more general introduction to the history, geography, people and culture of the Baltic states, see Facts about the Region at the front of the book.

GEOGRAPHY

Latvia, the middle Baltic state, is 63,700 sq km in area – a little smaller than the Irish Republic. Unlike the other two Baltic states, which are fairly compact in shape, Latvia is a lot wider from east to west than from north to south. A good half of Latvia's long, sweeping coast faces the Gulf of Rīga, a deep inlet of the Baltic Sea which is shielded from the open sea by the Estonian island of Saaremaa.

Latvia borders Estonia in the north, Russia and Belarus in the east, and Lithuania in the south. Rīga lies on the Daugava River, just inland from the Gulf of Rīga. Latvia has four regions: Vidzeme, the north-east; Latgale, the south-east; Zemgale, the centre; and Kurzeme, the west.

The Vidzeme Upland in eastern Latvia is the largest expanse of land with an elevation

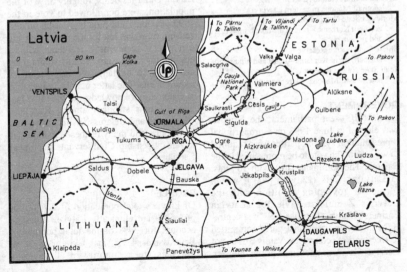

229

over 200 metres in the Baltics, with Latvia's highest point, Gaizina kalns (311 metres), topping it. The Latgale Upland in south-east Latvia reaches 289 metres at Lielais Liepukalns. The Kurzeme Upland in south-west Latvia manages only 184 metres at Krievu kalns near Priekule.

Borders

Latvia does not accept the incorporation into Russia in 1944 of its Abrene (Russian: Pytalovo) region – a 15-km-wide, 85-km-long slither of territory down its north-east border, immediately south of the Pechory region.

NATIONAL PARKS & RESERVES

Latvia has a single national park and a number of nature reserves. More information is provided in the regional chapters.

Gauja National Park
    920 sq km straddling the Gauja valley east of Rīga – castles, lovely valley scenery, wildlife centre, walking trails; park administration at Sigulda
Grīņi State Nature Reserve
    south of Pāvilosta in Kurzeme – bog area
Krustkalni State Nature Reserve
    south of Madona in eastern Latvia
Moricsala State Nature Reserve
    northern Kurzeme – part of the lake Usmas ezers and its shores
Slītere State Nature Reserve
    northern tip of Kurzeme – coast and hinterland
Teiči State Nature Reserve
    south-east of Madona –large bog area

GOVERNMENT

Latvia's 100-seat parliament, the Saiema, was elected in June 1993 on a proportional representation system: parties were required to win 4% of the vote to be represented in the Saiema. The dominant party, with 36 seats, is Latvijas Celš (Latvian Way), which formed a governing coalition with the Latvijas Zemnieku Savieniba (Latvian Farmers' Union). Latvijas Celš is a centre-right moderate-nationalist party committed to free-market economics. Valdis Birkavs of Latvijas Celš was chosen as prime minister,

while Guntis Ulmanis of Latvijas Zemnieku Savieniba, a great-nephew of the pre-WW II leader Kārlis Ulmanis, was given the more ceremonial role of president. Anatolijs Gorbunovs, a former communist leader who had also been the effective Latvian president from 1990 to 1993 and had led Latvijas Celš into the election, stepped down to the position of parliamentary speaker. The two leading opposition parties both have from 12 to 15 seats in the Saiema. One party is the right-wing Latvijas Nacionala Neatkarigas Kustiba (LNNK or Latvian National Independence Movement) – led by a German Latvian returnee, Joahims Zigerists – which takes a hard line on the citizenship issue. The second is Saskaņa Latvijai (Latvian Harmony), led by a former foreign minister Janis Jurkans, which has a moderate citizenship policy and enjoys the support of many Russian voters.

Citizenship

Citizens of the pre-1940 Latvian Republic and their descendants – including about 300,000 non-ethnic Latvians (mainly Russians) – are automatically citizens of modern Latvia. Other residents, roughly 35% of the population, were not allowed to vote in the 1993 elections, and final legislation on citizenship rules was left for the new Saiema to sort out. It seems most residents will be eligible for citizenship. As in Estonia there are likely to be language and residence requirements. The latter may be longer than in Estonia, but knowledge of the local language seems stronger among Russians, Ukrainians and Belarussians in Latvia than in Estonia, and many of these are expected to gain citizenship. Civil servants must speak Latvian.

PEOPLE

Of Latvia's total population of 2.7 million just 52% are ethnically Latvian. Russians account for 34% of the total population, Belarussians 4.5%, and Ukrainians 3.5%. Latvians are a minority in all seven of

Latvia's biggest cities including the capital, Rīga, which has a predominantly Russian population.

The Latvians and Lithuanians are the two surviving peoples of the Balt branch of the Indo-European ethno-linguistic group. The Balt peoples are thought to have spread into the south-eastern Baltic area around 2000 BC from the region which is now Belarus and neighbouring parts of Russia. (The term *Balt*, derived from the Baltic Sea, was first used last century to describe these peoples.) Those who stayed behind were assimilated, much later, by Belarussian or Russian Slavs (who are ethnically the Balts' nearest relatives). By the 13th century the Balts were divided into a number of tribal kingdoms.

The Latvians are descended from those tribes who were settled on the territory of modern Latvia, such as the Letts (or Latgals), the Selonians, the Semigallians, and the Cours. The Latgals, Semigallians and Cours gave their names to Latvian regions: Latgale, Zemgale and Kurzeme. The Selonians were settled between the Daugava River and northern Lithuania. During succeeding centuries of foreign rule these tribes (and to a large extent the Finno-Ugric Livs who inhabited northern coastal regions of Latvia) lost their separate identities and became merged in one Lettish, or Latvian, identity.

Up to 200,000 Latvians live in Western countries as a result of emigration around the turn of the 20th century and during and after WW II. There are approximately 100,000 Latvians in the USA, 33,000 in Australia, 18,000 in Canada, 12,000 in Germany, and 10,000 in Britain.

ARTS
Literature

Latvia's national epic – *Lāčplēsis* (The Bear Slayer), written by Andrējs Pumpurs in the mid-19th century – is based on traditional Latvian folk stories. The hero struggles against his enemy, a German Black Knight, only to drown in the Daugava River at the moment of final triumph. The anticipated rebirth of Lāčplēsis, however, leaves hope

for new freedom. The first Latvian novel, *Mērnieku Laiki* (The Time of the Land Surveyors), written in the 1860s and '70s by the brothers Reinis and Matiss Kaudzīte, has become a classic for its humorous portrayal of Latvian characters.

The towering figure in Latvian literature is Jānis Rainis (1865-1929), who Latvians say might have the acclaim of a Shakespeare or Goethe if he had written in a less obscure language. Rainis' criticisms of social and political oppression led to him spending much of his life in exile in Siberia and Switzerland. His leading works, all written in the first quarter of the 20th century, include the plays *Uguns un nakts* (Fire and Night) on the Lāčplēsis theme and *Jāzeps un viņa brāļi* (Joseph and his Brothers), and the poetry volumes *Gals un sākums* (The End and the Beginning) and *Piecas Dagdas skiču burtnīcas* (Dagda's Five Notebooks). Rainis' wife, Aspazija, was also a leading poet, playwright and social critic.

Rūdolfs Blaumanis (1863-1908) wrote psychologically penetrating novelettes and comic and tragic plays; among them, *Skroderdienas Silmačos* (Tailor's Days in Silmači) is still one of Latvia's most popular plays. Anna Brigadere (1861-1933) wrote much loved tales of rural life and fairy-tale dramas. Kārlis Skalbe (1879-1945) was another major writer of fairy tales.

Visual Arts

Jānis Rozentāls was really the first major Latvian painter. Around the turn of the century he painted scenes of peasant life and portraits, with some influence from Impressionism and Art Nouveau. Vilhelms Purvītis and Jānis Valters were the outstanding landscape artists of the time. Both – especially Purvītis – were influenced by Impressionism. Olegs Tillbergs is one of the most interesting modern Latvian artists. He collects and assembles garbage and other unwanted materials. His most controversial effort, in 1990, was an arrangement of coffins he had dug up from a cemetery.

Apparently they were empty. Ivars Poikans is another contemporary artist to watch for.

In the realm of film, Jūris Podnieks, who died young in 1992, produced some outstanding, haunting documentaries of life in the late Soviet era including: *Vai viegli būt jaunam?* (Is it Easy to be Young?), *Hallo, vai jūs mūs dzirdat?* (Hello, Do You Hear Us?), *Post Scriptum* and *Baltic Requiem*. The last two include very dramatic footage of the events of January 1991.

Music & Dance

Rock is very popular in Latvia and, like Estonia, there are big annual festivals (see Cultural Events).

Odis are the leading Latvian R&B outfit, while Bet Bet play a smooth (some say *too* smooth) Dire Straits/Travelling Wilburys-type rock. Livi are hard rockers from Liepāja. Kaspars Bindemanis is a flamboyant guitarist playing '50s and '60s rock.

Rīga was the Baltics' pre-eminent performing arts centre before WW I and between the world wars. Its ballet, which produced Mikhail Baryshnikov among others, goes back to the 1920s and was one of the best in the Soviet Union. The song composers Joseph Wihtol (Jāzeps Vītols) and Alfrēds Kalniņš are important early 20th century figures in classical music.

Facts for the Visitor

This chapter contains visitor information specific to Latvia. For details on obtaining visas for the Baltic states, Russia and Belarus and for more general information on travelling in the Baltic states see the introductory Facts for the Visitor chapter at the front of the book.

DIPLOMATIC MISSIONS

Latvian diplomatic missions are still being set up in many countries. Addresses and times of opening may change, so phone ahead before visiting.

Latvian diplomatic missions include:

Australia
    Consulate: PO Box 23, Kew, Victoria 3101 (☎ 03-499 6920)
Canada
    Consulate: 230 Clemow Ave, Ottawa, Ontario K1S 2B6 (☎ 613-238 6868)
Denmark
    Embassy: Rosbaeksvej 17, 2100 Copenhagen (☎ 39 27 60 00)
Estonia
    Embassy: Tõnismägi 10, Tallinn (☎ 22-681 668)
Finland
    Embassy: Bulevardi 5A-18, 00120 Helsinki (☎ 90-60 56 40)
France
    Embassy: 14 Boulevard Montmartre, 75009 Paris (☎ 1-34.80.90.76)
Germany
    Embassy: Adenaueralle 110, 5300 Bonn 1 (☎ 0228-26 4242)
Lithuania
    Embassy: Tumo-Vaižganto gatvė 2, Vilnius (☎ 22-220 558)
Norway
    Consulate: Beddingen 8, Aker Brygge, PO Box 1583 VIKA, N-0118 Oslo (☎ 22-28 91 31)
Russia
    Embassy: ulitsa Chaplygina 3, Moscow 103062 (☎ 095-921 07 91)
Sweden
    Embassy: Storgatan 38, S-11455 Stockholm (☎ 08-667 3414)
UK
    Embassy: 72 Queensborough Terrace, London W2 3SP (☎ 071-727 1698); due to move to 45 Nottingham Place, London W1, in 1994
USA
    Embassy: 4325 17th Street NW, Washington DC 20011 (☎ 202-726 8213)

CUSTOMS

Customs rules vary between the Baltic states and are subject to change. Some general points are given in the introductory Facts for the Visitor. If there is anything you are concerned about, contact a Latvian embassy or consulate for help.

Alcohol & Tobacco

You can import duty-free one litre of alcohol and 200 cigarettes.

Money

You can import and export duty-free any amount of hard currency.

Other Items

The import of pornography is banned. There are restrictions on exporting objects of cultural, historical or artistic value. A number of galleries and salons have special arrangements and their receipts will suffice at customs on departure. For other things you may need permission from the Culture Ministry at Elizabetes iela 18, Rīga (☎ 22-287 868).

Customs Information

The Customs Department is at Krišjāna Valdemara iela 1A, Rīga (☎ 22-226 246).

MONEY

Latvia's currency, the *lats* (plural: *lati*), was introduced in March 1993 alongside a transitional currency – the Latvian rouble (Latvijas rublis), which was due to disappear by October 1993. One lats was worth 200 Latvian roubles.

The lats is divided into 100 *santimi* (singular: *santims*). Though it's a floating currency, not tied in value to any other, the lats is expected to be fairly stable. Late 1993 exchange rates included:

US$1	=	0.63 lati
DM1	=	0.38 lati
UK£1	=	0.93 lati
C$1	=	0.46 lati
A$1	=	0.39 lati
1 Fmk	=	0.11 lati
1 SKr	=	0.08 lati

At the time of writing the denominations which have been issued are coins of 50 santimi, 1 lats and 2 lati; and notes of 5 lati (which will be the lowest denomination note). The 5-lati note shows an oak tree. The denominations to come are coins of 1 santims, 2 santimi, 5 santimi, 10 santimi and 20 santimi; and notes of 10 lati, 20 lati, 50 lati, 100 lati and 500 lati. The notes, printed in Germany, will depict Latvian wildlife, a farmhouse scene, the Daugava River, and the 19th century national awakener Krišjānis Barons. The reverse sides show traditional Latvian patterns and symbols. (On banknotes the word *latu* is used for the currency.)

The Latvian rouble, which the lats replaced, was introduced in May 1992. It circulated parallel to the Russian rouble till the latter ceased to be legal tender in July 1992. The lats joined the Latvian rouble in March 1993 with a few months of parallel circulation following before the Latvian rouble ceased to be legal tender. The Latvian rouble maintained its value over its year or so of existence, successfully shielding Latvia from the ongoing devaluation of the Russian rouble and its inflationary effects.

Latvian law requires prices to be quoted in lati, but other currencies can be used in the actual transaction.

NATIONAL HOLIDAYS

Latvian national holidays include Christian feast days, the Latvian National day, and even Mother's Day.

New Year's Day, 1 January
Good Friday
Easter Day – Easter Monday is also taken as a holiday by many
Labour Day, 1 May
Mothers' Day, second Sunday in May
Ligo (Midsummer festival), 23 June
Jāni or *Jānu Diena* (St John's Day), 24 June
National Day (anniversary of proclamation of Latvian Republic, 1918), 18 November
Christmas (Ziemsvētki), 25 December
Second Holiday, 26 December
New Year's Eve, 31 December

CULTURAL EVENTS

Latvia, in common with Estonia and Lithuania, celebrates a number of regular cultural events. The most important of these include the national song festival, Midsummer celebrations, and the Baltika folk festival. For some background to these events, see Cultural Events in the introductory Facts for the Visitor chapter at the front of the book.

Baltic Theatre Spring – drama festival; Rīga, April
Gadatirgus – big arts and crafts fair; Open-Air Ethnography Museum, Rīga, first weekend in June
Untamed Fashion Assembly – avant-garde fashion week; Rīga and Jūrmala, summer (dates vary)
Jūrmala Pop Festival – a contest not a festival, intended for TV not the public, with truly enormous ticket prices; Jūrmala, mid or late July
Liepājas Dzintars – rock festival, Liepāja, usually mid-August
Ascension Day – Roman Catholic processions, celebratory masses; Aglona, 14-16 August
Arsenāls – big international film festival, Rīga, mid or late September, even-numbered years
Bildes – lively week-long rock, folk, jazz & art festival featuring most of Latvia's top musicians and groups; Rīga, October-November
Lāčplēsis Day (Lāčplēšu Diena) – commemoration of dead heroes, named after Latvia's mythical warrior hero, whose name means 'Bear-slayer'; 11 November

MEDIA
Local-Language Press

The Latvian papers *Diena*, *Rigas Balss* and *Neatkariga Cina*, published four or five days a week, and the rural weekly *Lauku Avize* all sell from 70,000 to 160,000 copies per issue. Details of English-language newspapers and

magazines published in the Baltics are given in Facts for the Visitor, Media at the front of the book.

TV & Radio

The state TV channel, Latvijas Televīzija (LTV), shows CNN news in English at 5 pm. The independent NTV-5 on channel 7 has news about Latvia in English at 9.40 pm from Monday to Friday. Two Moscow channels, RTR and TsT, are also received in Latvia. In Rīga you can also get Sankt-Peterburg TV.

Radio Rīga broadcasts five minutes of news in English at 11.30 pm on 576 kHz,

1350 kHz, and 1422 kHz. The commercial Radio AA on 102.7 MHz FM plays the American Top 40 at 11 am on Sundays and relays Voice of America from midnight to 5 am.

FOOD

Latvians consume a lot of dairy products, eggs, potatoes, fish and grains, though you'll find plenty of meat in restaurants. *Šprotes* (sprats) crop up as a starter in many places. If they're *ar sīpoliem*, they'll be with onions. You may also find *siļķe* (herring), *līdaka* (pike), *zutis* (eel), *forele* (trout), or *lasis* (salmon). If fish is *cepts*, it's fried; if *sālīts* or *mazsālīts*, salted; if *kūpīnats*, smoked. Soups and sausage are also popular. *Žāvēta desa* is smoked sausage. In summer and autumn good use is made of many types of berry. Pies and tarts (*kūka*) also form an important part of the national diet. Cream is *krējums*, sour cream *skābais krējums*.

General information on eating in the Baltic states is given in the introductory Facts for the Visitor chapter at the front of the book. The Language Guide at the back of the book includes words and phrases you will find useful when ordering food and drink.

Rīga

Rīga has always been the major metropolis of the Baltic states; and today, with about 900,000 people, it has easily more big-city atmosphere than anywhere else in the region.

Set on a remorselessly flat plain divided only by the half-km-wide Daugava River, Rīga is less pretty than Tallinn or Vilnius and is also less quaint architecturally. But it has a touch more depth to its life than the other Baltic capitals.

Like them, it has a historic quarter – Vecrīga (Old Rīga) – that is the city's single major attraction, but it also has a more self-sufficient contemporary life, less dependent for its liveliness and bustle on tourists pulled in by its past. One Russian resident neatly summed up Rīga's attractions when explaining why she was happy to be returning there from a summer holiday in Poland and Kaliningrad: 'Rīga – it's civilisation!'. Despite the problems of transition from Soviet rule, you get the feeling that a new economic take-off is not far away in Rīga. Coca-Cola and McDonald's, among others, have chosen it as their Baltic headquarters.

Only just over a third of Rīgans are Latvians. Most of the rest are Russians – but there's less tension over that than you might expect, partly, perhaps, because the Latvians are so outnumbered but also because the Russian presence goes back quite a long way.

For the first six centuries of its existence Rīga was an almost exclusively German-peopled city, but Russians settled here in numbers in the first half of the 19th century, at least as early as Latvians. Today's Russian-population level, however, results mainly from the Soviet era, when Rīga became the industrial and commercial powerhouse of the USSR's Baltic region and many thousands migrated here to work in the new industries. Rīga was regarded as the most 'Western' city in the USSR, with a liberal arts and music scene that attracted people from all over the union.

This mixed-up past makes Rīga, today, a

fascinating blend of Latvian, German and Russian impressions in about equal measures. Few Germans live here now, but the German connections are clear from the old buildings (many now looking better-than-ever after restoration), from the numbers of German visitors and from the clear German economic interest today.

HISTORY

There was a Latgal or Liv fishing village on the site of modern Rīga and Scandinavian and Russian traders and raiders had paused here for centuries before German traders from Lübeck and Bremen first reconnoitred the mouth of the Daugava in the mid-12th century. In 1201 Bishop Albert von Buxhoevden from Bremen founded the first German fort in the Baltics here, as a bridge-head for the crusade against the northern heathens. Albert founded the Knights of the Sword, who made Rīga their base for subjugating Livonia. The first German settlements were at the southern end of the existing old city. Colonists from north Germany followed, and Rīga became the major city in the German Baltic, thriving from trade between Russia and the west and joining the Hanseatic League in 1282. The city's coat of arms still combines the key of Bremen with the towers of Hamburg – the two cities most instrumental in its founding. Furs, hides, honey and wax were among the products sold westward from Russia through Rīga.

Rīga's bishop, elevated to archbishop in 1252, became the leader of the church in the lands the Germans conquered, ruling a good slice of Livonia directly and further areas of Livonia and Estonia indirectly through his bishops. But there was always a contest for power between the church, the knights (who controlled most of the rest of Livonia and Estonia), and the German merchant-dominated city authorities, who managed to maintain a degree of independence from 1253 to 1420.

Rīga reached its early peak of prosperity around the beginning of the 16th century. Following the knights' collapse in the middle of that century, the city suffered attacks by Poles and Russians; after a brief spell of independence from 1561, it fell under Polish rule in 1582. Sweden captured it in 1621, but both Sweden and Poland allowed it autonomy. In the Swedish period, Rīga was, effectively, the second city of Sweden, and it was at this time that it first expanded beyond its fortified walls. In 1710 Russia took it from Sweden. Throughout this entire period, however, the old German nobility and merchants remained in real control.

In the Russian era Rīga grew into an important trading and industrial city, the capital of the province of Livonia. Its population jumped to 28,000 in 1794 and 60,000 by the 1840s. While the old part of city remained a preserve of Rīga's approximately 30,000 Germans, around it were spreading suburbs of wider, straighter streets with wooden houses, inhabited by the largest Russian community in the Baltic provinces as well as a growing number of Latvians. In

the 1840s the German traveller J G Kohl reported:

The Russians demand all the rights of citizenship, with seat and vote in the city colleges, the town council etc. The Germans resist these demands, declaring that the Russians know nothing about matters of this kind, and that their admission would be the ruin of the community. They point to their capitulation of 1710, according to which a Russian was never to become a citizen of Rīga, nay, was not even to be allowed to open the smallest shop within the city walls...

In fact, Russian traders – Kohl says many hundreds of small shops or booths – were already well entrenched in Old Rīga. The city walls were pulled down between 1857 and 1863 to assist the free flow of commerce. Rīga developed into the world's busiest timber port and Russia's third-greatest industrial city (after Moscow and St Petersburg). Russia's first cars would be built here. Rīga was also renowned for the quality of the Lithuanian and Belarussian hemp and flax which it exported to the outside world. The combustible nature of these materials made the boats (called *strusen*) on which they were brought downriver to Rīga something of a fire hazard – 'on account of the carelessness of the Russians, with respect to fire,' Kohl says, going on to relate one incident:

One evening...four burning *strusen* came floating down the river, straight towards the wooden bridges, where lay from 400 to 500 ships. All was in alarm. The bridges were torn up to let at least some of the ships escape...but the burning *strusen* were fast approaching, and the greatest loss seemed unavoidable, when, all at once, the four vessels slackened their pace, then stood still, and at length...floated slowly back up the river...The people shouted 'a miracle!' and some persisted that they had seen angels descend from heaven, and draw the ships back.

The fact, however, was, that the burning vessels on their way had warmed the air behind them, which produced a stream of cold air towards them, from all sides...Before them the greatest degrees of heat and cold met suddenly. At the time when the fire was strongest, therefore, the wind in front blew most strongly, and drove back the dreaded *strusen*.

Also in the 19th century, Latvians freed from serfdom in the countryside moved to the city and pushed into its trades, business, civil service, and intellectual circles, forming about a quarter of the population by the 1860s. The Rīga Latvian Association, formed in 1868, became the core of the Latvian national awakening, inspiring a Latvian national theatre, opera, encyclopedia and, in 1873, the first Latvian song festival. The number of Latvians in Rīga grew till it reached about half the city's population of half a million on the eve of WW I. There were also significant communities of Jews and Western merchants: the city's last mayor before the war, George Armitstead, came from an English merchant family.

Rīga was badly damaged in both world wars and was left with only 181,000 people at the end of WW I after evacuations and other ravages. The Germans departed after the Latvian land reform of the 1920s and Hitler's 'come home' call in 1939. In the Latvian independence era between the wars, Rīga was the centre chosen by Western diplomats, journalists and spies to eavesdrop on Stalin's Soviet Union; and flourishing nightclubs, restaurants and intellectual life earned it the nickname Little Paris.

During WW II, Rīga was occupied by the Germans from 1941 to 1944, and virtually all its Jewish community (estimated variously at 45,000 to 100,000) was exterminated. Thousands of Latvians left for the West towards the end of the war to avoid Soviet rule.

After the war, the city was turned into a leading Soviet technical and industrial centre. It became the USSR's main source of railway engines and carriages, producing half its mopeds and a third of its washing machines, as well as trams, radios, telephone exchanges, robots and computers. The city sprawled outwards as large numbers of migrants came to work for the new industries. But after independence, enterprises which had been leaders in the USSR found themselves out-of-date by comparison with Western products.

ORIENTATION

Rīga sprawls either side of the Daugava River, about 15 km inland from its mouth in the south-east corner of the Gulf of Rīga. The east bank holds almost all the interest. Old Rīga (Vecrīga), the historic heart of the city, stretches one km along this side of the river and 700 metres back from its banks.

Old Rīga's skyline is dominated by three steeples. From south to north these are: St Peter's (the tallest), the square bulk of the Dom (cathedral) tower, and the simpler St Jēkab's. Round most of the old city runs a wide band of 19th century parks and boulevards, and beyond that is 'New Rīga', beginning with the areas built up in the 19th and early 20th century, which have a mixed business and residential life. Further out are the newer, mainly residential suburbs and industrial enclaves.

The boundaries between these zones are clear to see if you trace the street running north-east from the October Bridge (Oktobra tilts) over the Daugava. First it cuts across the middle of the old city as a narrow, mainly pedestrianised artery called Kaļķu iela. Then, gaining the name Brīvības bulvāris (Freedom Boulevard), it widens to cross the ring of boulevards and parks and passes the Freedom Monument, an important landmark. At the towering Hotel Latvija, 1¼ km from the river, it enters the new town and becomes Brīvības iela. Further out still, en route to Sigulda, Pskov and St Petersburg, it becomes Brīvības gatve. (In the Soviet era, incidentally, it was called Ļeņina iela from one end to the other.)

The railway and bus stations are five-minutes walk apart on the south-east edge of Old Rīga. Many places to stay, too, are conveniently placed on the fringe of the old city.

INFORMATION
Money

There are exchange offices at Rīga airport and dotted throughout the central area in hotels, banks, shops, street kiosks and elsewhere. Look for the sign 'Valūtas Apmaiņa'. The Rīgas Komerc Banka (Rīga Commercial Bank) at Smilšu iela 6 in Old Rīga will change travellers' cheques from 9 am to 1 pm and 2 to 3.30 pm Monday to Friday, with commission charged only on cheques of more than US$50. When I last used this service the bank insisted on paying me out in cash US dollars, which I then had to change into local currency elsewhere.

Latvia Tours (see Travel Agencies) is the local American Express representative.

Post & Telecommunications

Rīga's head post, telephone and telegraph office, open 24 hours daily, is at Brīvības bulvāris 21, but the poste-restante service is at another large post office on Stacijas laukums, next to the railway station. Have poste-restante mail addressed like this example:

John SMITH
Poste Restante
Rīga 50
LV-1050
LATVIA

The Stacijas laukums office also has an international express-mail service for letters or parcels, as does DHL at Palasta iela 5.

Normal international telephone service in Latvia is primitive at the time of writing – basically, whether calling from a private phone or a public telephone office, you have to book the call, wait 24 hours, then wait some more when the appointed time rolls around. Direct-dial facilities were supposed to become generally available by the end of 1993, though there may still be queues at phone offices or a shortage of lines to slow things down.

In the meantime there are a couple of places in Rīga where you can make international calls quickly if you're prepared to pay. Best is the 'Telex, Fax, Telephone' office on Dzirnavu iela behind the Hotel Latvija. It's open from 9 am to 8 pm daily. One minute by phone (minimum three minutes) or fax (minimum four minutes) costs 0.65 lati to Europe, 1 lats elsewhere. You can receive faxes here, too, at 0.65 lati for two pages.

The telephone office at Brīvības bulvāris 21, more expensive for immediate phone calls, charges between 2 lati and 2.65 lati per page (not per minute) for immediate transmission of outgoing faxes but considerably less for its 'regular' fax service (faxes may not be sent till the next day). It charges less than the Dzirnavu office for incoming faxes – but, in my experience, has problems with its incoming lines.

Rīga's telephone code (for calls made from elsewhere within Latvia) is 22.

Foreign Diplomatic Missions

Foreign missions started setting up in Rīga after independence in 1991. A few were still looking for permanent premises, so they may move from the addresses given here. Some countries cover Latvia from their embassies in nearby countries, including: Austria, Iceland and the Netherlands from Stockholm; Australia from Copenhagen; New Zealand from Moscow; Ireland from Warsaw; and South Africa from Helsinki.

Belgium
    Embassy: Hotel Ridzene, Endrupa iela 1 (☎ 325 982)
Canada
    Embassy Office: Elizabetes iela 45/47 (☎ 333 355)
Denmark
    Embassy: Pils iela 11 (☎ 226 210)
Estonia
    Embassy: Nometņu iela 62 (☎ 601 014)
Finland
    Embassy: Teātra iela 9 (☎ 216 040)
France
    Embassy: Raiņa bulvāris 9 (☎ 212 878)
Germany
    Embassy: Basteja bulvāris 14 (☎ 229 096)
Israel
    Consulate: Strēlnieku iela 11/4 (☎ 332 778)
Italy
    Embassy: Teātra iela 9 (☎ 216 069)
Lithuania
    Embassy: Elizabetes iela 2 (☎ 321 519)
Norway
    Embassy: Zirgu iela 14 (☎ 216 744)
Poland
    Chargé d'Affaires: Elizabetes iela 2 (☎ 322 233)
Russia
    Embassy: Paegles iela 2 (☎ 285 842)
Sweden
    Embassy: Lāčplēša iela 13 (☎ 286 276)

LATVIA

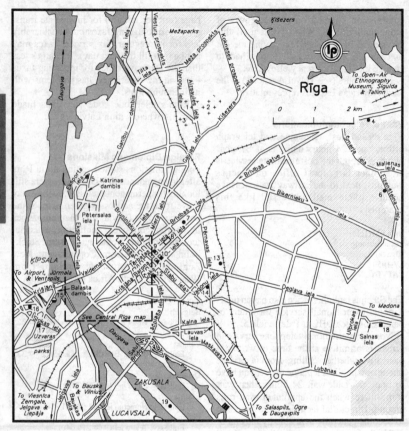

UK
    Embassy: Elizabetes iela 2 (☎ 320 737); expected to return to pre-WW II embassy at Raiņa bulvāris 2
USA
    Embassy: Raiņa bulvāris 7 (☎ 227 045)

Travel Agencies

There are numerous travel agencies in Rīga, offering outbound bookings as well accommodation, tours and other services within Rīga and around the Baltic states. The Association of Latvian Travel Agencies (☎ 327 254, fax 213 666) is at Torņa iela 9. TAS (☎ 216 201, fax 222 901) in Room 201 of the Hotel Rīga is a small, but competent agency which should be able to help you find middle or top-end accommodation when everywhere seems full. Latvia Tours (☎ 213 652, fax 213 666) is a major local agency which, among other things, sells tickets for the Mercuri (Rīga-Klaipėda-Kiel), Tallink (Tallinn-Helsinki), EstLine (Tallinn-Stockholm) and Viking Line (Helsinki-Stockholm) ferries. Its main office is at Grēcinieku iela 22/24, with ferry-ticket sales and car rentals from Peldu iela 25 nearby, but it also has an office in the Hotel de Rome. Baltic Tours (☎ 329 514) at Eksporta iela 1A

1 Brothers' Cemetery
2 Second Woodland Cemetery
3 Rainis Cemetery
4 Neste Petrol Station
5 Hotel Karavel
6 Motor Museum
7 Daugavas Sporta Namā
8 Sporta Pils
9 Alternative Ltd
10 Kino Nams
11 Viesnīca Viktorija &
     Restorāns Selga
12 Kooperativ Lido
13 Daugava Stadium
14 Neste Petrol Station
15 River Station
16 YMCA Tours Youth Hostel (Summer)
17 Viesnīca Tūrists
18 Viesnīca Plavnieki
19 TV Tower

(the sea-passenger port) sells tickets for Tallink, the Silja Line ferries between Finland and Sweden, and the Rīga-Stockholm and Rīga-Travemunde services. Another agency which may be useful for varied tasks is Celotajs (☎ 227 719) at Turgeņeva iela 19. FremadRiga (☎ 210 773) at R Vagnera iela 3, owned by FremadRejser of Copenhagen, claims to have been the first foreign travel agency to set up in the Baltic states. It deals mainly with business travellers and top-end tourists.

Media
Riga This Week (0.65 lati) and the similar *Riga Success Guide* have listings of places to stay and eat, things to see, entertainment and so on, though they're less on the ball than their Tallinn and Vilnius equivalents. The Tallinn-published *Baltic Independent* newspaper and *Baltic Outlook* and Rīga's own *Baltic Observer* are all well worth picking up. See the Media section in the introductory Facts for the Visitor chapter at the front of the book for more on some of these publications. The news kiosk in the lobby of Rīga Technical University (Rīgas Tehniskā Universitāte) at Kaļķu iela 1 sells some of them cheaper than their normal prices.

You can pick up British and German newspapers, the *International Herald Tribune*, *Time* and *Newsweek* at several places including the Hotel de Rome – which receives same-day British papers in the late evening (*The Guardian* or *The Times* is 1.30 lati) – and at Grāmatnīca Gaisma across the street.

See Latvia – Facts for the Visitor: Media for information on TV and radio broadcasts in English.

Bookshops
Rīga has several good bookshops where you're always likely to come across some titles in English, including guides or other material on Latvia. Grāmatnīca Gaisma on Kaļķu iela, opposite the Hotel de Rome, is one of the best; Centrālā Grāmatnīca at Aspazijas bulvāris 24, opposite the Hotel Rīga, is also good.

Maps
Globuss, next door to Centrālā Grāmatnīca, is the best shop for maps. An excellent 1:25,000 (1 cm = 250 metres) *Rīga City Map*, published in 1991, with a close-up of the city centre and keys in Latvian, English and Russian, is sold here and in kiosks and other bookshops for 0.10 lati. It shows bus, tram and trolleybus routes, too. There's also the *Rīgas un Jūrmalas Apkārtne* (1991), a 1:150,000 (1 cm = 1.5 km) map of Rīga's surroundings, which is useful for day trips out of the city. Globuss has close-up sheets at 1:75,000 (1 cm = 750 metres) of some parts of Latvia.

Health & Medical Services
Drinking tap water is not advisable unless you can boil it first, as residents do. Reputedly, over half the city's sewage still goes untreated into the Daugava. The City Clinical Hospital is at Bruņinieku iela 8. There's emergency dental service (☎ 274 546) at Stabu iela 9. Pharmacies at Elizabetes iela 21, Elizabetes iela 55 (in the Hotel Latvija), and R Vāgnera iela 15 sell some Western medicines. There's a homeopathic drugstore at Vaļņu iela 26.

Left Luggage

There are left-luggage rooms at the airport, the bus station and the railway station. At the bus station there are two, open slightly different hours between 5.30 am and 11 pm. The 24-hour left-luggage room (Rokas Bagāžas) at the railway station is downstairs in the long-distance side of the station. The official cost of storing your bag here is apparently related to its value, but 0.15 lati or so seems acceptable. There are also lockers (*automātiskas rokas bagāžas glabātuves*), open from 4 am to 1 am, at the rear of the main concourse.

Film & Photography

Kodak Express at Brīvības iela 40, opposite the Hotel Latvija, sells some Kodak film (but not Kodachrome) and other photographic supplies including batteries and will process print film in 24 hours for 0.25 lati a print. The Fuji shop at Vaļņu iela 11 in Old Rīga charges 1.30 lati, plus 0.20 lati for each print. It can also do four passport photos for 0.80 lati in 24 hours.

WALKING TOUR

A walk something like the following will give you a good introductory feel for Rīga. It will take about three hours nonstop at a fairly leisurely pace, but you could make a day of it with pauses at museums, galleries, cafés and so on that take your fancy. Start with a look at the northern half of Old Rīga, which centres on **Doma laukums** (but don't forget to explore a few smaller, crookeder byways). Then make your way to the riverside and maybe walk halfway over the **October Bridge** for a view of Old Rīga from the river. Return to the southern half of Old Rīga and take the lift up the tower of **St Peter's Church** for a view of Old Rīga from the sky. Wander south out of Old Rīga to the **market** on Prāgas iela, a focus of the city's modern life. Then head past the railway station, another of today's city hubs, to the **Freedom Monument**, set in the band of boulevards and parks. Have a wander round the parks and, if you still have the energy, head out to the streets to their east to have a

look at a more everyday, but still busy section of the city.

OLD RĪGA

Many centuries-old German buildings survive in the old city – in places, whole squares or rows have stood since the 17th century or earlier. Old Rīga is a protected zone of narrow, crooked, now mainly pedestrian-only streets, made prettier by restoration, and dotted with cafés and restaurants. Latvia's government and finance houses are still centred here today, but commerce has taken a back seat to conservation and restoration (which is ongoing). Old Rīga, therefore, sometimes feels unnaturally quiet, but exploring it is still a chief pleasure of the city. Kaļķu iela divides Old Rīga fairly neatly into two halves, each focusing on a towering church: the Dom (cathedral) in the north, St Peter's in the south.

The Dom

The brick cathedral known as Rīgas Doms (from the German: *Dom*, cathedral) towers beside Doma laukums, the major open space within the old city, and is surrounded by an unusual brew of architectural styles. Founded in 1211 as the seat of the Rīga bishop, the Dom is now a combined church, museum and organ-concert hall. Its opening hours as a museum are from 1 to 5 pm Tuesday to Friday and 10 am to 2 pm Saturday. Church services are held at noon on Sunday. In the Soviet era they were banned; the first service for over 30 years, in 1988, was a major event of the *perestroika* era.

Architecturally the Dom is an amalgam of styles from the 13th to 18th centuries: the east end, the oldest, has Romanesque features; the tower is 18th century Baroque; and much of the rest dates from a 15th century Gothic rebuilding. The floor and walls of the huge interior are dotted with old stone tombs – note the curious carved symbols on some of those on the north side, denoting the rank or post of the occupant. Eminent citizens would pay to be buried as near the altar as possible. In 1709, a cholera and typhoid outbreak which killed a third of Rīga's pop-

The Dom

ulation was blamed on a flood that inundated the cathedral's tombs. The pulpit dates from 1641 and the huge organ, which has 6768 pipes, from the 1880s. The **Museum of the History of Rīga & Navigation**, open daily except Monday and Tuesday, is housed in the cloister of the monastery attached to the cathedral.

Rīga Castle

The castle, on Pils laukums, dates from 1330 when it was built as the Livonian Order's headquarters and served as the residence of the order's grand master. Today the castle, after modifications down the centuries, looks much younger and not very castle-like from its inland side. You get a more turreted aspect from the river or the Vanšu Bridge. The castle houses the **Latvian History Museum** (Latvijas Vēstures Muzejs), the **Rainis Museum** of Literary and Art History (Raiņa Literatūras un Mākslas Vēstures Muzejs), and an unexciting Museum of Foreign Art, all reached through the same

door at Pils laukums 3. The history museum, up four flights of steps, spans the millennia from bronze body-ornaments more than 2000 years old to the present, including 1930s tourist maps in English. Galoshes, we learn, were a leading export of pre-WW II Latvia. This museum is open Wednesday and Friday from 1 to 7 pm and Thursday, Saturday and Sunday from 11 am to 5 pm. The Rainis Museum is named after Latvia's national poet but also covers theatre and other Latvian writers. It's open from 1 to 7 pm on Wednesday, and 11 am to 5 pm every other day except Sunday. At the north end of the castle is a pleasant sculpture garden.

Old Rīga North – other sights

Near the castle at Mazā Pils iela 17, 19 and 21 is a quaint row of houses known as the **Three Brothers** (Trīs brāli), one of which is now an art gallery. No 17 dates from the 15th century, which makes it the oldest house in Latvia. At the end of Mazā Pils iela is Jēkaba iela, where the interior of tall **St Jacob's Church** (Jēkaba baznīca) maintains its original 13th century form. This church is the seat of Rīga's Roman Catholic archbishop. Next door to St Jacob's at Jēkaba iela 11 is Latvia's **parliament**, a Florentine Renaissance-style building which was a focus of Latvian resistance to Soviet provocation in January 1991 and remained barricaded for over a year afterwards.

The picturesque **Swedish Gate** (Zviedru vārti) at the meeting of Torņa iela and Aldaru iela was built on to the city walls in 1698 during the Swedish period and is the only remaining old-city gate. The round, peaked **Powder Tower** (Pulvertornis) at the end of Torņa iela is a 14th century original and the only survivor of the 18 towers in the city wall. Nine Russian cannonballs from 17th and 18th century assaults are embedded in the tower's walls. After incarnations as a gunpowder store, prison, torture chamber and Soviet revolution museum, the tower is now the **Latvian War Museum** (Latvijas Kara Muzejs), open Thursday from noon to 7 pm and other days (except Monday) from 11 am to 6 pm. The museum has quite a lot of material, much of it suppressed in the Soviet era, on Latvian armed forces in the two world wars and the period between them.

The 19th century Gothic exterior of the **Great Guild Hall** (Lielā Ģilde) at Amatu iela 6 encloses a fine 1330 merchants' meeting hall, the Minsteres istaba, which is now the concert hall of the Latvia State Philharmonia. If you can't get in to look round the hall, consider attending a concert to see it. Look up here to see, atop the yellow-painted house on the other side of Meistaru iela, two lifelike **cat figures** seemingly stuck on the building's topmost pinnacles. A **plaza** with an outdoor art market opens out before it at the meeting of Meistaru iela and Kaļķu iela.

Latviešu Strēlnieku Laukums

The open space immediately east of the October Bridge is known as Latviešu strēlnieku laukums ('Latvian Riflemen Square'). It is dominated by a big, black statue of the said marksmen; a museum, behind the statue, is dedicated to them. The Latvian Riflemen were eight regiments formed in WW I to fight in the Russian imperial army. When the Bolshevik revolution rolled around, most of them supported it. They provided a kind of palace guard for Lenin and formed key units of the Red Army during the Russian civil war. But some sided against the Bolsheviks in the concurrent Latvian independence war. During the Soviet era the riflemen were known as the Latvian Red Riflemen and the museum, which along with the statue is a Soviet creation, gave a Soviet version of events.

Before WW II this square was called Rātslaukums (Town Hall Square). Its fine classical town hall and the magnificent 17th century House of Blackheads (Melngalvju nams), built for the Blackheads guild of unmarried merchants (who also had an important house in Tallinn), were both destroyed during or soon after WW II. There has been talk of demolishing the museum and re-creating the House of Blackheads.

From the square it's worth walking along

the riverside a little way, or out on to the bridge.

St Peter's Church

Red-brick, Gothic St Peter's (Pētera Baznīca) is the dominant feature of the southern half of Old Rīga. Don't miss the panoramic view from its famed spire, which has been built three times in the same Baroque form: originally in wood in the 1660s; again in wood in the 18th century, after being burnt down by lightning; and most recently in steel between 1967 and 1973, after the church had been burnt to a shell in 1941 (whether by attacking Germans or the retreating Red Army depends on who you consult). A wooden church was built here in 1209, but the body of the existing building dates mainly from the 15th century; the fine pink stone of the western façade is 17th century. The body, like the spire, was badly damaged by the Germans, and much restoration has taken place; it's now used as an exhibition hall. The way up the spire is by lift (0.07 lati), which ascends at fixed times listed as 'seansi' in the ticket office in the lobby.

Skārņu Iela & Mārstaļu Iela

A row of particularly pretty restored buildings faces the north side of St Peter's on Skārņu iela. No 10/16, originally a chapel of the Knights of the Sword's first Rīga castle built here in 1208, is now the absorbing **Museum of Applied Arts** (Dekoratīvi Lietišķās Mākslas Muzejs), full of fine Latvian work; it's open from 10 am to 6 pm daily, except Monday. The pottery and wall hangings are outstanding.

The building at No 22 is the **Eka Convent** (Ekes konventa), built in the 15th century and converted, in 1592, into a home for widows by the then mayor, N Eke. The Tourist Club of Latvia has its offices inside. Duck into the yard behind for a view of St Peter's rising above the roofs. Next door at No 24, **St John's Church** (Jāņa Baznīca) is a 13th to 19th century amalgam of Gothic, Renaissance and Baroque styles.

Further south at Mārstaļu iela 2/4, on the

corner of Audeju iela, is the 17th century **House of Johannes Reitern**, a rich merchant, with elaborate stonecarving. Mārstaļu iela 10, a 1727-33 **Protestant church**, is now a recording studio; and Mārstaļu iela 21 is the Baroque **House of Dannenstern**, another wealthy 17th century merchant.

Alberta laukums, a small square on the south edge of Old Rīga, was the site of Bishop Albert's original German settlement. There are several tall **medieval warehouses** on narrow streets which lead back into the old city from here – at Alksnāja iela 5, 7, 9 and 11 and Vecpilsētas iela 10 and 11.

PARKS & BOULEVARDS

East of Old Rīga's confined streets, the city opens out into a perfectly contrasting band of parks and wide boulevards laid out in the 19th century. Along the boulevards are many fine 19th and early 20th century buildings, some of the 'Eclectic' school which drew on a multitude of past styles, while others are flamboyant examples of *Jugendstil* (German Art Nouveau), which crops up all over Rīga – in fact more so here than in many German cities because of damage during WW II. Many of the ornate *Jugendstil* decorative motifs are on upper storeys, so don't forget to look up! The old defensive moat, known as the **City Canal** (Pilsētas kanāls), snakes through the parks and marks the line of the old-city walls which were knocked down in the mid-19th century.

Freedom Monument

The central landmark of the park ring is the Freedom Monument (Brīvības piemineklis) on Brīvības bulvāris, near the corner of Raiņa bulvāris. Paid for by public donations, the monument was erected in 1935 in the style you could describe as Thirties National Heavy, on a spot where a statue of Peter the Great had stood. Topped by a bronze female Liberty holding up three stars representing the major regions of Latvia – Kurzeme, Vidzeme and Latgale – it bears the inscription 'Tēvzemei un Brīvībai' ('For Fatherland and Freedom'). During the Soviet years the Freedom Monument was out of bounds, and

a statue of Lenin, facing the other way down Brīvības iela, was placed two blocks east. In the late 1980s and early '90s the Freedom Monument became a focus of the Latvian independence movement, starting on 14 June 1987 when 5000 rallied here illegally to commemorate the victims of Stalin's deportations. Several later rallies and marches focused on the monument, which also functioned as an unofficial centre for animated political debate. Since 1992 the guard of honour that stood at the monument before WW II has been revived.

North of Brīvības Bulvāris

The mound called **Bastejkalns** (Bastion Hill) beside Basteja bulvāris is what remains of one of the bastions of Old Rīga's fortifications. Beside the paths either side of the canal below Bastejkalns stand five red stone slabs – **Memorials to the Victims of 20 January 1991**. Edijs Riekstins, Sergey Kononenko, Vladimir Gomanovich, Andris Slapins and Gvido Zvaigzne were all killed or fatally wounded here when Soviet OMON troops stormed the Interior Ministry nearby at Raiņa bulvāris 6. Slapins and Zvaigzne were members of the film crew of the Latvian documentary maker Jūris Podnieks. No one who has seen the films *Baltic Requiem* or *Post Scriptum* will forget the last footage shot by Slapins that night or his gasped 'Keep filming...' as he lay dying.

Raiņa bulvāris was 'Embassy Row' during Latvian independence between the world wars and is approaching that status again, with the Stars and Stripes fluttering in front of No 7, France installed at No 9, and Britain expected to move back into its former premises at No 2. To the west, on Krišjāna Valdemāra iela, opposite the corner of Basteja bulvāris, the **National Theatre** is an interesting 1899-1902 Baroque building; Latvia's independence was declared here on 18 November 1918. To the north, Elizabetes iela 2 was the Latvian Communist Party headquarters. More recently it provided temporary homes for a few foreign embassies. It's now Rīga's **International Trade Centre**,

LATVIA

LATVIA

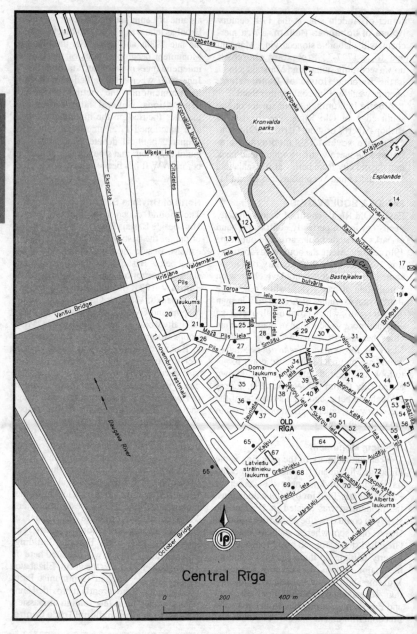

Central Rīga

0   200   400 m

LATVIA

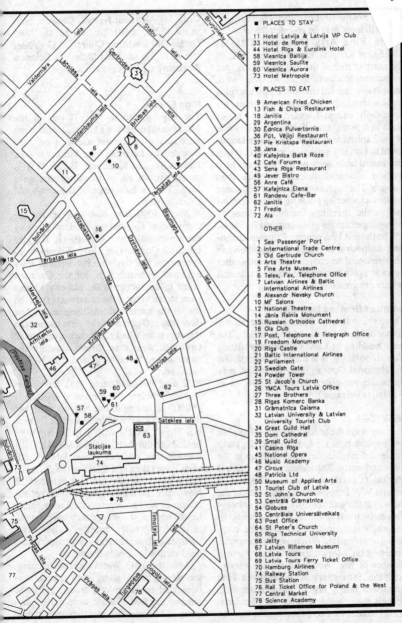

■ PLACES TO STAY

11 Hotel Latvija & Latvija VIP Club
33 Hotel de Rome
44 Hotel Rīga & Eurolink Hotel
58 Viesnīca Baltija
59 Viesnīca Saulīte
60 Viesnīca Aurora
73 Hotel Metropole

▼ PLACES TO EAT

9 American Fried Chicken
13 Fish & Chips Restaurant
18 Janitis
29 Argentina
30 Ēdnīca Pulvertornis
36 Pūt, Vējiņi Restaurant
37 Pie Kristapa Restaurant
38 Jana
40 Kafejnīca Baltā Roze
42 Cafe Forums
43 Sena Rīga Restaurant
49 Jever Bistro
56 Anre Café
57 Kafejnīca Elena
61 Randevu Cafe-Bar
62 Janitis
71 Fredis
72 Ala

OTHER

1 Sea Passenger Port
2 International Trade Centre
3 Old Gertrude Church
4 Arts Theatre
5 Fine Arts Museum
6 Telex, Fax, Telephone Office
7 Latvian Airlines & Baltic
  International Airlines
8 Alexandr Nevsky Church
10 MF Salons
12 National Theatre
14 Jānis Rainis Monument
15 Russian Orthodox Cathedral
16 Ola Club
17 Post, Telephone & Telegraph Office
19 Freedom Monument
20 Rīga Castle
21 Baltic International Airlines
22 Parliament
23 Swedish Gate
24 Powder Tower
25 St Jacob's Church
26 YMCA Tours Latvia Office
27 Three Brothers
28 Rīgas Komerc Banka
31 Grāmatnica Gaisma
32 Latvian University & Latvian
   University Tourist Club
34 Great Guild Hall
35 Dom Cathedral
39 Small Guild
41 Casino Rīga
45 National Opera
46 Music Academy
47 Circus
48 Patricia Ltd
50 Museum of Applied Arts
51 Tourist Club of Latvia
52 St John's Church
53 Centrālā Grāmatnica
54 Globuss
55 Centrālais Universālveikals
63 Post Office
64 St Peter's Church
65 Rīga Technical University
66 Jetty
67 Latvian Riflemen Museum
68 Latvia Tours
69 Latvia Tours Ferry Ticket Office
70 Hamburg Airlines
74 Railway Station
75 Bus Station
76 Rail Ticket Office for Poland & the West
77 Central Market
78 Science Academy

and some of the 1991 barricades from around the parliament may be re-erected here.

The **Fine Arts Museum** (Mākslas Muzejs) at Krišjāna Valdemāra iela 10A, on the north corner of the Esplanāde park, has permanent collections of Russian work downstairs and Latvian work upstairs, plus some interesting temporary exhibitions. It's open daily, except Tuesday, from 11 am or noon to 6 pm. On the Kalpaka bulvāris side of the Esplanāde is the **Jānis Rainis Monument** to Latvia's national poet who Latvians say would have been world famous if he'd written in a less obscure language than Latvian. The open area in front of this statue is often a gathering place for demonstrations and public meetings including, strangely enough, gatherings of disgruntled Russians.

The domed 19th century **Russian Orthodox cathedral** fronting Brīvības bulvāris only returned to church use recently, after years as a planetarium under Soviet rule, and is under restoration.

South of Brīvības Bulvāris

There's a colourful **flower market** on the corner of Merķeļa iela and Tērbatas iela. The main building of **Latvia University**, dating from 1866-1906, is at Raiņa bulvāris 9; and the **National Opera** (1860-63), which may be under reconstruction till 1996, is at Aspazijas bulvāris 3.

NEW RĪGA

In many ways the heart of everyday Rīga life lies beyond both the old city and the park-boulevard ring, in the areas built up in the 19th and early 20th century. The **Central Market** (Centrālais tirgus) – housed in several WW I zeppelin hangars, south of the railway at the south end of Old Rīga – always presents a lively scene and is a barometer of the city's standards of living. In the combined residential, office and commercial streets east of Elizabetes iela, where a number of low, wooden buildings survive from the 19th century. A wander round these areas will nearly always prove interesting, though there are few other specific landmarks to head for except perhaps the Russian

Orthodox **Alexandr Nevsky Church**, built in the 1820s, at Brīvības iela 56; the 1865 Gothic **Old Gertrude Church** at Gertrūdes iela 8; or the towering Stalin-era **Science Academy** on Turgeņeva iela.

Rīga Ghetto

The Rīga ghetto in WW II was in the Maskava suburb about a km south-east of the railway station. It was a 3/4-sq-km area bounded by Lāčplēša iela, Maskavas iela, Lauvas iela and Kalna iela. Before WW II many, but not all, of its inhabitants were Jews. There's little trace of the area's old character now.

About 5000 Jews had been among the thousands of Latvians deported to Siberia by the Soviet authorities in 1940-41. The city fell to the Germans on 1 July and new atrocities began that day with hundreds of Jews executed as 'retribution' for the Germans killed in the taking of the old city. Others were forced to scrub the bloodstains from the site of the battle with toothbrushes. A few days later 300 or more Jews were taken from the streets and locked in their synagogue. Grenades were then thrown through the windows and the building set on fire. No one survived.

Several thousand more Rīga Jews were murdered before the remaining thousands (34,000 according to one Nazi account, but that doesn't tally with other figures for pre-war Rīga's total Jewish population) were herded into the ghetto in October 1941. Half-starved, they endured forced labour until most were taken and killed at the Salaspils death camp outside the city between 30 November and 8 December. Latvian collaborators as well as Germans were responsible for the holocaust – indeed they have a reputation for greater cruelty. Other Jews transported from Germany took some of the dead victims' places in the ghetto.

After the 1943 Warsaw-ghetto uprising, the Rīga ghetto, along with others, was liquidated on Himmler's orders, but those inmates capable of work were moved to a camp in Mežaparks. Later they were pulled back to other camps with the retreating German forces.

SUBURBS
Motor Museum

Rīga Motor Museum (Rīgas Motormuzejs) is a long way out in the suburbs, but its unique and amusing collection is definitely worth the trip, even if you're no particular fan of cars or museums. It's at S Eizenšteina iela 6, eight km east of the old city along Brīvības iela, then two km south; it's open daily (except Monday) from 10 am to 6, 7 or 8 pm. Entry is about 0.08 lati.

The museum was opened in 1989, but its seeds go back to 1975 when a Latvian car enthusiast, Viktors Kulbergs, saved a very rare 16-cylinder 1938 German Auto Union racer from being scrapped in a Moscow factory. The racer is now on show with 100 or so other Eastern and Western cars, motorbikes and bicycles, all packed into the two floors of this modern, purpose-built museum. The collection ranges from an 1886 Daimler Motorkutsche (a genuine horseless carriage – maximum speed 16 km/h) to a 1984 Cadillac Fleetwood limo. Motorcycle enthusiasts can drool over the 1942 Harley-Davidson.

My favourites are the cars that once belonged to the Soviet luminaries Gorky, Stalin, Khrushchev and Brezhnev – complete with irreverent life-size figures of the men themselves. Stalin, pock-marked cheeks and all, sits regally in the back of his seven-tonne, 6005 cc armoured limousine. The car has 1.5-cm iron plating everywhere except on the eight-cm-thick windows. It drank a litre of petrol every 2½ km and had to be tested under machine-gun and grenade attack before the paranoid Uncle Joe dared to ride in it. Brezhnev sits, with appropriate surprise registering on his features, at the wheel of his crumpled Rolls-Royce Silver Shadow, written off in 1980 when he strayed from the safety of an official convoy into the path of a lorry.

In summer a shuttle bus runs to the museum a few times a day from beside the Orthodox cathedral on Brīvības bulvāris –

signs at the stop give the schedule. Alternatively, take bus No 21 from the Orthodox cathedral to the Pansionāts stop on Šmerļa iela in the suburb of Mežciems. The stop is opposite the corner of Eizenšteina iela, where a housing estate begins on the right, immediately after a stretch of road with woods on both sides. A sign on the corner points to the museum, half a km along Eizenšteina iela.

Latvian Ethnography Museum

The Latvian Open-Air Ethnography Museum (Latvījas etnogrāfiskais brīvdabas muzejs) is on the shore of Lake Jugla on the eastern edge of the city, at Brīvības gatve 440. Over 90 buildings from rural Latvia, mainly wooden and from the 18th and 19th centuries, have been assembled on a one-sq-km site here. They include churches, windmills, and farmhouses from Latvia's different regions, and they're furnished with thousands of artefacts to provide a record of

Latvian Windmill

LATVIA

bygone country life. On summer weekends, folk-dance performances are given, and museum staff wear national costumes. There's also a big crafts fair in early June (see Things to Buy). The museum is normally open 10 am to 5 pm daily from mid-May to mid-October, except the last day of the month. Take bus No 1 from opposite the Orthodox cathedral on Brīvības bulvāris.

Mežaparks & Cemeteries

Rīga's biggest park is **Mežaparks** (Woodland Park), about seven km north of the centre, beside the lake Ķīšezers. Here you'll find playgrounds, a zoo, the stage for the main concerts of Latvian song festivals, and pine woods. South of Mežaparks on Aizsaules iela, which branches off Gaujas iela, are three cemeteries: the **Rainis Cemetery** (Raiņa kapi), where Jānis Rainis, his wife (the feminist poet, Aspazija), and other Latvian cultural figures are buried; the large **Second Woodland Cemetery** (Meža kapi II), with a monument to the five dead of 20 January 1991; and the **Brothers' Cemetery** (Brāļu kapi), originally designed as the resting place of Latvian soldiers who died in WW I and the independence war, and notable for its many monuments and sculptures. Later, WW II dead (including some Soviet troops who died reconquering Latvia, and some Communist Party members) were buried in the Brothers' Cemetery, but for much of the Soviet period the cemetery was out-of-bounds and allowed to fall into disrepair. In 1993 the Latvian parliament decided to restore the cemetery to its pre-Soviet state and move the graves of about 200 Communist Party members elsewhere.

To reach the south end of Aizsaules iela, a few hundred metres from the cemeteries, take bus No 9 from opposite the Orthodox cathedral on Brīvības bulvāris to the Aizsaules iela stop on Gaujas iela, or tram No 4 or 11 going north-east on Krišjāna Barona iela to the Brāļu kapi stop on Gaujas iela. Tram No 11 continues to Mežaparks.

GALLERIES & EXHIBITIONS

There are numerous art galleries around town, varying in quality, and many of them are well worth a visit. They're listed in *Rīga This Week*, while temporary exhibitions are announced on posters and in the Upcoming Events section of *The Baltic Independent*.

RIVER TRIPS

The motorboats and hydrofoils that used to ply the rivers and lakes around Rīga seem to have floated away with the end of the Soviet era. They used to sail in summer from the jetty by the east side of the October Bridge to places like Mežaparks, Majori in Jūrmala, and out into the Gulf of Rīga. If they make a comeback they're worth a ride because, apart from anything else, they give you a fish's-eye view of the docks which line the Daugava most of the way to the sea. A Jūrmala ferry service from the sea-passenger terminal was advertised in 1992. Also possibly worth checking, though it's primarily intended for long-distance river craft, is the River Station (Upju stacija) on Balasta dambis, at the south end of Ķīpsala island, on the west side of Vanšu Bridge.

ORGANISED TOURS

The Tourist Club of Latvia (Latvijas Tūristu Klubs, LTK) (☎ 221 731 or 227 680) at Skārņu iela 22 (the historic Eka Convent building facing St Peter's Church), offers Old Rīga walking tours for about 5 lati and other excursions in and outside the city cheaper than most travel agents.

FESTIVALS

Rīga hosts dozens of annual and one-off festivals of many different types each year. See Cultural Events in the Latvia, Facts for the Visitor chapter and study the media and posters when you get there.

PLACES TO STAY – BOTTOM END
Hostels & Colleges

The *Latvian University Tourist Club* (Latvijas Universitātes Tūristu Klubs or LUTK) (☎ 223 114, fax 225 039 or 227 411) has decent rooms available in university hostels, both central and outlying, at a range of prices. The central rooms are very well located on the edge of Old Rīga and cost 4 to 6 lati per person, with shared toilet, shower and kitchen (all very clean); or 12.50 to 20 lati per person in 'suites' with their own facilities. Rooms with shared facilities in the Argo hostel, 20 minutes from the centre by bus, cost 3 lati per person. There's a student café across the street from the Argo. Contact the busy, but friendly club office in the university building at Raiņa bulvāris 19 (along the corridor to the right from the lobby). They like you to phone, fax or write (the postcode is LV-1098) in advance but are very unlikely to turn you away if you don't.

The hostel scene in Rīga is less developed than in Tallinn. Places seem to appear and disappear quickly – look for notices about current ones in the sea-passenger terminal or the railway station. The Latvian YMCA travel organisation, YMCA Tours Latvia (☎ 226 463, fax 224 785) of Pils iela 6, runs one hostel, for both men and women, that looks likely to continue – though it functions in summer only. This *YMCA Tours Youth Hostel* is at Kalnciema iela 10/12, west of the river. The building is normally a music and ballet college. The quite big double rooms are clean, light and bare and cost 7 lati per person including breakfast. Bathrooms and toilets are shared but clean. To get there, take tram No 4 or 5 from the Grēcinieku iela stop by the October Bridge and go five stops to the Kalnciema iela stop.

Private Homes

Patricia Ltd (☎ 284 868, fax 286 650) at Elizabetes iela 22-4A runs a 'Family Hotel & Tourist Information Service' which offers rooms in private flats all over Latvia, including Rīga, mostly between 4 and 7 lati per person, though some are 10 lati. An outfit called *Family Hotel Service Network* (☎ 212 743, ☎ & fax 283 595) advertises a similar service for an average 7 lati. *Gatve* (☎ 612 466) at Graudu iela 58 offers accommodation for 8 lati a day.

The *Tourist Club of Latvia* (Latvijas Tūristu Klubs, LTK) (☎ 221 731 or 227 680) at Skārņu iela 22, facing St Peter's Church, charges 8.50 to 10 lati per person for rooms

in private flats, with breakfast available for 1.30 lati or all meals for 7 lati. I have stayed in LTK homestays in other towns and enjoyed them.

Alternative Ltd (☎ 270 369 or 273 206, fax Finland 049-348 168) at Bruņinieku iela 29/31 offers rooms in what it says are 'good flats' – a few in the old city but most in the inner part of the new town – for 13 lati a person or 10 lati for stays of a week or more, including breakfast. Some of the flats can take up to five visitors.

See Private Homes under Accommodation in the Facts for the Visitor chapter at the front of the book for further agencies which can provide rooms in Rīga – and in other cities too.

Hotels

There are three cheapies across the road from the railway station and a fourth a km away up the same street. Both the *Viesnīca Aurora* (☎ 224 479) at Marijas iela 5, facing the station, and the *Viesnīca Saulīte* (☎ 224 546) round the corner at Merķeļa iela 12 have singles/doubles, usually with a washbasin in the room, for around 0.65/1.30 lati. The rooms are bare and in need of a lot of fresh air, but they're kept reasonably clean. The shared showers and toilets are a gamble. The *Viesnīca Baltija* (☎ 227 461), opposite the station at Raiņa bulvāris 33, on the corner of Marijas iela, has rooms from 0.40 lati per person (sharing with others) to 3.25 lati double with private bathroom but isn't welcoming to Westerners. The *Viesnīca Viktorija* (☎ 272 305), a km from the station at A Čaka iela 55 (the north-east continuation of Marijas iela), is more hospitable; it has a similar range of prices and its best rooms aren't bad at all, being clean and bright, with TV and private bathroom.

There are similar prices at two hotels in Rīga's outlying suburbs – the *Viesnīca Plavnieki* (☎ 137 040) at Salnas iela 26, about seven km east of the centre, and the *Viesnīca Zemgale* (☎ 622 714) at Valdeķu iela 66, about seven km south. The Plavnieki has some rooms with shower and toilet; to reach it take bus No 17 from the bus station or No 52 from the railway station to the Liepiņas stop on Deglava iela. Salnas iela is a block south. For the Zemgale, bus No 40 from Gogoļa iela behind the railway station terminates just past the south end of Valdeķu iela.

PLACES TO STAY – MIDDLE

There are only a couple of hotels in this bracket. One is the *Viesnīca Tūrists* (☎ 615 455), a large former Soviet trade-union-tourism hotel at Slokas iela 1, about a km west of the October Bridge. Clean enough, if fusty rooms with private shower and toilet go for 20 lati a single, 35 lati a double, which is quite a lot for what they are. There's a restaurant and cafeteria in the hotel. To get there take tram No 4 or 5 from the Grēcinieku iela stop by the October Bridge and go three stops to the Rainberga bulvāris stop.

More pleasant is the *Hotel Karavel* or *Jūrnieku Nams Karavella* (Karavella Sailors' House) (☎ 323 130), a tower block at Katrīnas dambis 27 in the Pētersala area, two km north of the old city. This is a fairly modern hotel run by the Latvian Shipping Company. Singles/doubles are 36/50 lati; they're clean and bright and half of them face the river. There's no restaurant – just three cafés – but there's said to be excellent food at the Sailors' Hall, a few minutes walk south down the street. Tram Nos 5 and 9 north along Aspazijas bulvāris and Kronvalda bulvāris in the city centre go to the Kinoteātris Kosmoss stop on the corner of Pētersalas iela and Katrīnas dambis, 500 metres south of the hotel.

PLACES TO STAY – TOP END

Rīga has two top-notch international hotels, as well as two typical ex-Intourist institutions, each with a separately run enclave of Western comfort within. All are central. Travel agents may be able to find you rooms in these places when the hotels themselves say 'full' – see the Rīga Information section.

The ex-Intourist *Hotel Latvija* (☎ 212 645 or 212 505, fax 283 595) is unmissable. Its 27 Soviet-built storeys poke uglily into the sky at Elizabetes iela 55, on the corner of

Brīvības iela. It has about 700 beds but still gets full. At least the views are good. Rooms are moderately sized, the service fair, and the eating options manifold. Singles/doubles are about 55/70 lati from mid-May to mid-September, and 43/56 lati at other times, breakfast included. Things will change because the Latvija is to be privatised and renovated. One not-so-crazy idea is to demolish it altogether and build something more in harmony with the rest of Rīga.

The *Hotel Rīga* (☎ 216 000, 216 285, fax 229 828), also ex-Intourist, is on the edge of Old Rīga at Aspazijas bulvāris 22. It's older (1956) and smaller (about 300 rooms) than the Latvija and gets similarly full in summer. It was renovated in the late 1980s. There's little to choose between its rooms and those in the Latvija, but the eating options are poorer here. Prices yo-yo but are normally below the Latvija's.

In 1992, 49 rooms occupying three floors of the Hotel Latvija were turned into the jointly Danish and Latvian-run *Latvija VIP Club* (☎ 221 611, fax Denmark 30 24 99 30), with 'three-star' rooms at 63/99 lati from May to September and 46/73 lati at other times, and 'four-star' rooms – Danish design, satellite TV, minibar – for 73/110 lati from May to September, 60/85 lati otherwise. Prices include an excellent breakfast, and the VIP Club has its own bar. The VIP Club office is in suite 1612. The Swedish-run *Eurolink Hotel* (☎ 216 317, fax Sweden 010-261 70 41) operates on a similar basis within the Hotel Rīga, where it occupies a whole floor of 50-odd rooms, renovated in 1992. There's also a brasserie. Rooms have cable TV and cost about 85/105 lati including breakfast.

The *Hotel de Rome* (☎ 216 268, fax Finland 049-348 175) at Kaļķu iela 28, looking out along Brīvības bulvāris, was the first genuinely new hotel in Rīga when it opened in 1991 – though it bears the name of a top hotel from the Latvian independence period. It's an elegant atrium hotel, designed with business people in mind – good service, direct-dial phones, colour TV and minibars in rooms, fax machines – but there's no reason anyone with around 100/125 lati to spare shouldn't enjoy one of its 90 rooms.

The 85-room *Hotel Metropole* (☎ 216 145 or 225 411, fax 216 140; international ☎ 882 0065, fax 882 0074 with no city code needed) at Aspazijas bulvāris 36 is the newest addition to the top-end scene. It's a Swedish-Latvian renovation of an old hotel that was renowned as a centre of espionage and intrigue in the 1930s. It's run by the same people as the Eurolink, with the same prices.

PLACES TO EAT
Fast Food

Rīga is the main *McDonald's* bridgehead in the Baltic states, with three branches due to open by 1994, so Westerners will have something familiar to fall back on.

American Fried Chicken at Tērbatas iela 33 in the new town will do you respectable fried chicken at 0.20 lati a piece, chips at 0.15 lati and coleslaw at 0.05 lati – open 7 am to 11 pm daily. The *Argentina* at Smilšu iela 3 in the old town is another reasonable fast-food café. *Janitis* (Little Johnny's) on Brīvības bulvāris and at Elizabetes iela 91 does good-value pizza. On Kronvalda bulvāris, opposite the side of the National Theatre, there's a *Fish & Chips Restaurant*, still without a proper name at the time of writing. The fish may not come in the conventional British or Australian fillets – but it's still fried fish, and the service is quick. A hunk of fried salmon (cepts lasis) will set you back about 0.75 lati. A serve of three pilchards (ceptas reņģes) or two fish cakes (zivu kūkas) or chips (kartupeli) is 0.15 lati. You can take away or sit down with your meal; opening hours are from 8 am to 8 pm Monday to Saturday and 11 to 6 pm Sunday.

Cheaper Restaurants

About the cheapest restaurant in central Rīga is the *Ēdnīca Pulvertornis* (Powder Tower Canteen) on Vaļņu iela in the old city, open 7 am to 6 pm daily except Sunday. A good fill-up here will set you back about 0.40 lati. You can just queue up and point to what you want. Offerings include soups, meat and veg dishes, beetroot salad, rice pudding and fruit salad. There's a separate counter for coffee and pastries. The queue will be much shorter if you lunch before noon or after 2 pm.

The unassuming *Restorāns* upstairs in the suburban half of the railway station, open from 11 am to 11 pm, serves perfectly respectable fare – for example beef stroganoff, mashed potato and beetroot for 0.55 lati.

The *Restorāns Selga* at A Čaka iela 55, in the same building as the Viesnīca Viktorija, one km from the railway station, offers, as one waiter put it, 'fish soup, cold fish, hot fish'. But it's good fish, with most main dishes in the 0.35 lati region and the most expensive a tasty fish kebab called shashlik Selga at 1.15 lati. The Selga is open from 11 am to 11 pm daily.

At Jauniela 25/29 near the Dom, *Pie Kristapa* is a large, lively, enjoyable and relatively inexpensive place with two sections: a fairly formal upstairs restaurant with live music and dancing, and a more-casual basement 'beer hall'. Both parts have exactly the same food menu and prices, with starters up to 0.40 lati and main dishes of meat, fish or chicken in the 0.40 to 1 lats range. Downstairs, the beer is local, not imported, and comes in large jugs – but you don't need to have them full. Unlike in some of the cruder beer halls in the Baltic states, women without men are unlikely to be harassed by drunken idiots here.

Across the street at Jauniela 18, *Pūt, Vējiņi* (Blow, Wind) is a small, quiet upstairs restaurant with quick service and good, well-priced food. The menu is in Latvian and Russian only, so you may need to ask the waiter's recommendation. I ended up with hors d'oeuvres followed by trout with a mushroom side dish, both very acceptable. Most main dishes are between 0.50 and 0.85 lati but starters – many of which, in the Russian style, are at least as substantial – may be a bit more. A reservation is advisable – best made in person, at about 11 am or noon for the same evening.

Also in Old Rīga, the *Cafe Forums* in the courtyard at Kaļķu iela 24 is a shiny waiter-service café-restaurant, with a cool jazz trio most nights. Opening hours are from noon to 6 pm and 7 pm to midnight. In the evenings you may need to get there early to avoid queueing. There's a 0.50 lati entry fee; a meat and veg dish plus a salad will cost you about 1.50 lati. Portions aren't huge but it's decent fare. Unfortunately, according to last-minute reports, the Forums has gone somewhat downhill – let's hope it recovers.

More Expensive Restaurants

The German-run *Jever Bistro*, at Kaļķu iela 6 in the old city, offers German beer, excellent German and Latvian food, and a jolly German atmosphere, from 11 am to 3 am. It's busy and very popular with Western tourists and business people – a good place to go if you want (and can afford) a dose of Western familiarity. Main dishes, from around 5 to 10 lati, are good and generous. There are also lighter meals like smoked Rīga sprats with fried potatoes for 3.50 lati. In summer get there early in the evening to avoid waiting to get in.

Jana at Šķūņu iela 16, near the Dom, is a tiny little restaurant serving excellent local and Western food, with main dishes around 2 lati. I had a good steak here. There are also lots of quite expensive starters and a long drinks menu. The waiters have a discreet, European manner. There are only about five tables, so you'd be advised to book for any meal in summer and for dinner in winter.

The *Sena Rīga* (Old Rīga) at Aspazijas bulvāris 22, beside the Hotel de Rome, will give you a decent meal for around 4 lati, not counting drinks. It's a popular cellar establishment, with four rooms in the styles of different Latvian regions. It's easier to get in at lunch time than in the evening. I enjoyed Vistas Gaļas Kotletes Kurzeme – a good chicken schnitzel with vegetables.

Another polished eatery with good food and reasonable prices is *Kooperativ Lido* at Lāčplēša iela 53 in the new town – open from noon to 6 pm and 8 pm to midnight.

For Chinese food try *Asia China* at Mārstaļu iela 6 – open from noon till midnight.

Hotel Restaurants None of Rīga's hotel restaurants has earned any major rave reviews yet. Most are adequate except those in the *Hotel Rīga*, where the service is still Soviet-style. The best breakfast buffet in town has to be the one at the *Amber Café* in the Hotel Latvija – you pay 4 lati for the privilege.

Cafés & Bars

Rīga has dozens of cafés, many of them dotted around the old city. In summer an open-air beer-and-sausage bar, with a dozen or so tables, sets up on Doma laukums – a pleasant place to watch the world go by for an hour or two.

My favourite Rīga café, worth queueing 20 minutes or so for, is the *Kafejnīca Baltā Roze* on Meistaru iela, near the corner of Kaļķu iela in the old city. This small upstairs café has quick counter service, really tasty snacks (for 0.10 to 0.35 lati) which you can build into a lunch, and good ice cream and coffee. Opening hours are from 9 am to 3 pm and 4.30 to 9 pm daily (Saturday and Sunday opening: 11 am).

Fredis on Audeju iela in the old city does good rolls, salads and beer. The *Anre* café at Aspazijas bulvāris 30 does good cakes and pastries, and also reasonable light meals like noodles and a few veg for 0.15 lati, or sausage and veg for 0.50 lati. The *Randevu Cafe-Bar* on Marijas iela, next to the Viesnīca Aurora, does reasonable light hot meals (karbonad and a couple of veg for around 0.50 lati); the *Kafejnīca Elena*, round the corner on Raiņa bulvāris, has good pancakes for about 0.35 lati a serve.

You can put together a tolerable daytime or evening meal fairly quickly in the *Hotel Rīga*'s first-floor snack bar, or the *Express Bar* in the Hotel Latvija (through the lobby of the Zaļā Zāle restaurant, then down a floor) for 0.65 lati or so. You don't have to be staying in the hotels to use these places. *Ala*, in a courtyard off Vecpilsētas iela, at the south end of the old city, is a pleasant place for a beer, with tables outside and a downstairs bar.

Market

Don't forget the large central market behind the bus station, which has plenty of fresh foods.

ENTERTAINMENT

Rīga has a lively entertainment and cultural scene. Two good what's-on poster sites are on the square where Kaļķu iela meets Meistaru iela in Old Rīga and on Basteja bulvāris opposite Smilšu iela. *The Baltic Independent* lists some events in its Upcoming Events section. The newspaper *Rīgas Balss* (evenings, Monday to Friday) is another information source.

Rīga stages a variety of festivals, especially in summer, from classical music or theatre to jazz or rock.

Rock, Blues & Jazz

Rīga is developing some lively nightlife. As everywhere, it's a changing scene but some of the following places should stay around for a while. Most are open weekends only, but the Ola, at Elizabetes iela 63, functions nightly, with live pop or rock from about 11 pm to 3 am. It gets good reports. About the best of the weekend places is the Kabata at Peldu iela 19 in the old city, a cosy basement club with a small dance floor and live blues or rock from 10 pm to 3 am – entrance costs 2 lati for non-members. The small Ave Sol club in the Kino nams (Film House) at A Čaka iela 67 has good jazz or acoustic rock on Saturday and Sunday nights – a ticket to the bar is 3 lati, a table (which should be booked in advance) 4.50 lati. The IMF club on Lāčplēša iela has a café-bar with acoustic bands, and a dance area upstairs with live rock or DJs. Entrance costs only 1 lats, but the club closes at 11 pm. The Cafe Forums (see Places to Eat) has a nice resident jazz trio.

Concerts by visiting bands are advertised on posters, which also state where tickets are sold, if you can decipher them. The Sporta Pils (Sports Palace) at Krišjāna Barona iela 75 and the Daugavas Sporta Namā (Daugava Sports House) at Krišjāna Barona iela 107 are two venues.

Discos

The student club of the Mūzikas Akadēmija (Music Academy) at Raiņa bulvaris 23 has music, dancing and drinks Wednesday to Friday from 9 pm to 5 am. The Vecrīga club on Vaļņu iela in the old city is a popular disco-cum-beer hall with a fairly young crowd. Entrance is 0.85 lati. The regular discos in the Mazā Ģilde (Small Guild) at Amatu iela 5 also attract a young crowd – dates are given on posters outside the building on the corner of Meistaru iela. The disco at Jauniela 29A in the old city, open Thursday to Sunday from 11 pm to 5 pm, has very loud music, a rough atmosphere and occasional fights.

Classical Music

The Latvia Philharmonia is a local leader in the field, and there's an acclaimed national symphony orchestra, too, plus lots of visiting orchestras, quartets and so on. The Philharmonia has concert halls at Kaļķu iela 11A and at Amatu iela 6 in the Great Guild (Lielā Ģilde), a medieval meeting hall. The box office at the Great Guild sells tickets for most classical concerts in Rīga. The Dom's acoustics, as well as its huge organ, are spectacular, and regular organ and other concerts are held there too. The ticket office opposite the cathedral's west door has schedules. The 17th century Vāgnera Zālē (Wagner Hall), at R Vāgnera iela 4, is used for chamber and solo concerts. The Mūzikas Akadēmija Lielajā Zāle (Music Academy Main Hall), at Krišjāna Barona iela 1, is another main concert venue.

Ballet & Opera

With the National Opera at Aspazijas bulvāris 3 under reconstruction, possibly until 1996, there's no proper home for the highly rated Rīga Ballet (Rīgas Balets), where Mikhail Baryshnikov made his name, or for Latvian opera. However the companies are likely to perform at other venues from time to time – study the posters.

Other Entertainment

Rīga has the only permanent circus in the

Baltic states – at Merķeļa iela 4. The Casino Rīga at Kaļķu iela 24 is open daily from 4 pm to 4 am, with entry costing 2 lati (including one free drink) and women admitted free on Monday and Wednesday. No jeans or trainers are permitted! There's a second casino in the Hotel Rīga.

Theatre is all in Latvian or Russian. The National Theatre at Kronvalda bulvāris 2 and the Arts Theatre (Dailes Teatris) at Brīvības iela 75 stage plays in Latvian, while the Russian Drama Theatre is at Kaļķu iela 16. Like ballet and opera, theatre shuts up shop from June to October.

Basketball (*basketbola*) and soccer are the most popular spectator sports – posters announce the big games. The Daugavas Sporta Namā (Daugava Sports House), at Krišjāna Barona iela 107, is the big basketball venue, while top soccer games are played at the Daugava Stadium (Daugavas Stadions) at Augšiela iela 1.

THINGS TO BUY

Rīga has lots of craft and souvenir shops, some selling goods of genuine quality – a major improvement on the Soviet years when good modern crafts could only be found in museums. You'll pass several shops in a stroll round the old city and the boulevards/parks area, but undoubtedly the best I have come across is MF Salons on Brīvības iela, half a block past the Hotel Latvija. Somehow much of the best Latvian craft work has found its way into this one shop: unique ceramics, paintings, prints, stained glass, leather work, and long and chunky amber necklaces for around 25 to 35 lati. The shop is open Monday to Friday from 10 am to 2 pm and 3 to 7 pm. The Russian Drama Theatre at Kaļķu iela 16 has a selling exhibition of good-quality art.

If you're in Rīga on the first weekend in June don't miss the Gadatirgus, an annual two-day crafts fair at the Open-Air Ethnography Museum, which draws buyers from all over the Baltic region. Several hundred artisans show and sell their wares. The event officially opens at 8 am on the Saturday – but you need to be there at 6 am for the very best goods.

Centrālais Universālveikals, near the Hotel Rīga, on the corner of Vaļņu iela and Audēju iela, is the main department store.

GETTING THERE & AWAY

This section concentrates on transport between Rīga and other places in Latvia, Estonia, Lithuania or Kaliningrad. More detail on links with countries outside the Baltic states, which include ferries to/from Sweden and Germany, flights to/from several Western and CIS cities, trains to/from Germany, Poland, Russia and Belarus, and buses to/from Poland and Russia is given in the Getting There & Away chapter.

Air

Estonian Air used to fly between Rīga and Tallinn, but at the time of writing this service had been stopped. Flights between Rīga and Kaunas are being talked about – but, to date, there's no mention of a Vilnius service. Check with Latvian Airlines.

The airport is at Skulte, 14 km west of the city centre. It has a restaurant, a couple of cafés, car-rental offices, a left-luggage office, exchange counters and a post office where you can make local or long-distance phone calls. The information kiosk sells city bus/tram/trolleybus tickets and telephone tokens. For flight information, ring ☎ 207 661 for flights to/from the west or ☎ 207 009 for flights to/from the east.

Airline ticket offices in Rīga include:

American TransAir
    Stabu iela 6 (☎ 293 702)
Baltic International Airlines
    Brīvības iela 54 (☎ 201 611)
    Pils laukums 4 (☎ 327 296)
    Airport (☎ 207 643)
CSA
    Airport (☎ 207 636)
Finnair
    Airport (☎ 207 010)
Hamburg Airlines
    Mārstaļu iela 12 (☎ 227 638)
Latvian Airlines
    Brīvības iela 54 (☎ 201 666, 201 677)
    Airport (☎ 207 372, 207 541)

Top: View over Rīga, Latvia (EV)
Left: The Dom, Rīga, Latvia (JN)
Right: Freedom Monument, Rīga, Latvia (EV)

Top: Meistaru iela, Rīga, Latvia (EV)
Left: Street scene, Old Rīga, Latvia (EV)
Right: Swedish Gate, Rīga, Latvia (JN)

Lot
   Airport (☎ 207 113)
Lufthansa
   Krišjāņa Barona iela 9 (☎ 285 614)
   Airport (☎ 207 183)
Rīga Airlines Express (RIAIR)
   Airport (☎ 207 325)
SAS
   Aspazijas bulvāris 36/38 (☎ 216 139)
   Airport (☎ 207 055)

Bus

Buses to/from other towns and cities use Rīga's main bus station *(autoosta)* at Prāgas iela 1, behind the railway embankment just beyond the south edge of the old city. Up-to-date timetables are posted up, with services listed under their final destination and the platform they depart from. There's an information office *(izzinu birojs)*, too, which may be able to tell you more than the timetables, particularly about buses in transit *(tranzīts)*; for instance, though only three or four daily services may be posted up for Šiauliai in Lithuania, there are actually about a dozen if you include buses for which Rīga-Šiauliai is only part of the route. Some routes are served by microbuses, which leave from out the front of the bus station, on Prāgas iela. Buses within the Baltic states and Kaliningrad (at times of full service, when there's no fuel shortage) include:

Bauska
   65 km, 1½ hours, 12 to 15 buses daily, 0.40 lati
Cēsis
   90 km, two hours, 10 buses daily, 0.55 lati
Daugavpils
   230 km, four hours, two or three buses daily, 1.65 lati
Jelgava
   40 km, one hour, up to 17 microbuses daily, 0.25 to 0.45 lati
Kaliningrad
   370 km, nine hours, one bus daily, 3 lati
Kaunas
   280 km, 5½ hours, five buses daily, 2.15 lati
Klaipēda
   310 km, six to seven hours, two buses daily, 2.50 lati
Kuldīga
   150 km, three to four hours, six buses daily, 1 lats

Liepāja
   220 km, 3½ hours direct, four to 4½ hours via Kalnciems; five to seven hours via Jelgava or Tukums; about 12 buses daily, 1.30 to 1.50 lati
Pärnu
   180 km, 3½ hours, seven buses daily, 1.25 lati
Rēzekne
   245 km, 4½ hours, two buses daily, 1.85 lati
Šiauliai
   130 km, 2½ to three hours, about 12 buses and one microbus daily, 1.30 lati
Sigulda
   50 km, one hour, four buses daily, 0.35 lati
Tallinn
   310 km, six hours, six buses daily, 2.15 lati
Valmiera
   120 km, 2½ hours, 10 buses or microbuses daily, 0.80 lati
Ventspils
   200 km, 3½ to five hours, about 12 buses daily, 1.30 to 1.50 lati
Vilnius
   290 km, six hours, four or five buses daily, 2.35 lati

Train

Rīga station, on Stacijas laukums at the south end of the park-and-boulevard ring, is divided into two parts, side by side, for long-distance trains (the left hand side as you face the station) and slower 'suburban trains' *(piepilsetas vilcienu)*, which may go as far as Jelgava, Krustpils or Valmiera and stop at virtually every station on the way. Timetables are clearly presented and the only difficulty you may have is in finding the right window to buy a ticket for a long-distance train – the system is explained below.

Suburban At the time of writing, it's only 0.40 lati to some of the furthest flung places served by suburban trains, such as Valmiera or Mazsalaca. Fare lists are posted by the ticket windows. They're worked out on a zonal basis; the huge colour wall chart in the suburban-ticket hall shows which stations are on which lines and which fare zones they fall into. Sigulda for instance is on the Sigulda-Cēsis-Valmiera line, in zone six. At times when inflation hasn't rendered all the coinage worthless, you can get tickets to some zones from machines in the ticket hall. You deposit the appropriate coins for your zone and press buttons for one-way (shown in Russian as *tuda*) or round-trip (*tuda i obratno*), full-fare (*polny*) or child (*detsky*).

Some main suburban stations are also served by long-distance trains on the way to places further afield. These trains are likely to be quicker, especially to the more distant suburban stations, but may have only couchette accommodation available and may require advance booking – for information and tickets, check with window 36 in the advance booking hall at the south end of the suburban part of the station.

There are five suburban lines out of Rīga:

Ķemeri-Tukums Line
  This is the line to take for Jūrmala. About one train an hour leaves for each of Ķemeri, Sloka and Tukums II between 4.25 am and midnight. All call at Majori.
Jelgava Line
  One or two trains an hour go to Jelgava between 5.20 am and 11.30 pm. Most long-distance trains to Ventspils, Šiauliai, Kaliningrad and Vilnius stop at Jelgava too.
Ogre-Krustpils Line
  This line follows the Daugava River inland to Krustpils, opposite Jēkabpils. Most trains only go as far as Ogre (eight between 4.40 and 9.05 am, six between 2.20 and 6.25 pm). A few others go on to Lielvārde, Aizkraukle or Krustpils. Long-distance trains heading to Daugavpils, Rēzekne, Zilupe, Moscow and elsewhere also take this line.
Sigulda-Cēsis-Valmiera Line
  There are five trains daily to Sigulda, two to Ieriķi, one to Cēsis and two to Valmiera. All call at Sigulda; Valmiera trains call at Cēsis. Long-distance trains to Lugaži, Valga, Tallinn, and St Petersburg also take this line, and those to Žīguri follow it to just past Ieriķi.
Saulkrasti-Rūjiena Line
  One to three trains an hour leave for varying destinations between 4.50 am and 11.15 pm.

Long-Distance Ticket windows marked 'Bilešu noformiēšana vilciena atiešanas dienā' in the long-distance part of the station are for same-day trips only. To buy a ticket for a long-distance train anywhere within the former USSR (including Latvia, Lithuania and Estonia) 24 or more hours before departure, go to the advance-booking windows (*iepriekšpārdošanas kases*), which have a

hall to themselves at the south end of the suburban part of the station – enter through a small doorway beside a row of phones. The wonderful discovery here is that window 36 is reserved for foreigners and has much shorter queues than the others – and charges the same prices! For tickets to Poland and the West, go under the bridge on Gogoļa iela, beside the station, then turn immediately left along a pedestrians-only street; a special booking office is on your left.

The daily *Baltic Express* between Tallinn and Warsaw comes through Rīga around midnight, southbound, and in the early morning, northbound. Its other stops include Kaunas and Tartu. The other main link with the other Baltic states is the *Seagull* train (Latvian: *Kaija*; Russian: *Chayka*) which trundles daily from Tallinn to Minsk, and vice versa, in 17½ hours, stopping at Tartu, Cēsis, Sigulda, Rīga, Jelgava, Šiauliai, Vilnius and a dozen-or-so other places en route. It comes through Rīga in the afternoon, both ways, and takes 7½ hours to/from Tallinn and six hours to/from Vilnius. There are also slower overnight trains to/from Tallinn and Vilnius via Kaunas, plus four or more other daily trains to/from Vilnius (terminating at Gomel, Lvov, Kiev or Simferopol). These make most of the same intermediate stops as the *Seagull*.

Fares are approximately 1 lats per 320 km in general seating or 1 lats per 215 km in compartment class. Other long-distance services from Rīga to places within the Baltic states include :

Cēsis
  90 km, five other trains daily terminating at Lugaži, Valga or St Petersburg
Daugavpils
  225 km, five trains daily (some terminating at Indra, Robežnieki or Voronezh), 3¼ to four hours
Ipiķi
  160 km, one train daily, four hours
Kaliningrad
  370 km, one train nightly, 9½ hours
Klaipēda
  280 km, one train nightly, 6½ hours (return train travels in afternoon)

Liepāja
    220 km, three trains daily, 4¾ to 5¾ hours
Rēzekne
    235 km, five to seven trains daily, most terminat-
    ing at Moscow or Zilupe, 2¾ to four hours
Šiauliai
    130 km, five to nine trains daily, terminating at
    Vilnius, Kaliningrad, Minsk, Simferopol, Kiev,
    Lvov, Gomel or Kharkov, two to 2½ hours
Sigulda
    50 km, six other trains daily terminating at
    Lugaži, Valga, Žīguri or St Petersburg
Valmiera
    115 km, five other trains daily, terminating at
    Lugaži, Valga or St Petersburg
Valga
    165 km, four other trains daily, terminating at
    Valga or St Petersburg, three to 3½ hours
Ventspils
    200 km, two trains daily, 4¼ hours
Võru
    215 km, two trains daily terminating at St Peters-
    burg, four hours

Car & Motorbike
The Finnish company Neste runs two 24-
hour petrol stations in Rīga, with 99-octane
and unleaded petrol. They're at Pērnavas iela
78 near the corner of Vagonu iela, two km
east of the railway station, and Brīvības
gatve 386 (the road to Sigulda, Pskov and
Tartu) in Jugla, eight km east of the city
centre. A third station is proposed at Ķekava,
on the Vilnius road, 20 km from the city
centre. The Pērnavas iela station also does
repairs and maintenance. The Auto Rīga
workshop at the Motor Museum (☎ 538 353)
does Volkswagen and Audi repairs.

Rental You can rent Russian cars at the Hotel
Rīga (☎ 216 516). Avis (☎ 207 353) and
Hertz (☎ 207 980) are both at the airport.
Check the various rates and deals they offer.
One of the best was a maxi-weekend rental
from Hertz – you could get a diesel-run VW
Polo or Ford Fiesta from Friday noon to
Monday 6 pm for around 85 lati, including
1500 free km (plus 0.12 lati for every extra
km). You can waive your damage-and-loss
liability for an extra 11 lati a day. Avis book-
ings can also be made at Latvia Tours (see
Travel Agencies in the Rīga Information

section), the Hotel Rīga and the Hotel de
Rome.

Boat
Rīga's sea-passenger port is at Eksporta iela
1, on the river about 1½ km downstream
(north) of the October Bridge. The Baltic
Line ferry to/from Stockholm, the Mercuri
ferries to/from Kiel, and the weekly
Travemunde ferry all dock here. For information on ticket outlets for these and other
ferries, see Travel Agencies in the Rīga
Information section.

Bicycle
The Latvian University Tourist Club (see
Places to Stay) is connected with the Baiļi
sports centre at Valmiera in Vidzeme and
may be able to arrange for bicycle tours
starting from Rīga.

GETTING AROUND
To/From the Airport
Rīga Airport (Lidosta Rīga) is at Skulte, 14
km west of the city centre. Bus No 22 runs
about every 20 minutes between the airport
and Arhitektu iela, off Raiņa bulvāris in the
city centre, next to the university building.
Tickets are sold at the information booth in
the airport terminal building. Taxi drivers
develop shark's teeth at the airport: you'll be
lucky to get one to take you to the city centre
for much less than 15 lati, even though the
official fare, at the time of writing, is under
1.50 lati.

City Transport
Most attractions are in the central area so you
only really need public transport – which
doesn't run through Old Rīga anyway –
when travelling to/from outlying parts. The
Rīga City Map shows the routes of the extensive bus, tram, trolleybus and route-taxi
system. The usual ticket-punching system is
used on buses, trams and trolleybuses.
Tickets were about 0.01 lati. On Sunday and
holidays you're supposed to punch two for
each trip. The fine for riding without punching a ticket is 0.40 lati. One central ticket-

selling kiosk is in the middle of Brīvības bulvāris at the junction of Raiņa bulvāris.

Taxi

Officially, taxis charged 0.08 lati to pick you up and 0.08 lati a km, but that rate is sure to go up. You also have to watch out for rip-offs. Insisting on the meter running is one way to avoid being cheated. Otherwise, fix a price before you get in. One main taxi rank near the city centre is at the railway station. You can call a taxi on ☎ 334 041.

Bicycle

The Tourist Club of Latvia (Latvijas Tūristu Klubs, LTK) (☎ 221 731 or 227 680), at Skārņu iela 22 in the old city, has bicycles to rent for looking around the city.

Around Rīga

The places in this section are easy day trips from Rīga – though Jūrmala is also a possible place to stay. Other places within day-trip reach from the capital, but further out, are covered in other chapters – such as Sigulda and Gauja National Park in the Vidzeme chapter and Bauska, Rundāle and Jelgava in the Zemgale chapter.

SALASPILS

Between 1941 and 1944 an estimated 45,000 Jews from Rīga and about 55,000 other people, including Jews from other Nazi-occupied countries and prisoners of war, were murdered in the Nazi concentration camp at Salaspils, 15 km south-east of Rīga. Giant, gaunt sculptures stand on the site as a memorial, and there's also a museum. The inscription on the huge concrete barrier at the entrance means 'Behind this gate the earth groans'.

Getting There & Away

From Rīga, take a suburban train on the Ogre-Krustpils line to Dārziņi (not Salaspils) station. A path leads from the station to the memorial (Latvian: *piemineklis*; Russian: *pamyatnik*) – about a 15-minute walk.

JŪRMALA

Jūrmala ('Seashore') is the combined name for a string of small towns and resorts stretching 20 km along the coast west of Rīga. Holiday-makers have been coming here since the 19th century. Jūrmala's long, sandy beaches are backed by dunes and pine woods, its shady streets lined with low-rise wooden houses. The beautifully fresh air and relaxed atmosphere make it a pleasant change from the city of Rīga. But don't come to swim: the Baltic waters are so polluted that there are official warnings against swimming. Waste from a factory that has been one of the chief culprits is now being treated, but there's still raw sewage from half of Rīga flowing into the sea at the mouth of the Daugava, just 15 km away.

The reasons Jūrmala's atmosphere has been quieter than usual in recent years, however, are political and economic, not environmental. In Soviet times 300,000 holiday-makers a year flooded into boarding houses, holiday homes and sanatoriums owned by trade unions and other institutions. Now the people and institutions can't afford to pay for the trips and, in any case, the ownership of the buildings is under question.

Orientation

Jūrmala lies between the coast, which faces north, and the Lielupe river which flows parallel to the coast, a km or two inland (it finally empties into the Gulf of Rīga just nine km west of the mouth of the Daugava). The main townships which make up Jūrmala are, from the east (Rīga) end: Lielupe, Bulduri, Dzintari, Majori, Dubulti, Jaundubulti, Pumpuri, Melluži, Asari, Vaivari, Kauguri (on the coast) and Sloka (two km inland), and finally Jaunķemeri (on the coast) and Ķemeri (six km inland). All except Kauguri and Jaunķemeri have railway stations. The busiest part is the four or five km between Bulduri and Dubulti, centred on Majori and Dzintari.

Majori's main street (and the centre of

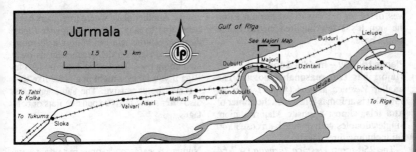

things, generally) is the one-km-long, pedestrians-only Jomas iela, across the main road from Majori station, then to the right. Here you'll find cafés, ice-cream stalls, galleries, shops and bars. Streets and paths lead through the woods on the left (north) to the beach.

Information
The 1988 Russian-language tourist map *Yurmala Turistskaya Skhema* is typically imprecise but does give a reasonable overall representation of the place.

The pharmacy at Jomas iela 76 in Majori sells some Western medicines.

Jūrmala has the Rīga telephone area code: 22. You drop the initial hyphenated digit from the numbers given here if dialling from within Jūrmala.

Things to See & Do
Walking the beach, dunes and woods and popping into a couple of cafés is reason enough to come to Jūrmala. The highest **dunes** are at Lielupe. In Majori, at Pliekšāna iela 7, north off Jomas iela, the poet Jānis Rainis' country cottage, where he died in 1929, is now a **museum** dedicated to him – open from 10 am to 5 pm daily except Tuesday. You can continue along Pliekšāna iela to the beach, or walk on to the east end of Jomas iela and approach the beach along busier Turaidas iela. At Turaidas iela 11, opposite the end of Jomas iela, there's an **art-exhibition hall** (*izstāžu zāle*).

Many of Jūrmala's sanatoriums are in the quiet streets behind the beach, from Majori

to Bulduri. Jūrmala's **History & Art Museum** (Vēstures un Mākslas Muzejs) is in a former church at Muzeja iela 13, almost opposite Dubulti station. Dubulti is the oldest of the Jūrmala settlements.

Quite a few art galleries are dotted around Majori – special exhibitions (*izstāde*) are advertised.

Places to Stay
Jūrmala is a very spread-out place; you may have to put in some legwork to find a room.

Places to Stay – bottom end
For cheaper private rooms and flats try some of the homestay agencies mentioned in Rīga – Places to Stay. One cheaper-end place worth a try is the *Vasaras Viesnīca Pumpuri* (Pumpuri Summer Hotel) (☎ 7-67 554) on Upes iela, Pumpuri, which consists of a few chalets and a couple of low blocks of rooms among trees, close to the beach. As its name indicates, it's only open in summer. To reach it from Pumpuri station, walk 350 metres towards the coast along Kronvalda iela, cross over Strelnieku prospekts, then turn left along Dubultu prospekts after another 150 metres. The second road on your right will be Upes iela. At Vaivari there's the reasonable-looking *Tūristu Bāze Vaivari* (Vaivari Tourist Base), a solid three-storey building in a secluded setting at Kauguru iela 49. From Vaivari station walk five minutes or so towards the coast till you reach the main road, Asaru prospekts. There's a sign to the tourist base, along a road that branches diagonally off Asaru prospekts, immediately

west of the big red Vaivari Sanatorium. From the sign it's a few hundred metres to the tourist base.

Places to Stay – middle & top end

Majori has two reasonable hotels. The smaller *Viesnīca Majori* (☎ 7-61 380, fax 336 200) is at Jomas iela 29, on the corner of Atrā iela, almost opposite Majori station. Singles/doubles with private bath cost 30/40 lati including three meals.

The 250-room *Viesnīca Jūrmala* (☎ 7-64 276, fax 7-61 455), in Soviet glass-and-concrete style at Jomas iela 47-49, charges 26/46 lati, or 35/46 lati with a sea view, without meals. It has a restaurant, three cafés and a casino – and also a branch (☎ 6-51 157) at Viļņu iela 3 in Lielupe.

In Soviet times, many visitors stayed in holiday homes or sanatoriums run by institutes, trade unions, factories and so on. Some of those intended for Communist Party high-ups are quite luxurious. Some of these places are opening up to general tourism. One, the *Zinatnes Nams* (☎ 7-51 205, fax 7-51 234) at Vikingu iela 3, a short walk from Lielupe station, has rooms with private bathroom for US$20/30, plus a restaurant, bar, and tennis

```
                    1  Pansionāts Rīgas Jūrmala
                    2  Dzintari Concert Hall
                    3  Rainis Museum
                    4  Viesnīca Majori
                    5  Viesnīca Jūrmala
                    6  Orients Restorāns
                    7  Art Exhibition Hall
                    8  Bistro
Majori              9  Pinguin
                   10  Majori Station
0    250   500 m   11  Jetty
```

Majori

courts. Another place where foreigners have been able to stay is the *Pansionāts Rīgas Jūrmala* at Jūras iela 7 in Majori, a 98-room showpiece right on the beach with its own swimming pool. Try Latvia Tours or TAS in Rīga if you fancy a night in a place like this – it will be expensive. The same agencies also offer some fairly expensive flats or cottages.

Places to Eat

Numerous cafés and some restaurants are dotted along Jomas iela in Majori and in the woods between it and the beach. The *Orients Restorāns* at Jomas iela 86, about 500 metres east of the Viesnīca Jūrmala, is among the best on this coast – and it's popular, so try to make a reservation for an evening meal. A table full of what Russians call zakuski – tasty salads, cold meats, smoked fish – followed by a hot shashlik (kebab) or fish dish with vegetables, plus a couple of brandies will set you back about 3.50 lati. There's also a *kafejnīca* and a *bārs* here. Side by side towards the station end of Jomas iela are a branch of the *Bistro* fast-food chain, also found in Tallinn and Pärnu, and one of the ubiquitous *Pinguin* ice-cream bars.

The *Jūrmala* restaurant in the Viesnīca Jūrmala is reasonable.

Entertainment

In summer there are discos several nights a week in and around Majori. They're advertised on posters. From June to August there's a summer season of concerts at the Latvia Philharmonia's Dzintari Concert Hall (Koncertzāle), at the beach end of Turaidas iela.

Getting There & Away

Train About three trains an hour run from Rīga to Jūrmala along the Ķemeri-Tukums line (see Rīga, Getting There & Away). They all stop at Majori, but not always at every other station, so check before boarding. The fare from Rīga to Majori is 0.07 lati for a journey of about 40 minutes.

River The hydrofoils which used to sail in

summer from Rīga to Majori, a one-hour trip with some also stopping at Lielupe, had, unfortunately, ceased operations at the time of writing. With luck they may restart. In Rīga they berthed at the jetty downstream from the east side of the October Bridge; and in Majori, just downstream from the railway station. A twice-daily summer ferry service, taking two hours each way for just under 1.30 lati, was advertised in 1992 from the 'Baltic ferry port' in Rīga – for information telephone ☎ 418 071 or 454 200.

Taxi There's a special Jūrmala taxi stand outside Rīga station.

Car Rental The Viesnīca Jūrmala has a car-rental service.

Getting Around

You can use the trains to move from one part of Jūrmala to another. There are also buses along the main roads (eg No 4 from Dubulti station to Sloka).

LATVIA

Vidzeme

Vidzeme is the northern half of eastern Latvia, the country's most scenically varied region. Its highlight is the valley of the Gauja River, part of it a national park, which contains some of the prettiest scenery in the Baltic states and is dotted with castles. Also in the region are the Vidzeme Upland, Latvia's highest region, and a long stretch of fairly unspoilt coast along the Gulf of Rīga.

THE COAST

The main road from Rīga to Pärnu and Tallinn runs pretty close to the shore of the Gulf of Rīga for much of the 115 km to the Estonian border. Soon after dividing from the Sigulda and Tartu road, 15 km from Rīga, it starts to run through some lovely wooded country, dotted with lakes and small villages with country churches. One such village, **Baltezers**, stands between two lakes, one on each side of the road. Most suburban trains on the Sigulda line stop at Baltezers station, three km south. At **Ādaži**, about five km further north, there's a small roadside *Grill Bārs & Picēria*. Another seven or eight km north, between the 509/277 and 510/276-km markers, is a *Kempings* with cabins in woods by a lake, on the west side of the road. You're only a few km, here, from the mouth of the Gauja.

At **Saulkrasti**, 45 km from Rīga, a 24-hour petrol and service station with a coffee shop, run by the Finnish company Neste, is likely to be open on the south side of town by the time you read this. Saulkrasti is a popular summer escape for Rīga residents. The road meets the open sea at a sandy beach on the north side of town. A little further north, inland from the road, is the cheap *Viesnīca Saulkrasti Priedes* (Saulkrasti Pines Hotel) and around 35 km north, at the 564/222-km sign, there's a turning to the *Kempings Meleki & Hotel Captains* on the coast a km or two south of the Vitrupe river.

Salacgrīva, at the mouth of the Salaca River, is where most northbound buses stop for a drinks break. The *Kafejnīca Pie Bocmaņa*, just into the town on Baznīcas iela, is pleasanter than the canteen by the bus stop, but you're unlikely to have time for it if you're on a bus. **Ainaži**, a small former shipbuilding town, is a km before the Estonian border. The main highway bypasses it inland, but buses usually detour along the old road into the town centre, where the old Maritime School is now a museum (Ainaži Jūrskolas Memorialais Muzejs), open daily from 10 am to 4 pm.

Getting There & Away

Buses north from Rīga to Pärnu and Tallinn follow this coastal road. Journey time is about one hour to Saulkrasti, 1¾ hours to Salacgrīva. There are also a few buses a day just as far as Saulkrasti or Ainaži, both from Rīga and from places in the Gauja valley like Sigulda, Cēsis and Valmiera. Suburban

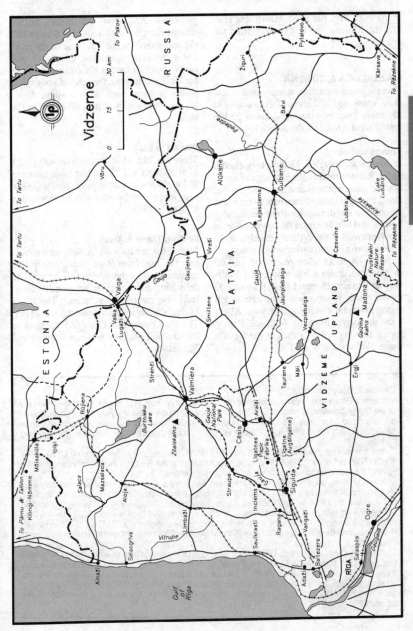

trains from Rīga run to Saulkrasti, but after that the Rūjiena line heads away from the coast.

MAZSALACA & RŪJIENA

There's some attractive scenery and a few spots renowned in Latvian folklore around the small town of Mazsalaca, about 55 km inland from Ainaži on the Salaca River.

Things to See

In Mazsalaca there's a 13th century church on the Rūjiena road on the east edge of town, but the main spots that attract visitors are along the right bank of the river, to the west. About one km downriver from the railway bridge, and two km from the town centre, is the **Werewolf Pine** (Vilkaču priede), reckoned to turn you into a werewolf if you crawl through its roots after muttering certain incantations under a full moon. The **Stairway of Dreams** (Sapņu kāpnes), about 300 metres north, is supposed to be able to tell young lovers how well suited they are. About a km downriver from the Werewolf Pine, a spring flowing out of a rock at the **Devil's Cave** (Velna ala) is said to have healing properties. And about 800 metres further downstream, the sandstone cliff **Sound Hill** (Skaņaiskalns) on the left bank of the river has some bizarre acoustic effects: if you stand about 50 metres back from the right bank in certain spots, the echo of your voice seems to come back, after a slight delay, louder – and not from the cliff but from the sky.

Places to Stay

There's an old, basic *Viesnīca* (Hotel) (☎ 51 235) at Rīgas iela 17, not far from the river in Mazsalaca; but at Rūjiena, about 20 km east, a new part-Swedish-run hotel was due to open in 1993.

Getting There & Away

Mazsalaca and Rūjiena are both on a suburban rail line from Rīga, though only one suburban train a day comes this far up. The daily long-distance train between Rīga and Ipiķi also reaches both stations. The Rīga-Mazsalaca fare in general seating is 0.40 lati. There are buses from Cēsis and Valmiera to Rūjiena and possibly between Rūjiena and Mazsalaca.

Canoe & Bicycle Trips

Vidzeme's Gauja and Salaca rivers are both good for canoeing – in particular the 220-km stretch of the Gauja between Vireši and Sigulda, which flows through some of Latvia's best scenery with nothing more hazardous than some fairly gentle rapids. There are riverside tent-camping sites dotted along this whole stretch, and above Valmiera the river flows through almost entirely unspoilt country.

You can set up a Gauja canoe trip through the Latvian University Tourist Club (LUTK) or the Tourist Club of Latvia (LTK), both in Rīga (see Activities in the Facts for the Visitor chapter at the front of the book for contact details), or other organisations.

The LUTK is good value and offers three basic trips depending on your preparedness: Vireši-Sigulda (nine days out of Rīga, eight of them on the river), Valmiera-Sigulda (six days out of Rīga, four on the river) and Valmiera-Cēsis (five days out of Rīga, 2½ on the river). The cost per person including equipment and food, and transport to/from Rīga is about 75 lati for the long route or 50 lati for the others (or even less if you provide your own food). The LUTK works with the Baiļi Sports Centre (Sporta Bāze Baiļi) at Valmiera (see Valmiera, Places to Stay) in organising these trips.

The Baiļi Centre also rents bicycles for touring, either on your own or with a guide. A guided trip, organised through the LUTK, would cost around 10 lati a day including bike, food and tent. Incidentally, the Baiļi's director, Valdis, is a tremendous person to contact if you're thinking of some adventure travel elsewhere in the ex-USSR, as he's young, friendly, English-speaking and full of experience and ideas for highly unusual trips in the Pamir Mountains, the Arctic, Lake Baykal and so on. ■

SIGULDA

With a string of medieval castles and legendary caves scattered along one of the prettiest stretches of the Gauja valley, Sigulda (formerly: Segewold), 50 km east of Rīga, is about the most popular tourist day trip from the capital. There's plenty to make a longer stay in this attractive part of Latvia enjoyable, including some good walks and other interesting places nearby such as Līgatne and Cēsis.

Sigulda stands on the south edge of a picturesque, steep-sided, wooded section of the Gauja valley. Though the name sometimes applied to the region, 'Latvian Switzerland', is a gross exaggeration, the landscape is certainly much more dramatic than in most other parts of the Baltic states. Sigulda is the main gateway to the 920-sq-km Gauja National Park (Gaujas nacionālais parks), which stretches north-eastward almost to Valmiera, extending some distance either side of the Gauja valley. Impressive wooded and agricultural landscapes, historic sites and a wildlife centre are among the national park's features. At Sigulda you enter the park as you descend the hill from the town to the river. In addition to its tourist attractions, Sigulda is a minor health resort and a winter sports centre, with a bobsleigh run snaking down into the valley.

History

Finno-Ugric Liv tribes inhabited the area as far back as 2000 BC, and by the 12th century they had built several wooden hilltop strongholds. But they were unable to prevent the German conquest in the early 13th century. In 1207, when the German crusaders were dividing up their spoils, the Gauja was chosen as the boundary in this area between the territories of the Knights of the Sword, who got the land south of the river, and of the archbishop of Rīga, who got the north side. Both built castles in prominent positions – as much to guard against each other, one suspects, as against any local uprising.

After being subject to numerous wars, particularly in the 16th to 18th centuries, Sigulda started to develop as a country resort with the building of the Pskov-Rīga railway in 1889. The Russian owner of the local estate, Prince Kropotkin, sold plots of land to wealthy Rīgans to build their own country houses.

Information

There was no functioning left-luggage office in either the train or the bus station when I last visited Sigulda – but if you ask the station managers nicely, they're likely to oblige. There's a post office at Pils iela 2 and a small department store at Paegles iela 3 on the corner of Pils iela. The Gauja National Park offices (☎ 22-974 006) are at Raiņa iela 15.

Sigulda Castles & Church

Only some bits of the knights' stronghold (Siguldas pilsdrupas), built between 1207 and 1226 among woods on the north-east edge of Sigulda town, have survived the numerous wars to which the area has been subject. The castle hasn't been repaired since the Great Northern War, but its ruins are perhaps more evocative because of that. There's a great view through the trees to the reconstructed Turaida Castle of the archbishop, on the far side of the valley.

On the way to the ruins from the town, you pass the 1225 Sigulda Church (Siguldas baznīca), rebuilt in the 17th and 18th centuries, and the 19th century New Sigulda Castle (Siguldas Jaunā pils), the former Kropotkin residence, now a cardiovascular sanatorium.

Krimulda Castle & Manor

On the north side of the valley, a track leads up from near the bridge to the ruined Krimulda Castle (Krimuldas pilsdrupas), built in 1255-73 and once used as a guesthouse for visiting dignitaries. A good way to reach it, or leave it, is the cable car which crosses the valley from Baumaņa iela in Sigulda. The big white building just west of the northern cable-car station is Krimulda Manor (Krimuldas muižas pils), built in 1854 and now a children's sanatorium.

Gūtmanis' & Viktors' Caves

In the bottom of the north side of the valley, Gūtmanis' Cave (Gūtmaņa ala) is covered with graffiti going back to the 16th century – including the coats of arms of long-gone hunters. The water of the stream flowing out of the cave is supposed to remove wrinkles, and the cave is named after a healer who allegedly cured the sick with water from it.

But this cave is most famous for its role in the tragic legend, apparently based on truth, of the local beauty Maija, the Rose of Turaida. Maija had been taken into Turaida Castle as a little girl when she was found among the wounded after a battle in 1601. She grew into a famous beauty courted by men from far and wide, but she loved Viktors, a gardener at Sigulda Castle. They would meet in this cave, halfway between the two castles. One day a particularly desperate Polish officer among Maija's suitors lured her to the cave by means of a forged letter in Viktors' handwriting. Maija offered to give the Pole the scarf from around her neck, which she said had magical protective powers, if he let her go. To prove the scarf's powers, she suggested he swing at her with his sword. Whether this was a bluff or she

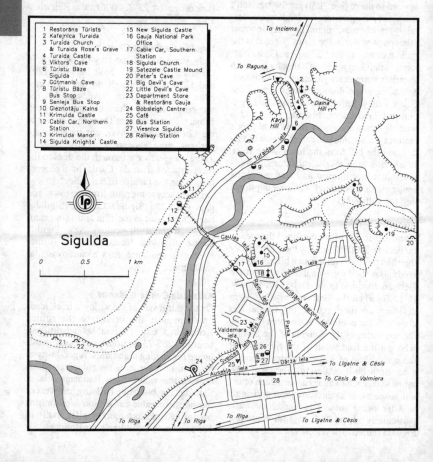

1 Restorāns Tūrists
2 Kafejnīca Turaida
3 Turaida Church
   & Turaida Rose's Grave
4 Turaida Castle
5 Viktors' Cave
6 Tūristu Bāze
   Sigulda
7 Gūtmanis' Cave
8 Tūristu Bāze
   Bus Stop
9 Senleja Bus Stop
10 Gleznotāju Kalns
11 Krimulda Castle
12 Cable Car, Northern
    Station
13 Krimulda Manor
14 Sigulda Knights' Castle
15 New Sigulda Castle
16 Gauja National Park
    Office
17 Cable Car, Southern
    Station
18 Sigulda Church
19 Satezele Castle Mound
20 Peter's Cave
21 Big Devil's Cave
22 Little Devil's Cave
23 Department Store
    & Restorāns Gauja
24 Bobsleigh Centre
25 Café
26 Bus Station
27 Viesnīca Sigulda
28 Railway Station

To Inciems
To Raguna
Daina Hill
Kārļa Hill
Turaidas iela

Sigulda

0   0.5   1 km

Gaujas iela
Livkalna iela
Krišjāņa Barona iela
Pils iela
Parka iela
Valdemāra iela
Sveices iela
Ausekļa iela
Dārza iela

To Ligatne & Cēsis
To Cēsis & Valmiera
To Riga
To Riga
To Riga
To Ligatne & Cēsis

really believed in the scarf isn't clear. Either way, the Pole duly took his swing – and killed her. And fled. The hapless Viktors found her body in the cave and was suspected of her murder until a friend of the Pole's spoke up to clear him.

Viktors' Cave (Viktora ala), a little further along the valley, was supposedly dug out by Viktors for Maija to sit and watch the castle gardens where he worked.

Turaida Castle & Around

The archbishops' castle (Turaidas pils), founded in 1214 on the site of a Liv stronghold, was blown up when lightning hit its gunpowder store in the 18th century. What you see today is mostly the result of recent rebuilding, which has made it the most complete of the Sigulda area's old castles and the most prominent feature on the southern escarpment of the valley. There's a museum within and good views from the 42-metre **Donjon Tower**, originally a last refuge from attack.

On the path between the castle and the road, near the small wooden **Turaida Church** (Turaidas Baznīcas), built in 1750 and now a museum, two lime trees shade a grave with the inscription 'Turaidas Roze 1601–1620'. Viktors himself is said to have buried Maija and planted one of the trees, then disappeared from the area without trace. The hillside behind the church is known as Daina Hill (Dainu kalns). The *daina* or poetic folk song is a major Latvian tradition, and the hillside is dotted with sculptures dedicated to Krišjānis Barons, the great collector and recorder of dainas. The whole castle area is open daily from 10 am to 5 pm – entry is 0.04 lati.

Kārļa Hill (Kārļa kalns), facing Turaida Castle across the ravine which the road ascends from the valley bottom, was another old Liv stronghold.

Walks

You'll get a good stretch of the legs if you walk to the main sites – Sigulda Castle, Gūtmanis' Cave and the Turaida Castle area. If you want goals for further exploration,

there are many other historic sites and caves with legends attached, up and down the valley. A good circular walk on the south side of the valley – about six km from and back to Sigulda Church – is to the **Satezele Castle Mound** (Satezeles pilskalns), a Liv stronghold; then to **Peter's Cave** (Pētera ala), on a steep bank of the Vējupīte river; and on to **Gleznotāju Kalns** (Artists' Hill), which has a 12-km panorama.

On the north bank you could walk downstream from the bridge to the **Little Devil's Cave** (Mazā Velnala) and **Big Devil's Cave** (Lielā Velnala), then return along the top of the escarpment to Krimulda Castle – about seven km. The Little Devil's Cave has a **Spring of Wisdom** (Gudrības avotiņš). The Big Devil's Cave has black walls from the fiery breath of a travelling demon who once sheltered for a day here to avoid sunlight.

Bungy Jumping

You can bungy jump from the bridge over the Gauja on summer weekends – 2 lati a jump!

Places to Stay

The *Viesnīca Sigulda* (☎ 22-972 263), in the town at Pils iela 6, is extremely bare and basic but charged only 0.90 lati for a double with private toilet. It must be ripe for taking over and upgrading. There are brighter and better rooms, for 4.25 lati a single or double with private bathroom, at the *Tūristu Bāze Sigulda* (Sigulda Tourist Base) (☎ 22-972 162) in the valley just below Turaida Castle, at Turaidas iela 4. The tourist base has a bar and small casino, but no restaurant. It's open year round. It was originally built for Soviet groups in the 1950s.

Places to Eat

The *Restorāns Tūrists*, opposite the entrance to the Turaida Castle grounds, looks better than the *Restorāns Gauja* next to the department store on the corner of Pils iela and Paegles iela in the town. The *Kafejnīca Turaida* in the Turaida Castle grounds, open daily from 10 am to 9 pm, has some reasonable snacks, as do the bus and train station

LATVIA

cafés. There's another café on Valdemara iela which might be worth checking out.

The *Restorāns Senīte*, 12 km along the road to Rīga, is said to better than any of these.

Getting There & Away
Bus To/from Rīga there should be four buses daily, taking one hour for 0.35 lati, but when I last visited Sigulda none of these were running – presumably because of the petrol shortage at that time. The rail service is more frequent, in any case. Other buses travel to/from Cēsis, Saulkrasti, Madona, Aizkraukle and, some days, Ogre.

Train Sigulda is on the Rīga-Tallinn-St Petersburg railway and is served by 10 suburban trains and eight long-distance trains to/from Rīga daily. Journey time is 45 minutes to 1¼ hours, and the fare in general seating is 0.15 lati. There are two or three suburban and seven long-distance trains daily to/from Cēsis and Valmiera. There are also direct trains once or twice daily to/from Tartu, Tallinn, St Petersburg, Vilnius and Minsk.

Getting Around
Walking is a good way to get around, as the atmosphere is fairly leisurely here. But you can save your legs by taking the cable car which crosses between Krimulda and the end of Baumaņa iela in Sigulda, or bus No 12 which runs from Sigulda bus station to Turaida and Krimulda a few times a day. The bus departure times are posted at the bus station; it takes about 50 minutes for the round trip to Krimulda and back. Get off at the Senleja stop for Gūtmanis Cave or the Tūristu Bāze stop for the Tūristu Bāze Sigulda.

LĪGATNE & AROUND
The stretch of the Gauja valley between Sigulda and Cēsis is in the heart of the national park, and there are a number of things to see and do even if you're not in a canoe – which is about the best way to experience the Gauja.

Deer

On the south side of the river, about 15 km north-east of Sigulda, there's a Latvian wildlife park – officially the **Līgatne Leisure & Study Park** (Līgatnes Atpūtas un Mācību Parks) – with elk, beaver, deer, bison and wild boar in sizeable open-air enclosures in the forest. A five-km motor circuit and a network of footpaths link a series of observation points, and there's a 20-metre-high observation tower with a fine panorama. Some of the animals are none too wild – the elk came trotting over for a snack when our car pulled up at their enclosure! The wildlife park is part of an 'Intensive Recreation Zone' within the national park, and one of the recreations is **horse riding**: a few hundred metres west of the motor-circuit entrance, you can rent a steed for a 4.8-km-circuit ride. There's also a 2.3-km **botanical path** marked out along here.

Several sections of steep bank line the Gauja either side of Līgatne. These would hardly rate a second glance in some parts of the world, but in a flat country like Latvia they're a big deal – and they get names. One on the north bank, almost opposite the wildlife park, is called **Katrīna**.

If you're continuing to Cēsis from the wildlife park, you don't have to return to the main road. Instead, you can head on through the settlement around **Līgatne paper factory**, which locals proclaim is the biggest paper factory in Latvia. Three or four km past the factory, in the valley bottom at Skalupji, is a large modern building which used to be a **Communist Party holiday home**. Here (wonder why?) the road ceases to be paved, and you have about 12 km of dirt and gravel before you reach the main road again, via Karļi. On the way there's a turning to **Kuku Klintis** (Kuku Rock), another section of steep bank on the Gauja. Then you cross a small tributary of the Gauja called the Amata. A footpath runs from here to Ieriķi, about 12 km south, on the railway and main road from Sigulda to Cēsis. The path follows the Amata much of the way.

The 16-metre sandstone bluff, **Zvārtas Iezis**, a couple of km up the Amata, is a popular local beauty spot. You can reach it by road if you turn right at the Krustkalni bus stop at a junction opposite a low, old inn building.

Places to Stay

There are several sites for tent campers, intended for hikers and canoeists, along the banks of the Gauja between Sigulda and Cēsis. They're mostly on the north bank, but there's one opposite the Katrina bank at Līgatne – and there are a couple more on the Amata between Zvārtas Iezis and the Gauja.

Getting There & Away

The way to the wildlife park can be confusing, partly because there are two Līgatne settlements. One, shown on maps as either Līgatne or Augšlīgatne (Upper Līgatne), is on the main Sigulda-Cēsis road 12 km from Sigulda; the other is six km north, around the Līgatne Paper Factory (Līgatnes Papir Fabrika). A sign in Līgatne main-road village indicates the turning to the paper factory and park. Turn left just as you enter the paper-factory village (if you reach the factory you have gone too far) and fork left at the Vidusskola bus stop after a few hundred

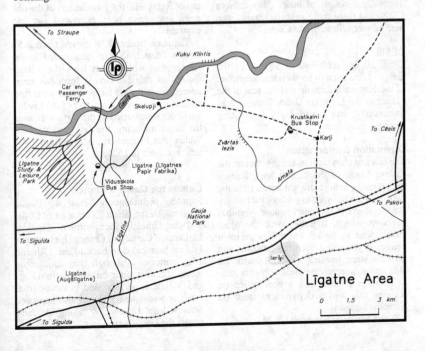

Līgatne Area

metres. About 1½ km further on, shortly before the road reaches a ferry crossing over the Gauja, turn sharp left. The wildlife park entrance is then on the left after two km.

Public transport to the area is poor. The nearest bus stop to the wildlife park is Gaujasmala, two km from the entrance, near the final turning to the park. But when I went, there didn't appear to be any buses going there from either Sigulda or Cēsis, and only a couple a day going to the paper factory (Fabrika Līgatne) from Cēsis. Things may improve as there was a petrol shortage at the time. Five buses daily are scheduled from Cēsis to Zvārtas Iezis, but this service, too, is erratic. You can always get a bus or suburban train to the Līgatne main road village or to Ieriķi, then walk or maybe hitch.

ARAIŠI

A 9th century island settlement in Lake Araiši (Araišu ezers), six km south of Cēsis, has been excavated and is open to visitors. There are a couple of buses daily to/from Cēsis, and three daily suburban trains stop here between Sigulda and Cēsis.

CĒSIS

Cēsis, 30 km north-east of Sigulda up the Gauja valley, used to be Wenden, a member of the Hanseatic League and the seat of the master of the Livonian Order. Today it's an unheralded, but surprisingly interesting medium-sized town.

Orientation & Information

The bus and train stations are together on the eastern fringe of the central area. Raunas iela, running almost straight ahead from the far side of the bus yard as you exit the railway station, leads to the main square, Vienības laukums which, together with the older streets down to the left, constitutes the town centre. If you cross Vienības laukums and take the street heading downhill on the far side you soon reach the castle, on your left.

There is a bank and a post office on Raunas iela and a department store on Vienības laukums.

The Cēsis telephone code is 241.

Castle, Museum & Park

Cēsis Castle (Cēsu Pils) was founded by the Knights of the Sword (who later became the Livonian Order) in 1209. Its dominant feature is two stout towers at the west end, looking over the castle park. To enter, you need to visit the extensive Regional History Museum (Cēsu Vēstures Muzejs) which is housed in the adjoining 19th century 'new castle' – open from 10 am to 5 pm daily except Monday. In the attractive park below the castle there is a small song bowl, a lake and a Russian church. Beside the park, on the far side from the church, is Latvia's oldest brewery.

Old Town

The old part of town, with a few narrow, crooked streets of mainly wooden buildings – not yet prettified like, say, the old city at Rīga – extends south from the bottom end of Vienības laukums. Just off this square, at the top of Rīgas iela, the foundations of the old town gates have been excavated and left exposed.

The main landmark of the old town is St John's Church (Svēta Jāņa baznīca) on Skolas iela, which dates from the 1280s, though its original Gothic form has been altered down the centuries. It has some fine stained glass. Several masters of the Livonian Order were buried by the north wall, near the altar, including the last capable one, Walter von Plettenberg, master from 1494 until his death in 1535.

Lielstraupe Castle & Church

Standing picturesquely beside the Brasla River at Straupe, about 25 km west of Cēsis, and the same distance north of Sigulda, Lielstraupe Castle and Church (Lielstraupes Pils un baznīca) date back to the 13th and 14th centuries – though they look more recent. There are four daily buses from Rīga and Valmiera, and the odd bus runs from Cēsis at weekends. You can also approach Straupe from Līgatne, by taking the ferry across the Gauja there.

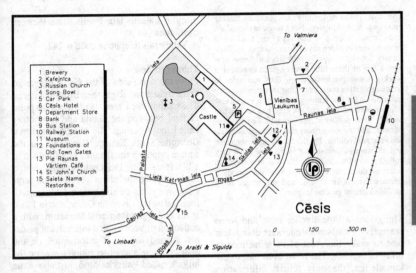

1 Brewery
2 Kafejnīca
3 Russian Church
4 Song Bowl
5 Car Park
6 Cēsis Hotel
7 Department Store
8 Bank
9 Bus Station
10 Railway Station
11 Museum
12 Foundations of
   Old Town Gates
13 Pie Raunas
   Vārtiem Café
14 St John's Church
15 Saieta Nams
   Restorāns

Cēsis

0   150   300 m

LATVIA

Places to Stay & Eat

The ageing *Cēsis Hotel* (☎ 22 392) at Vienības laukums 1 reopened in 1993 after renovation by a Danish company, which no doubt made it much more inviting, and dearer, than its previous Soviet-style incarnation.

The best restaurant in town is the *Saieta Nams Restorāns* at the bottom of Rīgas iela. It's open from 11 am to midnight every day and has music in the evenings. At the top end of Rīgas iela, *Pie Raunas Vārtiem* is a good cellar café. There's also a restaurant in the hotel.

Getting There & Away

Bus About 10 buses daily run to/from Rīga, taking two hours for 0.50 lati, and seven to/from Valmiera. There are also daily services to/from Saulkrasti, Limbaži, Ainaži, Valka, Rūjiena, Madona, Jaunpiebalga and Alūksne and buses a few days a week (including Saturday and Sunday) to/from Jēkabpils, Aizkraukle and Daugavpils.

Train There are three suburban and seven long-distance trains daily to/from Sigulda (30 to 45 minutes, 0.15 lati in general seat-

ing) and Rīga (1¼ to two hours, 0.30 lati). To/from Valmiera there are two suburban and seven long-distance trains each day (30 to 45 minutes, 0.10 lati). Direct trains run once or twice daily to/from Tartu, Tallinn, St Petersburg, Vilnius and Minsk.

VALMIERA

Valmiera (formerly: Wolmar), a similar-sized town to Cēsis about 30 km further north up the Gauja valley, just outside the national park, is less historic than Sigulda or Cēsis (most of its old town burnt down in 1944) but is still an interesting place on an attractive bend of the Gauja, with some useful accommodation possibilities.

J G Kohl, travelling rather forlornly through the remote Latvian countryside in the mid-19th century, found Valmiera 'at once cheerful and tranquil. The streets were wide and straight, the houses clean and handsome, and all the windows gleamed with lights, reminding the wayfarer of the comforts of the social circle'.

But in general, Kohl found rural Livonia (as the eastern half of Latvia and southern Estonia were known) about the hickest region he'd ever been in:

The small towns of Livonia...are gradually sinking into complete nothingness. Not a single branch of art, manufacture, science, or industry of any kind, could be mentioned in which any of these towns excel. Their literary activity is equally insignificant. Some time ago, a few of these little towns agreed to publish a weekly newspaper in common. They succeeded in scraping together some interesting matter, which they published in the first number, but the next week a new number was wanted, and all they had to say had already been published...they republished the first number, and the subscribers had to take it as a new and improved edition. The third week, however, came and all were in despair, for in no way could they collect matter for a third number; and, in order not to warm up the same dish a third time, the periodical declared itself insolvent, and the undertaking exploded amidst general laughter.

Things are a little livelier now, and some enterprising souls in Valmiera are doing their best to make the most of its attractions to bring in tourism. The town even has, to my knowledge, the only tourist information office, as such, in Latvia!

Orientation

The focus of matters is the road bridge over the Gauja, in the middle of town. Stacijas iela leads south from the bridge to the bus station, opposite the corner of Cēsu iela, after a hundred metres or so and the railway station after two km. The centre of town is on the north side of the bridge; the area rebuilt since WW II is ahead of you and to the left as you come off the bridge, while the little historic area is to the right, above the end of the bend of the Gauja.

Information

The museum at Bruņinieku iela 3 in the historic area runs a helpful tourist information service (☎ 32 733 daytime, 32 275 evenings). You can change money at the bank on Rīgas iela, in the northern half of town, a km west of the bridge. The central department store is at Rīgas iela, just ahead to your right as you come off the north side of the bridge. The market is at Tērbatas iela 8A near the centre: go north from the square in front of St Simeon's Church and turn right after crossing the small Ažkalna River. The phar-macy at Laicena iela 1 sells some Western medicines.

Valmiera's telephone code is 242.

Things to See

From the north side of the Gauja bridge go to the right along Rīgas then Bruņinieku iela. The small historic area stands here on a point of land between the Gauja and a tributary called the Ažkalna. The tall **St Simeon's Church** (Svētā Sīmaņa Baznīca), on the square opposite the theatre, was founded in 1283. It has a fine 19th century organ. A little further along the street are the not-very-extensive ruins of the **castle** (Pilsdrupas), founded by the Livonian Order, also in 1283; at the end is the **Regional Museum**, with a collection of very limited interest, but possibly a good source of information on the district. There's an observation tower on the hillock called **Valterkalniņš**, just above the meeting of the Ažkalna and the Gauja. Across a small bridge over the Ažkalna, a loop of land surrounded by the Gauja has been kept undeveloped as a woodland **park**.

Activities

The Sporta Bāze Baiļi has touring bicycles for rent and is also a base for canoe trips on the Gauja – see the following section and the Canoe & Bicycle Trips section at the start of this chapter.

Places to Stay & Eat

The tourist-information service at the museum can find you rooms in private homes for about 4 lati per person.

At the *Sporta Bāze Baiļi* (Baiļi Sports Centre), on the eastern outskirts of Valmiera, a couple of little self-contained wooden chalets for tourists were under construction. Though intended mainly for foreigners on canoe or cycle trips organised in conjunction with the Latvian University Tourist Club in Rīga (see the Canoe & Bicycle Trips section at the start of this chapter), they'll probably be open to anyone. There's also some dormitory accommodation here, and you could almost certainly pitch a tent, too. The centre has a friendly, young English-speaking director who plans to open a café-restaurant – but until that happens you'll need to bring your own food. The tourist-information service will be able to contact Baiļi for you in advance to find out what accommodation is available and what it will cost. To reach Baiļi, go about 1½ km south along Stacijas iela from the Gauja bridge, then turn left (east) along Kauguru iela and go about two km, mainly through woodland. The centre is easily identifiable by its tall ski jump.

A small three-room private hotel called the *Irina* is also due to open in Valmiera. It's at Palejas iela 8B and must be pretty comfortable because it'll be charging around 26 lati a single and 35 lati a double, including breakfast. Further small hotels are likely to follow – let's hope some will be cheaper. The only sizeable hotel in the town, the *Viesnīca Gauja* (☎ 22 165) at Tērbatas iela 2, on the square in front of St Simeon's Church, was closed awaiting renovation – by a Scandinavian company, it was hoped.

There's a restaurant in the department-store building at Rīgas iela 4 and a few cafés along Rīgas iela.

Getting There & Away
Bus There are about 10 buses or microbuses daily to/from Rīga, taking about 2½ hours for 0.80 lati, and seven buses to/from Cēsis; there are also services to/from Rūjiena, Valka, Ainaži, Rēzekne, Daugavpils and elsewhere.

Train There are two suburban and seven long-distance trains daily to/from Cēsis, Sigulda and Rīga (1¾ to three hours, 0.40 lati in general seating). Direct trains run once or twice daily to/from Tartu, Tallinn, St Petersburg, Vilnius and Minsk.

AROUND VALMIERA
The **Strenči Rapids** on the Gauja, four km below the town of Strenči and 15 km north-east of Valmiera, are reckoned to be the most scenic stretch of the entire river, with steep, high banks. **Zilaiskalns** (Blue Hill), 14 km west of Valmiera, and the lake **Burtnieku ezers**, about 23 km north, off the Mazsalaca road, are other local beauty spots. There's a lookout tower on top of Zilaiskalns.

VALKA
Valka, about 45 km north-east of Valmiera on the road and railway to Tartu in Estonia, is the Latvian (and smaller) part of the town of Valga/Valka, which is divided between Latvia and Estonia. A few buses go to Valka, and the odd train to nearby Lugaži, if you're curious about it, but there are no through-buses into or out of Estonia at the time of writing – only trains.

VIDZEME UPLAND
Between Cēsis and Madona, 80 km to its south-east, is the part-forest, part-farmed Vidzeme Upland (Vidzemes Augstiene), which is at its hilliest approaching Madona. Latvia's highest point, 311-metre Gaizina kalns, is 10 km west of Madona. There are a number of lakes in the upland, and the Gauja rises on the south side of Elka kalns hill near Māli. The Gauja basically flows in a big circle: first east through Jaunpiebalga and Lejasciems, then north past Vireši and Gaujiena (where there's a ruined 13th century castle) to form the Latvian-Estonian border for a stretch, before turning south-west through Strenči and Valmiera.

The Rīga-Rēzekne-Moscow trunk road crosses the upland from west to east and goes through Madona, but the north-south route from Cēsis to Madona (through Taurene and Vecpiebalga) is probably more scenic. There's a hotel at Madona. The Rīga-Pskov-St Petersburg road crosses to the north of the upland; there's a *Kempings* near Alūksne, 17 km south of the road not far from the Estonian border.

Getting There & Away
Buses reach into and cross the upland from Cēsis, Valmiera and Sigulda to the north, from Rēzekne to the south, and from Rīga to the west.

Latgale

Latgale is south-east Latvia, named after the Latgal (Lettish) tribes who were its inhabitants at the time of the German invasion in the 12th century. It's the main bastion of Roman Catholicism in Latvia, having been under Polish control from 1561 to 1772.

The Latgale Upland, in the far south-east corner, is a scenic lake district, with Rēzekne prominent among the medium-sized towns around its fringes. Daugavpils, to the south-west, is Latvia's second-biggest city and has a mainly Russian population. The Daugava River flows from Daugavpils to Rīga. A number of dams and hydro-electric schemes create artificial lakes along its length, and there are a few towns of mostly minor significance. Relatively few visitors come to this part of Latvia.

DAUGAVA VALLEY

The road and railway from Rīga to Daugavpils follow the north bank of the Daugava fairly closely. At **Lielvārde**, 50 km from Rīga, and **Aizkraukle** (formerly: Stučka), 80 km out, there are ancient castle mounds *(pilskalns)* of the pre-German inhabitants. The one at Aizkraukle is large and impressive. At **Koknese**, 95 km from Rīga, there's a 13th century knights' castle right on the river bank. At **Krustpils**, 140 km from Rīga, the railway divides, with the main line heading due east away from the river towards Rēzekne and Moscow and a branch continuing on up the river to Daugavpils. Krustpils forms a single town with **Jēkabpils** on the south bank. Krustpils has a 13th century castle and a 17th century church. In Jēkabpils are a 1769 church and a Regional Museum.

RĒZEKNE

Rēzekne (formerly: Rositten) is a pleasant country town of 43,000 people, 235 km east of Rīga, forming the north-western gateway to the Latgale Upland.

Orientation

After decades as Leņiņa iela, Rēzekne's long, straight main street has now had its pre-WW II name, Atbrīvošanas aleja (Liberation Avenue), restored. It runs 2½ km from just west of Rēzekne II railway station in the north of town to just west of the bus station in the south end.

The central square, with the Māra statue and the new building of the Hotel Latgale, is about two-thirds of the way down Atbrīvošanas aleja from the north, at the top of a hill running 800 metres down to the bus station. Rēzekne I railway station is in the south-west of town, 900 metres west along Brīvības iela from the foot of Atbrīvošanas aleja (about halfway, you have to fork left on to what looks like a minor road but is, in fact, still Brīvības iela).

The main Rīga-Moscow road bypasses Rēzekne to the north. The Daugavpils-Pskov-St Petersburg road goes through the middle as Atbrīvošanas aleja.

LATVIA

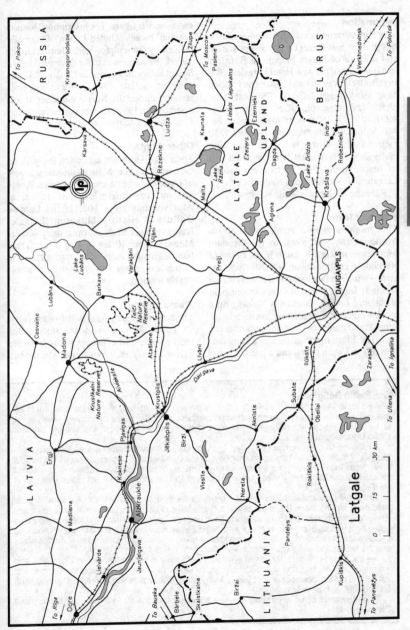

LATVIA

Information

There are currency-exchange windows in the bus station and Rezekne II railway station and a Bank of Latvia branch on Baznīcas iela, just east of the new Hotel Latgale building. Both railway stations and the bus station have left-luggage lockers. The post, telephone and telegraph office is 100 metres south of the hotel at Atbrīvošanas aleja 81. MF Salons at Atbrīvošanas aleja 84, 250 metres further down, is a quite interesting crafts shop. The market is in the south-east of town, about 300 metres east along Latgales iela from the bus station.

Rēzekne's telephone code is 246.

Statue of Māra

This monument is a symbol of Latvian freedom almost as potent as the Freedom Monument in Rīga. It stands in the centre of Rēzekne's central square on Atbrīvošanas aleja – which in fact looks as if it was created specially for the statue. It shows a woman, in traditional Latvian headdress, holding up a cross while two men look up, seemingly for support and guidance, from the ground at her feet. The Māra figure is seen as a combination of the Virgin Mary and a pre-Christian earth-mother figure. The inscription 'Vienoti Latvijai' means 'United Latvia'. Originally created by the sculptor Kārlis Jansons in the 1930s, the statue was twice destroyed by the Soviet authorities – once in 1940 or 1941 and again in the late 1940s, after it had been restored during the Nazi occupation. It was re-erected in 1992 at a ceremony attended by President Anatolijs Gorbunovs.

Other Sights

There's an Orthodox church in the park on the east side of the Māra statue and a couple of other churches around the centre. About 100 metres north of the statue, at Atbrīvošanas aleja 102, is the **Latgale Culture & History Museum** (Latgales Kulturvēstures Muzejs), open daily (except Monday) from 10 am to 4 or 5 pm. Three hundred metres south of the statue, then 250 metres east along Pils iela, there's an old **castle mound**.

Places to Stay

The new *Hotel Latgale* at Atbrīvošanas aleja 98, beside the central square, stood seemingly completed, but not yet quite open when I visited Rēzekne. It looks sure to be the best

---

Old Baltic Religions

Quite a lot is known about the pre-Christian religions of the Latvians and Lithuanians, who had many similarities to each other as both were members of the Balt group of peoples. Less seems to be known about the religion of the old Estonians, who came from the entirely different Finno-Ugric religious tradition.

Paralleling the importance of Latvian and especially Lithuanian among Indo-European languages, the old Latvian/Lithuanian religion apparently has many correspondences with Vedic ideas from India and ancient Iranian ideas. There are also similarities between the metrical structure of the Baltic folk rhymes known as *dainas* and the verses of the old Indian sacred text the *Rig Veda*.

To the old Latvians and Lithuanians the sky was a mountain and many of the leading gods lived on it, among them: Dievs the sky god, Saule the sun god (a female), Pērkons (Lithuanian: Perkūnas) the thunder god (who seems to have been particularly revered) and Mēness the moon god. There was also an earth mother figure called Zemes māte in Latvia and Žemyna in Lithuania. In Latvia the Christian Virgin Mary seems to have taken on many of the attributes of Zemes māte, and the two figures seem to be combined in the mythological figure of Māra. Also important were Laima the goddess of fate, the forest goddess (Meža māte in Latvia, Medeinė in Lithuania), and the guardian of wizards and sages (Latvian: Velns; Lithuanian: Velnias) who was transformed into the devil in the Christian scheme of things. Many lesser deities presided over natural phenomena and objects, or human activities.

This system of belief apparently still has a number of followers in Latvia, under the name Dievturība. ∎

LATVIA

Rēzekne

0   100   200 m

1 Latgale Culture
   & History Museum
2 Kafejnīca Rāzna
3 Town Hall
4 Māra Statue
5 Orthodox Church
6 Church
7 Hotel Latgale
8 Bank of Latvia
9 Post, Telephone
   & Telegraph Office
10 MF Salons
11 Castle Mound
12 Viesnīca Latgale
13 Bus Station
14 Market

To Rēzekne II Station,
Kārsava, Madona & Rīga

Brieža iela

Seiles iela

Baznīcas iela

Brālu

aleja

Skrindu

iela

Pils iela

Atbrīvošanas

Brīvības iela

To Rēzekne I
Station

Brīvības iela

To Ludza, Lake
Rāzna & Ezernieki

Latgales

iela

To Daugavpils

hotel in Latgale, with prices perhaps in the region of 20 lati or 26 lati a double – but I'm only guesstimating. I stayed in its shabby predecessor – the *Viesnīca Latgale* (☎ 22 180), at Brīvības iela 2, on the corner of Atbrīvošanas aleja, 200 metres west of the bus station. Though treated with much honour when the desk staff of one realised that a genuine 'Englishman' was seeking refuge in her hotel one snowy November Saturday night, I was unable to avoid a foreigner's price – 6.50 lati for a reasonable double with private bath. That will probably seem pretty reasonable if the viesnīca stays

in operation once the new hotel has opened its doors. Alternatively, try asking around for a private room.

Places to Eat

The *Hotel Latgale* is sure to have a decent restaurant. The restaurant in the old *Viesnīca Latgale* could do a reasonable meal of salad, soup, beefsteak and veg, dessert, mineral water and coffee for about 0.65 lati but may be closed by the time you get there. An alternative is the *Kafejnīca Rāzna*, open from noon to midnight, on the north side of the central square on Atbrīvošanas aleja.

Getting There & Away

For trips to/from Rīga or Daugavpils, trains are much more frequent than buses.

Bus The bus station is at Latgales iela 17, 200 metres east of Atbrīvošanas aleja in the south of the town. There are five or six buses daily to/from each of Daugavpils (two hours, 0.55 lati), Ludza and Kaunata near Lake Rāzna; there are also services at least daily to/from Rīga (4½ hours, 1.85 lati), Madona, Cēsis, Alūksne and Dagda, and most days to/from Valmiera.

Train Rēzekne I station, at the end of Brīvības iela in the south-west of town, is on the Vilnius-Daugavpils-Pskov-St Petersburg line with seven or eight trains in each direction daily (Vilnius five to six hours, Daugavpils two to 2½ hours, St Petersburg nine to 11 hours). Some of them go on to, or come from, Kaunas, Kaliningrad, Warsaw, Berlin, Lvov or Sofia. The fare to Daugavpils is about 0.30 lati in general seating.

Rēzekne II station, just east off Atbrīvošanas aleja about 1¾ km north of the town centre, is on the Rīga-Moscow line, with five to seven trains daily to/from Rīga (2¾ to four hours, 0.60 lati in general seating), three or four of them terminating at Moscow (13 hours) and most of the others at Zilupe, 60 km east of Rēzekne.

See the Getting There & Away chapter for more on trains travelling beyond the Baltic states.

Getting Around

Buses run pretty frequently up and down Atbrīvošanas aleja.

LATGALE UPLAND

The Latgale Upland (Latgales Augstiene) stretching south and south-east from Rēzekne is Latvia's lake district, a plateau-like area with literally thousands of lakes, large and small. They're mostly clean and shallow, though **Lake Drīdzis** (Dridzu ezers) is Latvia's deepest at 65 metres. **Lake Rāzna** (Rāznas ezers) covering 55 sq km has been Latvia's biggest lake since Lake Lubāns

(Lubānas ezers), further north-west, was partly drained by the Soviet authorities. Some of Latgale's prettiest scenery is around Lake Rāzna and between there and **Ezernieki** on the east side of the lake Ežezers. The highest point in the upland is 289-metre **Lielais Liepukalns**, three km east of the Lake Rāzna-Ezernieki road. From the Catholic church at **Pasiene**, eight km south of Zilupe and four km from the Russian border, there's a fine view across to the plains of Russia stretching endlessly eastward.

In **Ludza** on the northern fringe of the region, 25 km east of Rēzekne, there's a regional museum at Kuļņeva iela 2; and at **Krāslava** on the southern fringe, 45 km east of Daugavpils, there's a castle and an 18th century Catholic church.

Aglona

The twin-towered white church at Aglona, in the western part of the lake district, 35 km north of Krāslava and 45 km north-east of Daugavpils, is the leading Roman Catholic shrine in Latvia. It was built in 1699. Thousands gather here – some pilgrims coming long distances on foot – for Ascension Day in mid-August and a candlelight procession the night before. Trees around the church were uprooted to create a huge open space for a visit by Pope John Paul II in 1993.

Activities

The Latvian University Tourist Club (LUTK) or the Tourist Club of Latvia (LTK), both in Rīga (see Activities in Facts for the Visitor at the front of the book for contact details), could help you organise a canoe or bicycle trip through Latgale. There's a good group of interconnected lakes beginning with Lake Dridzis in the southern part of the upland.

Places to Stay

There are *Tourist Bases* (Tūristu Bāze) at Sauleskalns (Sun Hill), 15 km north of Krāslava near Lake Dridzis, and at Ezernieki. Tourist bases are essentially basic hotels, usually with canteens and shared bathrooms, built in the Soviet era to accommodate Soviet groups. If they have a room they're unlikely to turn you away. There should also be opportunities for wild camping. Otherwise there are the hotels at Rēzekne and Daugavpils, plus the basic *Viesnīca Krāslava* (☎ 256-21 449) at Raiņa iela 35 in Krāslava and another *Viesnīca* (☎ 257-22 490) at Stacijas iela 42 in Ludza. Patricia Ltd of Rīga (see Rīga Places to Stay) may be able to book you private-home accommodation.

Getting There & Away

A car or bicycle, or even a canoe (see Activities) is the ideal way to get around the Latgale Upland, as public transport is limited.

Bus The country was in the grip of a petrol shortage when I visited Latgale, so it's hard to gauge the true frequency of bus services in easier times, but you can expect the following minimal service, possibly with extra buses in summer:

From Rēzekne
  six buses daily to Ludza; six to Lake Rāzna and Kaunata; one to Malta and Dagda
From Daugavpils
  four buses daily to Krāslava and Dagda (one coming from Rīga and going on to Ezernieki Tourist Base); two to Aglona; buses to Dagda via Aglona, and Ludza via Dagda were cancelled when I visited but may restart
From Krāslava
  four buses daily to Dagda; reportedly, buses to Sauleskalns Tourist Base

Train Five or six trains daily in each direction run along both the northern fringe of the district, on the Rēzekne-Ludza-Zilupe line, and along the southern fringe, on the Daugavpils-Krāslava-Indra-Robežnieki line. Aglona station, on the Rēzekne-Daugavpils line, is 10 km north-west of Aglona village.

DAUGAVPILS

Daugavpils, Latvia's second-biggest city, dates from 1275 and has a chequered past in which it has, at various times, been called

Dünaberg by Germans, Borisoglebsk by Russians and Dvinsk by Poles. Today it's predominantly a drab, post-WW II Soviet creation – strangely interesting to visit for the view it gives you of another side of Baltic reality. It's also a gateway to the Latgale Upland. Situated on the north bank of the Daugava, 225 km upstream from Rīga, Daugavpils had 40,000 inhabitants before WW II, about two-thirds of them Latvians and one-third Russians or Poles. Now it has 130,000 people but only 10% to 15% of them are Latvians. The change has come because of industries sited here during the Soviet period, which attracted workers mainly from Russia. Because many of the industries were large, specialist, all-union plants performing a single service for the whole USSR – for example 4000 people devoted to making bicycle and tractor chains and 3500 to repairing one particular type of railway locomotive – Daugavpils has suffered badly from the break-up of the USSR and is even more economically depressed than other Latvian towns.

Orientation & Information

The rail station is at the east end of mostly pedestrianised Leņina iela (though this name looks like it might be on the way out, even in Russified Daugavpils) which leads to the central area, focused on the Gostinitsa Latvija hotel, 800 metres west. The bus station is on the corner of Viestura iela (which crosses Leņina iela halfway between the station and the hotel) and Lāčplēša iela, two blocks south of Leņina iela. The Daugava River skirts the south of the city centre; the main road bridge over it is at the west end of Karla Marksa iela, one block south of Lāčplēša iela.

There are left-luggage rooms in the railway and bus stations. The one in the railway station is downstairs.

Daugavpils' telephone code is 254.

City Centre

The downtown area is a typical Soviet city centre of straight streets, a couple of large squares, the odd park and a mixture of pre-

LATVIA

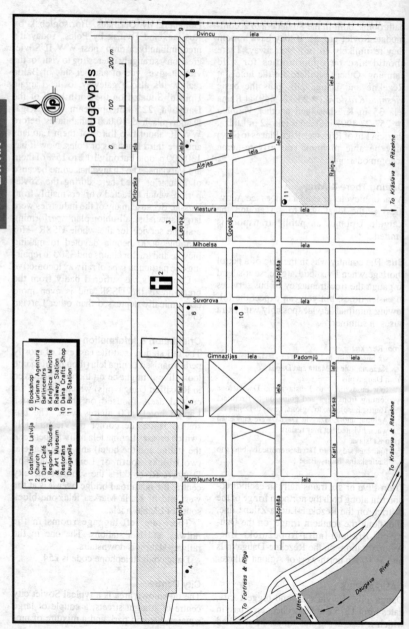

Daugavpils

0   100   200 m

Dvincu   iela

Rīga iela
Raiņa iela

To Krāslava & Rēzekne

Alejas   iela

Orlovska iela

Viestura   iela

Lencija iela
Gogoļa iela
Lāčplēša iela

Mihoelsa   iela

Suvorova   iela

Gimnāzijas   iela   Padomju   iela

Marksa iela

Karļa iela

Komjaunatnes   iela

Leņina iela
Lāčplēša iela

To Krāslava & Rēzekne

To Fortress & Rīga

To Utena

Daugava River

1 Gostiņīnīca Latvija
2 Church
3 Dart Café
4 Regional Studies
   & Art Museum
5 Restorans
   Daugavpils
6 Bookshop
7 Tūrisma Agentūra
   Baltincentrs
8 Kafejnīca Minotīte
9 Railway Station
10 Daina Crafts Shop
11 Bus Station

WW II and Soviet-era buildings – not unpleasant but not exactly exciting. The Gostinitsa Latvija hotel is the dominant landmark. There's a Russian church next to it across Suvorova iela, and a bookshop and the Daina crafts shop a block or two down Suvorova iela. The **Regional Studies & Art Museum** (Novadpētniecības un Mākslas Muzejs), open 11 am to 6 pm Tuesday to Saturday, is 3½ blocks west of the hotel on Leņina iela.

River & Fortress

The most remarkable feature I found in Daugavpils is a huge fortress (*cietoksnis*) built by Russia in the first half of the 19th century, on the north-west side of town, just past the railway bridge. You can walk to it along a fairly quiet riverside road – two km from the west end of Karla Marksa iela. Though the fortress was still occupied by the Russian army when I visited in 1992, I was able to go as far as the gate of the inner compound and to observe the fortress's enormous ramparts and earthworks. A monument by the entrance road tells us in Russian that the Tatar poet Musa Jalil languished here from September to October 1942, in what was then the Nazi concentration camp Stalag 340.

Places to Stay

The *Gostinitsa Latvija* (Russian for 'Hotel Latvia'), a big concrete-and-glass block in the centre of town on Leņina iela, has reasonable rooms with private bathroom for 3.20 lati a single, 4 lati a double. *Turisma Agentura Baltincentrs* at Leņina iela 65, 1½ blocks from the railway station, might be able to help with accommodation in private flats. See Private Homes under Accommodation in the Facts for the Visitor chapter at the front of the book for other agencies which may be able to organise rooms in Daugavpils.

Places to Eat

The *Gostinitsa Latvija* has an adequate res-

taurant and a reasonable *bufet* on one of the upper floors. The other main restaurant in town, also large and Soviet-style, is the *Restorāns Daugavpils* on Leņina iela, half a block west of the hotel. There are a couple of cafés on Leņina iela, too, and a reasonable, cheap canteen (*ednīca*) in the railway station.

Getting There & Away

Bus There's a useful information office in the bus station, open from 7 am to 7 pm. Two or three buses daily run to/from Rīga, taking four hours for 1.65 lati. There are daily Minsk and Warsaw services (see the Getting There & Away chapter) but only one bus a day to/from Vilnius – and it tends to get cancelled during petrol shortages. The other main bus services, all several times daily, are to/from Krāslava, Dagda, Jēkabpils and Rēzekne. Buses also run at least twice daily to/from Aglona and a few days a week to/from Cēsis and Valmiera.

Train Daugavpils is reached by Rīga-Indra, Rīga-Robežnieki and Rīga-Voronezh as well as Rīga-Daugavpils trains. In total there are five trains daily each way between Rīga and Daugavpils, taking 3¼ to four hours for 0.65 lati in general seating. Daugavpils is also on the Vilnius-Pskov-St Petersburg line with several trains daily in each direction (Vilnius three to 3½ hours, St Petersburg 11 to 13 hours). About nine trains daily run to/from Rēzekne on this line, taking two hours, and there are services once or twice a day to/from Kaunas (five hours), Šiauliai (four or five hours), Klaipēda (nine hours) and Kaliningrad (nine to 12½ hours). Other trains run to/from Moscow (16 hours), Warsaw (13 hours), Berlin (23 hours), Minsk (seven hours), Lvov (18 hours) and Sofia (46 hours) daily. See the Getting There & Away chapter for more on services beyond the Baltic states.

Getting Around

Tram No 1 runs from Dvincu iela a block north of the railway station to the central square in front of the Gostinitsa Latvija.

LATVIA

Zemgale

Zemgale is the region of central Latvia west of the Daugava River, between Rīga and the Lithuanian border. Low-lying (below sea level in parts) and watered by dozens of rivers, most of them flowing into the Lielupe, which enters the sea between Rīga and Jūrmala, it is Latvia's most fertile region. Zemgale is named after the Baltic Zemgal (Semigallian) tribes who lived here before the 13th century German conquest. The Semigallians, in fact, held out longer against the Germans than any other people living in the area which is now Latvia and Estonia, not being finally subdued till 1290. From the 16th to 18th centuries Zemgale formed part of the semi-independent Duchy of Courland, along with the Kurzeme region.

Most places in Zemgale can be reached on day trips, if quite lengthy ones, from Rīga. You pass through the region, in any case, if you're travelling between Rīga and Lithuania. The main road to Vilnius and Kaunas passes through Bauska; the railway, through Jelgava.

IECAVA

Iecava is a small, nondescript town 45 km south of Rīga on the road to Bauska and Vilnius. But about six km north of Iecava, on the east side of the road, is the *Brentis* motel, reportedly the best place to stay between Rīga and not far short of Vilnius. It's a modern place aimed at foreigners and wealthier locals, with a restaurant open from 8 am to 11 pm. There's no 'Brentis' sign, but by the road there is one of those bed symbols meaning 'hotel'.

BAUSKA

Bauska is a country town, with some textile industry, 65 km south of Rīga on the main Rīga-Vilnius road. It's a staging post on the way to Rundāle but worth a stop in its own right primarily to see its large castle.

Orientation

The town centre is on the south side of the main road bridge over the Mēmele River. The bus station is a km from the bridge on the road out towards Vilnius – half a km straight up the hill (Kalnu iela), then round to the left along Zalā iela.

Information

The post, telephone and telegraph office is next to the bus station, at Slimnīcas iela 9. The market is at Rūpniecības iela 11, along the third street to the right as you go up Kalna iela from the bridge. The pharmacy at Ratslaukums 1 sells some Western medicines.

Bauska's telephone code is 239.

Things to See

The **Bauska Castle** (Bauskas Pilsdrupas) is a km from the town centre on a hillock between the Mēmele and Mūsa rivers, on the western edge of town. From the bus station,

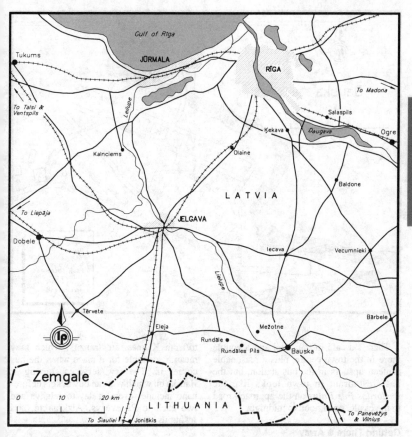

Gulf of Riga

Tukums

JŪRMALA

RĪGA

To Madona

To Talsi &
Ventspils

Salaspils

Lielupe

Ķekava

Daugava

Ogre

Kalnciems

Olaine

L A T V I A

Baldone

To Liepāja

JELGAVA

Dobele

Iecava

Vecumnieki

Lielupe

Tērvete

Bārbele

Eleja

Mežotne

Rundāle

Rundāles Pils

Bauska

Zemgale

0   10   20 km

L I T H U A N I A

To Šiauliai   Joniškis

To Panevėžys
& Vilnius

walk towards the centre along Zalā iela then
branch left along Uzvaras iela beside the
park at the top of Kalna iela. You can also
approach the castle along any street westward off Kalna iela. The castle was built
between 1443 and 1456 for the Livonian
knights and occasioned the first mention of
Bauska in historical documents, though the
place had been a Zemgal settlement previously. It's an imposing edifice, currently
being rebuilt for the first time since 1706,
when it was blown up during the Great
Northern War.

Around the town centre are a number of
low-rise 18th and 19th century houses.
There's a **regional museum** at Kalna iela 6,
open from Wednesday to Sunday 9 am to 5
pm.

Places to Stay & Eat

The *Viesnīca Bauska* (☎ 24 705), across the
way from the bus station at Slimnīcas iela 7,
is a typical Soviet-style place with 57 rooms.
Foreigners' prices haven't yet arrived here –
bare but serviceable singles/doubles with
private bathroom were 0.90/1.15 lati. But if
you want comfort in this part of Latvia, head
for the Brentis near Iecava.

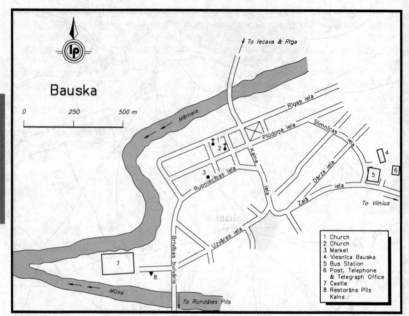

Bauska

0   250   500 m

To Iecava & Rīga

Mēmele

Rīgas iela

Plūdoņa iela

Kalna iela

Slimnīcas iela

Dārza iela

To Vilnius

Rūpniecības iela

Zaļā iela

Uzvaras iela

Brīvības bulvāris

Mūsa

To Rundāles Pils

1 Church
2 Church
3 Market
4 Viesnīca Bauska
5 Bus Station
6 Post, Telephone
   & Telegraph Office
7 Castle
8 Restorāns Pils
   Kalns

There's a café in the hotel and a couple more in the town centre, plus a reasonable canteen upstairs in the bus station, but the best restaurant in town looks like the *Restorāns Pils Kalns* on the approach road to the castle, open noon to midnight.

Getting There & Away

There's no railway to Bauska so you have to rely on buses. Normal Rīga-Bauska buses go 12 times daily starting at 6 am and take a tedious 1½ to 1¾ hours for a fare of 0.40 lati. Quicker are the few expresses which run from Monday to Saturday and the 10 or so daily long-distance buses passing through Bauska en route from Rīga to Panevėžys, Vilnius, Kaunas, Minsk and so on (these are listed as 'tranzīts' at Bauska). If you're going on from Bauska to Rundāle you should make an early start from Rīga.

Apart from the Rīga service, most buses at Bauska, including all those travelling to/from Vilnius and the single daily bus to/from Kaunas, are tranzīts, which may mean a scramble for a place when the bus comes in. The few services starting at Bauska on which you can buy tickets beforehand include several a day to Jelgava and two each to Panevėžys, Aizkraukle, and Jēkabpils.

RUNDĀLE

The 18th century Rundāle Palace (Rundāles Pils), 12 km west of Bauska, is the architectural highlight of provincial Latvia and a popular day trip from Rīga. It was designed for Baron Ernst Johann von Bühren (1690-1772), Duke of Courland, by Bartolomeo Rastrelli, the Baroque genius from Italy who created many of St Petersburg's finest buildings including the Winter Palace, and built in two phases – one in the 1730s, one in the 1760s.

Modern restoration work begun in the 1970s, when the palace had fallen into some disrepair, is now nearly completed. The existing period furnishings were bought or donated.

Of the palace's 138 rooms, the main reception rooms, upstairs in the east wing, are the most splendid, with marble and gilt wall decorations that conjure up the same opulence as the great tsarist palaces in Russia. These date from the second phase of work. The Gold Room (Zelta zāle) was the throne room: its ceiling paintings display the baron's virtues as a ruler. The White Room (Baltā zāle) was the ballroom. The main staircase in this wing, with multiple mirrors in its walls, is perhaps the outstanding original Rastrelli creation here, reminiscent of his wonderful Jordan Staircase in the Winter Palace. Decorative work by the Italians Francesco Martini and Carlo Zucchi and the German J M Graf, brought in during the second phase, is also found in the duke's apartments in the central part of the palace.

On the ground floor of the east wing you can visit the palace kitchens, while the west wing was the duchess's apartments. The ground floor of the palace also houses a museum of 15th to 20th century applied art from Latvia, Russia and Western Europe.

The palace and park are open from Wednesday to Sunday. Hours are 11 am to 6 pm from May to September, 11 am to 5 pm during other months.

Getting There & Away

Rundāle Palace is a km or so south off the Bauska-Eleja road. Unless you're on a tour or have your own transport, the best way to reach it is to get first to Bauska and take a bus from there. From Bauska you need a bus

---

From Russia with love

How the Italian master Bartolomeo Rastrelli came to build this splendid palace in such a remote corner of Europe, which wasn't even part of the Russian empire at the time, is a curious little tale. It begins with the marriage in 1710 of Anna Ioannovna, a niece of Russia's Peter the Great, to Frederick, Duke of Courland – no doubt an affair of state as Russia clawed its way into Poland's sphere of influence. In 1730, following Peter the Great's death, Anna of Courland found herself crowned empress of Russia, and she appointed the Baltic German baron Ernst Johann von Bühren (Latvian: Bīron) to handle her affairs of state.

Von Bühren had been something of a failed adventurer in Courland and Russia before becoming Anna's chief adviser (and lover) a few years before she succeeded to the Russian throne. With more interest in the trappings than the exercise of power, Anna handed over much of the management of the empire to von Bühren and a small clique of German advisers. Von Bühren's apparently heavy-handed and corrupt style soon made him unpopular with the Russian nobility, but as long as Anna ruled Russia, the baron's star waxed. When he decided he needed a new home to go with his new status, Anna dispatched Rastrelli to Courland, and in 1736 work began on the summer palace for von Bühren, at Rundāle. It proceeded quickly with as many as 1000 people working on it at one time.

In 1737 the Duke of Courland died heirless and, thanks to Russian influence, von Bühren was handed the dukedom. He then began work on an even grander Rastrelli-designed palace at Jelgava, intended as his main residence. Rundāle was put on the back burner – and came to a halt altogether in 1740 when Empress Anna died and von Bühren's enemies took their revenge, forcing him into exile for the duration of Empress Elizabeth's reign in Russia. Only in 1763 – with a German, Catherine the Great, now on the Russian throne – was von Bühren allowed to return and finish Rundāle, also restoring the parts that had decayed in his absence.

This time Rastrelli brought the Italians Francesco Martini and Carlo Zucchi, who had worked on the St Petersburg Winter Palace, to do the ceiling paintings. J M Graf, who had worked on Prussian royal palaces in Berlin, came to do the elaborate wall decorations. In contrast to Rastrelli's initial Baroque work, this second phase at Rundāle, completed in 1768, was in the newer Rococo style. Von Bühren was then able to enjoy the palace until 1795 when, in the third Partition of Poland, Courland became Russian territory, and Catherine gave Rundāle to one of her favourites, Subov. Von Bühren managed to shift most of the fixtures and fittings to some of his other estates in Germany. ∎

that's going to Rundāles Pils, not just Rundāle which is about 2½ km further west. There's a gap in bus services from Bauska to Rundāles Pils (and Rundāle for that matter) between 9 am and 12.30 pm, so if you want to reach Rundāle Palace in the morning, you should ideally aim to reach Bauska by 8 am and certainly by 8.30 am. Otherwise try to get there by noon to allow yourself at least a reasonable part of the afternoon at the palace.

There are also several buses a day between Rundāles Pils and Jelgava, 33 km north-west, so it's possible to approach it from there, too – or to go on to Jelgava after visiting the palace.

MEŽOTNE

About the same distance west of Bauska as Rundāle Palace but on the north side of the Lielupe river and approached by a different road from Bauska, **Mežotne Palace** was built in the classical style in 1797-1813. It's less grand than Rundāle, and restoration hasn't yet proceeded as far, but there are pleasant grounds with views of the Lielupe.

JELGAVA

Jelgava, 42 km south-west of Rīga, is the biggest town in Zemgale, with 75,000 people and a number of industries. Numerous rivers converge in the Jelgava area to make the Lielupe deep enough here for a harbour for seagoing vessels, even though its mouth is over 60 km away, between Rīga and Jūrmala. This helps to explain why, from the 16th to 18th centuries, Jelgava (then called Mitau), was the capital of the Duchy of Courland and its little overseas empire (see the introduction to the Kurzeme chapter). Afterwards, it was the capital of the Russian province of Courland and a place of renowned society and hospitality where gentry from all around, including some from the neighbouring province of Livonia (who preferred Jelgava to their own capital Rīga), would gather in winter. Jelgava is also notable for having produced three pre-WW II presidents of Latvia and even one of Lithuania.

Unfortunately, a lot of old Jelgava was wrecked in the two world wars, and it's not

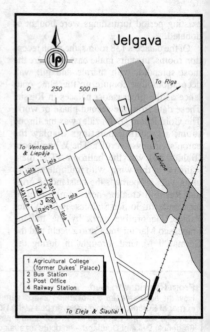

Jelgava

0   250   500 m

To Rīga

To Ventspils & Liepāja

Lielupe

Liela iela

Mātera iela

Pasta iela

Raiņa iela

1 Agricultural College (former Dukes' Palace)
2 Bus Station
3 Post Office
4 Railway Station

To Eleja & Siauliai

such an exciting place any more. Lovers of Rastrelli architecture, however, should stop here.

Orientation & Information

To reach the central square from the bus station, walk out on to Mātera iela, turn right (north), right again along Lielā iela at the first corner, and go 1½ blocks. From the railway station take the right-hand of the two roads leading ahead as you exit the station, and head north for 1½ km.

The main post office is on the corner of Pasta iela and Raiņa iela, a block west and a block south of the main square.

Jelgava's telephone code is 230.

Things to See

The 300-room **Baroque palace** of the dukes of Courland is on the east side of town, beside the main river bridge on the Rīga road. Walk 750 metres east from the central square to reach it. It has the unmistakable

Left: Gūtmanis' Cave, Sigulda, Latvia (CR)
Right: Līgatne Leisure & Study Park, Latvia (JN)
Bottom: Zvārtas Iezis sandstone bluff, Amata River, near Līgatne, Latvia (JN)

Top: Thirteenth century knight's castle, Koknese, Latvia (EV)
Middle: Gauja River, Latvia (MB)
Bottom: Winter scene, near Rīga, Latvia (EV)

touch of Bartolomeo Rastrelli and was, indeed, built to his designs, on the site of an earlier Livonian Order castle, in 1738-40 and 1763-72, for Duke Ernst Johann von Bühren (see the Rundāle section for more on Rastrelli and this duke). The palace, now an agricultural college, is soon to undergo its third restoration of the 20th century (the first two followed severe damage in 1919 and WW II). There's a pleasant park on the town side of the palace and a few more old buildings in the streets south and east of the main square.

Getting There & Away

Bus Up to 17 microbuses daily make the one-hour trip to/from Rīga for a fare of 0.25 to 0.45 lati. Other buses run to/from Rundāles Pils and Bauska about 10 times daily; Liepāja four times daily (four to 4½ hours); Ventspils twice daily (five hours); Talsi twice daily (three hours); Kuldīga once daily, except Sunday; Šiauliai about 10 times daily (two hours); and Kaunas about three times daily.

Train One or two suburban trains an hour run from Rīga to Jelgava and vice versa from about 5.20 am to 11.30 pm. The fare is 0.15 lati. Long-distance trains between Rīga and Liepāja, Ventspils, Šiauliai, Kaunas, Vilnius and Kaliningrad stop at Jelgava, too.

TĒRVETE

Tērvete, 35 km south-west of Jelgava and 15 km from the Lithuanian border, might be worth a detour if you have a car or bike but may not be easy to reach by bus. It was the capital of the 13th century Zemgal leader, Viesturs, and his successor, Namejs, who raided Rīga in 1280.

The ruined 14th century German **castle** at Tērvete stands on the site of the wooden Zemgal fortress. Also here is **Sprīdīši**, the house where the well-known Latvian children's writer Anna Brigadere who was a native of this region, spent her last years from 1922 to 1933. It's now preserved as a museum. Another attraction of Tērvete is a fine forest park, **Meža Ainavu Parks**, with numerous footpaths and lookout points.

Kurzeme

The western region of Latvia, with coasts on both the open Baltic Sea and the Gulf of Rīga, is known as Kurzeme (English: Courland; German: Kurland). Though Liepāja and Ventspils on the Baltic Sea are sizeable ports, Kurzeme as a whole is one of Latvia's least densely settled regions, with the northern part still heavily forested. The landscape is quite pretty, with surprising variety, though it never rises to any great altitude. Krīevu kalns on the Kursa Upland (Kurzemes augstiene), in the south, is Kurzeme's highest point at 184 metres.

In many ways Kurzeme is a region apart from the rest of Latvia, with its off-the-beaten-track location and a distinct history. It's named after the Cours (Latvian: Kursi; German: Kuren), a Balt people who lived here before the 13th century German invasion. They were a quite adventurous lot who would raid Scandinavia from time to time – and even, occasionally, join forces with the Vikings to attack bits of Britain. Their leader, Lamekins, accepted Christian baptism and made a separate peace with the pope in 1230 in order to avoid rule by the German knights – but the knights refused to accept this arrangement and eventually subjugated the Cours in the 1260s.

The Cours themselves ceased to exist as a separate people during the subsequent centuries of foreign rule, but Courland emerged as a player in the game of Colonies played by the later European powers. When the Livonian Order state collapsed under assault by Russia's Ivan the Terrible in the 16th century, the order's last master, Gotthard Kettler, salvaged Courland and neighbouring Zemgale as his own personal fiefdom. Though owing allegiance to Poland, this Duchy of Courland, as it was known, was for most purposes independent. Its capital was Jelgava (then called Mitau) in Zemgale. Duke Jakob, its ruler from 1640 to 1682, developed a sizeable and well-known navy, merchant fleet and shipbuilding industry,

and purchased two far-flung colonies: Tobago in the Caribbean (from Britain) and an island in the mouth of the Gambia River (from local African chiefs). He even laid plans to colonise Australia! His son Duke Frederick tried to make Jelgava into a northern Paris and married into the Russian royal family. The duchy was swallowed up by Russia in 1795 and governed as a province of the tsarist empire. It became part of independent Latvia after WW I.

Along with its coasts, ports, farms and forests, Kurzeme has two longish rivers – the Venta and the Abava – and some interesting old country towns, chief among them Kuldīga. All in all it's well worth the effort of finding your way there.

TUKUMS

The small town of Tukums is just north of the Rīga-Ventspils road, 65 km west of Rīga. It has a 1670 church, an old castle mound and a **Regional Studies & Art Museum**

LATVIA

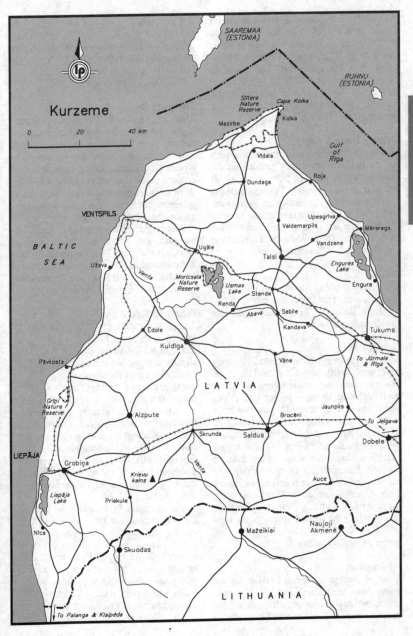

(Novadpētniecības un Mākslas Muzejs) with a good collection of 1920s and '30s Latvian art. There are good views reaching as far as the Gulf of Rīga, from 113-metre Milzukalns, five km north-east. The Kurzeme Tourist Association (☎ 231-25 145, fax 231-22 559), at Pils iela 16A in the town centre, may be able to help with information or arrangements for travel in Kurzeme.

Getting There & Away

You could combine a visit to Tukums with one to Jūrmala, since they're both on the same suburban rail line from Rīga. About one train an hour comes to Tukums. Tukums I station, the first you reach coming from the east, is nearer the town centre than Tukums II where the trains terminate. Some buses from Rīga to Talsi, Ventspils, Liepāja and elsewhere call at Tukums.

TALSI

The peaceful, pretty country town of Talsi, a few km north of the Rīga-Ventspils road, 120 km from Rīga, can be used as a base for exploring northern Kurzeme.

Orientation

Talsi is surprisingly hilly, as a shallow valley runs north-south down the middle of it. There are two lakes in the valley, one on the south edge of town, a bigger one (Vilku ezers) towards the north. The town centre is at the top of the valley's western slope, with the central square at the meeting of Krišjāna Valdemara iela and Lielā iela. From here Lielā iela slopes down the valley, past the southern lake, then up the eastern slope. To reach the central square from the bus station, walk a block south down Dundagas iela to the first traffic lights, go left along Puskaiša iela then take the second turning to the right which is Krišjāna Valdemara iela – altogether about 700 metres.

Information

You can change money at Latvijas Banka, going down the hill on Lielā iela. The post, telephone and telegraph office is on the central square at Lielā iela 4. The market is at Ezera iela 7, north off Lielā iela in the bottom part of town. There's a rather exaggeratedly named 'universalveikals' (department store) at Brīvības iela 17A, just up the hill southward from the central square.

The Talsi telephone code is 232.

Things to See

There's not a great deal to do except wander round and enjoy the quiet atmosphere and scenery. The lakes are good focal points. Talsi has quite a lot of one or two-storey wooden buildings dating from the 19th century or maybe earlier. Along Lielā iela there are a couple of souvenir shops and art galleries, a sculpture garden as you start to go up the east side of the valley, and an old-looking church at the top of the hill on the same side of town. A block past the church is the small **Talsi Regional Studies & Art Museum** (Talsu Novadpētniecības un Mākslas Muzejs) at Rožu iela 7, open daily, except Monday, from noon to 6 pm.

Places to Stay & Eat

The *Viesnīca Talsi* (☎ 22 689) at Kareivju iela 16 is the only hotel. It's a Soviet-era block of 95 rooms on four or five floors, slightly decrepit but reasonably clean. For a room with a cold shower you'll pay 6.50 lati a single, 10 lati a double. There's a café-bar but no restaurant. It's near the town centre but a little hard to find; from the corner of Puskaiša iela and Krišjāna Valdemara iela (see Orientation) go a short distance north along Krišjāna Valdemara iela and take the first road to the right, which is Kareivju iela. The hotel is at the end on the left; it had no name sign when I stayed, but the number, 16, was visible.

The best place for a meal is the *Restorāns Kurzeme*, upstairs at Brīvības iela 17A, just up the hill, southward, from the central square. Despite the forbidding exterior, service is friendly – and I got cucumber and tomato salad, a plate of cheese, karbonāde with potatoes and other vegetables, a dessert, coffee and mineral water for under 0.65 lati. The restaurant is open from noon to midnight. There's also a canteen (*ēdnica*)

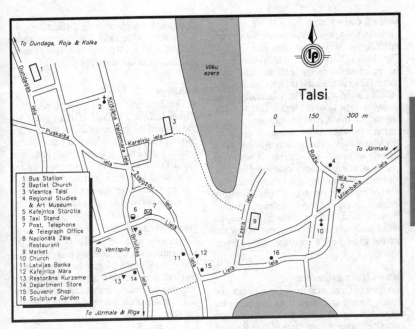

1 Bus Station
2 Baptist Church
3 Viesnīca Talsi
4 Regional Studies
   & Art Museum
5 Kafejnīca Stūrītis
6 Taxi Stand
7 Post, Telephone
   & Telegraph Office
8 Nacionālā Zāle
   Restaurant
9 Market
10 Church
11 Latvijas Banka
12 Kafejnīca Māra
13 Restorāns Kurzeme
14 Department Store
15 Souvenir Shop
16 Sculpture Garden

downstairs in the same building, open from 8 am to 7 pm. Another possibility, for light eats only, is the *Kafejnīca Māra* at Lielā iela 16. And don't forget the market on Ezera iela as a source of fresh food.

Getting There & Away

The pre-WW II maps in the *Latvijas Ceļu Karte* atlas show a railway through Talsi, but the track has been torn up. You can make out its old course behind the bus station, parallel to Dundagas iela. So the only long-distance public transport is bus. The bus station is at Dundagas iela 15, on the road leading north out of Talsi towards Dundaga and Valdemarpils.

To/from Rīga there are two direct microbuses and around 10 buses, via Tukums or Jūrmala, daily. The microbuses run only between Rīga and Talsi and take two hours. Most of the buses are in transit to/from Ventspils and make stops en route. They take 2¼ to 3¼ hours. The fare is 0.10 lati (a bit more in a microbus). Other bus services to/from Talsi include:

Jelgava
    two buses daily (transit), three hours
Kuldīga
    two buses daily (one in transit to/from Liepāja),
    two or 2½ hours
Liepāja
    one bus daily, 4½ hours
Roja
    six to eight buses daily, 45 minutes
Sabile
    one bus daily (transit), 45 minutes
Saldus
    three buses daily, 2½ hours
Ventspils
    nine buses daily (mostly transit), 1½ to two hours

NORTHERN KURZEME

You could visit the remote northern tip of Kurzeme in a day trip from Talsi, the nearest accommodation base, or on the way to/from Rīga and Talsi or even on the way to/from Ventspils.

Kolka & Cape Kolka

Kolka is Kurzeme's most northerly village, standing on the Gulf of Rīga just south of Cape Kolka (Kolkasrags), which is the dividing point between the gulf and the open Baltic. The village itself is pretty nondescript but it's a good starting place for walks along sandy beaches, over dunes and through forests. In the Soviet era the area was a military reserve, out of bounds to civilians. The 'cape' itself – the Latvian *rags* translates literally as 'horn' – is just the point where the line of beach and dunes changes direction. It's marked by nothing more than a couple of piles of concrete and stone blocks – possibly remnants of Soviet coastal defences. A short distance west, there's what looks like an abandoned military lookout post. A few km off the cape there's an island with a lighthouse.

Slītere Nature Reserve

For about 26 km west from Cape Kolka, the dunes, forests and other flora and fauna for up to five or 10 km behind the coast are protected in the Slītere State Nature Reserve (Slīteres Valsts Rezervāts). Wildlife includes deer, elk, buzzards and beaver. You're supposed to have a permit to enter the reserve, though the coastal road running up the Gulf of Rīga then west down to Ventspils goes right through it. Some coastal villages, including Kolka, are excluded from the reserve; others are included in it. Part of the southern boundary of the reserve runs close to the line of the 15-km-long, 35-metre-high Slītere Cliff. The Mazirbe-Dundaga and Kolka-Vīdale-Dundaga roads both ascend (or descend, depending which way you're going) the cliff line, with a lookout tower on the former.

Some of the villages along the reserve's north-facing coast contain the last remaining groups of Livs – the Finno-Ugric people who inhabited the coastal regions on the east and west sides of the Gulf of Rīga at the time of the 13th century German invasion. The Livs are now almost completely assimilated into the surrounding Latvian culture and language and seem certain to go the way of the Cours and disappear as a distinct people. According to the 1989 Soviet census there are just 135 Livs left, and very few of them still speak the Liv language.

Dundaga

At Dundaga, a village set among three lakes, 20 km in from the Gulf of Rīga coast via Vīdale, and 40 km north of Talsi, there's a 13th century castle with a legend almost identical to the one associated with Haapsalu Castle in Estonia – a maiden who was walled up alive and appears on full-moon nights. The poor lass's sin was apparently to have intruded upon a gnomes' wedding.

Places to Stay & Eat

The nearest hotel or similar is at Talsi. At Kolka there's a canteen, open on weekday lunch times, down the lane heading towards the coast from the bus stop. You can get some provisions – bread, cheese, tomatoes and the like – at the shop across the road from the bus stop.

Getting There & Away

Private transport is easily the most convenient, but there are buses too – if you can work out a way of using their schedules. The Tourist Club of Latvia (LTK) and the Celotajs travel agency offer reasonably priced day or two-day trips from Rīga to northern Kurzeme (see the Tours and Information sections of the Rīga chapter for contact details). If travelling by bus, always try to check return schedules before you set out. There's one morning and one lunch time bus from Rīga to Kolka (1.15 lati, 3½ hours) straight up the coast road through Engure, Mērsrags and Roja. It's quite a pretty trip through forest much of the way, with occasional coastal villages and the sea never far away. The two daily buses from Rīga to Kolka via Talsi and/or Vandzene take about 4½ hours and don't go till the afternoon. Only the first bus of the day gives you ample time at Kolka.

Bus services between Talsi, Dundaga and Kolka are also potentially useful. The schedules were like this: at 5.55 am on Monday,

Friday and Sunday a bus leaves Talsi for a four-hour round trip to Dundaga (45 minutes from Talsi), Kolka (1¾ hours), Mazirbe, Slītere and back through Dundaga to Talsi. At 4.25 pm Monday, Friday and Saturday a bus does the same trip in reverse. (These two buses are listed respectively as 'Kolka-Mazirbe' and 'Mazirbe-Kolka' at Talsi bus station.) At 7.50 am on Thursday and 12.35 pm on Monday, Wednesday and Friday a bus leaves Talsi for Dundaga; it takes about 50 minutes one way and comes back almost straight away. At 12.35 pm Thursday, Saturday and Sunday a bus leaves Talsi for Kolka; going back, it leaves Kolka for Talsi about 3 pm.

If you can't get a bus all the way through from where you are to where you want to go, you'll often be able to get there with a change at Roja, 45 minutes from Kolka (0.45 lati) and an hour from Talsi (0.50 lati).

There are at least five buses a day from Roja to Rīga (the last at 6 pm), six to eight a day to Talsi (up to 8 pm), and even one to Ventspils (at 2.15 pm, taking 3¼ hours). There's also a daily morning bus from Ventspils to Kolka, returning in the afternoon (currently at 2.25 pm from Kolka). It's scheduled to take a discouraging 4¼ hours each way. A bus leaves Kolka at 2 pm for Roja, Tukums and Jelgava.

THE ABAVA VALLEY

The Abava River from around Kandava to its confluence with the Venta is a canoe route, and both the LUTK and the LTK (see Activities in the Facts for the Visitor chapter at the front of the book for contact details) can arrange trips here. It's also quite possible for landbound travellers to visit the area.

Kandava has both the ruins of a Livonian Order castle and a mound once fortified by the ancient Cours, plus a 14th century stone bridge over the river and a 1736 church.

At **Sabile**, 14 km downstream (a few more if you're following the twists and turns of the river), is another ancient fortification mound and a 17th century church, plus good views from Vīna kalns (Wine Hill).

The **Abavas Rumba** is a small, pleasant waterfall four km downstream from Sabile, close to the Sabile-Renda road, while the **Rendas Rumba** just off the Abava at Renda, 20 km below Sabile, on a tributary called the Ivanda, is claimed to be Latvia's highest natural waterfall (which won't make it all that high!).

Kandava is only five km south of the main Rīga-Ventspils road, though its station on the Rīga-Ventspils railway is seven km north of the town. There's summer accommodation at the *Tūristu Bāze Kandava*. Buses run from Rīga, Talsi and Kuldīga, among other places, to Kandava and Sabile.

VENTSPILS

Ventspils (former German name: Windau), 200 km west of Rīga, is an industrial town of 50,000 people and Latvia's busiest port. If all you have heard of Ventspils is its alarming pollution record – 2% of children die in their first year, and gas masks have reportedly been issued to the survivors – the place comes as a pleasant surprise.

The interesting port and old-town area along the Venta River is under restoration, and there's a park-backed beach area south of the river mouth.

History

There was a Courish settlement before the Livonian Order founded a castle here in 1244. Ventspils was in the Hanseatic League from the 14th to 16th centuries, and in the 17th century Duke Jakob of Courland based his navy here. After a spell in the doldrums the town revived with the arrival of a railway from Rīga in the early 20th century.

In the Soviet era its ice-free harbour brought it considerable – if unwelcome – importance and attracted a gas pipeline, oil and gas refineries, an oil and chemical terminal, and ammonia and fertiliser plants. These in turn attracted a new workforce mainly from non-Latvian parts of the USSR.

Orientation

The Venta River flows up the east side of the town then turns west for its final 2½ km to the sea. The central area of Ventspils is south

LATVIA

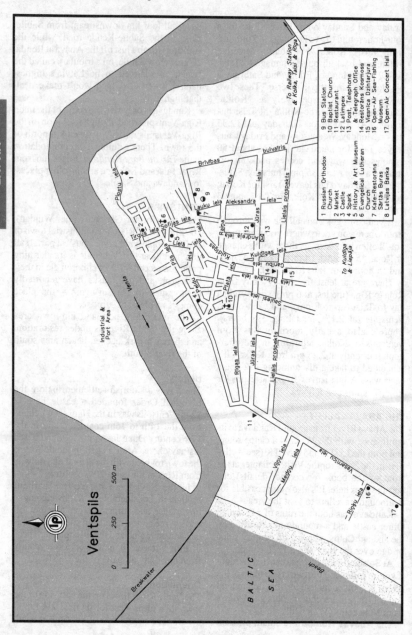

Ventspils

0   250   500 m

BALTIC SEA

Beach

Breakwater

Industrial & Port Area

Venta

To Railway Station & Kolka, Talsi & Rīga

To Kuldīga & Liepāja

Brīvības bulvāris

Lauku iela

Aleksandra iela

Raiņa iela

Lielais prospekts

Kuldīgas iela

Ganību iela

Dzintara iela

Saules iela

Plata iela

Pasta iela

Lielā iela

Sofijas iela

Tirgus iela

Pils iela

Pasta iela

Jūras iela

Andreja iela

Rīgas iela

Jūras iela

Lielais prospekts

Vasarnīcu iela

Vīnu iela

Medņu iela

Rīpku iela

1 Russian Orthodox Church
2 Market
3 Castle
4 Spark
5 History & Art Museum
6 Evangelical Lutheran Church
7 Kafe-Restorāns Sārtas Buras
8 Latvijas Banka
9 Bus Station
10 Baptist Church
11 Restaurant
12 Latimpex
13 Post, Telephone & Telegraph Office
14 Restorāns Kosmoss
15 Viesnīca Dzintarjūra
16 Open-Air Sea-Fishing Museum
17 Open-Air Concert Hall

of the river, about 1½ km in from the coast. The old part, nearest the river, is a bit of a maze. Its main street is Pils iela, running roughly east-west, parallel to the river and about 200 metres south of it. This was the real town centre until the Soviet navy took over the riverside area, and a new 'centre' was created around Ganību iela and Kuldīgas iela, 750 metres or so further south. The bus station, on Lauku iela, is about 300 metres south of the eastern part of Pils iela. The railway station is on the Rīga road, two km east of the centre, across the river.

Information

The bus station has a money-exchange office and a left-luggage room (*bagāžu glabātuve*) which is open from 9 am to noon and 1 to 6 pm Monday to Friday. You can also change money at the Latvijas Banka branch a short walk away (turn right along Lauku iela as you leave the bus station, then right again, and the bank is just along on the right), or at the Spark shop on Pils iela. The main post, telephone and telegraph office is on Jūras iela opposite the corner of Andreja iela, 100 metres east of Kuldīgas iela. There's an international telephone and fax service at Latimpex, Gertrūdes iela 26. The main shops are along Kuldīgas iela and Ganību iela in the 'new centre'. The odd handicrafts shop may appear in the old town.

The Ventspils telephone code is 236.

Old Town

You can get to all the main points of interest in the old town by wandering the length of Pils iela, with a few detours here and there. You wouldn't know from its run-down state that this area, along and just back from the river, was the centre of town in the pre-Soviet era. Ventspils used to have a proud waterfront, with hotels, smart port buildings and a long pedestrian promenade – and it aims to restore some of the past grandeur now that the dead hand of the Soviet navy has been prised away from this part of town.

You can reach Pils iela by turning right out of the bus station, left at the end of Lauku iela, then first right (Sofijas iela). After 150 metres this brings you to the **Evangelical Lutheran church** on the right. Cross over Pils iela, just past the church, and continue straight along Tirgus iela to the **market**, on your right. Immediately past the market, turn right along Skolas iela, which becomes Plostu iela and leads, after about 250 metres, to a pretty little **Russian Orthodox church**. Along the way there are views along the river and across to the industrial and transport installations on the north bank.

If you now return to Pils iela and head west along it, you soon reach a small square with the Ventspils **History & Art Museum** (Ventspils Vēstures un Mākslas Muzejs) on its far side at Akmeņu iela 3. The museum is open daily, except Monday, from noon to 6 pm. The **Castle** (Pils) is 450 metres further west along Pils iela. It's a shabby three-storey building with a tower, set back from the north side of the street – and must be high on the list of priorities for restoration. You can walk up the street beside it and round the back, where some excavation has been going on just outside the walls at the top of the river bank. The oldest streets in Ventspils are to the west of the castle. There's not much to see there, nowadays, except quite a lot of one-storey, wooden, fishing people's houses from the early 20th century or before. In a small riverside park there's a **Monument to Lost Sailors** which is a traditional lovers' meeting place.

Seafront & Parks

Ventspils' sandy, dune-backed **beach** stretches south from the river mouth, about two km west of the town centre. Some locals swim there. You can reach it along Viļņu iela or Medņu iela from Vasarnīcu iela – or take bus No 10 along Lielais prospekts from the Viesnīca Dzintarjura hotel.

Breakwaters poke a km or so out to sea from the mouth of the river to form Ventspils' **Sea Gates**, with a narrow entrance that is treacherous for shipping if there's any sea running. Since Latvian independence in 1991 it has been a popular pastime to walk or cycle from the north end of the beach to the lighthouse at the end of the southern breakwater – a previously illegal activity which still involves clambering through a gap in the wire fence separating the beach from the breakwater. There are good river views, and you can see the oil refinery and terminal on the north side of the river mouth.

Vasarnīcu iela, parallel to the beach about 700 metres inland, runs through an area of greenery and parks. Towards its south end, on the corner of Riņķu iela, is the Ventspils **Open-Air Sea-Fishing Museum** (Ventspils Jūras Zvejniecības Brīvdabas Muzejs) with a collection of venerable fishing craft and related and not-so-related items including an old windmill. It's open from 11 am to 6 pm daily, except Monday and Tuesday. A little further south on Vasarnīcu iela there's an **open-air concert hall**. Bus Nos 6 and 11 both come down here, about hourly, from Lielais prospekts opposite the Viesnīca Dzintarjura.

Places to Stay & Eat

There's only one hotel, the Soviet-era *Viesnīca Dzintarjura* (Amber Sea Hotel, ☎ 22 719) at Ganību iela 26, on the corner of Lielais prospekts, facing a park. It has about 70 rooms; doubles with private bathroom were 2.65 lati (the price is almost sure to rise for foreigners). I stayed in a homestay arranged through the Tourist Club of Latvia (LTK) in Rīga – see Private Homes under Accommodation in the Facts for the Visitor chapter at the front of the book for contact details. The hosts were English-speaking, hospitable, travel enthusiasts and only too happy to show me round the town – excellent people to visit if you're on the right kind of budget.

There's a café in the hotel where you could put a number of small dishes together to form a meal, but the best restaurant in town is the *Restorāns Kosmoss*, half a block north up Ganību iela. Other possibilities include the *Kafe-Restorāns Sārtās Buras* on Kuldīgas iela, opposite Sofijas iela, and a small place near the north end of Vasarnīcu iela almost opposite the end of Jūras iela. There's a reasonable *bufet* in the bus station.

Getting There & Away

Bus About 12 buses a day run to and from Rīga, taking 3½ to five hours depending on the route, and costing 1.30 to 1.50 lati. One goes via Kuldīga and about five via Talsi (both routes take 1½ hours and cost 0.80 lati). There are also two buses daily to/from Kuldīga; two to/from Talsi; one to/from each of Roja (3¼ hours) and Kolka (4¼ hours); two to/from Jelgava (4¾ to 5½ hours); and six to/from Liepāja (3¼ to 3¾ hours – some direct, some via Pāvilosta and some via Kuldīga). The daily service to/from Klaipėda via Kuldīga and Liepāja seemed to have been cancelled, but may reappear.

Train Trains run to and from Rīga morning and evening: a trip of 4¼ hours for 0.65 lati in general seating, the only class available. There's also one train daily each way to/from Liepāja, taking 3½ hours.

Getting Around

For a bus from the railway station to the town centre, turn right on your exit from the station and walk up to the roundabout, then turn right and walk down to the bus stop opposite the end of the railway tracks. Any bus from here will go to the centre.

VENTSPILS TO LIEPĀJA

There are high sandstone cliffs and a lighthouse on the coast at **Užava**, 21 km south of Ventspils. **Pāvilosta**, 70 km from Ventspils, is a small port at the mouth of the Saka River. Between these two places the road runs fairly close to the coast most of the way. The railway stays well inland for the entire 125 km from Ventspils to Liepāja.

KULDĪGA

Kuldīga, 150 km west of Rīga and 55 km south-east of Ventspils, is the most picturesque and historic small town in Kurzeme. Set on the Venta River, it has a number of old buildings and some pretty cottage gardens. It attracts quite a lot of local tourism.

History

Kuldīga was an important settlement of the

Cours and probably their capital at the time of the 13th century German invasion. Later Kuldīga (then called Goldingen) became an important stronghold of the Livonian Order. When the Duchy of Courland was founded in 1561, Kuldīga was briefly its capital. It suffered in the Great Northern War, at the beginning of the 18th century, and never really regained its former importance, which is why it remains a small country town today.

Orientation

The Venta River flows up the east side of town and is crossed by the bridge that leads out to the Rīga road. The old part of the town centre is within the half km west and south-west of the bridge. The newer part of the centre focuses on Pilsētas laukums, a further half km west along Liepājas iela. The bus station is on Stacijas iela, a km walk south-east of the old part.

Information

There's a left-luggage room *(bagažas telpa)* in the bus station, open from 6 am to 6 pm. The main post, telephone and telegraph office *(telekomunikācija centrs)* is at Liepājas iela 34. The department store is on

LATVIA

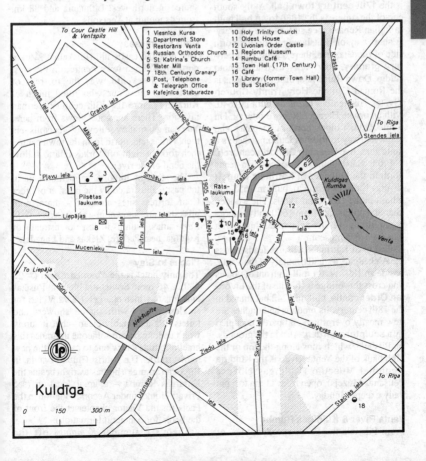

1 Viesnīca Kursa
2 Department Store
3 Restorāns Venta
4 Russian Orthodox Church
5 St Katrina's Church
6 Water Mill
7 18th Century Granary
8 Post, Telephone & Telegraph Office
9 Kafejnīca Staburadze
10 Holy Trinity Church
11 Oldest House
12 Livonian Order Castle
13 Regional Museum
14 Rumbu Café
15 Town Hall (17th Century)
16 Café
17 Library (former Town Hall)
18 Bus Station

Kuldīga

0   150   300 m

the north side of Pilsētas laukums, and there are other shops along Liepājas iela.

Kuldīga's telephone code is 233.

Old Town

A central point to start an exploration is **Rātslaukums**, the old town hall square, where Pasta, Tirgu, Liepājas and Baznīcas streets all meet. Kuldīga's **oldest house** stands here on the northern corner of Pasta iela; its '1670 – 1742 – 1982' sign tells the dates of its construction, reconstruction and renovation. The wooden building on the southern corner of Pasta iela, at Rātslaukums 5, is the **17th century town hall**. At the south end of the square is the **1860 town hall** built in Italian Renaissance style – now a library. A short way off Rātslaukums, on the north side of Liepājas iela, there's a big **18th century granary**, now partly used as a photo studio. Down Raiņa iela, off Liepājas iela, is the Roman Catholic **Holy Trinity Church** (Svētās Trisvienības baznīca), built in 1640, with an ornate Baroque/Rococo interior. On Smilšu iela, a block north of Liepājas iela, about halfway to Pilsētas laukums, there's a quite attractive **Russian Orthodox church**.

From Rātslaukums, Baznīcas iela leads north to the Lutheran **St Katrina's Church** (Svētās Katrīnas baznīca), built in 1655 and rebuilt in the 1860s and 1960s. The wooden altar and pulpit date from 1660 and the large organ from 1712. In Soviet times this church was used as a museum.

East of St Katrina's, a bridge leads across the Alekšupīte, a small tributary of the Venta, beside an 1807 **water mill**. In front of you as you cross this bridge is the site of the **Livonian Order castle**, built in 1242 but ruined in the 18th century. Its mounds and ditches are now mostly overgrown and partly occupied by a **sculpture garden**. Also in the grounds, on Pils iela, which runs along the top of the high bank of the Venta River, is the **Kuldīga Regional Museum** (Kuldīgas Novada Pētīšanas Muzejs), open from 11 am to 5 pm daily except Monday.

Venta River & Kuldīgas Rumba

From Pils iela there's an excellent view of the 100-metre-wide Venta, crossed by its long road bridge built in the 1870s. A short distance upstream of the bridge, directly below the castle, is the well known Kuldīgas Rumba waterfall, only a metre or two high but stretching the whole width of the river, and pretty enough to be big news in a flat country like Latvia, where any waterfall is a rarity. It's popular with fishers and swimmers, and when there's not too much water flowing you can walk across the top of the fall – altogether, a refreshing place to end a walk round the old part of Kuldīga.

The Venta at this point is 258 km from its source in north-west Lithuania and 88 km from its mouth at Ventspils.

Cour Fortresses

The large old castle hill (Pilskalns) 2½ km north of Kuldīga town centre, on the west bank of the Venta, was the fortress of Lamekins, the Cour who ruled much of Kurzeme before the 13th century German invasion. There are good views from here. You can get to it by following Ventspils iela then Virkas iela, north from the town centre, then forking right off Virkas iela to follow the bend of the river.

The strategic importance of the Venta in the past is illustrated by the number of other Cour fortress sites along it – three more pilskalns are shown in the *Latvijas Ceļu Karte* atlas, within 30 km downstream of Kuldīga, near Padure, Zlēkas and Lagzdene.

Places to Stay

The only hotel is the *Viesnīca Kursa* (☎ 22 430), a 46-room Soviet-era block at Pilsētas laukums 6, which charges 1.25/2.50 lati for singles/doubles with shared showers and toilets. It's reasonably clean – but it surely won't be long before someone upgrades this hotel or builds a new one to cater to the new tourist traffic. The Tourist Club of Latvia, in Rīga, can arrange a homestay right beside the Kuldīgas Rumba – a great location (see Private Homes under Accommodation in the Facts for the Visitor chapter at the front of the book for contact information).

There's a summer *Kempings* off the

Ventspils road. It's 1½ km east off the road, signposted about 13 km from Kuldīga, half a km past the Nabas Ezers bus stop.

Places to Eat

The *Kafejnīca Staburadze*, at Liepājas iela 8, has a ground-floor café, open till 7 pm, where you could combine a number of small dishes to make a meal, and an upstairs restaurant with a live band, open till midnight. The other restaurant is the *Restorāns Venta* on the north side of Pilsētas laukums. There's a pleasant open-air café beside the Alekšupīte on Pasta iela, and the *Viesnīca Kursa* also has a café. The *Rumbu* café on Pils iela overlooks the Kuldīgas Rumba – a great location, but it had hardly anything to eat or drink when I visited.

Getting There & Away

There are no trains, only buses. Six run daily to/from Rīga, taking three to four hours for 1 lats. There are five or six a day to/from both Ventspils (1½ hours, 0.80 lati) and Liepāja (two hours, 1 lats); two to/from Talsi (two to 2½ hours); and one to/from Jelgava, except on Sunday. Only a few buses start or end their runs at Kuldīga – most are in transit.

LIEPĀJA

With 115,000 people, Liepāja, 220 km from Rīga on the Baltic coast, is Latvia's third-biggest city. Like Ventspils it has an ice-free harbour. Though lacking in big attractions Liepāja (former German name: Libau) is an amiable enough place with a reasonable hotel. Latvia's major rock festival, Liepājas Dzintars (Amber of Liepāja), is held here every summer, usually in mid-August.

History

Liepāja is mentioned as being founded by the Livonian Order in the mid-13th century, but there's said to have been a fishing village here before that. Development didn't really take off till the deepening of the harbour and arrival of a railway in the 19th century. It became a communications centre, with an undersea cable to Copenhagen laid in the 1860s, and a passenger shipping service to

North America before WW I. Between the world wars there were ship-repairing and aircraft-building industries.

Orientation

Liepāja stands on the two to three-km wide neck of land between 18-km-long Liepāja Lake (Liepājas ezers) and the sea. The city straddles the narrow channel flowing from the lake to the sea. The city centre and most residential areas are south of the channel, and the industrial areas are on the north side.

The rail and bus stations are together at the north end of Rīgas iela, on the north side of the channel, about a km from the main bridge. The main street through the city centre begins on the south side of this bridge and runs south till it eventually meets the main road south to the Lithuanian border. It goes through a variety of names starting as Lielā iela, then Tirgoņu iela, then Kuršu iela. Liepāja's beach stretches a long way south from the river mouth, one to 1½ km west of Lielā or Tirgoņu iela.

Information

There are left-luggage lockers in the combined bus and rail station. The main post and telegraph office is on the corner of Pasta iela and Radio iela, a block west of Lielā iela. The pharmacy in the large Kurzeme store, at the south end of Lielā iela, sells some Western medicines. The travel agency, Turisma Firma Ligo, or the Liepāja Tūristu Klubs, together on Graudu iela just south of the corner of Kurmajas prospekts, may be able to help with information or arrangements.

Liepāja's telephone code is 234.

City Centre

There's one of the interesting **MF Salons** group of art and handicrafts shops at the north end of Lielā iela, just south of the bridge. The large Lutheran **Holy Trinity Church** (Svētās Trisvienības baznīca), on the east side of Lielā iela 300 metres further south, was built in 1742-58 and has a fine interior. Other main buildings on Lielā iela include the Viesnīca Liva hotel a little further along, and the **Teacher Training Institute**

(Liepājas Pedagoģiskais Institūts) on the west side.

About 700 metres from the bridge, Lielā iela becomes **Tirgoņu iela**, which is pedestrianised and has a few fancy-looking shops – but actually I found nothing of note in them. More interesting are the busy main **market** (*tirgus*) and **flea market** (*mantu tirgus*), a block further south on the same street (here called Kuršu iela). You may not find anything to buy here, but observing what the local people are buying and selling is always an eye-opener. Across Kuršu iela from the markets is the Roman Catholic **St Joseph's cathedral** (Svēts Jāzepa katedrāla).

Beach Area

Between the main street and the beach, the architecture is mostly wooden two-storey houses, some of quite original design – a neighbourhood that must once have been attractive and may become so again, but is for the moment rather shabby. You can reach the beach by following Jūras iela west from the north end of Lielā iela, by the bridge. Jūras iela becomes Kurmajas prospekts, which leads to the beach. Graudu iela, beside

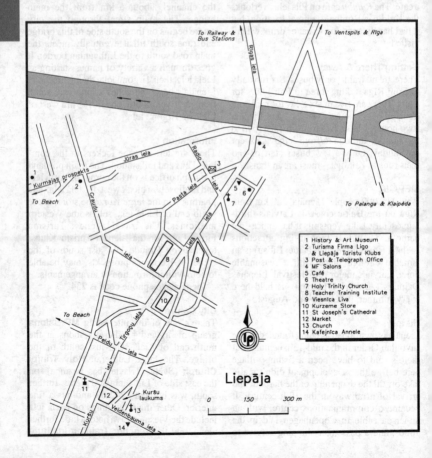

1 History & Art Museum
2 Turisma Firma Ligo & Liepāja Tūristu Klubs
3 Post & Telegraph Office
4 MF Salons
5 Café
6 Theatre
7 Holy Trinity Church
8 Teacher Training Institute
9 Viesnīca Līva
10 Kurzeme Store
11 St Joseph's Cathedral
12 Market
13 Church
14 Kafejnīca Annele

Liepāja

0   150   300 m

the Teacher Training Institute on Lielā iela, also leads to the start of Kurmajas prospekts.

On the north side of Kurmajas prospekts is the **Liepāja History & Art Museum** (Liepājas Vēstures un Mākslas Muzejs), whose collection includes some carved amber ornaments 1500 years old. At the end of Kurmajas prospekts is a big **monument** to sailors and fishers who have died at sea. The **beach**, backed by dunes and a **park** strip, is long, clean and sandy. But no one seems to swim, which may be connected with reports that several hundred thousand tonnes of toxic waste and unexploded bombs were dumped off Liepāja by the Soviet navy after WW II, with their protective casings expected to start decomposing in the 1990s.

Places to Stay

The only hotel in the city is the *Viesnīca Liva* (☎ 20 139) at Lielā iela 11. Refurbishment has started but had yet to reach the rooms when I visited. Clean singles/doubles with private bathroom and TV cost 8/12 lati. A possible alternative, if you have your own transport, is what looks like a good new hotel with a restaurant, by the Rīga road at Alande, 12 km east of Liepāja.

See Private Homes under Accommodation in the Facts for the Visitor chapter at the front of the book for agencies which may be able to provide rooms in private homes in Liepāja (and other towns too). Locally, the Turisma Firma Ligo travel agency or the Liepāja Tūristu Klubs (see Information) may be able to help if you want private accommodation.

Places to Eat

The *restorāns* in the *Viesnīca Liva* will give you some of the better meals in town. The *Kafejnīca Annele* on Veidenbauma iela, behind the market, has a slightly bigger range of fare than the coffee, ice cream, juice and pastries which is all that's available in most Liepāja cafés. Don't forget the main market on Kuršu iela as a source of fresh food. There's a smaller market just off Rīgas iela,

the approach road to the bus and rail stations. The Kurzeme shop on Lielā iela has a reasonably good food section.

Getting There & Away

You'll probably have to make a connection in Liepāja if you're travelling from Kurzeme to Lithuania or vice versa. Buses are the only cross-border transport although there are trains between Liepāja and Rīga and Ventspils. Liepāja's railway station, at the north end of Rīgas iela, doubles as booking hall for the buses, whose terminus is immediately outside.

Air Liepāja has an airport and, at the time of writing, Latvian Airlines flies to/from St Petersburg three times a week for a foreigner's fare of 44 lati one way. Flights to/from Minsk and Kiev may start. The Latvian Airlines office is at Radio iela 12/14 (☎ 23 455 or 24 288).

Bus There are about 12 buses daily to/from Rīga, taking 3½ hours direct, four to 4½ hours via Kalnciems, five to 5½ hours via Jelgava, and seven hours via Tukums, for a fare of 1.30 to 2.80 lati. Other services to/from Liepāja include:

Kaliningrad: two buses daily, 7½ or 9½ hours
Klaipėda: six buses daily, 2¾ hours
Kuldīga: five or six buses daily, two hours
Talsi: one bus daily, 4½ hours
Palanga: five or more buses daily, 1¾ hours
Ventspils: six buses daily, 3¼ to 3¾ hours

Train There are three daily trains to/from Rīga, taking 4¾ to 5¾ hours for 0.70 lati in general seating; and one daily train to/from Ventspils, taking 3½ hours.

Getting Around

Tram No 1 from Rīgas iela outside the rail and bus stations will take you straight down the main street. If you get off in front of the Kurzeme department store on Lielā iela, shortly beyond the Viesnīca Liva, you'll be just about in the centre of things.

LATVIA

Lithuania

Facts about the Country

Lithuania (Lietuva), the southernmost Baltic state, is in many ways the most vibrant, as it showed the world by its daring, emotional drive for independence. Lithuania owes much to the rich cultural currents of central Europe; with neighbouring Poland it once shared an empire stretching from the Baltic Sea almost to the Black Sea, and it still shares the Roman Catholicism which sets it apart from its Baltic neighbours.

Vilnius, the historic, lively capital, is the obvious base for visitors. But Lithuania has other sizeable cities such as Kaunas, briefly its capital this century, and the seaport Klaipėda, formerly the German town Memel. Other intriguing places include the Neringa sandspit on the coast, the strange Hill of Crosses near Šiauliai, and the forests and castles of the south.

This chapter contains information specific to Lithuania. For a more general introduction to the history, geography, people and culture of the Baltic states see Facts about the Region at the front of the book.

GEOGRAPHY

Lithuania is the biggest of the three Baltic states, covering an area of 65,200 sq km. It borders Latvia in the north, Belarus in the south-east, and Poland and the Kaliningrad Region in the south-west. Vilnius lies in the south-east of the country, an oddly off-centre location explained by the fact that Lithuania used to stretch much further to the south and east than it does now. Its four main regions are Aukštaitija (Upper Lithuania), the east; Žemaitija (Lower Lithuania), the west; Dzūkija, the south; and Suvalkija or Sūduva, the south-west.

Lithuania's Baltic coast extends only about 100 km, half of which lies along the extraordinary Courland Spit (Lithuanian: Neringa; Russian: Kurshskaya kosa) – a sandbar 98 km long and up to 66 metres high, but nowhere more than four km wide wide. It's the most unusual natural feature of the Baltic states and well worth a visit. Behind Neringa is the wide (up to 35 km) Courland Lagoon, one of a series of lagoons protected

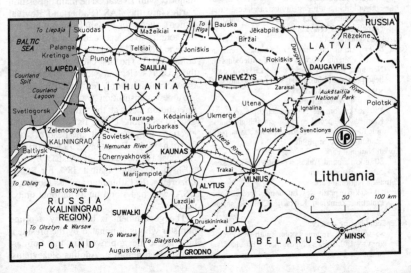

Lithuania

307

by sandbars round this south-east corner of the Baltic Sea. It has a single narrow opening to the sea at its north end, by the Lithuanian port of Klaipėda.

Lithuania is a predominantly flat country, though it has two broad bands of territory which often exceed 150 metres above sea level. One is down the whole eastern quarter of the country, straddling the border with Belarus. It reaches its highest levels in the Medininkų Upland in the south-east (where the country's highest point, 294-metre Juozapinės, is located) and the Švenčionių Upland in the north-east. The second band is the Žemaitija Upland which spreads over much of the north-west and reaches a height of 234 metres.

NATIONAL PARKS & RESERVES

Lithuania has five national parks and a number of nature reserves dotted throughout the country. The highlight is the Kuršių Nerija National Park on the outstanding Neringa sandspit. More information on some of the parks can be found in the regional sections.

Aukštaitija National Park
  300 sq km in north-east Lithuanian lake district near Ignalina – lakes, rivers, forest, walking, canoeing; park centre at Palūšė

Dzūkija National Park
  550 sq km of the Varėna-Druskininkai forest in south Lithuania – forests, historic settlements on Nemunas River at Merkinė and Liškiava; park headquarters at Marcinkonys, accommodation at spa town of Druskininkai

Kuršių Nerija National Park
  180 sq km on the Neringa sandspit south of Klaipėda – a special environment of high dunes, pine forests, beaches, lagoon and sea coasts; park headquarters at Smiltynė

Trakai National Park
  80 sq km around Trakai, west of Vilnius – lakes, castles, historic town

Žemaitija National Park
  200 sq km in north-west Lithuania – forests, Lake Plateliai, Žemaičių Kalvarija Catholic shrine centre

Čepkeliai Nature Reserve
  85 sq km on Belarus border south of Marcinkonys – Lithuania's biggest marsh, bird habitat, forest

Kamanos Nature Reserve
  36 sq km, west of Naujoji Akmenė in north-west Lithuania near Latvian border – upland bogs, bird, plant and mammal habitat; limited access

Viešvilė Nature Reserve
  west of Jurbarkas, south-west Lithuania – 32 sq km of river basin, forest and marshland

Žuvintas Nature Reserve
  54 sq km around Žuvintas Lake near Marijampolė, south-west Lithuania – important bird and plant habitat

GOVERNMENT

Lithuania's parliament is the Seimas. In the first post-independence general election, held in two rounds in October and November 1992, 71 of the 141 seats were reserved for candidates who won an overall majority in their electorates, and 70 were awarded on a proportional-representation basis according to the parties' share of the popular vote. The second round of voting took place only in those electorates which didn't produce an overall majority the first time round.

The LDDP (Lithuanian Democratic Labour Party), born from the democratic, pro-independence wing of the old Lithuanian Communist Party, won a narrow overall majority with 73 seats. The main opposition parties are the TAS (Fatherland Revival Union), successor to Sajūdis which had led the country to independence, with 30 seats, and the LKDP (Lithuanian Christian Democratic Party). The first cabinet chosen after the LDDP's election victory was broadly based, containing only four LDDP members.

A new constitution was approved in a referendum held at the same time as the general election. Under its terms, popular elections for a president, the head of state, were held in February 1993. Algirdas Brazauskas, the leader of the LDDP, won 60% of the votes against 38% for Stasys Lozoraitis, the Lithuanian ambassador to the USA, who had stood on a 'national unity' ticket.

The government is headed by a prime minister who is nominated by the president but has to be approved by the Seimas. Brazauskas' nominee, Adolfas Šleževičius, an LDDP member, was approved in March 1993.

Citizenship

By the citizenship law of December 1991, all residents who lived in Lithuania before 3 November 1989 were granted citizenship. People who have moved there since will have to stay 10 years before they can become citizens. Non-ethnic Lithuanians have to pass a language test to get jobs dealing with the public.

PEOPLE

Lithuania has the most ethnically homogenous population of the three Baltic states, with Lithuanians accounting for 80% of the 3.68 million people. About 9% are Russian and 7% Polish.

The modern Lithuanians are the descendants of the Balt tribes who inhabited roughly the area of modern Lithuania. They are thought to have spread into the southeastern Baltic area, along with other Balt tribes who settled modern Latvia, Poland and the Kaliningrad Region, from the south and east about 2000 BC. By the 13th century the tribes in Lithuania were basically two groups – now referred to as Lithuanians (in the south-east) and Samogitians (in the north-west). Some of the Yotvingians or Sūduviai, a Balt people who lived in the region which is now south-west Lithuania and north-east Poland, were assimilated by the Lithuanians. Another Balt people, the Old Prussians, who inhabited the area that became known as East Prussia (the modern Kaliningrad Region and neighbouring areas of northern Poland) were almost exterminated (and were finally assimilated) by the Germans who conquered their territory in the 13th century.

The Lithuanian diaspora is by far the biggest of any of the peoples of the Baltic states, mainly due to emigration for political and economic reasons in the 19th and early 20th century and also around the time of WW II. There are now an estimated 800,000 Lithuanians in the USA with the main concentration in Chicago. Other Lithuanian communities are scattered all around the world including Canada, South America, Britain and Australia.

ARTS
Literature

The first major fiction in Lithuanian was the poem *Metai* (The Seasons) by Kristijonas Donelaitis, describing the life of serfs in the 18th century. A high mark in the 19th century was Antanas Baranauskas' poem *Anykščių šilelis* (Anykščiai Pine Forest), written in 1860-61, which uses the forest as a symbol of Lithuania and bemoans its cutting down by foreign landlords.

From 1864 Lithuanian literature was severely handicapped by Russia's insistence on the Cyrillic alphabet for Lithuanian publishing. Jonas Mačiulis, known as Maironis, was the poet of the Lithuanian national revival. His nationalist, romantic *Pavasario balsai* (Voices of Spring), published in 1895, was the start of modern Lithuanian poetry. Vincas Mykolaitis-Putinas, a priest who left the priesthood in the 1930s, is probably the leading literary figure of the 20th century. He wrote poetry as well as prose but his outstanding work is *Altorių šešėly* (In the Altars' Shadow), a three-volume novel.

Lithuania's intimate relations with Poland down the centuries give it a share of the credit for some of the best of Polish literature, too. Several major Polish writers grew up in Lithuania and regarded themselves as partly Lithuanian in one way or another. Among them are Adam Mickiewicz, inspiration of 19th century Polish nationalists, whose great poem *Pan Tadeusz* begins: 'Lithuania, my fatherland...', and the contemporary writers Czesław Miłosz (winner of the 1980 Nobel prize) and the novelist Tadeusz Konwicki. Miłosz, a poet, essayist and critic has, among many other things, translated Lithuanian *dainas* into French and written about the Soviet occupation of the Baltic states in the last chapter of *The Captive Mind* which looks at ways in which intellectuals sell out to oppressive communist regimes.

Visual Arts

Mikalojus Konstantinas Čiurlionis (1875-1911) achieved international recognition with his romantic and symbolic paintings in gentle, lyrical tones. A depressive genius, he was also a major composer. There's a good book on his life and work by the former Lithuanian president Vytautas Landsbergis (see Books in the Facts for the Visitor chapter at the front of the book).

Two artists who achieved major standing, though their work is not specifically Lithuanian, were the Vilnius-bred Jews Isaak Levitan (a landscape painter who holds an important place in Russian 19th century art) and Jacques Lipchitz (a 20th century sculptor). One contemporary artist to look out for is Romas Dalinkievičius who composes pictures based on old runic symbols.

Folk Art

An interesting Lithuanian folk-art tradition is that of carving large wooden crosses or suns, saints' figures or weathercocks on tall poles and placing them at crossroads, in cemeteries or village squares, or at the sites of extraordinary events. Vincas Svirskis (1835-1916) is reckoned to be the master of this form; there's a fine collection of his carvings in the State Museum in Vilnius. In the Soviet period, such work – with its religious overtones – was banned, but it survived to amazing effect at the Hill of Crosses near Šiauliai.

Music

Lithuania is the jazz headquarters of the Baltics, and Vilnius has a good little live-jazz scene. Two musicians you should particularly look out for are the sparkling pianist Gintautas Abarius and the more cerebral saxophonist Petras Vyšniauskas. On the rock scene, Foje, with an original Indian-influenced sound, may make a big name; while Bix play brassy, danceable music.

The Romantic, folk-influenced Lithuanian Mikalojus Konstantinas Čiurlionis is probably the Baltic states' leading composer from earlier periods. Two of his major works are the symphonic poems *Miške* (In The Forest) and *Jūra* (The Sea), written between 1900 and 1907, but he also wrote a lot of piano pieces.

Facts for the Visitor

This chapter contains visitor information specific to Lithuania. For details on obtaining visas for the Baltic states, Russia and Belarus and for more general information on travelling in the Baltic states see the introductory Facts for the Visitor chapter at the front of the book.

DIPLOMATIC MISSIONS

Lithuanian diplomatic missions are still being set up in many countries. Addresses and times of opening may change, so phone ahead before visiting.

Lithuanian diplomatic missions include:

Australia
    Consulate: 26 Jalanga Crescent, Aranda, ACT, 2614 (☎ 062-53 2062)
Belgium
    Embassy: Rue Maurice Lietart 48, 1150 Brussels (☎ 02-7722750)
Canada
    Consulate: 235 Yorkland Blvd, Suite 502, Willowdale, Ontario M2J 4Y8 (☎ 416-494 8313)
Czech Republic
    Embassy: Janakova 6, 16000 Prague 6 (☎ 02-311 01 94)
Denmark
    Embassy: Bernstorffsvej 214, DK-2920 Charlottelund, Copenhagen (☎ 31 63 62 07)
Estonia
    Embassy: Vabaduse väljak 10, EE0100 Tallinn (☎ 22-666 634)
France
    Ambassador: 14 Boulevard Montmartre, Paris 75009 (☎ 1-48.01.00.33)
Germany
    Embassy: Argelander Strasse 108A, Bonn 1 (☎ 0228-914 9113)
Italy
    Embassy: Piazza Asti 25, 00182 Rome (☎ 06-686 7855)
Latvia
    Embassy: Elizabetes iela 2, LV-1340 Rīga (☎ 22-321 519)
Norway
    Consulate: Stranden 3, Aker Brygge, 0250 Oslo 2 (☎ 22-83 35 10)
Poland
    Embassy: al J Ch Szucha 5, 00-580 Warsaw (☎ 0-2-6253410)

Russia
    Embassy: Borisoglebsky pereulok 10, Moscow 121069 (☎ 095-291 26 43)
Sweden
    Embassy: Strandvagen 53, 11523 Stockholm (☎ 08-667 1134)
Ukraine
    Embassy: vulitsya Gorkoho 22, 252024 Kiev (☎ 044-227 1042)
UK
    Embassy: 17 Essex Villas, London W8 7BP (☎ 071-938 2481)
USA
    Embassy: 2622 16th St NW, Washington DC 20009 (☎ 202-234 5860)
    Consulate: 41 West 82nd St, New York, NY 10024 (☎ 212-582 1345)

CUSTOMS

Customs regulations vary between the Baltic states and are subject to change. Some general pointers are given in the Facts for the Visitor chapter at the front of the book. Contact a Lithuanian embassy or consulate for information if there is anything you are concerned about.

Alcohol & Tobacco

You can import duty-free one litre of alcoholic drinks over 40% volume and two litres of wine or champagne. You cannot export more than two-minimum-monthly-salaries' worth of alcohol and tobacco (at the time of writing that means about 40 litų).

Money

Hard currency must be declared on entry, but there's no limit. You can't take out more than you brought in.

Other Items

You can't import or export precious stones or metals without special permission. Exporting 'cultural objects' requires Cultural Heritage Inspectorate permission. Cultural objects over 30 years old also attract 200% duty. There's export duty on more than 20 litres of petrol.

Customs Information

The Customs Department is at Jakšto gatvė 1/25, Vilnius (☎ 22-613 027).

MONEY

Lithuania introduced its own currency, the *litas*, in June and July 1993. The litas is divided into 100 *cento* (singular: *centas*). The plurals of litas and centas are *litai* and *centai* for numbers from two to nine inclusive and for 102 to 109, 202 to 209, 302 to 309 and so on; but, *litų* and *cento* from 10 to 100, 110 to 200, 210 to 300 and so on; and, litas and centas again for 101, 201, 301 etc. Decimal fractions use litų and cento. In late 1993, exchange rates included:

US$1	=	4.25 litų
DM1	=	2.63 litų
UK£1	=	6.05 litų
C$1	=	2.99 litų
A$1	=	2.56 litų
1 Fmk	=	0.69 litų
1 SKr	=	0.49 litų

The denominations initially released were coins of 1 centas, 2 centai, 5 centai, 10 cento, 20 cento, 50 cento, one litas, two litai and five litai; and notes of 10 litų, 20 litų, 50 litų and 100 litų. Notes of 500 litų and 1000 litų were expected later. The design for the 10-litų note shows the Lithuanian aviators Steponas Darius and Stasys Girėnas, who died in 1933 when their plane crashed in a German forest as they tried to fly nonstop from New York to Kaunas.

The litas is Lithuania's sole legal tender. The Lithuanian transitional currency used during the phasing-out of the Russian rouble, the *talonas* ('coupon'), ceased to be legal tender with the introduction of the litas. Trading in Western currencies was outlawed in August 1993 – but that doesn't prevent some taxi drivers from asking to paid in dollars.

The talonas had slipped steadily in value from around 250 to US$1 in October 1992 to nearly 500 to US$1 in mid-1993. After repeated postponements of the litas, the Bank of Lithuania chairman, Vilius Baldišis, resigned in spring 1993 amid reports that the new banknotes, printed in the US, were too easy to forge and would have to be printed again. Despite the reprint, significant numbers of forged banknotes found their way into circulation after the litas was finally introduced.

There were two series of talonai, both bearing pictures of animals. The first, known as Vagnorkės after the prime minister who introduced them, Gediminas Vagnorius, began life in 1991; it was paid into wage packets as coupons redeemable for certain scarce goods to restrict the sale of those goods to non-residents. The coupons soon started to be used as a currency in their own right. The second series, smaller in size and known as Žvėriukai (Little Animals), was introduced in spring 1992 to combat a shortage of Russian roubles, still Lithuania's main currency at the time. The rouble ceased to be legal tender in October 1992, leaving both sets of talonai circulating together.

NATIONAL HOLIDAYS

In addition to the usual Christian feast days, Lithuania also has two national holidays which celebrate its independent nationhood. Details follow:

New Year's Day, 1 January
Independence Day (Nepriklausomybės diena; anniversary of 1918 independence declaration), 16 February
Easter Day
Easter Monday
Mothers' Day, first Sunday in May
Statehood Day (commemoration of coronation of Grand Duke Mindaugas, 13th century), 6 July
All Saints' Day, 1 November
Christmas (Kalėdos), 25 & 26 December

CULTURAL EVENTS

Like Estonia and Latvia, Lithuania celebrates a number of regular cultural events. The most important of these include the national song festival, Midsummer celebrations and the Baltika folk festival. For some background to these events see Cultural

Events in the introductory Facts for the Visitor chapter at the front of the book.

Lithuanian cultural events include:

Horse Races – on Sartų Lake near Utena if frozen, otherwise in the town; first Saturday of February

Užgavėnės (Mardi Gras) – animal, bird and beast masquerades in towns and villages of Žemaitija

St Kazimieras' Day – Lithuania's patron saint's day, 4 March, with the Kaziukas crafts fair in Vilnius around this date

Birštonas Jazz Festival – very popular spring jazz event with top Lithuanian and foreign musicians; Birštonas, usually three days around late March, even-numbered years

Easter – a busy time in Lithuanian churches

Skamba Skamba Kankliai – folk music and dance festival; Vilnius old town, last week of May

Vilnius Jazz Festival – one of Eastern Europe's leading contemporary jazz gatherings; Vilnius, autumn (usually October)

Vėlinės (All Souls' Day) – commemoration of the dead with visits to cemeteries; 2 November

MEDIA
Local-Language Press

Lietuvos Rytas, *Respublika* and *Lietuvos Aidas* sell over 100,000 copies. Details of English-language newspapers and magazines published in the Baltics are given in the Media section of the Facts for the Visitor chapter at the front of the book.

LIETUVOS
rytas

TV & Radio

Lithuanian state TV has two channels, LTV-1 and LTV-2. Russian RTR is also generally received. In Vilnius most sets can be tuned to a British satellite channel which is beamed down by a dish on the parliament building, originally set up so that Lithuanians could receive real news during the January 1991 crisis when Soviet troops occupied the Vilnius TV installations. Polish TV is also

received in Vilnius and other border regions. A new commercial station, Baltic TV, started up in 1993.

Radio Vilnius broadcasts 30 minutes of English-language news about Lithuania at 10 pm on 666 kHz. There's also Lithuanian news in English on the independent music-and-news station Radiocentras (101.0 MHz) at 2 pm. In Vilnius, Voice of America broadcasts continuously in English on 105.6 MHz.

FOOD

Dairy products and potatoes are mainstays of the ordinary Lithuanian diet, though meat and other vegetables are standard fare in restaurants. Common dairy products include *varškė* (curd) and *grietinė* (sour cream). Pancakes seem particularly popular here, and there are special names for various types including: *blyneliai* (small pancakes), *varškėčiai* (curd pancakes), and *bulviniai blynai* which are pancakes made with grated potato. Common Lithuanian starters include *silkė* (herring), *šprotai* (sprats), mushrooms and salads.

Lithuania has a number of idiosyncratic specialities and you should have a go at one or two of them. You're unlikely to forget your first encounter with a *cepelinas* (Zeppelin) – an airship-shaped parcel of a glutinous substance alleged to be potato dough, with a wad of cheese, meat, or mushrooms in the centre. Another local favourite is *virtinukai*: small, ravioli-like dumplings stuffed with cheese, curd, fruit, mushrooms or meat. Then there's that old standby, the *balandėlė*: a stuffed cabbage roll, which may be cheered up with jam (*džemas*). *Troškinys* is a type of meat stew-cum-soup. *Šaltibarščiai* is a beetroot, cucumber and sour cream soup usually eaten cold. Boiled potatoes can accompany it.

General information on eating in the Baltic states is given in the introductory Facts for the Visitor chapter at the front of the book. The Language Guide at the back of the book includes words and phrases you will find useful when ordering food and drink.

Vilnius

The greenest and prettiest of the three Baltic capitals, Vilnius (population: 590,000) lies 290 km inland on the Neris River, among a series of small hills. While Tallinn is arguably the most picturesque of the three cities and Rīga the most metropolitan, Vilnius is the most fun. Its people are generally warmer and less reserved, and life, on the whole, less formal. Vilnius also has a more international flavour than the other capitals – partly because of the influence of the big Lithuanian diaspora and partly because it has always been more open to central Europe and the outside world, especially through Catholic Poland, in whose history it has a prominent place and of which it was actually a part as recently as 1939.

Vilnius' varied array of central-European Catholic architecture (contrasting with the German influence on the other Baltic capitals) also contributes to its more light-hearted atmosphere. The large old part of the city is a warren of winding streets, hidden courtyards and dozens of old churches and is endlessly intriguing to explore. Vilnius' modern history is dramatic: there are reminders of its once-flourishing Jewish community, all but wiped out in WW II, and of its pivotal role in the campaign for Baltic independence from the USSR. Please allow yourself plenty of time to explore this fascinating city.

HISTORY

Legend has it that Vilnius was founded in the 1320s when the Lithuanian grand duke Gediminas, camping here on a hunting trip, dreamt of an iron wolf that howled with the voices of 100 wolves – meaning that he must build an impregnable city, as mighty as the howl of 100 wolves. In fact, the site had been occupied at least 1000 years before and, with river access to the Baltic and Black seas, may well have been a political and trade centre before Gediminas' time.

Fourteenth century Vilnius was built on Gediminas Hill, with its upper and lower castles and townspeople's houses all protected by a moat, walls and towers against the knights of the Teutonic Order, who attacked at least six times between 1365 and 1402.

The knights' defeat by joint Lithuanian-Polish forces at Grünwald, in 1410, ushered in a period of prosperity in which Vilnius extended south from Gediminas Hill into what's now the Old Town, and many Gothic buildings went up. Merchant and artisan guilds were formed. The castles were rebuilt, and the cathedral founded inside the lower one. Following attacks by Tatars from the south, a 2.4-km-long defensive wall was built, between 1503 and 1522, around the new part of town, south of Gediminas Hill.

Sixteenth century Vilnius was one of the biggest cities in eastern Europe, with a population around 25,000, and blossomed with fine buildings in the late Gothic and Renaissance styles. It was increasingly Polish-dominated as the two states moved to formal union and Lithuanian gentry became, in effect, Polish gentry. Polish Jesuits founded Vilnius University in 1579 and made the city a bastion of the Catholic Counter-Reformation. Lithuania sank into a subordinate position in the Polish-Lithuanian state in the 17th century, and Vilnius gained a place in Poland's 'golden age'. Under Jesuit influence, Baroque architecture made a big impact.

Nineteenth century Vilnius became a refuge of Polish and Polonised Lithuanian gentry dispossessed by the region's new Russian rulers, which made it a focus of the Polish national revival, in which the Vilnius-bred poet Adam Mickiewicz was a leading inspiration. The 1830-31 and 1863-64 Polish uprisings didn't take off here, but Vilnius University was closed by the tsarist authorities in any case.

In the second half of the century the city grew quite quickly as railways arrived and industry developed. Vilnius had also become a very important Jewish city, with around 70,000 or 80,000 Jews in its 160,000 population at the turn of the century, earning it the nickname 'Jerusalem of Lithuania'. So strong was Polish influence, meanwhile, that the first language of most of the non-Jewish inhabitants, even if they regarded themselves as Lithuanian, was Polish. At the same time, many Poles and Jews emigrated to the USA.

In the 20th century, Vilnius has changed hands about a dozen times. Germany occupied it for 3½ years in WW I. When the subsequent, confused, Soviet/Polish/Lithuanian fighting died down, Vilnius found itself in an isolated corner of Poland, cut off from trade with both Lithuania and Russia. Economically it went backward. Nevertheless, it developed into a prominent centre of Jewish culture. Vilnius was now, essentially, a Polish and Jewish city, with its streets named in Polish, and Lithuanians a small minority in the population – if perhaps not quite as small as the 1% claimed by Polish statistics of the time!

The knight on horseback has been a national symbol of Lithuania since the 14th Century

Stalin handed Vilnius to Lithuania after the Red Army walked into Poland in 1939, but WW II saw another three-year German occupation. Nearly all the Vilnius Jews were killed in its ghetto or in the nearby Paneriai death camp. Vilnius' population fell from 209,000 to 110,000, and the city was badly damaged in the six-day battle in which the Red Army recaptured it towards the end of the war.

Many of its Poles – including virtually all the middle and upper classes – moved or were deported to Poland between 1945 and 1958. Those who stayed in Vilnius were mostly Belarussian speakers of peasant origins, whose communities had been Polonised in the 19th century, at least to the extent of worshipping in Polish-speaking Catholic churches.

The new residential and industrial suburbs which sprung up around Vilnius were filled by Lithuanians who moved in from the countryside and other towns and by immigrant Russians and Belarussians. Russians and Poles each account for about 100,000 of the city's population today; Belarussians, for 30,000.

Vilnius was the chief focus of Lithuania's push for independence from the Soviet Union in the late 1980s and early 1990s. Particularly dramatic and tragic events took place here in January 1991, when Soviet troops trying to destabilise the situation stormed the city's TV installations, killing 13 among the crowds gathered to defend them and wounding many more.

ORIENTATION

The centre of Vilnius is on the south side of the Neris River, and its heart is Katedros aikštė, an open square with the cathedral on its north side and Gediminas Hill (Gedimino kalnas) rising behind it. South of Katedros aikštė are the streets of the Old Town (senamiestis); to the west, Gedimino prospektas cuts straight across the newer part of the centre. The rail and bus stations are just beyond the south edge of the Old Town, 1½ km from Katedros aikštė. Hotels are mostly dotted around the central area or its fringes.

INFORMATION
Travellers' Information

The friendly Lithuanian Youth Hostels people run a year-round, budget-travel information office (fax 260 631) in room 407, Kauno gatvė 1A, 400 metres from the rail and bus stations. The postal address is PO Box 12, 2000 Vilnius. Among other things, this office can make bookings for several hostels in Vilnius and around Lithuania (including in Kaunas, Palanga, Juodkrantė, Aukštaitija National Park, Molėtai and Jūžintai); help you set up bike or canoe trips; and give advice on ways of crossing to/from Poland, the Kaliningrad Region or Belarus.

The Lithuanian Travellers' Union (☎ 627 118), at Didžioji gatvė 11, is a nongovernment organisation offering 'information and consultation on various aspects of travelling in Lithuania'. It organises hiking, cycling, boating and camping trips, and its members favour 'ecologically clean rivers, lakes and forests'. It has branches in many provincial towns and may be able to help with accommodation, too.

Money

Check exchange rates and commissions before you part with your money. Balticbank at Gedimino prospektas 15 had good rates for cash. It's open from 9.30 am to 1 pm and 2 to 3.30 pm Monday to Friday. The exchange desk in the central post office at Gedimino prospektas 7 also has reasonable rates – open from 8 am to 8 pm Monday to Friday, and 11 am to 7 pm Saturday, Sunday and holidays. You can change travellers' cheques at Lietuvos Bankas at Gedimino prospektas 6, from 9 am to 12.30 pm Monday to Friday, or Vilniaus Bankas at Gedimino prospektas 14, from 9 am to 12.30 pm and 2.30 to 5 pm Monday to Friday. Another Vilniaus Bankas building, next door at No 12, is open the same hours, and will give cash advances to Visa card holders (charges at the time of writing are US$2.75 plus 0.33%). Bankas Hermis at Jogailos gatvė 9/1 has average rates but, in my experience, short queues and good hours – 9 am to 8 pm Monday to Friday, and 9 am to 5 pm Saturday. The exchange desk in the Hotel Lietuva is open from 9 am to 3 pm Saturday and Sunday, as well as longish weekday hours. There are also exchange desks at the airport and railway station and in some shops and other hotels.

Post & Telecommunications

The central post office (Centrinis Paštas) at Gedimino prospektas 7, open from 8 am to 8 pm Monday to Friday and 11 am to 7 pm Saturday and Sunday, has telephone and telegram facilities, too. But the Telecommunications Centre at Vilniaus gatvė 33 is a better place to go for phone calls or telegrams – it's always open for phone calls to anywhere in the world and from 8 am to 11 pm daily for telegrams. When queues are short (which they usually are) you only have to wait a few minutes for your call. The Telecommunications Centre, along with the Lietuva and Draugystė hotels and one or two other places, also has international direct-dial card phones – you can buy cards on the spot. But these calls were dearer than the regular rates, at about 7 litų a minute to Western Europe. In addition, the centre has working pay phones for calls within Vilnius and inter-city pay phones (*tarpmiestiniai telefonai automatai*) for calls to elsewhere in Lithuania and to the other Baltic states and the ex-USSR. Like post offices, it also has a window selling the coins and tokens (*žetonas*) that you need for these calls.

Also at the Telecommunications Centre are post, telex and fax services. The fax desk, open from 10 am to noon and 2 to 4 pm Monday to Friday, charges 20 litų for three minutes to Western Europe for immediate transmission or 6.50 litų for same-day transmission. Rates to North America are about double these. You can also receive faxes cheaply here. The Hotel Lietuva service bureau has a fax service open longer hours, but it's about three times the cost. The best fax service is said to be at the Telegraph & Data Transmission Centre (Telegrafo ir duomenų perdavimo centras) at Universiteto gatvė 14 – open 24 hours, seven days a week.

There are international express-mail services for letters or parcels at the post office at Vokiečių gatvė 7, and at DHL, Barboros Radvilaitės gatvė 1.

The telephone code for Vilnius (for calls originating from elsewhere within Lithuania) is 22.

Foreign Diplomatic Missions
Some embassies are still looking for permanent buildings, so may move from the addresses given here. Some countries cover Lithuania from their embassies in nearby countries, including: Australia, Austria, Iceland and Spain from Copenhagen; New Zealand from Moscow; Ireland from Warsaw; the Netherlands from Stockholm; and South Africa from Helsinki.

Canada
    Embassy Office: Hotel Draugystė, Čiurlionio gatvė 84 (☎ 661 731)
Denmark
    Embassy: Kosciuškos gatvė 36 (☎ 628 028)

Estonia
    Embassy: Turniškių gatvė 20 (☎ 769 848)
Finland
    Embassy: Klaipėdos gatvė 6 (☎ 221 621)
France
    Embassy: Daukanto aikštė 3/8 (☎ 222 979)
Germany
    Embassy: Sierakausko gatvė 24 (☎ 660 188)
Italy
    Embassy: Žygimantu gatvė 9 (☎ 661 751)
Latvia
    Embassy: Tumo-Vaižganto gatvė 2 (☎ 220 558)
Norway
    Embassy: Poškos gatvė 59 (☎ 732 553)
Poland
    Embassy: Aušros Vartų gatvė 7 (☎ 224 444)
Russia
    Embassy: Juozapavičiaus gatvė 11 (☎ 351 763)
Sweden
    Embassy: Jogailos gatvė 10 (☎ 226 467)
UK
    Embassy: Antakalnio gatvė 2 (☎ 222 070)
USA
    Embassy: Akmenų gatvė 6 (☎ 223 031)

Travel Agencies
Several travel agencies in Vilnius offer outbound bookings as well as accommodation, tours and other services within Lithuania and the other Baltic states.

Lithuanian Tours (☎ 353 931, ☎ & fax 351 815), at Šeimyniškių gatvė 18, can book you into some of the more expensive Vilnius hotels at short notice if you're having problems finding a room. Balticorp (☎ 220 303, fax 226 368), at Gedimino prospektas 26-217, specialises in air tickets to worldwide destinations. Other agents which may be helpful include Liturimex (☎ 226 063, fax 621 770) at Gedimino prospektas 14; TL Travel (☎ 635 244, fax 262 276) in Room 510, Kauno gatvė 1A; and Okto-Piligrimas (☎ 630 706, fax 224 952) at Ševčenkos gatvė 19.

Media
The best single investment you can make in Vilnius is a copy of the English-language city guide *Vilnius In Your Pocket*, updated five times a year, which is as good as any publication of this type I've seen anywhere in the world. It's sold at hotels, bookshops and various other spots around town and

LITHUANIA

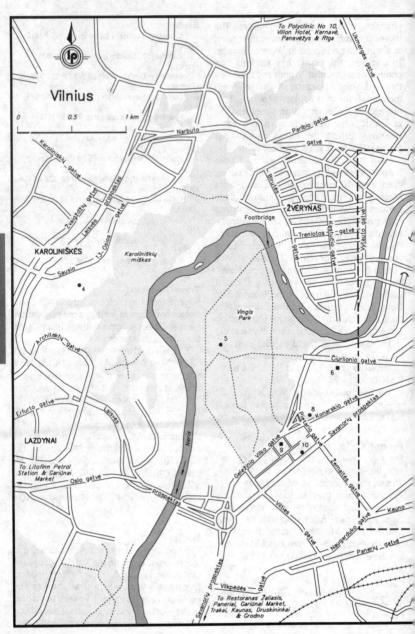

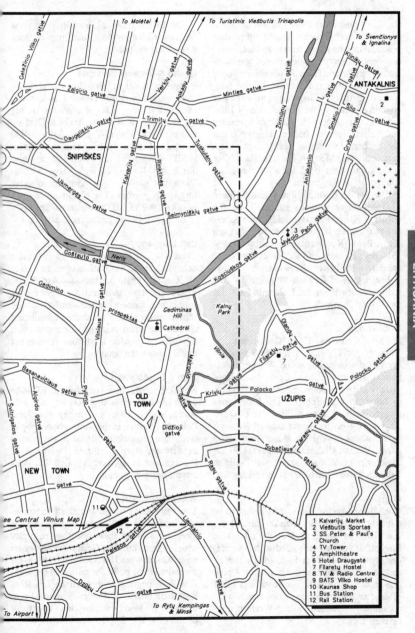

LITHUANIA

1 Kalvarijų Market
2 Viešbutis Sportas
3 SS Peter & Paul's
   Church
4 TV Tower
5 Amphitheatre
6 Hotel Draugystė
7 Filaretų Hostel
8 TV & Radio Centre
9 BATS Vilko Hostel
10 Kaunas Shop
11 Bus Station
12 Rail Station

shouldn't cost more than 5 litai – excellent value for comprehensive and up-to-date practical info on places to stay and eat, entertainment, money exchange, travel, communications and more. Even the photos are good! The *Baltic News* is a weekly Vilnius-published English-language newspaper covering events in the Baltic states – Lithuania's equivalent of the *Baltic Independent* and *Baltic Observer*, both of which you can also get here. *Lithuanian Weekly* covers Lithuania only. See Media in Facts for the Visitor at the front of the book for a little more on some of these publications.

The British Council library in the House of Teachers at Vilniaus gatvė 39, on the corner of Klaipėdos gatvė, has British papers and magazines. If you want to buy Western press, Penki Kontinentai bookshop, also at Vilniaus gatvė 39, and the Hotel Draugystė are two of the better places to try.

For details of English-language TV and radio broadcasts see the Lithuania Facts for the Visitor chapter.

Bookshops

Penki Kontinentai (Five Continents), at Vilniaus gatvė 39, is a foreign-languages bookshop also selling some Western newspapers and magazines. Other bookshops usually sell a few maps, guides, photo essays or other titles in English. The better ones include the bookshops at Pilies gatvė 10 and 22; the one on the south side of Šv Jono gatvė, about 50 metres along from Pilies gatvė; Vaga at Gedimino prospektas 50, on the corner of Vilniaus gatvė; and Žinija at Vilniaus gatvė 22, which has some bargains.

Maps

Every time I go to Vilnius there seems to be a newly published city map on sale. I have six different ones, several with keys in English. If you're confronted with a choice, one with a street index is decidedly useful, and date of publication is a key factor – pick one from 1991 or later, as Soviet-era maps often contain deliberate errors which were presumably intended to keep Western spies on their toes.

The Pilies gatvė 22 bookshop had the *Lietuvos Keliai* national road map in stock when I last visited.

Health & Medical Services

Vilnius tap water smells pretty vile at times, and I suggest you don't drink it unless you can boil it first. Two pharmacies selling Western medicines are Apotheke at Didžioji gatvė 13 and Pharm-Tech at Šeimyniškių gatvė 21. The only private clinic in Vilnius is SBT Private Clinic (☎ 468 583) in polyclinic No 10 at Šeškinės gatvė 24, off Ukmergės gatvė in the northern suburbs. English is spoken. There's an emergency hospital (☎ 269 262) at Šiltnamių kelias 29 in Lazdynai. For an ambulance, call 03.

Left Luggage

There's a left-luggage room in the main ticket hall at the bus station, open from 6 to 10.30 am, 11 am to 3.30 pm, and 4 to 11 pm. There are also two left-luggage rooms *(saugojimo kamera)* at the nearby railway station, either side of the stairs immediately outside the main entrance. Between them they should provide a 24-hour service but double-check the opening hours.

Film & Photography

Kodak Express, in a courtyard at Sv Jono gatvė 13, does one-hour processing and sells some Kodak film and other supplies. Polaroid Express, in the Vilnius bookshop at Gedimino prospektas 13 and in the central department store (Centrinė Universalinė Parduotuvė) at Ukmergės gatvė 16, does instant passport photos.

WALKING TOUR

You can't hope to get round all the main places of interest in Vilnius on one walk, as there are a lot of them and they're pretty widely spread out. The **Gedimino Tower** on top of **Gediminas Hill** (Gedimino kalnas) is a good starting point for an initial exploration. Walk up the path through the park from **Katedros aikštė** (Cathedral Square). From the top of the tower there are views over most of the city: the Old Town stretches to the

Top: Clock tower & Cathedral, Vilnius, Lithuania (CR)
Left: Gedimino tower, Vilnius, Lithuania (CR)
Right: Old Town Hall, Kaunas, Lithuania (GZ)

Top: Hill of Crosses, Šiauliai, Lithuania (JN)
Bottom: Canoeing in Aukštaitija National Park, Lithuania (LG)

south, Gedimino prospektas cuts west through the newer part of the centre, **Three Crosses Hill** (Trijų kryžių kalnas) stands to the east, and the river stretches north.

From here, descend to Katedros aikštė and have a look in the **cathedral**, then dive into the Old Town. Pilies gatvė, Didžioji gatvė, and Aušros Vartų gatvė form the main single axis of the Old Town, but the essence of exploring it is to ramble as the fancy takes you, picking a few points of interest from the sections that follow.

Try to save some time after your initial wander in the Old Town for a walk along Gedimino prospektas, through the newer part of central Vilnius to the **parliament**. From here you might even go for a stroll in **Vingis Park** (Vingio parkas) or cross the river to the north to visit the **State Museum**. Another area you shouldn't miss (but you'll probably have to save it for another day) is north and east of the cathedral – where you'll find museums, Three Crosses Hill and **SS Peter & Paul's Church**.

GEDIMINAS HILL & KATEDROS AIKŠTĖ

Gediminas Hill (Gedimino kalnas) and Katedros aikštė (Cathedral Square), below it, are the focal points of the city. The Old Town stretches to their south; Gedimino prospektas leads west across the New Town.

Gediminas Hill

This mound, rising 44 metres behind the cathedral, was the natural bastion on which early Vilnius was founded. Walk up the path through the park from Katedros aikštė. The **Gedimino Tower** (Gedimino bokštas), the single, brick tower flying the national flag atop the hill was part of the 14th century defences of the upper of the two Vilnius castles. On top of the tower is an **observation platform**. Inside is the **Vilnius Castle Museum** (Vilnius pilies muziejus), open 11 am to 5 pm daily except Tuesday, with exhibits on old Vilnius that show you the extent of the castles, of which little remains now. The lower castle was round the western foot of the hill, and the cathedral was included within it.

Katedros Aikštė

Katedros aikštė, the open space at the foot of Gediminas Hill dominated by the white bulk of Vilnius Cathedral, was the scene of most of the mass gatherings during Lithuania's independence campaign. In the 19th century, markets and fairs were held here. Before that, the square and the cathedral were within the precincts of the lower castle, destroyed by the Russians in the early 19th century. A moat ran round what's now the square's perimeter – roughly where Vrublevskio and Šventaragio streets are today – and ships could sail almost up to the cathedral door. Within the moat was a ring of walls and towers, the only remaining parts of which are the **clock tower** standing alone near the west end of the cathedral (a favourite rendezvous point in the city) and a few excavated remains behind the cathedral.

Off the east end of the square, bordered by the little Vilnia River, is a 600-metre stretch of **parks**, some of which are surprisingly little frequented.

Cathedral This most important national symbol was used only as a picture gallery during the Soviet era. It was reconsecrated in 1989, and mass is now said in Lithuanian at least five times daily.

The site was originally used for the worship of Perkūnas, the old Lithuanian thunder god, and a pagan altar still stands somewhere in the basement. The first wooden cathedral was built here in the 13th or 14th century. The present grander edifice was originally constructed under Grand Duke Vytautas in the 15th century. It was initially in Gothic style, but has been rebuilt so often in pursuit of changing architectural fashions that its old form is unrecognisable. The most important restoration was done between 1783 and 1801, when the outside was completely redone in the classical style that remains today. The statues on the south side facing the square are of Lithuanian dukes, those on the north side are of apostles and saints. The interior retains more of its original aspect, though the entrances to the side chapels were harmonised in the late 18th century.

The chief showpiece is the **Chapel of St Kazimieras** at the east end of the south aisle, which was created in 1623-36 with a Baroque cupola, coloured marble and granite on the walls, white stucco sculptures, and fresco scenes from the life of St Kazimieras, the country's patron saint, who was a 15th century Lithuanian grand duke. The remains of several members of the old Lithuanian royalty and high nobility lie beneath the chapel.

Museums

The **Lithuanian History & Ethnography Museum** (Lietuvos Istorijos ir Etnografijos muziejus), in a long, low, old arsenal building 100 metres north of the cathedral, takes you from prehistoric amber ornaments to the pre-WW II independence period. There are good sections on costume and folk art. It's open 11 am to 6 pm daily except Tuesday.

The **Decorative & Applied Arts Museum** (Taikomosios dailės muziejus), in another old arsenal at Arsenalo gatvė 3 at the northern foot of Gediminas Hill, has an exceptional collection of furniture, tapestries, jewellery and ceramics from the 15th century onwards. Don't miss the 20th century work upstairs. The museum is open from 11 am to 7 pm, except Monday and Tuesday.

OLD TOWN

The area stretching 1½ km south from Katedros aikštė was built up in the 15th and 16th centuries, and its narrow, winding streets, hidden courtyards and amazing number of old churches retain the feel of bygone centuries. It's an area to come back to and wander in several times if you can: you'll find something new and surprising every time. Some buildings have been polished to a pristine state they never knew in the past; others remain evocatively dilapidated. The Old Town's main axis is along Pilies gatvė, Didžioji gatvė, and the northern half of Aušros Vartų gatvė. Its approximate boundary, starting from Katedros aikštė, runs along Stuokos-Gucevičiaus, Liejyklos, Vilniaus, Trakų, Pylimo, Bazilijonų, Šv Dvasios, Bokšto, Maironio, Barboros Radvilaitės, and Šventaragio streets – an area of roughly three-quarters of a sq km.

Pilies Gatvė

Pedestrianised Pilies gatvė (Castle Street) is the main entrance to the Old Town from Katedros aikšte, with a little gaggle of bright tourist shops. Until the 19th century the street was divided from what's now the square by the lower castle wall which ran across its north end. Only a gate in the wall connected the two. Notice the 15th to 17th century brickwork of Nos 4, 12 and 16 towards the north end of the street.

Vilnius University

The central buildings of the university form most of the block between Pilies gatvė and Universiteto gatvė. Founded by Jesuits in 1579 on the instigation of the Polish king, Stefan Batory, in the Counter-Reformation, the university was run by Jesuits for two centuries and became one of the greatest centres of Polish learning. It produced many notable scholars in the 17th and early 19th centuries, but was closed by the Russians in 1832 and didn't reopen till 1919. Today it has about 14,000 students.

The 12 linked courtyards can be entered by numerous passages and gates from the surrounding streets. The southern gate on Šv Jono gatvė brings you into the Didysis or Skarga Courtyard, where you'll find **St John's Church** (Šv Jono bažnyčia), which was founded in 1387 well before the university arrived. It now has an outstanding 18th century Baroque main facade and a fine interior. In the Soviet era it was used as a 'museum of scientific thought'. Its 17th and 18th century **bell tower**, standing separately on the south side of the courtyard, is a feature in the Vilnius skyline. The galleries around three sides of this courtyard are in the early 17th century Mannerist style which formed the transition from Renaissance to Baroque.

The arch through the 16th century building opposite St John's leads to the Pocobuto Courtyard, with an old two-domed **observ-**

atory whose late 18th century facade is adorned with reliefs of the zodiac. The other main courtyard, reached through the passage from the north side of the Didysis Courtyard, is the Sarbievijus Courtyard. Some of the halls and chambers on the east side of this courtyard have interesting artwork – among them the 1st-floor lobby of the Lithuanian Studies Centre with modern murals by Petras Repšys, partly based on early pagan Lithuanian motifs. Each panel depicts traditions associated with a different month of the year.

Daukanto Aikštė

The exit from the university's Sarbievijus Courtyard to Universiteto gatvė brings you out opposite the former **Bishops' Palace** on Daukanto aikštė, rebuilt in the classical Russian-Empire style early in the 19th century. Once the residence of Vilnius bishops, the palace was later used by Russian governors and, during the Napoleonic Wars, by both Napoleon when he was advancing on Moscow and by his Russian adversary, General Mikhail Kutuzov, when he was chasing Napoleon back to Paris. In Soviet times it became the Art Workers' Culture Palace (Menininkų rūmai), and on my last visit it also housed the French Embassy – though the embassy was expected to move to another Old Town building where the writer Stendhal once spent a few nights.

At the west end of Daukanto aikštė is a pleasant, secluded public garden. The Baroque **Holy Cross Church** (Šv Kryžiaus bažnyčia) at the north-west corner of the square is used as an organ-concert hall, the Mažoji baroko salė.

East of Pilies Gatvė

Mickiewicz Museum The old rooms of the Polish Romantic poet Adam Mickiewicz (1798-1855), at Bernardinų gatvė 11, are now the Adam Mickiewicz Memorial Apartment, open Friday from 2 to 6 pm and Saturday from 10 am to 2 pm. Mickiewicz grew up near Vilnius and studied at its university from 1815 to 1819 before being exiled, in 1824, for anti-Russian activities. The exhibits trace his life and career. Much

of his work, which inspired Polish nationalists through the 19th century, is set in the Vilnius region. It's a measure of how intertwined Lithuanian and Polish history are that Mickiewicz's poem, *Pan Tadeusz*, which ranks as Poland's national Romantic epic masterpiece, begins: 'Lithuania, my fatherland...'!

St Michael's & St Ann's Churches Opposite the east end of Bernardinų gatvė is the 17th century St Michael's Church (Šv Mykolo bažnyčia) at Volano gatvė 13, now an architecture museum. Members of the noble Sapieha family, which had it built, are mummified in the vaults beneath, and it's possible to see them.

Across Maironio gatvė stands the fine, brick, 16th century St Ann's Church (Šv Onos bažnyčia), the jewel of Lithuanian Gothic architecture with its sweeping curves and delicate pinnacles. Napoleon reportedly wished he could take it back to Paris with him. The buildings adjoining St Ann's, including the austere church behind it, were part of a mostly 16th century **Bernardine monastery** (like St Michael's) and also part of the Old Town's defensive wall.

Didžioji Gatvė

Rotušės Aikštė Didžioji gatvė (Main Street) is the southward continuation of Pilies gatvė. Towards its south end it widens into Rotušės aikštė (Town Hall Square), which was, for a long time, one of the centres of Vilnius life. Markets were held here from the 15th century, when this was a crossroads from which roads led to Moscow, Kraków and Rīga. The old Town Hall in the middle of the square – now the **Lithuanian Art Museum** (Lietuvos dailės muziejus), showing 19th century Lithuanian work – has stood since at least the early 16th century, but its classical exterior dates from 1785-99. The **Contemporary Art Centre** (Šiuolaukinio Meno Centras), behind the Town Hall at Vokiečių gatvė 2, displays avant-garde art – for which it has attracted hostility from established or conservative artists who feel

LITHUANIA

they are neglected – and also has a sculpture garden, café, and arts and crafts shop.

St Kazimieras' Church Vilnius' oldest Baroque church, the large St Kazimieras' Church (Šv Kazimiero bažnyčia), almost opposite the Astorija hotel, was built by the Jesuits in 1604-15. Its dome and cross-shaped ground plan, influenced by the Jesuits' Il Jesu Church in Rome, defined a new style for 17th century Lithuanian churches. Under tsarist rule St Kazimieras' – which is dedicated to Lithuania's patron saint – was taken over by the Russian Orthodox Church and given an onion dome (removed in 1942); under Soviet rule it spent two decades as a museum of atheism.

Aušros Vartų Gatvė

North End Aušros Vartų gatvė leads south from St Kazimieras'. At No 73 near its north (lower) end, on the west side, there's a fine late-Baroque archway known as the **Basilian Gates**, which forms the entrance to the decrepit Basilian monastery complex. On the east side of the street, just above the 16th century house which now contains the Med-ininkai restaurant, is the big, pink, domed, 17th century **Holy Spirit Church** (Šv Dvasios cerkvė), the chief Russian Orthodox church of Lithuania. The amazingly preserved bodies of three 14th century martyrs – SS Anthony, Ivan and Eustachius – lie in a chamber at the foot of a flight of steps in front of the altar. The Catholic **St Teresa's Church** (Šv Teresės bažnyčia), on the east side of the street above the Holy Spirit Church, is early Baroque (1635-50) outside and more elaborate late Baroque inside.

Gates of Dawn At the top of Aušros Vartų gatvė, the Gates of Dawn (Aušros Vartai) are, in fact, themselves a single gate tower – the only one of the original nine in the town wall that's still intact. This was once the start of the Moscow road. Shortly before the gate, a door on the east side of the street gives on to a staircase which leads up to a little 18th century chapel directly over the gate arch. This houses a supposedly miracle-working

icon of the Virgin, reputed to have been souvenired from the Crimea by Grand Duke Algirdas in 1363, though more probably dating from the 16th century. It is particularly revered by the Polish community, to whom the chapel is known as the Ostrabramska. It attracts a constant bustle of people coming, going and saying prayers. The icon was repainted in the 17th or 18th century. Notice the quite different appearances of the northern and southern faces of the tower. One of the few surviving lengths of the Old Town wall leads east from here.

Artillery Bastion

If you follow the old wall round from the Gates of Dawn on to Šv Dvasios gatvė, then continue north, you reach the Artillery Bastion (Artilerijos bastėja) at Bokšto gatvė 20. This 17th century fortification, with a collection of old weaponry and armour, is open as a museum from 11 am to 7 pm daily, except Tuesday.

Jewish Vilnius

One of Europe's most important Jewish communities once flourished in the Old Town of Vilnius. A few years ago there was hardly any outward sign of this, so thoroughly had the Soviet authorities obliterated its memory, after the Nazis had annihilated the Jewish community itself. Between the 1950s and '70s even the city's Jewish graves were desecrated: tombstones were used as paving stones and one Jewish cemetery became the Žalgiris football stadium. Since independence the city council has started returning tombstones to the existing Jewish community and has promised to build some memorials. A national Jewish Museum has opened, and information on Vilnius' Jewish past is much easier to come by.

History Jews lived in Vilnius almost from its founding by Gediminas, who invited them here. Their numbers apparently reached 3000, in a city population of 15,000, in the mid-17th century. In the 18th century it was a Vilnius rabbi and scholar, Gaon, who led the opposition to the widespread Jewish mystical movement Hassidism. In the 19th century the Vilnius Jewish community grew, and the city became a centre of development of the European Jewish language, Yiddish. The famous landscape artist Isaak Levitan and, later, the sculptor Jacques Lipchitz were Vilnius Jews. Despite emigration, the city's Jewish population peaked on the eve of WW I at nearly 100,000 out of a total of 235,000.

Between the world wars, with Vilnius a provincial outpost of Poland, the Jewish community of 60,000 to 80,000 faced discrimination and poverty, but Vilnius blossomed into the Jewish cultural hub of eastern Europe. In 1925 it was chosen ahead of the other Yiddish centres, Warsaw and New York, as the headquarters of the Yiddish-language scientific-research institute YIVO (which stood west of the Old Town on what's now Vivulskio gatvė, opposite the end of Šviesos gatvė). Jewish schools, libraries, literature and theatre flourished. There were over 100 synagogues and prayer houses and six daily Jewish newspapers.

Jewish Quarter & Ghettos The Jewish quarter lay in the streets west of Didžioji gatvė. Today the street names Žydų ('Jews') and Gaono are among the few explicit reminders of this. The main synagogue, founded in the 16th century, and its famous library stood just about where the west end of Žydų gatvė is now, with a nursery school on its site.

Virtually all Vilnius' Jewish organisations, except communist ones, were dissolved when the Soviet Union took over eastern Poland in September 1939. Many Jewish leaders were deported. Meanwhile Polish Jews fleeing the Nazis arrived here as refugees. Vilnius fell to the Nazis two days after their invasion of the USSR on 22 June 1941. About 35,000 Jews – almost half those in the city – were murdered at the Paneriai death camp (see the Around Vilnius section) in the next three months, before a ghetto was established in a small area north of Vokiečių gatvė, which was the heart of the Jewish quarter. This first ghetto was liquidated after

46 days and its inhabitants killed at Paneriai; a larger one, south of Vokiečių gatvė, lasted until the general liquidation of ghettos on Himmler's orders in 1943, when 26,000 people were killed at Paneriai and 8000 transported to Estonia. The single gate of the main ghetto stood at what's now the south end of Rūdininkų gatvė. About 6000 Vilnius Jews escaped, one way or another. Survivors say that Lithuanian sidekicks acted at least as cruelly and mercilessly in the Vilnius holocaust as their German masters.

The central reservation on Vokiečių gatvė and the roadway down its eastern side were created after WW II in place of buildings of the Jewish quarter which had stood there previously. The contrast between the old buildings on the west side of the street and the Stalin-era ones on the east is clear. Sources differ on whether the original buildings were destroyed by Nazi or Soviet hands.

Jewish Museum Today there are about 5000 or 6000 Jews in Vilnius, most newcomers since WW II. One of the few ghetto survivors still here has helped to found the admirable Lithuanian State Jewish Museum (Lietuvos valstybinis žydų muziejus) which currently has two sections near each other which both open from 10 am to 5 pm Monday to Friday. The branch at Pamėnkalnio gatvė 12 (actually up the first little street on the south side of Pamėnkalnio gatvė as you go from Pylimo gatvė) provides a general record (with many photographs) of Vilnius' Jewish history and the holocaust in Lithuania. The branch at Pylimo gatvė 4 contains relics of the great synagogue, blown up along with its adjoining library in 1944. The eventual aim is to open a bigger museum at Naugarduko gatvė 10/2.

Synagogue Modern Vilnius' only synagogue is at Pylimo gatvė 39. It was originally built in 1894 for the wealthy. It survived because the Nazis used it as a medical store.

Old Town – West
In case you hadn't realised the importance of the Church in bygone centuries, there are no

LITHUANIA

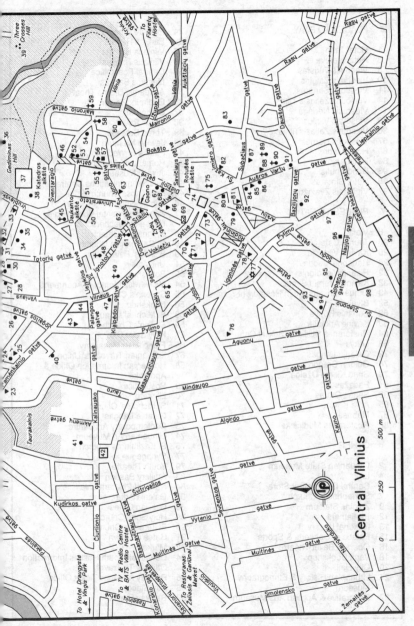

Central Vilnius

LITHUANIA

■ PLACES TO STAY

1	Hotel Taffo
3	Hotel Lietuva
5	Viešbutis Turistas
10	Viešbutis Žalgiris
11	Viešbutis Šarūnas
14	Viešbutis Žaliasis Tiltas
17	Viešbutis Neringa
19	Viešbutis Vilnius
30	Viešbutis ŽaliasisTiltas
57	Viešbutis Narutis
60	Hotel Mabre
80	Hotel Astorija
93	Bendrabutis
96	Hotel Gintaras
97	Viešbutis Žvaigždė

▼ PLACES TO EAT

8	Viola
23	Tauras Café
25	Kavinė Viktorija
28	Raudona-Juoda
32	Piceria Vidudienis
33	Kavinė Literatų Svetainė
43	Lithuanian Jersualem Restaurant
52	Blyninės
62	Senasis Rūsys
63	Kavinė Arkadija
64	Restoranas Stikliai & Stikliai Cafe
66	Lokys
72	Galerija Langas
76	Golden Dragon
78	Seno Kiemo Užeiga
81	Pasažas
82	Senas Grafas
85	Arka Kavinė
87	Idabasar
88	Restoranas Medininkai

OTHER

2	Lithuanian State Museum
4	LAL
6	Central Department Store
7	St Raphael's Church
9	Žalgiris Stadium
12	Parliament
13	National Library
15	Palace of Concerts & Sports
16	Opera & Ballet Theatre
18	Vaga Bookshop
20	City Hall
21	Lithuanian History & Ethnography Museum
22	Decorative & Applied Arts Museum

24	Pergalė Cinema
26	Bankas Hermis
27	Vilniaus Bankas
29	Vilniaus Bankas
31	Central Post Office
34	Lietuvos Bankas
35	Academic Drama Theatre
36	Gedimino Tower
37	Cathedral
38	Clock Tower
39	Three Crosses
40	Jewish Museum
41	Palace of Weddings
42	Romanovs' Church
43	Jewish Museum
44	Telecommunications Centre
45	Holy Cross Church
46	Vilbara Shop
47	Penki Kontinentai Bookshop & House of Teachers
48	St Ignatius' Church
49	St Catherine's Church
50	Bishops' Palace
51	University
53	Bookshop
54	Mickiewicz Memorial Apartment
55	St John's Church
56	Bookshop
58	St Michael's Church
59	St Ann's Church
61	Holy Spirit Church
65	Franciscan Monastery
67	Lithuanian Travellers' Union
68	Norwegian Information Office & Apotheke
69	Post Office
70	Litinterp
71	St Nicholas' Church
72	Galerija Langas
73	Contemporary Art Centre
74	Lithuanian Art Museum
75	St Kazimieras' Church
77	Synagogue
79	Youth Theatre
83	Artillery Bastion
84	National Philharmonia
85	Galerija Arka
86	Basilian Gates
89	Holy Spirit Church
90	St Teresa's Church
91	Gates of Dawn
92	Market
94	Lithuanian Youth Hostels Information Office & TL Travel
95	Railway Advance Ticket Office
98	Bus Station
99	Railway Station

less than four sizeable Catholic church-and-monastery complexes, all created by different monastic orders, within 200 metres of the corner of Vilniaus and Dominikonų streets. All date chiefly from the 17th and 18th century Baroque era. Among them, the **Holy Spirit Church** (Šv Dvasios bažnyčia) at the corner of Dominikonų and Šv Ignoto streets is now one of Vilnius' chief Polish churches. Once attached to a Dominican monastery, it has a splendid gold and white interior. The twin towers of **St Catherine's Church** (Šv Kotrynos bažnyčia), once part of a Benedictine monastery at Vilniaus gatvė 30, are a Vilnius landmark. The other monasteries are the **Jesuit Noviciate** with **St Ignatius' Church** (Šv Ignoto bažnyčia) on Šv Ignoto gatvė and the **Franciscan monastery** on Trakų gatvė. The fine little **St Nicholas' Church** (Šv Mikalojaus bažnyčia), on Šv Mikalojaus gatvė, is much older – it's Lithuania's oldest Gothic church, dating from 1320 (before Lithuania's conversion) and was founded by German merchants.

EAST OF GEDIMINAS HILL
Three Crosses
The white Three Crosses (Trys kryžiai) overlooking the Old Town from Three Crosses Hill (Trijų kryžių kalnas), just east of Gediminas Hill, are old Vilnius landmarks. Crosses are said to have stood here since the 17th century in memory of three monks who were martyred by crucifixion on this spot. The current crosses, erected in 1989, are replicas of the three which were knocked down and buried by the Soviet authorities after WW II. You can walk up to them through Kalnų Park from Kosciuškos gatvė.

SS Peter & Paul's Church
The outside of SS Peter & Paul's Church (Šv Petro ir Povilo bažnyčias) at the east end of Kosciuškos gatvė is plain, but the interior is a sea of sparkling-white Baroque stucco which has been moulded into thousands of sculptures and reliefs of plants, animals, and real and mythical people – broken here and there by touches of gilt, paintings and col-

oured statues. Most of the decoration was done by Italian sculptors between 1675 and 1704. The church was founded by the Lithuanian noble, Mykolas Kazimieras Pacas, whose tomb is on the right of the porch as you enter. If you don't want to walk, trolleybus No 2, 3 or 4 will take you there from the Gedimino stop on Vrublevskio gatvė, near the cathedral.

NEW TOWN
The area known as the New Town (naujamiestis) stretches 1½ to two km west of the cathedral and the Old Town. It was mostly built up in the 19th century.

Gedimino Prospektas
The main street of modern Vilnius runs west from the cathedral to the river. Its 1¾-km length is dotted with shops, a theatre, banks, hotels, offices and a few park squares. Laid out in 1852, it has had 11 name changes since, reflecting the nationalities and political tendencies of Vilnius' rulers. The Russian tsarist authorities named it after St George, the Poles after Mickiewicz, the Soviet rulers first after Stalin, then Lenin.

Savivaldybės Aikštė The existing city hall is on the east side of this square at the corner of Vilniaus gatvė; government offices occupy the north side. Above Vilniaus gatvė, down towards the river, is the large modern Opera & Ballet Theatre.

Lukiškių Aikštė A number of government buildings surround Lukiškių aikštė, which used to have a statue of Lenin in the centre. The building facing this square on the corner of Tumo-Vaižganto gatvė and Gedimino prospektas used to be the headquarters of the Lithuanian KGB (and during the Nazi occupation, the Gestapo). Part of it is due to be opened up as a Museum of Lithuanian Genocide.

Parliament Only a few slabs now remain as reminders of the barricades erected at the west end of Gedimino prospektas in January

LITHUANIA

Barricades near Lithuania's Parliament, 1991

1991 to protect Lithuania's parliament (Aukščiausiosios Tarybos rūmai) from marauding Soviet troops. Thousands of people gathered inside and outside the building on 13 January 1991, just as they gathered at the TV & Radio Centre and the TV tower. Inside parliament, President Landsbergis declared: 'This could be the last session of the Parliament of the Lithuanian Republic. We have done everything we can and now we must stand with our people and see it to the end.' In the event, parliament was not attacked, but one of those present died of heart failure when the attack on the TV tower began. The barricades, and the trenches to the north of the parliament building, were left in place until December 1992.

The satellite dish on the roof of parliament was set up in January 1991 to bring US TV reports on Lithuania to the people of Vilnius after Soviet troops had taken over the Lithuanian TV installations. For over a year afterwards, parliamentary security guards used it to help relay British and German TV programmes into Vilnius homes. Eventually protests from the Catholic Church over the supposedly obscene content of some Western films put a stop to this. The classical building next to parliament is the national library.

Trolleybus No 7 from the railway station, or No 3 from the Gedimino stop on Vrublevskio gatvė near the cathedral, will take you along Jasinskio gatvė, a block south of Gedimino prospektas. For parliament, get off at the Tiltas stop just before the river or the Liubarto stop just after it.

South of Gedimino Prospektas

There are good views from the Soviet-era **Palace of Weddings** (Santuokų rūmai) in the park off Kalinausko gatvė at the top of Taurakalnis, the hill climbing up to the south of Gedimino prospektas. Just south of the Palace of Weddings, on Basanavičiaus gatvė, is the **Romanovs' Church**, an interesting Russian Orthodox church built in 1913. A little further down Basanavičiaus gatvė, at No 42, is a daily flower market.

Vingis Park

Just over a km south-west of parliament, at the west end of Čiurlionio gatvė, is the pleasant, wooded Vingis Park (Vingio parkas). It's surrounded on three sides by the Neris and has a big stage which is the usual setting for the Lithuanian Song Festival. If you don't want to walk all the way from the city centre, take trolleybus No 7 from the railway station or No 3 from the Gedimino stop on Vrublevskio gatvė near the cathedral to the Kęstučio stop (the second after the bridge over the river), then walk over the footbridge from the end of Treniotos gatvė.

TV & Radio Centre

Like the more distant TV Tower, the Television & Radio Centre at the corner of Konarskio gatvė and Pietario gatvė, near the south-east edge of Vingis Park, was stormed by Soviet tanks and troops in the early hours of 13 January 1991. One man was killed. Groups of wooden crosses stand outside the centre as memorials to the martyrs of Lithuania's independence campaign.

LITHUANIA

NORTH OF THE RIVER

St Raphael's Church (Šv Rapolo bažnyčia), on the north side of the Žaliasis tiltas (Green Bridge) over the Neris, has quite a fine Baroque interior. Beyond the Hotel Lietuva on Ukmergės gatvė is the **Lithuanian State Museum** (Lietuvos valstybės muziejus) with many very interesting exhibits including, on my last visit, collections of Lithuanian regional folk costumes; carved wooden crosses, saints, suns and weathercocks from the 19th and early 20th centuries (a major folk art form); and displays on Lithuanians in America, the anti-Nazi and anti-Soviet resistance in the 1940s and '50s, Lithuanians exiled in Siberia, and the historic events of 1991. The museum is open from 11 am to 7 pm daily, except Monday and Tuesday. In the Soviet era this was the Revolution Museum of the Lithuanian Soviet Socialist Republic!

TV TOWER

Vilnius' 326-metre-high Television Tower (Televizijos bokštas) is in the suburb of Karoliniškės, across the river west of Vingis Park. Here, on 13 January 1991, Soviet tanks, armoured personnel carriers and troops killed 12 people and wounded many more as they fought through the crowd which had gathered to defend the tower after the troops' disruptive activities of the previous days. Lithuanian TV kept broadcasting until the troops came through the tower door. Its director announced: 'The tower and studios are being attacked by the Red Army. But we will celebrate victory in the end.' A few carved wooden crosses now stand as memorials to the victims.

The tower is visible from parts of the city centre, but if you want to get right up to it, take trolleybus No 16 from the railway station or No 11 from Lukiškių aikštė to the Televizijos Bokštas stop on Laisvės prospektas. The tower is on Sausio 13-Osios gatvė (13 January Street) which is still marked as Sudervės gatvė on many maps. A visit here also takes you into the heart of some of Vilnius' Soviet-era high-rise suburbs.

ART GALLERIES

There are many galleries in Vilnius. Work in most of them is for sale but you're quite free just to look. What's on show ranges from 'tourist' art to serious avant-garde work. Lithuanian and some foreign avant-garde artists are exhibited at the Contemporary Art Centre (Šiuolaukinio Meno Centras) at Vokiečių gatvė 2 in the Old Town. Some of the other higher-quality galleries are Langas at Ašmenos gatvė 8; Arka at Aušros Vartų gatvė 7; Vartai at Vilniaus gatvė 39 (in the House of Teachers); and the Russian Gallery at Bokšto gatvė 4/2. The Photographic Society gallery at Didžioji gatvė 19 has some interesting shows, too.

GARIŪNAI

Gariūnai is the big free-for-all market held daily, except Monday, up to about 11 am, just off the Kaunas road, on the western fringe of Vilnius. Poles are among the main traders and Gariūnai is where Lithuanians come to get things the shops don't sell – a fascinating insight into the country's real economy. Many of the goods are from China, Turkey and Poland – few are from the West. Minibuses marked 'Gariūnai' or 'Gariunų Turgus' ferry shoppers from the railway station approach road for 1 litas from early morning. A taxi is about 12 litų. In your own vehicle take a turning marked 'Lazdynai', 11 km along Savanorių prospektas from Vilnius centre; the market will soon come into view on your left; or head out of town along Oslo gatvė, which becomes Gariūnų gatvė, until you reach the market on your right.

FESTIVALS

Study *Vilnius In Your Pocket*, posters and other media in Vilnius for information on Vilnius' many festivals. Two festivals with an especially Lithuanian flavour are the Kaziukas crafts fair held around St Kazimieras' Day, 4 March, and the Skamba Skamba Kankliai folk music and dance festival in the old city in the last week of May.

PLACES TO STAY – BOTTOM END

There's already quite a range of accommodation choices in all price brackets, but new places are opening up all the time. *Vilnius In Your Pocket* keeps tabs on new developments.

Campsites

The *Turistinis Viešbutis Trinapolis* (see Places to Stay – middle) has some small summer bungalows mainly used by Polish and Russian groups, with shared toilets and showers. You might also be able to pitch a tent here.

Out of town *Rytų Kempingas* (☎ 22-544 287, fax 22-220 172) at Rukainiai, 25 km east of Vilnius just off the Minsk road, has three or four-person cabins, space for tents, and a café. It's open in summer only.

Hostels & Colleges

Lithuanian Youth Hostels (Lietuvos Jaunimo Nakvynės Namai) (☎ 756 650, fax 260 631) of PO Box 12, Vilnius 2000, runs what it calls the *Green Shelter Camping Hostel* or the *Alternative Green Summer Hostel* (☎ 445 140) for low-budget foreign travellers from about April to September in Vingis Park. This excellent venture made a successful start in 1992 and 1993. Accommodation from June to August is in surprisingly comfortable six-person ex-Red-Army tents pitched near the song amphitheatre in the park. In the other months, it's in the amphitheatre building itself. Breakfast and bedding are provided. No charge is demanded, but a donation is requested and most people give about 12 to 15 litų a night.

What's special about this place is the organisers' positive passion for helping visitors explore Lithuania, particularly its countryside. They don't force anything on you but they can rent you bikes, help set up canoe trips in Aukštaitija National Park and tell you about several other cheap hostels around Lithuania. They can also take you for unusual and fascinating walks round Vilnius' Old Town, which are very well worth your time. See the Vingis Park section earlier in this chapter for trolleybus routes to the park. The Lithuanian Youth Hostels year-round

budget-travel information office in room 407, Kauno gatvė 1A, 400 metres from the rail and bus stations, can also help with bookings for other hostels in Vilnius and throughout Lithuania (see the Information section in this chapter).

The *Filaretų Hostel* (☎ 696 627 or 696 585) at Filaretų gatvė 17 in the Užupis area, just under one km east of the old city, has two to four-bed rooms with toilet and shower for 20 or 25 litų per person including breakfast. There are great views over the old city on the walk down from the hostel. Another good cheapie is the *Bendrabutis* (Hostel) in the building of the Lithuanian Energy & Electrification Board (Lietuvos Vyriausioji Gamybinė Energetikos ir Elektrifikacijos Valdyba) at Šv Stepono gatvė 11, 500 metres from the railway station. Don't ask me why, but foreign budget travellers are welcome here in three-bed rooms with their own TV, bathroom and kitchen, which cost just 8 litų for the room. This may be too good to last, and there aren't very many rooms – but so far, so good.

The *Vilko Hostel* or *BATS Hostel* (☎ 661 692, or 765 518 from 7 pm to 8 am only, fax 261 435) is at Geležinio Vilko gatvė 27, opposite the south edge of Vingis Park, about 2½ km west of the city centre. It's run by BATS (Baltic Accommodation & Travel Service) which also has places at Kaunas and near Trakai. You pay 40 litų (32 litų with an IYHF card) for a place in one of four three-bed rooms sharing showers and a toilet, on the ground floor of a block of flats. The rooms are OK – bare but big enough, with table, chairs and a cupboard – but the place is a bit damp and airless and there are no common areas for fellow travellers to get together. Still, it's comfortable enough and seemingly a secure place to lay your head. To get there take trolleybus No 15 or 16 from the railway station or No 4 or 12 from the Gedimino stop on Vrublevskio gatvė, near the cathedral, to the Kaunas stop by the Kaunas shop on Savanorių prospektas (the fifth stop from the station, the seventh or eighth from Gedimino). Walk north through the blocks of flats till you come out on

Geležinio Vilko gatvė, where the park will be on the far side of the road. Go to the reception window in the main lobby of No 27.

Vilnius University Student Representation (Vilniaus Universiteto Studentų Atstovybė or VUSA) (☎ 614 414, ☎ & fax 617 920), in the Pocobuto Courtyard of the main university buildings at Universiteto gatvė 3, can offer rooms in a university hotel or student block, about a 20-minute trolleybus ride from the centre. Most have their own toilet and basin and share a shower with two other rooms. Ask them to tell you about student eateries near where you'll be staying. Prices per person slide from around 45 litų for the first and second nights to around 35 litų for the 10th and later nights. VUSA would like to be contacted in advance but probably won't turn you away if you arrive at short notice.

Private Homes

Viešbutis Ekspresas (Express Hotel) (☎ 261 717), which operates from a kiosk beside the railway station taxi stand, offers rooms in private flats, mostly in the suburbs, for about 10 litų a head per night. *Nakvynė* (☎ 634 823, fax 637 732), at Kauno gatvė 8, offers rooms with families at about 4 litų per person. *Kooperatyvas Viešnagė* with desks at the airport and in the LAL office does the same sort of business; it also has branches in Moscow and St Petersburg which might be useful if you're going there. Viešnagė's phone number seems to change every time you turn round; at the last check it was ☎ 752 375.

See Places to Stay – middle for information on more expensive homestay accommodation. *Vilnius In Your Pocket* may list yet more possibilities.

Hotels

The *Viešbutis Sportas* (☎ 748 953) at Bystričios gatvė 13, two km north-east of the cathedral, is a large, slightly decayed Soviet-era hotel where you can get a reasonable double with bathroom and TV for 20 litų, or rooms sharing facilities for less. There's a canteen where you can fill up for 2 litai or so. Take trolleybus No 2, 3 or 4 from the Gedimino stop on Vrublevskio gatvė near the cathedral, five stops to the Minskas stop on Antakalnio gatvė; walk east along Tramvajų gatvė and turn left (north) along Grybo gatvė at the end, after two blocks; Bistryčios gatvė is then the first on the right.

Convenient for rail and bus travellers and big enough (200 rooms) to have vacancies, but without many other plus points, is the *Hotel Gintaras* (☎ 624 157) which is on Naujoji gatvė in front of the railway station (though its address is Sodų gatvė 14). Unless they decide to hit you with a foreigner's price, which will be in the 80 to 120 litų region (and definitely not worth paying), you should get a small, faded room with private bathroom for about 8 litai a single, 15 litų a double; better 'lyux' rooms are 12/24 litų. Security here seems notably slack.

At the *Viešbutis Žvaigždė* (☎ 619 626), near the Gintaras at Pylimo gatvė 63, a bed in a shared four to six-bed room is yours for around 5 litai. But most of the customers are from Russia, Central Asia or Caucasia and you may find the reception reluctant to take foreigners. Start by asking in Russian: 'Yist mi-ESS-toh?' ('Is there a place?'). The small *Viešbutis Narutis* (☎ 622 882), in the Old Town at Pilies gatvė 24, used to be a fair bet among the cheapies, with singles/doubles with shared facilities costing up to 32/40 litų. But it's closed for renovation at the time of writing and, in such a prime location, is likely to emerge more expensive.

PLACES TO STAY – MIDDLE
Private Homes

Litinterp (☎ 612 040, fax 220 331) at Vokiečių gatvė 10-15 runs a group of attractive, modern, pine-panelled houses round a courtyard in the Old Town, where you can get bed and breakfast for 60 litų single, 100 litų double (less after the first night). In each house one floor is reserved entirely for the guests.

Mr Vaclovas Sakalauskas (☎ 352 032 or 613 580), a friendly ex-diplomat, can fix you a comfortable flat in Vilnius with or without

LITHUANIA

a resident family for about 100/150 litų single/double in the city centre, or 85/100 litų a few minutes' bus ride out. With a family, you may be asked an extra 10 litų per person for breakfast. I stayed in one of Mr Sakalauskas' flats on one visit to Vilnius; it was comfortable, clean, spacious, and a minute's walk from the cathedral, in a building classified as an architectural monument – much better value than many more expensive hotels.

The *Norwegian Information Office* (☎ 224 140), in a courtyard at Didžioji gatvė 13, can reportedly arrange accommodation for tourists (who needn't be Norwegian) for about 60 litų a night.

Several organisations based elsewhere can also arrange homestays in Vilnius – see Accommodation in Facts for the Visitor at the front of the book.

Hotels

Probably the best value in this range are the cheaper rooms in the *Hotel Astorija* – see Places to Stay – top end. Otherwise there's the large and central *Viešbutis Vilnius* (☎ 624 157, 623 665) at Gedimino prospektas 20, which has bare but clean and quite sizeable singles/doubles sharing showers and toilets for 65/110 litų, or with private facilities for 105/210 litų or 170/340 litų.

The *Turistinis Viešbutis Trinapolis* (Trinapolis Tourist Hotel) (☎ 778 735), among woods near the river at Verkių gatvė 66, five km north of the centre, has singles/doubles with private shower for 105/170 litų in four-storey blocks. The hotel is mostly used by Polish and Russian tour groups and has a canteen-type restaurant and a bar. Trolleybus No 5 from the railway station, or No 5 or 6 from the Universalinė Parduotuvė stop on the north side of the Žaliasis bridge, will take you within 10-minutes walk of the hotel. Get off when they diverge to the right off Verkių gatvė.

PLACES TO STAY – TOP END

Many of Vilnius' better hotels are often full, so try to book ahead. At short notice Lithuanian Tours (see Travel Agencies in the

Vilnius Information section) can get you into some of them at or near the desk price.

Old Town & Gedimino Prospektas

The *Viešbutis Žaliasis Tiltas* has two good central locations and 70 quite pleasant, clean rooms with TV and private bathroom, at what, for Vilnius, are moderate prices of around 175/245 litų single/double. The locations are Vilniaus gatvė 2 (☎ 615 460), which was once a Communist Party hangout, and Gedimino prospektas 12 (☎ 615 450). For reservations phone or fax ☎ 221 716. The *Viešbutis Neringa* (☎ 610 516, fax 614 160), at Gedimino prospektas 23, charges 250/300 litų for comfortable but uninspiring singles/doubles. It's very heavily booked, as is the large *Hotel Draugystė* (☎ 662 711, fax 263 101), 2¼ km west of the centre at Čiurlionio gatvė 84, which was once the top Communist Party hotel and now houses a few embassies. Rooms in the Draugystė cost 210 litų single, 300 to 380 litų double.

Rates at the Norwegian-run *Hotel Astorija* (☎ 629 914, fax 220 097) at Didžioji gatvė 35, overlooking St Kazimieras' Church in the Old Town, range from 125/166 litų for smallish rooms with basin or toilet only to 540 litų for larger ones with attached bathroom. There are 37 rooms in all. All have TV and satellite telephone and are well kept, as is this pleasantly pre-Soviet-built hotel in general. Prices include continental breakfast.

The *Hotel Mabre* (☎ 614 162, fax 613 086, German-speaking management) at Maironio gatvė 13, on the eastern edge of the Old Town, consists of four excellent multi-level apartments in a modernised former monastery building. For single/double use the cost is 315/530 litų including breakfast, but the apartments can hold up to five.

North of the River

There's a clutch of top-end hotels north of the river, mostly within a 15-minute walk of the cathedral. The *Viešbutis Šarūnas* (☎ 353 888, fax 290 072) at Raitininkų gatvė 4, east of the Žaliasis bridge, is a modern place built by the Lithuanian basketball star Šarūnas Marčiulionis. It has 26 stylish and comfortable rooms for 270/340 litų. The *Viešbutis Žalgiris* (☎ 353 428, fax 353 933), nearby at Šeimyniškių gatvė 21A, has 26 clean rooms ranging from 140 to 220 litų for singles and 320 to 490 litų for doubles.

West of the Žaliasis bridge the towering 330-room *Hotel Lietuva* (☎ 356 665 or 356 092, fax 356 270) at Ukmergės gatvė 20 is Vilnius' biggest. The Lietuva has been a chief haunt of Western tour groups since the Soviet era and, on my last visit, some features of that time, including prostitution, remained. There's also a reputation for theft. But the hotel's pending privatisation, with new, Western ownership likely, should change that. Meanwhile the views are good; the staff, in general, helpful; and there's a selection of bars and cafés where you can get a drink or snack at most times of day. Rooms are comfortable enough and cost 324/396 litų including breakfast.

The 100-room *Viešbutis Turistas* (☎ 733 200, fax 353 161), at Ukmergės gatvė 14 in the shopping precinct next to the Hotel Lietuva, was built for a lower grade of Soviet-era tourist than the Lietuva – East Germans, Hungarians, trade-union groups from the West and so on. In 1993 it was taken over by Dutch owners who began a complete overhaul of the place, despite some nightmarish obstacles placed in their path by the bureaucracy and the mafia. At the time of writing rooms with private bath are 140/195 litų.

About 1¼ km further west at Saltoniškių gatvė 56, the *Hotel Taffo* (☎ 351 136) used to belong to the government cultural department but is being renovated by Swedes, which will probably make it one of the better places in town. Rooms are 125/230 litų at the time of writing.

Out of town

The 73-room *Villon Hotel* (☎ 22-651 385 or 22-505 100, fax 22-651 385), a Lithuanian-British joint venture opened in 1993 on the Rīga road, 19 km north of Vilnius, looks set to outstrip anywhere in the city for facilities. Aimed primarily at Western business travellers, it's set between two lakes and has a

restaurant, nightclub, casino, swimming pool, riding, sauna, fishing, boating, hairdresser and a shuttle bus to/from the city. Single/double rooms are 187/332 litų. There are also de luxe rooms and apartments up to about 600 litų. Everything is tasteful and modern, with lots of pine. Prices include breakfast. The postal address is PO Box 2590, 2015 Vilnius.

PLACES TO EAT

Vilnius has a limited (though growing) number of places where you can get a full meal, but lots of places where you can drop in for a drink, a snack or a light meal. Consult *Vilnius In Your Pocket* for the latest tips on what's new and good.

The markets on Bazilijonų gatvė (not far from the railway station) and at Kalvarijų gatvė 61 are useful sources of fresh foods like fruit and cheese, and also colourful places to visit, with numbers of traders from southern states of the ex-USSR such as Georgia and Azerbaijan. Alcohol is sold cheaper in numerous kiosks and shops than in bars and cafés. Gėrimai at Kauno gatvė 1 is a shop specialising in alcohol and it stays open from 1 pm to 1 am.

Old Town

Cheap Restaurants There are a couple of places where you can get a reasonable meal for local prices, but you may have to put up with some pretty lacklustre waiters. One is the *Lokys* (Bear) at Stiklių gatvė 8. There are four or five rooms here, some of them underground. In one, a large stuffed bear watches you dine. The Lokys specialises in game dishes from the Lithuanian forests like elk rissoles or boar sausages, but you can play safe with pork chop etc, if you like. Either way the fare's passable but not spectacular. Main dishes, with accompanying vegetables, are around 1.50 to 2.50 litų; starters are mostly 1 litas or less. The menu is in several languages including English. Another cellar establishment, with good food and similar prices, is the *Senasis Rūsys*, nearby at Šv Ignoto gatvė 16. This place has a vaguely Russian flavour, so there's an emphasis on starters. A third possibility is the *Restoranas Medininkai* at Aušros Vartų gatvė 4, yet another cellar restaurant but with a gloomier air and poor service.

Expensive Restaurants The best restaurants are aimed at Westerners, and you'll pay Western prices in most of them. The best known and most expensive is the *Restoranas Stikliai* (☎ 627 971) at Gaono gatvė 7. When opened in the early Gorbachev years, this was just about the only class eatery in the Baltic states, and it lists President Mitterrand of France, Queen Margaret of Denmark and Princess Caroline of Monaco among its past guests. Though the food's still very good, portions were decidedly smaller on my most recent visit than on my first (in 1989). Main courses include trout, veal and steak and there are choices for vegetarians. Italian pancakes are a tasty dessert. There's an English-language menu; three typical courses will come to around 80 litų including service charge – more with drinks. The atmosphere is refined, with bow-tied waiters (you don't have to dress up yourself, but dirty clothes get dirty looks). The Stikliai is open daily, from noon to midnight; for the evening, book by phone from 10 am (English is spoken).

Fortunately, the Stikliai also runs the much less formal *Stikliai Cafe* round the corner at Stiklių gatvė 18, which serves up equally good and substantial food for much less – though still a lot by local standards, of course. A starter of assorted fish, followed by soup, a main dish such as chicken, pork chop, pizza or cheeseburger and a dessert of pancakes with nuts in chocolate sauce will set you back 25 litų or so. There's cappuccino, too. Hours are from noon to 10 pm on Saturday, and 9 am to 10 pm other days.

The *Idabasar* (☎ 628 484) at Subačiaus gatvė 3 is another good two-section establishment: it has an upstairs restaurant and a cheaper downstairs 'cellar bar'. Both serve reliable, tasty, mainly German food in large German portions. A typical meal will cost 50 to 75 litų upstairs, less downstairs where the service is actually a bit better. There's an English menu but the only beer is imported.

Both sections are open from 11 am or noon to 1 am.

A third quality place is the *Corner Café* in the Hotel Astorija at Didžioji gatvė 35. Don't bother coming here for lunch, when only expensive snacks are on offer; but from 6 to 11 pm you can get an excellent dinner with good service – for instance bliny (pancakes) for 8 litai to 35 litų depending whether you order them with sour cream or caviar, chicken soup for 8 litai, and steak with potatoes and vegetables for 35 litų. The café is at the end of an upstairs corridor in the hotel – ask directions at the reception.

The *Senas Grafas* at Šv Kazimiero gatvė 3, off Didžioji gatvė, specialises in fondues. A meal is likely to cost 80 litų or more. The *Golden Dragon* (☎ 262 701), a couple of blocks west of the Old Town at Aguonų gatvė 10, is Vilnius' only Chinese restaurant. The food is reportedly erratic. A meal is usually under 40 litų. The Golden Dragon is open from noon to 8 pm on Sunday, and noon to 3 pm and 5.30 to 10 pm on other days except Wednesday, when it is closed.

In late 1993 the first new Jewish restaurant in Vilnius in a long, long time opened at Pylimo gatvė 4. Called *Lithuanian Jerusalem* it serves French, Lithuanian and fish dishes as well as kosher food; there's French wine, too. A meal is likely to cost 100 litų or more.

Cafés & Bars One of the best Old Town cafés is the little *Seno Kiemo Užeiga* in a courtyard at Pylimo gatvė 44 (you can also enter the courtyard from Ligoninės gatvė). The few tables are always busy and a friendly atmosphere reigns. If you're hungry, order a karštas sumuštinis (1.25 litų) which turns out to be a long, hot, tasty cheese-and-tomato-sauce open sandwich. There are also cakes, other snacks, good coffee and tea, and alcoholic drinks including fruit liqueurs (likeriai) at 1.25 litų a 50-gram shot. The Seno Kiemo Užeiga is open from 1 to 9 pm.

Two cafés where you can get fairly filling snacks are the *Kavinė Arkadija* at Šv Jono gatvė 3 and *Pasažas* at Arklių gatvė 12. The Arkadija's offerings include blyneliai (small pancakes) or a small befstroganas for 1.50 litų each, salads and decent coffee. It's open from 10 am to 4 pm daily and 5 to 10 pm daily, except Monday. Pasažas has more blyneliai and other hot dishes like balandeliai (stuffed cabbage rolls), troškynis (meat soup) and karbonadas (grilled meat), all between 1.25 litų and 2 litai. It's open from noon or 2 pm to 10 pm daily, except Monday.

If pancakes are what you really fancy, there are other places too. One even specialises in them, though it has a surprisingly glum atmosphere: *Blyninės* at Pilies gatvė 8 (open daily from 9 am to 6, 7 or 8 pm, but there's no sign – look for the purple curtains). You take a seat at the horseshoe-shaped counter and order a serve of blynai with a choice of apple (obuoliai), meat (mėsa), curd (varškė), cheese (sūris), jam (džemas) or sour cream (grietinė), all for around 1 litas. There's a handy bread (duona) shop next door, by the way. The clean and modern *Baltų Ainiai*, open from 10 am to 6 pm daily (except Sunday) at Savičiaus gatvė 12 (off Didžioji gatvė), has more pancakes, good coffee, and a Lithuanian speciality which you really ought to try just once – cepelinai, zeppelin-shaped parcels of a glutinous substance alleged to be grated potato, with a wad of cheese or meat or maybe mushrooms in the centre.

The *Geležinis Vilkas II* in the Contemporary Arts Centre at Vokiečių gatvė 2 has good salads and rice dishes (with friendly service), though it's only open from 11 am to 7 pm daily.

On Universiteto gatvė, the *Kavinė Alumnatas* at No 4 and the *Menininkai* at No 8 are both popular with students. There are also a couple of interesting cafés and bars connected to art galleries: the *Arka Kavinė* at Aušros Vartų gatvė 7, full of young, fashionable, arty types and the *Langas* at Ašmenos gatvė 8 which has a cosy café and is working on a wine bar.

Gedimino Prospektas

One uncomplicated central place to feed is the *Piceria Vidudienis*, at Gedimino pros-

pektas 5, where solid, bread-like, one-person 'pizzas' cost around 1.70 litų. Varieties include su daržovėmis (cheese, ham or sausage, and vegetables), Virdžinija (cheese, tomato, sausage), and su grybais (with mushrooms). Opening hours are from 10 am or noon to 9 pm.

For a proper meal head for the *Raudona-Juoda* (Red-Black) restaurant tucked away, close by, at Gedimino prospektas 14. The food and the menu are Lithuanian, but the waiters will translate for you. This good, smart eatery aims for Lithuanians as well as foreigners, as the prices indicate. Most starters are around 2 litai and main courses about 5 litai.

Back at Gedimino prospektas 1 (the cathedral end) the *Kavinė Literatų Svetainė* has a long tri-lingual menu and you can get a fair meal of salads, meat with vegetables, and a dessert for around 4 litai. At Gedimino prospektas 23, next to the Neringa hotel, the *Kavinė Neringa* will do a reasonable meal for a similar price.

A block south of Gedimino prospektas at Pamėnkalnio gatvė 7 (at the rear of the Pergalė Cinema building), the *Kavinė Viktorija* has good service and good food – šašlykas (shish kebab), karbonadas or bifštekas, all around 2.50 litų; salads including kalmarų (squid) about 1 litas. It's open from noon to 4 pm and 5 to 10 pm Monday to Friday, 2 to 10 pm Saturday.

Elsewhere

If you're staying at the Vingis Park or Vilko (BATS) hostels, you could do worse than get breakfast in the restaurant of the *Draugystė Hotel* at Čiurlionio gatvė 84. An omelette, two cheese-filled pancakes, plus juice and tea cost me about 2.50 litų. The *Hotel Lietuva* has at least six eateries. The 1.70 litų karbonadas I had in lobby-floor bistro was revolting, but there's better, if dearer fare in the *Juodasis Baras*, open from 2 pm to midnight, along the corridor. The restaurant on floor 22 is only open at night and has a floor show and disco, for which you pay a few litai on top of the meal price – which is around 15 litų for a fair spread. The *Light Hall* serves

LITHUANIA

breakfast, while down in the bowels are the *Seklyčia*, with Lithuanian specialities, and the *Didžioji Salė*, with another evening floor show.

Not far from the Lietuva at Kalvarijų gatvė 3, the *Viola* restaurant has excellent Armenian food but a grumpy Soviet hangover of a doorman and a too-loud band.

Vilnius' most surprising eating experience is the *Restoranas Žaliasis* (☎ 653 233), similar in style and quality to the Stikliai but cheaper. It's located at Jankiskių gatvė 43A which is about the last place you'd expect to find a classy restaurant, as it's an old office building on an industrial estate on the southwest edge of the city. Little English is spoken, but try to muddle through with a telephone reservation in any case. The menu is in Lithuanian. We gave the thumbs-up to kijevo kotletas (chicken Kiev) and bifštekas angliškai ('English beefsteak' – not beef, but respectable). If you're very hungry order two or three starters, as portions could be bigger – but, even so, a three-course meal with a drink is unlikely to exceed 25 litų. Jankiskių gatvė is north-west off the main Kaunas road, Savanorių prospektas, seven km from the city centre, opposite the suburb of Žemieji Paneriai. You may have to bargain with a taxi driver to bring you here – and book the same driver to take you back, as there's little passing traffic!

ENTERTAINMENT

Vilnius In Your Pocket has a pretty good entertainment section, and the evening paper *Vakarinės Naujienos* may also help you work out what's on. In addition to regular events, Vilnius hosts lots of cultural festivals of many varieties – they're listed in *Vilnius In Your Pocket*.

Jazz, Blues, Rock & Pop

Vilnius has an excellent little jazz and blues scene, with music in cafés or galleries several evenings a week. The scene is changeable of course, so check *Vilnius In Your Pocket* or the *Baltic Independent* Upcoming Events section for details. There's a major contemporary and avant-garde jazz festival held in the city every autumn, usually in October. Local jazz musicians to look out for include the internationally known saxophonist Petras Vyšniauskas and the pianist Gintautas Abarius. At the time of writing, probably the best jazz evenings are Wednesday, Friday and Saturday at the Galerija Langas at Ašmenos 8, where there's some wild dancing, and Saturday at 5 pm in the Galerija Arka at Aušros Vartų gatvė 7. You need to book ahead for the Arka. There's also jazz every second Saturday at the Leandra café at Labdariu gatvė 10, and on Friday nights in the House of Teachers at Vilniaus gatvė 39. For the teachers' house, book between 5 and 7 pm, Wednesday to Friday, in room 216 of the same building.

There's blues in the Tauras café at Pamėnkalnio gatvė 38 on Wednesday evenings, and the Kavinė Viktorija at Pamėnkalnio gatvė 7 on Saturday evenings. A main venue for rock and pop gigs is the Palace of Concerts & Sports (Koncertų ir Sporto rūmai) at Rinktinės gatvė 1.

Classical Music, Opera & Ballet

The Lithuania Chamber Orchestra, the Kaunas State Choir (Kauno Valstybinis Choras) and the Lithuanian State Symphony Orchestra (Lietuvos Valstybinis Simfoninis Orkestras) all have good reputations. Big concerts are usually given at the modern Opera & Ballet Theatre at Vienuolio gatvė 1, whose resident companies perform a wide range of mainly classical opera and ballet in repertory. Unfortunately the theatre's acoustics are notoriously bad and some of its best artists have been lured by higher earnings in other countries.

You can catch piano and other solo concerts at the Conservatoire (Lietuvos Muzikos Akademija) at Gedimino prospektas 42, and chamber music in the Art Workers' Palace (Menininkų rūmai) at Daukanto aikštė 3/8. There are organ concerts every Saturday and Sunday evening in the Holy Cross Church, alias the Small Baroque Hall (Mažoji baroko salė), a nice little church with good acoustics at Daukanto aikštė 1.

Tickets for most classical concerts are sold

at the National Philharmonia (Nacionalinė Filharmonija) ticket office at Aušros Vartų gatvė 5. Only the most expensive are above 2 litai. The usual regular sequence of events is interrupted from about mid-June to mid-September when the main performing ensembles take holidays or go on tour. At this time there are still quite a few one-off events, however.

Theatre

The main theatres, both staging a variety of Lithuanian and foreign plays in Lithuanian, are the Academic Drama Theatre (Akademinis dramos teatras) at Gedimino prospektas 4 and the currently more popular Youth Theatre (Jaunimo teatras) at Arklių gatvė 5. There are also one or two smaller or experimental theatre groups, plus the Russian Drama Theatre at Basanavičiaus gatvė 13.

THINGS TO BUY

Vilnius has lots of craft shops with some good pottery, leather work, cast iron, amber jewellery and paintings in amongst some pretty ordinary stuff. Prices vary, so shop around.

Tautodailės Galerija, upstairs in the Kavinė Arkadija building at Šv Jono gatvė 3, is one with a good range of high quality work. Dailė Centrinis Salonas at Vokiečių gatvė 2 has wide-ranging stocks.

For amber, Sage at Aušros Vartų gatvė 15 has probably the biggest stocks, while Verba at Savičiaus gatvė 10 is among the cheapest places. Dailė, next door to the Kavinė Literatų Svetainė at the cathedral end of Gedimino prospektas, and Magnus, at the corner of Jogailos gatvė and Pamėnkalnio gatvė, both have some interesting pottery. Vilnius ir Dailė, at Barboros Radvilaitės gatvė 6, specialises in paintings of Lithuanian cityscapes and landscapes.

The Melodija music shop at Tilto gatvė 15 has a fair range of local jazz and other recordings. The main department store is the Centrinė Universalinė Parduotuvė at Ukmergės gatvė 16, in the precinct by the Hotel Lietuva. This is a place to look at what

the locals have to live with, as much as to buy anything for yourself.

There are a number of shops specialising in imported Western goods like packaged food, alcohol, tobacco, domestic appliances and clothes. These often have better stocks than other shops and can be useful if you crave some familiar foodstuff like chocolate, packaged cheese etc, but are generally more expensive. Among the more useful ones are Vilbara at Pilies gatvė 2 and Londvil at Vokiečių gatvė 6.

GETTING THERE & AWAY

This section deals chiefly with transport between Vilnius and other places in Lithuania, Latvia, Estonia or the Kaliningrad Region. Except for information on Vilnius ticket sources, detail on services to/from other countries (which include flights to/from several Western and CIS cities and trains and buses to/from Denmark, Germany, Poland, Russia and Belarus), is given in the Getting There & Away chapter.

Air

LAL flies to/from Palanga between three and 12 times a week at the time of writing, depending on the season. It's a half-hour flight and the foreigner's fare is 300 litų one way.

The only other flights inside the Baltic states, so far, are to/from Tallinn four times weekly with Estonian Air. Currently this costs 510 litų (US$120) one way or 1020 litų (US$240) return if you buy the ticket in Vilnius (from LAL); in Tallinn you'll pay at least US$190 for a 'superpex' return, which is cheaper than the one-way fare of US$258.

If you're buying an international air ticket in Vilnius, it's worth trying Balticorp (see the Vilnius Information section) and maybe one or two other travel agents to see if they can do anything cheaper than the airlines themselves.

The airport (Aerouostas) is four km south of the centre in the suburb of Kirtimai. Renovated in 1992-93, it has a café and restaurant, a good-value duty-free shop and a cur-

LITHUANIA

rency-exchange office. For information call ☎ 669 481 (international) or ☎ 630 201.

Airline offices in Vilnius include:

Air Lithuania
    Gedimino prospektas 1/1 (☎ 227 710)
Austrian Airlines
    Airport (☎ 662 000)
Hamburg Airlines
    c/o LAL, Ukmergės gatvė 12 (☎ 752 550)
    Airport (☎ 669 481)
LAL
    Ukmergės gatvė 12 (☎ 752 588)
    Airport (☎ 669 481)
Lot
    Airport: Room 104, Hotel Skrydis(☎ 630 195)
Lufthansa
    Airport (☎ 636 049)
Malev
    c/o LAL, Ukmergės gatvė 12 (☎ 752 550)
    Airport: Room 103, Hotel Skrydis (☎ 630 810)
SAS
    Airport (☎ 662 000)
Swissair
    Airport (☎ 662 000)
Taffo
    Room 15, Mickevičiaus gatvė 29 (☎ 351 136)

Bus

The long-distance bus station (*autobusų stotis*) is just south of the Old Town at Sodų gatvė 22, next to the railway station. The main ticket hall is on the right as you enter. Schedules are clearly displayed both here (where white letters on a red background indicate a coach, green letters a microbus), and on the platform, but it's best to confirm what they tell you at the helpful 'Informacija' window in the booking hall. There's a left-luggage room in the booking hall too.

Out on the platform, the left-hand side is for buses to nearby destinations (including Trakai). On these, you pay on board. For the longer-distance red buses on the right-hand side, you need a ticket unless the bus is in transit, in which case you may have to scrum for a seat when it pulls in. Buses to destinations within the Baltic states and Kaliningrad Region include:

Alytus
    115 km, 2¼ hours, 20 buses daily, 2.50 litų

Anykščiai
    115 km, 2¼ hours, six or seven buses daily,
    2.50 litų
Bauska
    225 km, 4¼ hours, four buses daily, 4.80 litų
Druskininkai
    125 km, 2½ hours, four direct buses daily,
    2.50 litų
Ignalina
    110 km, 2½ hours, two buses daily, 2.30 litų
Kaliningrad
    350 km, 8¼ hours, two or three buses daily via
    Kaunas and Chernyakhovsk, or Jurbarkas and
    Sovietsk, 7.40 litų
Kaunas
    100 km, two hours, about 30 buses daily, 2.10 litų
    (also 12 microbuses daily in 1¾ hours from out
    front of the bus station)
Klaipėda
    310 km, five hours, 16 to 18 buses daily, 6.80 litų
Lazdijai
    150 km, three hours, four to eight buses daily,
    3.20 litų
Molėtai
    75 km, 1½ hours, up to nine buses daily, 1.70 litų
Palanga
    340 km, six hours, three to seven buses daily,
    7.20 litų
Panevėžys
    140 km, 2¼ hours, about 30 buses daily, 3 litai
Rīga
    290 km, six hours, four buses daily, 6.40 litų
Šiauliai
    220 km, 4½ hours, about 18 buses daily by
    various routes, 5.10 litų
Tallinn
    600 km, 12 hours, one bus nightly, 12 litų
Trakai
    30 km, 3/4 hour, 10 buses daily between 8.30 am
    and 8 pm, 0.60 litų

Tickets to Poland & the West The bus station booking hall has a separate window for tickets to Poland and the West, including the weekly Copenhagen bus, with a chart showing when each bus has vacant seats: 'vietų yra' means 'there are places'; 'vietų nėra' means 'no places'. Same-day tickets are sold from 7.30 am to noon and 1 to 11 pm, advance tickets from 8 am to 12 noon and 1 to 5.30 pm.

Tickets for the Orbis bus to Warsaw and for some buses to Gdańsk, which all depart from the Hotel Lietuva, are sold by Turistinė Firma Erelis (☎ 225 392), in the lobby of the Pergalė cinema at Pamenkalnio gatvė 7/8, from 11 am to 3 pm Monday to Friday, at the time of writing.

Train

The railway station *(geležinkelio stotis)* is just south of the Old Town at Geležinkelio gatvė 16.

Ticket Outlets There are different ticket offices for different types of destination.

Local Tickets for local trains – which basically means those starting and ending their journeys within the eastern half of Lithuania or at Daugavpils in Latvia, and includes most trains to Kaunas – are sold from their own ticket hall in a separate building to the left as you face the main station building. There are timetables for these trains here, too.

Long-Distance in the ex-USSR Tickets for long-distance trains within the former USSR – which means trains to or from Šeštokai, Šiauliai, Klaipėda and elsewhere in the western half of Lithuania, as well as Latvia, Estonia, Belarus, Russia (including Kaliningrad), Ukraine and other ex-Soviet states – are sold up to 24 hours before departure at a special advance-sales office at Šopeno gatvė 3, 250 metres from the station. Its sign says 'Geležinkelio Kasos' and it's open from 8 am to 8 pm Monday to Saturday

and 8 am to 5 pm Sunday. Even though queues at this office are sometimes slow (they tend to be shorter early or late in the day), they're usually a lot better than at the station itself, where you have to buy your ticket if departure is within 24 hours. Timetables are slightly better presented at the advance-sales office than at the station. A typical timetable entry at either place might read '80 greit Kaliningradas-Sankt Peterburgas 22.23 kasdien', which means that train No 80, fast, starting at Kaliningrad and terminating at St Petersburg, leaves Vilnius at 10.23 pm daily. Intermediate stops aren't shown.

The advance-sales office also has an information window (at the left-hand end as you go in) which can answer queries and tell you what places are available on a particular train, so you know whether it's worth queueing for a ticket.

Outside the ex-USSR Tickets to places outside the former USSR are sold only at the Travel Bureau (Kelionių Biuras) (☎ 356 225) in the sunken courtyard beside the Hotel Lietuva, at Ukmergės gatvė 20; it's open from 9 am to 1 pm daily, and again from 2 to 6 pm Monday to Saturday, and 2 to 4 pm on Sunday. Ask here about tickets to Warsaw using the *Baltic Express* from Kaunas or Šeštokai. If you're planning just to take the

Flower Power

There's an old saying from the Soviet days that goes something like: 'It's impossible, but if you really want it...' Traveller Derek Emson from the UK was treated to a classic example of the ingenuity that this implies (and of the Baltic peoples' frequent willingness to help foreigners) when he went down to Vilnius bus station to get a ticket to Warsaw:

I got into conversation with a young Lithuanian medical student whose name, Šinšinaitis, sounded like it had come out of a medical book itself. The queue at the ticket office was long and hardly moving, so he said he would help me.

The door into the ticket office was unlocked so he entered and closed it behind him. Some minutes later he emerged saying we had to buy a rose. 'A rose, what for?' I asked myself as we went outside the bus station to a flower stall. Šinšinaitis explained that we had to buy one for the woman in the ticket office because then she would sell me a ticket straight away. 'I'll get her two,' I said, thinking it might make the deal an absolute certainty. 'No, you must buy one, three or five,' he said. 'Oh, OK, get three.'

There was an uneasy silence as we waited outside the door, which had been locked during our absence. But soon two women came along with a key to let themselves in and Šinšinaitis slipped in with them. He emerged once again, only this time accompanied by a middle-aged woman, who was smiling radiantly and clutching three roses in one hand and a ticket in the other. ∎

Šeštokai-Suwałki train into Poland, you can get Vilnius-Šeštokai and Šeštokai-Suwałki tickets here for a combined 51 litų – much more than you'd pay buying direct from the railways, but then you might not be able to get both tickets direct from the railways (see the Getting There & Away chapter for why). The problematic sector is Šeštokai-Suwałki itself, so you might see if the Kelionių Biuras will sell you a ticket for that on its own and still save by getting the Vilnius-Šeštokai ticket from the railways.

Services The quickest link with the other Baltic capitals is the *Seagull* (Lithuanian: Žuvėdra; Russian: Chayka) which trundles daily from Minsk to Tallinn, and vice-versa, in 17½ hours, stopping at Vilnius, Šiauliai, Rīga, Sigulda, Tartu and a dozen or so other places en route. Northward it comes through Vilnius in mid-morning; southward, in the evening. It takes six hours to/from Rīga and 13½ hours to/from Tallinn. There's also a slower overnight train to/from Rīga via Kaunas, plus two or three other daily trains to/from Rīga making the same intermediate stops as the *Seagull*. The Vilnius-Rīga fare in compartment class is 6.30 litų. In general, fares on long-distance trains are about 4 litai for 250 km in compartment class. On local trains it's currently 0.40 litų for every 65 km. Other services from Vilnius within the Baltic states or Kaliningrad Region include:

Daugavpils
  175 km, six local and seven long-distance trains (terminating at St Petersburg) daily, three to 3½ hours
Druskininkai
  125 km, four local trains daily, 3¼ to 4¼ hours
Ignalina
  110 km, six local and seven long-distance trains (terminating at St Petersburg) daily, two hours
Kaliningrad
  350 km, six long-distance trains daily, 5¼ to 6¼ hours
Kaunas
  100 km, 15 local and nine or 10 long-distance trains (most terminating at Šeštokai, Klaipėda, Rīga or Kaliningrad) daily, 1¼ to 2¼ hours
Klaipėda
  350 km, one morning and one overnight long-distance train daily, 6¾ or 9¾ hours

Rēzekne
  265 km, seven long-distance trains daily (terminating at St Petersburg), 5½ to six hours
Šeštokai
  190 km, one long-distance train daily, 3¼ hours
Šiauliai
  200 km, about eight long-distance trains daily (most terminating at Mažeikiai, Rīga or Tallinn), 4½ hours
Trakai
  30 km, seven local trains daily, 40 minutes

Car & Motorbike

The Litofinn 24-hour petrol station at Erfurto gatvė 41 in the western suburb of Lazdynai is part-owned by the Finnish company Neste and has higher-grade and unleaded petrol (and a good café). Litofinn was due to open a second outlet about 11 km north of the city centre on the Panevėžys and Rīga road by late 1993. *Vilnius In Your Pocket* has information on other outlets and on repairs and service.

Rental The Eva car rental firm (☎ 649 428 or 649 419, fax 643 419) at Jačionų gatvė 14 has Volvos and Audis from 200 litų a day plus 1.25 litų a km, or 500 litų a day with unlimited km. Its Ladas are cheaper – they tend to be booked up well ahead, but it's worth a try. Balticar (☎ 460 998, fax 758 924) also has Ladas. Avis (☎ 733 226, fax 353 161) is at the Viešbutis Turistas, Ukmergės gatvė 14.

Bicycle

Lithuanian Youth Hostels (see Information and Places to Stay) can rent bikes to its guests for touring outside Vilnius.

GETTING AROUND
To/From the Airport

Vilnius Airport (Aerouostas) is four km south of the centre off Dariaus ir Girėno gatvė in the suburb of Kirtimai. Bus No 1 runs between the airport and railway station about 35 times a day (the first bus from the station is at 5.50 am, the last at 11.50 pm). Bus No 2 runs between the airport and the north-western suburb of Šeškinė via the Žaliasis (Green) bridge over the Neris, just north of the city centre, and the Hotel

Lietuva. You can buy flat-rate public transport tickets at some of the kiosks in the airport. A taxi from the airport to the city centre should be about 2 litai but you'll probably be asked up to 20 times as much and will have to bargain – 5 litai, or 10 litų at most, should be acceptable.

City Transport

Trolleybuses provide most of the public transport in and around the centre; buses tend to serve more outlying areas. Most routes run from about 5.30 or 6 am to about midnight. From the railway and bus stations, trolleybus Nos 2 and 5 go up Pylimo gatvė and Jogailos gatvė to Savivaldybės aikstė on Gedimino prospektas; No 2 then continues to the Gedimino stop on Vrublevskio gatvė by the cathedral, and on up Kosciuškos gatvė to the north-east suburb of Antakalnis; No 5 goes over the river and north up part of Kalvarijų gatvė (you can use it for the Lietuva and Turistas hotels). If you're staying in or near the centre, you'll really only need transport for outlying sights since the city centre and Old Town form a compact, walkable area. Bus and trolleybus tickets are about 6 centai at the time of writing; one kiosk selling them is at the east end of the railway station forecourt, with the sign 'Bilietai važiuoti miesto transportu'. The usual ticket-punching system is used on buses and trolleybuses. The fine for riding without punching a ticket is 80 cento.

Taxi

Taxis officially cost 50 cento a km, at the time of writing, but more often than not the meter is 'not working' and you have to agree a fare in advance. Two or three times the official rate should be acceptable. Two useful taxi ranks are on Katedros aikštė and in front of the old Town Hall on Didžioji gatvė. You can order a cab on ☎ 228 888. State taxis – usually large Volga cars – tend to be less cutthroat than private cabs.

Bicycle

Lithuanian Youth Hostels (see Information and Places to Stay) has a few bikes available for its guests.

Around Vilnius

There are three obvious day trips from Vilnius – two pleasant, the other appalling.

PANERIAI

The WW-II Nazi death camp of Paneriai is 10 km south-west of central Vilnius. Over 100,000 people were murdered here between July 1941 and July 1944: some 70,000 of them were Jews from Vilnius and around. About half the city's Jewish population – some 35,000 people – had already been massacred here by the end of the first three months of the German occupation (June to September 1941). Lithuanian accomplices reportedly did at least as much of the killing as their German masters. It's a gruesome place, made more so by its closeness to the Paneriai marshalling yards with their echoes of the way in which so many Jews were transported to their deaths by the Nazis.

The entrance to the wooded site is marked by a memorial, the **Panerių Memorialas**, with text in Hebrew, Lithuanian and Russian which now specifically states that 70,000 of the victims here were Jews. In the Soviet period the victims were all referred to simply as 'Soviet citizens'. A path leads down to the small but terrible **Paneriai Museum** (Panerių muziejus), open from 11 am to 6 pm daily (except Tuesday), and two monuments – one Jewish, one Soviet. From here other paths lead to a number of grassed-over pits among the trees where, according to signs on the spot, from December 1943 the Nazis burnt the exhumed bodies of their victims in order to hide the evidence of their crimes. One of the deeper pits, according to its sign, was where they kept those who were forced to dig up the corpses and pulverise the bones.

Getting There & Away

Bus No 8 from Vilnius railway station runs to Aukštieji Paneriai about every 15 minutes

Around Vilnius

No 8 there. Some suburban trains also run from Vilnius to Paneriai station which is on Agrastų gatvė, a couple of hundred metres east of the footbridge already mentioned.

TRAKAI

The old Lithuanian capital, Trakai, with its two lakeside castles, is 30 km west of Vilnius. Gediminas may have made it his capital in the 1320s; Kęstutis certainly made it his base later in the 14th century. The castles were built to fend off the German knights. Today Trakai is a small, quiet town in an attractive country area of numerous lakes and islands, and probably the most popular day trip from Vilnius.

Orientation

Most of the town stands on a two-km-long, north-pointing tongue of land between Lake Luka to its east and Lake Totoriškių to its west. A third lake, Lake Galvė, opens out from the north end of the peninsula. From the railway station at the south end of town, Vytauto gatvė leads 400 metres north to a square where you'll find the bus station, then continues north up the peninsula for about 1¼ km till it becomes Karaimų gatvė.

Peninsula Castle

The ruins of Trakai's peninsula castle are towards the north end of town, in a park close to the eastern shore of the peninsula. It's thought to have been built in 1362-82 by Grand Duke Vytautas' father, Kęstutis. Turn down Kęstučio gatvė, off Karaimų gatvė, to reach it.

Karaites

The peninsula is dotted with old wooden cottages, many of them built by the Karaites (Karaimai), a Judaist sect originating in Baghdad and adhering only to the Law of Moses, some of whom were brought to Trakai from the Crimea by Vytautas around 1400 to serve as bodyguards. Some 150 Karaites still live in Trakai. Karaimų gatvė 22, on the west side, is a small Karaites museum, and there's an early 19th century

throughout the day. It follows Savanorių prospektas, the main Kaunas road, out of town for some distance then, after Savanorių prospektas climbs a hill and bends right, the bus turns left on to Galvės gatvė, the main road to Trakai, Druskininkai and Grodno (Lithuanian: Gardinas). After almost a km it turns left again along Vilijos gatvė and stops at the end, near a footbridge over the Paneriai marshalling yards. Get off the bus, cross the footbridge, and turn right along the street on the far side of the rail tracks, Agrastų gatvė, which leads straight to the site, about 900 metres away.

If you're not starting from the Vilnius railway station area, take any transport that will go down Savanorių prospektas such as trolleybus No 4 or 12 from the Gedimino stop by the cathedral or the Savivaldybės stop on Gedimino prospektas. Get off at the Vaduvos stop (just after a railway bridge over the road and just before the turning to the left to Žemieji Paneriai), and pick up bus

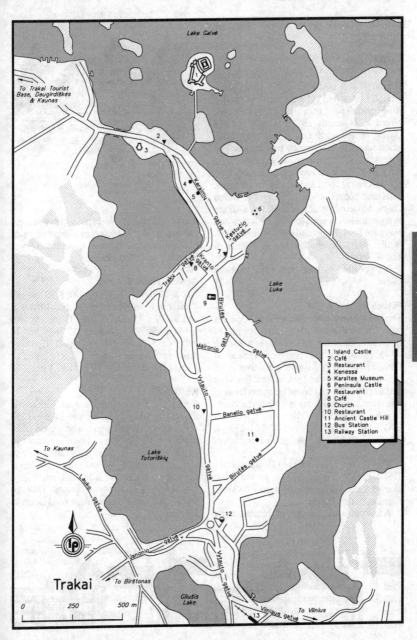

LITHUANIA

1 Island Castle
2 Café
3 Restaurant
4 Kenessa
5 Karaites Museum
6 Peninsula Castle
7 Restaurant
8 Café
9 Church
10 Restaurant
11 Ancient Castle Hill
12 Bus Station
13 Railway Station

Lake Galvé

To Trakai Tourist
Base, Daugirdiškės
& Kaunas

Karaimų gatvė

Kęstučio gatvė

Trakų gatvė

Kranto gatvė

Lake Luka

Birutės gatvė

Maironio gatvė

Vytauto gatvė

Banelio gatvė

Lake Totoriškių

To Kaunas

Birutės gatvė

Vytauto gatvė

Lauko gatvė

Janonio gatvė

Trakai

To Birštonas

Gilušis Lake

Vilniaus gatvė

To Vilnius

0   250   500 m

Kenessa (Karaite prayer house) along the street at No 30.

Island Castle

The painstakingly restored, red-brick, Gothic island castle probably dates from around 1400 when Vytautas found he needed stronger defences than the peninsula castle afforded. It stands on an island in Lake Galvė, off the north end of Karaimų gatvė, and is linked to the shore by footbridges. The triangular outer courtyard is separated by a moat from the main tower, which has a cavernous central court and a range of galleries, halls and rooms, some housing the Trakai Castle Museum, which is open from 10 am to 6 pm daily, except Monday. Concerts and plays are held in the castle in summer – look at the entertainment listings in *Vilnius In Your Pocket*.

It's possible to take boat trips on Lake Galvė.

Places to Stay & Eat

The Nakvynė private room service in Vilnius (see Vilnius Places to Stay) also has places in Trakai. There's a *BATS hostel* (☎ 238-73 437) about 12 km west of Trakai at Daugirdiškės. It looks quite attractive, is set next to pine woods and near a lake, has a bar and satellite TV, and could be a good base if you want to spend a day or two in the countryside. The price is 40 litų a night. Contact BATS (☎ 22-627 793, fax 22-261 435) at Aguonų gatvė 10 in Vilnius for more information.

The *Trakai Tourist Base* (Turistinė Bazė Trakuose) (☎ 238-51 745) is on the north side of Lake Galvė off the road to Vievis, four km out of Trakai.

A few cafés and a couple of restaurants are

Island Castle

dotted along the Vytauto gatvė-Karaimų gatvė axis. The *Kibininė*, in a small wooden house near the Karaite museum, serves Karaite pies called kibinai.

Getting There & Away

About 10 buses daily, between 8.30 am and 8 pm, run from Vilnius bus station to Trakai and back, a 45-minute trip. There are also seven trains daily, taking 40 minutes. In either case it's advisable to check departure times in advance – there are few buses or trains between around 10 am and 4 pm.

KERNAVĖ

Kernavė, 35 km north-west of Vilnius, is thought to have been the site of the 1253 coronation of Mindaugas, who united Lithuania for the first time. There are four old castle mounds, in rural surroundings, and archaeologists are uncovering a medieval town nearby. Kernavė is in the Neris valley, reached by a minor road through Dūkštos from Maišiagala on the main road north to Ukmergė.

Eastern & Southern Lithuania

The eastern and southern corners of Lithuania are rural. North-east of Vilnius begins a lakeland region that continues east into Belarus and north into Latvia. It includes the Aukštaitija National Park, Lithuania's oldest. West and south of the park stretches the 900-sq-km Labanoras-Pabradė forest, the second biggest in Lithuania. The biggest is the Druskininkai-Varėna forest, 1500 sq km in Lithuania's far south, an area known as Dzūkija. Druskininkai is a pleasant forest resort on the Nemunas River. Dzūkija is known for its folk songs, festivals of which are held in the summer. Neither the east nor the south of Lithuania has any very big towns.

AUKŠTAITIJA NATIONAL PARK

The Aukštaitija National Park (Aukštaitijos Nacionalinis Parkas), founded in 1974, includes a major part of the labyrinth of lakes scattered over far-eastern Lithuania. A little over 30 km from north to south and up to 20 km from east to west, the park is an attractive area with pine forest covering much of the land between the 100 lakes. Elk, deer and wild boar inhabit the forests. There are good panoramas from the 155-metre hill, Ledakalnis. Canoeing and camping along the lakes and the rivers that connect them is a popular activity, and there are walking trails and roads, too. You can rent canoes at the Kaltanėnai Youth Hostel. Lake Dringis is the biggest lake and Lake Tauragnas the deepest. Lake Baluošas has seven islands including one with its own small lake. The Žeimena is reckoned to be the most beautiful river. The Lithuanian Youth Hostels people in Vilnius, among others, can help you fix up a canoe trip in the park.

In addition to the natural attractions of the area there are numerous sites of human interest, among them several ancient **fortification mounds** (*piliakalnis*), such as the Taurapilio mound on the south shore of Lake Tauragnas, and some quaint old wooden

architecture including a fine 1757 **church and bell tower** at Palūšė. There's a **museum of beekeeping** at Stripeikiai.

The park centre (☎ 229-52 891 or 229-47 477) is at Palūšė on Lake Lūšiai, four km west of Ignalina at a fairly central point in the waterways network. Ignalina has a nuclear power station which, with two Chernobyl-type RBMK reactors, is feared to be a second Chernobyl disaster waiting to happen, though there have been some safety improvements with Swedish help. Ignalina generates over half Lithuania's electricity, even when other power stations aren't shut down by fuel shortages. There's talk of building a third, non-RBMK, reactor. Ignalina is just outside the eastern boundary of the national park.

Places to Stay

There's a *Youth Hostel* (☎ 217-44 368 or 217-44 399) in an old school in Kaltanėnai

Eastern Lithuania

0   15   30 km

village, near Lake Žeimenys in the southern part of the park. The cost is about 12 litų a night.

Kaltanėnai is on the Žeimena River near its outflow from Lake Žeimenys, and the hostel has canoes for rent at 17 litų a day. The Lithuanian Youth Hostels office in Vilnius can make bookings and tell you how to get there (see the Vilnius Information section for contact details).

There's also a *Tourist Base* at Palūšė with cheap accommodation, plus a dozen or so *tent camping sites* scattered elsewhere in the park.

Getting There & Away

A train to Ignalina, 110 km from Vilnius, then a local bus or a taxi from there, is the best approach to the park if you don't have your own transport. Six local trains (most terminating at Daugavpils in Latvia) and seven long-distance trains (terminating at St Petersburg) connect Ignalina with Vilnius daily. It's a two-hour trip. There are just two buses between Vilnius and Ignalina daily at the time of writing.

MOLĖTAI

The small town of Molėtai, 75 km north of

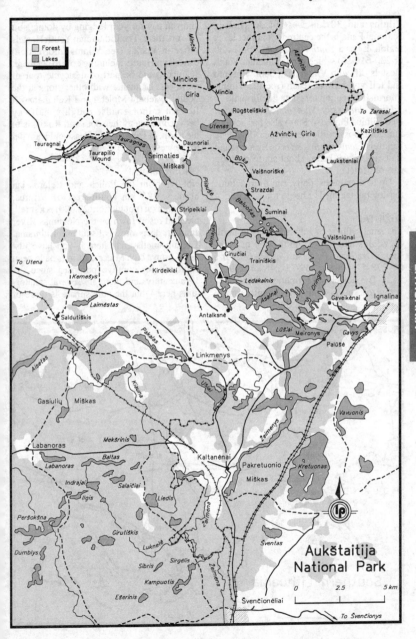

LITHUANIA

Aukštaitija
National Park

Vilnius and 30 km west of Aukštaitija National Park, is the centre for another lakes region. It has a *Youth Hostel* (☎ 230-51 830 or 230-61 560) which the Lithuanian Youth Hostels office in Vilnius can book you into and tell you how to reach (see the Vilnius information section for contact information). *Vilnius University Student Representation* (see Vilnius Places to Stay) also has accommodation possibilities in the area. There's a handful of *tent camping sites* on Siesartis and Baltieji Lakajai lakes, about six to nine km east of Molėtai.

Up to nine buses, daily, run from Vilnius to Molėtai, taking 1½ hours for 1.70 litų.

JŪŽINTAI
The small village of Jūžintai, 135 km north of Vilnius and 70 km north-west of Aukštaitija National Park, has a *Youth Hostel* (☎ 278-51 696 or 239-72 248 or 239-37 952). The hostel is a farmhouse being converted to a small pottery and ceramics centre,

and you pay for your lodging by doing a bit of work there. The Lithuanian Youth Hostels office in Vilnius (see Vilnius Information) can tell you more, including how to get there. Jūžintai could be part of a bicycle tour of north-east Lithuania with other stops at the youth hostels in Molėtai and Kaltanėnai. It lies on minor roads, roughly halfway between Utena to the south and Rokiškis to the north, or Dusetos to the east and Kamajai to the west.

DRUSKININKAI
Not far from the Polish and Belarussian borders, 125 km south-west of Vilnius, Druskininkai (population: 22,000) is a small, pleasant resort town on the Nemunas River amid the deep forests of southern Lithuania. The air smells great here if you have just come from a city. Mineral springs have been exploited for curative purposes since the 19th century, and there are several sanatoriums here – but the atmosphere is more of

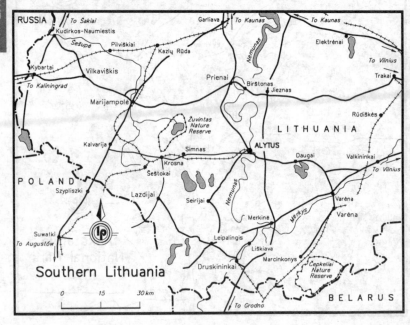

Southern Lithuania

relaxation and leisure than of medicine. Druskininkai is also well known as the home town of the outstanding Lithuanian Romantic painter and composer Mikalojus Kon-stantinas Čiurlionis (1875-1911).

Orientation

A focal point to get your bearings is the crossroads overlooking Druskininkai's lake, where Kudirkos gatvė, coming into town from the south-east, crosses Čiurlionio gatvė. The Viešbutis Turistas hotel is on Kudirkos gatvė a block north-west of this crossroads. In the opposite direction, the bus and rail stations are 450 and 750 metres away, respectively, on the south-eastward continuation of Kudirkos gatvė, called Gardino gatvė. Coming out of either station, turn left along the road to reach the centre of town. Čiurlionio gatvė, Kudirkos gatvė and the pedestrianised avenue Vilniaus aleja, parallel to Kudirkos gatvė a block to its south-west, are the most important streets. The Nemunas River loops round the north side of town.

Information

There are coin-operated baggage lockers at the rail and bus stations. There's a bank at Kudirkos gatvė 31, and currency-exchange offices on Taikos gatvė across the street from the Viešbutis Turistas and at Vilniaus aleja 26. The post, telephone and telegraph office is on Kudirkos gatvė, half a block south-east of the Viešbutis Turistas. The market is at Čiurlionio gatvė 133A, and there are shops scattered along Čiurlionio gatvė and Vilniaus aleja.

The Druskininkai telephone code is 233.

Walking Tours

A gentle stroll around the town is as pleasant a thing to do as any. Vilniaus aleja is lined with parks for much of its 800-metre length and you can quickly reach the tree-lined banks of the Nemunas, with its wide sweeping curves, from the northern half of Vilniaus aleja. A large stylised **statue of Čiurlionis**, which is more or less a symbol of Druskininkai, stands at the north end of Kudirkos gatvė.

There are walking routes marked from where the small Ratnyčia stream enters the Nemunas about 300 metres east of the statue. Another route is the five-km Saulės Takas (Sun Path) through the pines from the spa health park on Sausoji gatvė (which is off Gardino gatvė, opposite the bus station) to an old **water mill** in Jaskoniu village. You can also walk the shores of the lake by Čiurlionio gatvė, and reach another bend of the Nemunas from the far west end of that street.

Čiurlionis Museum

Čiurlionis lived for most of his childhood in this house at what's now Čiurlionio gatvė 41, about 400 metres west of Kudirkos gatvė. The house is now the Čiurlionio Memorialinis Muziejus, open from noon to 6 pm daily (except Monday and the last Tuesday of each month). Piano and chamber concerts are held here in summer.

The exhibits cover both Čiurlionis' life and his work. His father was the Druskininkai church organist. Though Čiurlionis' musical and artistic career first took him away from Druskininkai at the age of 13 or 14, and he spent much of his often unhappy adult life in Warsaw, Leipzig, Vilnius and elsewhere, he repeatedly returned to Druskininkai for solace and inspiration.

It's an interesting reflection on the condition of Lithuania in the late 19th century that Čiurlionis, who became a leading figure in the Lithuanian national revival, grew up speaking Polish at home and being taught in Russian at Druskininkai village school!

Forest Museum

Girios Aidas (Echo of the Forest) at Čiurlionio gatvė 102, about two km east of the Kudirkos gatvė corner, is an unusually carved two-storey wooden house, supported by a single pedestal, which contains a forest museum with exhibits on forest fauna and the forester's craft. It's open the same days and hours as the Čiurlionis museum.

LITHUANIA

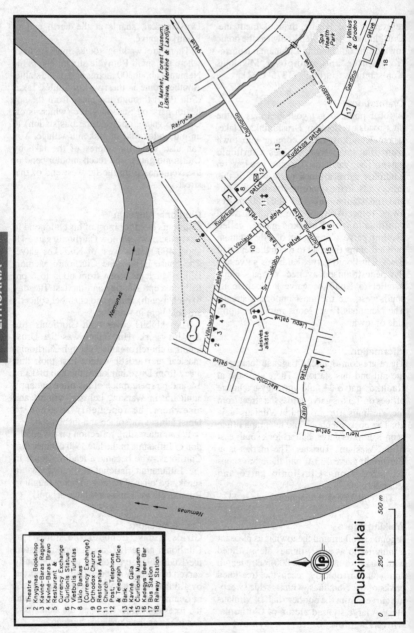

Druskininkai

1 Theatre
2 Knygynas Bookshop
3 Kavinė-Baras Raganė
4 Kavinė-Baras Bravo
5 Restaurant &
6 Currency Exchange
7 Čiurlionis Statue
8 Viešbutis Turistas
9 Ukio Bankas
   (Currency Exchange)
10 Orthodox Church
11 Restoranas Astra
12 Church
13 Post, Telephone
   & Telegraph Office
14 Bank
15 Kavinė Galia
16 Čiurlionis Museum
17 Kadagys Beer Bar
18 Bus Station
19 Railway Station

0   250   500 m

Places to Stay & Eat

The only hotel is the plain *Viešbutis Turistas* (☎ 52 566 or 51 345) at Kudirkos gatvė 41. The rooms are faded; the plumbing, leaky; and the electrical fittings, hazardous; but you pay only 6 litų per person for rooms with private bathroom. Its restaurant, the *Kavinė Turistas*, is ordinary but passable, with meat-and-veg main courses around 1.70 litų.

A much brighter, if louder place to eat is the modern, in fact positively space-age *Restoranas Astra* at Vilniaus aleja 10, with tables on three banked tiers either side of a dance floor. The Astra is open from noon to 5 pm and 6.30 pm to midnight daily, except Monday. There's another reasonable-looking restaurant (at No 26) and several cafés and bars along Vilniaus aleja.

Getting There & Away

There are four direct buses and four local trains daily to/from Vilnius. The buses are quicker at about 2½ hours against 3¼ to 4¼ hours for a train. But avoid buses taking indirect routes such as via Varėna, which take quite a lot longer. There are about 12 daily buses to/from Kaunas taking two to three hours (most via Alytus); 10 to/from Lazdijai; two to/from Jurbarkas; one or two to/from Šiauliai; and one each to/from Klaipėda, Kaliningrad, Rīga and even Ignalina.

For buses to/from Poland and Belarus see the Getting There & Away chapter. There's also a train to/from Grodno (Lithuanian: Gardinas) in Belarus in the afternoon, taking 1¼ hours.

AROUND DRUSKININKAI

The pleasantly sited village of **Liškiava**, 10 km north-east of Druskininkai, on the left bank of the Nemunas, has remnants of a 14th century hilltop castle which figures in several Lithuanian folk tales. The small town of **Merkinė**, a similar distance further down the Nemunas at its confluence with the Merkys River, also dates back to the 14th century. In Merkinė is another castle hill, with fine river views, plus an impressive church and gate-cum-bell tower dating

partly from the 17th and partly from the 19th centuries; it's on Osmolskio gatvė a short distance down the hill from the bus stop in the centre of town. Both Liškiava and Merkinė fall within the 550-sq-km **Dzūkija National Park**, designated in 1991, whose headquarters (☎ 260-53 637) is at Marcinkonys. Some 85% of the park is forest. Between Marcinkonys and the Belarus border is the **Čepkeliai Nature Reserve**, protecting Lithuania's biggest marsh. The reserve's headquarters (☎ 260-44 686) are at Marcinkonys.

Getting There & Away

In summer there are boats along the Nemunas between Druskininkai and Liškiava. Otherwise there are four or five buses daily between the two places. There are also a few buses a day from Druskininkai to Merkinė and vice versa. A whole lot more buses – including all those between Druskininkai and Vilnius and most of those between Druskininkai and Alytus or Kaunas – stop at the Merkinė crossroads (Merkinės kryžkelė), two km east of Merkinė town centre.

THE SOUTH-WEST

Lazdijai, 43 km north-west of Druskininkai, is the nearest town to the infamous border on the road to Suwałki in Poland. It has a basic hotel, the *Viešbutis Žibintas* (☎ 268-51 983) at Nepriklausomybės aikštė 6.

Mute Swan

LITHUANIA

Šeštokai, 18 km north of Lazdijai, is one end of another infamous Lithuania-Poland route, the Šeštokai-Suwałki railway. When (and if) the new road border between Kalvarija and Budzisko (Poland) is opened, the main approach to it will run through **Marijampolė**, where there's the *Viešbutis Sūduva* (☎ 243-70 345) at Basanavičiaus aikštė 8.

Žuvintas Lake, 30 km north of Lazdijai and 20 km south-east of Marijampolė, and

---

A Day on Mars

I travelled from Vilnius to Warsaw by the Šeštokai- Suwałki route with an Aussie companion, met on Vilnius station while awaiting the train for the first leg to Šeštokai. Julian rapidly became a firm friend, not least because he had a small supply of Mars bars. I had misguidedly relied on Vilnius market being open early enough to provide food for the trip, and had ended up with nothing. Julian had bought a ticket to Šeštokai at Vilnius station, but I was following what turned out to be outdated advice that a dollar here and a dollar there, handed to the conductor, would do instead of tickets.

I wasn't too upset by the fine – equivalent to US$1.20 – for travelling from Vilnius to Šeštokai without a ticket. Julian and I agreed that at Šeštokai, I would run for the ticket office while he would take both our packs and grab seats on the train to Suwałki. I found a throng of about 20 people around the ticket office. No one moved an inch for the next hour and a half. Whether the clerk was ignoring us altogether, or one of the customers was buying all the tickets then reselling them for a 'commission', I never fathomed.

With 10 minutes left before departure, I gave up and wandered through another door of the station building to find half a dozen Central Asians huddled around a wad of passports. *'Bilety?'* ('Tickets?') I chanced. No one even bothered to look up. Outside, I found Julian struggling towards me with both our packs. The conductors wouldn't let him on the train without tickets. Reviewing the alternatives (wait here till tomorrow; go back to Vilnius; try to find a bus), we decided to try to wangle our way on to the train, somehow. Back we went, this time to find no conductors in sight and no one else remotely interested in who was getting on or off the train. We settled into a corner of the corridor and shared half the last Mars bar.

Even standing room was at a premium on this cross-border sector. Every seat was stacked with baggage and the passengers were stuffed into the corridors. After another small fine for the sector from Šeštokai to the border, and several long halts in the middle of nowhere, we entered Poland. That meant Polish ticket inspectors too. Unimpressed by Western passports, the English language or feigned incomprehension, they made it clear to us, with the aid of gestures and numbers written in their notebooks, that we had to pay 28,000 złoty (about US$2) each for the fare from the border to Suwałki, plus fines of 300,000 złoty (US$22) each, or else they would impound our passports or something else equally unhelpful. Now I understood why several other passengers had locked themselves in the toilet when these officials appeared.

With hunger and the morning's early start now taking their effect, I protested loudly in an aggrieved mixture of English and pidgin Russian that I had queued 1½ hours for a ticket and the queue hadn't moved; it certainly wasn't my fault that I hadn't got a ticket. The inspectors briefly moved on in pursuit of other quarry, but soon returned to us with the hieroglyphic '$10' in a notebook and the whispered words *'bez kvitantsia'* ('without receipt'). A fair compromise, we reckoned, and paid up, then celebrated with the final half Mars.

Our train pulled into Suwałki just as our 'connection' to Warsaw was pulling out. We ran to the ticket office anyway and found ourselves second in the queue. Soon we were joyfully clutching tickets to the Polish capital. We deciphered from a conductor that the train leaving any minute for somewhere called Sokółka would take us in the Warsaw direction, and boarded it. I noticed many of the Central Asians from the previous train boarding a bus outside the station.

The rest of the trip went something like this: departed Suwałki 15.39; arrived Sokółka 17.39; departed Sokółka 18.14; arrived Białystok 18.55; departed Białystok 19.35, along with all the Central Asians, who now reappeared, still struggling with the same gigantic baggage; arrived Warsaw Central 22.07 after a long, tortuous conversation with a Belarussian who wanted us to help him export essence of bee-sting, allegedly an aphrodisiac, to the West; arrived Warsaw youth hostel 22.55, five minutes before closing, to be told 'house full'. We gasped '...But we've come from Vilnius...by Šeštokai and Suwałki...', to which they responded 'Ah...have a seat...', and found us a room. ∎

its extensive surrounding marshes form the **Žuvintas Nature Reserve** which, though troubled by pesticide pollution, is an important breeding ground for birds (including the mute swan). Thousands of migrating geese stop at the lake in autumn. The nature reserve's office (☎ 235-49 540) is in the village of Simnas, south of the reserve. Cheap dormitory accommodation is reportedly available. The Poilsis travel agency (☎ 235-52 562, fax 235-53 259) at Pulko gatvė 4, Alytus, offers trips to the reserve.

Getting There & Away

Buses run to Marijampolė and Kalvarija from Kaunas, and to Lazdijai from Druskininkai, Kaunas and Vilnius. Trains run to Šeštokai from Kaunas and Vilnius. For detail on the crossings into Poland, see the Bus, Train and Car & Motorbike sections in the Getting There & Away chapter.

The crossing into the Kaliningrad Region between Kybartai (40 km west of Marijampolė) and Nesterov is reportedly meant for commercial traffic, though that may not mean that private vehicles are banned.

The road into the Kaliningrad Region from Kudirkos-Naumiestis, further north, is definitely to be avoided as it leads into a Russian military-training zone.

Central Lithuania

Three of Lithuania's five biggest towns lie in a triangle in the centre of the country: Kaunas and Panevėžys in the low-lying Nemunas and Nevėžis valleys, and Šiauliai on the eastern side of north-west Lithuania's Žemaitija Upland. Kaunas is the biggest non-capital city in the Baltic states and an important, quite attractive place – though less exciting than Vilnius. Near Šiauliai stands perhaps the strangest monument in all the Baltic states: the Hill of Crosses, a place of pilgrimage for people from all over Lithuania.

KAUNAS

Lithuania's second city is 100 km west of Vilnius at the confluence of the Nemunas and Neris rivers. About 90% of Kaunas' 420,000 people are ethnic Lithuanian, and it's often considered a more 'Lithuanian' and nationalist city than Vilnius, which has a higher proportion of Russians in its population and many Polish associations in its past. Kaunas also has a reputation as a bastion of the entrepreneurial spirit and a hotbed of post-Soviet mafia and other wheeler-dealers.

Kaunas was the national capital during Lithuania's period of independence between WW I and WW II, when Vilnius had been taken over by Poland. Founded in the 11th century, it grew up around its castle on the point of land between the two rivers and from the 13th to 15th centuries was in the front line against the Teutonic Order on Lithuania's western frontier. After the order was decisively defeated by the Lithuanians and Poles at Grünwald, in 1410, Kaunas became a successful river-trade town of the 15th and 16th centuries. German merchants were influential here, and there was a Hanseatic League office, but Kaunas was never controlled by Germans, as Estonian and Latvian cities were. Its strategic position is, no doubt, the main reason why it's said to have been reduced to ashes 13 times before WW II, in which it received one more battering. Today

it's still a river port as well as Lithuania's chief industrial city and a cultural centre. It has a sizeable student population, some fine architecture, museums and galleries, and a quite attractive setting.

Orientation

The old part of the city centres on Rotušės aikštė (Town Hall Square) on the point of land between the two rivers. Pedestrianised Vilniaus gatvė runs 700 metres east from Rotušės aikštė to meet the city's main axis, Laisvės alėja, also mainly pedestrianised, which then heads two km dead straight to the east.

The life of modern Kaunas, including most of the shops, galleries, museums, places to eat, and the main hotels, revolves around Laisvės alėja and Donelaičio gatvė which is parallel to it a block north. The bus and rail stations are 900 metres and 1¼ km, respectively, south of the east end of Laisvės alėja, down Vytauto prospektas.

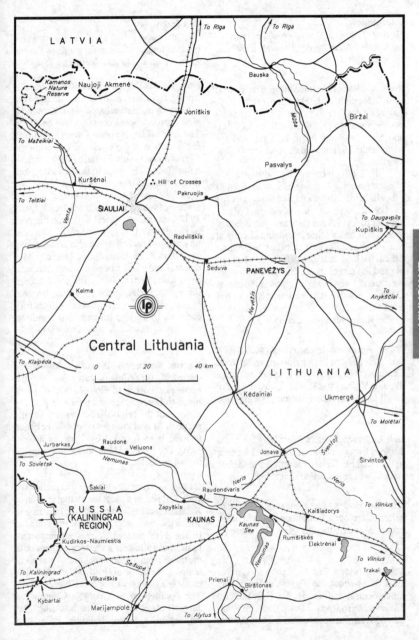

LITHUANIA

Information

Money There are numerous currency-exchange offices along Laisvės alėja and Vilniaus gatvė.

Post & Telecommunications The central post, telegraph and telephone office is at Laisvės alėja 102. It's open for postal business Monday to Friday from 8 am to 8 pm. and Saturday from 8 am to 3 pm and for phone calls 24 hours a day, apart from a few short breaks.

In the lobby, there are long-distance pay phones (tarpmiestiniai telefonai automatai) for calls within Lithuania and the rest of the ex-USSR. Ask at the telephone office counter for the tokens (žetonas) you need for these. You order other international calls at the counter. There's another telephone office, for long-distance calls within Lithuania and the rest of the ex-USSR, a bit further west along Laisvės alėja, opposite the end of Oželkienės gatvė. The Viešbutis Lietuva has a fax service.

The Kaunas telephone code is 27.

Travel Agencies Interservisas (☎ 251 089, fax 226 109) at Betygalos gatvė 2, A K Ceponis (☎ or fax 203 604) of Laisvės alėja 99, and Visata (☎ 227 441) of Miško gatvė 16 all handle accommodation bookings and tours.

Left Luggage There's a left-luggage room at the railway station, in the tunnel leading to the outer platforms, and another at the bus station, where it's called 'bagažinė'.

Museum Hours Most Kaunas museums and galleries are open from noon to 6 pm daily, except Monday, though a few also close on Tuesday.

Other Services The bookshop at Laisvės alėja 81 is about the biggest in town. The most central market is the Geležinkelio Turgavietė (Railway Market) at Čiurlionio gatvė 29, almost opposite the railway station.

Old Town

Vilniaus gatvė is lined with a few attractive old buildings, but the main sights of the old town are on and around Rotušės aikštė.

Rotušės Aikštė The old **central square** is a pretty sight, with many of the 15th and 16th century German merchants' houses around it now restored. Some contain cafés or shops. The fine, white, Baroque former **town hall** in the middle of the square, dating from the 17th century, is now a Palace of Weddings – a function it was given in the Soviet period. It also contains a ceramics museum.

In the square's south-west corner stands a **statue of Maironis** (Jonas Mačiulis; 1862-1932), the Kaunas priest who was the poet of Lithuania's late 19th and early 20th century national revival. His works were banned by Stalin. The **Lithuanian Literary Museum** is in the house behind, where Maironis lived from 1910 to 1932. The south side of the square is dominated by a twin-towered Jesuit church, college and monastery complex from the 17th and 18th centuries, now back in church use after years as a school.

Kaunas Cathedral Kaunas' single-towered cathedral, on Vilniaus gatvė just off the north-east corner of Rotušės aikštė, owes much to Baroque reconstruction, especially inside, but the original 15th century Gothic shape of its windows remains. It's reckoned to have been founded by Vytautas around 1410. The **tomb of Maironis** stands outside the south wall.

Castle A reconstructed tower and sections of wall, and part of a moat are all that remain of Kaunas Castle (Kauno pilis), the hub around which the town originally grew up. Founded in the 11th century, it was an important bastion of Lithuania's western borders until the threat from the German knights was eliminated at the Battle of Grünwald in 1410. The castle is a short walk north of Rotušės aikštė. The boarded-up St George's Church (Šv Jurgio bažnyčia), beside it, is a fine 15th century brick Gothic building. From here you can walk along the bank of the Neris towards its meeting with the Nemunas.

House of Perkūnas & Vytautas Church At Aleksotas gatvė 6, off the south-east corner of Rotušės aikštė, the unusual brick House of Perkūnas (Perkūno namas) was built in the 16th century as trade offices, on the site of a former temple to the Lithuanian thunder god, Perkūnas. There's a small museum inside. Just beyond, on the river bank, is the Gothic Vytautas Church (Vytauto bažnyčia), built of brick by Vytautas about 1400. Its tower and spire are reminiscent of the pre-WW II appearance of Kaliningrad's cathedral.

Lookout Point There's a good panorama of both old and new Kaunas from the hill across the Nemunas from the Vytautas Church. Cross the bridge and mount the hill either by the funicular railway (*funikulierius*) or by the steps beside it. A ride on the funicular costs one bus ticket (you can buy this from the conductor). A right turn from the top of the funicular leads to the lookout point a short distance away.

New Town
Kaunas expanded east from the old town in the 19th century, and the new town fairly soon became the real city centre.

Laisvės Alėja This two-km-long mainly vehicle-free artery (its name means Freedom Avenue) is pleasantly tree-lined and contains a good number of Kaunas' shops, but is architecturally dull. Towards its west end stands a **statue of Vytautas**. In 1972 a student, Romas Kalanta, burnt himself to death in the park facing the statue, as a protest against Soviet occupation, sparking riots which were perhaps the earliest major public protests against Soviet rule. There are remnants of an old defensive wall and tower on the west side of this park. The Philharmonia building, a block north of the Vytautas statue at Sapiegos gatvė 5, was Lithuania's Parliament when Kaunas was the capital between WW I and WW II.

The Merkurijus department store at Laisvės alėja 60 was sometimes used as a film set in the Soviet period because it had some of the best-stocked shelves in the USSR. The **Russian Orthodox church** on Nepriklausomybės aikštė (Independence Square), built in 1895, is the dominant feature of the east end of Laisvės alėja. Also on Nepriklausomybės aikštė is the **Žilinskas Gallery** (Mykolo Žilinsko dailės galerija) showing modern Lithuanian art.

Vienybės Aikštė This square (Unity Square) straddles Donelaičio gatvė a block north of Laisvės alėja. On its south side, flanking the north end of Daukanto gatvė, are the main buildings of Kaunas Technological University (Kauno technologijos universitetas), which has 14,000 students, and Vytautas Magnus University (Vytauto Didžiojo universitetas), refounded in 1989 by an emigré Lithuanian, Lucija Baškauskaite, with around 2000 students. On the north side of Donelaičio gatvė is a cluster of monuments to Lithuanian freedom including two lines of busts of national heroes, an eternal flame flanked by some fine carved crosses and, at the east end of the lines of busts, Kaunas' **Freedom Monument** (Laisvės paminklas), first erected in 1928, hidden during the Stalin era, and put back in place in 1989.

The north side of the square is occupied by a building housing the **Vytautas the Great War Museum** (Vytauto Didžiojo karo muziejus) and the M K Čiurlionis Art Museum (M K Čiurlionio dailės muziejus). The latter, entered from the north side of the building facing Putvinskio gatvė, is Kaunas' leading museum and has good collections of the paintings of Mikalojus Konstantinas Čiurlionis (1875-1911), one of Lithuania's greatest artists and composers, plus 17th to 20th century Lithuanian folk art and 16th to 20th century European applied art. Across the street, at Putvinskio gatvė 64, is Kaunas' very popular '**Devil Museum**' ('Velnių muziejus'), officially the A Žmuidzinavičius Art Collection Museum (A Žmuidzinavičiaus kūrinių ir rinkinių muziejus) – a worldwide collection of hundreds of devil

LITHUANIA

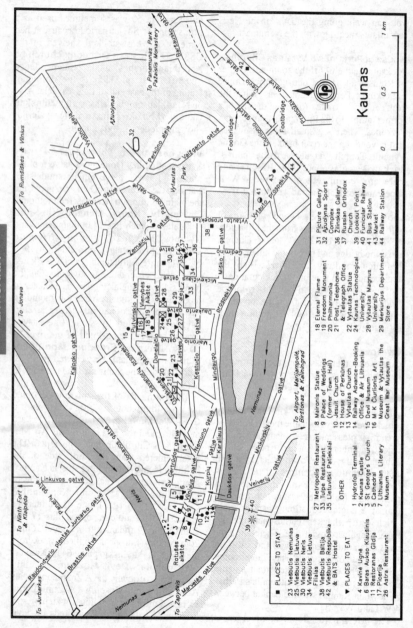

Kaunas

0   0.5   1 km

PLACES TO STAY
23 Viešbutis Nemunas
25 Viešbutis Lietuva
30 Viešbutis Neris
34 Viešbutis Lietuva
38 Filialas
38 Viešbutis Baltija
42 Viešbutis Respublika
    & BATS Hostel

PLACES TO EAT
4   Kavinė Ugnė
6   Baras Auksō Klausinis
5   Restoranas Gildija
17 Pica rija
26 Astra Restaurant
27 Metropolis Restaurant
33 Tulpe Restaurant
35 Lietuviški Patiekalai

OTHER
1   Hydrofoil Terminal
2   Kaunas Castle
3   St George's Church
5   St Michael's Cathedral
7   Lithuanian Literary
    Museum
8   Maironis Statue
9   Palace of Weddings
    (former Town Hall)
10 Jesuit Church
12 House of Perkūnas
13 Vytautas Church
14 Railway Advance-Booking
    Office & Air Lithuania
15 Devil Museum
16 M K Čiurlionis Art
    Museum & Vytautas the
    Great War Museum
18 Eternal Flame
19 Freedom Monument
20 Philharmonia
21 Post, Telephone Office
    & Telegraph Office
22 Vytautas Statue
24 Kaunas Technological
    University
28 Vytautas Magnus
    University
29 Merkurijus Department
    Store
31 Picture Gallery
32 Ažuolynas Sports
    Complex
36 Žilinskas Gallery
37 Russian Orthodox
    Church
39 Lookout Point
40 Funicular Railway
41 Bus Station
43 Market
44 Railway Station

statuettes gathered by the artist Antanas Žmuidzinavičius (1876-1966).

Kaunas' Picture Gallery (Paveikslų galerija) at Donelaičio gatvė 16, three blocks east of Vienybės aikštė, has mainly Western art including work by Rubens, Cézanne, Goya, Picasso and Matisse.

Parks

Wooded parkland covers much of the hilly area just east of the city centre. The small hillside Vytautas Park (Vytauto parkas) occupies the slope up from the end of Laisvės aleja. The lovely Ąžuolynas (Oak Wood) stretches more than a km east from the stadium near the top of the rise. Panemunas Park (Panemunės parkas), on the south side of the river about 1½ km further east, is mostly pine woods. You can reach it by bus No 29 going south down Vytauto prospektas, which takes a roundabout southern route, or by taking trolleybus No 5, 6 or 7 east from the railway station for three km, then walking a km south on Gravrogkų gatvė to cross the river to the park.

Ninth Fort & Jewish Ghetto

The Ninth Fort (written 'IX Fortas' in Lithuanian), at Žemaičių plentas 73 on Kaunas' north-west outskirts, was built in the late 19th century and used by the Russians in a failed attempt to defend their western frontiers against Germany in WW I. In WW II the Nazis turned it into a death camp. An estimated 80,000 people, including most of Kaunas' Jewish population, were murdered here. One of the prison buildings remains, and the site of the mass grave is marked by stark, monumental sculptures. The museum at the site entrance pointedly had material on Soviet atrocities and deportations, as well as Nazi horrors, when I visited. Bus No 45 goes to the Ninth Fort from the railway station. It stops by the roundabout at the east end of the Neris bridge, near the old town, on the way.

The Kaunas Jewish ghetto in WW II lay on the west bank of the Neris, within the area bounded by Jurbarko, Panerių and Demokratų streets. Much of it is derelict.

Pažaislis Monastery

This fine example of 17th century Baroque architecture stands about nine km east of the city centre near the shores of the Kaunas Sea (Kauno marios), the large artificial lake created by damming the Nemunas on the east side of Kaunas for hydro-electricity. Its highlight is the monastery church with a 50-metre-high cupola and a sumptuous interior, modelled on a Venetian design, with pink and black marble brought from Kraków in Poland and frescoes on the walls and ceilings. There are pleasant gardens, too. The monastery has had a chequered history, passing from Catholic to Orthodox then back to Catholic hands before being used as a psychiatric hospital for part of the Soviet era. It has been under restoration since the 1960s. To get there, take trolleybus No 5 from the railway station or from Donelaičio gatvė in the city centre to its terminus on Masiulio gatvė, a few hundred metres before the monastery.

Places to Stay – bottom end

There are two cheap central hotels. The *Viešbutis Baltija* (☎ 223 639), at Vytauto prospektas 71, charges 8/13.50 litų for reasonable singles/doubles with private shower and toilet. The older *Viešbutis Nemunas* (☎ 223 102) at Laisvės alėja 88 has large-ish rooms with TV, toilet and basin for 9.75/19.50 litų, but in the room I was offered the toilet hadn't been cleaned. Showers are shared.

The *Viešbutis Lietuva Filialas* (☎ 221 791) at Laisvės alėja 35, an annexe of the top-end Viešbutis Lietuva, quoted me 20/24.50 litų for singles/doubles with private bath and TV, or 34 litų for a suite – but these prices might escalate if management realises there's a foreigner interested.

BATS (Baltic Accommodation & Travel Service) (☎ 748 972) has a good place at Prancūzų gatvė 59, about a 1¼-km walk east of the railway station. It's poorly served by public transport and there are no restaurants nearby, but the accommodation is pretty good. It's actually a middle-range hotel, the *Viešbutis Respublika*, normally charging 100 to 125 litų a night, but if you say you're from BATS, or better still get the BATS or Lithuanian Youth Hostels people in Vilnius to book ahead for you, you'll be charged about 40 litų per person. I had an entire suite of bedroom, bathroom and kitchen, with fine upper-storey views, to myself for 40 litų this way. Breakfast is available on the top floor. From the railway station walk east along Čiurlionio gatvė, which becomes Baršausko gatvė, cross the second footbridge over the railway (don't be tempted by the first), climb the steps on the far side and go a block straight ahead to Prancūzų gatvė. Turn left along Prancūzų gatvė; No 59 is the second nine-storey building on the left and its entrance is at the back.

Simpleksas (☎ 294 556, fax 203 647) at Putvinskio gatvė 49 can arrange bed and breakfast in private homes. The *Tourist Club of Latvia* (see Rīga – Places to Stay) is another organisations which can arrange accommodation in private homes in Kaunas. Also try some of the agents listed under Private Homes in the Accommodation section of the introductory Facts for the Visitor chapter.

For student accommodation try the *Student Representation* (studentų atstovybė) office (☎ 223 191) at Vytautas Magnus University (Vytauto Didžiojo universitetas), at Daukanto gatvė 28.

Places to Stay – top end
Probably the best hotel is the *Viešbutis Lietuva* (☎ 205 992, fax 206 269), centrally placed at Daukanto gatvė 21, a pre-Soviet establishment with sizeable rooms for 170/230 litų. There's no restaurant in-house, only a snack bar, but the large Metropolis restaurant is next door. The *Viešbutis Neris* (☎ 204 224, 203 863, fax 205 289), also central at Donelaicio gatvė 27, is newer with 180 moderately sized rooms at similar prices. It has its own restaurant.

Places to Eat
Kaunas still hasn't fully recovered from Soviet restaurant-blight. Restaurants and cafés tend to cluster along Laisvės alėja and

Vilniaus gatvė and near Rotušės aikštė. There are quite a lot of them, but too many have limited and disappointing fare. It's generally a question of wandering along and seeing which place repels least.

There's one life-saver, however: the *Picerija* (Pizzeria) at Donelaičio gatvė 66 beside Vienybės aikštė. You couldn't claim that what's served up here has the Italian touch – the base is thick and bread-like and the toppings have none of the classic pizza tang – but when you're wondering where on earth you can fill your stomach half-tastily without having to grapple with surly doormen, aloof waiters or a long wait, this place is a godsend. Several varieties are on offer, all for around 1 litas: su silkė is with herring; dešra, sausage; pikantiška dešra, savoury sausage (it comes with egg too); mėsa, meat; and grybais, with mushrooms. All have plenty of cheese. If you're really hungry order two. The Piceria's hours are from 10 am to 7.30 pm on Monday, 10 am to 9 pm Tuesday to Friday, and 11 am to 9 pm Saturday and Sunday.

The *Metropolis* at Laisvės alėja 68 on the corner of Daukanto gatvė is one of the best large restaurants – it has a rock group and dancing in the evenings and a meal will cost around 15 to 20 litų. The *Astra,* half a block west of the Metropolis, is cheaper, popular and quite quick though the choice of food is fairly limited. Another possibility is the *Tulpe* restaurant half a block east of the Metropolis at Laisvės alėja 49.

The *Viešbutis Neris* has a large glittering cavern of a restaurant with a variety show of some kind late in the evening and exceptionally ordinary food at about 8 litai a meal. I had to repeat the starter for a third course to try to fill up, as there were no desserts available. What made the occasion enjoyable however were the airs of the manager who resembled a cross between Joan Collins and Cruella de Vil of *101 Dalmatians.* A mere extension of her finger nails towards the appointed table was all she deemed necessary in the way of customer relations as she led diners across the room in her golden two-piece and dangling furs.

The *Viešbutis Baltija* has another large, musical restaurant where you can get a reasonable meal for around 4 to 6 litų. For Lithuanian specialities try *Lietuviški Patiekalai* at the corner of Laisvės alėja and Nepriklausomybės aikštė.

A block from Rotušės aikštė in the old town, the *Baras Aukso Kiaušinis* on Vilniaus gatvė, at the corner of Daukšos gatvė, serves (sadly without much cheer) cheery little egg-liqueur-based cocktails and a few light bites. The *Kavinė Ugnė* at Rotušės aikštė 23, on the north side of the square, has outdoor tables in a courtyard in summer. The *Restoranas Gildija* at Rotušės aikštė 2 is reputed to be one of Kaunas' best restaurants – its atmosphere was dead when I looked in one lunch time, but it's probably more appealing at busier times. It's open from noon to 11 pm daily, except Monday when it closes at 6 pm. There's a beer cellar, the *Aludė Gildija*, next door.

Entertainment

The main classical concert hall is the Kaunas Philharmonic (Kauno Filharmonija) at Sapiegos gatvė 5. The ticket office is open from 2 to 7 pm. Visiting ensembles from Vilnius and elsewhere quite often perform here, as do local ones, among which the Kaunas State Choir (Kauno Valstybinis Choras) has a high reputation. Organ and chamber music concerts are given in the former Orthodox cathedral on Nepriklausomybės aikštė. The Kaunas State Drama Theatre (Valstybinis dramos teatras), at Laisvės alėja 71, has one of Lithuania's most original theatre companies.

Keep your eyes open for signs announcing games of Kaunas' Žalgiris basketball team, which has won Soviet and European championships and supplied three of Lithuania's Olympic bronze-medal team in 1992.

The leading sports venue is the Ąžuolynas sports-hall/stadium complex (Ąžuolyno sporto kompleksas) at Perkūno alėja 5.

Discos crop up on Friday and Saturday nights at places like Vytautas Magnus University, the Ąžuolynas sports hall and elsewhere.

Things to Buy

The more interesting craft shops include Dailė at Rotušės aikštė 27 and on the corner of Laisvės alėja and Daukanto gatvė; and Dailės Salonas, on Vytauto prospektas next to the Viešbutis Baltija.

Getting There & Away

This section deals with transport within the Baltic states and the Kaliningrad Region. Bus and rail connections to/from other countries are covered in the Getting There & Away chapter.

Air The privately owned Air Lithuania (Aviakompanija Lietuva) flies to/from Palanga at least twice a week, as well as to cities in Finland, Sweden, Germany, Hungary and the Czech Republic. It's office (☎ 229 706) is at Šv Gertrūdos gatvė 7. Flights may start to/from Rīga, Tallinn, Moscow, St Petersburg or Minsk with LAL, Latvian and other airlines. LAL is on ☎ 228 176. The airport is on top of the hill, across the river, south of the old town.

Bus Kaunas bus station is at Vytauto prospektas 24. There's a useful 'Informacija' window in the booking hall. Services from Kaunas include:

Birštonas
  40 km, one hour, about 20 buses daily
Druskininkai
  130 km, two to three hours, about 12 buses daily (most via Alytus)
Ignalina
  200 km, four hours, three or four buses daily
Jurbarkas
  85 km, 1½ hours, several buses daily
Kaliningrad
  250 km, six hours, three buses daily via Marijampolė and Chernyakhovsk, or Jurbarkas and Sovietsk
Kalvarija
  75 km, 1½ hours, about six buses daily
Klaipėda
  210 km, three to 3½ hours, about 12 direct buses daily
Lazdijai
  100 km, two hours, four or five buses daily
Marijampolė
  55 km, one to 1½ hours, about 15 buses daily

Palanga
    230 km, 3½ hours. about 10 buses daily from 1
    June to 10 September; one bus daily at other
    times
Panevėžys
    110 km, two hours, 20 to 25 buses daily
Pärnu
    445 km, 9½ hours, one bus daily
Rīga
    280 km, 5½ hours, five buses daily
Šiauliai
    140 km, three hours, 10 to 12 buses daily
Sovietsk
    150 km, three to 3½ hours, two or three buses
    daily
Tallinn
    575 km, 12 hours, one bus daily
Vilnius
    100 km, two hours, about 30 buses daily (also 12
    microbuses, daily, in 1¾ hours)

Train Kaunas station is at Čiurlionio gatvė
16, at the south end of Vytauto prospektas.
Window Nos 1 and 2 sell tickets for any train.
Window Nos 3, 4 and 5, the 'priemiestiniai
kasos' at the west end of the station, only sell
tickets for 'local' trains (which include the
majority of those to Vilnius). There's an
advance-booking office (Geležinkelio
kasos), for tickets more than 24 hours before
departure, near the old town at Šv Gertrūdos
gatvė 7, open daily except Sunday.

About 15 local and nine or 10 long-distance trains make the trip to/from Vilnius
daily. The two types are shown on separate
timetables. The journey is usually about two
hours, but a few trains make it in less, the
quickest being 1¼ hours. The long-distance
trains mostly terminate at Moscow, St
Petersburg, Kharkov or Gomel eastbound,
and Klaipėda, Rīga or Kaliningrad westbound.

The *Baltic Express*, travelling between
Warsaw and Tallinn via Rīga and Tartu, also
passes through Kaunas (see the introductory
Getting There & Away chapter), as does the
Vilnius-Šeštokai train which connects with
the daily Šeštokai-Suwałki train into Poland.
There is a special window in the Šv Ger-
trūdos gatvė booking office for tickets to
Poland, open Monday to Friday from 9 am
to 2 pm and 3 to 5 pm. There are also three

other trains a day from Kaunas to Šeštokai
and vice versa.

To/from Klaipėda there's one train nightly
each way, taking eight hours; to/from Rīga
there's one train nightly each way, taking
5½ hours; to/from Kaliningrad there are five
to seven trains daily each way, taking 3½ to
4½ hours; to/from Šiauliai there are three or
four trains daily, taking about four hours.

Car Neca (☎ 201 928) at Donelaičio gatvė
26 advertises cars to rent. Some of the travel
agencies mentioned in the Information
section also advertise car rentals.

Hydrofoil From about May to September
you can travel daily by *Raketa* hydrofoil
along the Nemunas to Nida – and to Klaipėda
at weekends – an unusual and appealing way
of reaching Lithuania's coast. The craft leave
Kaunas about 8 am and get back in the evening. It's about a four-hour trip to Nida, five
hours to Klaipėda, and the one-way fare is
about 6.50 litų. I've heard of foreigners
being asked 10 times as much, but you
shouldn't have to put up with that. The terminal (☎ 261 348) is at Raudondvario plentas
107, on the north side of the Nemunas about
half a km west of the mouth of the Neris. You
can get there by bus No 11 from the Kaunas
Castle terminal on Jonavos gatvė, or trolleybus No 7 from the railway station or
westbound on Kęstučio gatvė in the city
centre or from the roundabout on the east
side of the Neris bridge. Get off at the
Kaspinas stop on Raudondvario plentas (the
second stop on the west side of the Neris
bridge) and walk a little further along to a
turning marked 'Prieplauka' ('Dock') to the
left (south), opposite a petrol station. The
terminal is a grey concrete building with a
tower, near the river bank, a few hundred
metres away.

Getting Around
Buses and trolleybuses go almost everywhere. The orange-covered *Kauno turistinė
schema* map shows their routes. Key central
services, linking the rail and bus stations
with the city centre and the old town, include

trolleybus Nos 1, 3, 5 and 7 which all go north from the railway station along Vytauto prospektas, west along Kęstučio gatvė and Nemuno gatvė, then north on Birštono gatvė. In the other direction they head east along Šv Gertrūdos gatvė, Ožeškienės gatvė and Donelaičio gatvė, then south down Vytauto prospektas to the railway station.

You can call a taxi on ☎ 777 775 or 777 777.

AROUND KAUNAS
Rumšiškės
The **Lithuanian Country Life Museum** at Rumšiškės, 20 km east of Kaunas about two km off the Vilnius road, is well worth a visit for its large and interesting collection of 18th and 19th century Lithuanian country buildings (mainly wooden) and artefacts. Several entire 'farmsteads' have been set up. They're spread over a nearly two-sq-km site near the Kaunas Sea (Kauno marios). On summer Sundays there are folklore performances, and there's a tavern in the grounds.

To get there take a Vilnius-bound bus from Kaunas (or a Kaunas-bound bus from Vilnius), get off at the Rumšiškės turning and walk.

Birštonas
Forty km south of Kaunas on the Nemunas, the small spa town of Birštonas (population: 4000) is unremarkable except for the highly popular jazz festival it holds over about three days in spring, in even-numbered years, which brings out Lithuania's top jazz musicians and many of their fans. The most recent event was held in late March. There's a historical museum at Vytauto gatvė 9. The *Viešbutis Nemunas* (☎ 210-56 345) is at Algirdo gatvė 3 and the *Viešbutis Turistas* (☎ 210-56 331) at Turistų gatvė 1. There are a couple of restaurants on Algirdo gatvė.

Zapyškis
There's a gem of a little 16th century **Gothic church**, red brick with a very tall, pointed roof, in fields by the south bank of the Nemunas near Zapyškis, 18 km west of Kaunas. Zapyškis is on the Šakiai road.

Kaunas to Jurbarkas
The 85-km road west from Kaunas to the town of Jurbarkas follows the north bank of the Nemunas fairly closely. The Nemunas was once an important trade route and, at one stage, this region also lay in the frontier lands between Lithuania and the territory of the Teutonic Order, so it's not surprising that quite a few castles were built along here. The main ones to look for are at **Raudondvaris**, (eight km from Kaunas); **Veliuona**, where there are two castle mounds and fine Nemunas valley views (50 km from Kaunas); and **Raudonė**, an impressive 17th century towered castle (60 km from Kaunas).

If you have your own transport this could be a pleasant trip out from Kaunas or an alternative route towards the coast. If not, you should be able to reach one or two of the castles using the moderately frequent Kaunas-Jurbarkas bus service.

ŠIAULIAI
Šiauliai (population: 145,000), 140 km north of Kaunas and 80 km west of Panevėžys, is Lithuania's fourth-biggest city and the main centre of the north-western region of Žemaitija, known to history as Samogitia. The real magnet of the Šiauliai area is the strange **Hill of Crosses**, 10 km north of the town off the Rīga road. If the Hill of Crosses is all you're interested in here, you could visit it in a day's drive between any of the main Lithuanian cities or Rīga, if you have your own vehicle. If you're travelling by public transport you may need to spend a night in Šiauliai (unless you're coming from Rīga or going on there afterwards) as you have to get to Šiauliai first, then get a bus out to the Hill of Crosses, then another bus back into town to catch your onward transport.

History
The Šiauliai region played an important role in the fortunes of medieval Lithuania and its enemies. It was at, or not too far from the modern city that, in 1236, the Knights of the Sword, returning north from a raid in Samogitia, were decisively defeated at the Battle of Saulė. The victors were

LITHUANIA

Samogitians together with (depending on whose account you read) either Semigallians from what's now part of Latvia, to their north, or other allies from what's now Lithuania. The knights' grand master, Volquin, was killed; the following year, the order was forced to reorganise as a branch of the Teutonic Order. The Teutonic Order finally occupied Samogitia in 1398, but a Samogitian rebellion in 1408 led to a joint Lithuanian and Polish campaign against the knights and the decisive defeat of the knights at Grünwald in 1410.

Šiauliai was a relatively big town by the mid-15th century. Much of it was consumed by a fire in 1872 and today's town mostly dates from after that.

Orientation

Central Šiauliai isn't too spread out and is quite walkable. The main north-south street is Tilžės gatvė, with the bus station towards its south (lower) end and the tall SS Peter & Paul's Church on Pergalės aikštė towards its north end, almost a km away. To the south, Tilžės gatvė becomes the road to Sovietsk and Kaliningrad; to the north it becomes the Rīga road. The main east-west axis is Vilniaus gatvė, which crosses Tilžės gatvė 300 metres south of the church and is pedestrianised for over half a km either side. A small clock tower in the little square where the two streets meet is a good orientation point and favourite local meeting place.

Information

There are left-luggage lockers at the railway station. There are currency-exchange offices in the bus station and on the west side of Tilžės gatvė immediately south of the corner of Vilniaus gatvė, and a branch of the Lietuvos Bankas (Bank of Lithuania) half a block west of the post office on Aušros alėja. The main post, telephone and telegraph office is at Aušros alėja 42, two blocks west of SS Peter & Paul's Church. The Šiauliai travel firm (☎ 34 509, fax 38 461) at Varpo gatvė 22A, and Paralele (☎ 38 810, fax 36 724) at Vytauto gatvė 145 offer accommodation and local tours.

Knygos at Vilniaus gatvė 213 is a quite well-stocked bookshop. Dailė at Vilniaus gatvė 136, facing the clock tower, sells handicrafts. The department store is at Vilniaus gatvė 206, and the market is on Turgaus gatvė.

The Šiauliai telephone code is 214.

Town Centre

The chief landmark is the white **SS Peter & Paul's Church** (Šv Petro ir Povilo bažnyčia) overlooking Pergalės aikštė at the north end of the town centre. It has what's claimed to be Lithuania's highest spire (64 metres) and, standing on a hilltop, it is visible from some distance away. It's a fine Renaissance-style building dating from the early 17th century, though with some reconstruction down the years, most recently in the 1950s. **St George's Church** down on Dubijos gatvė near the railway station, was, as its appearance indicates, originally Russian Orthodox (it was built for the local Russian garrison in 1909) but is now Catholic.

Šiauliai has a collection of unusual museums if you're in the mood for them. They cover history and ethnography (the Aušra muziejus at Aušros alėja 47); bicycles (the Dviračių muziejus at Vilniaus gatvė 139); cats (Žuvininkų gatvė 18); and photography (Vilniaus gatvė 140). The first three are open Wednesday to Sunday, from 11 am to 5, 6 or 7 pm; the last Thursday to Monday, from noon to 7 pm. There's an exhibition hall, the Parodu rumai, at Vilniaus gatvė 245.

Hill of Crosses

The Hill of Crosses (Kryžių kalnas) is 10 km north of Šiauliai, 1½ km east off the road to Joniškis and Rīga. This is a place of national pilgrimage: a two-humped hillock covered in a forest of thousands upon thousands of crosses – large and tiny, expensive and cheap, wood and metal. There are crosses festooned with dozens of smaller crosses, and crosses with heaps of little crosses at their feet. Some are devotional, to accompany prayers, others are memorials. Some are finely carved folk-art masterpieces.

The hillock is said to have been originally

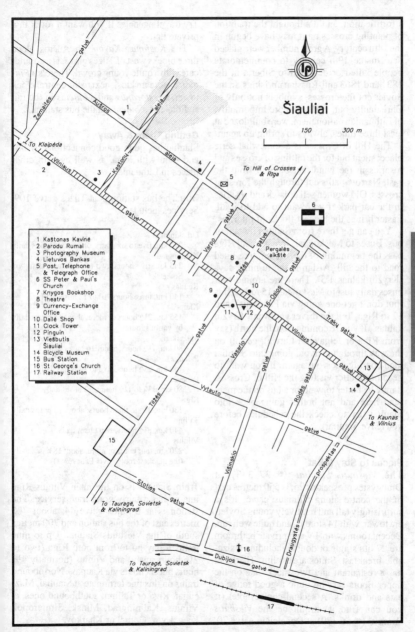

Šiauliai

0   150   300 m

1 Kaštonas Kavinė
2 Parodu Rumai
3 Photography Museum
4 Lietuvos Bankas
5 Post, Telephone
   & Telegraph Office
6 SS Peter & Paul's
   Church
7 Knygos Bookshop
8 Theatre
9 Currency-Exchange
   Office
10 Dailė Shop
11 Clock Tower
12 Pinguin
13 Viešbutis
   Šiauliai
14 Bicycle Museum
15 Bus Station
16 St George's Church
17 Railway Station

To Klaipėda

To Hill of Crosses
& Rīga

Pergalės
aikštė

To Kaunas
& Vilnius

To Tauragė, Sovietsk
& Kaliningrad

To Tauragė, Sovietsk
& Kaliningrad

LITHUANIA

a fortification, and it's thought the tradition of planting crosses on it may have begun in the 14th century. A great number were placed here in the 19th century to commemorate people killed or deported to Siberia in the 1831 and 1863 anti-Russian uprisings. In the Soviet era the crosses, symbols not only of Christianity but, perhaps more importantly, of Lithuanian nationalism, were bulldozed at least three times, always to spring up again.

The Hill of Crosses is a somewhat eerie place: silent but for the rattling of crosses and rosaries in the wind that bites in from the east. Narrow paths cut through the forest of crosses. Old women sell crosses and rosaries in the car park if you want to add to it all. Easter brings the biggest flocks of pilgrims.

You can get there from Šiauliai by taxi or bus. Buses to Meškuičiai, Joniškis and Rīga pass the beginning of the 1½-km tree-lined road to the hill. A sign at the turning says 'Kryžių kalnas 1.5'. There are around four buses daily just to Meškuičiai, 15 to Joniškis (but don't get one going via Pakruojis), and 12 to Rīga. Tell the driver you want 'Kryžių kalnas'. If you're coming from the north (say from Rīga or Jelgava in Latvia), get off on the way through to avoid going into Šiauliai then coming back out again. If you want to head north after visiting the Hill of Crosses, it may be better to wait for a bus on the main road here and not bother going back into Šiauliai (try to check the schedules before you leave Šiauliai).

Places to Stay & Eat
The *Viešbutis Šiauliai* (☎ 37 333), at Draugystės prospektas 25, is 550 metres east of the centre along Vilniaus gatvė. It's a surprisingly tall and relatively young Soviet-era tower, with 14 storeys, and quite well run. Decent rooms with TV and private bathroom are 27 litų single or double including a sizeable breakfast. Suites are 50 litų. The hotel has a restaurant and two snack bars on the upper floors serving quite a good range of eats and drinks. A second-choice hotel (if you can find it) might be the *Viešbutis Salduvė* (☎ 56 179) at Donelaičio gatvė 70.

Try travel agencies if you want a room in a private flat.

The *Kaštonas Kavinė* on Aušros alėja, three blocks west of Tilžės gatvė, is a popular café with a quite young crowd. There's a *Pinguin* ice-cream kiosk next to the central clock tower, a *restoranas* and a *bufetas* in the rail station, and a *bufetas* in the bus station.

Getting There & Away
Šiauliai has quite good connections by bus and train with Rīga, as well as with other places in Lithuania.

Bus The bus station is at Tilžės gatvė 109. Services include:

Druskininkai
    270 km, five to six hours, one or two buses daily
Kaliningrad
    245 km, five hours, two to four buses daily via Sovietsk
Kaunas
    140 km, three hours, 10 to 12 buses daily
Klaipėda
    155 km, 2½ hours or more, about 15 buses daily by various routes
Mažeikiai
    80 km, 1½ hours, about 16 buses daily
Palanga
    150 km, 2½ hours, five to 12 buses daily
Panevėžys
    80 km, 1¼ to 1½ hours, 12 buses daily
Rīga
    130 km, 2½ to three hours, about 12 buses daily
Tallinn
    440 km, 8½ hours, two buses daily
Vilnius
    220 km, four hours or more, about 18 buses daily (the quickest route is via Panevėžys)

Train Šiauliai is on the main Vilnius-Rīga line so has a fairly good train service. The station is at Dubijos gatvė 44, about 700 metres east of the bus station and 700 metres south of the Viešbutis Šiauliai. Up to nine trains a day go to/from both Rīga (two to 2½ hours away) and Vilnius (normally 4½ hours but six hours via Kaunas). Northbound trains on this line terminate at Šiauliai, Mažeikiai, Rīga or Tallinn; southbound ones, at Vilnius, Kaliningrad, Minsk, Simferopol, Kiev, Lvov, Gomel or Kharkov.

Other train services to/from Šiauliai include:

Daugavpils: three trains daily, 4½ to 5½ hours
Kaliningrad: two trains daily, 6½ to 7½ hours
Kaunas: three or four trains daily, four hours
Klaipėda: five trains daily, three to four hours
Sovietsk: one or two trains daily, 3½ hours
Tallinn: two trains daily, 10 hours

PANEVĖŽYS

Panevėžys, 140 km north of Vilnius on the Nevėžis River and on the main road to Rīga, is Lithuania's fifth city, with 125,000 people. The road from Vilnius crosses the western edge of the Aukštaitija Upland, unremarkable but with some long vistas. Panevėžys is a drab, industrial place full of Soviet-era buildings. There's a **regional museum** at Vasario 16-Osios gatvė 23, open daily (except Monday) from noon to 8 pm, and a **folk-art museum** at Respublikos gatvė 56.

Places to Stay & Eat

If you need somewhere to stop the night, there's a reasonable hotel, the *Viešbutis Nevėžis* (☎ 254-35 117), at Laisvės alėja 26, charging around 13/16.50 litų for singles/doubles with private bathroom. The hotel has a restaurant and there are one or two other eateries along Laisvės alėja.

The *Viešbutis Rambynas* (☎ 254-61 007) at Respublikos gatvė 34 is cheaper: suites costing 16.50 litų are the only rooms with private bathroom. Another cheaper possibility is the *Viešbutis Upytė* (☎ 254-66 747) at Respublikos gatvė 38.

Getting There & Away

There are buses to/from Vilnius (about 30 daily, taking 2¼ hours), Kaunas (20 to 25 daily, two hours), Šiauliai (12 daily, one to 1½ hours), Bauska (six daily, two to 2½ hours), Rīga (four or five daily, about four hours) and elsewhere. The bus station is at Savanorių aikštė 5. The Šiauliai-Daugavpils railway runs through Panevėžys, too, with three daily trains each way, one eastbound continuing to Moscow and one westbound to Klaipėda and Kaliningrad. The station is on Stoties gatvė.

Western Lithuania

Lithuania has a short (under 100 km), but attractive coastline. Palanga is the main seaside resort and, in summer, has probably the most light-hearted atmosphere you'll find anywhere in the Baltic states. Klaipėda, at the mouth of the 100-km-long Courland Lagoon (Kuršių marios), is Lithuania's historic third city and major port.

South of Klaipėda stretches the Baltic states' most unusual natural feature – the Courland Spit, known to the Lithuanians as Neringa or the Kuršių nerija. This is an anorexically thin finger of sand, 98 km long, but nowhere more than four km wide, dividing the Courland Lagoon from the open Baltic Sea. It's a place with a touch of magic, composed entirely of sand dunes up to 66 metres high. Its northern half is Lithuanian territory, its southern half Russian. A paved road runs down its length from Smiltynė, the northern tip opposite Klaipėda, to Zelenogradsk in the Kaliningrad Region. In the Lithuanian half there is accommodation at Smiltynė and at two small fishing villages, Juodkrantė and Nida, which double as holiday resorts.

At the time of the German crusades in the 13th century, what's now coastal Lithuania was, like western Latvia, inhabited by a Baltic people called the Cours. The Cours long ago lost their distinct identity but their name lives on in the two outstanding geographical features of the region: the Courland Lagoon and the Courland Spit.

Klaipėda Today, published in parallel-text English and German by the team which produces the excellent *Vilnius In Your Pocket*, is a very useful practical guide to the whole Lithuanian coast.

ŽEMAITIJA UPLAND

North-west Lithuania, historically called Samogitia, is today known as Žemaitija, or Lower Lithuania, in contrast to the north-east of the country which is Aukštaitija (Upper Lithuania). This distinction can hardly be one of altitude since Žemaitija is only slightly lower than Aukštaitija. But, confusingly, in a part of the world that's really pretty low (altitude-wise) all over, keen eyes have observed that the middle part of Žemaitija is a bit less low than the rest. So they call it Žemaičių aukštuma, which means – you guessed it – Upper Lower Lithuania. To reduce confusion, it's more commonly rendered as Žemaitija Upland.

The Kaunas-Klaipėda road crosses the southern edge of this upland, passing within 13 km of its highest point, Medvėgalis (234 metres).

Plungė

Plungė, on the Klaipėda-Kretinga-Šiauliai railway, and just off the Palanga-Kretinga-Šiauliai road, is one of the main towns of the area. It has a hotel, the *Viešbutis Gandinga* (☎ 218-52 345), at Minijos gatvė 4.

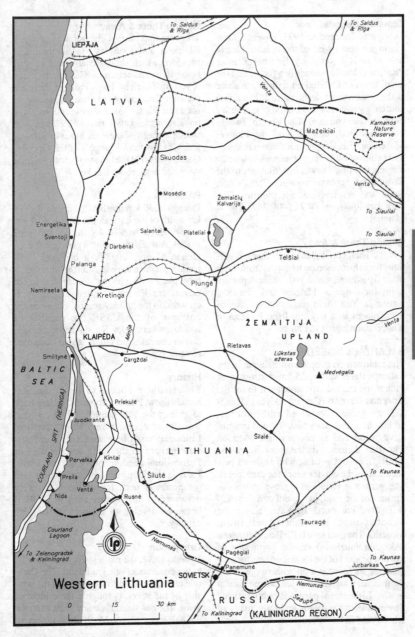

Žemaitija National Park

This park, declared in 1991, covers 200 sq km in the north-west of the upland. Nearly half of it is covered by fir forests. Lake Plateliai (Platelių ežeras) is a focus, and the small town of Plateliai on its western shore is the main visitor destination. It has a fine church, a yacht club and a number of holiday homes where you might find a room. Twenty km to the north-east, just off the Plungė-Mažeikiai road, Žemaičių Kalvarija is a popular centre of Catholic worship, with some 20 chapels forming a seven-km 'Stations of the Cross' route, commemorating Christ's life, death and resurrection, for pilgrims. The park headquarters (☎ 218-48 343) are at Plateliai.

Getting There & Away

See the Klaipėda, Palanga and Šiauliai sections for information on transport from those places to Plungė, which is the main departure point for buses to Plateliai and Žemaičių Kalvarija. You could reach one or other of these places in a day trip from Palanga or Klaipėda, changing at Plungė.

SALANTAI & MOSĖDIS

The main reason people visit Salantai in the Salantas River valley, 25 km north-west of Plungė, on the road to Skuodas, is to see the **Orvydas Garden** (Orvydų sodyba). This is a large garden decorated with grottoes, arches, huts and many fantastic and imaginative wood and stone carvings, often on Christian themes. All the work is by one family, named Orvydas, who suffered persecution in the Soviet years for their pains. The garden is visible as a grove of trees to the east of the road, just south of Salantai.

Twelve km north of Salantai, on the Skuodas road, is another small town, Mosėdis. The goal here is the **Rock Museum** (Akmenų muziejus) on the north side of town, a product of the local fondness for rock gardens. Its focus is a pit with an obelisk in the middle, which is regarded as a monument to the Lithuanian partisans who resisted Soviet rule in the 1940s and '50s, many of whom died in this area.

Getting There & Away

There are four buses daily each way between Klaipėda and Skuodas via Salantai and Mosėdis, which should enable you to visit both places and return to Klaipėda in a day if you time it right. From Palanga there are occasional excursions to Mosėdis in summer for under 5 litai – ask at the excursions kiosk on Kretingos gatvė beside Palanga bus station. Otherwise there are buses to Salantai and Mosėdis from Plungė. For the Orvydas Garden get off at the last stop before Salantai town and walk about one km.

PALANGA

Palanga is 30 km north of Klaipėda and 18 km south of the Latvian border, on a 10-km sandy beach backed by dunes and pine woods. A small town with a permanent population of only 20,000, it becomes Lithuania's premier seaside resort in summer, a busy place with a happy atmosphere. In the Soviet era Palanga tended to get overcrowded in the holiday season, but since the collapse of the USSR the number of holidaymakers from Russia and other ex-Soviet countries has fallen. It's an attractive, likeable place.

History

Though there appear to be no ancient remains now, Palanga apparently dates back to at least the 12th century. Lying on what was, for centuries, a very short stretch of Lithuanian coast between German or Prussian territory to the south and German or Polish-dominated territory to the north, Palanga has often been Lithuania's only port (or potential port, for it was completely destroyed by the Swedish army in 1710). It began to develop as a resort in the 19th century.

Orientation

Vytauto gatvė, the main street, runs parallel to the coast about one km inland. The Catholic church at Vytauto gatvė 51, on the west side of the street, is roughly the middle of town. The bus station is a few steps east of it on Kretingos gatvė. Most other places of

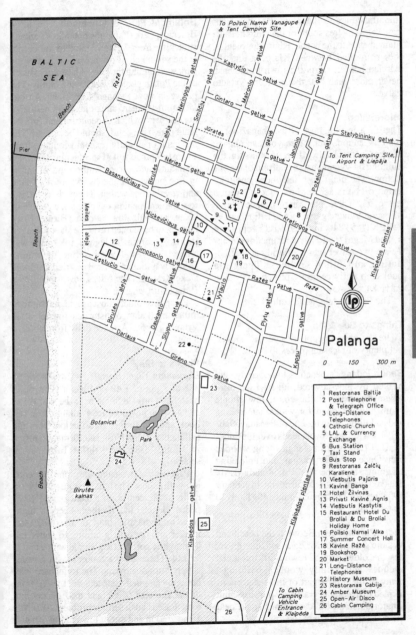

LITHUANIA

BALTIC
SEA

Beach

Pier

Beach

Beach

To Poilsio Namai Vanagupė
& Tent Camping Site

To Tent Camping Site,
Airport & Liepāja

Statybininkų gatvė

Kastyčio gatvė

Neringos aleja

Smiltelių gatvė

Cintaro gatvė

Vaironio gatvė

Jūratės gatvė

Nėries gatvė

Basanavičiaus gatvė

Birutės aleja

Mickevičiaus gatvė

Kęstučio gatvė

Simpsonio gatvė

Meilės aleja

Birutės aleja

Daukanto gatvė

Dariaus ir Girėno gatvė

Silupo gatvė

Vytauto gatvė

Kretingos gatvė

Ražės gatvė

Ražė

Pylių gatvė

L.Jononio gatvė

Potelos gatvė

Klaipėdos plentas

Kapsu gatvė

Botanical
Park

Birutės
kalnas

Klaipėdos plentas

Palanga

0   150   300 m

To Cabin
Camping
Vehicle
Entrance
& Klaipėda

1 Restoranas Baltija
2 Post, Telephone
  & Telegraph Office
3 Long-Distance
  Telephones
4 Catholic Church
5 LAL & Currency
  Exchange
6 Bus Station
7 Taxi Stand
8 Bus Stop
9 Restoranas Žalčių
  Karalienė
10 Viešbutis Pajūris
11 Kavinė Banga
12 Hotel Žilvinas
13 Privati Kavinė Agnis
14 Viešbutis Kastytis
15 Restaurant Hotel Du
   Broliai & Du Broliai
   Holiday Home
16 Poilsio Namai Alka
17 Summer Concert Hall
18 Kavinė Ražė
19 Bookshop
20 Market
21 Long-Distance
   Telephones
22 History Museum
23 Restoranas Gabija
24 Amber Museum
25 Open-Air Disco
26 Cabin Camping

importance are to the south. Basanavičiaus gatvė, 150 metres south of the church, is the main avenue to the beach. Klaipėdos plentas, the main road between Klaipėda and the Latvian border, skirts the town to the east, never more than 750 metres from Vytauto gatvė.

Information

There's a left-luggage office (bagažinė) in the bus station. One place you can change money is the LAL office, upstairs in the building on Vytauto gatvė out front of the bus station. The main post, telephone and telegraph office is across the street at Vytauto gatvė 53. There are long-distance phone offices at Vytauto gatvė 39 and Biliūno gatvė 1. REK (☎ 54 840, fax 51 709) at Žvejų gatvė 47 and Mega (☎ 52 770) at Klaipėdos plentas 72 are two travel agents offering accommodation and other services. There's a bookshop fairly centrally placed at Vytauto gatvė 84.

The Palanga telephone code is 236.

Things to See & Do

There are only a couple of specific 'sights' but plenty of pleasant places to stroll.

Beach Palanga's beach is long, sandy, and backed by pine-covered dunes. Like elsewhere along the Baltic coast, few people swim, but it's good for walks, sunbathing and paddling. From the end of Basanavičiaus gatvė, a wide boardwalk leads over the dunes to what remains of Palanga's long wooden pier. Once used for loading and unloading seagoing ships, the pier was already partly decayed before a freak hurricane, in January 1993, reduced it to bare stumps. It's likely to be restored.

Older Part of Town Between the beach and Vytauto gatvė, south of Basanavičiaus gatvė, lies the older part of town with tree-lined avenues and mainly wooden buildings, many of them now part of the sanatoriums formed in the Soviet era. Other purpose-built sanatoriums and holiday homes stand near the coast to the north of the town.

Botanical Park & Museums The large Botanical Park (Palangos botanikos parkas), stretching from Vytauto gatvė to the beach, at the south end of town, was originally the park surrounding the late 19th century palace of the Polish noble Tyszkiewicz family. The palace is now Palanga's excellent **Amber Museum** (Gintaro muziejus) and neither it nor the park, which is beautiful and (off the main paths) peaceful, should be missed. The museum, open daily (except Monday) from 11 am to 7 pm, is full of spectacular examples of natural and carved amber and of information on what amber is, where it's found and what's done with it. The park includes a rose garden (behind the palace), a couple of lakes, and **Birutės kalnas** (Birutė Hill), thought to have once been the site of a pagan shrine. According to legend, the shrine was tended by vestal virgins one of whom, Birutė, was kidnapped and married by Grand Duke Kęstutis. The hill is now topped by a 19th century chapel.

Palanga's other museum is its **history museum** (Palangos istorijos muziejus) at Vytauto gatvė 23A , open daily from noon to 5 pm.

Places to Stay

Lithuanian Youth Hostels (☎ 54 488, or 53 388 at 3 pm or 8.40 pm) has a year-round hostel in a private home near the sea. Bikes and a swimming pool are available. You can book and get further information from the Lithuanian Youth Hostels information office in Vilnius (see the Vilnius Information section).

Palanga has two campsites: one for tents, one with cabins. The tent *Camping* is 2½ km north of the centre, in a field beside Klaipėdos plentas, the Klaipėda-Liepāja highway, immediately south of the 69/29-km marker and opposite a turning to Darbėnai. The nightly cost for two people with a tent is 15 litų. There are washrooms with a water supply but no showers. The toilets are vile, but you can pitch your tent well away from them. The size of the site also means that road noise is not a serious problem. Bus Nos 1 and 2 go in and out of town along Vytauto gatvė (which borders the west side of the site) once or twice an hour; the most central stop to get on or off is on Poželos gatvė, at the back of the bus station.

The cabin *Camping* (or *Kemping*, depending which sign you look at) is at the south end of town. The vehicle entrance is from Klaipėdos plentas. People on foot can enter by a path that leads about 150 metres east through the woods from Vytauto gatvė; turn in just over a km south of the Gabija restaurant and about 350 metres past the open-air disco. The cost here is 2.30 litų per person without a car, 2.55 litų with. There are about 100 cabins of varied shapes and sizes: a three-person cabin is one large-ish room with a private toilet but sharing not-very-clean showers. Blankets are provided and sheets 'can be'.

The *Viešbutis Pajūris* (☎ 53 345) in the town centre at Basanavičiaus gatvė 9 is a basic, worn-out place, which until not long ago was the only hotel in town open to casual customers. The cheapest rooms are about 10.50/16 litų a single/double for foreigners. They're tolerably clean, though the shared showers and toilets are less so. Better rooms with private bathrooms go up to 17/47.50 litų single/double.

Fortunately for those looking for a bit more comfort, some of the holiday homes once reserved for members of Soviet organisations are opening up to general custom. One is the *Poilsio namai Alka* (Alka Holiday Home) (☎ 56 277) on the corner of Daukanto gatvė and Simpsonio gatvė, which has bright, clean rooms with private bathroom, and in some cases sitting room, for about 60/120 litų. Another is the *Hotel Žilvinas* (☎ 58 876) near the west end of Kęstučio gatvė, which has the added plus of bicycles to rent for its customers – but rooms here are more than 200 litų. The *Du Broliai* (Two Brothers) holiday home (☎ 51 270) at Daukanto gatvė 15, between the Alka and the Pajūris, has rooms with private bath at 60 litų per person including breakfast.

The former Jūratė holiday home at Mickevičiaus gatvė 8 has been converted into the small, privately run *Viešbutis*

Kastytis (☎ 53 504) with reportedly comfortable roooms. North of the centre at Vytauto gatvė 171 there's the *Poilsio namai Vanagupė* (☎ 58 201, fax 58 307), built in 1982, with over 100 rooms on six floors. It belongs to the Lithuanian Shipping Company and ranks as one of the best holiday homes in Palanga, with saltwater swimming pools.

For accommodation in private homes try travel agencies such as REK or Mega (see the Information section). About 14 km north of Palanga on the Liepāja highway, signs indicate a hotel or holiday home and a campsite at Energetika, on the coast north of Sventoji. An ambitious Lithuanian-Dutch development is planned for a former Soviet army base near the coast at Nemirseta, eight km south of Palanga. Four motel buildings are planned around a winter garden, a zoo and a pool, with 200 cottages and riding stables in the nearby forest.

Places to Eat

About the best and most expensive place to eat in Palanga is the *Restaurant Hotel Du Broliai*, open from 1 to 11 pm daily, at Daukanto gatvė 15 (the entrance is at the back of the building). The food and service are good and the surroundings pleasant. You order at the counter and your choices are brought to your table. A good choice of salads and desserts at around 4 litai each is laid out for you to choose from, but the rest of the menu is written on a blackboard in Lithuanian – you can get help to translate it. Main courses such as karbonadas, schnitzel, or fish (all with vegetables) are around 15 litų. The blueberries and ice cream dessert is delicious.

Also good is the cosy little *Restoranas Žalčių Karalienė* on Basanavičiaus gatvė. Starters cost up to 2.50 litų for a plate of cold meats, and main courses are in the 3 litai region. The *Kavinė Banga*, a few doors up the street, is a bigger, less carefully tended restaurant, while the *Restoranas Baltija* at Vytauto gatvė 98 (near the bus station) and the *Restoranas Gabija* at Vytauto gatvė 40 combine food with drinking, loud music and

LITHUANIA

dancing in the time-honoured (or rather dis-honoured) Soviet manner.

Palanga has a lot of cafés to drop into for coffee, tea, a snack or a drink, including a handful just back from the beach. One of the brightest is the *Kavinė Ražė* just off Vytauto gatvė by the tiny Ražė River that flows through the town centre. There are small pancakes here for 80 cento each. You can get inexpensive light meals at the *Privati Kavinė Agnis* in the middle of the block between Daukanto, Simpsonio, Birutės and Micke-vičiaus streets.

The *Viešbutis Pajūris* has a tolerable res-taurant where a typical main course of bifshtekas (which here seems to mean a meatball) with a few veg and a salad is about 1.25 litų – though this is less tolerable when it's the only item available for breakfast!

Entertainment

Palanga holds summer music festivals which may cover pop, light classical, chamber music or other modes. The Lithuanian State Symphony Orchestra and other leading ensembles also give summer concerts. The posters around town will help you work out what's on. The main venue is the Summer Concert Hall (Vasaros koncertų salė) at Vytauto gatvė 43. The Restoranas Gabija had what was said to be a good live group when I was in Palanga. Regular open-air discos are held at a site 700 metres down Vytauto gatvė from the Gabija.

Things to Buy

The flea market beside the market on Plytų gatvė has about the biggest range of amber jewellery you'll find anywhere in the Baltic states.

Getting There & Away

You can reach Palanga by road or air. Ser-vices tend to be more frequent in the summer season – roughly early June to mid-Septem-ber – than at other times of year. Kretinga, 10 km east, is the nearest railway station, served by at least four daily trains to/from Klaipėda, two each to/from Vilnius and

Šiauliai, and one each to/from Kaliningrad and Rīga.

Air There are three to 12 LAL flights a week to/from Vilnius, depending on the season. The one-way fare is 300 litų. The LAL office (☎ 53 331 or 53 031) is upstairs in the build-ing on Vytauto gatvė out front of the bus station, opposite the main post office. Air Lithuania flies to/from Kaunas and Kristianstad, Sweden, twice a week. It plans extra flights to/from Kaunas and flights to/from Hamburg. Its nearest ticket office at the time of writing is at Daukanto gatvė 23-2 in Klaipėda (☎ 261-10 665). There are also flights to/from Moscow (see the Getting There & Away chapter). The airport is six km from the town centre on the main road north.

Bus The bus station is on Kretingos gatvė just east of Vytauto gatvė in the centre of town. For information beyond what the post-ed schedules tell you, ask in the dispatcher's office, up the steps just inside the main door of the ticket hall. Services include:

Kaliningrad: two buses daily, six hours
Kaunas: one to 10 buses daily, 3½ hours
Klaipėda: about 30 buses daily, 45 minutes
Kretinga: up to 30 buses daily, 20 minutes
Liepāja: five or more buses daily, 1¾ hours
Rīga: two buses daily in the summer season,
    5½ hours
Šiauliai: five to 12 buses daily, 2½ hours
Tallinn: one bus a day Friday to Monday in summer
    season, 12 hours
Vilnius: three to seven buses daily, six hours

Getting Around

Bus No 2 runs to/from the airport (aerouos-tas) roughly every hour from 6 am to 10 pm. Timetables are posted at its town centre stop on Poželos gatvė behind the bus station. Bus No 1 runs the length of the town via the same stop on Poželos gatvė, but is erratic and in-frequent. The main taxi stand is also on Poželos gatvė behind the bus station.

KLAIPĖDA

The port of Klaipėda, the third-biggest city in Lithuania, with 205,000 people, is 315 km west of Vilnius, beside the narrow strait where the Courland Lagoon opens into the Baltic Sea. Though most of the city now dates from after WW II (in which much of it was wrecked) it's an interesting and quite attractive place. It has a long, curious, and mostly German history (which draws thousands of German tourists every year) and an unusual geographical situation with the appeal of the Courland Spit (Lithuanian: Neringa) just a five-minute ferry ride away.

History

There was probably a fishing village settled by ancient Balts at the mouth of the Danės River before the German crusaders arrived in the region, but Klaipėda has been a predominantly German town, called Memel, for nearly all its history. A castle was founded here in 1252 by the Livonian Order and transferred, along with its surrounding settlement, to the Teutonic Order in 1328. Memel was the northernmost town of the territory ruled by the Teutonic Order till the 16th century, then of the order's successor state, the Duchy of Prussia, and from 1871 to WW I of a united Germany that stretched as far west as the borders of France and Switzerland. The town has been destroyed several times by war, beginning with a number of occasions during the struggles between the Teutonic Order and Lithuania in the 13th and 14th centuries. In 1678 it was reduced to ashes by Sweden. Up to the 17th century, brick or stone houses were forbidden lest they provide any cover for attackers.

By WW I, after economic development through the timber trade and shipbuilding in the 18th and 19th centuries, Memel had about 30,000 inhabitants, about half of them German and half of them Lithuanian.

Under the Treaty of Versailles at the end of WW I, the town, the northern half of the Neringa peninsula, and a strip about 150 km long and 20 km wide along the east side of the Courland Lagoon and the north side of the Nemunas River, were separated from Germany as an 'international territory', with an autonomous government and a French garrison. This 'Memel Territory' remained in a kind of stateless limbo till January 1923 when Lithuanian troops marched in, drove the French out, and annexed it. In 1925 Memel officially became Klaipėda for the first time.

Hitler annexed the territory in March 1939 – his last land grab before WW II began. In January 1945 whole sections of the town were razed to the ground by the bombardment leading to its capture by the Red Army. Most of the population had already been evacuated. Only a handful of Germans live in or around Klaipėda today.

After WW II, Klaipėda was rebuilt, repopulated (mainly by Lithuanians and Russians) and developed into an important Soviet city on the back of shipbuilding and a fishing fleet that ranges as far as the Pacific Ocean.

Orientation

The Danės River flows westward across the city centre to enter the Courland Lagoon four km from the open Baltic Sea. The key street axis is the single, long, north-south main street, called Herkus Manto gatvė north of the river, Tiltų gatvė for its first 600 metres south of the river, and then Taikos prospektas. The heart of the old part of town lies within the 400 metres south of the river, mostly west of Tiltų gatvė. In this area note that Turgaus gatvė (Market St) leads not to Turgaus aikštė (Market Square), which is 350 metres further south, but to Teatro aikštė (Theatre Square). Most hotels, the rail and bus stations, and many other services are north of the river.

Smiltynė, the northern tip of the Neringa peninsula, lies about half a km off the mouth of the Danės, across the narrow channel which forms the north end of the Courland Lagoon.

Information

Money You can change money at the Lietuvos Bankas at Turgaus gatvė 1, on the corner of Teatro aikštė, from 9.30 am to 1 pm Monday to Friday. Outside opening hours, unofficial money-changers hang around outside. There are also two other banks on

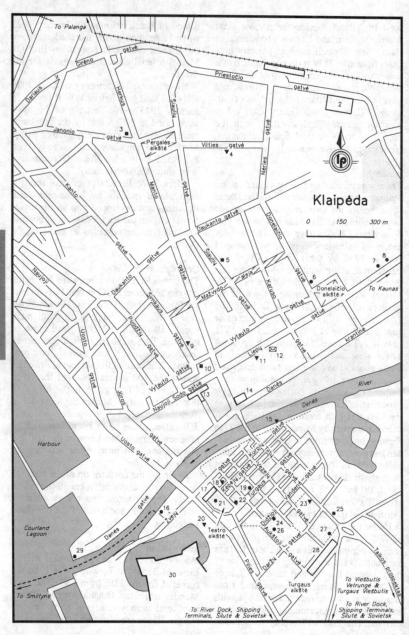

To Palanga

Priestočio gatvė

1

2

Giréno gatvė

Herkaus

Danaus

ir

Janonio gatvė

3

Pergalés aikštė

Šiltų gatvė

Néries gatvė

Vilties gatvė

4

Kento gatvė

Mantō gatvė

Klaipėda

0   150   300 m

Daukanto gatvė

Donelaičio gatvė

Šaulių

5

Naujoji gatvė

Daukanto gatvė

Simkaus gatvė

Mažvydo aleja

Karaus gatvė

6

Donelaičio aikštė

7 8

To Kaunas

Puodžių gatvė

Uosto gatvė

Vytauto gatvė

9

Liepų gatvė

12

krantinė

11

10

Danés

River

Vytauto gatvė

Naujoji Sodo gatvė

13

14

Danés

Jūros gatvė

15

Harbour

Kurpių gatvė

Turgaus gatvė

Vežėjų gatvė

Uosto gatvė

gatvė

Vandens gatvė

Courland
Lagoon

Danés

17

18

19

22

23

25

Kepėjų gatvė

21

24

16
Žvejų

20

Teatro
aikštė

Didžioji gatvė

26

27

28

29

30

Aukštoji gatvė

Pilies gatvė

Galvų gatvė

Taikos prospektas

Turgaus
aikštė

To Viešbutis
Vetrungé &
Turgaus Viešbutis

To River Dock,
Shipping Terminals,
Silutė & Sovietsk

To Smiltyne

To River Dock, Shipping
Terminals, Silutė & Sovietsk

■ PLACES TO STAY

3 Viešbutis Baltija
5 Viešbutis Pamarys
10 Viešbutis Viktorija

▼ PLACES TO EAT

4 Trio Café
9 Restoranas Prūsija
11 Clock Museum & Antika Café
15 Meridianas Restaurant
18 Restoranas Žilinskas
20 Astra Café
23 Restoranas Neptūnas

OTHER

1 Railway Station
2 Bus Station
6 Conservatoire
7 Gurda Shop
8 Picture Gallery
12 Post, Telephone & Telegraph Office
13 Viešbutis Klaipėda
14 Musical Theatre
16 Smiltynė Ferry Dock
17 Klaipėda Theatre
19 Dailė Shop
21 Simon Dach Fountain
22 Lietuvos Bankas
24 Lithuania Minor History Museum
25 Vilbara Shop
26 Exhibition Gallery
27 Centrinis Knygynas
28 Market
29 Smiltynė Ferry Dock
30 Old Castle

Turgaus gatvė and currency-exchange offices in the Klaipėda and Pamarys hotels. You may have difficulty changing currencies other than Deutschmarks and US dollars anywhere except the bank.

Post & Telecommunications The central post, telegraph and telephone office is at Liepų gatvė 16, 300 metres east of Herkus Manto gatvė. It's open from 9 am to 7 pm Monday to Friday, and from 9 am to 5 pm Saturday and Sunday. You can make international phone calls fairly quickly here. The building has a clock tower and a fine wood-panelled interior. You can also make international phone calls and send faxes at Prestižas, Liepų gatvė 30. Fax Biuras at Naujoji Uosto gatvė 22 has a marginally cheaper fax service. There are pay phones for long-distance calls within the ex-USSR (tarpmiestinis telefonas automatas) on Herkus Manto gatvė at the corner of Liepų gatvė.

The Klaipėda telephone code is 261.

Travel Agencies Barta (☎ 19 317, fax 19 955) at Liepų gatvė 54 and Turistas (☎ 93 087 or 14 488) at Žvejų gatvė 8 both offer accommodation bookings and excursions.

Left Luggage There's a left-luggage room, open till 11 pm, at the bus station, and lockers at the railway station.

Shops & Market Centrinis Knygynas on Turgaus aikštė is a main bookshop. The main market (turgavietė) stretches a couple of hundred metres west from here. Vilbara, half a block north on Tiltų gatvė, and Intershop on Naujoji Sodo gatvė, next to the Viešbutis Klaipėda, sell mainly packaged foods, tobacco, drinks and other goods imported from the West. Gurda, next to the Picture Gallery on Liepų gatvė, and Dailė, at Turgaus gatvė 7, are among the more interesting art and craft shops.

Old Town
Much of central Klaipėda was wrecked in WW II, so there are only bits of the German town left. Some of the oldest part, between the river and Turgaus aikštė, has retained (or been restored to) something like its old appearance. This area is mainly vehicle-free and interesting to wander round, with a number of craft and antique shops and art galleries. Along Kurpių gatvė and Kepėjų gatvė, east of Tiltų gatvė, and other narrow streets in the few blocks immediately south of the river are a number of restored **old houses**. You can rent **rowing boats** on the south bank, on the west side of the Tiltų gatvė bridge.

The main focus of the old town is the

broad **Teatro aikštė** (Theatre Square), west of Tiltų gatvė. On its north side stands the fine classical-style **Klaipėda Theatre** built in 1857, damaged in WW II, and since restored. Hitler stood on the theatre balcony and proclaimed the *anschluss* (connection) of Memel to Germany to crowds in the square in 1939.

In front of the theatre stands the **Simon Dach Fountain**, named after the 17th century German poet, born in Klaipėda, who became the focus of a well-known circle of Königsberg writers and musicians. On a pedestal in the middle of the fountain stands a **statue of Aennchen von Tharau**. The girl in question was the subject of a famous German wedding and love song, originally written in the East Prussian dialect. The words of the song used to be ascribed to Dach, but it's now thought that another member of the same Königsberg circle, the composer and cathedral organist Johann Albert, wrote them. The original early 20th century statue and fountain, symbols of Memel, did not survive WW II, but replicas were put in place in 1989 by an Aennchen von Tharau Society founded in Germany for the purpose. One verse of the song inscribed on the pedestal goes (in a non-dialect version):

Aennchen von Tharau, mein Reichthum, mein Gut,
Du meine Seele, mein Fleisch und mein Blut!

(Aennchen from Tharau, my wealth, my fortune,
You are my soul, my flesh and my blood!)

Before WW II, Klaipėda's market used to stretch west from Teatro aikštė to the far (west) side of Pilies gatvė. West of Pilies gatvė you can make out the site of Klaipėda's old **castle**, south of Žvejų gatvė and still protected by its moat which has an outlet into the south side of the Danės.

The **Exhibition Gallery** (Parodų rumai) at Aukštoji gatvė 3, two blocks south of Teatro aikštė, is partly housed in a converted fish warehouse in the exposed-timbers style known as *fachwerk*, which was typical of old Memel. There are a few more **fachwerk** **buildings** around this part of town: Pilies gatvė 19 is a fine one. Round the corner from the Exhibition Gallery, on Didžioji Vandens gatvė, is the **Lithuania Minor History Museum** (Mažosios Lietuvos Istorijos muziejus), open Wednesday to Sunday, from 11 am to 7 pm. (Lithuania Minor is a name given by Lithuanians to the Klaipėda and Kaliningrad regions, which were German-ruled but had significant Lithuanian populations.)

North of the River

There's a **riverside park** along the north bank of the Danės, immediately east of the Tiltų gatvė/Herkus Manto gatvė bridge. Klaipėda's **Picture Gallery** (Paveikslų galerija) and sculpture garden is at Liepų gatvė 33, 750 metres east of Herkus Manto gatvė. It's open Wednesday to Sunday, from noon to 6 pm. There's a **Clock Museum** (Laikrodžių muziejus) at Liepų gatvė 12, open from noon to 6 pm daily, except Monday. Liepų gatvė was once, for a brief inglorious spell, called Adolf-Hitler-Strasse. Herkus Manto gatvė was Hermann-Göring-Strasse.

Smiltynė

Smiltynė, the narrow north end of the 98-km Neringa sandspit, is Klaipėda's playground, which partly explains the paucity of parks in the city itself. Here are beaches, high dunes, pine forests, and a collection of exhibitions and museums. Smiltynė is easy to reach, with regular ferries making the five-minute crossing from Klaipėda. On hot summer weekends people pour across in their thousands, and the beaches become absolutely packed. The main ferry run, from the Danės River in Klaipėda, arrives at Landing No 1 (I-oji perkėla) on the east side of Smiltynė, two km from the tip of the peninsula. The road south down the peninsula to Nida and Kaliningrad begins here. See the Getting Around section later in this chapter for more information on the ferries.

Also at Smiltynė are a couple of places to stay and eat (see the relevant sections for detail), a yacht club and the office of the

Kuršių Nerija National Park, which covers most of the Lithuanian part of Neringa.

Exhibitions On the east side of Smiltynė, between Landing No 1 and the Sea Museum, & Aquarium, are three exhibitions with a local flavour. The Kuršių Nerija Nature Museum (Kuršių nerijos gamtos muziejaus ekspozicija), 200 metres from Landing No 1, gives an introduction to the flora, fauna and landscape of Neringa. Seven hundred metres further north is a 'garden of veteran fishing boats' ('žvejybos laivai-veteranai') – four craft perched on wooden stands looking rather forlornly towards the water. Next along is an Ethnographic Coastal Fishing Settlement (Etnografinė pajūrio žvejo sodyba) – a small collection of old, wooden, fisherfolk's houses.

Sea Museum & Aquarium Smiltynė's main showpiece is 1½ km north of Landing No 1. It's set in a large 19th century German fort. The Sea Museum & Aquarium (Jūrų muziejus ir akvariumas) has penguins, seals, sea lion performances at 12 noon and 4 pm, an aquarium with fish from coral reefs as well as the Courland Lagoon and the Baltic Sea, a coral and shell display, and a section tracing the history of ship design.

At the time of writing, opening hours in June, July and August are from 11 am to 7 pm daily, except Monday; in April, May and September, from 11 am to 7 pm daily, except Monday and Tuesday; and from October to March, from 11 am to 5 or 6 pm daily, except Monday and Tuesday. Admission is 20 cento. Feeding times include: seals in the moat, 11 am and 2.30 pm; seals in pool No 2, 11.30 am and 3 pm; penguins, 11.30 am and 3.30 pm; coral fish and turtles, noon; sea lions, 12.30 and 4.30 pm.

Work on the fortress in which it's all housed, which was intended to protect Klaipėda from naval attack, began in the 1860s. But, by the end of the 19th century, advances in military technology had rendered it obsolete before it ever fired a shot in anger. In WW II the Germans used it as an ammunition store then blew it up in 1945 as

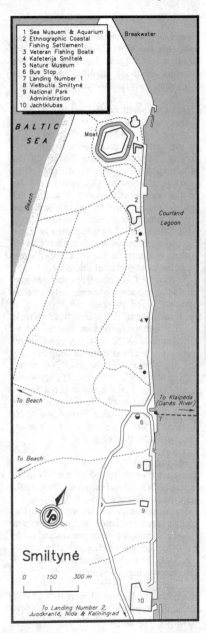

1 Sea Musuem & Aquarium
2 Ethnographic Coastal Fishing Settlement
3 Veteran Fishing Boats
4 Kafeterija Smiltelė
5 Nature Museum
6 Bus Stop
7 Landing Number 1
8 Viešbutis Smiltynė
9 National Park Administration
10 Jachtklubas

LITHUANIA

the Red Army was moving in to take Klaipėda. It was reconstructed for its present job in the 1970s but is suffering from a lack of funds, which means that some of the collections are being depleted and that the dolphinarium remains unfinished.

Beaches A sandy beach fronts the Baltic all the way down the west side of Smiltynė. It's often pretty blowy here, and the combination of sun and wind produces some fine tans among Klaipėda residents. Dozens of low windbreaks have been constructed from intertwined branches in the dunes so that people can sunbathe without getting chilled by the wind. Seen from above or below, these are reminiscent of a seabird nesting colony, with little knots of people dotted here and there over the landscape. Some topless sunbathing – a rarity in the Baltic states – goes on in the more secluded shelters.

Sections of beach signposted 'Moterų pliažas' are meant for women only; sections marked 'Vyrų pliažas' are for men. A 'bendras pliažas' is a mixed beach. Tracks lead through the forest from the east side of the peninsula to the west. If you follow the track straight ahead from Landing No 1, or the one veering off the road 300 metres further south, it's about one km across the peninsula and you'll come out on a general beach. Further north the distance is less, further south it's greater. From Landing No 2 (II-oji perkėla), 2½ km south, it's nearly two km across the peninsula.

Places to Stay

There are both cheap and quite costly hotels in Klaipėda itself and across the water in the semi-rural surroundings of Smiltynė. For rooms in private homes try travel agents, or contact agencies listed in the the Private Homes section of Accommodation in the Facts for the Visitor chapter at the front of the book, or make enquiries in Vilnius or elsewhere before you come.

Klaipėda The *Viešbutis Viktorija* (☎ 13 670) at Šimkaus gatvė 12, near the Viešbutis Klaipėda, has singles/doubles for 6/9 litai.

The rooms are bare and faded and the shared toilets and showers grubby. The *Viešbutis Baltija* (☎ 14 967) about 800 metres further north at Janonio gatvė 4, on the corner of Herkus Manto gatvė, is a bit better, but the showers and toilets are still shared. Rooms are up to 17/25 litų.

Two other bottom-end places worth trying in desperation are south of the city centre: the *Viešbutis Vetrungė* (☎ 54 801) at Taikos prospektas 28 has rooms with private bathrooms for about 25 litų, while the *Turgaus Viešbutis* (☎ 75 002) at Taikos prospektas 80A, used by market traders, has rooms between about 5 litai and 10 litų.

The best hotel in town is the *Viešbutis Klaipėda* (☎ 19 960 or 16 971, fax 53 911) at Naujoji Sodo gatvė 1. It's a modern brick building with a 12-storey central tower, just north of the Danės River, beside Herkus Manto gatvė. Clean, bright rooms with private bathrooms that have bathtubs as well as showers cost 170/255 litų including breakfast. There are excellent views from the upper storeys. The hotel has a good restaurant, a coffee shop and a news kiosk, and is used by most tour groups.

The *Viešbutis Pamarys* (☎ 19 943 or 19 939) at Šiaulių gatvė 28, a block east of Herkus Manto gatvė, about 700 metres north of the river, charges 110/125 litų and is another modern place in good condition, though the rooms are a bit more worn. Some share a bathroom with one or two others.

Smiltynė The *Viešbutis Smiltynė* (☎ 91 149 or 91 166), 300 metres down the coast from the ferry landing, has singles/doubles for 125 litų with private shower, or lyux rooms with sitting room and bathroom for 145 litų. It's an old-fashioned building with sizeable rooms, but it's a pity it faces the city docks across the strait, not the open sea. Breakfast is included. The *Jachtklubas* (Yacht Club), 700 metres further down the same coast, has small, worn, but tolerable rooms with wash basin for 5 litai single or double in a wooden building overlooking its small harbour. There are communal toilets and hot showers.

Elsewhere

At Melnragė, near the coast four km north of the city centre, the modern *Viešbutis Morena* (☎ 261-98 456) at Audros gatvė 8A, has 17 reportedly clean, tasteful and pleasant rooms with private bath. Singles/doubles are about 100/200 litų.

Places to Eat

The restaurant in the *Viešbutis Klaipėda* is one of the best in town. Get there early – say about 6.30 pm – for a peaceful and swift dinner before the tour groups come in. There's a long multi-lingual menu and a lot of it is 'on'. One hungry night I enjoyed three starters, a beef and vegetables main course, two pancakes, dessert and coffee for just 4 litai. A German beer was an extra 2.50 litų. In the morning, breakfast is served till 10 am, but it may be a meagre one if you appear much later than 9 am.

Another good central restaurant is the *Restoranas Prūsija* at Šimkaus gatvė 6, with friendly service and decent food – open till midnight. Also good is the *Restoranas Žilinskas* at Kurpių gatvė 1, which has live jazz nightly except Monday. It's above a theatre.

The *Meridianas*, a restaurant in a former sailing ship moored on the river by the Herkus Manto gatvė bridge, is better at lunch time than in the evening, when heavy drinking and loud music are the priorities. Ditto the *Neptūnas* down the street at Tiltų gatvė 18.

Better than such restaurants are some of the growing number of cafés and bars serving meals. These include the *Deutscher Club* at Daukanto gatvė 24, a little enclave of German food, beer and prices; the *Antika* at Liepų gatvė 12 with good food and good service in elegant surroundings; the *Arka* at Liepų gatvė 20, which does spicy Central Asian dishes; the *Trio* at Vilties gatvė 12; and the *Juoda-Balta* at Herkus Manto gatvė 15.

The *Kavinė* in the Viešbutis Pamarys is OK for snacks or light meals – there are pancakes (blyneliai) for 40 cento each, or an omelette for 60 cento. Also good for pancakes is the *Astra* café at Pilies gatvė 14, which also serves cepelinai.

There are one or two bars – seedy with drunks in the evening – in the old town.

At Smiltynė there are cafés at the Viešbutis Smiltynė and the Yacht Club, plus the *Kafeterija Smiltelė*, 500 metres north of the ferry landing, open from 11 am to 2 pm and 3 to 6 pm Wednesday to Sunday.

Entertainment

In summer, members of Klaipėda's small German community put on a weekly folksong performance for the diners in the Viešbutis Klaipėda restaurant. The Drama Theatre (Dramos teatros) is at Teatro aikštė 2. Klaipėda's Conservatoire (Music Academy) has a concert hall at Donelaičio gatvė 4, and the city's Musical Theatre (Muzikinis teatras) is at Danės krantinė 19, on the corner of Herkus Manto gatvė, just north of the river.

Getting There & Away

This section concentrates on services within the Baltic states and the Kaliningrad Region. Information on trains to/from Russia, buses to/from Belarus, and more on the ships to/from Germany is given in the Getting There & Away chapter.

Klaipėda's rail and bus stations are 150 metres apart on Priestočio gatvė, about 1½ km north of the river and 750 metres east of Herkus Manto gatvė. The rail station has an unusual tall, helmeted clock tower. Both stations have 'Informacija' windows.

Air The nearest airport is at Palanga. LAL (☎ 30 409) has a booking office at Taikos prospektas 107 in Klaipėda. Air Lithuania (☎ 10 665) is at Daukanto gatvė 23-2.

Bus The Klaipėda-Kaunas-Vilnius road is among the best in the Baltics, and the 16 to 18 daily buses to/from Vilnius take about five hours, while the 12 or so daily buses to/from Kaunas take three to 3½ hours.

Most buses to Juodkrantė, Nida and Kaliningrad depart not from the main bus station, but from ferry landing No 1 at

Smiltynė. Their theoretical schedules are posted up at the stop at Smiltynė, but it's better to ask at the 'Informacija' window at the bus station.

Services to/from Klaipėda include:

Druskininkai
    one bus daily, 5½ hours
Juodkrantė
    two or three buses daily from the bus station, one hour; 11 or 12 buses daily from Smiltynė, 30 minutes
Jurbarkas
    nine or 10 buses daily, 2½ hours
Kaliningrad
    one to three buses daily from the bus station via Sovietsk, five hours; six daily from Smiltynė via Nida, 3½ to four hours
Liepāja
    six buses daily, 2¾ hours
Mažeikiai
    10 buses daily, 2½ to three hours
Nida
    two or three buses daily from the bus station, 1½ to two hours; 11 or 12 buses daily from Smiltynė, 1¼ hours
Palanga
    about 30 buses daily (mostly local bus No 11), 45 minutes
Rīga
    two buses daily, six or seven hours
Šiauliai
    about 15 buses daily by various routes, 2½ hours or more
Sovietsk
    four buses daily, two hours
Tallinn
    one bus a day Friday to Monday in summer season, 13 hours

Train There's one night and one day train each way to/from Vilnius via Šiauliai. The night train also goes via Kaunas. Travelling times are: Vilnius 6¾ hours (afternoon) or 9¾ hours (overnight), Kaunas eight hours, Šiauliai three or four hours. There are also three other daily trains to/from Šiauliai, one to/from Rīga (6½ hours), one or two to/from Kaliningrad (3½ to 4½ hours), four to/from Sovietsk (2¼ hours), and others to/from Skuodas, Kretinga, Šilutė and Mažeikiai.

Hydrofoil & Ship From about May to September there's a weekend hydrofoil service using the Courland Lagoon and Nemunas River to/from Kaunas via Nida. The trip is about five hours and the one-way fare about 6.50 litų. Ask hotels and travel agents for information on schedules, tickets and departure points.

See the Getting There & Away chapter for schedules and fares on the ferries to/from Kiel and Mukran in Germany. For information and bookings on the Kiel ferry in Klaipėda contact Litma, the Lithuanian Maritime Agency (☎ 55 549, fax 16 681 or 53 466), at Perkėlos gatvė 10 or PO Box 667, Klaipėda 5815. For the Mukran ferry contact Deutsche Seereederei-Lines (☎ 55 052, fax 57 377) or Trans-Expedition Service Agency Vesttrans (☎ 55 922, fax 12 272 or 13 836) at Kalvos gatvė 4. Klaipėda currently has no purpose-built ferry terminal. Currently dockings are a few km south of the city on the east bank of the Courland Lagoon. Take the Sovietsk road south from the centre and follow the 'Tarptautinė perkėla' signs. Bus No 18 from the city centre goes to the Mukran terminal at least.

Getting Around
Bus Bus Nos 1 and 8 from the Geležinkelio Stotis stop outside the railway station run south to Pergalės aikštė then down Herkus Manto gatvė through the city centre to the Turgus stop on Taikos prospektas, just past the market.

Smiltynė Ferries The main Smiltynė ferry normally leaves from the south bank of the Danės River, on Žvejų gatvė, 100 metres west of the Naujoji Uosto gatvė/Pilies gatvė bridge. It docks at Landing No 1 (I-oji perkėla) on Smiltynė, the start of the road to Nida, 1½ km south of the sea museum and aquarium.

Timetables are posted at the ticket office; at the time of writing sailings are half-hourly from 6.30 am to 8.30 pm, then 9.30, 10.30 and 11 pm. Return sailings from Smiltynė are 15 minutes later. The crossing takes five minutes. The return fare is 20 cento for a passenger, 1.25 litų for a motorbike and 3 litai for a car. There's room for perhaps half a dozen cars and trucks on board.

Top: Palanga resort architecture, Lithuania (JN)
Bottom: Carving shop, Juodkrantė, Lithuania (JN)

Top: Old fisherfolk's house, Nida, Lithuania (JN)
Bottom: Dunes at Nida, Lithuania (JN)

Sometimes in summer the ferry sails from the north side of the mouth of the Danės, at the end of Danės gatvė, 500 metres west of the Naujoji Uosto gatvė/Pilies gatvė bridge. A few times a day in summer there are also sailings direct to the sea museum on the days when the museum is open.

Another ferry service – recommended for motorists – sails half-hourly from 8.15 am to 7.45 pm from the River Dock (upių prieplauka), three km south of the mouth of the Danės, to Landing No 2 (II-oji perkėla) on Smiltynė, 2.5 km south of Landing No 1. Bus No 1 continues down to the River Dock from its stops in Klaipėda city centre (see the previous Bus section). Get off at the II Perkėla stop.

COURLAND LAGOON – EAST COAST

If you have your own transport it would be interesting to explore the low-lying, marsh-dotted east side of the Courland Lagoon, which, like Klaipėda and Neringa, was historically Prussian/German territory. There are views of the high white dunes of Neringa across the lagoon. The Nemunas River splits into a delta to enter the lagoon, with the town of Rusnė lying at the point where the main stream divides into three – the Atmata, the Pakalnė and the Skirvytė. The main town of the region, with 22,000 people, is Šilutė (former German name: Heydekrug) which is on the Klaipėda-Sovietsk road and railway. It has a hotel, the *Viešbutis Nemunas* (☎ 241-52 345) at Lietuvininkų gatvė 70.

Probably the most intriguing point to head for is Ventė, on the tip of the south-pointing promontory due west of Šilutė. A Teutonic Order castle was built here in the 1360s to protect shipping in the area, but both it and its church collapsed within a couple of hundred years. In the church's case at least, this was due to the severity of the storms on this isolated point – as is indicated by Ventė's German name, Windenburg (Windy Castle). The church was rebuilt but wrecked again by storms in 1702. Its stones were used to build the church at Kintai, 10 km north, a few years later. So bad can the weather be off Ventė that, until the 1870s, river craft sometimes

had to spend whole winters in Rusnė waiting for the storms to abate before they could proceed north to Klaipėda. The problem was solved by the building of the König Wilhelm Canal (now the Klaipėdos kanalas) from the Minija River, a tributary of the Atmata branch of the Nemunas, to Klaipėda.

A surfaced road runs down to Ventė from Kintai, 10 km north. It's a sparsely inhabited area, with just a few fisherfolk's houses and a lighthouse at the tip, which can be either beautifully tranquil or beautifully wild. The many birds which nest out here are under protection.

Neringa (Courland Spit)

The typical Baltic coastal scent of mingled ozone and pine is at its headiest on Neringa, the Lithuanian half of the Courland Spit, where you are never more than two km from a coast, and usually much closer. There's a real 'different world' feeling on this isolated 98-km thread of sand between the Courland Lagoon and the Baltic Sea, held together by pine forests inhabited by elk, deer and wild boar. The place is held in great affection not only by Lithuanians and Russians but also by the many Germans who once enjoyed holidays here. Neringa was Prussian or German territory till WW I; the northern half was annexed by Lithuania along with the rest of the Memel Territory in 1923, but remained a retreat for Germans till WW II. It's probably less changed since then than anywhere else in the northern half of the old East Prussia, which gives it a magnetic attraction for returning German exiles. During the Soviet era the holiday accommodation was more or less reserved for communist apparatchiks and their families.

The main settlement on Lithuanian Neringa is Nida, just north of the Russian border. Like the handful of other settlements, Nida is on the sheltered lagoon coast and began life as a fishing village. Nida and Juodkrantė further north now also function as laid-back resorts. The good, sandy

LITHUANIA

beaches are all on the west coast of the spit, where the waters can get quite rough as it faces the widest part of the Baltic Sea. Don't bathe in the lagoon, which is polluted, and check locally on the cleanliness of the west-side waters.

Neringa is also called the Kuršių nerija in Lithuanian, and is known to Germans as the Kurische Nehrung. It was formed 5000 or 6000 years ago as sand accumulated in shallow waters near the coast. Its trees were originally a mixture of deciduous and conif-erous, but heavy felling in the 16th and 17th centuries removed most of the deciduous forests. It also led to severe sand shifting which buried numerous villages. Reforesta-tion to stabilise the sands began in the 19th century.

Today much of the Lithuanian part of the spit has been declared the **Kuršių Nerija National Park**. You can get information on the park and organise a guided tour if you should want one, at the park office a couple of hundred metres south of the Viešbutis Smiltynė. There's a fee of 80 cento per person and 4.50 litų per car to enter the park, payable at a checkpoint eight km down the road from Smiltynė.

Smiltynė is covered in the Klaipėda section as it really functions as part of that city.

JUODKRANTĖ
The small, quiet village of Juodkrantė (former German name: Schwarzort) is 20 km south of Smiltynė on the east (lagoon) coast of Neringa, and the first settlement you come to travelling south from there. It consists of three separate little clusters. At the north end there's an area around a pretty little fishing harbour known as the Gintari įlanka (Amber Bay). The central part, a km south, focuses on a bunch of holiday homes, and here you'll also find a couple of shops, a post office, a canteen-and-bar called the *Kavinė Naglis*, and the main bus stop and pier. A km further south there's a little villagey area with a church and sports field. Juodkrantė has quite a number of prettily painted, old wooden cottages – with colourful gardens in summer.

Neringa is about 1½ km wide here and the forest is among the loveliest on the penin-sula, with some fine walks. Numerous paths and tracks wander through it or cross to the west coast; the two main cross-tracks, the Nidos kelias and the Pašto kelias, start from the back of the central part of the village.

There are good views from the hill Raganos kalnas half a km inland from the northern part of the village. A track called the 'promenada' leads north to it from the central area. The forests around Juodkrantė are also among the better places on the peninsula for spotting elk, which tend to emerge from cover in early morning and evening.

A short way up a side road between the central and southern parts of the village is the **Witches' Hill Museum** (Raganų kalno muziejus), with a display of wooden carv-ings, a favourite Lithuanian folk art. Beneath four tall, carved pillars, is a quite interesting little carvings and souvenir shop. There's a good little bookstall in the Poilsio namai Ąžuolynas.

Places to Stay
Lithuanian Youth Hostels has a place at Juodkrantė charging 16 litų a night per person – for further information and book-ings contact the Lithuanian Youth Hostels information office in Vilnius (see the Vilnius Information section).

One place you can ask for a room in a private home is the shop by the Witches' Hill Museum – the man there said he could fix people up for about 20 litų. In a rather differ-ent price bracket is the *Poilsio namai Ąžuolynas* (Oak Forest Holiday Home ☎ 259-53 110), next to the church in the south-ern part of the village, which is partly run by the German travel firm Rautenberg Reisen. It's a nice place if you can afford it: a com-fortable, modernised single with full board costs around 200 litų a day. There are rooms in a similar price bracket at the *Poilsio namai Santauta* (☎ 259-53 167) at Kalno gatvė 26 in the central part of the village (take the first turn to the right, south of the bus stop, to reach it). Some other holiday homes might have cheaper rooms available – there are about a dozen in the central part of the village.

Getting There & Away
Eleven or 12 buses a day, in each direction between Smiltynė and Nida, come through Juodkrantė. About half of them are coming from, or going on to Kaliningrad. From Juodkrantė it's half an hour to Smiltynė, 50 minutes to Nida. There are also two or three buses daily to/from Klaipėda bus station.

JUODKRANTĖ TO NIDA
Shortly south of Juodkrantė the road switches from the east side of the peninsula to the west. Between the two main settlements are two even smaller villages, Pervalka and Preila, both on the east coast and reached by side roads from the main road. The peninsula is less forested south of Juodkrantė and there are some high, steep dunes between Juodkrantė and Pervalka. The highest dune on the whole peninsula, 66 metres, is near Preila.

NIDA
With its unique natural environment, this combination of old-fashioned fishing village and mildly fashionable small resort is one of the most attractive places on the Baltic coast. Nida (former German name: Nidden) is the biggest settlement on the Lithuanian half of Neringa, but it's still a small place, with a permanent population that couldn't exceed a couple of thousand, supplemented by the vacationers who come to its dozen or so holiday homes in summer. It lies on the lagoon side of the peninsula, 48 km from Klaipėda and just three km from the Russian border; it has a sizeable harbour. Just to the south stand some of the most impressive dunes on the peninsula, while a fine Baltic beach is less than a two-km walk across the peninsula through the woods.

Originally a fishing village, Nida attracted a colony of mainly East Prussian artists from the late 19th century. It developed as a tourist resort and there were five hotels by the 1930s, when the writer Thomas Mann had a summer home built here. Judging by the high quality of its more recent housing, Nida looks as though it must have enjoyed some kind of elite status among resorts during the Soviet period.

Orientation & Information
The settlement is very spread out by ex-Soviet standards and straggles nearly two km along the coast, but the hub, where Nida's few shops and other services are concentrated, is the south end, behind the harbour. Three roads link the village to the main road, which is nearer the west side of the peninsula than the east at this point. The southernmost of these, which you'll probably take if you're coming from Kaliningrad, is Taikos gatvė which leads straight to the village heart. Coming from the north you'll probably enter Nida along Kuverto gatvė. Turn right at the end along Pamario gatvė to reach the centre.

You can change money in the post office, which is on Taikos gatvė, or in the branch of the Lietuvos Akcinis Inovacinis Bankas in the village centre.

The Nida telephone code is 259.

Things to See & Do
The main things to do here are go for walks, relax and enjoy yourself. You might pick up a ride of some kind at the harbour, where quite a lot of yachts put in. On land you can basically go in three directions from the harbour – north, west or south.

North There's a pleasant waterfront promenade stretching for over a km and a road leading a couple of km further on. A bit over a km from the harbour, the street Skrudzdynės gatvė comes down close to the waterfront. A flight of steps leads up the bank beside it to the **Thomas Mann House** (Tomo Mano namelis), which the German writer had built and spent the summers of 1930, 1931 and 1932 in. It's open as a museum now. Back towards the centre, on the inland side of the road, 200 metres from the corner of Kuverto gatvė, a path leads up to a little red-brick church with a peaceful woodland cemetery.

LITHUANIA

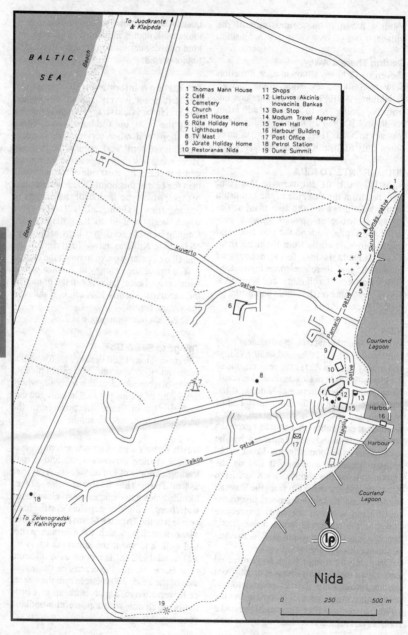

BALTIC
SEA

Beach

To Juodkrantė
& Klaipėda

1 Thomas Mann House	11 Shops
2 Café	12 Lietuvos Akcinis
3 Cemetery	Inovacinis Bankas
4 Church	13 Bus Stop
5 Guest House	14 Modum Travel Agency
6 Rūta Holiday Home	15 Town Hall
7 Lighthouse	16 Harbour Building
8 TV Mast	17 Post Office
9 Jūratė Holiday Home	18 Petrol Station
10 Restoranas Nida	19 Dune Summit

Beach

Kuverto gatvė

Skrudžolynės gatvė

Pamario gatvė

Courland
Lagoon

Naglių gatvė

Taikos gatvė

Harbour

Harbour

Courland
Lagoon

To Zelenogradsk
& Kaliningrad

Nida

0   250   500 m

LITHUANIA

West All westward routes lead ultimately to the beach on the far side of the peninsula. One good one is to turn right (north) off Taikos gatvė opposite the post office. The street you're now on bends sharply left after 150 metres and climbs. Just over 400 metres up the hill, a path leads up to a lighthouse on the right, on the highest point in the area. If you continue 700 metres along the path behind the lighthouse you'll come out on a good, straight path leading down to the main road and to the beach, 400 metres beyond the road.

The beach is long, wide, sandy, beautiful and, at times, windswept. A sign as you approach indicates that nude bathers should turn left for their own stretch of beach.

South South from the harbour are two or three streets of old-fashioned fishing cottages with pretty gardens. Beyond them a path leads through a wooded area and starts to climb up the spectacularly high bare dunes that you can see from the village. A flight of steps enables people to climb without destroying the dune. From the top of the steps a track leads directly to the highest point, where there are great views to both coasts, the forests to the north, and a mixture of sand and forests to the south. You can explore in any direction from here but bear in mind that the Kaliningrad border is only about two km south (though there seemed to be nothing off the road to mark it when I visited).

Places to Stay

The house across the road from the church on Pamario gatvė functions as a cheap *guest house*, though there's no sign outside. In summer you'll probably see a few guests' cars pulled up outside it. The cost – unless foreigners' prices rear their ugly heads – is around 2.50 litų a night, slightly more for your own shower or toilet. The Modum travel agency in the village centre offers rooms in private flats for about 55 litų per person.

The *Jūratė* (☎ 52 618) at Pamario gatvė

3 is a holiday home now operating partly as a hotel. It's open year round and has good, quite big, slightly old-fashioned rooms with private bath for around 65 litų per person including breakfast. Other meals are available. Other holiday homes may be able to provide rooms too. They're dotted around near the village centre and back along Taikos gatvė and Kuverto gatvė. Two to try, as some German groups stay in them, are the *Rūta* (☎ 52 367) at Kuverto gatvė 15, a grey building with a flat, red-brown roof, about 600 metres back from Pamario gatvė, and the *Auksinės Kopos* (☎ 52 212) at Kuverto gatvė 17. Doubles in the Rūta are around 120 litų.

Places to Eat

With most visitors on full-board arrangements in their holiday homes, Nida appears to have only one restaurant – the *Restoranas Nida* in the village centre just north of the shops. Fortunately, it can cater for a variety of needs. On the ground floor there's a cheap canteen, open from 8 am to 7 pm Monday to Friday, and from 9 am to 6 pm Saturday and Sunday, where you can fill up on tolerable food for about 3 litai. One floor up is the main waiter-service restaurant, open till midnight and with loud music in the evenings. On the top floor is a café-bar with an open-air terrace.

There are a number of café-cum-bars dotted around the place. One of the best, with good coffee and cakes, is right in the village centre facing the town hall.

Getting There & Away

You can reach Nida by bus or private vehicle from Klaipėda, or Smiltynė at the northern tip of Neringa, or Kaliningrad via Zelenogradsk. The Lithuanian border post is on the main road, immediately south of the petrol station at the corner of Taikos gatvė. The Russian post is 2½ km further south.

Bus There are 11 or 12 buses daily to/from Smiltynė, taking 1¼ hours; two or three buses daily from Klaipėda bus station (1½ to two hours); and six to/from Zelenogradsk

LITHUANIA

(1½ hours), and Kaliningrad (2½ hours). Last departures from Smiltynė to Nida and vice-versa are normally about 8.30 pm, though there may be one or two later buses between 1 June and mid-September. At the time of writing, buses leave Nida for Kaliningrad at 8.20 am and 12.20, 2.05, 5, 8.45 and 10 pm. Departures from Kaliningrad to Nida and Smiltynė are at 7, 8.15 and 11.15 am and 3, 4.10 and 6 pm.

Hydrofoil From about May to September you can travel daily by *Raketa* hydrofoil from Kaunas to Nida (and back) along the Nemunas River and across the Courland Lagoon. Departure from Kaunas is in the morning, from Nida in the afternoon. It's about a four-hour trip costing 6.50 litų one way – provided you don't get hit with a foreigner's fare. The hydrofoils also continue to/from Klaipėda at weekends.

Kaliningrad Region

Kaliningrad Region
Калининградская область

Sometimes referred to as the 'fourth Baltic state', the Kaliningrad Region is an *oblast* (region) of Russia wedged between Lithuania and Poland and separated from the rest of Russia. From the 13th century until 1945, the Kaliningrad Region was German, part of the core territory of the Teutonic knights and their successors, the dukes and kings of Prussia. Its capital, now named Kaliningrad after an early Soviet leader, was the famous German city Königsberg.

This chapter contains information specific to the Kaliningrad Region. For a broader introduction to its history, geography, people and culture see the Facts about the Region chapter at the front of the book. For details on obtaining Russian visas for the Kaliningrad Region (and visas for the Baltic states and Belarus) and for more general visitor information see the introductory Facts for the Visitor chapter at the front of the book.

GEOGRAPHY

The Kaliningrad Region is 15,100 sq km in area. The city of Kaliningrad stands on the Pregolya River, which collects most of the waters of the Kaliningrad Region and enters the Kaliningrad Lagoon just west of the city.

The southern half of the Courland Lagoon (Russian: Kurshsky zaliv) and the Courland Spit (Russian: Kurshskaya kosa) are within the Kaliningrad Region. The region also includes the northern half of another sandbar-lagoon pairing stretching down into Poland, with the lagoon mouth at Baltiysk.

The Kaliningrad Region is mostly low and gently rolling, but reaches an elevation of 200 metres in the south-east near the Polish and Lithuanian borders.

GOVERNMENT

The Kaliningrad Region is one of the several dozen *oblasty* (regions) into which Russia is divided. Like other oblasty, it has its own *soviet* (local assembly) with powers over some of its affairs, but it's also answerable to Moscow. Recently the Kaliningrad Region has declared itself a free port (local companies are exempt from import and export duty), but as Moscow's most westward territory, the region still remains heavily militarised.

PEOPLE

The Kaliningrad Region has seen even bigger ethnic changes than the Baltic states since WW II. Virtually its entire pre-WW II German population were evacuated or fled to Germany during the war or were shot or deported to Siberia after it. They were replaced with people from the USSR, mainly Russia. In the last few years some ethnic Germans from Russia (mainly from the Volga region) have made their way there, too.

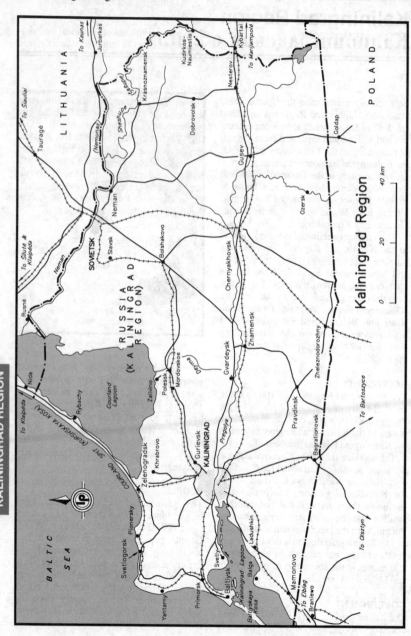

DIPLOMATIC MISSIONS

Because the Kaliningrad Region is part of Russia, you need a Russian visa to go there. Full details on obtaining Russian visas can be found in Facts for the Visitor at the front of the book.

Russian embassies include:

Australia
78 Canberra Ave, Griffith, ACT 2603 (☎ 062-95 9474)
Canada
52 Range Rd, Ottawa, Ontario K1N 8G5 (☎ 613-236 7220)
Denmark
Kristianiagade 3, 2100 Copenhagen (☎ 31 38 23 70)
Estonia
Pikk 19, Tallinn (☎ 22-443 014)
Finland
Vuorimiehenkatu 6, 00140 Helsinki (☎ 90-66 14 49)
France
40-50 Boulevard Lannes, 75016 Paris (☎ 1-45.04.05.50)
Germany
Waldstrasse 42, W-5300 Bonn 2 (☎ 0228-31 2085)
Latvia
Paegles iela 2, Rīga (☎ 22-285 842)
Lithuania
Juozapavičiaus gatvė 11, Vilnius (☎ 22-351 763)
Norway
Drammensveien 74, 0271 Oslo-1 (☎ 22-55 32 78)
Poland
Ulica Belwederska 49, Warsaw (☎ 0-22-213453)
Consulate: ulica Batorego 15, Gdańsk (☎ 0-58-411088)
Sweden
Kungsgatan 48, 11135 Stockholm (☎ 08-208 652)
UK
5 Kensington Palace Gardens, London W8 (☎ 071-229 8027)
USA
1825 Phelps Place NW, Washington DC 20008 (☎ 202-332 1483)

CUSTOMS

You can take in half a litre of hard liquor or one litre of wine, plus modest amounts of other things except weapons or illegal drugs. But large quantities of anything sellable may be suspect. There are restrictions and duties on exporting articles of historical and cultural value, some of which require a Culture Ministry permit.

MONEY

The official currency of the Kaliningrad Region is the Russian rouble, worth around one-tenth of one US cent (that is, R1000 = US$1) at the time of writing. But Western currencies are legal tender, too, and as people are only too keen to get their hands on US dollars or Deutschmarks, you may have to pay in these currencies for some things. Some shops and businesses will accept nothing but hard currency.

NATIONAL HOLIDAYS

Russian national holidays include:

New Year's Day, 1 January
Russian Orthodox Christmas Day, 7 January
International Women's Day, 8 March
Labour Day Holiday, 1 & 2 May
Victory Day (commemorating victory in WW II), 9 May
October Revolution Anniversary, 7 & 8 November

Kaliningrad
Калининград

Kaliningrad (former German name: Königsberg) is a far from lovely city, but strangely absorbing. Today the capital and main city of the Kaliningradskaya oblast (Kaliningrad Region) of Russia, it was an almost entirely German city from 1255 to 1945, and for much of that time was the chief metropolis of Prussia – the state which grew from its south-east Baltic origins to become the crux of a united Germany in the 19th century.

The fascination of the place is the contrast between the Soviet-style city that's here today and the utterly different German city which was here just half a century ago. Huge areas of Königsberg, including most of the centre, were totally wrecked by British bombing in 1944 and the Red Army's successful assault in 1945. After WW II the new Soviet authorities levelled most of the ruins and built a completely new city. They also brought in a whole new population of Russians to replace the Germans who had all been evacuated, killed or deported. The city was renamed after Mikhail Kalinin, a Stalin loyalist who survived the purges and was the formal head of the Soviet state from 1919 almost until his death in 1946.

Soviet-built Kaliningrad is a city of very drab architecture, semi-desolate open spaces where nothing has been rebuilt, and awful pollution – the traffic fumes are thick, and the Pregolya River flowing through the city's heart is black as pitch and really stinks. Kaliningrad's people, however, are surprisingly jolly and friendly.

Königsberg must have been, if nothing else, far more pleasing to the eye than Kaliningrad. What makes Kaliningrad such a poignant place is that just enough remnants of Königsberg survive to just give a taste of what it used to be like, and of its 700-year history. The shell of the old Gothic cathedral, the ornately turreted, red-brick city gates and the dilapidated Luisenwahl woodland park, in their bizarre contrast with the Soviet apartment blocks or seas of semi-desolate space around them, tell the story of their city's unique and dreadful transformation better than any number of history books could.

Kaliningrad was not opened to Western tourists until 1991, launching a flood of German returnee groups – about 50,000 people in 1991, 60,000 in 1992. Border controls on the Kaliningrad Region's border with Lithuania were tightened in 1992-93,

Where is Prussia?

The original Prussians were a Baltic people, related to the Lithuanians and Latvians, who inhabited the south-east hinterland of the Baltic Sea roughly from the Vistula River in modern Poland to the Nemunas River along today's Lithuania/Kaliningrad Region border (see map opposite). They were wiped out and/or assimilated by the German crusading knights of the Teutonic Order, who took over their territory in the 13th century. The knights also took over Pomerelia, an adjoining area stretching about 100 km west of the lower reaches of the Vistula, in the 14th century. Poland then drove the Teutonic Order out of Pomerelia and some western parts of its earlier territory in the 15th century, leaving it in control of what was basically the territory the order had taken from the Prussians in the 13th century, minus a few bites in its southern half.

This knightly territory was transformed into the Duchy of Prussia, ruled by the successors of the knights' last leader in the 16th century. It amounted more or less to what are now the Kaliningrad Region and a similar-sized chunk of Poland immediately to the south (minus the aforesaid bites, but plus a strip along the north bank of the Nemunas and the east side of the Courland Lagoon). Its capital was Königsberg.

In the 17th century, the Duchy of Prussia became linked through royal marriage to the extensive north-German state of Brandenburg, centred on Berlin, and at the start of the 18th century Brandenburg's ruler was crowned the Prussian king. In the late 18th century, Prussia-Brandenburg took over large sections of a disintegrating Poland, including Pomerelia which became known as West Prussia. The former Duchy of Prussia, with its lost 'bites' restored, correspondingly came to be called East Prussia.

By the early 19th century, the whole Prussia-Brandenburg bloc was going by the single name Prussia, and after further territorial gains later that century Prussia stretched all the way from Memel (now Klaipėda, Lithuania) to the borders of Belgium and Luxembourg. This Prussia pulled in a variety of lesser states to create a united Germany in the late 19th century.

With Germany's defeat in WW I, most of the old West Prussia was handed to a reborn Poland, while Danzig (now Gdańsk) and its surrounds around the mouth of the Vistula became a free port. This meant that East Prussia was separated from the rest of Germany. Hitler temporarily reunited them in 1941, but after the Red Army swept through in 1945 East Prussia was divided between the USSR, which got its northern half (the modern Kaliningrad Region), and Poland, which got the southern half.

Germans refer to the Kaliningrad Region as *Das nördliche Ostpreussen* (Northern East Prussia). ∎

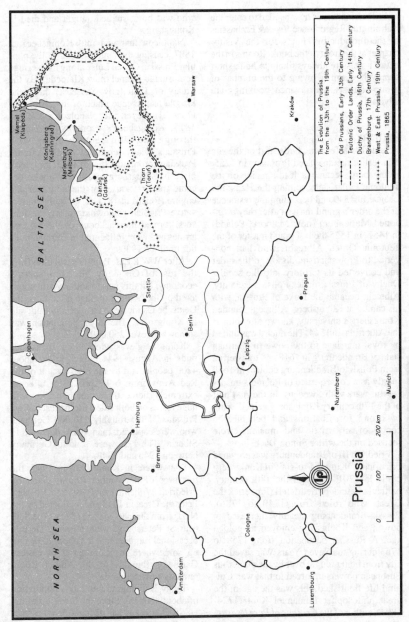

The Evolution of Prussia
from the 13th to the 19th Century:

········ Old Prussians, Early 13th Century

– – – Teutonic Order Lands, Early 14th Century

········ Duchy of Prussia, 16th Century

——— Brandenburg, 17th Century

+++++ West & East Prussia, 19th Century

——— Prussia, 1865

Warsaw

Kraków

Memel
(Klaipeda)

Königsberg
(Kaliningrad)

Marienburg
(Malbork)

Thorn
(Toruń)

Danzig
(Gdańsk)

BALTIC SEA

Stettin

Prague

Copenhagen

Berlin

Leipzig

Nuremberg

Hamburg

Munich

Bremen

Prussia

Cologne

NORTH SEA

Amsterdam

Luxembourg

0   100   200 km

KALININGRAD REGION

and a Russian visa is now needed to enter the Kaliningrad Region – see Visas & Embassies in the introductory Facts for the Visitor chapter at the front of the book. Rooms in the better hotels are always likely to be in short supply in summer owing to the number of group tourists, so advance bookings are advisable.

HISTORY

Founded as a Teutonic Order fort on the site of a fort of the displaced Prussians in 1255, Königsberg became a leading city of the Teutonic Order state, joining the Hanseatic League in 1340 and becoming the residence of the order's grand masters after they abandoned Marienburg (now Malbork, Poland) in 1457. In 1525 the last grand master of the Teutonic Order, Albrecht, who had converted to Protestantism, dissolved the order and converted its territory into the secular Duchy of Prussia, under Polish suzerainty. Albrecht became the Duke of Prussia, with his capital at Königsberg. Albrecht founded Königsberg's university, known after him as the Albertina, in 1544. The duchy was united by royal marriage to the powerful German state of Brandenburg in 1618 and transferred from Polish to Brandenburg control in 1660 (partly as a consequence of Poland's unsuccessful wars with Sweden). In the first half of the 17th century Königsberg gained a ring of strong fortifications and became the centre of an artistic and musical circle focused on the writer Simon Dach.

Friedrich III of Brandenburg was crowned Friedrich I, 'King in Prussia', in Königsberg castle in 1701. Through the 18th century, particularly under Friedrich II (Frederick the Great, who ruled from 1740 to 1786), Prussia-Brandenburg steadily increased in power, and Königsberg enjoyed its golden age. A Russian occupation from 1758 to 1763 during the Seven Years War saved the city from being fought over by the numerous European powers involved in that war. Cultural life flourished: this was the age of the great philosopher Immanuel Kant (1724-1804), author of the *Critique of Pure Reason*,

who was born, studied, taught and died in Königsberg.

Napoleon marched into Königsberg in 1807, causing the famous flight of the popular Prussian Queen Luise along the Neringa peninsula to Memel (now Klaipėda). By the Treaty of Tilsit (now Sovietsk) that year, Prussia had to cede much of its territory to France. However, after Napoleon's defeat in 1815, Königsberg's economy developed through the 19th century along with Prussia's steady territorial gains. Another Prussian coronation, that of Wilhelm I, took place in Königsberg in 1861. Wilhelm became the first kaiser of the new German empire (Reich) in 1871. The highly conservative Prussian landowning class, the Junkers, formed the backbone of the kaisers' armies and were influential in German politics until the 1930s.

After WW I, East Prussia's isolation from the rest of Germany hit Königsberg's economy, but this was to some extent countered by the holding of huge trade fairs, the Deutsche Ostmesse, on a specially built site in Königsberg. The city's population was somewhere over 250,000.

Königsberg was wrecked by British air raids in August 1944, which killed about 4200 people, and by the final assault of the Red Army from 6-9 April 1945, after an extremely fierce three-month battle, with huge losses on both sides, for the rest of East Prussia. Of the roughly 110,000 Germans who were captured, many were deported to Siberia. The rest were sent to Germany between 1946 and 1948.

Somewhere in Königsberg in 1945, the treasures of the Amber Room, given by Friedrich Wilhelm I of Prussia to Russia's Peter the Great in 1713 and plundered by the Nazis from the tsars' palace at Tsarskoe Selo near St Petersburg, went missing. Despite occasional rumours that it's about to be dug up somewhere in Kaliningrad or eastern Germany, the fate of the Amber Room remains a mystery today.

Today Kaliningrad city has a population of about 400,000. Since the break-up of the USSR in 1991 it has declared itself a free-trade zone in the hope of becoming a major trading nexus between Russia and the West. The bulk of Western interest is coming from Poland and Germany. There's plenty of evidence of a flourishing free-enterprise mentality among some sections of the local population. After decades of Soviet spin on their city's history, which attempted to obliterate most of its German past, Kaliningrad people are also developing an interest in the real story. Some refer to their city as 'König' and there's even talk of giving it back its old name officially.

ORIENTATION

Leninsky prospekt, a broad south-north avenue, is the main artery of Kaliningrad, running three km from the bus station and the main railway station, the Yuzhny Vokzal (South Station), to the suburban Severny Vokzal (North Station) on ploshchad Pobedy. About halfway it crosses the Pregolya River and the island on which the shell of Kaliningrad's cathedral – a major landmark – stands. Just north of the river, Leninsky prospekt passes through Tsentralnaya ploshchad, with the Gostinitsa Kaliningrad hotel and the unmistakable House of Soviets.

Other important arteries include Moskovsky prospekt, the main east-west thoroughfare, which passes beneath Leninsky prospekt between the Pregolya and Tsentralnaya ploshchad; ulitsa Chernyakhovskogo, heading east from ploshchad Pobedy, past the central market to the Amber Museum in the Dohna Tower on ploshchad Vasilevskogo; and prospekt Mira, winding west from ploshchad Pobedy to Kalinin Park.

INFORMATION
Tourist Information

There's no tourist office as such, but main hotels will usually be able to answer basic questions.

Money

Deutschmarks and US dollars, in that order, are the favoured foreign currencies here, and you can use them to pay direct for some things. Places you can change money include the advance-booking hall in the Yuzhny Vokzal; the main hotels; Investbank at Leninsky prospekt 28, across the road from the Gostinitsa Kaliningrad; another Investbank branch on ulitsa Ivannikova off ulitsa Chernyakhovskogo; and Amberkönigbank on the southern half of Leninsky prospekt between ulitsa Portovaya and ulitsa Polotskaya. The best rates I found were in the floating Hotel Baltinvest.

There's also a black market. People hanging around in or outside the Gostinitsa Kaliningrad, for instance, may offer you a better exchange rate thanthebanks, but always beware of rip-offs.

Post & Telecommunications

The head post, telephone and telegraph office (pochtamt) is in an extraordinarily out-of-the-way location at ulitsa Kosmonavta Leonova 22, about 700 metres north of prospekt Mira. Trolleybus Nos 1 and 3 come up here from the Yuzhny Vokzal via Leninsky prospekt, ulitsa Teatralnaya and prospekt Mira, as does bus No 101 from prospekt Mira. The postal section is open from 9 am to 9 pm Monday to Friday, 10 am to 6 pm Saturday and Sunday; the telephone and telegraph sections, 24 hours daily. You can make long-distance calls to other towns within the Kaliningrad Region, the Baltic states or the rest of the former USSR, both here and at another more central telephone office at ulitsa Teatralnaya 13/19, off the northern part of Leninsky prospekt. The ulitsa Teatralnaya office is open round the clock daily and has telegram facilities too. There's also a telephone and telegraph office beside the Yuzhny Vokzal.

The Gostinitsa Kaliningrad has an international telephone, fax and telex office. It's pretty busy. There's a srochniy (urgent) service for phone calls at more than double the normal costs.

The telephone code for Kaliningrad city is 22 if you're dialling from within the Kaliningrad Region, but 0112 if you're dialling from elsewhere.

KALININGRAD REGION

KALININGRAD REGION

Media

You may find the odd German newspaper in hotels, but not much else unless you can read Russian. *Kaliningradskaya Pravda* comes out daily.

Bookshops

There are quite a lot of bookshops but little in anything but Russian. Posters, cards and art books, however, don't require much verbal understanding. Two of the biggest bookshops are Znanie at Leninsky prospekt 103, and Svetoch at ulitsa Zarayskaya 19, just east of the House of Soviets.

Maps

See Maps in the introductory Facts for the Visitor chapter for details of an up-to-date Kaliningrad city map published by Verlag Gerhard Rautenberg of Germany. This map may become available in Kaliningrad, but the only city map available locally when I visited was the *Kaliningradskaya turist-skaya skhema*, which is more of a diagram than a map and will mislead you all over the place if you try to find your way round by it. It does, however, enable you to work out the rough whereabouts of most streets and dozens of marked features. It comes in two versions – one (grey and blue) in Russian only, the other (orange) in Russian and German. The German title is *Touristen Plan Kaliningrad Königsberg*. Hotels are the best place to look for it – the only place I found the two-language version was the Hotel Baltinvest.

Health & Medical Services

Seek help in your hotel in the first instance, if you're in one. There's emergency service at the hospital at Klinicheskaya ulitsa 74. You can phone 03 for emergency medical help. For Western medicines you could try hotels or the the hard-currency shop next to the Gostinitsa Kaliningrad.

Left Luggage

There's a left-luggage room *(kamera khranenia)* at the Yuzhny vokzal, open daily from 6.30 am to midnight with breaks from 9.30 to 10 am, 1 to 2 pm and 7.30 to 8 pm.

WALKING TOUR

Kaliningrad's sights are fairly spread out but the following route of about 4½ km will take you around the heart of the city and some of its most interesting spots in half a day or so. Public transport can save your legs (and lungs) on some stretches.

Starting from the **cathedral** on its island in the Pregolya, head north past the **House of Soviets** on Tsentralnaya ploshchad, along the bank of the **Prud Nizhny** (Lower Pond), perhaps calling in at the **History & Art Museum**, to the **Amber Museum** in the Dohna Tower. Then go west along ulitsa Chernyakhovskogo to the **market** and **ploshchad Pobedy** (trams can help you along this bit). By now you've covered about three km.

Head back south down Leninsky prospekt, by trolleybus if you like. You can stop in at the **Bunker Museum** on ulitsa Universitetskaya just before you get back to Tsentralnaya ploshchad. An extension for the energetic is to head out west along **prospekt Mira** from ploshchad Pobedy.

CATHEDRAL

The gaunt red-brick shell of Kaliningrad's cathedral stands at the heart of the city, on the island at the meeting of the two arms of the Pregolya. You can walk on to the island from Oktyabrskaya ulitsa at its east end or by steps down from the Leninsky prospekt bridge over the river. The cathedral is very much a symbol of the city, representing its German past but also, in its ruined state, a permanent reminder of the Soviet conquest in 1945. No longer is it the towering landmark that it used to be, as the Soviet buildings forming its backdrop are at least as tall as the cathedral, but the semi-desolate open spaces now surrounding it, in place of the narrow streets that used to crowd the island and the north bank of the river, leave it an isolated dignity. There are plans to restore the cathedral but they face difficulties of finance and the fact that its foundations are slowly sinking. There are also plans for a German company to develop the island with a hotel, shopping centre and office blocks, which would be a very nice twist of history.

The cathedral was built in the 14th century in the Gothic style. Several bishops, grand masters of the Teutonic Order and other leading figures from Königsberg history were buried inside. Originally there were two towers at the west end but they burnt down in 1544 and only the southern one was rebuilt. Before the cathedral's destruction in 1944, the tower was topped by a pointed spire rather like a taller version of the one on the Vytautas Church in Kaunas.

The **tomb of Immanuel Kant**, the great 18th century philosopher who was born, studied and taught in Königsberg, remains on the outer north side of the cathedral. It was restored after WW II and a roof added to its columned surround. There's a small **sculpture park** with statues of Russian and Soviet cultural figures on the south bank of the island, to the west of the cathedral.

STOCK EXCHANGE

The fine, blue, Italian Renaissance-style building on the south bank of the Pregolya, a little further west than the cathedral, is the old Stock Exchange (Torgovaya birzha), built in the 1870s. As the sign on its roof says, it became the Sailors' Culture Palace (Dvorets Kultury Moryakov) under Soviet rule.

TSENTRALNAYA PLOSHCHAD

Tsentralnaya ploshchad (Central Square), on the mound above the north bank of the Pregolya, is an apt centrepiece for post-WW II Kaliningrad – a typical wide Soviet city square surrounded by drab buildings, among them the Gostinitsa Kaliningrad, and dominated by the upright-H-shaped **House of Soviets** (Dom Sovietov) which has been described as the ugliest creation of Soviet architecture (which is some achievement).

The House of Soviets, still unfinished and perhaps never to be completed, was originally meant as a kind of city hall, but more recently there has also been talk of making it

a business centre. Many people reckon dynamite is what it most needs. Its construction began after the blowing up, in the 1960s, of Königsberg Castle, which had stood for over 700 years just west of the site of the House of Soviets, covering much of what's now Tsentralnaya ploshchad.

The castle was really where Königsberg began, founded about 1260 by the Teutonic Order as a redoubt against the rebelling Prussians. (It replaced a temporary wooden fort built in 1255 on the site of Prussian fortifications which were probably on the site of the House of Soviets.) The grand master of the Teutonic Order resided in the castle after abandoning Marienburg to the Poles in 1457. The order's successors from 1525, the dukes of Prussia, greatly expanded the castle. It was wrecked in the 1944 bombing and 1945 shelling, but its remains stood for another 24 years.

The buildings behind the east side of the House of Soviets include Kaliningrad's **Palace of Weddings** (Dvorets brakosochetaniy).

BUNKER MUSEUM

The first opening on the right as you go north up Leninsky prospekt from Tsentralnaya ploshchad leads into a square that was called Paradeplatz in German times but doesn't seem to have its own name today. However, the street along its north side is named ulitsa Universitetskaya, after the building of Kaliningrad University which stands towards its east end.

Down a flight of steps in the centre of the square is the **Bunker Museum** (Muzey-Blindazh), the German command post during the Red Army's assault on Kaliningrad. This now strangely quiet set of rooms lining an underground passage contains models, maps, photos and other material recounting the four-day Soviet storming of the city in April 1945. Room 13 is left as it was at 9 pm on 9 April when the German commander, General Otto Lasch, and Soviet officers Janovsky and Kruglov signed the surrender document in it. The Bunker

KALININGRAD REGION

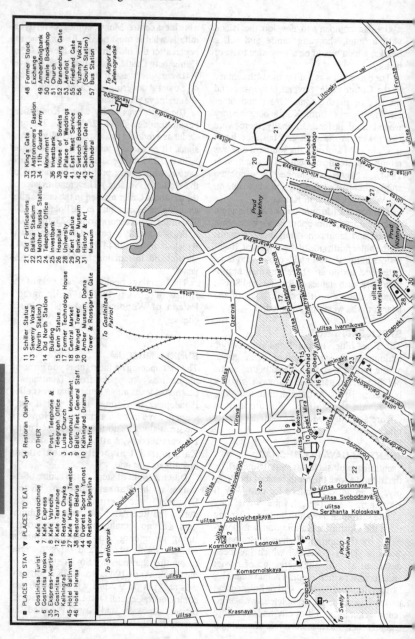

■ PLACES TO STAY

1 Gostinitsa Turist
6 Gostinitsa Moskva
35 Ekspress-Kvartira
37 Gostinitsa
45 Hotel Baltinvest
46 Hotel Hansa

▼ PLACES TO EAT

4 Kafe Vostochnoe
7 Kafe Express
8 Kafe Vstrecha
12 Kafe Teatralnoe
16 Restoran Olsha
27 Kafe Kamenny Tsvetok
38 Restoran Belarus
44 Dvorets Sporta Yunost
48 Restoran Brigantina
54 Restoran Olshtyn

OTHER

2 Post, Telephone &
   Telegraph Office
3 Luisa Church
5 Cosmonaut Monument
9 Baltic Fleet General Staff
   Tower
10 Kaliningrad Drama
    Theatre
11 Schiller Statue
13 Severny Vokzal
    (North Station)
14 Old North Station
    Building
15 Lenin Statue
18 Former Technology House
19 Central Market
20 Amber Museum, Dohna
    Tower & Rossgarten Gate
21 Old Fortifications
22 Baltika Stadium
23 Mother Russia Statue
24 Telephone Office
25 Investbank
26 Hospital
28 University
29 Kant Statue
30 Bunker Museum
31 History & Art
    Museum
32 King's Gate
33 Astronomers' Bastion
34 11th Guards Army
    Monument
36 House of Soviets
39 House of Soviets
40 Palace of Weddings
41 East West Service
42 Svetoch Bookshop
43 Sackheim Gate
47 Cathedral
48 Former Stock
    Exchange
49 Amberkönigbank
50 Znanie Bookshop
51 Church
52 Brandenburg Gate
53 Aeroflot
55 Friedland Gate
56 Yuzhny Vokzal
    (South Station)
57 Bus Station

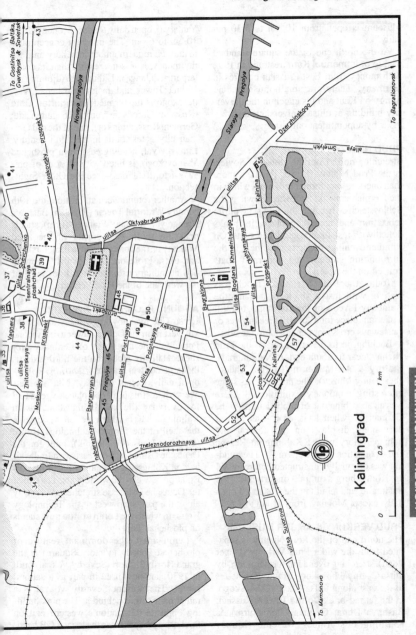

KALININGRAD REGION

Museum is open from 10 am to 5.30 pm daily.

At the north end of the square stands a **statue of Immanuel Kant**, restored in 1992 with money from East Prussian emigrés in Germany. There's a small museum and library on Kant and his epoch in the university building at ulitsa Universitetskaya 2 – visits by appointment only.

PRUD NIZHNY

Stretching north from the House of Soviets is the Prud Nizhny (Lower Pond), a more than one-km-long former mill pond which in the German era – when it was known as the Schlossteich – became the city's favourite relaxation and recreation place, its banks dotted with restaurants and dance spots. On summer evenings concerts were held in the surrounding gardens and lanterned boats cruised on the waters.

Today the Prud Nizhny is much less festive, with just a single restaurant (the Kamenny Tsvetok on the east bank), but still a pleasant place for a stroll. Three bridges or causeways cross from one bank to the other.

Backing on to the east bank of the Prud Nizhny, near its south end, is Kaliningrad's **History & Art Museum** (Istoriko-Khudozhestvenny Muzey). The museum has some interesting temporary exhibitions – there was an absorbing one of applied art from the German era when I visited it – as well as permanent displays on the natural and human history of the Kaliningrad Region and a collection of Soviet-era art. The building was originally constructed before WW I as Königsberg's main concert hall, the Stadthalle, and rebuilt in the 1980s. It's open daily, except Monday, from 11 am to 7 pm.

PRUD VERKHNY & AMBER MUSEUM

The north end of the Prud Nizhny is separated from the wider Prud Verkhny (Upper Pond), stretching over a km further north, by ulitsa Chernyakhovskogo. About 100 metres to the east along ulitsa Chernyakhovskogo, in the fat red-brick **Dohna Tower** (Russian: Bashnya Dona; German: Dohnaturm), is Kaliningrad's Amber Museum (Muzey

Yantarya), open daily (except Monday) from 10 am to 6 pm. The museum concentrates mainly on modern amber jewellery and, for my money, is less interesting than its counterpart at Palanga in Lithuania. Adjoining the Dohna Tower and facing ploshchad Vasilevskogo is the turreted **Rossgarten Gate** (Russian: Gorodskie vorota Rosgartenskie; German: Rossgärter Tor), one of the old German city gates, built in the 19th century. Litovsky val, heading east from ploshchad Vasilevskogo, is lined with a series of pre-WW I fortifications – see the Other Sights section.

Another rotund German bastion, the 19th century **Wrangel Tower** (Russian: Bashnya Vrangelya; German: Wrangel-Turm), stands near the south-west corner of the Prud Verkhny on the corner of ulitsa Proletarskaya and ulitsa Profesora Baranova. It's now in Soviet military use. Parkland lines most of the west side of the Prud Verkhny.

AROUND PLOSHCHAD POBEDY

Ulitsa Chernyakhovskogo leads about 1½ km west from the Dohna Tower to ploshchad Pobedy at the north end of Leninsky prospekt. Halfway along, on the north side, is the large **central market** (*tsentralny rynok*), open daily, except Monday. Like markets everywhere, this is a good place to get a feel for everyday life and living standards in Kaliningrad. Its northern section is housed in the shell of the former Technology House (German: Haus der Technik), built for the Deutsche Ostmesse, a big east-west trade fair held in Königsberg to counter East Prussia's isolation between the world wars. The site of the Deutsche Ostmesse stretched all the way along the park strip west of the Technology House to where the **Lenin statue** now stands on ploshchad Pobedy.

Lenin apart, the dominant feature of ploshchad Pobedy (Victory Square) is the grand **North Station** (Severny Vokzal) built in 1930, and now used in part as a sailors' hostel. The present Severny Vokzal is a rather paltry affair behind it. The pink building opposite the station's western exit on Sovietsky prospekt was the local KGB headquarters. Kaliningrad's city hall is on the south side of ploshchad Pobedy, with the Restoran Chayka at its rear. A large heroic **statue of Mother Russia** dominates the park just south of here, between Leninsky prospekt and ulitsa Teatralnaya.

ALONG PROSPEKT MIRA

Prospekt Mira winds west from ploshchad Pobedy. The fine building overlooking the west end of the little park, on the north side of its first stretch, is the General Staff of the Russian Baltic Fleet. About 400 metres from ploshchad Pobedy, west along prospekt Mira, is the **Kaliningrad Drama Theatre**, first built in 1927 and restored (not identically) in 1980. Opposite is a **statue** of the German playwright Friedrich Schiller, which has stood hereabouts since 1936. By the theatre, prospekt Mira turns right, passing the Baltika Stadium on the site of a former park, Walter-Simon-Platz, and a little later on the right the **Kaliningrad Zoo**, which dates back to the 1890s.

About 400 metres beyond the zoo, on the south side of prospekt Mira, opposite the corner of ulitsa Kosmonavta Leonova, is a tall **Cosmonaut Monument**, and a further 400 metres along is the main entrance to the **Kalinin Park** of Culture & Rest (PKiO im Kalinina), formerly the Luisenwahl, a favourite Königsberg park. The park now has a funfair, café, domino and cards pavilion, and disco, as well as the 1901 **Luise Church** (tserkov Luizy), now a puppet theatre, and a sadly shabby treed section with a stream running through it. Though originally named after the wife of a teacher who owned the land in the 18th century, the park was long associated with Queen Luise of Prussia whose statue stood here till 1945.

OTHER SIGHTS

Kaliningrad is dotted with a couple of dozen more old bastions and remnants of the fortifications built up from the 17th century on. Königsberg had an imposing defensive ring about two km out from its castle.

Perhaps most interesting are the old gates

in this ring, which are red brick and quite picturesque. One is the Rossgarten Gate on ploshchad Vasilevskogo (see the Prud Verkhny & Amber Museum section). From ploshchad Vasilevskogo, Litovsky val curves to the south, just inside the line of the pre-WW I defensive works, to the **King's Gate** (Russian: Gorodskie vorota Korolevskie; German: Königstor) at the east end of ulitsa Frunze, after just over one km, and the **Sackheim Gate** (Russian: Gorodskie vorota Zakkhaymskie; German: Sackheim Tor) on Moskovsky prospekt after 1½ km.

South of the river are the **Brandenburg Gate** (Russian: Gorodskie vorota Brandenburgskie; German: Brandenburger Tor) on ulitsa Bagrationa, just west of the Yuzhny Vokzal, and the **Friedland Gate** (Russian: Gorodskie vorota Fridlyandskie; German: Friedländer Tor) at the east end of prospekt Kalinina, 1½ km from the station. The park along the south side of prospekt Kalinina was itself a section of the old fortifications.

One particularly large bastion, not open to visitors, is the **Astronomers' Bastion** (Russian: Bastion Astronomichesky; German: Astronomische Bastion) on Gvardeysky prospekt. In the park south of the Astronomers' Bastion is an **obelisk monument** at the mass grave of 1200 Soviet soldiers of the 11th Guards Army who died in the 1945 assault. This is the best known of the city's many monuments and graveyards for Soviet troops.

There's a fine 20th century red-brick **neo-Gothic church**, modelled on some of the old churches from the Teutonic Order period, at ulitsa Bogdana Khmelnitskogo 63A, east off the southern part of Leninsky prospekt.

PLACES TO STAY – BOTTOM END
Private Homes

There are a couple of agencies offering rooms in private flats but you can't always be certain they'll accept Westerners. Such businesses also have a habit of moving their offices, so keep an eye open for signs at places like the rail and bus stations. *Ekspress-Kvartira* (☎ 467 446) in a dowdy little office at ulitsa Vagnera 58-1A, about 500 metres west of Tsentralnaya ploshchad, offers rooms in private flats for US$0.65 per person but may up the price to US$1.50 or so for foreigners. If you're on your own, you may find yourself sharing a room with someone else. The office is friendly enough but only Russian is spoken. A Russian visa was asked for, but not insisted on, when I enquired here.

Koop Visit or *Visit Kvartira* (☎ 441 362), which has an office inside the Aeroflot office on ploshchad Kalinina, charges US$0.45 per person but doesn't seem keen on foreigners. People hanging around the Gostinitsa Kaliningrad may also offer to find you private accommodation – I was quoted US$4.50 a person but you could try bargaining.

Hotels & Campsite

The *Gostinitsa Kaliningrad* (☎ 469 440), on Tsentralnaya ploshchad on the corner of Leninsky prospekt (its address is Leninsky prospekt 81), has singles/doubles with private bathroom for US$5/6 for foreigners, or 'lyux' rooms (with a sitting room) for US$15 to US$20. It's nothing very special, but because of its central location it's sometimes fully booked. Locals pay about a quarter of the foreigner's prices.

The large *Gostinitsa Moskva* (☎ 272 089) at prospekt Mira 19, about 400 metres west of ploshchad Pobedy, has reasonable rooms (a bit ageing but adequately clean) at a variety of prices depending mainly on whether they have a private bathroom or not. I had a single with a TV, sharing a shower and toilet with one other room, for US$5. Singles using toilet and shower on the corridor are US$4, and doubles are about 30% dearer than singles. I had to show my passport but not my visa when I checked in.

The *Gostinitsa Patriot* (☎ 275 023), three km north of the city centre at Ozernaya ulitsa 25A, has doubles with private bathroom for US$6.50. There's a café in the building. Take tram No 6 or 10 north up ulitsa Gorkogo from the central market; Ozernaya ulitsa is the first street on the right after ulitsa Gorkogo crosses a bridge over the railway (the nearest tram stop is a bit past the Gorkogo/Ozernaya corner). Walk 200 or 300 metres along Ozernaya ulitsa then turn into the side road beside house No 25 on the north side. Keep going through a couple of unpromising yards till you see the newish nine-storey slab of the Patriot ahead.

The *Gostinitsa Baltika* (☎ 437 977) is seven km east of the centre on Moskovsky prospekt at Zaozerie. This 10-storey block has doubles with private bathroom for US$12 and is used by some German tour groups. There is a restaurant and café-bar in the building. There's also a *Kemping*, with cabins, next door. A taxi to the hotel from the city centre is about US$0.75 and takes about 10 minutes – it's on the left not long after you cross the ring road, Bolshaya Okruzhnaya ulitsa. Bus No 25 goes to the hotel once or twice an hour; its stops in the city centre include the southbound Kinoteatr Rossia stop on Gvardeysky prospekt, just off ploshchad Pobedy, and the eastbound Grazhdanproekt stop on Moskovsky prospekt east of the Oktyabrskaya ulitsa corner.

PLACES TO STAY – MIDDLE & TOP END

In 1992 and 1993 two resting cruise ships were moored on naberezhnaya Bagramyana, the north bank of the Pregolya, just west of the Leninsky prospekt bridge, to alleviate the shortage of Western-tourist-standard accommodation in Kaliningrad. They may stay in use for some time, as no large new hotels seem to be in the offing on land. Their cabins are small but have private shower and toilet. If you don't mind keeping your porthole shut to lock out the smell of the Pregolya, these floating hotels are a reasonable choice, being centrally located, comfortable enough, and with their own good restaurants. They're very similar but the *Hotel Baltinvest*, alias the *Semyon Budyonny*, the further of the two from Leninsky prospekt, is considerably cheaper at US$21/37 for singles/doubles including breakfast. The *Hotel Hansa* (☎ 433 806 or 433 737) on the *Georgy Dimitrov* charges about US$34/61, again including breakfast. The Hansa takes credit cards and has a postal address – naberezhnaya Bagramyana 6.

The *Gostinitsa Turist* (☎ 460 801) at ulitsa A Nevskogo 53, about 2½ km north-east of the centre, was renovated in 1991 and takes quite a few German groups. Rooms for independent travellers if available, are US$37/49 and have private bathroom and TV. The hotel has its own restaurant. You can get there by tram No 8 from ploshchad Vasilevskogo, or bus No 11 from any stop on Leninsky prospekt, ulitsa Chernyakhovskogo or ploshchad Vasilevskogo, or bus No 2, 17 or 32 from ulitsa Chernyakhovskogo or ploshchad Vasilevskogo – the hotel is about one km along ulitsa A Nevskogo from ploshchad Vasilevskogo.

All three hotels say they require their guests to have Russian visas.

The Russian state company for foreign tourism, Intourist, has a small hotel for up to 30 group tourists, the *Hotel Der Dohna*, entered through the Ama shop at ploshchad Vasilevskogo 2. Intourist didn't start operating in Kaliningrad until the city was opened up to Western tourism. Intourist's office (☎ 228 482) is in Room 111 of the Dom Ofizerov (Officers' House) on the south side of ulitsa Kirova, just off Sovietsky prospekt and near the Severny Vokzal.

PLACES TO EAT

For a good feed you can hardly beat the restaurants on the floating *Hotel Baltinvest* and *Hotel Hansa*, which serve good Western as well as Russian food. The Baltinvest has one restaurant for roubles and one for hard currency, with the former much the better value though its menu is handwritten in Russian only. In the rouble restaurant a good three or four-course meal can cost under US$1.50. The only slight catch is that there are no cheap drinks – even mineral water is imported and costs US$0.45. The Hotel Hansa insists on hard currency. At dinner it has two set menus at around US$7.50 and US$9.50 – the cheaper one might be soup, a big serve of fried chicken and vegetables, and a slice of gateau; or four good slices of

cold beef, a fish and vegetables main course, and ice cream – plus a sizeable lettuce, cucumber and tomato salad in each case. A beer is US$1.25.

Right in front of the Hotel Hansa is the large *Dvorets Sporta Yunost* (Youth Sports Palace), whose *bufet* – no signs, just enter and walk along the passage to the left – is popular with locals. It attracts quite a variety of customers, with rock videos (not too loud), good service, and food that's nothing spectacular but at least corresponds to what the menu says (in Russian only). When I ate here, there was a choice between chicken (tsyplyonok), stuffed pepper (perets farshirovany) or eskalop for the main course, all between US$0.45 and US$0.60, plus a few sweet desserts and salads (including caviar) at US$0.30 to US$0.45.

Hotel restaurants provide some of the better fare elsewhere. The *Restoran Moskva*, entered from the street down the side of the Gostinitsa Moskva, will do you a good beef stroganoff main course for just US$0.30, or spicy Georgian chicken tabaka for US$0.65, or a shashlik (kebab) for US$0.40. Dinner in the *Gostinitsa Turist* restaurant is about US$6.

Two restaurants reckoned among the best in town, but not recommended for those who don't like very loud dance music with their food, are the *Restoran Olshtyn* at ulitsa Olshtynskaya 1, near the Yuzhny Vokzal, and the *Restoran Brigantina* in the old stock exchange, now the Sailors' Culture Palace (Dvorets Kultury Moryakov), at Leninsky prospekt 83. The Olshtyn also has a popular café on its ground floor. The *Restoran Chayka* on ploshchad Pobedy is in a similar vein.

Quieter, totally unpretentious, and conveniently central is the *Restoran Belarus* at ulitsa Zhitomirskaya 14, facing the west side of Tsentralnaya ploshchad. A tomato salad, meat-and-veg main course and a soft drink will set you back about US$0.75. The Belarus is open from noon to 4 pm and 5 to 10 pm. The restaurant in the *Gostinitsa Kaliningrad* across the road is pretty ordinary but its café on floor 3 is a good place for a quiet drink or snack. It does grilled chicken at US$0.60 a portion, also small salads at US$0.10 to US$0.20 or so – open from 8 am to 3 pm and 5 pm to midnight.

The *Kafe Kamenny Tsvetok* on the east side of the Prud Nizhny is smart and clean, with rock videos and just nine tables around a dance floor. It gets busy in the evenings and you need to book at noon for an evening meal, but at lunch time you're likely to get a table without booking. However the food is neither generous in quantity nor anything special in taste, and not all the items on the only semi-legible Russian menu are on. I settled for a small salad, sturgeon (osetrina), ice cream and coffee which cost under US$1. Opening hours are noon to 4.30 pm and 6 to 11 pm.

Another place serving pretty ordinary meals to the accompaniment of rock videos is the *Kafe Teatralnoe* at Teatralnaya ulitsa 38. Main courses are from US$0.30 to US$0.60, beer (German only) is US$0.50. The menu is hand-written and hard to decipher. A bit further west, the *Kafe Vstrecha* at prospekt Mira 10 serves – very slowly – grilled chicken. It has two rooms with separate street entrances. A little further along prospekt Mira on the corner of ulitsa Grekova, the *Kafe Express* lives up to its name with quick counter service for snacks such as buterbrody (open sandwiches), cakes, juice and coffee. The *Kafe Vostochnoe* at prospekt Mira 76, just before the corner of ulitsa Komsomolskaya, has a reportedly decent little tea-house, the *Chaykhana*, next door.

Another café supposed to be pleasant, but closed when I visited, is the *Kafe Solnechny Kamen* in the Rossgarten Gate. There's a tolerable canteen in the Yuzhny Vokzal.

ENTERTAINMENT

Choices are pretty limited unless you fancy one of the restaurants with dance music (Russian pop), a play in Russian at the drama theatre, or a film in Russian at one of the cinemas (kinoteatry). The occasional rock concert is announced on posters.

THINGS TO BUY

Kaliningrad's shops are disappointing. Their main clusters are along the southern half of Leninsky prospekt and along prospekt Mira. Even amber, which is mined on the coast at Yantarny, seems to be in short supply. Two of the main amber and jewellery shops – Rubin, at Leninsky prospekt 40, and Yantar, at prospekt Mira 53 – both have sparse selections. Khudozhestvenny Salon at Leninsky prospekt 10 and another shop of the same name at ulitsa 9 Aprelya 5 sell crafts and souvenirs. For records, tapes and musical instruments try Akkord at prospekt Mira 14 and Melodia at Leninsky prospekt 38. Some of the bookshops are worth a look – see the Information section. There's a quite large hard-currency shop with imported Western goods on Tsentralnaya ploshchad next door to the Gostinitsa Kaliningrad. Stamp collectors should visit the Filatelia shop at ulitsa Grekova 12 on the corner of prospekt Mira – open daily from 10 am to 2 pm and 3 to 7 pm. The flea market held at the central market on ulitsa Chernyakhovskogo on Saturday and Sunday mornings is worth a visit for interest's sake, even if you don't find anything to buy.

GETTING THERE & AWAY

This section focuses on transport within the Kaliningrad Region and to/from Lithuania, Latvia and Estonia. The growing number of transport links to/from other countries, including the rest of Russia and the CIS, are covered in the introductory Getting There & Away chapter – except for information on ticket outlets in Kaliningrad, which is given here.

Kaliningrad's long-distance transport hub is ploshchad Kalinina at the south end of Leninsky prospekt, where the main railway station (the Yuzhny Vokzal), the bus station (*avtovokzal*), and the main Aeroflot office are located.

Air

There are currently no flights to/from anywhere else in the Kaliningrad Region or the Baltic states, but you can fly to several CIS cities. Scheduled flights to Poland, Denmark and Germany are also in prospect. Aeroflot's main office (☎ 446 666 or 446 657) is on the north side of ploshchad Kalinina. Apart from a daily break for lunch from 1 to 2 pm, it's open from 9 am to 7 pm on Mondays, 8 am to 7 pm Tuesday to Friday, and 8 am to 5 pm on Saturdays and Sundays. Timetables, at the time of writing, are still all in Moscow time (*Moskovskoe vremya*), though they don't always say so. There's also an air ticket window in the Gostinitsa Kaliningrad lobby.

The airport is at Khrabrovo, about 22 km north of the city, east off the Zelenogradsk road. You must check in at least 40 minutes before departure – otherwise Aeroflot reserves the right not to let you on the flight. See Getting Around for information on the airport bus service.

Bus

The bus station is towards the east end of ploshchad Kalinina. Buses run to/from main points in Lithuania, Latvia and Estonia as well as within the Kaliningrad Region. They include:

Baltiysk
50 km, 1½ hours, one or two buses an hour, US$0.15
Chernyakhovsk
90 km, two to 2½ hours, eight or more buses daily, US$0.30
Druskininkai
330 km, seven hours, one bus daily, US$0.80
Gusev
115 km, three hours, four buses daily, US$0.40
Kaunas
250 km, six hours, three buses daily, via Chernyakhovsk and Marijampolė, or Sovietsk and Jurbarkas, US$0.65
Klaipėda (via Zelenogradsk and Nida)
130 km, 3½ hours, six buses daily (terminating at Smiltynė), US$0.35
Klaipėda (via Sovietsk)
210 km, five hours, one to three buses daily (terminating at Klaipėda bus station), US$0.55
Liepāja
305 km, 7½ to 9½ hours, two buses daily via Sovietsk and Klaipėda, US$0.75
Mamonovo
55 km, 1½ hours, eight buses daily, US$0.15
Nida
80 km, 2½ hours, six buses daily, US$0.25
Palanga
235 km, six hours, two buses daily, US$0.60
Pärnu
560 km, 11 hours, one bus nightly, US$1.40
Rīga
370 km, nine hours, one bus daily via Sovietsk and Šiauliai, US$0.85
Šiauliai
245 km, five hours, two to four buses daily via Sovietsk, US$0.65
Sovietsk
115 km, three to 3½ hours, eight or more buses daily, US$0.40
Svetly
25 km, one hour, bus No 105 four or five times hourly from 5.30 am to 10.30 pm, US$0.15 (also stops on ulitsa Teatralnaya, just east of prospekt Mira)
Tallinn
690 km, 13½ hours, one bus nightly, US$1.75
Vilnius
350 km, 8¼ hours, two or three buses daily via Chernyakhovsk and Marijampolė, or Sovietsk and Jurbarkas, US$0.90
Yantarny
45 km, 1½ hours, six buses daily, US$0.15
Zelenogradsk
30 km, 50 minutes, six buses daily, US$0.15

For information on bus routes and frequencies to/from Poland, the rest of Russia, and Belarus, see the introductory Getting There & Away chapter. Tickets to Belarus are sold at the bus station. For Poland, tickets were sold at window 11 in the bus station from 9 to 10 am, 11 am to 1.50 pm and 2.20 to 4.30 pm. Advance tickets only were sold at window 7 in the Aeroflot office from 9 am to 3.30 pm and at the Hotel Kaliningrad. Look for the signs saying 'ВРеспублику Польша' or 'На Польшу'. The company operating the buses to Poland is König Auto (☎ 430 480). Moscow and St Petersburg buses were advertised by the organisation Turism (☎ 446 656, 442 352) of ulitsa Sudostroitelnaya 13.

Train

Kaliningrad's two important stations are the Yuzhny Vokzal (South Station) on ploshchad Kalinina, and the Severny Vokzal (North Station) just off ploshchad Pobedy. All long-

KALININGRAD REGION

distance and some local trains (to nearby towns) use the Yuzhny Vokzal only; other local trains use the Severny Vokzal only; yet other local trains use both stations. The Yuzhny Vokzal is sometimes referred to as the Passazhirsky Vokzal (Passenger-train Station); this distinguishes it from the Severny Vokzal, because the trains that stop at the Severny Vokzal are not classed as 'passenger' trains but as 'suburban' (*prigorodny*) trains.

Train timetables are given in local time (*mestnoe vremya*).

Long-Distance Trains Buy your tickets as far in advance as you can. There's a railway ticket window in the Gostinitsa Kaliningrad lobby which is convenient and not too busy. The Yuzhny Vokzal has an advance-booking hall (*kassy predvaritelnoy prodazhi*) for long-distance tickets bought 24 hours or more before departure, down the steps to the left inside the main entrance. It's open from 8 am to 1 pm and 2 to 8 pm daily, except Sunday when it closes at 6 pm. Tickets to Poland are sold here too – look for signs saying 'В Республику Польша' or 'На Польшу'.

The advance-booking hall also has a chart showing what types of seats are available for which trains on which dates. Trains are listed by their numbers (which are given on time-tables): 'К' means kupeynyy, platskartnyy and obshchiy seats are all available; 'П' means only platskartnyy and obshchiy are available; 'О' means only obshchiy is available; a dash means the train's booked out. Ticket windows for same-day trips are round to the right once you have entered the station – and often have long queues.

Fares from Kaliningrad are low – just US$0.55 to Vilnius and US$0.65 to Rīga in compartment (*kupeynyy*) class, for instance, at the time of writing. Soft class is available on some 'fast' trains to Kaunas, Vilnius, Minsk, Moscow and St Petersburg.

Long-distance trains from Kaliningrad to other places within the Kaliningrad Region and the Baltic states include:

Chernyakhovsk
 90 km, eight to 10 trains daily, terminating at Klaipėda, Rīga, Vilnius, Moscow, St Petersburg, Kharkov or Gomel, 1½ to two hours (also see Local Trains)
Gusev
 115 km, five to seven trains daily, terminating at Vilnius, Moscow, St Petersburg, Kharkov or Gomel, two to 2½ hours (also see Local Trains)
Kaunas
 240 km, five to seven trains daily, terminating at Vilnius, Moscow, St Petersburg, Kharkov or Gomel, 3½ to 4½ hours
Klaipėda
 235 km, one or two trains daily, terminating at Moscow or Klaipėda, 3½ to 4½ hours
Rīga
 370 km, one train nightly, terminating at Rīga, 9½ hours
Šiauliai
 290 km, two trains daily, terminating at Rīga or Moscow, 6½ to 7½ hours
Sovietsk
 140 km, two or three trains daily, terminating at Klaipėda, Rīga or Moscow, 3½ hours (also see Local Trains)
Vilnius
 350 km, six trains daily, terminating at Vilnius, Moscow, St Petersburg or Gomel, 5¼ to 6¼ hours

Services to 'mainland' Russia and other countries including Belarus, Ukraine and Poland are covered in the introductory Getting There & Away chapter.

Local Trains There's a fairly good 'suburban' (prigorodnyy) train service between Kaliningrad and several towns in the Kaliningrad Region including Zelenogradsk, Svetlogorsk, Gvardeysk, Chernyakhovsk, Gusev, Nesterov, Mamonovo, Bagrationovsk, Gurievsk, Polessk, Sovietsk, and Baltiysk (which is a restricted zone – see the Around Kaliningrad section). Gvardeysk, Chernyakhovsk, Gusev, Nesterov and Sovietsk are also served by some long-distance trains.

Most trains to Zelenogradsk and Svetlogorsk – there are a couple of dozen a day to each place – start at the Yuzhny Vokzal but stop at the Severny Vokzal, too; the rest go from the Severny Vokzal only – for more detail see the Svetlogorsk and Zelenogradsk sections. The four daily local trains to Sovietsk all start from the Yuzhny Vokzal: three call at the Severny Vokzal, too, and go via Gurievsk and Polessk, the other goes via Chernyakhovsk and doesn't call at the Severny Vokzal. Trains to all the other places mentioned go from the Yuzhny Vokzal only. There are six daily to Mamonovo and two or three to Bagrationovsk.

You can buy tickets at the station a few minutes before departure. Fares are low – only US$0.15 even as far as Sovietsk.

Taxi
Taxis are worth considering for out-of-town trips. Use the basic city rate of about US$0.10 a km to help you work out a fair price.

Car & Motorbike
The main road entry point into the Kaliningrad Region from Lithuania is at Sovietsk (from Panemunė, Lithuania). The road down the Courland Spit (Kurshskaya kosa) from Klaipėda to Zelenogradsk is an attractive alternative. The crossing between Kybartai (Lithuania) and Nesterov is said to be meant for commercial traffic, though that may not mean private cars cannot use it. One route into the Kaliningrad Region definitely to be avoided is the one from Kudirkos-Naumiestis, north of Kybartai, which leads into a military training zone.

A four-lane highway to the Polish border in the Elblag direction was due to open about the time this book was published, and a second new crossing is reportedly being readied between Goldap (Poland) and Gusev.

Sea
See the introductory Getting There & Away for information on ferry and hydrofoil services between the Kaliningrad Region and Poland, Germany and potentially elsewhere. At the time of writing most of these use the port of Svetly, 25 km west of Kaliningrad city. (Information on buses to Svetly is given in the Bus section.) In Kaliningrad, tickets

for the Alexandr Line service are sold by East West Service (Istvest-Servis) (☎ 468 438) at ulitsa Frunze 6. Tickets for the Baltic Foils service are sold at the port at Svetly 1½ hours before departure; the railway or Aeroflot booking windows in the Gostinitsa Kaliningrad may also sell them.

GETTING AROUND
To/From the Airport
An airport bus runs to/from Kaliningrad bus station two or three times an hour. The first departure from Kaliningrad is at 6 am and the last at 9 pm. The trip takes about 50 minutes. Tickets, sold on the bus, are US$0.15, plus US$0.05 for any baggage you put in the baggage compartment.

City Transport
Public Transport Trams, trolleybuses and buses cover the city pretty thoroughly but they can get crowded. The usual ticket-punching system is used; tickets are sold by some kiosks around town but also by some drivers, who are easier to locate.

Some services stop on the Yuzhny Vokzal forecourt, but the surest place to get transport north from near the Yuzhny Vokzal or the bus station is the Prospekt Kalinina stop at the far north-east corner of ploshchad Kalinina, just north of the corner of prospekt Kalinina itself. Tram Nos 2 and 3 from here go all the way up Leninsky prospekt to ploshchad Pobedy, stopping at the Gostinitsa Kaliningrad on the way. No 3 continues west from ploshchad Pobedy along prospekt Mira to the PKiO Kalinina (Kalinin Park). Trolleybus No 4 from the Prospekt Kalinina stop goes up Leninsky prospekt to the Gostinitsa Kaliningrad, then turns west along ulitsa Teatralnaya and prospekt Mira, also reaching the PKiO Kalinina. Other useful routes include:

Tram No 1
    PKiO Kalinina, prospekt Mira, ploshchad Pobedy, ulitsa Chernyakhovskogo, Proletar-skaya ulitsa

Tram No 4

PKiO Kalinina, prospekt Mira, ploshchad Pobedy, ulitsa Chernyakhovskogo, ploshchad Vasilevskogo, ulitsa 9 Aprelya, ulitsa Frunze

Tram No 5

Sovietsky prospekt, ploshchad Pobedy, ulitsa Chernyakhovskogo, ploshchad Vasilevskogo, ulitsa 9 Aprelya, ulitsa Oktyabrskaya

Tram No 8

ulitsa 9 Aprelya, ploshchad Vasilevskogo, ulitsa A Nevskogo

Tram No 10

Prospekt Kalinina stop, Leninsky prospekt, ulitsa Shevchenko (doesn't stop near Gostinitsa Kaliningrad), ulitsa 9 Aprelya, ploshchad Vasilevskogo, ulitsa Chernyakhovskogo, ulitsa Gorkogo

Trolleybus No 1

ploshchad Kalinina, prospekt Lenina, Gostinitsa Kaliningrad, ulitsa Teatralnaya, prospekt Mira, ulitsa Kosmonavta Leonova, Sovietsky prospekt

Trolleybus Nos 3 and 6

ploshchad Kalinina, prospekt Lenina, Gostinitsa Kaliningrad, ulitsa Teatralnaya, prospekt Mira, PKiO Kalinina (No 3 detours off prospekt Mira up ulitsa Kosmonavta Leonova to the head post office before returning down ulitsa Komsomolskaya)

Taxi Taxis are common and cheap. There's a rank outside the Yuzhny Vokzal. It costs about US$0.20 from either station to the Gostinitsa Kaliningrad.

Other Destinations

The 15,100 sq km of the Kaliningrad Region are mostly low-lying and gently rolling, though the land rises in the south, exceeding 200 metres in the far south-east. There's a lot of farmland, plus about 20% woodland and some marshes. Many of the roads are lined with avenues of trees mostly planted during the German period. There's also some attractive coast, which includes the two seaside resorts of Svetlogorsk and Zelenogradsk, both of them easy day trips from Kaliningrad, and the southern half of the 98-km Courland Spit (Kurshskaya kosa) stretching up the west side of the Courland Lagoon from Zelenogradsk to Klaipėda. (The northern half of the spit is in Lithuania,

where it's called Neringa.) Inland in the Kaliningrad Region are a number of former German towns, all with new Russian names and populations and mostly new Russian buildings. Many of them were fought over at least as fiercely as Kaliningrad itself in 1945. They're mostly of moderate interest to outsiders except to the Germans who used to live there. Here and there stands the occasional decrepit German church or ruined castle as a relic of the past.

The total population of the region, including Kaliningrad city, is about 900,000 civilians plus somewhere between 200,000 and 500,000 military – such has been its strategic importance since WW II. You're unlikely to have problems with officialdom going anywhere in the Kaliningrad Region except the naval port of Baltiysk and perhaps Yantarny, and just possibly the Polish border area until that's opened up to general traffic.

The main road-border point between the Kaliningrad Region and Lithuania is at Sovietsk. The Zelenogradsk-Klaipėda road along the Courland Spit is a scenic alternative. There's also a road border between Nesterov and Kybartai in the east, though that is reportedly meant for commercial traffic. Avoid the road into the Kaliningrad Region from Kudirkos-Naumiestis, north of Kybartai – it leads into a Russian military training zone. A new highway to the Polish border in the Elblag direction was due to open in 1993, and another new crossing is reportedly being prepared between Gusev and Goldap (Poland).

SVETLOGORSK
Светлогорск

Svetlogorsk (former German name: Rauschen) is a pleasantly treed coastal town, 35 km north-west of Kaliningrad city. The beach, backed by high, steep slopes, is narrower than the one at Zelenogradsk, but the town is more interesting to wander round. It began to develop as a resort with the building of the railway from Kaliningrad at the beginning of the 20th century. Svetlogorsk retains quite a lot of the appearance of old Rauschen, with its tree-lined streets and numbers of small, wooden houses, some of them used in the Soviet era for sanatoriums or holiday homes for Soviet workers and officials. The number of visitors has dropped since the collapse of the USSR and Svetlogorsk is now a pleasantly relaxed place.

Orientation

Svetlogorsk is a slightly confusing place owing to its two railway stations – Svetlogorsk I and Svetlogorsk II – between which the track does a 180° loop. The important thing is to know which station you have got off at. Svetlogorsk II on ulitsa Lenina, at the end of its own branch line, is much nearer the beach and the centre of things than Svetlogorsk I. Svetlogorsk I – the first station you reach coming from Kaliningrad – is about 1½ km inland, on the main line from Kaliningrad through to Yantarny and Primorsk. It has a small 'Svetlogorsk I' sign on top of one of the station buildings on the right-hand side of the

tracks if you're coming from the Kaliningrad direction. There's a taxi stand beside Svetlogorsk I.

Information

The post office is on ulitsa Ostrovskogo off ulitsa Oktyabrskaya. There's a telephone and telegraph office nearby on ulitsa Gagarina. Ulitsa Gagarina is also the location of the small *univermag* (department store). There's a small market just off ulitsa Oktyabrskaya opposite the water tower.

Svetlogorsk's telephone code is 2533; numbers have only four digits.

Things to See & Do

A walk along the sandy **beach** itself, particularly westwards from Svetlogorsk, is one of the best things to do. A **chair lift** *(funikuler)* runs down to the beach from the north side of Svetlogorsk II station (a ride costs about US$0.01).

Ulitsa Lenina on the south side of

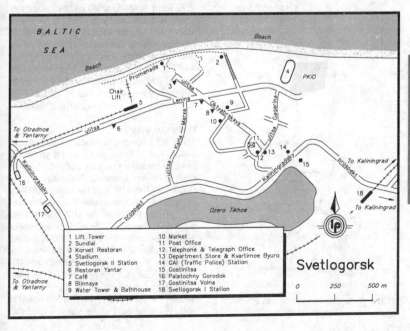

1 Lift Tower	10 Market
2 Sundial	11 Post Office
3 Korvet Restoran	12 Telephone & Telegraph Office
4 Stadium	13 Department Store & Kvartirnoe Byuro
5 Svetlogorsk II Station	14 GAI (Traffic Police) Station
6 Restoran Yantar	15 Gostinitsa
7 Café	16 Palatochny Gorodok
8 Blinnaya	17 Gostinitsa Volna
9 Water Tower & Bathhouse	18 Svetlogorsk I Station

Svetlogorsk

0   250   500 m

Svetlogorsk II station runs roughly parallel to the coast. If you follow it eastwards for 450 metres you reach its corner with ulitsa Oktyabrskaya, the main boulevard of the resort. About 150 metres inland from this corner along ulitsa Oktyabrskaya are the 25-metre **water tower** and the curious red-tile-domed *Jugendstil* (Art Nouveau) **bathhouse** which adjoins it. Both structures are symbols of the town and even appeared on a Soviet postage stamp in the 1960s. In a wooded park near here (though I didn't manage to track them down) are four **sculptures** by the renowned German Hermann Brachert (1890-1972) including the well known *Water Carrier* (Wasserträgerin), a marble figure of a bare-breasted woman carrying a pitcher of water on her head. Brachert

The *Water Carrier* by Hermann Brachert (Svetlogorsk)

had a house at Otradnoe (former German name: Georgenswalde), a couple of km west along the coast from Svetlogorsk, to which he retreated when the Nazis came to power. When the Germans fled East Prussia in face of the oncoming Red Army, Brachert had to leave a lot of his work behind. There are plans to turn his former home into a museum.

Two hundred metres north from the ulitsa Lenina corner, ulitsa Oktyabrskaya reaches the top of a zig-zag path down to the beach. Not far from the foot of this path is an ugly beach landmark: the tower of the lift that carries people up and down from Svetlogorsk's military sanatorium.

About 200 metres east along ulitsa Lenina from the ulitsa Oktyabrskaya corner, is another small crossroads where a left (north) turn takes you to the main steps down to the beach. On the beach promenade near the bottom of these steps is a very large and colourful **sundial**. Still further along ulitsa Lenina is a sports stadium and a **park** of culture & rest (PKiO), with a small funfair.

A long **lake**, Ozero Tikhoe, stretches beside Kaliningradsky prospekt in the lower part of the town between the two stations. In summer you can hire rowing boats at its west end. One of Svetlogorsk's most striking pre-war houses – a turreted, blue-and-white painted edifice on Kaliningradsky prospekt shortly beyond the east end of the lake – is now occupied by the GAI traffic police.

Places to Stay

There are a few possibilities. Some German groups stay at Svetlogorsk, and if you book through Intourist you may get put here if it can't give you a room in Kaliningrad. The *Gostinitsa Volna* (☎ 3005) at Kaliningradsky prospekt 68A has reasonable double rooms with private bathroom for US$5.50. It's set back from the west side of the road, about 300 metres south of the ulitsa Lenina corner. There's also a small, very basic-looking *Gostinitsa* at the other end of Kaliningradsky prospekt, just past the east end of the lake. One place Intourist uses is the *Pansionat Stroitel* (☎ 2533-3381) a faded Soviet-style holiday home on Frunze ulitsa, Otradnoe, three km west of central Svetlogorsk. It's one to be avoided if you can, with peeling wallpaper, flaking paint and years of stains on the carpets. A taxi from Svetlogorsk is about US$0.20. A minor saving grace is that it has a restaurant of sorts and a tiny café-bar. Otradnoe railway station is beside the Stroitel. Other holiday homes and sanatoriums are likely to open their doors to tourists but maybe initially only to groups. The *Pansionat Yantarny* is used for accommodation by one German tour company, as is another hotel, the *Gostinitsa Baltika*, said to be not far from the beach, which has rooms with private shower and toilet.

There's a campsite, the *Palatochny Gorodok*, at Kaliningradsky prospekt 72, reached by a track leading off the road beside the railway crossing on the corner of ulitsa Lenina. There are a few cabins, room for tents, and some grotty toilets and washrooms. There's a *Kvartirnoe Byuro*, for rooms in private homes, beside the univermag on ulitsa Gagarina.

Places to Eat

The story is not inspiring. One of the more reliable places is *Blinnaya* on ulitsa Oktyabrskaya, just north and across the road from the water tower. It serves pancakes, rice pudding, fried chicken and small tomato salads – open from 8 am to 4 pm and 5 to 8 pm. The *Korvet Restoran* at the coast end of ulitsa Oktyabrskaya can do a tolerable meal; in the evening there's loud dance music. The same goes for the *Restoran Yantar* on ulitsa Lenina, just west of Svetlogorsk II station, which is about the liveliest place in town. The *Gostinitsa Volna* has a restaurant, also with a live band, but in the food line it can't manage much more than a couple of small salads and a piece of thin chicken and potatoes. The large, modern *Restaurant Exim* at Otradnoe doesn't seem to open till 10 pm. You may be able to talk your way into just eating without paying for the variety show, which starts at 11 pm.

There's a café that stays open late on the corner of ulitsa Lenina and ulitsa Oktyabr-

skaya, and a couple of snack and drink bars on the beach.

Getting There & Away

There are around 20 to 25 trains a day from Kaliningrad to Svetlogorsk. Direct trains (via Pereslavskoe) take about one hour; those going via Zelenogradsk take about 1½ hours. The fare is about US$0.05. About one-third of the trains start from the Severny Vokzal in Kaliningrad and don't go through the Yuzhny Vokzal; the others start from the Yuzhny Vokzal but also stop at the Severny Vokzal. All go to Svetlogorsk I station and most – but not the last couple of trains at night – go on to Svetlogorsk II, which is more convenient for most things. Timetables indicate which stations trains start and terminate at, but if you can't work them out it's easy enough to find someone who'll help you. From the end of May to mid-September there are extra trains on Saturdays and Sundays, and timetables have a separate section for those days.

Around 10 trains a day go from Svetlogorsk to Zelenogradsk. Most start at Svetlogorsk II and also stop at Svetlogorsk I, but a few run only from Svetlogorsk I. Most are going on to Kaliningrad but a couple terminate at Zelenogradsk.

Getting Around

The town is small enough to walk around, especially if you arrive at Svetlogorsk II station. There are buses but their routes and schedules are well nigh incomprehensible. Taxis are cheap and fairly easy to find, although only a few are allowed into the central part of the resort area. One taxi stand is by Svetlogorsk I station. Taxis – or private cars willing to act as taxis – also wait by the bus stop on the corner of ulitsa Lenina and Kaliningradsky prospekt.

Only residents are allowed to drive private cars into the resort area. There are car parks (*avtostoyanky*) by the Palatochny Gorodok campsite and the Kaliningradsky prospekt railway crossing near Svetlogorsk I station.

ZELENOGRADSK
Зеленоградск

Thirty km north of Kaliningrad, Zeleno-gradsk (former German name: Cranz) is the most popular beach spot of the Kaliningrad Region and has been since the mid-19th century. On sunny summer weekends thousands of people disgorge from Kaliningrad trains at Zelenogradsk station to enjoy a day on the long, wide, sandy beach. Though there are still a number of old houses in Zelenogradsk, it has lost most of the charm it apparently had in the German era. The seafront promenade (naberezhnaya) is dotted with semi-derelict buildings which contrast strangely with the jovial mood of its weekend visitors.

Orientation & Information

The rail and bus stations are side by side on the south side of ulitsa Lenina, the main east-west street running through the town. To reach the beach, cross ulitsa Lenina and take any street heading north. The beach is about 200 metres ahead.

There's a busy little market immediately east of the railway station. The post office faces the market on the street at its far end. The telephone and telegraph office is on the corner of ulitsa Lenina 80 metres north of the post office – alternatively you can reach it by walking 200 metres east along ulitsa Lenina from the stations. A further 400 metres east along ulitsa Lenina is Blick, by far the best handicrafts shop I found in the Kaliningrad Region, with some quality Russian wares – matryoshka nesting dolls, blue-and-white Gzhel pottery, enamelled wooden Palekh boxes painted with intricate scenes, and gold, red and black painted wooden spoons, mugs etc from Khokhloma. You can change money at Blick and at the Kafe Vstrecha, 200 metres west of Blick along ulitsa Lenina.

Things to See & Do

If you walk east along ulitsa Lenina from the

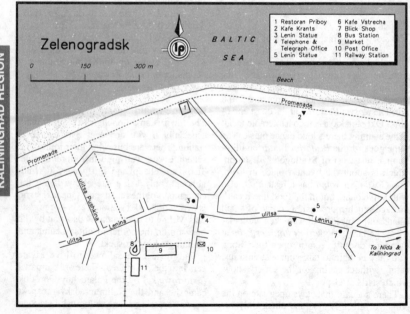

1 Restoran Priboy	6 Kafe Vstrecha
2 Kafe Krants	7 Blick Shop
3 Lenin Statue	8 Bus Station
4 Telephone &	9 Market
Telegraph Office	10 Post Office
5 Lenin Statue	11 Railway Station

Zelenogradsk

BALTIC

SEA

Beach

Promenade

Promenade

ulitsa Pushkina

Lenina

ulitsa

ulitsa   Lenina

To Nida & Kaliningrad

Left: House of Soviets, Kaliningrad (JN)
Right: Kaliningrad Cathedral ruins (JN)
Bottom: Street market, Kaliningrad (JN)

Top: A hot Sunday at Zelenogradsk beach, Kaliningrad Region (JN)
Left: Water tower & bathhouse, Svetlogorsk, Kaliningrad Region (JN)
Right: Silver-painted Lenin, Zelenogradsk Sanatorium, Kaliningrad Region (JN)

stations, after 200 metres you reach a small square with a Lenin statue (the telephone and telegraph office is on the south side of this square). Further along ulitsa Lenina there's another, silver-painted, Lenin in the grounds of the Zelenogradsk Sanatorium, which occupy much of the area between here and the seafront promenade.

The beach stretches a long, long way, particularly to the east, and you can have a good stretch of the legs and lungs along here.

Places to Stay & Eat
The German travel firms Schnieder Reisen and Ost-Reise Service lodge some groups in the *Sanatory Chayka* (Chayka Sanatorium) which has rooms with private shower and toilet.

The large concrete *Restoran Priboy* on the beach has both a restaurant section, open from noon to 11 pm, and a downstairs canteen *(stolovaya)* where you can feed quickly. About 350 metres further east along the promenade is the *Kafe Krants*, another stolovaya. There's also the *Kafe Vstrecha* on ulitsa Lenina about 550 metres west of the stations.

Getting There & Away
About 20 trains a day, plus a few extra on summer Saturdays and Sundays, run from Kaliningrad to Zelenogradsk, a trip of 30 to 40 minutes for a fare of US$0.05. Slightly more than half of them start from Kaliningrad's Yuzhny Vokzal and also call at the Severny Vokzal on the way out of the city; the others run only from the Severny Vokzal. About 10 trains a day run from Zelenogradsk to Svetlogorsk I, most continuing on to Svetlogorsk II.

There are also about 12 buses a day to/from Kaliningrad, plus six daily each way to/from the Lithuanian town of Smiltynė at the northern tip of the Courland Spit, opposite Klaipėda. The Smiltynė buses stop at places along the Courland Spit such as Lesnoy, Rybachy, Morskoe and, over the Lithuanian border, Nida and Juodkrantė.

SOVIETSK
Советск
Sovietsk (former German name: Tilsit) on the Neman River (Lithuanian: Nemunas) is the busiest road crossing point between the Kaliningrad Region and Lithuania, lying on the main Kaliningrad-Rīga road and connected by good roads to Kaunas, Vilnius and Klaipėda. With about 50,000 people, it's the second-biggest town in the Kaliningrad Region. It's famous as the scene of the 1807 Treaty of Tilsit during the Napoleonic Wars, when Napoleon, having defeated Prussia at the battles of Jena and Auerstädt, dictated severe peace terms to the Prussian king, Friedrich Wilhelm III, on a barge anchored in the Neman. Prussia had to pay large sums to France, cede half of its territory and accept an occupation of much of what was left. The tables were fully turned eight years later when Prussian forces took part in Napoleon's final defeat at Waterloo.

Things to See
The symbolic landmark of the town today is the **Queen Luise Bridge** over the Neman, with its stone portal which survived WW II. (The bridge itself was rebuilt in 1948 after being blown up by the retreating Germans in 1944). The bridge is named after the wife of Friedrich Wilhelm III, who made an unsuccessful appeal to Napoleon for clemency to Prussia at Tilsit in 1807.

The town centre is a mixture of old German buildings, including some in *Jugendstil* (Art Nouveau), and newer Soviet ones. The main street, ulitsa Pobedy, runs from the bridge to the town's biggest square. Off the square is a lake which used to be the mill pond of Tilsit Castle, burnt down in 1876, some remains of which are still in place by the lake. A Soviet tank monument has replaced a well-known statue of an elk which, before WW II, stood opposite the Sovietsk Drama Theatre, built in the 1890s.

Places to Stay & Eat
There's a hotel, the *Gostinitsa Rossia* (☎ 261-75 372), on ploshchad Lenina, behind the Lenin monument. Some rooms at

Queen Luise Bridge, Sovietsk

least have private shower and toilet. The *Restoran Rossia* is nearby in a former German bank building at ulitsa Lunacharskogo 2.

Getting There & Away

Sovietsk's train and bus stations are on ulitsa Gorkogo, where a big Russian military barracks also stands. Eight or more buses run daily between Kaliningrad and Sovietsk, many of them on their way to/from places across the border including Šiauliai, Klaipėda, Kaunas, Vilnius, Liepāja, Rīga and Tallinn. Kaliningrad-Sovietsk is a three to 3½-hour trip costing US$0.40. Two or three long-distance trains daily, en route between Kaliningrad Yuzhny Vokzal and Rīga, Moscow or Klaipėda, stop at Sovietsk. There are also four daily local trains to/from Kaliningrad Yuzhny Vokzal – three via Kaliningrad Severny Vokzal and Polessk; one via Chernyakhovsk. The trip is about 3½ hours. Fare in general seating is US$0.15, in kupeynyy US$0.30.

BALTIYSK
Балтийск

The naval port of Baltiysk (former German name: Pillau), on the north side of the

Kaliningrad Lagoon's narrow opening to the sea, is a restricted area. Intourist in Kaliningrad says the military-connected organisation Baltgarant (☎ 22-219 717) can arrange visits. There are nine trains daily from Kaliningrad's Yuzhny Vokzal to Baltiysk.

YANTARNY
Янтарный

About 25 km north of Baltiysk and 10 km south-west of Svetlogorsk, Yantarny (former German name: Palmnicken) is the source of most of the world's amber *(yantar)*. Over 90% of world production is mined from deposits on the coast here. There's no public access to the workings, or the beach to their south, but there's a point north of the town centre on Yantarny's main street, Sovietskaya ulitsa, where you can get a view over them. The amber-bearing earth is pumped through pipelines to be cleaned in another part of the town. A number of old buildings remain in the town, which has been mining the amber since the 19th century, including an 1892 neo-Gothic church.

Trains to Pokrovskoe, Primorsk and Baltiysk from Svetlogorsk I station stop at Yantarny – there are six a day – but ticket clerks aren't supposed to sell tickets to Yantarny to people without special documents. It may be possible to tag along with a tour group that's going there from one of the Kaliningrad hotels.

KURSHSKAYA KOSA
Куршская коса
The Kurshskaya kosa is the Russian half of the 98-km long, two to four-km wide Courland Spit, which divides the Courland Lagoon (Kurshsky zaliv) from the Baltic. The Kurshskaya kosa shares the same dramatic landscape as the northern, Lithuanian half – high sand dunes, pine forests, an exposed western coast and a calmer lagoon coast.

A few fishing-cum-holiday villages, contrasting in their untidy Russian state with those on the Lithuanian part of the peninsula, dot the eastern coast. The main ones, from south to north, are Lesnoy (former German name: Sarkau), Rybachy (former German name: Rossitten) and Morskoe (former German name: Pillkoppen) which is just six km short of the Lithuanian border.

Six buses a day from Kaliningrad via Zelenogradsk take the road up the peninsula to Smiltynė at its northern tip, opposite Klaipėda. It's about 1¾ hours from Kaliningrad to Rybachy, the biggest settlement in the Russian half.

GURIEVSK, MORDOVSKOE & POLESSK
Гурьевск, Мордовское и Полесск
The towns of Gurievsk and Polessk and the village of Mordovskoe are north-east of Kaliningrad on the A190 road, a possible route to Sovietsk.

The main point of interest in Gurievsk (former German name: Neuhausen), 10 km from central Kaliningrad, is its 14th century church. Though wrecked inside since WW II and plundered for its roof tiles and some of its bricks, this is still an imposing example of Teutonic Order architecture, with its tall brick Gothic tower, stone lower walls and wide, spreading roof. The road to the church

leads to the right (east) from behind the main monument in the town. Not far from the church are the ruins of the 13th century Neuhausen Castle, once a summer residence and hunting lodge for the dukes of Prussia. The offices of a collective farm now stand on the site.

Thirty km further along the A190, there's another old church at Mordovskoe (former German name: Gross Legitten), which is also called Turgenevo on some maps. This church was built around 1400 but again has fallen – or been pushed – into disrepair in recent decades. At Polessk (former German name: Labiau), 10 km beyond Mordovskoe, are scanty remains of a 13th century Teutonic Order castle by the Deyma River – damaged by a fire in the 1960s and since plundered for building materials. A road runs five km north from Polessk to the shore of the Courland Lagoon at Zalivino (former German name: Rinderort).

Getting There & Away
Bus No 103 from Kaliningrad goes to Gurievsk. Three daily local trains from both Kaliningrad stations stop at Gurievsk and Polessk, but not Mordovskoe, on their way to Sovietsk. The first two leave around 7.15 and 9.20 am.

There should also be buses to Polessk, which would stop at Mordovskoe. You could even consider taking a taxi out to these places from Kaliningrad – the usual fare in the city is about US$0.10 a km.

GVARDEYSK, CHERNYAKHOVSK & GUSEV
Гвардейск, Черняховск и Гусев
These are the main towns along the road and railway that lead from Kaliningrad to the Lithuanian border between Nesterov and Kybartai. All three have been almost completely rebuilt since WW II. Formerly Gvardeysk was called Tapiau, Chernyakhovsk was Insterburg, and Gusev was Gumbinnen.

There are basic hotels in Chernyakhovsk

KALININGRAD REGION

and Gusev, with rooms around US$1.50 a person. The one in Gusev is called the *Gostinitsa Rossia*.

All three towns are served by buses and trains from Kaliningrad. Most trains and some buses between Vilnius, Kaunas and Kaliningrad also come through. See Kaliningrad Getting There & Away for details.

BALGA
Балга

The 14th century Teutonic Order fort of Balga stands on the coast of the Mys Severny (North Cape) on the east side of the Kaliningrad Lagoon, about 40 km south-west of Kaliningrad. It's in an isolated spot and you'd need to have your own vehicle, or be in a tour group, to reach it.

Language Guide

Knowing a few words and phrases in the local languages will help you find your way around and will also help you break the ice with the local people. This guide introduces you to the alphabet and pronunciation of each of the Baltic languages and Russian and includes some words and phrases you will find useful on your travels.

ESTONIAN

Like Finnish, Estonian is a Finno-Ugric language, which sets it apart from Latvian, Lithuanian and Russian, which are all in the Indo-European language family. It's a very Nordic-sounding language with lots of deep 'oo's and 'uu's. The south, particularly the south-east, of the country has some dialect differences from the north. You're unlikely to get far with learning Estonian in a short visit – its nouns decline through no less than 14 cases – but the odd word goes down well.

Alphabet & Pronunciation
Estonian lacks a few letters of the English alphabet but has some extra ones of its own. Its alphabet is as follows:

a b d e f g h i j k l m n o p r s š z ž t u v õ ä ö ü

Note that **š** is counted as a separate letter from **s**, **ž** from **z**, **õ** and **ö** from **o**, **ä** from **a**, and **ü** from **u**. The alphabetical order becomes important if you're using a dictionary or any other alphabetical list: for instance words beginning **ä** are listed near the end, not after **a**. The letters are generally pronounced as in English except:

a	is pronounced like the 'u' in 'cut'
b	like 'p'
g	like 'k'

j	like the 'y' in 'yes'
š	is pronounced 'sh'
ž	as the 's' in 'pleasure'
õ	somewhere between the 'e' in 'bed' and the 'u' in 'fur'
ä	as the 'a' in 'cat'
ö	like the 'u' in 'fur' but with rounded lips
ü	like a short 'yoo'
ai	like the 'i' in 'bite'
ei	like the 'ay' in 'day'
oo	like the 'a' in 'water'
uu	like the 'oo' in 'boot'
öö	like the 'u' in 'fur'

LATVIAN

Latvian is one of only two surviving languages of the Baltic branch of the Indo-European language family (the other is Lithuanian). Even more than Estonians, the speakers of Latvian regard their language as an endangered species: only just over half the people in the country, and just over a third of the inhabitants of the capital, Rīga, speak it as their first language. The east and west of the country have some dialect differences from standard central Latvian.

Latvian and Lithuanian share quite a lot of words but are not quite close enough to each other to be mutually intelligible. They separated from each other about the 7th century AD.

Alphabet & Pronunciation
The Latvian alphabet is as follows:

a b c č d e f g ģ (Ģ) h i j k ķ l ļ m n ņ o p r s š t u v z

Note that **č**, **ģ**, **ķ**, **ļ**, **ņ**, **š** and **ž** are counted as separate letters from **c**, **g**, **k**, **l**, **n**, **s** and **z**. The letters are generally pronounced as in English except:

c	is pronounced 'ts'
č	as 'ch'
ǵ	as the 'j' in 'jet'
j	as the 'y' in 'yes'
ķ	as 'ch'
ļ	as the 'lli' in 'billiards'
ŋ	as the 'ni' in 'onion'
o	as the 'a' in 'water'
š	as 'sh'
ž	as the 's' in 'pleasure'
ai	as the the 'i' in 'pine'
ei	as the 'ai' in 'pain'
ie	as the 'ea' in 'ear'

The sign ‾ has the effect of lengthening the vowel it is placed over:

ā	is pronounced like the 'a' in 'barn'
ē	like the 'a' in 'bare'
ī	like the 'e' in 'he'
ū	like the 'oo' in 'boot'

LITHUANIAN

Lithuanian is one of only two surviving languages of the Baltic branch of the Indo-European language family (the other is Latvian). Because many of its forms have remained unchanged longer than those of other Indo-European languages (which cover most of Europe and a fair bit of Asia) Lithuanian is very important to linguistic scholars. It's certainly a subtle and refined language, as a look through a Lithuanian dictionary will show.

Nor is it averse to hurried borrowings from other tongues where necessary, as Lithuanian phrases like *ping pong klubas* and *marketingo departamento direktorius* demonstrate. Žemaičiai or Low Lithuanian, spoken in the west, is a separate dialect from Aukštaičiai or High Lithuanian, spoken in the rest of the country.

Alphabet & Pronunciation
The Lithuanian alphabet is as follows:

a b c č d e f g h i/y j k l m n o p r s š t u v z ž

The i and y are partly interchangeable and y comes straight after i in alphabetical lists. Note that č, š and ž are separate letters from c, s and z. The letters are generally pronounced as in English except:

c	is pronounced as 'ts'
č	as 'ch'
y	between the 'i' in 'tin' and the 'ee' in 'feet'
j	as the 'y' in 'yes'
o	like the 'oa' in 'boat'
š	as 'sh'
ž	as the 's' in 'pleasure'
ei	like the 'a' in 'hay'
ie	like the 'ye' in 'yet'
ui	like the 'wi' in 'win'

The signs ‾, ˙, and ˛ all have the general effect of lengthening the vowel they go with:

ą	is pronounced like the 'a' in 'father'
ę	like the 'ai' in 'air'
į	like the 'ee' in 'feet'
ų	like the 'oo' in 'boot'
ū	like the 'oo' in 'boot'
ė	like the 'a' in 'late'

RUSSIAN

Russian belongs to the Slavic branch of the Indo-European language family. The Slavic languages are the closest relatives to the Baltic languages: Lithuanian and Latvian. Russian uses the Cyrillic alphabet (see chart opposite).

Lonely Planet's *Russian Phrasebook* by James Jenkin is a good introduction to the Russian language, detailing many useful words and phrases.

Cyrillic Alphabet

Letter	Transliteration	Pronunciation
А, а	A, a	if stressed, like the 'a' in 'father' if unstressed, like the 'a' in 'about'
Б, б	B, b	like the 'b' in 'but'
В, в	V, v	like the 'v' in 'van'
Г, г	G, g	like the 'g' in 'god'
Д, д	D, d	like the 'd' in 'dog'
Е, е	Ye, e	if stressed, like the 'ye' in 'yet' if unstressed, like the 'ye' in 'yeast'
Ё, ё	Yo, yo	like the 'yo' in 'yore'
Ж, ж	Zh, zh	like the 's' in 'measure'
З, з	Z, z	like the 'z' in 'zoo'
И, и	I, i	like the 'ee' in 'meet'
Й, й	Y, y	like the 'y' in 'boy'
К, к	K, k	like the 'k' in 'kind'
Л, л	L, l	like the 'l' in 'lamp'
М, м	M, m	like the 'm' in 'mad'
Н, н	N, n	like the 'n' in 'not'
О, о	O, o	if stressed, like the 'o' in 'more' if unstressed, between the 'a' in hang and the 'u' in hung
П, п	P, p	like the 'p' in 'pig'
Р, р	R, r	like the 'r' in 'rub' (but rolled)
С, с	S, s	like the 's' in 'sing'
Т, т	T, t	like the 't' in 'ten'
У, у	U, u	like the 'oo' in 'fool'
Ф, ф	F, f	like the 'f' in 'fan'
Х, х	Kh, kh	like the 'ch' in 'Bach'
Ц, ц	Ts, ts	like the 'ts' in 'bits'
Ч, ч	Ch, ch	like the 'ch' in 'chin'
Ш, ш	Sh, sh	like the 'sh' in 'shop'
Щ, щ	Shch, shch	like the 'shch' in 'fresh chips'
ъ		('hard sign')
Ы, ы	Y, y	like the 'i' in 'ill'
ь		('soft sign')
Э, э	E, e	like the 'e' in 'end'
Ю, ю	Yu, yu	like the 'u' in 'use'
Я, я	Ya, ya	if stressed, like the 'ya' in 'yard' if unstressed, like the 'ye' in 'yearn'

ENGLISH	ESTONIAN	LATVIAN
Greetings & Civilities		
Hello.	Tere.	Labdien *or* Sveiki.
Good morning.	Tere hommikust.	Labrīt.
Good day/Good afternoon.	Tere päevast.	Labdien.
Good evening.	Tere õhtust.	Labvakar.
Good night.	Head ööd.	Ar labu nakti.
Goodbye.	Head aega (HEY-ahd EI-gah) *or* Nägemiseni.	Uz redzēšanos *or* Labi atā.
Excuse me.	Vabandage.	Atvainojiet.
Useful Words & Phrases		
Yes.	Jah.	Jā.
No.	Ei.	Nē.
Please.	Palun.	Lūdzu.
Thank you.	Tänan *or* Aitäh ('thanks').	Paldies.
There is/are...	Ole...	Ir...
There isn't/aren't...	Ei Ole...	Nav...
Where?	Kus?	Kur?
Do you speak English?	Kas teie räägite Inglise keelt?	Vai jūs runājat Angliski?
I don't speak Estonian/Latvian/ Lithuanian/Russian.	Mina ei räägi Eesti keelt.	Es Nerunāju Latviski.
I don't understand.	Ma ei saa aru.	Es nesaprotu.
Do you speak Russian?	—	—
How much?	Kui palju?	Cik?
cheap	odav	lēts
expensive	kallis	dārgs
Getting Around		
airport	lennujaam	lidosta
railway station	raudteejaam	dzelzceļa stacija
train	rong	vilciens
bus station	bussijaam	autoosta
bus	buss	autobuss
port	sadam	osta
taxi	takso	taksometrs
tram	tramm	tramvajs
trolleybus	trollibuss	trolejbuss
stop (eg bus stop)	peatus	pietura
petrol	bensiin	benzīns *or* degviela

LITHUANIAN	RUSSIAN	RUSSIAN PRONUNCIATION
Labas or Sveikas.	Здравствуйте.	ZDRAST-vooy-tye
Labas rytas.	Доброе утро.	DOH-bra-yuh OO-tra
Laba diena.	Добрый день.	DOH-bry dyehn
Labas vakaras.	Добрый вечер.	DOH-bry VYECH-er
Labanakt.	Спокойной ночи.	spa-KOY-nay NOCH-i
Sudie or Viso gero.	До свидания.	das-fi-DA-nya
Atsiprašau.	Извините.	iz-vi-NEE-ti-yeh
Taip.	Да.	da
Ne.	Нет.	nyet
Prašau.	Пожалуйста.	a-ZHAHL-stuh
Ačiū.	Спасибо.	spuh-SEE-ba
Yra...	Есть...	yist
Nėra...	Нет...	nyet
Kur?	Где?	gdyeh?
Ar kalbate Angliškai?	Вы говорите по-анг лийски?	vih ga-var-EE-tye pa-an-GLEE-ski?
Aš nekalbu Lietuviškai.	Я не говорю по-русски.	ya nye ga-var-YOO pa-ROOSS-ki
Aš nesuprantu.	Я не понимаю.	ya nye pa-ni-MA-yu
—	Вы говорите по-русски?	vih ga-var-EE-tye pa-ROOSS-ki?
Kiek?	Сколько?	SKOL-kah?
pigus	дешёвый	desh-YOV-y
brangus	дорогой	da-ra-GOY
aerouostas	аэропорт	ah-EH-ra-port
geležinkelio stotis	вокзал	vahk-ZAHL
traukinys	поезд	PO-yezd
autobusų stotis	автовокзал	af-tah-vahk-ZAHL
autobusas	автобус	uf-TOH-boos
uostas	порт	port
taksi	такси	tak-SI
tramvajus	трамвай	tram-VAY
troleibusas	троллейбус	trahl-YEY-buss
stotelė	остановка	asta-NOHV-kuh
benzinas	бензин	ben-ZIN

ENGLISH	ESTONIAN	LATVIAN
Where & When?		
departure/departure time	väljub *or* väljumine	atiet *or* atiešanas laiks
arrival/arrival time	saabub *or* saabumine	pienāk *or* pienākšanas laiks
every day	iga päev	katru dienu
even dates	—	pārdatums
odd dates	—	nepārdatums
except	välja arvatud	izņemot
not running/cancelled	ei sõida	nekursē *or* atcelts
through/via	läbi *or* kaudu	caur
Train & Bus Types		
express	ekspress	ekspresis
fast	kiir	ātrs
fast train	kiirrong	ātrvilciens
passenger train	reisirong	pasažieru vilciens
diesel train	diiselrong	dīzeļvilciens
suburban or local (train or bus)	linnalähedane	piepilsētu
electric train	elektrirong	elektrovilciens
transit (bus)	transiit	tranzīts
Tickets		
ticket	pilet	biļete
ticket office	piletikassa *or* kassa	kase
advance-booking office	eelmüügikassa	iepriekšpārdošanas kases
Train Classes		
soft class/deluxe	luksus	mīksts *or* grezns *or* luksus
sleeping carriage (soft class)	magamisvagun	guļamvagons
compartment (class)	kupee	kupeja
Signs		
open	avatud *or* lahti	atvērts
closed	suletud *or* kinni	slēgts
break (eg for lunch)	vaheaeg	pārtraukums
street	tänav	iela
square	väljak or plats	laukums
avenue or boulevard	puiestee	prospekts *or* bulvāris
road	tee	ceļš
highway	maantee	lielceļš

LITHUANIAN	RUSSIAN	RUSSIAN PRONUNCIATION
išvyksta or išvykimo laikas	отправление	at-prav-LIN-ia
atvyksta or atvykimo laikas	прибытие	pri-BEET-i-ye
kasdien	ежедневно	yezh-ed-NYEV-nay
porinėm	чётным	CHOT-nim
neporinėm	нечётным	nye-CHOT-nim
išskyrus	кроме	KRO-my
nekursuoja	отменён	at-min-YON
per	через	CHYER-ez
ekspresas	экспресс	ex-PRYESS
greitas	скорый	SKOH-ri
greitasis traukinys	скорый поезд	SKOH-ri PO-yezd
keleivinis traukinys	пассажирский поезд	passa-ZHIR-ski PO-yezd
dizelinis traukinys	дизельный поезд	DEEZ-el-ny PO-yezd
priemiestinis or vietinis	местный or	MYEST-ny or
	пригородный	PREE gor-ad-ny
elektrinis traukinys	электричка	el-ek-TREECH-ka
pravažiuojantis	транзитный	tran-ZEET-ny
bilietas	билет	bil-YET
kasa	касса	KASS-ah
išankstinio bilietų pardavimo kasa	кассы предварителбной продажи билетов	KASS-y prid-vah-REET-il-noy pra-DAZH-y bil-YET-ahv
minkštas or liuksusas	мягкий or люкс	MYAG-ky or li-OOKS
miegamasis	спальный вагон	SPAHL-ny va-GOHN
kupė	купейный	kup-EY-ny
atidarytas	открыт	aht-KRIT
uždarytas	закрыт	zuh-KRIT
pertrauka	перерыв	pi-ri-REEV
gatvė	улица	OOL-it-suh
aikštė	площадь	PLOSH-id
prospektas or bulvaras	проспект or бульвар	prahs-PYEKT or BOOL-vahr
kelias	дорога	da-ROHG-ah
plentas	шоссе	sha-SEH

ENGLISH	ESTONIAN	LATVIAN
Around Town		
city centre	kesklinn	centrs
hotel	hotell	viesnīca
room	tuba	istaba
currency exchange	valuutavahetus	valūtas apmaiņa
bank	pank	banka
post office	postkontor	pasts
stamp	mark	pastmarka
telephone	telefon	telefons
shop	kauplus *or* pood	veikals
market	turg	tirgus
department store	kaubamaja	universālveikals
castle	loss	pils
church	kirik	baznīca
Food		
restaurant	restoran	restorāns
café	kohvik	kafejnīca
canteen/cafeteria	söökla	ēdnīca
snack bar	einelaud	bufete
bread	leib	maize
butter	või	sviests
starters	eelroad	uzkoda
caviar	kalamari	kaviārs *or* ikri
salad	salat	salāti
sausage	vorst	desa
cheese	juust	siers
soup	supp	zupa
pancake	pannkook	pankūka
fish	kala	zivs
meat (red)	liha	mēsa
meat or main dishes	liharoad	gaļas ēdieni *or* otrie ēdieni
national dishes	rahvusroad	nacionālie ēdieni
kebab	šašlõkk	šašlīks
grilled 'chop'	karbonaad	karbonāde
'beefsteak'	biifsteek	bifšteks
beef stroganoff	biifstrogonoff *or* böfstrooganov	bifštroganovs

LITHUANIAN	RUSSIAN	RUSSIAN PRONUNCIATION
centras	центр города	tsyentr ga-ROHD-uh
viešbutis	гостиница	guh-STEE-nit-suh
kambarys	комната	KOHM-na-tuh
valiutos keitimas	обмен валюты	ab-MYEN val-YOOT-uh
bankas	банк	bank
paštas	почта	POCH-ta
pašto ženklas	почтовая марка	pach-TOHV-aya MARK-a
telefonas	телефон	ti-li-FON
parduotuvė	магазин	ma-ga-ZIN
turgus	рынок	REE-nak
universalinė parduotuvė	универсальный	u-ni-vyer-SAL-ny
	магазин	ma-ga-ZIN
pilis	замок	ZAHM-ak
bažnyčia	церков	TSYER-kav
restoranas	ресторан	ryest-ah-RAHN
kavinė	кафе	ka-FEH
valgykla	столовая	sta-LOH-vuh-yuh
bufetas	буфет	bu-FYET
duona	хлеб	khlyep
sviestas	масло	MAHS-luh
užkandis	закуски	za-KOOSS-ki
ikrai	икра	i-KRA
salotos *or* mišrainė	салат	suh-LAHT
dešra	колбаса	kal-bass-AH
sūris	сыр	seer
sriuba	суп	soop
blynas	блин	blin
žuvis	рыба	RIH-buh
gaļa	мясо	MYASS-uh
mėsos patiekalai	горячие	gah-ri-ACH-i-yeh
	блюда	BLYOOD-ah
nacionaliniai patiekalai	национальные	nahts-ya-NAHL-ni-yeh
	блюда	BLYOOD-ah
šašlykas	шашлык	shash-LUYK
karbonadas	—	—
bifštekas	бифштекс	bif-SHTEKS
befstrogenas	бефстроганов	byef-STROH-guh-nof

ENGLISH	ESTONIAN	LATVIAN
chicken	kana	vista
vegetables	köögivili	saknes *or* dārzeņi
potato	kartul	kartupelis
mushroom	seen	sēne *or* šampinjons
desserts	magusroad	saldie ēdieni
ice cream	jäätis	saldējums
fruit	puuvili	augļi
bill	arve	rēķins

Drinks

bar	baar	bārs
water	vesi	ūdens
mineral water	mineralveesi	minerāl ūdens
juice	mahl	sula
tea	tee	tēja
coffee	kohv	kafija
milk	piim	piens
sugar	suhkur	cukurs
beer	õlu	alus
vodka	valge viin	degvīns
brandy	konjak	konjaks
champagne	šampus	šampanietis
wine	vein	vīns

Days & Months

today	täna	šodien
yesterday	eile	vakar
tomorrow	homme	rīt
Sunday	pühapäev	svētdiena
Monday	esmaspäev	pirmdiena
Tuesday	teisipäev	otrdiena
Wednesday	kolmapäev	trešdiena
Thursday	neljapäev	ceturtdiena
Friday	reede	piektdiena
Saturday	laupäev	sestdiena

The days of the week are often abbreviated to their first one or two letters in timetables etc. In Latvian and Lithuanian note the difference between PR (Monday) and P (Friday); in Latvian, between SV (Sunday) and S (Saturday); and in Lithuanian, between S (Sunday) and Š (Saturday).

LITHUANIAN	RUSSIAN	RUSSIAN PRONUNCIATION
vištiena	курица	KOO-rit-suh
daržovės	овощи	OH-va-shchi
bulvė	картофель	karr-TOFF-el
grybas	гриб	greeb
saldumynai	сладкие блюда	SLAT-kye BLYOO-dah
ledai	мороженое	mah-ROZH-in-ay
vaisiai	фрукты	FROOK-ti
sąskaita	счёт	shyot
baras	буфет	buf-YET
vanduo	вода	va-DAH
mineralinis vanduo	минеральная вода	mi-ni-RAL-nuh-yuh va-DAH
sultys	сок	sohk
arbata	чай	chay
kava	кофе	KOF-yeh
pienas	молоко	ma-la-KOH
cukrus	сахар	SAKH-arr
alus	пиво	PEE-vah
degtinė	водка	VOHT-kuh
konjakas	коняк	kahn-YAHK
šampanas	шампанское	sham-PAN-ska-yuh
vynas	вино	vi-NOH
šiandien	сегодня	sye-VOHD-nya
vakar	вчера	fchi-RAH
rytdiena	завтра	ZAHV-tra
sekmadienis	воскресенье	vas-kri-SYEN-yuh
pirmadienis	понедельник	pa-nyi-DYEL-nik
antradienis	вторник	FTOR-nik
trečiadienis	среда	sri-DA
ketvirtadienis	четверг	chit-VERK
penktadienis	пятница	PYAT-nit-suh
šeštadienis	суббота	su-BOHT-uh

ENGLISH	ESTONIAN	LATVIAN
January	januar	janvāris
February	veebruar	februāris
March	märts	marts
April	aprill	aprīlis
May	mai	maijs
June	juuni	jūnijs
July	juuli	jūlijs
August	august	augusts
September	september	septembris
October	oktoober	oktobris
November	november	novembris
December	detsember	decembris

Numbers

one	üks ('yooks')	viens
two	kaks	divi
three	kolm	trīs
four	neli	četri
five	viis	pieci
six	kuus	seši
seven	sitse	septiņi
eight	kaheksa	astoņi
nine	üheksa	deviņi
ten	kümme	desmit
eleven	üsteist	vienpadsmit
twelve	kaksteist	divpadsmit
thirteen	kolmteist	trīspadsmit
fourteen	neliteist	četrpadsmit
fifteen	viisteist	piecpadsmit
sixteen	kuusteist	sešpadsmit
seventeen	seitseteist	septiņpadsmit
eighteen	kaheksateist	astoņpadsmit
nineteen	üheksateist	deviņpadsmit
twenty	kakskümmend	divdesmit
twenty-five	kakskümmendviis	divdesmitpieci
thirty	kolmkümmend	trīsdesmit
forty	nelikümmend	četrdesmit
fifty	viiskümmend	piecdesmit
sixty	kuuskümmend	sešdesmit

LITHUANIAN	RUSSIAN	RUSSIAN PRONUNCIATION
sausis	январь	YAN-var
vasaris	февраль	FIV-ral
kovas	март	marrt
balandis	апрель	ap-RIL
gegužė	май	my
birželis	июнь	i-YUN
liepa	июль	i-YUL
rugpjūtis	август	AV-gust
rugsėjis	сентябрь	sin-TYA-br
spalis	октябрь	ahk-TYA-br
lapkritis	ноябрь	na-YA-br
gruodis	декабрь	di-KA-br
vienas	один	ah-DYIN
du	два	dva
trys	три	tree
keturi	четыре	chi-TIR-yeh
penki	пять	pyats
šeši	шесть	shehst
septyni	семь	syem
aštuoni	восемь	VOSS-yem
devyni	девять	di-YEY-vits
dešimt	десять	di-YEY-sits
vienuolika	одинадцать	ad-YEEN-at-sats
dvylika	двенадцать	dvi-NAHT-sats
trylika	тринадцать	tri-NAHT-sats
keturiolika	четырнадцать	chi-tir-NAHT-sats
penkiolika	пятнадцать	pit-NAHT-sats
šešiolika	шестнадцать	shess-NAHT-sats
septyniolika	семнадцать	sim-NAHT-sats
aštuoniolika	восемнадцать	voss-im-NAHT-sats
devyniolika	девятнадцать	di-yey-vit-NAHT-sats
dvidešimt	двадцать	DVAHT-sats
dvidešimt penki	двадцать пять	DVAHT-sats pyats
trisdešimt	тридцать	TREET-sats
keturiasdešimt	сорок	SOR-ak
penkiasdešimt	пятьдесят	pi-di-SYAHT
šešiasdešimt	шестьдесят	shess-di-SYAHT

ENGLISH	ESTONIAN	LATVIAN
seventy	seitsekümmend	septiņdesmit
eighty	kaheksakümmend	astoņdesmit
ninety	üheksakümmend	deviņdesmit
one hundred	sada	simts

Emergency & Medical

toilet	tualett	tualete
chemist's	apteek	aptieka
doctor	arst	ārsts
hospital	haigla	slimnīca
ambulance	esmaabi	ātrā palīdzība
police	politsei	policija

LITHUANIAN	RUSSIAN	RUSSIAN PRONUNCIATION
septyniasdešimt	семьдесят	sim-di-SYAHT
aštuoniasdešimt	восемьдесят	VOSS-im-di-syaht
devyniasdešimt	девяносто	di-vi-NOSS-tah
šimtas	сто	stoh
tualetas	туалет	twal-YET
vaistinė	аптека	ap-TYEK-a
gydytojas	врач	vrach
ligoninė	больница	bahl-NIHT-sa
greitoji pagalba	амбулатория	am-bu-la-TOR-i-ya
policija	милиция	mi-LIT-sia

Appendix – Alternative Place Names

The following abbreviations are used:

(Eng) English
(Est) Estonian
(Finn) Finnish
(Ger) German
(Lat) Latvian
(Lith) Lithuanian
(Pol) Polish
(Russ) Russian
(Sov) Soviet name
(Swed) Swedish
(Uk) Ukrainian

Aizkraukle – Stučka (Sov)
Augustów – Augustavas (Lith)
Aukštaitija – Upper Lithuania (Eng)

Baltic Sea – Baltijas jūra (Lat), Baltijos jūra (Lith), Baltiyskoe More (Russ), Itämeri (Finn), Läänemeri (Est), Morze Bałtyckie (Pol), Östersjön (Swed), Ostsee (Ger)
Baltiysk – Pillau (Ger)
Bagrationovsk – Preussisch Eylau (Ger)
Bartoszyce – Bartoshitse (Russ)
Belarus – Baltarusija (Lith), Baltkrievija (Lat), Belorussia (Eng)
Białystok – Belostok (Russ)
Braniewo – Branevo (Russ), Braunsberg (Ger)

Cēsis – Võnnu (Est), Wenden (Ger)
Chernovtsy – Černovcai (Lith), Chernivtsy (Uk)
Chernyakhovsk – Insterburg (Ger)
CIS – SNG (Russ)
Courland Lagoon – Kurisches Haff (Ger), Kurshsky zaliv (Russ), Kuršių marios (Lith)
Courland Spit – Kurische Nehrung (Ger), Kurshskaya kosa (Russ), Kuršių nerija or Neringa (Lith)

Daugava – Düna (Ger), Zapadnaya Dvina (Russ)
Daugavpils – Borisoglebsk (Russ), Daugpilis (Lith), Dünaburg (Ger), Dvinsk (Pol)
Denmark – Dania (Russ), Danija (Lith), Dānija (Lat), Taani (Est)

Elblag – Elbing (Ger), Elblong (Russ)
England – Anglia (Russ), Anglija (Lat, Lith), Inglismaa (Est)
Estonia – Eesti (Est), Estija (Lith), Estland (Ger), Estonia (Russ), Igaunija (Lat), Viro (Fin)

Finland – Finlyandia (Russ), Somija (Lat), Soome (Est), Suomija (Lith)

Gauja – Koiva (Est)
Germany – Germania (Russ), Saksamaa (Est), Vācija (Lat), Vokietija (Lith)
Great Britain – Didžioji Britanija (Lith), Lielbritānija (Lat), Suurbritannia (Est), Velikobritania (Russ)
Grodno – Gardinas (Lith)
Gurievsk – Neuhausen (Ger)
Gusev – Gumbinnen (Ger)
Gvardeysk – Tapiau (Ger)

Helsinki – Helsingfors (Ger, Swed)
Hiiumaa – Dagö (Ger, Swed)

Ivangorod – Jaanilinn (Est)

Jelgava – Mitau (Ger)
Juodkrantė – Schwarzort (Ger)

Kaliningrad – Kaliningradas or Karaliaučius (Lith), Königsberg (Ger)
Kaliningrad Lagoon – Frisches Haff (Ger), Kaliningradsky zaliv or Vislinsky zaliv (Russ), Vistula Lagoon (Eng), Zalev Wiślany (Pol)
Kaunas – Kowno (Ger)
Kharkov – Charkovas (Lith), Kharkiv (Uk)
Kiel – Kylis (Lith)
Kiev – Kiiv (Uk), Kijeva (Lat), Kijevas (Lith)
Klaipėda – Memel (Ger)
Kuldīga – Goldingen (Ger)
Kuressaare – Arensburg (Ger), Kingissepa (Sov)
Kurzeme – Courland (Eng), Kurland (Ger), Kuršas or Kuržemė (Lith)

Lake Peipus – Chudskoe Ozero (Russ), Peipaus ežeras (Lith), Peipsi järv (Est)
Lake Pskov – Pihkva järv (Est), Pskovskoe Ozero (Russ)
Latvia – Läti (Est), Latvia (Russ), Latvija (Lat, Lith), Lettland (Ger)
Lazdijai – Łazdijaj (Pol)
Lesnoy – Sarkau (Ger)
Liepāja – Libau (Ger), Liepoja (Lith)
Lithuania – Leedu (Est), Lietuva (Lat, Lith), Litauen (Ger), Litva (Russ), Litwa (Pol)

Marijampolė – Kapsukas (Sov)
Mamonovo – Heiligenbeil (Ger)
Mordovskoe – Gross Legitten (Ger), Turgenevo (Russ)
Morskoe – Pillkoppen (Ger)
Moscow – Maskava (Lat), Maskva (Lith), Moskva (Est, Russ)

436

Nemunas – Memel or Njemen (Ger), Neman (Russ)
Nida – Nidden (Ger)

Olsztyn – Allenstein (Ger), Olshtyn (Russ), Olštynas (Lith)
Otradnoe – Georgenswalde (Ger)

Palanga – Polangen (Ger)
Pärnu – Pernau (Ger), Pērnava (Lat), Piarnu (Lith)
Pechory – Petseri (Est)
Poland – Lenkija (Lith), Polija (Lat), Polsha (Russ)
Polessk – Labiau (Ger)
Pregolya – Pregel (Ger)
Pskov – Pihkva (Est), Pleskau (Ger), Pleskava (Lat), Pskovas (Lith)

Rēzekne – Rossitten (Ger)
Rīga – Riia (Est), Riika (Fin), Ryga (Lith, Pol)
Rūjiena – Ruhja (Est)
Russia – Krievija (Lat), Rossia (Russ), Rusija (Lith), Venemaa (Est)
Rybachy – Rossitten (Ger)

Saaremaa – Ösel (Ger, Swed)
St Petersburg – Leningrad (Sov), Pietari (Fin), Sankt-Peterburg (Russ), Sanktpeterburga (Lat), St Peterburg (Est)
Salacgriva – Salatsi (Est)
Šeštokai – Szestokai (Ger)
Šiauliai – Šauļi (Lat), Shaulyay (Russ)
Sigulda – Segewold (Ger)
Šilutė – Heydekrug (Ger)
Sovietsk – Tilsit (Ger)
Suwałki – Suvalkai (Lith), Suvalki (Russ)

Svetlogorsk – Rauschen (Ger)
Svetly (Kal) – Svetlyj (Lith), Świetly (Pol), Zimmerbude (Ger)
Sweden – Rootsi (Est), Shvetsia (Russ), Švedija (Lith), Zviedrija (Lat)

Tallinn – Talinas (Lith), Tallina (Lat), Tallinna (Fin), Reval (Ger)
Tartu – Dorpat (Ger), Tartto (Fin), Tērbata (Lat)

USA – ASV (Amerikas Savienotās Valstis – Lat), JAVD(Jungtinės Amerikos Valstijos – Lith), SShA (Soedinyonnye Shtaty Ameriki – Russ)

Valga – Walk (Ger)
Valmiera – Volmari (Est), Wolmar (Ger)
Ventė – Windenburg (Ger)
Ventspils – Windau (Ger)
Vienna – Vīne (Lat), Viena (Lith)
Viljandi – Fellin (Ger)
Vilnius – Vilna (Fin, Ger), Viļņa (Lat), Wilno (Pol)
Voronezh – Voroneža (Lat)

Warsaw – Varšava (Lat), Varshava (Russ), Varssavi (Est), Varšuva (Lith), Warschau (Ger)

Yantarny – Palmnicken (Ger)

Zalivino – Rinderort (Ger)
Zelenogradsk – Cranz (Ger)
Žemaitija – Lower Lithuania or Samogitia (Eng)
Zemgale – Semigallia (Eng)

Index

ABBREVIATIONS

Est – Estonia
Lat – Latvia

Lith – Lithuania
Kal – Kaliningrad Region

Russ – Russia

MAPS

Aukštaitija National Park (Lith) 349
Baltic States & Kaliningrad Region 10
Bauska (Lat) 286
Cēsis (Lat) 273
Daugavpils (Lat) 282
Druskininkai (Lith) 352
Estonia 115
  North-East Estonia 153
  South-East Estonia 164
  South-West Estonia 216
  West Estonia & the Islands 185
German Rule 15
Haapsalu (Est) 188
Hiiumaa (Est) 195
Jelgava (Lat) 288
Jūrmala (Lat) 261
Kaliningrad Region 394
Kaliningrad (Kal) 402-403
Kärdla (Est) 199
Kaunas (Lith) 360
Klaipėda (Lith) 378

Kuldīga (Lat) 299
Kuressaare (Est) 211
Lahemaa National Park (Est) 155
Latvia 229
  Kurzeme Region 291
  Latgale Region 277
  Vidzeme Region 265
  Zemgale Region 285
Līgatne Area (Lat) 271
Liepāja (Lat) 302
Lithuania 307
  Central Lithuania 357
  Eastern Lithuania 348
  Southern Lithuania 350
  Western Lithuania 371
Majori (Lat) 262
Narva (Est) 159
Nida (Lith) 388
Otepää (Est) 176
Palanga (Lith) 373
Pärnu (Est) 218
Prussia (Kal) 397
Rēzekne (Lat) 279
Rīga (Lat) 240

Central Rīga (Lat) 246-247
Saaremaa & Muhu (Est) 203
Šiauliai (Lith) 367
Sigulda (Lat) 268
Smiltynė (Lith) 381
Svetlogorsk (Kal) 413
Swedish & Polish Control 19
Tallinn (Est) 126-127
  Around Tallinn (Est) 150
  Central Tallinn (Est) 130
Talsi (Lat) 293
Tartu (Est) 168-169
Trakai (Lith) 345
Ventspils (Lat) 296
Viljandi (Est) 225
Vilnius (Lith) 318-319
  Around Vilnius (Lith) 344
  Central Vilnius (Lith) 326-327
Vormsi (Est) 193
Võru (Est) 180
Who Was Who 13
Zelenogradsk (Kal) 416

TEXT

Maps references are in **bold** type
*See also Country and Capital City Entries

Aa (Est) 158
Aadma (Est) 201
Abrene Region (Lat) 230
Accommodation 65-69
Adavere (Est) 163
Ādaži (Lat) 264
Aglona (Lat) 280
Ähijärv (Est) 182
Ainaži (Lat) 264
Air Travel
  To/From the Baltic States 78-85
  Within the Baltic States 104-105
  Air Travel Glossary 80-81

Aizkraukle (Lat) 276
Äksi (Est) 174
Altja (Est) 156
Alūksne (Lat) 275, 280
Alytus (Lith) 355
Amber 12, 73, 374-376, 404, 408, 418
Angla (Est) 207
Annimatsi (Est) 177
Antsla (Est) 182
Araiši (Lat) 272
Asari (Lat) 260
Asuküla (Est) 192
Augšlīgatne, see Ligatne
Aukštaitija National Park (Lith) 308, 347-348, **349**

Balga (Kal) 420
Baltezers (Lat) 264

Baltic Glint (Est) 154, 158
Baltic Sea 191
Baltika Folklore Festival 50
Baltiysk (Kal) 418
Bargaining 47
Bauska (Lat) 284-286, **286**
Bicycling, see Cycling
Bird-watching 193, 202, 355
Birštonas (Lith) 365
Boat Travel, see Sea Travel and Sailing
Books 55-58
Brazauskas, Algirdas 26
Bulduri (Lat) 260
Bungy Jumping (Lat) 269
Bus Travel
  Local 111
  To/From the Baltic States 85-88

Within the Baltic States
    105-106
Business Hours 48-49

Camping 66
Canoeing 64-65,
    Estonia 179
    Latvia 266, 280, 295
    Lithuania 332, 347
Car, see Driving
Čepkeliai Nature Reserve (Lith)
    308, 353
Cēsis (Lat) 272-273,**273**
Chernyakhovsk (Kal) 419-420
Čiurlionis, Mikalojus
    Konstantinas 310, 351, 359
Climate 28-30, 47-48
Costs 46-47
Courland Lagoon 370, 385, 393
Courland Spit 370, 385-390,
    393, 412, 419
Credit Cards 45
Crime 63
Currency Exchange 46
Customs* 45
Cycling 64, 109-110
    To/From the Baltic States 97
    Within the Baltic States
        Estonia 179, 197, 198, 206,
        Latvia 266, 280,
        Lithiuania 332, 350, 374

Dagda (Lat) 280
Dārziņi (Lat) 260
Daugavpils (Lat) 281-283, **282**
Daylight Saving 55
Dejevo (Est) 213
Diby (Est) 192
Dirhami (Est) 190
Drīdzis, Lake (Lat) 280
Drinks 71-72
Driving 95
    Car Rental 108, 147-148, 259
    Fuel 109, 147, 259
    Insurance 95
    Licences 44, 95
    Road Rules 108
    To/From the Baltic States
        95-97
    Vehicle Ferries 95-96
    Within the Baltic States
        107-109
Druskininkai (Lith) 350-353,
    352
Dubulti (Lat) 260
Dūkštos (Lith) 346
Dundaga (Lat) 294-295
Dusetos (Lith) 350
Dzintari (Lat) 260

Dzūkija National Park (Lith)
    308, 353

Economy 32-33
Eikla (Est) 207
Electricity 55
Eleja (Lat) 287
Elva (Est) 177
Emmaste (Est) 202
Endla Nature Reserve (Est)
    161-162
Engure (Lat) 294
Entertainment* 72-73
Environment 31-32, 151, 158,
    160, 215, 347
Estonia 115-226, **115, 153, 164,
    185, 216**
    g itizenship 117
    Customs 119
    Embassies 119
    Festivals 121, 154, 220
    Food 122
    Geography 115-116
    Government 116-117
    Literature 117
    Media 121-122
    Money 120
    National Holidays 120-121
    National Parks 116, 152-157,
        161-162, 193, 202
    Population 117
    Radio 121-122
    TV 121-122
    Visual Arts 118
Ethnic Groups
    Belarussians 34, 315
    Estonians 35, 117, 202
    Germans 34, 36
    Jews 22-23, 34, 248-249, 260,
        315-316, 324-325, 343, 361
    Karaites 344
    Latvians 35, 231
    Lithuanians 35, 309
    Livs 294
    Poles 34, 315-316
    Russians 34, 123, 158, 237,
        315
    Setus 183
    Swedes 187, 190, 192,
        200
    Ukrainians 34
Ezernieki (Lat) 280

Fauna 30-31
Fax 54
Female Travellers 62-63
Ferries, see Sea Travel
Festivals* 49-50
Flora 30-31

Folk Culture 36-37
Food* 69-71

Gariūnai (Lith) 331
Gauja National Park (Lat) 230,
    267
Gaujasmala (Lat) 272
Gaujiena (Lat) 275
Gediminas 16, 314, 344
Geography* 27-28
Grīņi State Nature Reserve
    (Lat) 230
Gurievsk (Kal) 419
Gusev (Kal) 419-420
Gvardeysk (Kal) 419-420

Häädemeeste (Est) 223
Haanja (Est) 181
Haapsalu (Est) 184-190, **188**
Haeska (Est) 192
Haldi (Est) 202
Handicrafts 73
Hanila (Est) 194
Hanseatic League 16, 124, 160,
    163, 215, 225, 237, 295, 356,
    398
Harju (Est) 202
Health 61-63
Hiiumaa (Est) 194-202, **195**
Hill Of Crosses (Lith) 365,
    366-368
Hino Järv (Est) 183
Hitching 97, 110
Holidays, see under country
    entries
Holstre-Nõmme (Est) 226
Homestays 67-69
Horse Riding (Lat) 270
Hosby (Est) 190
Hostels 66-67
Hullo (Est) 192

Iecava (Lat) 284
Ignalina (Lith) 347
Indra (Lat) 281
Ivangorod (Russ) 158

Jakobson, Carl Robert 223
Järve (Est) 158, 209
Jaundubulti (Lat) 260
Jaunpiebalga (Lat) 275
Jaunķemeri (Lat) 260
Jēkabpils (Lat) 276
Jelgava (Lat) 288-289, **288**
Joaveski (Est) 154
Jogaila 16-17
Jõgeva (Est) 173
Jõhvi (Est) 158
Jūrmala (Lat) 260-263, **261**

Juodkrantė (Lith) 386-387
Jurbarkas (Lith) 365
Jūžintai (Lith) 350

Kaali (Est) 207
Kääriku (Est) 177
Kaarma (Est) 207-208
Kabli (Est) 223
Kahutsi (Est) 206
Käina (Est) 201
Kaliningrad (Kal) 395-412,
    402-403
    Bookshops 400
    Entertainment 408
    Getting Around 411-412
    Getting There & Away
        408-411
    History 398-399
    Information 399
    Left Luggage 400
    Maps 400
    Media 400
    Medical Services 400
    Money 399
    Music 118
    National Holidays 395
    Orientation 399
    Places to Eat 407-408
    Places to Stay 405-407
    Post, Telephone & Fax 399
    Shopping 408
    Things to See & Do 400
Kaliningrad Lagoon 393
Kaliningrad Region 393-420,
    394
    Customs 45, 395
    Embassies 395
    Geography 393
    Government 393
    Money 395
    People 393
Kallaste (Est) 174
Kaltanėnai (Lith) 347
Kalvarija (Lith) 96, 354, 372
Kamajai (Lith) 350
Kamanos Nature Reserve (Lith)
    308
Kandava (Lat) 295
Kanepi (Est) 177
Kant, Immanuel 398, 401, 404
Kärdla (Est) 198-200, **199**
Karilatsi (Est) 178
Karja (Est) 207
Karujärv (Est) 213
Karuse (Est) 194
Käsmu (Est) 156
Kassari (Est) 201-202
Kaugatuma (Est) 213
Kauguri (Lat) 260

Kauksi (Est) 161
Kaunas (Lith) 365-356, **360**
Kaunata (Lat) 280
Kayaking, see Canoeing
Keila (Est) 190
Ķemeri (Lat) 260
Kernavė (Lith) 346
Kernu (Est) 151
Kihelkonna (Est) 213
Kihnu (Est) 224
Kiidjärve (Est) 178
Kintai (Lith) 385
Klaipėda (Lith) 22, 377-385, **378**
Kloogaranna (Est) 149
Knights of the Sword 13-15,
    124, 133, 163, 184, 204, 206,
    224, 226, 236, 244, 267, 272,
    365
Kodasoo (Est) 151, 156
Koeru (Est) 162
Koguva (Est) 206
Kohtla-Järve (Est) 157-158
Koidula, Lydia 117, 136, 219
Koknese (Lat) 276
Kolga (Est) 156
Kõljala (Est) 207
Kolka (Lat) 294
Königsberg, See Kaliningrad
Kõõgumägi (Est) 183
Kõpu (Est) 200
Kõrgessaare (Est) 200
Krabi (Est) 182
Krāslava (Lat) 280
Kretinga (Lith) 370
Kreutzwald, Friedrich Reinhold
    117, 167, 179
Krustkalni State Nature Reserve
    (Lat) 230
Krustpils (Lat) 276
Kudirkos-Naumiestis (Lith) 355
Kuivastu (Est) 205
Kuldīga (Lat) 298-301, **299**
Kunda (Est) 157
Kuremaa (Est) 174
Kuressaare (Est) 208-212, **211**
Kurgja (Est) 223
Kurkse (Est) 151
Kurshskaya Kosa, see Courland
    Spit
Kuršių Nerija National Park
    (Lith) 308, 386
Kurzeme Region (Lat) 290-303,
    291
Kuutsemägi (Est) 177
Kybartai (Lith) 355

Laar, Mart 26, 116
Lahemaa National Park (Est)
    116, 152-157, **155**

Laikmaa, Ants 191
Laimjala (Est) 207
Laiuse (Est) 174
Landsbergis, Vytautas 25-26
Language 39, 421-435
    Estonian 421
    Latvian 421
    Lithuanian 422
    Russian 422
    Useful Words & Phrases
        424-435
Latgale Region (Lat) 276-283,
    277
Latgale Upland (Lat) 280-283
Latvia 229-289, **229**
    Citizenship 230
    Customs 233
    Dance 232
    Embassies 233
    Festivals 234
    Food 235
    Geography 229-230
    Government 230
    Literature 231
    Media 234
    Money 233-234
    Music 232
    National Holidays 234
    National Parks 230, 294
    Population 230-231
    Radio 235
    TV 235
    Visual Arts 231-232
Laulasmaa (Est) 149
Laundry 55
Lavassaare (Est) 223
Lazdijai 96, (Lith) 353
Left Luggage 55
Lehtma (Est) 200
Leisi (Est) 207
Lejasciems (Lat) 275
Lesnoy (Kal) 419
Lielupe (Lat) 260
Lielvārde (Lat) 276
Liepāja (Lat) 301-303, **302**
Līgatne (Lat) 270-272, **271**
Lihula (Est) 193-194
Liškiava (Lith) 353
Literature* 37
Lithuania 307-390, **307, 348,
    350, 357, 371**
    Citizenship 309
    Customs 311
    Embassies 311
    Festivals 312-313
    Folk Art 310
    Food 313
    Geography 307-308
    Government 308-309

Literature 309-310
Media 313
Money 312
Music 310
National Holidays 312
National Parks 308
Population 309
Radio 313
TV 313
Visual Arts 310
Liu (Est) 224
Livonia 14
Livonian Order 15-18, 157, 215, 272, 285, 289, 299, 301, 377
Local Transport
  Bus 111
  Tram 111
  Trolleybus 111
  Taxis 111
Lõhavere (Est) 226
Lohusalu (Est) 149
Lohusuu (Est) 161
Loksa (Est) 156
Lubans, Lake 280
Lublin, Treaty Of 17
Ludza (Lat) 280, 281
Lugaži (Lat) 275
Luidja (Est) 202
Luts, Oskar 118, 167, 174
Luua (Est) 174

Maardu (Est) 151
Madona (Lat) 275
Mafia 63
Mäha (Est) 176
Maironis (Jonas Mačiulis) 37, 309, 358
Maišiagala (Lith) 346
Majori (Lat) 260, **262**
Māli (Lat) 275
Malta (Lat) 281
Mändjala (Est) 210
Mann, Thomas 387
Maps 58-59
Marcinkonys (Lith) 353
Marijampolė (Lith) 354
Märjamaa (Est) 215
Matsalu Nature Reserve (Est) 116, 193
Mažeikiai (Lith) 368
Mazirbe (Lat) 295
Mazsalaca (Lat) 266
Media* 59-61
Mehikoorma (Est) 174
Melluži (Lat) 260
Melnragė (Lith) 383
Memel, see Klaipėda
Merkinė (Lith) 353
Mērsrags (Lat) 294

Metsküla (Est) 207
Mežotne (Lat) 288
Mickiewicz, Adam 309, 315, 323
Midsummer Festival 50
Mindaugas 16, 346
Misso (Est) 183
Mõisaküla (Est) 213
Molėtai (Lith) 350
Molotov-Ribbentrop Pact 22, 50
Money* 45-46
Mõniste (Est) 182
Mõntu (Est) 213
Mordovskoe (Kal) 419
Moricsala State Nature Reserve (Lat) 230
Morskoe (Kal) 419
Mosėdis (Lith) 372
Motorbike, see Driving
Muhu (Est) 206, **203**
Muhu Island (Est) 194
Munamägi, Battle of 181
Muratsi (Est) 210
Mustoja (Est) 156
Mustvee (Est) 161
Muuksi (Est) 154, 56

Narva (Est) 158-161, **159**
Nasva (Est) 210
National Parks & Reserves
  Aukštaitija National Park (Lith) 308, 347-348, **349**
  Čepkeliai Nature Reserve (Lith) 308, 353
  Dzūkija National Park (Lith) 308, 353
  Gauja National Park (Lat) 230, 267
  Kuršių Nerija National Park (Lith) 308, 386
  Lahemaa National Park (Est) 116, 152-157, **155**
  Trakai National Park (Lith) 308
  Endla Nature Reserve (Est) 116, 161-162
  Grīņi State Nature Reserve (Lat) 230
  Kamanos Nature Reserve (Lith) 308
  Krustkalni State Nature Reserve (Lat) 230
  Matsalu Nature Reserve (Est) 116, 193
  Moricsala State Nature Reserve (Lat) 230
  Nigula State Nature Reserve (Est) 116
  Slītere Nature Reserve (Lat) 294, 230

Teiči State Nature Reserve (Lat) 230
Väinameri Nature Reserve (Est) 116, 202
Viešvilė Nature Reserve (Lith) 308
Viidumäe State Nature Reserve (Est) 116
Vilsandi State Nature Reserve (Est) 116
Žemaitija National Park (Lith) 308, 372
Žuvintas Nature Reserve (Lith) 308, 355
Natturi (Est) 156
Neringa, see Courland Spit
Nesterov (Kal) 355
Newspapers* 59-61
Nida (Lith) 387-390, **388**
Nigula Bog (Est) 223
Nigula State Nature Reserve (Est) 116
Noarootsi Peninsula (Est) 190
Nõmmeveski (Est) 154
Nurste (Est) 202

Ogre (Lat) 270
Õngu (Est) 202
Ontika (Est) 158
Orissaare (Est) 206
Orjaku (Est) 201
Ösel-Wiek Bishopric 184, 191, 204, 208, 215
Österby (Est) 191
Otepää (Est) 174-177, **176**

Padise (Est) 149
Paganamaa (Est) 182
Paide (Est) 161
Palade (Est) 198
Palamuse (Est) 174
Palanga (Lith) 372-376, **373**
Paldiski (Est) 149
Palmse (Est) 154
Palūšė (Lith) 347
Paneriai (Lith) 343-344
Panevėžys (Lith) 369
Panga Bank 213
Pangodi Järv (Est) 177
Pärase (Est) 206
Parila (Est) 192
Parks, see National Parks
Pärnu (Est) 215-223, **218**
Pasiene (Lat) 280
Päts, Konstantin 21-22, 223
Pāvilosta (Lat) 298
Pechory (Russ) 116, 183
Peipus, Lake 161, 174
Pervalka (Lith) 387

Peter the Great 18, 124, 135, 149, 160, 164, 165
Petseri, see Pechory
Photography 61
Piirisaar (Est) 174
Pirita (Est) 135, 139
Piusa River 182
Plateliai (Lith) 372
Plungė (Lith) 370
Pöide (Est) 206
Polessk (Kal) 419
Põltsamaa (Est) 163
Põlva (Est) 178-179
Population* 33
Post 50-51
Poste Restante 51
Preila (Lith) 387
Prussia 14, 18-20, 377, 393, 395, 396, 398, 417, **397**
Pskov, Lake (Est) 174
Public Transport, see Local Transport, Bus Travel, Sea Travel and Train Travel
Pühajärv (Est) 175
Puise (Est) 192
Pumpuri (Lat) 260
Pürksi (Est) 191
Purtse (Est) 157

Rainis, Jānis 231, 243, 248, 250, 261
Ramsi (Est) 226
Rannametsa (Est) 223
Rannamõisa (Est) 151
Rannu (Est) 177
Räpina (Est) 174
Raudondvaris (Lith) 365
Raudonė (Lith) 365
Rāzna, Lake (Lat) 280
Religion 38-39
    Old Baltic Religions 278
Reserves, see National Parks
Rēzekne (Lat) 276-280, **279**
Ridala (Est) 191-192
Rīga (Lat) 236-260, **240**, **246-247**
    Bookshops 241
    Embassies 239-240
    Entertainment 255-256
    Getting Around 259-260
    Getting There & Away 256-259
    History 236-238
    Information 238-242
    Left Luggage 242
    Maps 241
    Media 241
    Medical Services 241
    Orientation 238

Photography 242
    Places to Eat 253-255
    Places to Stay 250-253
    Post, Telephone & Fax 239
    Rīga Ghetto 248-249
    Shopping 256
    Things to See & Do 242
    Tours 250
    Travel Agencies 240-241
Riisipere (Est) 190
Ristna (Est) 200
Road Rules 108
Robežnieki (Lat) 281
Rocca Al Mare (Est) 136
Roja (Lat) 294
Rokiškis (Lith) 350
Rõuge (Est) 182
Ruhnu (Est) 224
Rūjiena (Lat) 266
Rukainiai (Lith) 332
Rummu (Est) 149
Rumpo Peninsula (Est) 192
Rumšiškės (Lith) 365
Rundāle (Lat) 286-288
Rusnė (Lith) 385
Ruunavere (Est) 151
Ruusmä (Est) 182
Rybachy (Kal) 419

Saadjärv (Est) 173
Sääre (Est) 213
Sääre Tirp (Est) 201
Saaremaa (Est) 202-214, **203**
Säätse (Est) 183
Sabile (Lat) 295
Sagadi (Est) 156
Saia (Est) 210
Sailing 65, 110
    To/From the Baltic States 101, 148, 205, 210, 213
Saksby (Est) 192
Salacgrīva (Lat) 264
Salantai (Lith) 372
Salaspils (Lat) 260
Sanatoriums 69
Sangaste Loss (Est) 176
Sauleskalns (Lat) 280
Saulkrasti (Lat) 264
Sauna 65
Sea Travel
    To/From the Baltic States 97-101
    see also Sailing
Setumaa (Est) 183
Shopping 73-74
Šiauliai (Lith) 365-369, **367**
Siesartis (Lith) 350
Sigulda (Lat) 267-270, **268**
Sillamäe (Est) 158

Šilutė (Lith) 385
Simnas (Lith) 355
Skiing 65, 163, 174
Skuodas (Lith) 372
Slītere Nature Reserve (Lat) 230, 294
Smiltynė (Lith) 380-381, **381**
Song Festivals 49-50
Sõru (Est) 202
Sõrve Peninsula (Est) 213-214
Souvenirs 73-74
Sovietsk (Kal) 417-418
St Kazimieras 17, 322, 324
Stalag-351 (Est) 178
State Reserves, see National Parks
Straupe (Lat) 272
Strenči (Lat) 275
Stripeikiai (Lith) 347
Sutu (Est) 207, 210
Suur Munamägi (Est) 181-182
Suuremõisa (Est) 197
Suurjärv (Est) 182
Svetlogorsk (Kal) 412-415, **413**
Sviby (Est) 192

Tabivere (Est) 173
Taebla (Est) 191
Taevaskoja (Est) 178-179
Tagavere (Est) 206
Tahku (Est) 223
Tahkuna Peninsula (Est) 200
Tallinn (Est) 123-151, **126-127**, **130**, **150**
    Beaches 149
    Bookshops 128
    Embassies 125-128
    Entertainment 143-145
    Festivals 137
    Getting Around 148-149
    Getting There & Away 145-148
    History 123-124
    Information 124-129
    Left Luggage 129
    Maps 128
    Media 128
    Medical Services 129
    Orientation 124
    Photography 129
    Places to Eat 141-143
    Places to Stay 137-141
    Post, Telephone & Fax 125
    Shopping 145
    Travel Agencies 128
    Things to See & Do 129
Talsi (Lat) 292-293, **293**
Tamme (Est) 182

Tammsaare, Anton Hansen 118, 135, 136, 161
Tartu (Est) 163-173, **168-169**
Taurene (Lat) 275
Taxis 111
Tehumardi (Est) 213
Teiči State Nature Reserve (Lat) 230
Telegrams 54
Telephones 51-54
Telephone Codes 53
Tērvete (Lat) 289
Teutonic Order 14-17, 124, 161, 314, 356, 366, 377, 385, 393, 398, 401, 419, 420
Tilsit, Treaty of 398, 417
Time 55
Tipping 47
Tohvri (Est) 202
Toila (Est) 158
Toilets 55
Tona (Est) 183
Toolse (Est) 157
Torgu (Est) 211, 212
Tori (Est) 223
Tourism 33
Tourist Offices 48
Tours 102
Traffic Rules, see Road Rules
Train Travel
    To/From the Baltic States 88-94
    Within the Baltic States 106-107
Trakai (Lith) 344-346, **345**
Trakai National Park (Lith) 308
Tram 111
Trolleybus 111
Travel Agencies 75-78
Travellers' Cheques 45
Triigi (Est) 207
Tsirguliina (Est) 176
Tuhkana (Est) 207
Tuksi (Est) 190
Tukums (Lat) 290-292

Ukmergė (Lith) 346
Ulmanis, Kārlis 21-22
Undva (Est) 214
Unemployment 33
Utena (Lith) 350
Uulu (Est) 220
Uuri (Est) 156

Užava (Lat) 298

Vääna-Jõesuu (Est) 149
Vääna-Viti (Est) 151
Vahtseliina (Est) 182
Vaibla (Est) 226
Väinameri Nature Reserve (Est) 116, 202
Vaivari (Lat) 260
Valga (Est) 177, 178, 275
Valgu (Est) 202
Valjala (Est) 206, 207
Valka (Lat) 177, 275
Valmiera (Lat) 273-275
Vandzene (Lat) 294
Vargamäe, see Vetepere
Värska (Est) 183
Vasknarva (Est) 161
Vastseliina Castle (Est) 182-183
Vatku (Est) 156
Vecpiebalga (Lat) 275
Veere (Est) 213
Veliuona (Lith) 365
Ventė (Lith) 385
Ventspils (Lat) 295-298, **296**
Verijärv (Est) 179
Vetepere (Est) 161
Vīdale (Lat) 294
Vidzeme Region (Lat) 264, **265**
Vidzeme Upland (Lat) 275
Viešvilė Nature Reserve (Lith) 308
Vihula (Est) 156
Viidu (Est) 214
Viidumäe (Est) 213, 214
Viidumäe State Nature Reserve (Est) 116
Viiratsi (Est) 226
Viitna (Est) 152
Viivikonna (Est) 158
Viki (Est) 213
Viljandi (Est) 224-226, **225**
Vilnius (Lith) 314-346, **318-319**, **326-327**, **344**
    Bookshops 320
    Embassies 317
    Entertainment 338-339
    Festivals 331
    Getting Around 342-343
    Getting There & Away 339-342
    History 314-316
    Information 316-320

Jewish History 324-325
Left Luggage 320
Maps 320
Media 317-320
Medical Services 320
Money 316
Orientation 316
Photography 320
Places to Eat 335-338
Places to Stay 331-335
Post, Telephone & Fax 316-317
Shopping 339
Things to See & Do 320
Travel Agencies 317
Vilsandi State Nature Reserve (Est) 116
Vireši (Lat) 275
Virtsu (Est) 194, 205
Viru Bog (Est) 156
Virve (Est) 156
Visas 40-44
Viskoosa, see Kõrgessaare
Võhma (Est) 156, 213
Von Baer, Karl Ernst 166, 167
Võõpsu (Est) 183
Võporzova (Est) 183
Vormsi (Est) 192, **193**
Võrtsjärv (Est) 177
Võru (Est) 179-181, **180**
Võsu (Est) 156
Vytautas the Great 16-17, 321, 344, 358, 359

Women Travellers 62-63
Work 64

Yantarny (Kal) 418-419

Zalivino (Kal) 419
Zapyškis (Lith) 365
Zelenogradsk (Kal) 416-417, **416**
Žemaičių Kalvarija, see Kalvarija
Žemaitija National Park (Lith) 308, 372
Žemaitija Upland (Lith) 370-372
Zemgale Region (Lat) 284-289, **285**
Zilupe (Lat) 280
Žuvintas Nature Reserve (Lith) 308, 355
Zvārtas Iezis (Lat) 271

Lonely Planet guides to Europe

Eastern Europe on a shoestring
This guide has opened up a whole new world for travellers – Albania, Bulgaria, Czechoslovakia, eastern Germany, Hungary, Poland, Romania and former republics of Yugoslavia.
'...a thorough, well-researched book. Only a fool would go East without it.' – *Great Expeditions*

Mediterranean Europe on a shoestring
Details on hundreds of galleries, museums and architectural masterpieces and information on outdoor activities including hiking, sailing and skiing. Information on travelling in Albania, Andorra, Cyprus, France, Greece, Italy, Malta, Morocco, Portugal, Spain, Tunisia, Turkey and former republics of Yugoslavia.

Scandinavian & Baltic Europe on a shoestring
A comprehensive guide to travelling in this region including details on galleries, festivals and museums, as well as outdoor activities, national parks and wildlife. Countries featured are Denmark, Estonia, the Faroe Islands, Finland, Iceland, Latvia, Lithuania, Norway and Sweden.

Western Europe on a shoestring
This long-awaited guide covers all of Western Europe's well-loved sights and provides routes for cycling and driving tours, plus details on hiking, climbing and skiing. All the travel facts on Andorra, Austria, Belgium, Britain, France, Germany, Ireland, Italy, Liechtenstein, Luxembourg, Netherlands, Portugal, Spain and Switzerland.

Dublin – city guide
Where to enjoy a pint of Guinness and a plate of Irish stew, where to see spectacular Georgian architecture or experience Irish hospitality – Dublin city guide will ensure you won't miss out on anything.

Finland – travel survival kit
Finland is an intriguing blend of Swedish and Russian influences. With its medieval stone castles, picturesque wooden houses, vast forest and lake district, and interesting wildlife, it is a wonderland to delight any traveller.

Greece – travel survival kit
Famous ruins, secluded beaches, sumptuous food, sun-drenched islands, ancient pathways and much more are covered in this comprehensive guide to this ever-popular destination.

Hungary – travel survival kit
Formerly seen as the gateway to eastern Europe, Hungary is a romantic country of music, wine and folklore. This guide contains detailed background information on Hungary's cultural and historical past as well as practical advice on the many activities available to travellers.

Iceland, Greenland & the Faroe Islands – travel survival kit
Iceland, Greenland & the Faroe Islands contain some of the most beautiful wilderness areas in the world. This practical guidebook will help travellers discover the dramatic beauty of this region, no matter what their budget.

Ireland – travel survival kit
Ireland is one of Europe's least 'spoilt' countries. Green, relaxed and welcoming it does not take travellers long before they feel at ease. An entertaining and comprehensive guide to this troubled country.

Italy – travel survival kit
Italy is art – not just in the galleries and museums. You'll discover it's charm on the streets and in the markets, in rustic hill-top villages and in the glamorous city boutiques. A thorough guide to the thousands of attractions of this ever-popular destination.

Poland – travel survival kit
With the collapse of communism, Poland has opened up to travellers, revealing a rich cultural heritage and unspoiled beauty. This guide will help you make the most of this safe and friendly country.

Switzerland – travel survival kit
Ski enthusiasts and chocolate addicts know two excellent reasons for heading to Switzerland. This travel survival kit gives travellers many more; jazz, cafés, boating trips...and the Alps of course!

USSR – travel survival kit
Invaluable advice on getting around and beating red tape for individual and group travellers alike. This comprehensive guide includes an unsanitised historical background and complete information on art and culture. Over 130 reliable maps, and all place names are given in Cyrillic script. (includes the independent states)

Trekking in Greece
Mountainous landscape, the solitude of ancient pathways and secluded beaches await those who dare to extend their horizons beyond Athens and the antiquities. Covers the main trekking regions and includes contoured maps of trekking routes.

Trekking in Spain
Aimed at both overnight trekkers and day hikers, this guidebook includes useful maps and full details on hikes in some of Spain's most beautiful wilderness areas.

Also available:
Eastern Europe phrasebook
Discover the most enjoyable way to get around and make friends in Bulgarian, Czech, Hungarian, Polish, Romanian and Slovak.

Mediterranean Europe phrasebook
Ask for directions to the galleries and museums in Albanian, Greek, Italian, Macedonian, Maltese, Serbian & Croatian and Slovene.

Scandinavian Europe phrasebook
Find your way around the ski trails and enjoy the local festivals in Danish, Finnish, Icelandic, Norwegian and Swedish.

Western Europe phrasebook
Show your appreciation for the great masters in Basque, Catalan, Dutch, French, German, Irish, Portuguese and Spanish (Castilian).

Russian phrasebook
This indispensable phrasebook will help you get information, read signs and menus, and make friends along the way. Includes phonetic transcriptions and Cyrillic script.

Lonely Planet Guidebooks

Lonely Planet guidebooks cover every accessible part of Asia as well as Australia, the Pacific South America, Africa, the Middle East, Europe and parts of North America. There are five series: *travel survival kits*, covering a country for a range of budgets; *shoestring guides* with compact information for low-budget travel in a major region; *walking guides*; *city guides* and *phrasebooks*.

Australia & the Pacific
Australia
Bushwalking in Australia
Islands of Australia's Great Barrier Reef
Fiji
Melbourne city guide
Micronesia
New Caledonia
New Zealand
Tramping in New Zealand
Papua New Guinea
Bushwalking in Papua New Guinea
Papua New Guinea phrasebook
Rarotonga & the Cook Islands
Samoa
Solomon Islands
Sydney city guide
Tahiti & French Polynesia
Tonga
Vanuatu
Victoria

South-East Asia
Bali & Lombok
Bangkok city guide
Cambodia
Indonesia
Indonesia phrasebook
Laos
Malaysia, Singapore & Brunei
Myanmar (Burma)
Burmese phrasebook
Philippines
Pilipino phrasebook
Singapore city guide
South-East Asia on a shoestring
Thailand
Thai phrasebook
Vietnam
Vietnamese phrasebook

North-East Asia
China
Beijing city guide
Mandarin Chinese phrasebook
Hong Kong, Macau & Canton
Japan
Japanese phrasebook
Korea
Korean phrasebook
Mongolia
North-East Asia on a shoestring
Seoul city guide
Taiwan
Tibet
Tibet phrasebook
Tokyo city guide

West Asia
Trekking in Turkey
Turkey
Turkish phrasebook
West Asia on a shoestring

Middle East
Arab Gulf States
Egypt & the Sudan
Arabic (Egyptian) phrasebook
Iran
Israel
Jordan & Syria
Yemen

Indian Ocean
Madagascar & Comoros
Maldives & Islands of the East Indian Ocean
Mauritius, Réunion & Seychelles

Mail Order

Lonely Planet guidebooks are distributed worldwide. They are also available by mail order from Lonely Planet, so if you have difficulty finding a title please write to us. US and Canadian residents should write to Embarcadero West, 155 Filbert St, Suite 251, Oakland CA 94607, USA; European residents should write to Devonshire House, 12 Barley Mow Passage, Chiswick, London W4 4PH; and residents of other countries to PO Box 617, Hawthorn, Victoria 3122, Australia.

Indian Subcontinent
Bangladesh
India
Hindi/Urdu phrasebook
Trekking in the Indian Himalaya
Karakoram Highway
Kashmir, Ladakh & Zanskar
Nepal
Trekking in the Nepal Himalaya
Nepali phrasebook
Pakistan
Sri Lanka
Sri Lanka phrasebook

Africa
Africa on a shoestring
Central Africa
East Africa
Trekking in East Africa
Kenya
Swahili phrasebook
Morocco, Algeria & Tunisia
Arabic (Moroccan) phrasebook
South Africa, Lesotho & Swaziland
Zimbabwe, Botswana & Namibia
West Africa

Central America
Baja California
Central America on a shoestring
Costa Rica
La Ruta Maya
Mexico

North America
Alaska
Canada
Hawaii

Europe
Baltic States & Kaliningrad
Dublin city guide
Eastern Europe on a shoestring
Eastern Europe phrasebook
Finland
Greece
Hungary
Iceland, Greenland & the Faroe Islands
Ireland
Italy
Mediterranean Europe on a shoestring
Mediterranean Europe phrasebook
Poland
Scandinavian & Baltic Europe on a shoestring
Scandinavian Europe phrasebook
Switzerland
Trekking in Spain
Trekking in Greece
USSR
Russian phrasebook
Western Europe on a shoestring
Western Europe phrasebook

South America
Argentina, Uruguay & Paraguay
Bolivia
Brazil
Brazilian phrasebook
Chile & Easter Island
Colombia
Ecuador & the Galápagos Islands
Latin American Spanish phrasebook
Peru
Quechua phrasebook
South America on a shoestring
Trekking in the Patagonian Andes

The Lonely Planet Story

Lonely Planet published its first book in 1973 in response to the numerous 'How did you do it?' questions Maureen and Tony Wheeler were asked after driving, bussing, hitching, sailing and railing their way from England to Australia.

Written at a kitchen table and hand collated, trimmed and stapled, *Across Asia on the Cheap* became an instant local bestseller, inspiring thoughts of another book.

Eighteen months in South-East Asia resulted in their second guide, *South-East Asia on a shoestring*, which they put together in a backstreet Chinese hotel in Singapore in 1975. The 'yellow bible' as it quickly became known to backpackers around the world, soon became *the* guide to the region. It has sold well over half a million copies and is now in its 7th edition, still retaining its familiar yellow cover.

Today there are over 120 Lonely Planet titles in print – books that have that same adventurous approach to travel as those early guides; books that 'assume you know how to get your luggage off the carousel' as one reviewer put it.

Although Lonely Planet initially specialised in guides to Asia, they now cover most regions of the world, including the Pacific, South America, Africa, the Middle East and Europe. The list of *walking guides* and *phrasebooks* (for 'unusual' languages such as Quechua, Swahili, Nepalese and Egyptian Arabic) is also growing rapidly.

The emphasis continues to be on travel for independent travellers. Tony and Maureen still travel for several months of each year and play an active part in the writing, updating and quality control of Lonely Planet's guides.

They have been joined by over 50 authors, 54 staff – mainly editors, cartographers, & designers – at our office in Melbourne, Australia, 10 at our US office in Oakland, California and another three at our office in London to handle sales for Britain, Europe and Africa. In 1992 Lonely Planet opened an editorial office in Paris. Travellers themselves also make a valuable contribution to the guides through the feedback we receive in thousands of letters each year.

The people at Lonely Planet strongly believe that travellers can make a positive contribution to the countries they visit, both through their appreciation of the countries' culture, wildlife and natural features, and through the money they spend. In addition, the company makes a direct contribution to the countries and regions it covers. Since 1986 a percentage of the income from each book has been donated to ventures such as famine relief in Africa; aid projects in India; agricultural projects in Central America; Greenpeace's efforts to halt French nuclear testing in the Pacific and Amnesty International. In 1993 $100,000 was donated to such causes.

Lonely Planet's basic travel philosophy is summed up in Tony Wheeler's comment, 'Don't worry about whether your trip will work out. Just go!'